# GENERAL MOTORS
## FULL-SIZE VANS
## 1967-86 REPAIR MANUAL

MW00559250

CHILTON'S

Covers all U.S. and Canadian models of
Chevrolet/GMC 1/2, 3/4 and 1 ton Vans including
Cutaway and Motor Home Chassis;
gasoline and diesel engines

by **Thomas A. Mellon**, A.S.E., S.A.E.

CHILTON Automotive Books

PUBLISHED BY **HAYNES NORTH AMERICA**. Inc.

Haynes

APAA
AUTOMOTIVE
PARTS &
ACCESSORIES
ASSOCIATION MEMBER

Manufactured in USA
© 1997 Haynes North America, Inc.
ISBN 0-8019-8977-9
Library of Congress Catalog Card No. 97-65604
4567890123 9876543210

**Haynes Publishing Group**
Sparkford Nr Yeovil
Somerset BA22 7JJ England

**Haynes North America, Inc**
861 Lawrence Drive
Newbury Park
California 91320 USA

ABCDE
FGHIJ
KLMNO

# Contents

# Contents

## 7 DRIVE TRAIN

## 8 SUSPENSION AND STEERING

## 9 BRAKES

## 10 BODY AND TRIM

## GLOSSARY

## MASTER INDEX

## SAFETY NOTICE

Proper service and repair procedures are vital to the safe, reliable operation of all motor vehicles, as well as the personal safety of those performing repairs. This manual outlines procedures for servicing and repairing vehicles using safe, effective methods. The procedures contain many NOTES, CAUTIONS and WARNINGS which should be followed, along with standard procedures to eliminate the possibility of personal injury or improper service which could damage the vehicle or compromise its safety.

It is important to note that repair procedures and techniques, tools and parts for servicing motor vehicles, as well as the skill and experience of the individual performing the work vary widely. It is not possible to anticipate all of the conceivable ways or conditions under which vehicles may be serviced, or to provide cautions as to all possible hazards that may result. Standard and accepted safety precautions and equipment should be used when handling toxic or flammable fluids, and safety goggles or other protection should be used during cutting, grinding, chiseling, prying, or any other process that can cause material removal or projectiles.

Some procedures require the use of tools specially designed for a specific purpose. Before substituting another tool or procedure, you must be completely satisfied that neither your personal safety, nor the performance of the vehicle will be endangered.

Although information in this manual is based on industry sources and is complete as possible at the time of publication, the possibility exists that some car manufacturers made later changes which could not be included here. While striving for total accuracy, the authors or publishers cannot assume responsibility for any errors, changes or omissions that may occur in the compilation of this data.

## PART NUMBERS

Part numbers listed in this reference are not recommendations by Haynes North America, Inc. for any product brand name. They are references that can be used with interchange manuals and aftermarket supplier catalogs to locate each brand supplier's discrete part number.

## SPECIAL TOOLS

Special tools are recommended by the vehicle manufacturer to perform their specific job. Use has been kept to a minimum, but where absolutely necessary, they are referred to in the text by the part number of the tool manufacturer. These tools can be purchased, under the appropriate part number, from your local dealer or regional distributor, or an equivalent tool can be purchased locally from a tool supplier or parts outlet. Before substituting any tool for the one recommended, read the SAFETY NOTICE at the top of this page.

## ACKNOWLEDGMENTS

Portions of materials contained herein have been reprinted with the permission of General Motors Corporation, Service Technology Group.

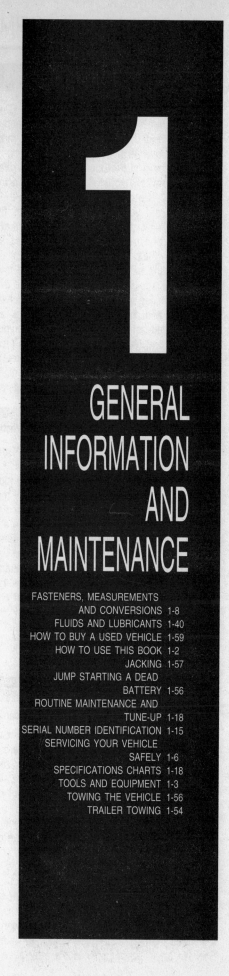

1

GENERAL
INFORMATION
AND
MAINTENANCE

## HOW TO USE THIS BOOK

Chilton's Total Car Care manual for the Chevrolet and GMC Vans is intended to help you learn more about the inner workings of your vehicle while saving you money on its upkeep and operation.

The beginning of the book will likely be referred to the most, since that is where you will find information for maintenance and tune-up. The other sections deal with the more complex systems of your vehicle. Operating systems from engine through brakes are covered to the extent that the average do-it-yourselfer becomes mechanically involved. This book will not explain such things as rebuilding a differential for the simple reason that the expertise required and the investment in special tools make this task uneconomical. It will, however, give you detailed instructions to help you change your own brake pads and shoes, replace spark plugs, and perform many more jobs that can save you money, give you personal satisfaction and help you avoid expensive problems.

A secondary purpose of this book is a reference for owners who want to understand their vehicle and/or their mechanics better. In this case, no tools at all are required.

### Where to Begin

Before removing any bolts, read through the entire procedure. This will give you the overall view of what tools and supplies will be required. There is nothing more frustrating than having to walk to the bus stop on Monday morning because you were short one bolt on Sunday afternoon. So read ahead and plan ahead. Each operation should be approached logically and all procedures thoroughly understood before attempting any work.

All sections contain adjustments, maintenance, removal and installation procedures, and in some cases, repair or overhaul procedures. When repair is not considered practical, we tell you how to remove the part and then how to install the new or rebuilt replacement. In this way, you at least save the labor costs. Backyard repair of some components is just not practical.

### Avoiding Trouble

Many procedures in this book require you to "label and disconnect . . . ." a group of lines, hoses or wires. Don't be lulled into thinking you can remember where everything goes — you won't. If you hook up vacuum or fuel lines incorrectly, the vehicle will run poorly, if at all. If you hook up electrical wiring incorrectly, you may instantly learn a very expensive lesson.

You don't need to know the official or engineering name for each hose or line. A piece of masking tape on the hose and a piece on its fitting will allow you to assign your own label such as the letter A or a short name. As long as you remember your own code, the lines can be reconnected by matching similar letters or names. Do remember that tape will dissolve in gasoline or other fluids; if a component is to be washed or cleaned, use another method of identification. A permanent felt-tipped marker can be very handy for marking metal parts. Remove any tape or paper labels after assembly.

### Maintenance or Repair?

It's necessary to mention the difference between maintenance and repair. Maintenance includes routine inspections, adjustments, and replacement of parts which show signs of normal wear. Maintenance compensates for wear or deterioration. Repair implies that something has broken or is not working. A need for repair is often caused by lack of maintenance. Example: draining and refilling the automatic transmission fluid is maintenance recommended by the manufacturer at specific mileage intervals. Failure to do this can ruin the transmission/transaxle, requiring very expensive repairs. While no maintenance program can prevent items from breaking or wearing out, a general rule can be stated: MAINTENANCE IS CHEAPER THAN REPAIR.

Two basic mechanic's rules should be mentioned here. First, whenever the left side of the vehicle or engine is referred to, it is meant to specify the driver's side. Conversely, the right side of the vehicle means the passenger's side. Second, most screws and bolts are removed by turning counterclockwise, and tightened by turning clockwise.

Safety is always the most important rule. Constantly be aware of the dangers involved in working on an automobile and take the proper precautions. See the information in this section regarding SERVICING YOUR VEHICLE SAFELY and the SAFETY NOTICE on the acknowledgment page.

### Avoiding the Most Common Mistakes

Pay attention to the instructions provided. There are 3 common mistakes in mechanical work:

1. Incorrect order of assembly, disassembly or adjustment. When taking something apart or putting it together, performing steps in the wrong order usually just costs you extra time; however, it CAN break something. Read the entire procedure before beginning disassembly. Perform everything in the order in which the instructions say you should, even if you can't immediately see a reason for it. When you're taking apart something that is very intricate, you might want to draw a picture of how it looks when assembled at one point in order to make sure you get everything back in its proper position. We will supply exploded views whenever possible. When making adjustments, perform them in the proper order; often, one adjustment affects another, and you cannot expect even satisfactory results unless each adjustment is made only when it cannot be changed by any other.

2. Overtorquing (or undertorquing). While it is more common for overtorquing to cause damage, undertorquing may allow a fastener to vibrate loose causing serious damage. Especially when dealing with aluminum parts, pay attention to torque specifications and utilize a torque wrench in assembly. If a torque figure is not available, remember that if you are using the right tool to perform the job, you will probably not have to strain yourself to get a fastener tight enough. The pitch of most threads is so slight that the tension you put on the wrench will be multiplied many times in actual force on what you are tightening. A good example of how critical torque is can be seen in the case of spark plug installation, especially

where you are putting the plug into an aluminum cylinder head. Too little torque can fail to crush the gasket, causing leakage of combustion gases and consequent overheating of the plug and engine parts. Too much torque can damage the threads or distort the plug, changing the spark gap.

There are many commercial products available for ensuring that fasteners won't come loose, even if they are not torqued just right (a very common brand is Loctite®). If you're worried about getting something together tight enough to hold, but loose enough to avoid mechanical damage during assembly, one of these products might offer substantial insurance. Before choosing a threadlocking compound, read the label on the package and make sure the product is compatible with the materials, fluids, etc. involved.

3. Crossthreading. This occurs when a part such as a bolt is screwed into a nut or casting at the wrong angle and forced. Crossthreading is more likely to occur if access is difficult. It helps to clean and lubricate fasteners, then to start threading with the part to be installed positioned straight in. Then, start the bolt, spark plug, etc. with your fingers. If you encounter resistance, unscrew the part and start over again at a different angle until it can be inserted and turned several times without much effort. Keep in mind that many parts, especially spark plugs, have tapered threads, so that gentle turning will automatically bring the part you're threading to the proper angle, but only if you don't force it or resist a change in angle. Don't put a wrench on the part until it's been tightened a couple of turns by hand. If you suddenly encounter resistance, and the part has not seated fully, don't force it. Pull it back out to make sure it's clean and threading properly.

Always take your time and be patient; once you have some experience, working on your vehicle may well become an enjoyable hobby.

## TOOLS AND EQUIPMENT

▶ **See Figures 1, 2, 3, 4, 5, 6, 7, 8, 9, 10, 11, 12 and 13**

Naturally, without the proper tools and equipment it is impossible to properly service your vehicle. It would also be virtually impossible to catalog every tool that you would need to perform all of the operations in this book. Of course, It would be unwise for the amateur to rush out and buy an expensive set of tools on the theory that he/she may need one or more of them at some time.

The best approach is to proceed slowly, gathering a good quality set of those tools that are used most frequently. Don't be misled by the low cost of bargain tools. It is far better to spend a little more for better quality. Forged wrenches, 6 or 12-point sockets and fine tooth ratchets are by far preferable to their less expensive counterparts. As any good mechanic can tell you, there are few worse experiences than trying to work on a vehicle with bad tools. Your monetary savings will be far outweighed by frustration and mangled knuckles.

Begin accumulating those tools that are used most frequently: those associated with routine maintenance and tune-up. In addition to the normal assortment of screwdrivers and pliers, you should have the following tools:

• Wrenches/sockets and combination open end/box end wrenches in sizes from ⅛-¾ in. or 3mm-19mm (depending on whether your vehicle uses standard or metric fasteners) and a ¹³⁄₁₆ in. or ⅝ in. spark plug socket (depending on plug type).

➡**If possible, buy various length socket drive extensions. Universal-joint and wobble extensions can be extremely useful, but be careful when using them, as they can change the amount of torque applied to the socket.**

• Jackstands for support.
• Oil filter wrench.
• Spout or funnel for pouring fluids.
• Grease gun for chassis lubrication (unless your vehicle is not equipped with any grease fittings — for details, please refer to information on Fluids and Lubricants found later in this section).
• Hydrometer for checking the battery (unless equipped with a sealed, maintenance-free battery).
• A container for draining oil and other fluids.
• Rags for wiping up the inevitable mess.

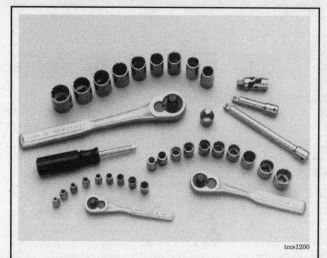

tccs1200

**Fig. 1 All but the most basic procedures will require an assortment of ratchets and sockets**

In addition to the above items there are several others that are not absolutely necessary, but handy to have around. These include Oil Dry® (or an equivalent oil absorbent gravel — such as cat litter) and the usual supply of lubricants, antifreeze and fluids, although these can be purchased as needed. This is a basic list for routine maintenance, but only your personal needs and desire can accurately determine your list of tools.

After performing a few projects on the vehicle, you'll be amazed at the other tools and non-tools on your workbench. Some useful household items are: a large turkey baster or siphon, empty coffee cans and ice trays (to store parts), ball of twine, electrical tape for wiring, small rolls of colored tape for tagging lines or hoses, markers and pens, a note pad, golf tees (for plugging vacuum lines), metal coat hangers or a roll of mechanics's wire (to hold things out of the way), dental pick or similar long, pointed probe, a strong magnet, and a small mirror (to see into recesses and under manifolds).

A more advanced set of tools, suitable for tune-up work, can be drawn up easily. While the tools are slightly more sophisticated, they need not be outrageously expensive. There are

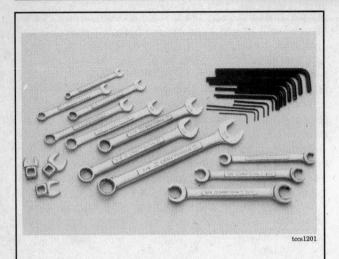

**Fig. 2 In addition to ratchets, a good set of wrenches and hex keys will be necessary**

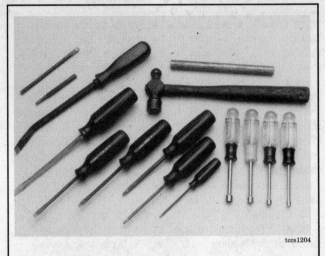

**Fig. 5 Various drivers, chisels and prybars are great tools to have in your toolbox**

**Fig. 3 A hydraulic floor jack and a set of jackstands are essential for lifting and supporting the vehicle**

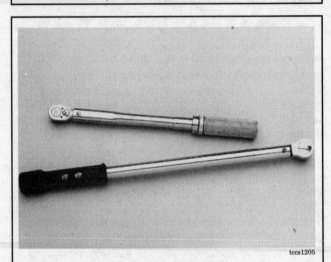

**Fig. 6 Many repairs will require the use of a torque wrench to assure the components are properly fastened**

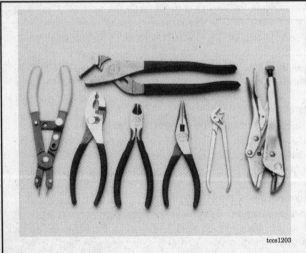

**Fig. 4 An assortment of pliers, grippers and cutters will be handy for old rusted parts and stripped bolt heads**

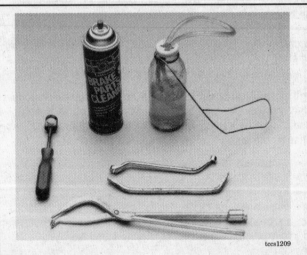

**Fig. 7 Although not always necessary, using specialized brake tools will save time**

**Fig. 8 A few inexpensive lubrication tools will make maintenance easier**

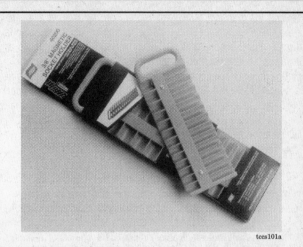

**Fig. 11 Tools available from specialty manufacturers such as Lisle® are designed to make your job easier . .**

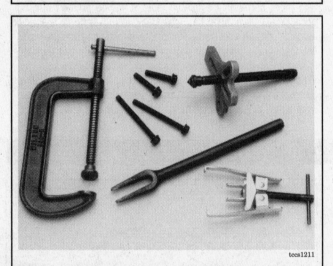

**Fig. 9 Various pullers, clamps and separator tools are needed for many larger, more complicated repairs**

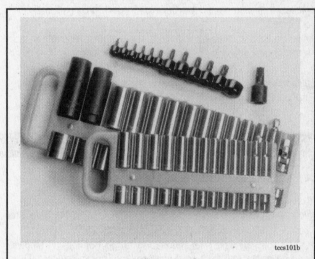

**Fig. 12 . . . these Torx® drivers and magnetic socket holders are just 2 examples of their handy products**

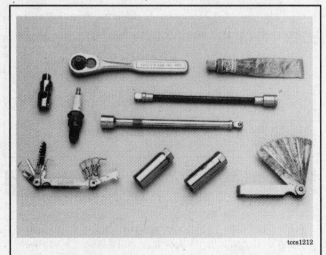

**Fig. 10 A variety of tools and gauges should be used for spark plug gapping and installation**

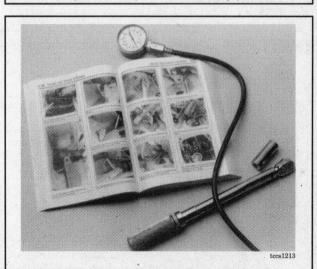

**Fig. 13 Proper information is vital, so always have a Chilton Total Car Care manual handy**

several inexpensive tach/dwell meters on the market that are every bit as good for the average mechanic as a professional model. Just be sure that it goes to a least 1200-1500 rpm on the tach scale and that it works on 4, 6 and 8-cylinder engines. (If you have one or more vehicles with a diesel engine, a special tachometer is required since diesels don't use spark plug ignition systems). The key to these purchases is to make them with an eye towards adaptability and wide range. A basic list of tune-up tools could include:

- Tach/dwell meter.
- Spark plug wrench and gapping tool.
- Feeler gauges for valve or point adjustment. (Even if your vehicle does not use points or require valve adjustments, a feeler gauge is helpful for many repair/overhaul procedures).

A tachometer/dwell meter will ensure accurate tune-up work on vehicles without electronic ignition. The choice of a timing light should be made carefully. A light which works on the DC current supplied by the vehicle's battery is the best choice; it should have a xenon tube for brightness. On any vehicle with an electronic ignition system, a timing light with an inductive pickup that clamps around the No. 1 spark plug cable is preferred.

In addition to these basic tools, there are several other tools and gauges you may find useful. These include:

- Compression gauge. The screw-in type is slower to use, but eliminates the possibility of a faulty reading due to escaping pressure.
- Manifold vacuum gauge.

- 12V test light.
- A combination volt/ohmmeter
- Induction Ammeter. This is used for determining whether or not there is current in a wire. These are handy for use if a wire is broken somewhere in a wiring harness.

As a final note, you will probably find a torque wrench necessary for all but the most basic work. The beam type models are perfectly adequate, although the newer click types (breakaway) are easier to use. The click type torque wrenches tend to be more expensive. Also keep in mind that all types of torque wrenches should be periodically checked and/or recalibrated. You will have to decide for yourself which better fits your purpose.

## Special Tools

Normally, the use of special factory tools is avoided for repair procedures, since these are not readily available for the do-it-yourself mechanic. When it is possible to perform the job with more commonly available tools, it will be pointed out, but occasionally, a special tool was designed to perform a specific function and should be used. Before substituting another tool, you should be convinced that neither your safety nor the performance of the vehicle will be compromised.

Special tools can usually be purchased from an automotive parts store or from your dealer. In some cases special tools may be available directly from the tool manufacturer.

## SERVICING YOUR VEHICLE SAFELY

▶ **See Figures 14, 15, 16 and 17**

It is virtually impossible to anticipate all of the hazards involved with automotive maintenance and service, but care and common sense will prevent most accidents.

The rules of safety for mechanics range from "don't smoke around gasoline," to "use the proper tool(s) for the job." The trick to avoiding injuries is to develop safe work habits and to take every possible precaution.

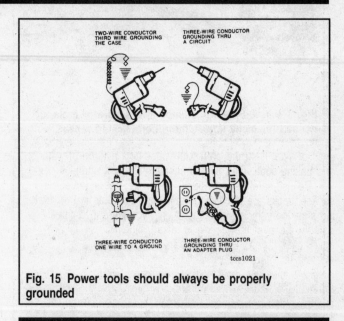

Fig. 15 Power tools should always be properly grounded

## Do's

- Do keep a fire extinguisher and first aid kit handy.
- Do wear safety glasses or goggles when cutting, drilling, grinding or prying, even if you have 20-20 vision. If you wear glasses for the sake of vision, wear safety goggles over your regular glasses.
- Do shield your eyes whenever you work around the battery. Batteries contain sulfuric acid. In case of contact with the

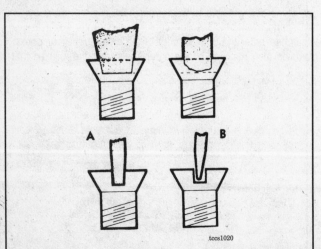

Fig. 14 Screwdrivers should be kept in good condition to prevent injury or damage which could result if the blade slips from the screw

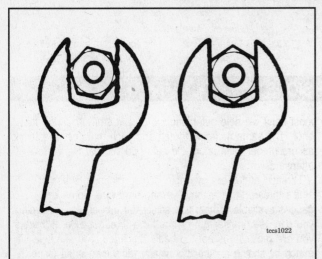

**Fig. 16 Using the correct size wrench will help prevent the possibility of rounding off a nut**

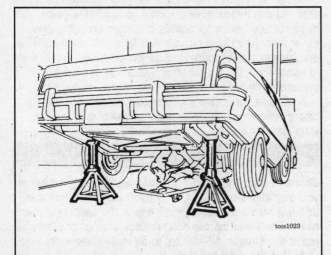

**Fig. 17 NEVER work under a vehicle unless it is supported using safety stands (jackstands)**

eyes or skin, flush the area with water or a mixture of water and baking soda, then seek immediate medical attention.

• Do use safety stands (jackstands) for any undervehicle service. Jacks are for raising vehicles; jackstands are for making sure the vehicle stays raised until you want it to come down. Whenever the vehicle is raised, block the wheels remaining on the ground and set the parking brake.

• Do use adequate ventilation when working with any chemicals or hazardous materials. Like carbon monoxide, the asbestos dust resulting from some brake lining wear can be hazardous in sufficient quantities.

• Do disconnect the negative battery cable when working on the electrical system. The secondary ignition system contains EXTREMELY HIGH VOLTAGE. In some cases it can even exceed 50,000 volts.

• Do follow manufacturer's directions whenever working with potentially hazardous materials. Most chemicals and fluids are poisonous if taken internally.

• Do properly maintain your tools. Loose hammerheads, mushroomed punches and chisels, frayed or poorly grounded electrical cords, excessively worn screwdrivers, spread wrenches (open end), cracked sockets, slipping ratchets, or faulty droplight sockets can cause accidents.

• Likewise, keep your tools clean; a greasy wrench can slip off a bolt head, ruining the bolt and often harming your knuckles in the process.

• Do use the proper size and type of tool for the job at hand. Do select a wrench or socket that fits the nut or bolt. The wrench or socket should sit straight, not cocked.

• Do, when possible, pull on a wrench handle rather than push on it, and adjust your stance to prevent a fall.

• Do be sure that adjustable wrenches are tightly closed on the nut or bolt and pulled so that the force is on the side of the fixed jaw.

• Do strike squarely with a hammer; avoid glancing blows.

• Do set the parking brake and block the drive wheels if the work requires a running engine.

## Don'ts

• Don't run the engine in a garage or anywhere else without proper ventilation — EVER! Carbon monoxide is poisonous; it takes a long time to leave the human body and you can build up a deadly supply of it in your system by simply breathing in a little every day. You may not realize you are slowly poisoning yourself. Always use power vents, windows, fans and/or open the garage door.

• Don't work around moving parts while wearing loose clothing. Short sleeves are much safer than long, loose sleeves. Hard-toed shoes with neoprene soles protect your toes and give a better grip on slippery surfaces. Jewelry such as watches, fancy belt buckles, beads or body adornment of any kind is not safe working around a vehicle. Long hair should be tied back under a hat or cap.

• Don't use pockets for toolboxes. A fall or bump can drive a screwdriver deep into your body. Even a rag hanging from your back pocket can wrap around a spinning shaft or fan.

• Don't smoke when working around gasoline, cleaning solvent or other flammable material.

• Don't smoke when working around the battery. When the battery is being charged, it gives off explosive hydrogen gas.

• Don't use gasoline to wash your hands; there are excellent soaps available. Gasoline contains dangerous additives which can enter the body through a cut or through your pores. Gasoline also removes all the natural oils from the skin so that bone dry hands will suck up oil and grease.

• Don't service the air conditioning system unless you are equipped with the necessary tools and training. When liquid or compressed gas refrigerant is released to atmospheric pressure it will absorb heat from whatever it contacts. This will chill or freeze anything it touches. Although refrigerant is normally non-toxic, R-12 becomes a deadly poisonous gas in the presence of an open flame. One good whiff of the vapors from burning refrigerant can be fatal.

• Don't use screwdrivers for anything other than driving screws! A screwdriver used as an prying tool can snap when you least expect it, causing injuries. At the very least, you'll ruin a good screwdriver.

• Don't use a bumper or emergency jack (that little ratchet, scissors, or pantograph jack supplied with the vehicle) for anything other than changing a flat! These jacks are only intended for emergency use out on the road; they are NOT designed as a maintenance tool. If you are serious about maintaining your vehicle yourself, invest in a hydraulic floor jack of at least a 1½ ton capacity, and at least two sturdy jackstands.

## FASTENERS, MEASUREMENTS AND CONVERSIONS

### Bolts, Nuts and Other Threaded Retainers

▶ See Figures 18, 19, 20 and 21

Although there are a great variety of fasteners found in the modern car or truck, the most commonly used retainer is the threaded fastener (nuts, bolts, screws, studs, etc). Most threaded retainers may be reused, provided that they are not damaged in use or during the repair. Some retainers (such as stretch bolts or torque prevailing nuts) are designed to deform when tightened or in use and should not be reinstalled.

Whenever possible, we will note any special retainers which should be replaced during a procedure. But you should always inspect the condition of a retainer when it is removed and replace any that show signs of damage. Check all threads for rust or corrosion which can increase the torque necessary to achieve the desired clamp load for which that fastener was originally selected. Additionally, be sure that the driver surface of the fastener has not been compromised by rounding or other damage. In some cases a driver surface may become only partially rounded, allowing the driver to catch in only one direction. In many of these occurrences, a fastener may be installed and tightened, but the driver would not be able to grip and loosen the fastener again. (This could lead to frustration down the line should that component ever need to be disassembled again).

If you must replace a fastener, whether due to design or damage, you must ALWAYS be sure to use the proper replacement. In all cases, a retainer of the same design, material and strength should be used. Markings on the heads of most bolts will help determine the proper strength of the fastener. The same material, thread and pitch must be selected to assure proper installation and safe operation of the vehicle afterwards.

Thread gauges are available to help measure a bolt or stud's thread. Most automotive and hardware stores keep gauges available to help you select the proper size. In a pinch, you can use another nut or bolt for a thread gauge. If the bolt you are replacing is not too badly damaged, you can select a match by finding another bolt which will thread in its place. If you find a nut which threads properly onto the damaged bolt, then use that nut to help select the replacement bolt. If however, the bolt you are replacing is so badly damaged (broken or drilled out) that its threads cannot be used as a gauge, you might start by looking for another bolt (from the same assembly or a similar location on your vehicle) which will thread into the damaged bolt's mounting. If so, the other bolt can be used to select a nut; the nut can then be used to select the replacement bolt.

In all cases, be absolutely sure you have selected the proper replacement. Don't be shy, you can always ask the store clerk for help.

### ✳✳WARNING

**Be aware that when you find a bolt with damaged threads, you may also find the nut or drilled hole it was threaded into has also been damaged. If this is the case, you may have to drill and tap the hole, replace the nut or otherwise repair the threads. NEVER try to force a replacement bolt to fit into the damaged threads.**

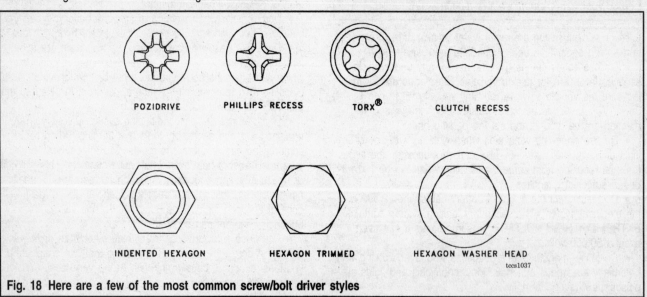

POZIDRIVE    PHILLIPS RECESS    TORX®    CLUTCH RECESS

INDENTED HEXAGON    HEXAGON TRIMMED    HEXAGON WASHER HEAD

tccs1037

Fig. 18 Here are a few of the most common screw/bolt driver styles

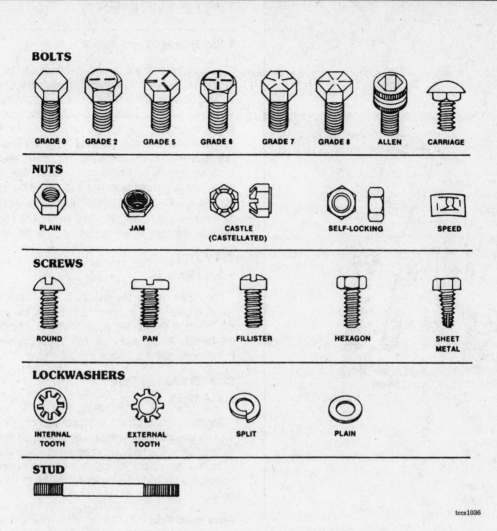

**Fig. 19 There are many different types of threaded retainers found on vehicles**

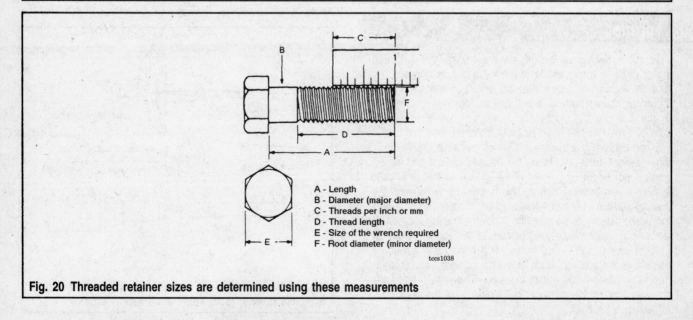

A - Length
B - Diameter (major diameter)
C - Threads per inch or mm
D - Thread length
E - Size of the wrench required
F - Root diameter (minor diameter)

tccs1038

**Fig. 20 Threaded retainer sizes are determined using these measurements**

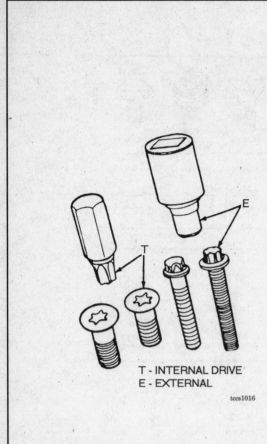

T - INTERNAL DRIVE
E - EXTERNAL

tccs1016

**Fig. 21 Special fasteners such as these Torx® head bolts are used by manufacturers to discourage people from working on vehicles without the proper tools**

## Torque

Torque is defined as the measurement of resistance to turning or rotating. It tends to twist a body about an axis of rotation. A common example of this would be tightening a threaded retainer such as a nut, bolt or screw. Measuring torque is one of the most common ways to help assure that a threaded retainer has been properly fastened.

When tightening a threaded fastener, torque is applied in three distinct areas, the head, the bearing surface and the clamp load. About 50 percent of the measured torque is used in overcoming bearing friction. This is the friction between the bearing surface of the bolt head, screw head or nut face and the base material or washer (the surface on which the fastener is rotating). Approximately 40 percent of the applied torque is used in overcoming thread friction. This leaves only about 10 percent of the applied torque to develop a useful clamp load (the force which holds a joint together). This means that friction can account for as much as 90 percent of the applied torque on a fastener.

## TORQUE WRENCHES

▶ **See Figures 22 and 23**

In most applications, a torque wrench can be used to assure proper installation of a fastener. Torque wrenches come in various designs and most automotive supply stores will carry a variety to suit your needs. A torque wrench should be used any time we supply a specific torque value for a fastener. A torque wrench can also be used if you are following the general guidelines in the accompanying charts. Keep in mind that because there is no worldwide standardization of fasteners, the charts are a general guideline and should be used with caution. Again, the general rule of "if you are using the right tool for the job, you should not have to strain to tighten a fastener" applies here.

### Beam Type
▶ **See Figure 24**

The beam type torque wrench is one of the most popular types. It consists of a pointer attached to the head that runs the length of the flexible beam (shaft) to a scale located near the handle. As the wrench is pulled, the beam bends and the pointer indicates the torque using the scale.

### Click (Breakaway) Type
▶ **See Figure 25**

Another popular design of torque wrench is the click type. To use the click type wrench you pre-adjust it to a torque setting. Once the torque is reached, the wrench has a reflex signalling feature that causes a momentary breakaway of the torque wrench body, sending an impulse to the operator's hand.

### Pivot Head Type
▶ **See Figures 25 and 26**

Some torque wrenches (usually of the click type) may be equipped with a pivot head which can allow it to be used in areas of limited access. BUT, it must be used properly. To

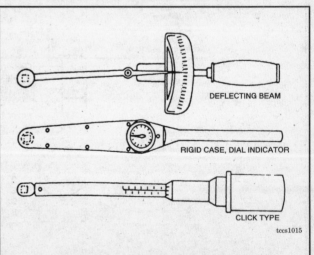

DEFLECTING BEAM

RIGID CASE, DIAL INDICATOR

CLICK TYPE

tccs1015

**Fig. 22 Various styles of torque wrenches are usually available at your local automotive supply store**

## Standard Torque Specifications and Fastener Markings

In the absence of specific torques, the following chart can be used as a guide to the maximum safe torque of a particular size/grade of fastener.

- There is no torque difference for fine or coarse threads.
- Torque values are based on clean, dry threads. Reduce the value by 10% if threads are oiled prior to assembly.
- The torque required for aluminum components or fasteners is considerably less.

### U.S. Bolts

| SAE Grade Number | 1 or 2 | | | 5 | | | 6 or 7 | | |
|---|---|---|---|---|---|---|---|---|---|
| Number of lines always 2 less than the grade number. | | | | | | | | | |
| Bolt Size (Inches)—(Thread) | **Maximum Torque** | | | **Maximum Torque** | | | **Maximum Torque** | | |
| | Ft./Lbs. | Kgm | Nm | Ft./Lbs. | Kgm | Nm | Ft./Lbs. | Kgm | Nm |
| ¼ — 20 | 5 | 0.7 | 6.8 | 8 | 1.1 | 10.8 | 10 | 1.4 | 13.5 |
| — 28 | 6 | 0.8 | 8.1 | 10 | 1.4 | 13.6 | | | |
| 5/16 — 18 | 11 | 1.5 | 14.9 | 17 | 2.3 | 23.0 | 19 | 2.6 | 25.8 |
| — 24 | 13 | 1.8 | 17.6 | 19 | 2.6 | 25.7 | | | |
| ⅜ — 16 | 18 | 2.5 | 24.4 | 31 | 4.3 | 42.0 | 34 | 4.7 | 46.0 |
| — 24 | 20 | 2.75 | 27.1 | 35 | 4.8 | 47.5 | | | |
| 7/16 — 14 | 28 | 3.8 | 37.0 | 49 | 6.8 | 66.4 | 55 | 7.6 | 74.5 |
| — 20 | 30 | 4.2 | 40.7 | 55 | 7.6 | 74.5 | | | |
| ½ — 13 | 39 | 5.4 | 52.8 | 75 | 10.4 | 101.7 | 85 | 11.75 | 115.2 |
| — 20 | 41 | 5.7 | 55.6 | 85 | 11.7 | 115.2 | | | |
| 9/16 — 12 | .51 | 7.0 | 69.2 | 110 | 15.2 | 149.1 | 120 | 16.6 | 162.7 |
| — 18 | 55 | 7.6 | 74.5 | 120 | 16.6 | 162.7 | | | |
| ⅝ — 11 | 83 | 11.5 | 112.5 | 150 | 20.7 | 203.3 | 167 | 23.0 | 226.5 |
| — 18 | 95 | 13.1 | 128.8 | 170 | 23.5 | 230.5 | | | |
| ¾ — 10 | 105 | 14.5 | 142.3 | 270 | 37.3 | 366.0 | 280 | 38.7 | 379.6 |
| — 16 | 115 | 15.9 | 155.9 | 295 | 40.8 | 400.0 | | | |
| ⅞ — 9 | 160 | 22.1 | 216.9 | 395 | 54.6 | 535.5 | 440 | 60.9 | 596.5 |
| — 14 | 175 | 24.2 | 237.2 | 435 | 60.1 | 589.7 | | | |
| 1 — 8 | 236 | 32.5 | 318.6 | 590 | 81.6 | 799.9 | 660 | 91.3 | 894.8 |
| — 14 | 250 | 34.6 | 338.9 | 660 | 91.3 | 849.8 | | | |

### Metric Bolts

| Relative Strength Marking | 4.6, 4.8 | | | 8.8 | | |
|---|---|---|---|---|---|---|
| Bolt Markings | | | | | | |
| Bolt Size Thread Size x Pitch (mm) | **Maximum Torque** | | | **Maximum Torque** | | |
| | Ft./Lbs. | Kgm | Nm | Ft./Lbs. | Kgm | Nm |
| 6 x 1.0 | 2–3 | .2–.4 | 3–4 | 3–6 | .4–.8 | 5–8 |
| 8 x 1.25 | 6–8 | .8–1 | 8–12 | 9–14 | 1.2–1.9 | 13–19 |
| 10 x 1.25 | 12–17 | 1.5–2.3 | 16–23 | 20–29 | 2.7–4.0 | 27–39 |
| 12 x 1.25 | 21–32 | 2.9–4.4 | 29–43 | 35–53 | 4.8–7.3 | 47–72 |
| 14 x 1.5 | 35–52 | 4.8–7.1 | 48–70 | 57–85 | 7.8–11.7 | 77–110 |
| 16 x 1.5 | 51–77 | 7.0–10.6 | 67–100 | 90–120 | 12.4–16.5 | 130–160 |
| 18 x 1.5 | 74–110 | 10.2–15.1 | 100–150 | 130–170 | 17.9–23.4 | 180–230 |
| 20 x 1.5 | 110–140 | 15.1–19.3 | 150–190 | 190–240 | 26.2–46.9 | 160–320 |
| 22 x 1.5 | 150–190 | 22.0–26.2 | 200–260 | 250–320 | 34.5–44.1 | 340–430 |
| 24 x 1.5 | 190–240 | 26.2–46.9 | 260–320 | 310–410 | 42.7–56.5 | 420–550 |

tccs1098

**Fig. 23 Standard and metric bolt torque specifications based on bolt strengths — WARNING: use only as a guide**

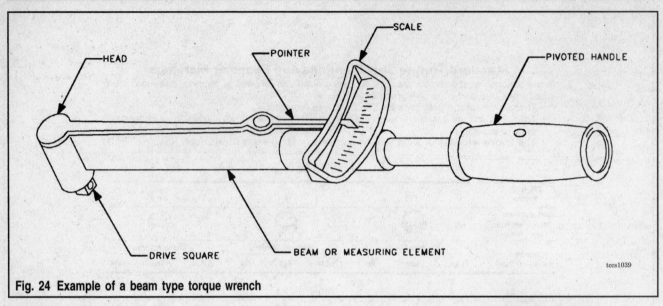

**Fig. 24 Example of a beam type torque wrench**

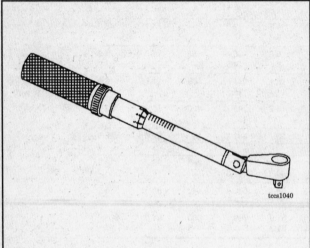

**Fig. 25 A click type or breakaway torque wrench — note this one has a pivoting head**

hold a pivot head wrench, grasp the handle lightly, and as you pull on the handle, it should be floated on the pivot point. If the handle comes in contact with the yoke extension during the process of pulling, there is a very good chance the torque readings will be inaccurate because this could alter the wrench loading point. The design of the handle is usually such as to make it inconvenient to deliberately misuse the wrench.

➡️ It should be mentioned that the use of any U-joint, wobble or extension will have an effect on the torque readings, no matter what type of wrench you are using. For the most accurate readings, install the socket directly on the wrench driver. If necessary, straight extensions (which hold a socket directly under the wrench driver) will have the least effect on the torque reading. Avoid any extension that alters the length of the wrench from the handle to the head/driving point (such as a crow's foot). U-joint or Wobble extensions can greatly affect the readings; avoid their use at all times.

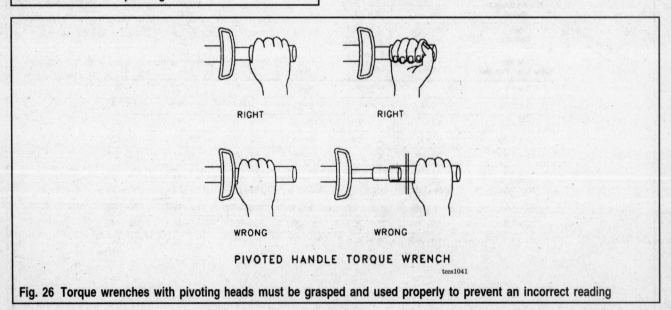

PIVOTED HANDLE TORQUE WRENCH

**Fig. 26 Torque wrenches with pivoting heads must be grasped and used properly to prevent an incorrect reading**

### Rigid Case (Direct Reading)

▶ See Figure 27

A rigid case or direct reading torque wrench is equipped with a dial indicator to show torque values. One advantage of these wrenches is that they can be held at any position on the wrench without affecting accuracy. These wrenches are often preferred because they tend to be compact, easy to read and have a great degree of accuracy.

## TORQUE ANGLE METERS

▶ See Figure 28

Because the frictional characteristics of each fastener or threaded hole will vary, clamp loads which are based strictly on torque will vary as well. In most applications, this variance is not significant enough to cause worry. But, in certain applications, a manufacturer's engineers may determine that more precise clamp loads are necessary (such is the case with many aluminum cylinder heads). In these cases, a torque angle method of installation would be specified. When installing fasteners which are torque angle tightened, a predetermined seating torque and standard torque wrench are usually used first to remove any compliance from the joint. The fastener is then tightened the specified additional portion of a turn measured in degrees. A torque angle gauge (mechanical protractor) is used for these applications.

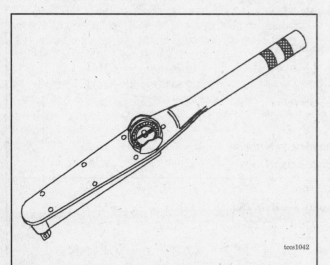

Fig. 27 The rigid case (direct reading) torque wrench uses a dial indicator to show torque

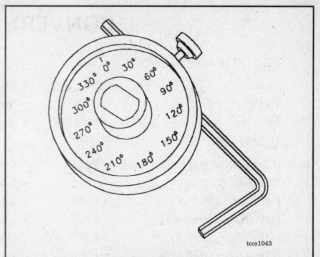

Fig. 28 Some specifications require the use of a torque angle meter (mechanical protractor)

## Standard and Metric Measurements

▶ See Figure 29

Throughout this manual, specifications are given to help you determine the condition of various components on your vehicle, or to assist you in their installation. Some of the most common measurements include length (in. or cm/mm), torque (ft. lbs., inch lbs. or Nm) and pressure (psi, in. Hg, kPa or mm Hg). In most cases, we strive to provide the proper measurement as determined by the manufacturer's engineers.

Though, in some cases, that value may not be conveniently measured with what is available in your toolbox. Luckily, many of the measuring devices which are available today will have two scales so the Standard or Metric measurements may easily be taken. If any of the various measuring tools which are available to you do not contain the same scale as listed in the specifications, use the accompanying conversion factors to determine the proper value.

The conversion factor chart is used by taking the given specification and multiplying it by the necessary conversion factor. For instance, looking at the first line, if you have a measurement in inches such as "free-play should be 2 in." but your ruler reads only in millimeters, multiply 2 in. by the conversion factor of 25.4 to get the metric equivalent of 50.8mm. Likewise, if the specification was given only in a Metric measurement, for example in Newton Meters (Nm), then look at the center column first. If the measurement is 100 Nm, multiply it by the conversion factor of 0.738 to get 73.8 ft. lbs.

# CONVERSION FACTORS

## LENGTH–DISTANCE

| | | | | |
|---|---|---|---|---|
| Inches (in.) | x 25.4 | = Millimeters (mm) | x .0394 | = Inches |
| Feet (ft.) | x .305 | = Meters (m) | x 3.281 | = Feet |
| Miles | x 1.609 | = Kilometers (km) | x .0621 | = Miles |

## VOLUME

| | | | | |
|---|---|---|---|---|
| Cubic Inches (in3) | x 16.387 | = Cubic Centimeters | x .061 | = in3 |
| IMP Pints (IMP pt.) | x .568 | = Liters (L) | x 1.76 | = IMP pt. |
| IMP Quarts (IMP qt.) | x 1.137 | = Liters (L) | x .88 | = IMP qt. |
| IMP Gallons (IMP gal.) | x 4.546 | = Liters (L) | x .22 | = IMP gal. |
| IMP Quarts (IMP qt.) | x 1.201 | = US Quarts (US qt.) | x .833 | = IMP qt. |
| IMP Gallons (IMP gal.) | x 1.201 | = US Gallons (US gal.) | x .833 | = IMP gal. |
| Fl. Ounces | x 29.573 | = Milliliters | x .034 | = Ounces |
| US Pints (US pt.) | x .473 | = Liters (L) | x 2.113 | = Pints |
| US Quarts (US qt.) | x .946 | = Liters (L) | x 1.057 | = Quarts |
| US Gallons (US gal.) | x 3.785 | = Liters (L) | x .264 | = Gallons |

## MASS–WEIGHT

| | | | | |
|---|---|---|---|---|
| Ounces (oz.) | x 28.35 | = Grams (g) | x .035 | = Ounces |
| Pounds (lb.) | x .454 | = Kilograms (kg) | x 2.205 | = Pounds |

## PRESSURE

| | | | | |
|---|---|---|---|---|
| Pounds Per Sq. In. (psi) | x 6.895 | = Kilopascals (kPa) | x .145 | = psi |
| Inches of Mercury (Hg) | x .4912 | = psi | x 2.036 | = Hg |
| Inches of Mercury (Hg) | x 3.377 | = Kilopascals (kPa) | x .2961 | = Hg |
| Inches of Water ($H_2O$) | x .07355 | = Inches of Mercury | x 13.783 | = $H_2O$ |
| Inches of Water ($H_2O$) | x .03613 | = psi | x 27.684 | = $H_2O$ |
| Inches of Water ($H_2O$) | x .248 | = Kilopascals (kPa) | x 4.026 | = $H_2O$ |

## TORQUE

| | | | | |
|---|---|---|---|---|
| Pounds–Force Inches (in–lb) | x .113 | = Newton Meters (N·m) | x 8.85 | = in–lb |
| Pounds–Force Feet (ft–lb) | x 1.356 | = Newton Meters (N·m) | x .738 | = ft–lb |

## VELOCITY

| | | | | |
|---|---|---|---|---|
| Miles Per Hour (MPH) | x 1.609 | = Kilometers Per Hour (KPH) | x .621 | = MPH |

## POWER

| | | | | |
|---|---|---|---|---|
| Horsepower (Hp) | x .745 | = Kilowatts | x 1.34 | = Horsepower |

## FUEL CONSUMPTION*

| | | |
|---|---|---|
| Miles Per Gallon IMP (MPG) | x .354 | = Kilometers Per Liter (Km/L) |
| Kilometers Per Liter (Km/L) | x 2.352 | = IMP MPG |
| Miles Per Gallon US (MPG) | x .425 | = Kilometers Per Liter (Km/L) |
| Kilometers Per Liter (Km/L) | x 2.352 | = US MPG |

*It is common to covert from miles per gallon (mpg) to liters/100 kilometers (1/100 km), where mpg (IMP) x 1/100 km = 282 and mpg (US) x 1/100 km = 235.

## TEMPERATURE

| | |
|---|---|
| Degree Fahrenheit (°F) | = (°C x 1.8) + 32 |
| Degree Celsius (°C) | = (°F – 32) x .56 |

tccs1044

**Fig. 29 Standard and metric conversion factors chart**

## SERIAL NUMBER IDENTIFICATION

### Vehicle

▶ See Figure 30

The vehicle identification number (VIN) on models through 1978 is on a plate fastened to the left door frame. On 1979 and later models, the VIN. plate is mounted on the driver's side of the instrument panel, and is visible through the windshield. The gross vehicle weight (GVW) or maximum safe total weight of the vehicle, cargo, and passengers is usually also given on the plate through 1978.

### 1967-69 MODELS

The first letter is the chassis type: G for van. The second letter identifies the engine: S for 6-cyl. and E for V8. The first number gives the load capacity (GVW) range: 1 for under 5,600 lbs. (2542 kg), 2 for over 5,500 lbs. (2497 kg). The second and third numbers are the cab to axle measurement code. The fourth and fifth numbers (letters for GMC) are a body style code. The sixth number is the last digit of the model year: 9 for 1969. The next number indicates the assembly plant. The remaining numbers are the vehicle's individual serial number.

### 1970-71 MODELS

The first letter is the chassis type: G for van. The second letter identifies the engine: S for 6-cyl. and E for V8. The first number gives the load capacity (GVW) range: 1 for under 5,500 lbs. (2497 kg), 2 for 5500-8,100 lbs. (2497-3677 kg), and 3 for 6,700-10,000 lbs. (3041-4540 kg The next number or two numbers indicates the body style: 5 for van, 26 for Cus-

tom Sportvan, and 36 for Deluxe Sportvan. The next number is the last digit of the model year: as 1 for 1971. The next letter indicates the assembly plant. The remaining numbers are the vehicle's individual serial number.

### 1972-80 MODELS

The first letter indicates a Chevrolet (C) or GMC (T) vehicle. The second letter is the chassis type: G for van. The third letter identifies the engine. For 1972, it was S for 6-cyl. and E for V8. For 1973-80, it is:

- Q — 250 six through 1975
- D — 250 six from 1976
- N — 262 4 bbl V6
- T — 292 six
- U — 305 V8
- X — 307 V8
- V — 350 2 bbl V8
- Y, L — 350 4 bbl V8
- U — 400 V8 through 1976
- R — 400 V8 from 1977

The first number gives the load capacity range: 1 for ½ ton (453.59 kg), 2 for ¾ ton (608.38 kg), and 3 for 1 ton (907.18 kg). The second number is 5 for van body. The third number is the last digit of the model year: as 6 for 1976. The next letter indicates the assembly plant. The remaining numbers are the vehicle's individual serial number.

### 1981-86 MODELS

▶ See Figure 31

Beginning in 1981 a new 17 digit code is used. The interpretation is the same as previous years except that the engine code is the eighth digit. Additional engines/codes include the 305 V8 (F and H codes); a 350 V8 (P code); a W-code 454 V8 and a Chevrolet built 379 cu. in. V8 diesel, in both C and J codes.

### Engine

▶ See Figures 32, 33 and 34

The engine number is located as follows:
- 6 Cylinder: On a pad on the right hand side of the cylinder block, at the rear of the distributor.
- V8: The engine number is found on a pad at the front of the right side cylinder head.

The engine number is broken down as follows: Example — F1210TFA:
- F — Manufacturing Plant. F-Flint and T-Tonawanda
- 12 — Month of Manufacture (December)
- 10 — Day of Manufacturer (Tenth)
- T — (1970 and later) Truck engine
- FA — Transmission and Engine Combination

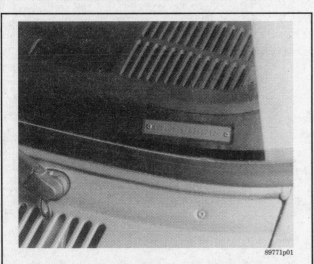

89771p01

**Fig. 30 The Vehicle Identification Number (VIN) is visible through the windshield — 1979 and later models**

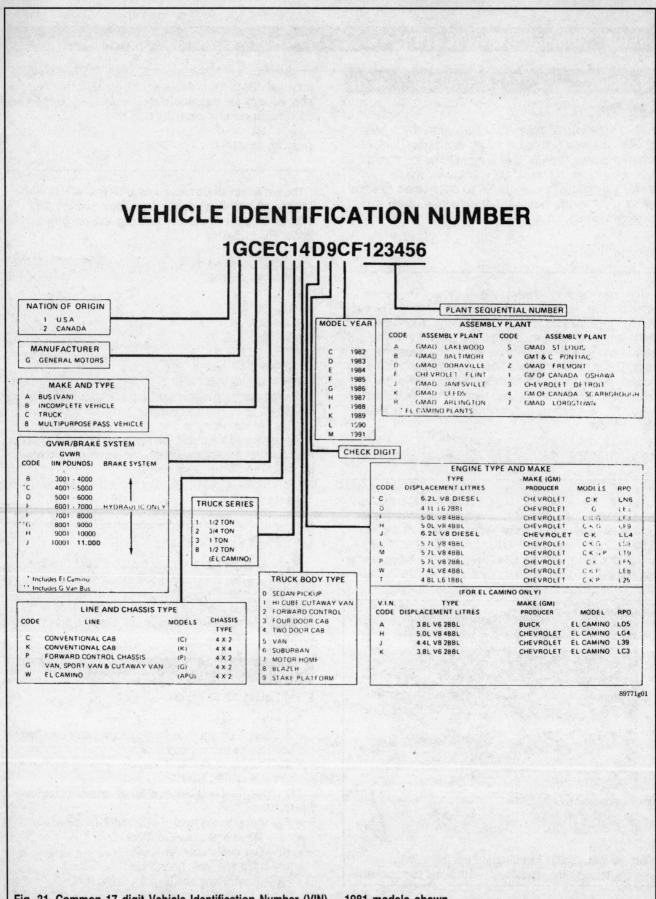

Fig. 31 Common 17 digit Vehicle Identification Number (VIN) — 1981 models shown

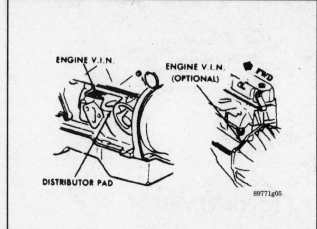

**Fig. 32 Common engine identification number location — inline six engines**

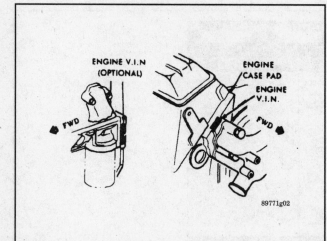

**Fig. 33 Common engine identification number location — V8 gasoline engines**

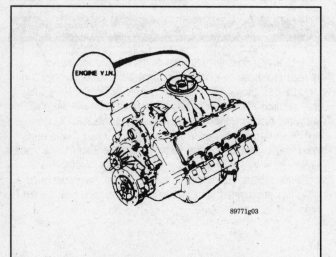

**Fig. 34 Common engine identification number location — 379 diesel engines**

## Transmission

▶ **See Figures 35 and 36**

The Muncie or Saginaw 3-speed manual transmission serial number is located on the lower left side of the case adjacent to the rear of the cover. The 3-speed Tremec transmission has the number on the upper forward mounting flange.

The 4-speed transmission is numbered on the rear of the case, above the output shaft. The Turbo Hydra-Matic 350 serial number is on the right rear vertical surface on the fluid pan. The Turbo Hydra-Matic 400 is identified by a light blue plate attached to the right side, which is stamped with the serial number. The Powerglide transmission (through 1972 only) is stamped in the same location as the Turbo Hydra-Matic 350.

## Drive Axle

The drive axle serial number is stamped on the axle shaft housing, where it connects to the differential housing, on 1974 and later models. On 1974 and earlier models the drive axle serial number is located on the bottom flange of the differential housing.

## Service Parts Identification Plate

▶ **See Figure 37**

The service parts identification plate, commonly known as the option list, is usually located on the inside of the glove compartment door. On some vans, you may have to look for it on an inner fender panel. The plate lists the vehicle serial number, wheelbase, all Regular Production Options (RPOs) and all special equipment. Probably, the most valuable piece of information on this plate is the paint code, a useful item when you have occasion to need paint.

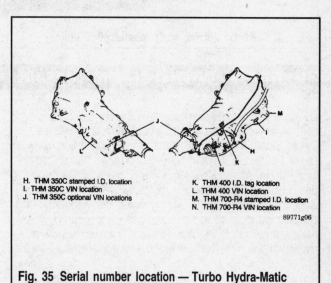

H. THM 350C stamped I.D. location
I. THM 350C VIN location
J. THM 350C optional VIN locations

K. THM 400 I.D. tag location
L. THM 400 VIN location
M. THM 700-R4 stamped I.D. location
N. THM 700-R4 VIN location

**Fig. 35 Serial number location — Turbo Hydra-Matic 350, 400 and 700 transmissions**

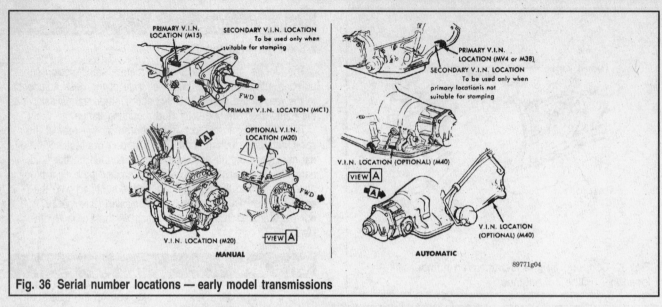

**Fig. 36 Serial number locations — early model transmissions**

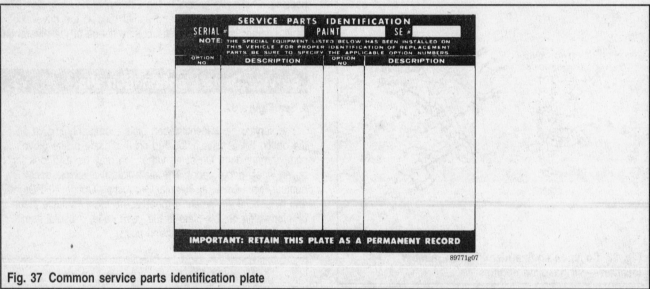

**Fig. 37 Common service parts identification plate**

## ROUTINE MAINTENANCE AND TUNE-UP

Proper maintenance and tune-up is the key to long and trouble-free vehicle life, and the work can yield its own rewards. Studies have shown that a properly tuned and maintained vehicle can achieve better gas mileage than an out-of-tune vehicle. As a conscientious owner and driver, set aside a Saturday morning, say once a month, to check or replace items which could cause major problems later. Keep your own personal log to jot down which services you performed, how much the parts cost you, the date, and the exact odometer reading at the time. Keep all receipts for such items as engine oil and filters, so that they may be referred to in case of related problems or to determine operating expenses. As a do-it-yourselfer, these receipts are the only proof you have that the required maintenance was performed. In the event of a warranty problem, these receipts will be invaluable.

The literature provided with your vehicle when it was originally delivered includes the factory recommended maintenance schedule. If you no longer have this literature, replacement copies are usually available from the dealer. A maintenance schedule is provided later in this section, in case you do not have the factory literature.

MAINTENANCE COMPONENT LOCATIONS
350 V8 (1984 SHOWN)

1. Engine coolant reservoir
2. Receiver/Drier
3. Engine oil filler cap/tube
4. Engine oil dipstick
5. Automatic transmission fluid dipstick
6. Air cleaner/distributor (under engine cover)
7. Windshield washer/fluid reservoir
8. Power steering pump reservoir/dipstick
9. Brake master cylinder reservoir
10. Battery
11. Heater hoses
12. Radiator cap

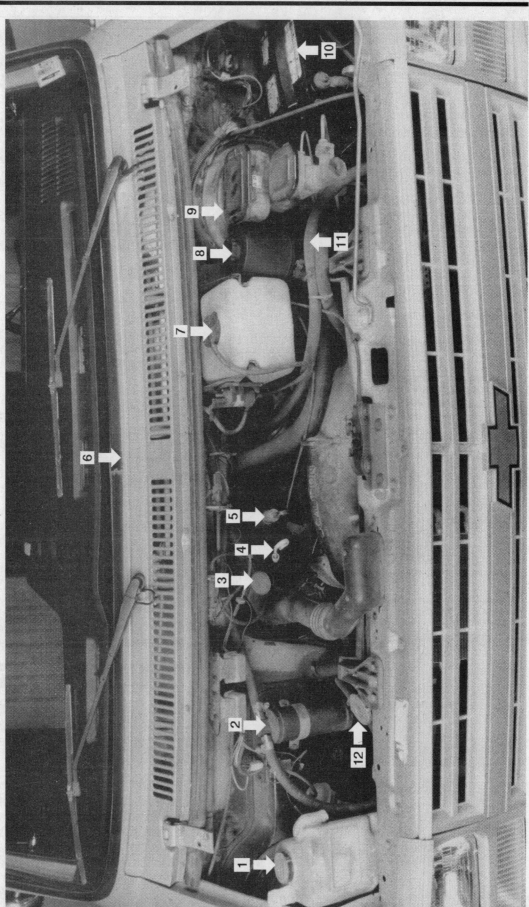

89771p90

## Air Cleaner

### REMOVAL & INSTALLATION

#### Paper Element Type
▶ **See Figures 38, 39, 40, 41 and 42**

Loosen the wing nut on top of the cover and remove the cover. The element should be replaced when it has become oil saturated or filled with dirt. If the filter is equipped with a foam wrapper, remove the wrapper and wash it in kerosene or similar solvent. Shake or blot dry. Saturate the wrapper in engine oil and squeeze it tightly in an absorbent towel to remove the excess oil.

Leave the wrapper moist. Clean the dirt from the filter by lightly tapping it against a workbench to dislodge the dirt particles. Wash the top of the air cleaner housing and wipe it dry.

Fig. 38 Remove the air cleaner cover . . .

Fig. 39 . . . then remove the air filter element

Fig. 40 If equipped, remove the crankcase ventilation filter

If equipped, replace the crankcase ventilation filter, located in the air filter housing if it appears excessively dirty. Replace the oiled wrapper on the air cleaner element and reinstall the element in the housing, repositioning it 180° from its original position.

➡ **Inverting the air cleaner cover for increased intake air volume is not recommended. This causes an increase in intake noise, faster dirt buildup in both the air cleaner element and the crankcase ventilation filter, and poor cold weather driveability.**

#### Oil Bath Type
▶ **See Figures 43 and 44**

To service the optional (through 1971) oil bath type air cleaner, remove the wing nut at the top and remove the cover and element. Drain all of the oil from the reservoir. Clean all of the parts and dry thoroughly, but do not use compressed air on the element.

Reinstall the reservoir and fill to the mark with SAE 50 engine oil (above freezing) or SAE 20 engine oil (below freezing). Install the element in the reservoir and replace the cover and tighten the wing nut.

## Fuel Filter

### REMOVAL & INSTALLATION

#### Gasoline Engines
▶ **See Figure 45**

The fuel filter should be serviced at the interval given on the Maintenance Interval chart. Two types of fuel filters are used, a bronze type and a paper element type. Inline fuel filters may be used on some engines which should be changed at the same time as the filter in the carburetor body. Filter replacement should be attempted only when the engine is cold. Additionally, it is a good idea to place some absorbent rags under the fuel fittings to catch the gasoline which will spill out when

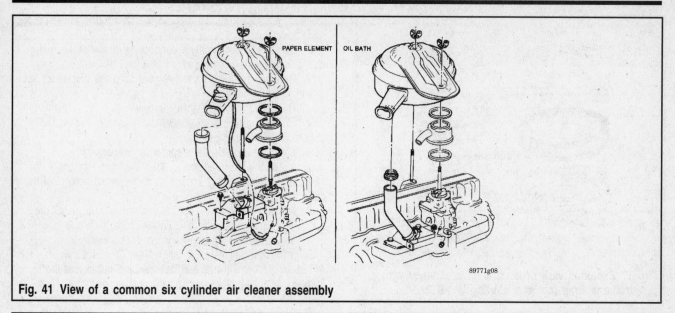

Fig. 41 View of a common six cylinder air cleaner assembly

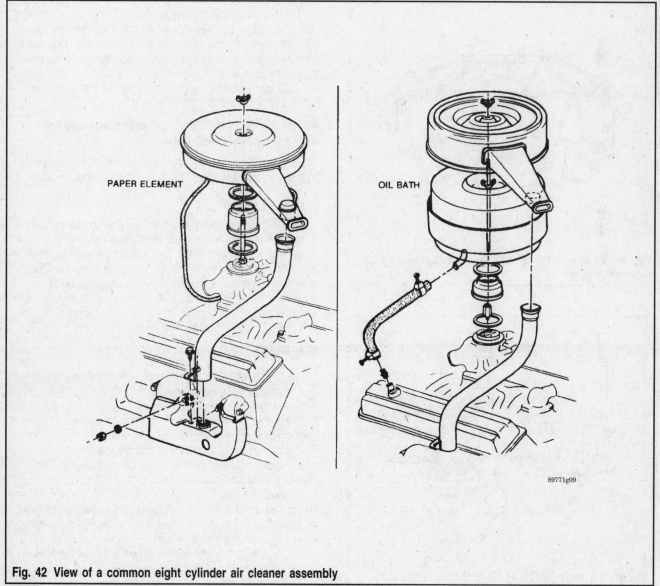

Fig. 42 View of a common eight cylinder air cleaner assembly

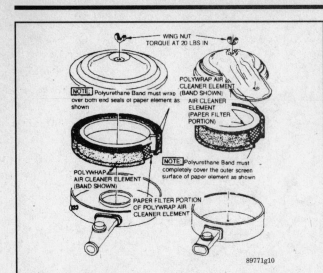

**Fig. 43 Exploded view of an air cleaner element with a polyurethane wrap (optional starting in 1972)**

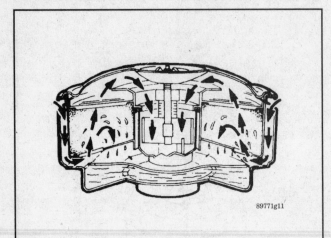

**Fig. 44 Air flow in the oil bath air cleaner assembly (optional through 1971)**

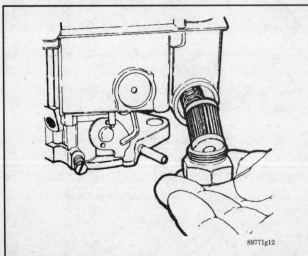

**Fig. 45 The paper fuel filter element can be found in the inlet fitting**

the lines are loosened. To replace the filter found in the carburetor body:

1. Disconnect the fuel line connecting at the intake fuel filter nut. Plug the opening to prevent loss of fuel.

2. Remove the intake fuel filter nut from the carburetor with a 1 in. (25mm) wrench.

3. Remove the filter element and spring.

4. Check the element for restrictions by blowing on the cone end. Air should pass freely.

5. Clean or replace the element, as necessary.

6. Install the element spring, then the filter element in the carburetor. Bronze filters should have the small section of the cone facing out.

7. Install a new gasket on the intake fuel nut. Install the nut in the carburetor body and tighten securely.

8. Install the fuel line and tighten the connector.

Some trucks may have an inline filter. This is a can shaped device located in the fuel line between the pump and the carburetor. It may be made of either plastic or metal. To replace the filter:

9. Place some absorbent rags under the filter. Remember, it will be full of gasoline when removed.

10. Use a pair of pliers to expand the clamp on one end of the filter, then slide the clamp down past the point to which the filter pipe extends in the rubber hose. Do the same with the other clamp.

11. Gently twist and pull the hoses free of the filter pipes. Remove and discard the old filter.

➡**Most replacement filters come with new hoses that should be installed with a new filter.**

12. Install the new filter into the hoses, slide the clamps back into place, and check for leaks with the engine idling.

### 6.2L Diesel Engines

The 1983 diesels utilize two fuel filters: a primary canister type screw-on filter, located on the chassis right hand under body cross sill forward of the fuel tank, and a clip-on secondary filter mounted on the rear of the intake manifold. The 1984-86 models use a combination fuel filter and water separator. These filters should be serviced at the regular intervals specified in the Maintenance chart. See Diesel Fuel System in Section 5 for more information.

### *1983 MODELS*

▶ **See Figures 46 and 47**

1. Remove the engine cover.

2. Remove the air cleaner and place a rag under the filter.

3. Unstrap the lower bail on the filter to relieve fuel pressure in the filter.

4. Unstrap the upper bail and remove the filter.

5. Before installing the new filter, insure that both filter mounting plate fittings are clear of dirt.

6. Install the new filter, snap the upper bail clamp only. Any time the secondary filter is removed or replaced, the air must be purged from the filter to prevent the engine from stalling or excessive cranking time to restart.

7. Disconnect the pink electrical wire from the injection pump to prevent the engine from starting.

8. Crank the engine (for 10 seconds max.) until the fuel is flowing at the lower fitting.

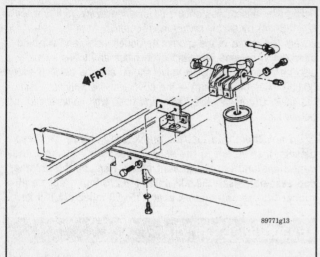

**Fig. 46 Exploded view of the primary fuel filter — 1983 6.2L diesel engines**

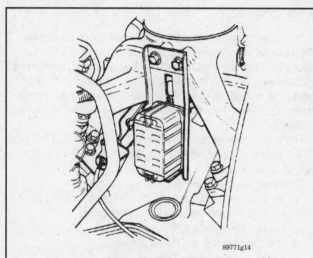

**Fig. 47 Exploded view of the secondary fuel filter — 1983 6.2L diesel engines**

9. If the fuel is not observed for 10 seconds, wait 15 seconds and repeat Step 8.

10. When fuel is observed at the lower fitting, connect the lower bail clamp.

11. Reconnect the pink wire on the injection pump and install the air cleaner.

12. Start the engine and allow it to idle for several minutes to purge the remaining air. Check for fuel leaks.

13. Remove the rag and reinstall the engine cover.

### 1984-86 MODELS

▶ See Figure 48

1. Drain the fuel from the fuel filter by opening both the air bleed and the water drain valve allowing the fuel to drain out into an appropriate container.

2. Remove the fuel tank cap to release any pressure or vacuum in the tank.

3. Unstrap both bail wires with a screwdriver and remove the filter.

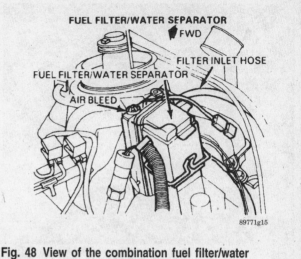

**Fig. 48 View of the combination fuel filter/water separator — 1984 6.2L diesel engines**

4. Before installing the new filter, insure that both filter mounting plate fittings are clear of dirt.

5. Install the new filter, snap into place with the bail wires.

6. Close the water drain valve and open the air bleed valve. Connect a ⅛ in. (3mm) I.D. hose to the air bleed port and place the other end into a suitable container.

7. Disconnect the fuel injection pump shut off solenoid wire.

8. Crank the engine for 10-15 seconds, then wait one minute for the starter motor to cool. Repeat until clear fuel is observed coming from the air bleed.

➡ If the engine is to be cranked, or starting attempted with the air cleaner removed, care must be taken to prevent dirt from being pulled into the air inlet manifold which could result in engine damage.

9. Close the air bleed valve, reconnect the injection pump solenoid wire and replace the fuel tank cap.

10. Start the engine, allow it to idle for 5 minutes and check the fuel filter for leaks.

## PCV Valve

### REMOVAL & INSTALLATION

▶ See Figures 49 and 50

The PCV valve is located on top of the valve cover or on the intake manifold. Its function is to purge the crankcase of harmful vapors through a system using engine vacuum to draw fresh air through the crankcase. It reburns crankcase vapors, rather than exhausting. Proper operation of the PCV valve depends on a sealed engine.

Engine operating conditions that would indicate a malfunctioning PCV system are rough idle, oil present in the air cleaner, oil leaks or excessive oil sludging.

The simplest check for the PCV valve is to remove it from its rubber grommet on top of the valve cover and shake it. If it rattles, it is functioning. If not, replace it. In any event, it should be replaced at the recommended interval whether it rattles or not. While you are about it, check the PCV hoses for

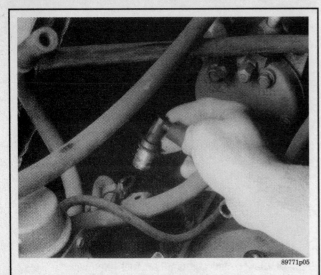

Fig. 49 Removing the PCV valve from the valve cover

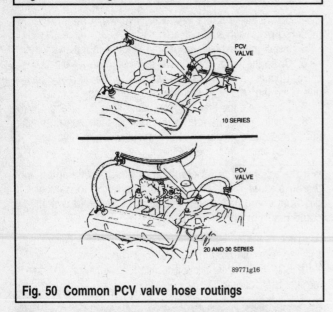

Fig. 50 Common PCV valve hose routings

breaks or restrictions. As necessary, the hoses should also be replaced.

## Crankcase Depression Regulator and Flow Control Valve

### SERVICING

**Diesel Engines**
▶ See Figure 51

The Crankcase Depression Regulator (CDR), found on 1982 and later diesels is designed to scavenge crankcase vapors in basically the same manner as the PVC valve on gasoline engines. The valves are located either on the left rear corner of the intake manifold (CDR). On this system there are two ventilation filters, one per valve cover.

The filter assemblies should be cleaned every 15,000 miles (24,135 km) by simply prying them carefully from the valve covers (be aware of the grommets underneath), and washing them out in solvent. The ventilation pipes and tubes should also be cleaned. The CDR valve should also be cleaned every 30,000 miles (48,270 km) — the cover can be removed from the CDR. Dry each valve, filter, and hose with compressed air before installation.

➡**Do not attempt to test the crankcase controls on these diesels. Instead, clean the valve cover filter assembly and vent pipes and check the vent pipes. Replace the breather cap assembly every 30,000 miles (48,270 km). Replace all rubber fittings as required every 15,000 miles (24,135 km).**

## Evaporative Canister

### SERVICING

▶ See Figure 52

The only regular maintenance that need be performed on the evaporative emission canister is to regularly change the filter and check the condition of the hoses. If any hoses need replacement, use only hoses which are marked EVAP. No other type should be used. Whenever the vapor vent hose is replaced, the restrictor adjacent to the canister should also be replaced.

The evaporative emission canister is located on the left side of the engine compartment, with a filter located in its bottom. Not all vans have one.

To service the canister filter:
1. Note the installed positions of the hoses, tagging them as necessary, in case any have to be removed.
2. Loosen the clamps and remove the canister.
3. Pull the filter out and throw it away.
4. Install a new canister filter.
5. Install the canister and tighten the clamps.
6. Check the hoses.

## Battery

### GENERAL MAINTENANCE

All batteries, regardless of type, should be carefully secured by a battery hold-down device. If this is not done, the battery terminals or casing may crack from stress applied to the battery during vehicle operation. A battery which is not secured may allow acid to leak out, making it discharge faster; such leaking corrosive acid can also eat away components under the hood. A battery that is not sealed must be checked periodically for electrolyte level. You cannot add water to a sealed maintenance-free battery (though not all maintenance-free batteries are sealed), but a sealed battery must also be checked for proper electrolyte level as indicated by the color of the built-in hydrometer "eye."

Keep the top of the battery clean, as a film of dirt can help completely discharge a battery that is not used for long periods. A solution of baking soda and water may be used for

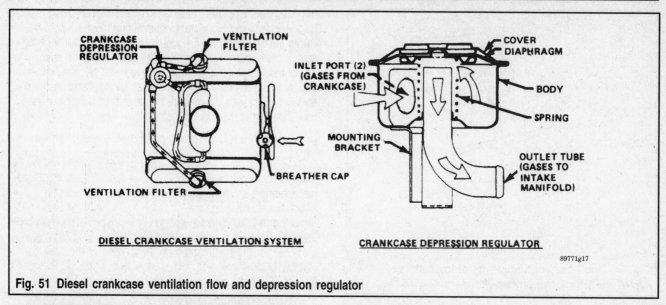

DIESEL CRANKCASE VENTILATION SYSTEM

CRANKCASE DEPRESSION REGULATOR

89771g17

**Fig. 51 Diesel crankcase ventilation flow and depression regulator**

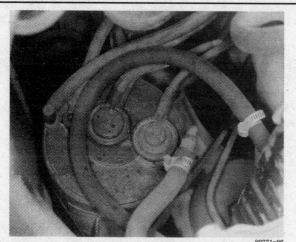

89771p06

**Fig. 52 Common evaporative canister used on most full size vans**

cleaning, but be careful to flush this off with clear water. DO NOT let any of the solution into the filler holes. Baking soda neutralizes battery acid and will de-activate a battery cell.

### ❊❊CAUTION

**Always use caution when working on or near the battery. Never allow a tool to bridge the gap between the negative and positive battery terminals. Also, be careful not to allow a tool to provide a ground between the positive cable/terminal and any metal component on the vehicle. Either of these conditions will cause a short circuit leading to sparks and possible personal injury.**

Batteries in vehicles which are not operated on a regular basis can fall victim to parasitic loads (small current drains which are constantly drawing current from the battery). Normal parasitic loads may drain a battery on a vehicle that is in storage and not used for 6-8 weeks. Vehicles that have additional accessories such as a cellular phone, an alarm system or other devices that increase parasitic load may discharge a

battery sooner. If the vehicle is to be stored for 6-8 weeks in a secure area and the alarm system, if present, is not necessary, the negative battery cable should be disconnected at the onset of storage to protect the battery charge.

Remember that constantly discharging and recharging will shorten battery life. Take care not to allow a battery to be needlessly discharged.

## BATTERY FLUID

▶ See Figures 53, 54, 55 and 56

### ❊❊CAUTION

**Battery electrolyte contains sulfuric acid. If you should splash any on your skin or in your eyes, flush the affected area with plenty of clear water. If it lands in your eyes, get medical help immediately.**

The fluid (sulfuric acid solution) contained in the battery cells will tell you many things about the condition of the battery.

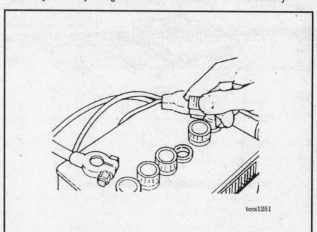

tccs1251

**Fig. 53 On non-maintenance free batteries, the level can be checked through the case on translucent batteries; the cell caps must be removed on other models**

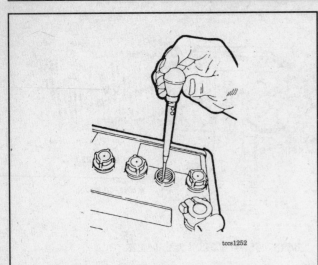

**Fig. 54 Check the specific gravity of the battery's electrolyte with a hydrometer**

| Specific Gravity Reading | Charged Condition |
|---|---|
| 1.260–1.280 | Fully Charged |
| 1.230–1.250 | ¾ Charged |
| 1.200–1.220 | ½ Charged |
| 1.170–1.190 | ¼ Charged |
| 1.140–1.160 | Almost no Charge |
| 1.110–1.130 | No Charge |

89771g20

**Fig. 56 Battery state of charge at room temperature chart**

Because the cell plates must be kept submerged below the fluid level in order to operate, maintaining the fluid level is extremely important. And, because the specific gravity of the acid is an indication of electrical charge, testing the fluid can be an aid in determining if the battery must be replaced. A battery in a vehicle with a properly operating charging system should require little maintenance, but careful, periodic inspection should reveal problems before they leave you stranded.

### Fluid Level

Check the battery electrolyte level at least once a month, or more often in hot weather or during periods of extended vehicle operation. On non-sealed batteries, the level can be checked either through the case on translucent batteries or by removing the cell caps on opaque-cased types. The electrolyte level in each cell should be kept filled to the split ring inside each cell, or the line marked on the outside of the case.

If the level is low, add only distilled water through the opening until the level is correct. Each cell is separate from the others, so each must be checked and filled individually. Distilled water should be used, because the chemicals and minerals found in most drinking water are harmful to the battery and could significantly shorten its life.

If water is added in freezing weather, the vehicle should be driven several miles to allow the water to mix with the electrolyte. Otherwise, the battery could freeze.

Although some maintenance-free batteries have removable cell caps for access to the electrolyte, the electrolyte condition and level on all sealed maintenance-free batteries must be checked using the built-in hydrometer "eye." The exact type of eye varies between battery manufacturers, but most apply a sticker to the battery itself explaining the possible readings.

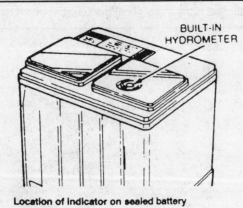

Location of indicator on sealed battery

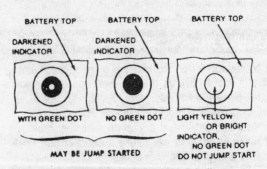

Check the appearance of the charge indicator on top of the battery before attempting a jump start; if it's not green or dark, do not jump start the car

tccs1253

**Fig. 55 A typical sealed (maintenance-free) battery with a built-in hydrometer — NOTE that the hydrometer eye may vary between battery manufacturers; always refer to the battery's label**

When in doubt, refer to the battery manufacturer's instructions to interpret battery condition using the built-in hydrometer.

➡Although the readings from built-in hydrometers found in sealed batteries may vary, a green eye usually indicates a properly charged battery with sufficient fluid level. A dark eye is normally an indicator of a battery with sufficient fluid, but one which may be low in charge. And a light or yellow eye is usually an indication that electrolyte supply has dropped below the necessary level for battery (and hydrometer) operation. In this last case, sealed batteries with an insufficient electrolyte level must usually be discarded.

### Specific Gravity

As stated earlier, the specific gravity of a battery's electrolyte level can be used as an indication of battery charge. At least once a year, check the specific gravity of the battery. It should be between 1.20 and 1.26 on the gravity scale. Most auto supply stores carry a variety of inexpensive battery testing hydrometers. These can be used on any non-sealed battery to test the specific gravity in each cell.

The battery testing hydrometer has a squeeze bulb at one end and a nozzle at the other. Battery electrolyte is sucked into the hydrometer until the float is lifted from its seat. The specific gravity is then read by noting the position of the float. If gravity is low in one or more cells, the battery should be slowly charged and checked again to see if the gravity has come up. Generally, if after charging, the specific gravity between any two cells varies more than 50 points (0.50), the battery should be replaced as it can no longer produce sufficient voltage to guarantee proper operation.

On sealed batteries, the built-in hydrometer is the only way of checking specific gravity. Again, check with your battery's manufacturer for proper interpretation of its built-in hydrometer readings.

## CABLES

♦ See Figures 57, 58, 59, 60, 61 and 62

Once a year (or as necessary), the battery terminals and the cable clamps should be cleaned. Loosen the clamps and remove the cables, negative cable first. On batteries with posts on top, the use of a puller specially made for this purpose is recommended. These are inexpensive and available in most auto parts stores. Side terminal battery cables are secured with a small bolt.

Clean the cable clamps and the battery terminal with a wire brush, until all corrosion, grease, etc., is removed and the metal is shiny. It is especially important to clean the inside of the clamp (an old knife is useful here) thoroughly, since a small deposit of foreign material or oxidation there will prevent a sound electrical connection and inhibit either starting or charging. Special tools are available for cleaning these parts, one type for conventional top post batteries and another type for side terminal batteries.

Before installing the cables, loosen the battery hold-down clamp or strap, remove the battery and check the battery tray. Clear it of any debris, and check it for soundness (the battery tray can be cleaned with a baking soda and water solution).

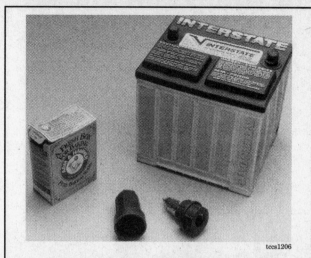

Fig. 57 Maintenance is performed with household items and with special tools like this post cleaner

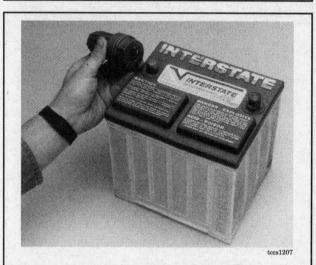

Fig. 58 The underside of this special battery tool has a wire brush to clean post terminals

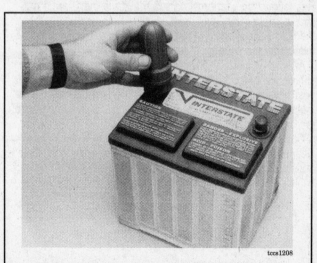

Fig. 59 Place the tool over the terminals and twist to clean the post

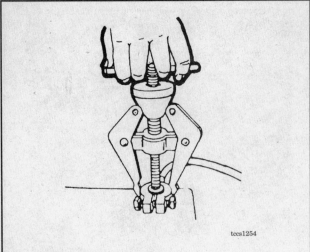

**Fig. 60 A special tool is available to pull the clamp from the post**

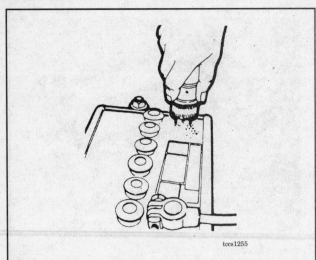

**Fig. 61 Clean the battery terminals until the metal is shiny**

Rust should be wire brushed away, and the metal given a couple coats of anti-rust paint. Install the battery and tighten the hold-down clamp or strap securely. Do not overtighten, as this can crack the battery case.

After the clamps and terminals are clean, reinstall the cables, negative cable last; DO NOT hammer the clamps onto post batteries. Tighten the clamps securely, but do not distort them. Give the clamps and terminals a thin external coating of grease after installation, to retard corrosion.

Check the cables at the same time that the terminals are cleaned. If the cable insulation is cracked or broken, or if the ends are frayed, the cable should be replaced with a new cable of the same length and gauge.

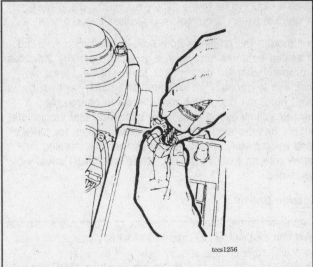

**Fig. 62 The cable ends should be cleaned as well**

## CHARGING

### ❊❊CAUTION

The chemical reaction which takes place in all batteries generates explosive hydrogen gas. A spark can cause the battery to explode and splash acid. To avoid serious personal injury, be sure there is proper ventilation and take appropriate fire safety precautions when connecting, disconnecting, or charging a battery and when using jumper cables.

A battery should be charged at a slow rate to keep the plates inside from getting too hot. However, if some maintenance-free batteries are allowed to discharge until they are almost "dead," they may have to be charged at a high rate to bring them back to "life." Always follow the charger manufacturer's instructions on charging the battery.

## REPLACEMENT

When it becomes necessary to replace the battery, select one with a rating equal to or greater than the battery originally installed. Deterioration and just plain aging of the battery cables, starter motor, and associated wires makes the battery's job harder in successive years. The slow increase in electrical resistance over time makes it prudent to install a new battery with a greater capacity than the old.

## Heat Riser

### OPERATION

The heat riser is a thermostatically or vacuum operated valve in the exhaust manifold. Not all engines have one. It closes when the engine is warming up, to direct hot exhaust gases to the intake manifold, in order to preheat the incoming fuel/air mixture. It it sticks shut, the result will be frequent stalling during warmup, especially in cold and damp weather. If it sticks open, the result will be a rough idle after the engine is warm. There is only one heat riser on a V8. The heat riser should move freely. If it sticks, apply GM Manifold Heat Control Solvent or something similar (engine cool) to the ends of the shaft. Sometimes rapping the end of the shaft sharply with a hammer (engine hot) will break it loose. If this fails, components must be removed for further repairs.

## Belts

## INSPECTION

▶ **See Figures 63, 64, 65, 66 and 67**

Inspect the belts for signs of glazing or cracking. A glazed belt will be perfectly smooth from slippage, while a good belt will have a slight texture of fabric visible. Cracks will usually start at the inner edge of the belt and run outward. All worn or damaged drive belts should be replaced immediately. It is best to replace all drive belts at one time, as a preventive maintenance measure, during this service operation.

## REMOVAL & INSTALLATION

▶ **See Figures 68, 69, 70, 71, 72 and 73**

1. Loosen the driven accessory's pivot and mounting bolts.
2. Move the accessory toward or away from the engine until the tension is correct. You can use a wooden hammer handle, or broomstick, as a lever, but do not use anything metallic, such as a prybar.
3. Tighten the bolts and recheck the tension. If new belts have been installed, run the engine for a few minutes, then recheck and readjust as necessary.

It is better to have belts too loose than too tight, because overtight belts will lead to bearing failure, particularly in the water pump and alternator. However, loose belts place an ex-

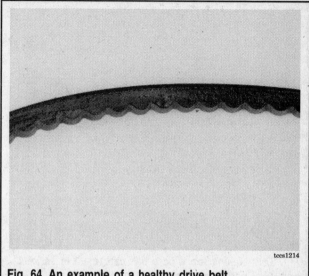

Fig. 64 An example of a healthy drive belt

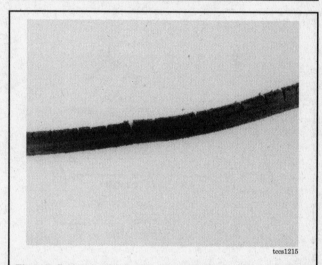

Fig. 65 Deep cracks in this belt will cause flex, building up heat that will eventually lead to belt failure

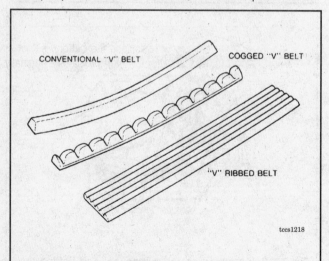

Fig. 63 There are typically 3 types of accessory drive belts found on vehicles today

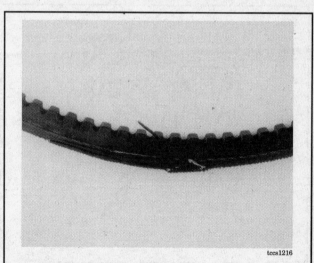

Fig. 66 The cover of this belt is worn, exposing the critical reinforcing cords to excessive wear

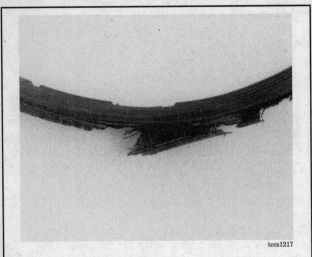

Fig. 67 Installing too wide a belt can result in serious belt wear and/or breakage

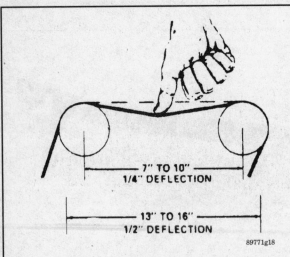

Fig. 68 A gauge is recommended, but you can check belt tension with thumb pressure

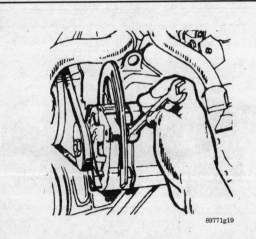

Fig. 69 Loosen the component's mounting and adjusting bolts slightly to remove or adjust the belt(s)

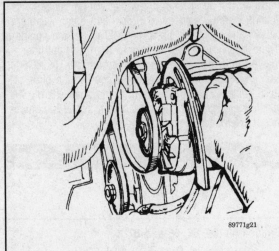

Fig. 70 Push the component toward the engine and slip off the belt

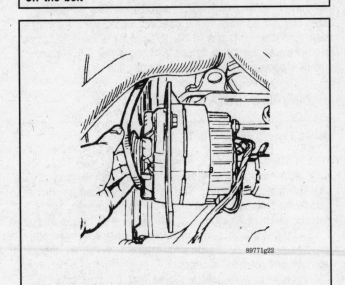

Fig. 71 Slip the new belt over the pulley

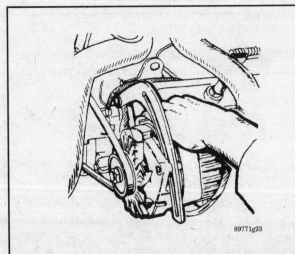

Fig. 72 Pull outward on the component and tighten the mounting bolts

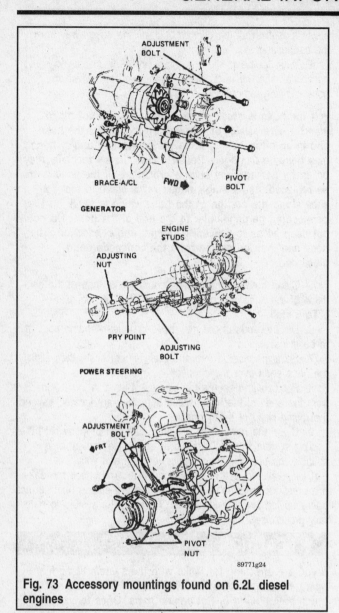

**Fig. 73 Accessory mountings found on 6.2L diesel engines**

tremely high impact load on the driven component due to the whipping action of the belt.

## Hoses

### INSPECTION

▶ **See Figures 74, 75, 76 and 77**

Upper and lower radiator hoses along with the heater hoses should be checked for deterioration, leaks and loose hose clamps at least every 15,000 miles (24,000 km). It is also wise to check the hoses periodically in early spring and at the beginning of the fall or winter when you are performing other maintenance. A quick visual inspection could discover a weakened hose which might have left you stranded if it had remained unrepaired.

Whenever you are checking the hoses, make sure the engine and cooling system are cold. Visually inspect for cracking, rotting or collapsed hoses, and replace as necessary. Run

your hand along the length of the hose. If a weak or swollen spot is noted when squeezing the hose wall, the hose should be replaced.

### REMOVAL & INSTALLATION

1. Remove the radiator pressure cap.

### ❊❊CAUTION

**Never remove the pressure cap while the engine is running, or personal injury from scalding hot coolant or steam may result. If possible, wait until the engine has cooled to remove the pressure cap. If this is not possible, wrap a thick cloth around the pressure cap and turn it slowly to the stop. Step back while the pressure is released from the cooling system. When you are sure all the pressure has been released, use the cloth to turn and remove the cap.**

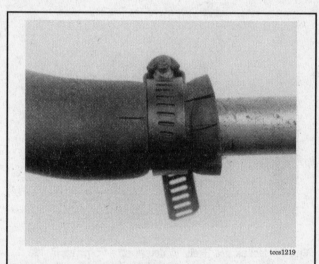

tccs1219

**Fig. 74 The cracks developing along this hose are a result of age-related hardening**

tccs1220

**Fig. 75 A hose clamp that is too tight can cause older hoses to separate and tear on either side of the clamp**

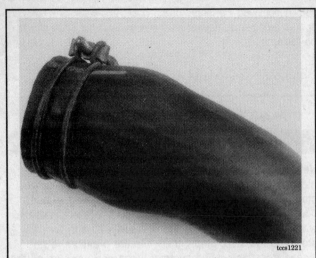

**Fig. 76 A soft spongy hose (identifiable by the swollen section) will eventually burst and should be replaced**

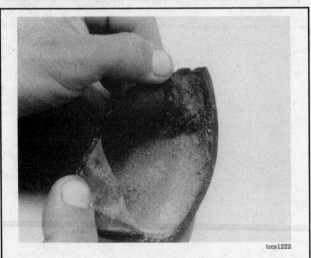

**Fig. 77 Hoses are likely to deteriorate from the inside if the cooling system is not periodically flushed**

2. Position a clean container under the radiator and/or engine draincock or plug, then open the drain and allow the cooling system to drain to an appropriate level. For some upper hoses, only a little coolant must be drained. To remove hoses positioned lower on the engine, such as a lower radiator hose, the entire cooling system must be emptied.

## ✳✳CAUTION

**When draining coolant, keep in mind that cats and dogs are attracted by ethylene glycol antifreeze, and are quite likely to drink any that is left in an uncovered container or in puddles on the ground. This will prove fatal in sufficient quantity. Always drain coolant into a sealable container. Coolant may be reused unless it is contaminated or several years old.**

3. Loosen the hose clamps at each end of the hose requiring replacement. Clamps are usually either of the spring tension type (which require pliers to squeeze the tabs and loosen) or of the screw tension type (which require screw or hex driv-

ers to loosen). Pull the clamps back on the hose away from the connection.

4. Twist, pull and slide the hose off the fitting, taking care not to damage the neck of the component from which the hose is being removed.

➡**If the hose is stuck at the connection, do not try to insert a screwdriver or other sharp tool under the hose end in an effort to free it, as the connection and/or hose may become damaged. Heater connections especially may be easily damaged by such a procedure. If the hose is to be replaced, use a single-edged razor blade to make a slice along the portion of the hose which is stuck on the connection, perpendicular to the end of the hose. Do not cut deep so as to prevent damaging the connection. The hose can then be peeled from the connection and discarded.**

5. Clean both hose mounting connections. Inspect the condition of the hose clamps and replace them, if necessary.

**To install:**

6. Dip the ends of the new hose into clean engine coolant to ease installation.

7. Slide the clamps over the replacement hose, then slide the hose ends over the connections into position.

8. Position and secure the clamps at least ¼ in. (6.35mm) from the ends of the hose. Make sure they are located beyond the raised bead of the connector.

9. Close the radiator or engine drains and properly refill the cooling system with the clean drained engine coolant or a suitable mixture of ethylene glycol coolant and water.

10. If available, install a pressure tester and check for leaks. If a pressure tester is not available, run the engine until normal operating temperature is reached (allowing the system to naturally pressurize), then check for leaks.

## ✳✳CAUTION

**If you are checking for leaks with the system at normal operating temperature, BE EXTREMELY CAREFUL not to touch any moving or hot engine parts. Once temperature has been reached, shut the engine OFF, and check for leaks around the hose fittings and connections which were removed earlier.**

## Air Conditioning

➡**Be sure to consult the laws in your area before servicing the air conditioning system. In most areas, it is illegal to perform repairs involving refrigerant unless the work is done by a certified technician. Also, it is quite likely that you will not be able to purchase refrigerant without proof of certification.**

### SAFETY PRECAUTIONS

There are two major hazards associated with air conditioning systems and they both relate to the refrigerant gas. First, the refrigerant gas (R-12) is an extremely cold substance. When exposed to air, it will instantly freeze any surface it comes in contact with, including your eyes. The other hazard relates to fire. Although normally non-toxic, the R-12 gas becomes highly poisonous in the presence of an open flame. One good whiff of the vapor formed by burning R-12 can be fatal. Keep all forms of fire (including cigarettes) well clear of the air conditioning system.

Because of the inherent dangers involved with working on air conditioning systems and R-12 refrigerant, these safety precautions must be strictly followed.

• Avoid contact with a charged refrigeration system, even when working on another part of the air conditioning system or vehicle. If a heavy tool comes into contact with a section of tubing or a heat exchanger, it can easily cause the relatively soft material to rupture.

• When it is necessary to apply force to a fitting which contains refrigerant, as when checking that all system couplings are securely tightened, use a wrench on both parts of the fitting involved, if possible. This will avoid putting torque on refrigerant tubing. (It is also advisable to use tube or line wrenches when tightening these flare nut fittings.)

➡**R-12 refrigerant is a chlorofluorocarbon which, when released into the atmosphere, can contribute to the depletion of the ozone layer in the upper atmosphere. Ozone filters out harmful radiation from the sun.**

• Do not attempt to discharge the system without the proper tools. Precise control is possible only when using the service gauges and a proper A/C refrigerant recovery station. Wear protective gloves when connecting or disconnecting service gauge hoses.

• Discharge the system only in a well ventilated area, as high concentrations of the gas which might accidentally escape can exclude oxygen and act as an anesthetic. When leak testing or soldering, this is particularly important, as toxic gas is formed when R-12 contacts any flame.

• Never start a system without first verifying that both service valves are properly installed, and that all fittings throughout the system are snugly connected.

• Avoid applying heat to any refrigerant line or storage vessel. Charging may be aided by using water heated to less than 125°F (50°C) to warm the refrigerant container. Never allow a refrigerant storage container to sit out in the sun, or near any other source of heat, such as a radiator or heater.

• Always wear goggles to protect your eyes when working on a system. If refrigerant contacts the eyes, it is advisable in all cases to consult a physician immediately.

• Frostbite from liquid refrigerant should be treated by first gradually warming the area with cool water, and then gently applying petroleum jelly. A physician should be consulted.

• Always keep refrigerant drum fittings capped when not in use. If the container is equipped with a safety cap to protect the valve, make sure the cap is in place when the can is not being used. Avoid sudden shock to the drum, which might occur from dropping it, or from banging a heavy tool against it. Never carry a drum in the passenger compartment of a vehicle.

• Always completely discharge the system into a suitable recovery unit before painting the vehicle (if the paint is to be baked on), or before welding anywhere near refrigerant lines.

• When servicing the system, minimize the time that any refrigerant line or fitting is open to the air in order to prevent moisture or dirt from entering the system. Contaminants such as moisture or dirt can damage internal system components. Always replace O-rings on lines or fittings which are disconnected. Prior to installation coat, but do not soak, replacement O-rings with suitable compressor oil.

## GENERAL SERVICING PROCEDURES

▶ **See Figures 78 and 79**

➡**It is recommended, and possibly required by law, that a qualified technician perform the following services.**

The most important aspect of air conditioning service is the maintenance of a pure and adequate charge of refrigerant in the system. A refrigeration system cannot function properly if a significant percentage of the charge is lost. Leaks are common because the severe vibration encountered underhood in an automobile can easily cause a sufficient cracking or loosening of the air conditioning fittings; allowing, the extreme operating pressures of the system to force refrigerant out.

The problem can be understood by considering what happens to the system as it is operated with a continuous leak. Because the expansion valve regulates the flow of refrigerant to the evaporator, the level of refrigerant there is fairly constant. The receiver/drier stores any excess refrigerant, and so a loss will first appear there as a reduction in the level of liquid. As this level nears the bottom of the vessel, some refrigerant vapor bubbles will begin to appear in the stream of liquid supplied to the expansion valve. This vapor decreases the capacity of the expansion valve very little as the valve opens to compensate for its presence. As the quantity of liquid in the condenser decreases, the operating pressure will drop there and throughout the high side of the system. As the R-12 continues to be expelled, the pressure available to force the liquid through the expansion valve will continue to decrease, and, eventually, the valve's orifice will prove to be too much of a restriction for adequate flow even with the needle fully withdrawn.

At this point, low side pressure will start to drop, and a severe reduction in cooling capacity, marked by freeze-up of the evaporator coil, will result. Eventually, the operating pressure of the evaporator will be lower than the pressure of the atmosphere surrounding it, and air will be drawn into the system wherever there are leaks in the low side.

Because all atmospheric air contains at least some moisture, water will enter the system and mix with the R-12 and the oil. Trace amounts of moisture will cause sludging of the oil, and corrosion of the system. Saturation and clogging of the filter/drier, and freezing of the expansion valve orifice will eventually result. As air fills the system to a greater and greater extent, it will interfere more and more with the normal flows of refrigerant and heat.

From this description, it should be obvious that much of the repairman's focus in on detecting leaks, repairing them, and then restoring the purity and quantity of the refrigerant charge. A list of general rules should be followed in addition to all safety precautions:

• Keep all tools as clean and dry as possible.

• Thoroughly purge the service gauges/hoses of air and moisture before connecting them to the system. Keep them capped when not in use.

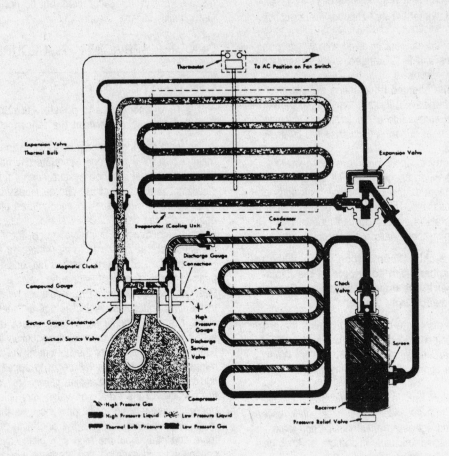

**Fig. 78 Schematic of an early air conditioning system's operation**

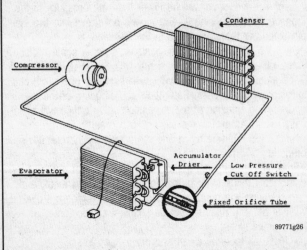

**Fig. 79 Schematic of the Cycling Clutch Orifice Tube (CCOT) system operation**

• Thoroughly clean any refrigerant fitting before disconnecting it, in order to minimize the entrance of dirt into the system.

• Plan any operation that requires opening the system beforehand, in order to minimize the length of time it will be exposed to open air. Cap or seal the open ends to minimize the entrance of foreign material.

• When adding oil, pour it through an extremely clean and dry tube or funnel. Keep the oil capped whenever possible. Do not use oil that has not been kept tightly sealed.

• Use only R-12 refrigerant. Purchase refrigerant intended for use only in automatic air conditioning systems.

• Completely evacuate any system that has been opened for service, or that has leaked sufficiently to draw in moisture and air. This requires evacuating air and moisture with a good vacuum pump for at least one hour. If a system has been open for a considerable length of time it may be advisable to evacuate the system for up to 12 hours (overnight).

• Use a wrench on both halves of a fitting that is to be disconnected, so as to avoid placing torque on any of the refrigerant lines.

• When overhauling a compressor, pour some of the oil into a clean glass and inspect it. If there is evidence of dirt, metal particles, or both, flush all refrigerant components with clean refrigerant before evacuating and recharging the system. In addition, if metal particles are present, the compressor should be replaced.

• Schrader valves may leak only when under full operating pressure. Therefore, if leakage is suspected but cannot be located, operate the system with a full charge of refrigerant and look for leaks from all Schrader valves. Replace any faulty valves.

### Additional Preventive Maintenance

#### USING THE SYSTEM

The easiest and most important preventive maintenance for your A/C system is to be sure that it is used on a regular basis. Running the system for five minutes each month (no matter what the season) will help assure that the seals and all internal components remain lubricated.

#### ANTIFREEZE

▶ See Figure 80

In order to prevent heater core freeze-up during A/C operation, it is necessary to maintain a proper antifreeze protection. Use a hand-held antifreeze tester (hydrometer) to periodically check the condition of the antifreeze in your engine's cooling system.

➡**Antifreeze should not be used longer than the manufacturer specifies.**

#### RADIATOR CAP

For efficient operation of an air conditioned vehicle's cooling system, the radiator cap should have a holding pressure which meets manufacturer's specifications. A cap which fails to hold these pressures should be replaced.

#### CONDENSER

Any obstruction of or damage to the condenser configuration will restrict the air flow which is essential to its efficient opera-

**Fig. 80 An antifreeze tester can be used to determine the freezing and boiling levels of the coolant**

tion. It is therefore a good rule to keep this unit clean and in proper physical shape.

➡**Bug screens which are mounted in front of the condenser (unless they are original equipment) are regarded as obstructions.**

#### CONDENSATION DRAIN TUBE

This single molded drain tube expels the condensation, which accumulates on the bottom of the evaporator housing, into the engine compartment. If this tube is obstructed, the air conditioning performance can be restricted and condensation buildup can spill over onto the vehicle's floor.

## SYSTEM INSPECTION

➡**R-12 refrigerant is a chlorofluorocarbon which, when released into the atmosphere, can contribute to the depletion of the ozone layer in the upper atmosphere. Ozone filters out harmful radiation from the sun.**

The easiest and often most important check for the air conditioning system consists of a visual inspection of the system components. Visually inspect the air conditioning system for refrigerant leaks, damaged compressor clutch, compressor drive belt tension and condition, plugged evaporator drain tube, blocked condenser fins, disconnected or broken wires, blown fuses, corroded connections and poor insulation.

A refrigerant leak will usually appear as an oily residue at the leakage point in the system. The oily residue soon picks up dust or dirt particles from the surrounding air and appears greasy. Through time, this will build up and appear to be a heavy dirt impregnated grease. Most leaks are caused by damaged or missing O-ring seals at the component connections, damaged charging valve cores or missing service gauge port caps.

For a thorough visual and operational inspection, check the following:

1. Check the surface of the radiator and condenser for dirt, leaves or other material which might block air flow.

2. Check for kinks in hoses and lines. Check the system for leaks.

3. Make sure the drive belt is under the proper tension. When the air conditioning is operating, make sure the drive belt is free of noise or slippage.

4. Make sure the blower motor operates at all appropriate positions, then check for distribution of the air from all outlets with the blower on **HIGH**.

➡**Keep in mind that under conditions of high humidity, air discharged from the A/C vents may not feel as cold as expected, even if the system is working properly. This is because the vaporized moisture in humid air retains heat more effectively than does dry air, making the humid air more difficult to cool.**

5. Make sure the air passage selection lever is operating correctly. Start the engine and warm it to normal operating temperature, then make sure the hot/cold selection lever is operating correctly.

## DISCHARGING, EVACUATING AND CHARGING

Discharging, evacuating and charging the air conditioning system must be performed by a properly trained and certified mechanic in a facility equipped with refrigerant recovery/recycling equipment that meets SAE standards for the type of system to be serviced.

If you don't have access to the necessary equipment, we recommend that you take your vehicle to a reputable service station to have the work done. If you still wish to perform repairs on the vehicle, have them discharge the system, then take your vehicle home and perform the necessary work. When you are finished, return the vehicle to the station for evacuation and charging. Just be sure to cap ALL A/C system fittings immediately after opening them and keep them protected until the system is recharged.

## Tires and Wheels

Common sense and good driving habits will afford maximum tire life. Fast starts, sudden stops and hard cornering are hard on tires and will shorten their useful life span. Make sure that you don't overload the vehicle or run with incorrect pressure in the tires. Both of these practices will increase tread wear.

➡**For optimum tire life, keep the tires properly inflated, rotate them often and have the wheel alignment checked periodically.**

Inspect your tires frequently. Be especially careful to watch for bubbles in the tread or sidewall, deep cuts or underinflation. Replace any tires with bubbles in the sidewall. If cuts are so deep that they penetrate to the cords, discard the tire. Any cut in the sidewall of a radial tire renders it unsafe. Also look for uneven tread wear patterns that may indicate the front end is out of alignment or that the tires are out of balance.

## TIRE ROTATION

▶ **See Figures 81 and 82**

Tires must be rotated periodically to equalize wear patterns that vary with a tire's position on the vehicle. Tires will also wear in an uneven way as the front steering/suspension system wears to the point where the alignment should be reset.

Rotating the tires will ensure maximum life for the tires as a set, so you will not have to discard a tire early due to wear on only part of the tread. Regular rotation is required to equalize wear.

When rotating "unidirectional tires," make sure that they always roll in the same direction. This means that a tire used on the left side of the vehicle must not be switched to the right side and vice-versa. Such tires should only be rotated front-to-rear or rear-to-front, while always remaining on the same side of the vehicle. These tires are marked on the sidewall as to the direction of rotation; observe the marks when reinstalling the tire(s).

Some styled or "mag" wheels may have different offsets front to rear. In these cases, the rear wheels must not be used up front and vice-versa. Furthermore, if these wheels are equipped with unidirectional tires, they cannot be rotated unless the tire is remounted for the proper direction of rotation.

➡**The compact or space-saver spare is strictly for emergency use. It must never be included in the tire rotation or placed on the vehicle for everyday use.**

## TIRE DESIGN

▶ **See Figure 83**

For maximum satisfaction, tires should be used in sets of four. Mixing of different types (radial, bias-belted, fiberglass belted) must be avoided. In most cases, the vehicle manufacturer has designated a type of tire on which the vehicle will perform best. Your first choice when replacing tires should be to use the same type of tire that the manufacturer recommends.

When radial tires are used, tire sizes and wheel diameters should be selected to maintain ground clearance and tire load capacity equivalent to the original specified tire. Radial tires should always be used in sets of four.

### ✳✳CAUTION

**Radial tires should never be used on only the front axle.**

When selecting tires, pay attention to the original size as marked on the tire. Most tires are described using an industry size code sometimes referred to as P-Metric. This allows the exact identification of the tire specifications, regardless of the manufacturer. If selecting a different tire size or brand, remember to check the installed tire for any sign of interference with the body or suspension while the vehicle is stopping, turning sharply or heavily loaded.

### Snow Tires

Good radial tires can produce a big advantage in slippery weather, but in snow, a street radial tire does not have sufficient tread to provide traction and control. The small grooves of a street tire quickly pack with snow and the tire behaves like a billiard ball on a marble floor. The more open, chunky tread of a snow tire will self-clean as the tire turns, providing much better grip on snowy surfaces.

To satisfy municipalities requiring snow tires during weather emergencies, most snow tires carry either an M + S designation after the tire size stamped on the sidewall, or the designation "all-season." In general, no change in tire size is necessary when buying snow tires.

Most manufacturers strongly recommend the use of 4 snow tires on their vehicles for reasons of stability. If snow tires are fitted only to the drive wheels, the opposite end of the vehicle may become very unstable when braking or turning on slippery surfaces. This instability can lead to unpleasant endings if the driver can't counteract the slide in time.

Note that snow tires, whether 2 or 4, will affect vehicle handling in all non-snow situations. The stiffer, heavier snow tires will noticeably change the turning and braking characteris-

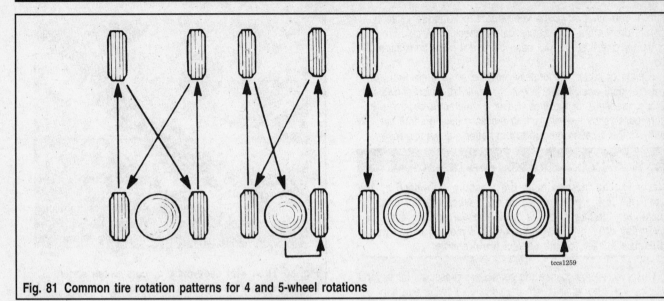

**Fig. 81 Common tire rotation patterns for 4 and 5-wheel rotations**

**Fig. 82 Unidirectional tires are identifiable by sidewall arrows and/or the word "rotation"**

METRIC TIRE SIZES

P 155    80 R 13
TIRE TYPE    RIM DIAM.
P- PASSENGER    ASPECT RATIO    (INCHES)
T- TEMPORARY    (SECTION HEIGHT)    12
C- COMMERCIAL    (SECTION WIDTH) × 100    13
    70    14
    75
    80

SECTION WIDTH
(MILLIMETERS)    CONSTRUCTION TYPE
145    R - RADIAL
155    B - BIAS-BELTED
ETC    D - DIAGONAL (BIAS)

SECTION
WIDTH

SECTION
HEIGHT

**Fig. 83 P-Metric tire coding**

tics of the vehicle. Once the snow tires are installed, you must re-learn the behavior of the vehicle and drive accordingly.

➡ **Consider buying extra wheels on which to mount the snow tires. Once done, the "snow wheels" can be installed and removed as needed. This eliminates the potential damage to tires or wheels from seasonal removal and installation. Even if your vehicle has styled wheels, see if inexpensive steel wheels are available. Although the look of the vehicle will change, the expensive wheels will be protected from salt, curb hits and pothole damage.**

## TIRE STORAGE

If they are mounted on wheels, store the tires at proper inflation pressure. All tires should be kept in a cool, dry place. If they are stored in the garage or basement, do not let them stand on a concrete floor; set them on strips of wood, a mat or a large stack of newspaper. Keeping them away from direct moisture is of paramount importance. Tires should not be stored upright, but in a flat position.

## INFLATION & INSPECTION

▶ **See Figures 84, 85, 86, 87, 88, 89, 90, 91 and 92**

The importance of proper tire inflation cannot be overemphasized. A tire employs air as part of its structure. It is designed around the supporting strength of the air at a specified pressure. For this reason, improper inflation drastically reduces the tires's ability to perform as intended. A tire will lose some air in day-to-day use; having to add a few pounds of air periodically is not necessarily a sign of a leaking tire.

Two items should be a permanent fixture in every glove compartment: an accurate tire pressure gauge and a tread depth gauge. Check the tire pressure (including the spare) regularly with a pocket type gauge. Too often, the gauge on the end of the air hose at your corner garage is not accurate because it suffers too much abuse. Always check tire pressure when the tires are cold, as pressure increases with temperature. If you must move the vehicle to check the tire inflation, do not drive more than a mile before checking. A cold tire is generally one that has not been driven for more than three hours.

A plate or sticker is normally provided somewhere in the vehicle (door post, hood, tailgate or trunk lid) which shows the proper pressure for the tires. Never counteract excessive pressure build-up by bleeding off air pressure (letting some air out). This will cause the tire to run hotter and wear quicker.

### ❈❈CAUTION

**Never exceed the maximum tire pressure embossed on the tire! This is the pressure to be used when the tire is at maximum loading, but it is rarely the correct pressure for everyday driving. Consult the owner's manual or the tire pressure sticker for the correct tire pressure.**

Once you've maintained the correct tire pressures for several weeks, you'll be familiar with the vehicle's braking and handling personality. Slight adjustments in tire pressures can fine-

**Fig. 86 Tires with deep cuts, or cuts which show bulging should be replaced immediately**

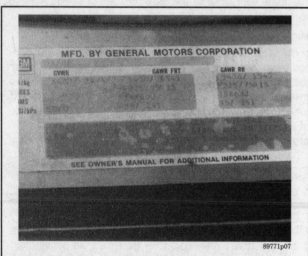

**Fig. 84 Proper tire pressures can usually be found listed on the door jamb**

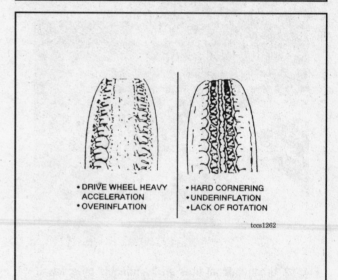

- DRIVE WHEEL HEAVY ACCELERATION
- OVERINFLATION

- HARD CORNERING
- UNDERINFLATION
- LACK OF ROTATION

**Fig. 87 Examples of inflation-related tire wear patterns**

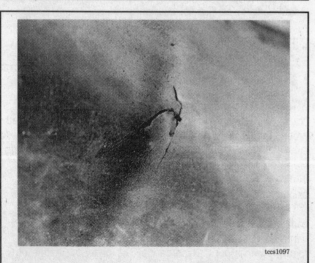

**Fig. 85 Tires should be checked frequently for any sign of puncture or damage**

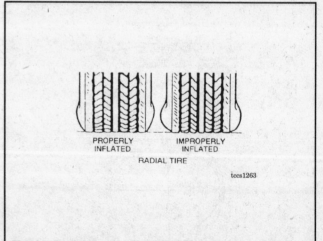

PROPERLY INFLATED    IMPROPERLY INFLATED

RADIAL TIRE

**Fig. 88 Radial tires have a characteristic sidewall bulge; don't try to measure pressure by looking at the tire. Use a quality air pressure gauge**

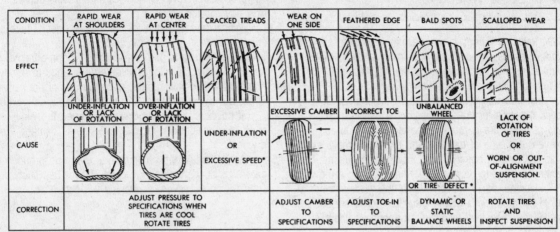

| CONDITION | RAPID WEAR AT SHOULDERS | RAPID WEAR AT CENTER | CRACKED TREADS | WEAR ON ONE SIDE | FEATHERED EDGE | BALD SPOTS | SCALLOPED WEAR |
|---|---|---|---|---|---|---|---|
| EFFECT | | | | | | | |
| CAUSE | UNDER-INFLATION OR LACK OF ROTATION | OVER-INFLATION OR LACK OF ROTATION | UNDER-INFLATION OR EXCESSIVE SPEED* | EXCESSIVE CAMBER | INCORRECT TOE | UNBALANCED WHEEL OR TIRE DEFECT * | LACK OF ROTATION OF TIRES OR WORN OR OUT-OF-ALIGNMENT SUSPENSION. |
| CORRECTION | | ADJUST PRESSURE TO SPECIFICATIONS WHEN TIRES ARE COOL ROTATE TIRES | | ADJUST CAMBER TO SPECIFICATIONS | ADJUST TOE-IN TO SPECIFICATIONS | DYNAMIC OR STATIC BALANCE WHEELS | ROTATE TIRES AND INSPECT SUSPENSION |

*HAVE TIRE INSPECTED FOR FURTHER USE.

**Fig. 89 Common tire wear patterns and causes**

tune these characteristics, but never change the cold pressure specification by more than 2 psi. A slightly softer tire pressure will give a softer ride but also yield lower fuel mileage. A slightly harder tire will give crisper dry road handling but can cause skidding on wet surfaces. Unless you're fully attuned to the vehicle, stick to the recommended inflation pressures.

All tires made since 1968 have built-in tread wear indicator bars that show up as ½ in. (13mm) wide smooth bands across the tire when 1/16 in. (1.5mm) of tread remains. The appearance of tread wear indicators means that the tires should be replaced. In fact, many states have laws prohibiting the use of tires with less than this amount of tread.

You can check your own tread depth with an inexpensive gauge or by using a Lincoln head penny. Slip the Lincoln penny (with Lincoln's head upside-down) into several tread grooves. If you can see the top of Lincoln's head in 2 adjacent grooves, the tire has less than 1/16 in. (1.5mm) tread left and should be replaced. You can measure snow tires in the same manner by using the "tails" side of the Lincoln penny. If you can see the top of the Lincoln memorial, it's time to replace the snow tire(s).

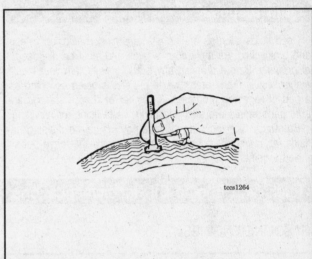

**Fig. 91 Accurate tread depth indicators are inexpensive and handy**

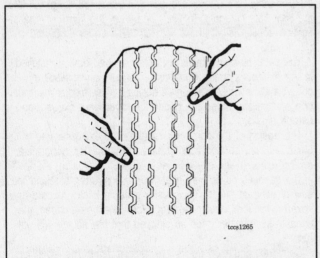

**Fig. 90 Tread wear indicators will appear when the tire is worn**

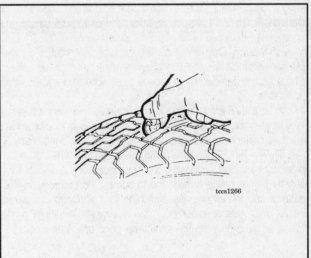

**Fig. 92 A penny works well for a quick check of tread depth**

## CARE OF SPECIAL WHEELS

If you have invested money in magnesium, aluminum alloy or sport wheels, special precautions should be taken to make sure your investment is not wasted and that your special wheels look good for the life of the vehicle.

Special wheels are easily damaged and/or scratched. Occasionally check the rims for cracking, impact damage or air leaks. If any of these are found, replace the wheel. But in order to prevent this type of damage and the costly replacement of a special wheel, observe the following precautions:

• Use extra care not to damage the wheels during removal, installation, balancing, etc. After removal of the wheels from the vehicle, place them on a mat or other protective surface. If they are to be stored for any length of time, support them on strips of wood. Never store tires and wheels upright; the tread may develop flat spots.

• When driving, watch for hazards; it doesn't take much to crack a wheel.

• When washing, use a mild soap or non-abrasive dish detergent (keeping in mind that detergent tends to remove wax). Avoid cleansers with abrasives or the use of hard brushes. There are many cleaners and polishes for special wheels.

• If possible, remove the wheels during the winter. Salt and sand used for snow removal can severely damage the finish of a wheel.

• Make certain the recommended lug nut torque is never exceeded or the wheel may crack. Never use snow chains on special wheels; severe scratching will occur.

## FLUIDS AND LUBRICANTS

### Fluid Disposal

Used fluids such as engine oil, transmission fluid, antifreeze and brake fluid are hazardous wastes and must be disposed of properly. Before draining any fluids, consult with your local authorities; in many areas waste oil, etc. is being accepted as a part of recycling programs. A number of service stations and auto parts stores are also accepting waste fluids for recycling.

Be sure of the recycling center's policies before draining any fluids, as many will not accept different fluids that have been mixed together.

### Fuels and Engine Oil Recommendations

#### GASOLINE ENGINES

##### All 1967-74 Models; 1975 and Later Models Without Catalytic Converter

Chevrolet and GMC trucks are designed to operate on regular grades of fuel (1967-71) commonly sold in the U.S. and Canada. In 1972-74 (and 1975 later models without catalytic converter), unleaded or low-lead fuels of approximately 91 octane (Research Octane) or higher are recommended. General Motors recommends the use of low-leaded or unleaded fuels (0-0.5 grams per gallon) to reduce particulate and hydrocarbon pollutants.

Use of a fuel which is too low in anti-knock quality will result in spark knock. Since many factors affect operating efficiency, such as altitude, terrain and air temperature, knocking many result even though you are using the recommended fuel. If persistent knocking occurs, it may be necessary to switch to a slightly higher grade of gasoline to correct the problem. In the case of late model engines, switching to a premium fuel would be an unnecessary expense. In these engines, a slightly higher grade of gasoline (regular) should be used only when persistent knocking occurs. Continuous or excessive knocking may result in engine damage.

➡Your engine's fuel requirement can change time, mainly due to carbon buildup, which changes the compression ratio. If you engine pings, knocks, or runs on, switch to a higher grade of fuel and check the ignition timing as soon as possible. If you must use unleaded fuel, sometimes a change of brands will cure the problem. If is is necessary to retard the timing from specifications, don't change it more than about 4°. Retarded timing will reduce power output and fuel mileage, and it will increase engine temperature.

##### 1975 and Later Models With Catalytic Converter

Chevrolet and GMC trucks with Gross Vehicle Weight Ratings (GVWR) which place them in the heavy duty emissions class do not require a catalytic converter. However, almost all 1975 and later light duty emissions trucks have a catalytic converter. The light duty classification applies to all trucks with a GVWR under 6,000 lbs. (2724 kg) through 1978, except for 1978 trucks sold in California. 1978 California models and all 1979 models with GVWR's under 8,500 lbs. (3859 kg) fall into the light duty category. In 1980 and later, the light duty classification applies to all trucks with GVWR's under 8,600 lbs. (3904 kg).

The catalytic converter is a muffler shaped device installed in the exhaust system. It contains platinum and palladium coated pellets which, through catalytic action, oxidize hydrocarbon and carbon monoxide gases into hydrogen, oxygen, and carbon dioxide.

The design of the converter requires the exclusive use of unleaded fuel. Leaded fuel renders the converter inoperative, raising exhaust emissions to legal levels. In addition, the lead in the gasoline coats the pellets in the converter, blocking the flow of exhaust gases. This raises exhaust back pressure and severely reduces engine performance. In extreme cases, the exhaust system becomes so clocked that the engine will not run.

Converter equipped trucks are delivered with the label "Unleaded Fuel Only" placed next to the fuel gauge on the instrument panel and next to the gas tank filler opening. In general, any unleaded fuel is suitable for use in these trucks as long as the gas has an octane rating or 87 or more. Octane ratings are posted on the gas pumps. However, in some cases, knocking may occur even though the recommended fuel is being used. The only practical solution for this is to switch to a slightly higher grade of unleaded fuel, or to switch brands of unleaded gasoline.

## DIESEL ENGINES

Diesel engine pick-ups require the use of diesel fuel. Two grades of diesel fuel are manufactured, #1 and #2, although #2 grade is generally the only grade available. Better fuel economy results from the use of #2 grade fuel. In some northern parts of the U.S., and in most parts of Canada, #1 grade fuel is available in winter, or a winterized blend of #2 grade is supplied in winter months. If #1 grade is available, it should be used whenever temperatures fall below +20°F (7°C). Winterized #2 grade may also be used at these temperatures. However, unwinterized #2 grade should not be used below +20°F (7°C). Cold temperatures cause unwinterized #2 grade to thicken (it actually gels), blocking the fuel lines and preventing the engine from running.

Do not use home heating oil or gasoline in the diesel pickup. Do not attempt to thin unwinterized #2 diesel fuel with gasoline. Gasoline line or home heating oil will damage the engine and void the manufacturer's warranty.

## Engine

### OIL RECOMMENDATIONS

▶ See Figures 93 and 94

The SAE grade number indicates the viscosity of the engine oil, or its ability to lubricate under a given temperature. The lower the SAE grade number, the lighter the oil; the lower the viscosity, the easier it is to crank the engine in cold weather.

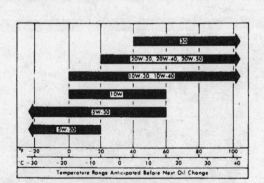

NOTES: 1. SAE 5W and 5W-20 are not recommended for sustained high speed driving.
2. SAE 5W-30 is recommended for all seasons in Canada

89771g27

**Fig. 93 Gasoline engine recommended oil viscosities**

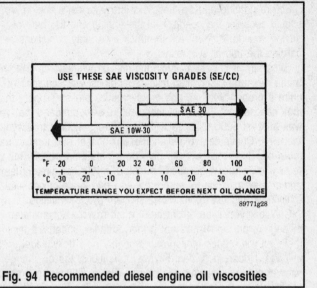

89771g28

**Fig. 94 Recommended diesel engine oil viscosities**

The API (American Petroleum Institute) designation indicates the classification of engine oil for use under given operating conditions. Only oils designated for "Service SF" should be used. These oils provide maximum engine protection. Both the SAE grade number and the API designation can be found on the top of a can of oil.

➡**Non-detergent should not be used.**

Oil viscosities should be chosen from those oils recommended for the lowest anticipated temperatures during the oil change interval.

The multi-viscosity oils offer the important advantage of being adaptable to temperature extremes. They allow easy starting at low temperatures, yet give good protection at high speeds and engine temperatures. This is a decided advantage in changeable climates or in long distance driving.

Diesel engines also require SF engine oil. In addition, the oil must qualify for a CC rating. The API has a number of different diesel engine ratings, including CB, CC, and CD.

➡**1981 and later diesel engines can use either SF/CC or SF/CD rated oils.**

The diesel engines in the Chevrolet and GMC trucks require SF/CC rated oil. DO NOT use an oil if the designation CD appears anywhere on the oil can. Use SF/CC engine oil only. Do not use an oil labeled only SF or only CC. Both designations must appear.

For recommended oil viscosities, refer to the chart. 10W-30 grade oils are not recommended for sustained high speed driving.

Single viscosity oil (SAE 30) is recommended for sustained high speed driving.

### SYNTHETIC OIL

There are excellent synthetic and fuel-efficient oils available that, under the right circumstances, can help provide better fuel mileage and better engine protection. However, these advantages come at a price, which can be three or four times the price per quart of conventional motor oils.

Before pouring any synthetic oils into your car's engine, you should consider the condition of the engine and the type of driving you do. Also, check the truck's warranty conditions regarding the use of synthetics.

Generally, it is best to avoid the use of synthetic oil in both brand new and older, high mileage engines. New engines require a proper break-in, and the synthetics are so slippery that they can prevent this. Most manufacturers recommend that you wait at least 5000 miles (8045 km) before switching to a synthetic oil. Conversely, older engines are looser and tend to use more oil. Synthetics will slip past worn pats more readily than regular oil, and will be used up faster. If your car already leaks and/or uses oil (due to worn parts and bad seals or gaskets), it will leak and use more with a slippery synthetic inside.

Consider your type of driving. If most of your accumulated mileage is on the highway at higher, steadier speeds, a synthetic oil will reduce friction and probably help deliver fuel mileage. Under such ideal highway conditions, the oil change interval can be extended, as long as the oil filter will operate effectively for the extended life of the oil. If the filter can't do its job for this extended period, dirt and sludge will build up in your engine's crankcase, sump, oil pump and lines, no matter what type of oil is used. If using synthetic oil in this manner, you should continue to change the oil filter at the recommended intervals.

Trucks used under harder, stop-and-go, short hop circumstances should always be serviced more frequently, and for these cars synthetic oil may not be a wise investment. Because of the necessary shorter change interval needed for this type of driving, you cannot take advantage of the long recommended change interval of most synthetic oils.

## Engine

### OIL LEVEL CHECK

▶ **See Figures 95, 96 and 97**

The engine oil should be checked on a regular basis, ideally at each fuel stop. If the van is used for trailer towing or for heavy duty use, it would be safer to check it more often.

When checking the oil level it is best that the oil be at operating temperature, although checking the level immediately after stopping will give a false reading because all of the oil will not yet have drained back into the crankcase. Be sure that the van is resting on a level surface, allowing time for the oil to drain back into the crankcase.

1. Open the hood or engine compartment and locate the dipstick. Remove it from the tube. The oil dipstick is located on the passenger's side of 6 cylinder engines and on the driver's side of V8s.

2. Wipe the dipstick with a clean rag.

3. Insert the dipstick fully into the tube, and remove it again. Hold the dipstick horizontally and read the oil level. The level should be between the "FULL" and "ADD OIL" marks. If the oil level is at or below the "ADD OIL" mark, oil should be added as necessary. Oil is added through the capped opening on the valve cover(s). See Oil and Fuel Recommendations for proper viscosity and oil to use.

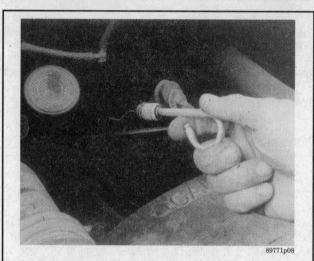

Fig. 95 Remove the engine oil dipstick and check the oil level

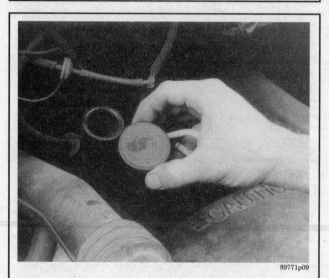

Fig. 96 If necessary, remove the oil filler cap . . .

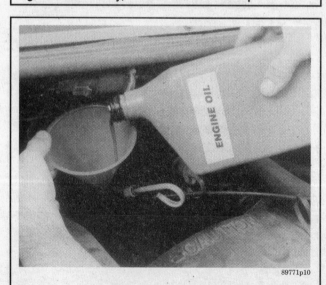

Fig. 97 . . . and add the proper amount and grade of oil

4. Replace the dipstick and check the level after adding oil. Be careful not to overfill the crankcase. There is about 1 quart between the marks.

## OIL & FILTER CHANGE

▶ **See Figures 98 and 99**

Engine oil should be changed according to the schedule in the Maintenance Interval Chart. Under conditions such as:
- Driving in dusty conditions
- Continuous trailer pulling or RV use
- Extensive or prolonged idling
- Extensive short trip operation in freezing temperatures (when the engine is not thoroughly warmed up)
- Frequent long runs at high speeds and high ambient temperatures
- Stop-and-go service such as delivery trucks

the oil change interval and filter replacement interval should be cut in half. Operation of the engine in severe conditions

**Fig. 98 Look for the API oil identification label when choosing your engine oil**

**Fig. 99 Before installing a new oil filter, lightly coat the rubber gasket with clean oil**

such as a dust storm may require an immediate oil and filter change.

Chevrolet and GMC recommended changing both the oil and filter during the first oil change and the filter every other oil change thereafter. For the small price of an oil filter, it's cheap insurance to replace the filter at every oil change. One of the larger filter manufacturers points out in its advertisements that not changing the filter leaves one quart of dirty oil in the engine. This claim is true and should be kept in mind when changing your oil.

➡**The oil filter on the diesel engines must be changed every oil change.**

To change the oil, the truck should be on a level surface, and the engine should be at operating temperature. This is to ensure that the foreign matter will be drained away along with the oil, and not left in the engine to form sludge. You should have available a container that will hold a minimum of 8 quarts of liquid, a wrench to fit the old drain plug, a spout for pouring in new oil, and a rag or two, which you will always need. If the filter is being replaced, you will also need a band wrench or filter wrench to fit the end of the filter.

➡**If the engine is equipped with an oil cooler, this will also have to be drained, using the drain plug. Be sure to add enough oil to fill the cooler in addition to the engine.**

1. Position the truck on a level surface and set the parking brake or block the wheels. Slide a drain pan under the oil drain plug.
2. From under the truck, loosen, but do not remove the oil drain plug. Cover your hand with a rag or glove and slowly unscrew the drain plug.

### ✳✳CAUTION

**The engine oil will be HOT. Keep your arms, face and hands clear of the oil as it drains out.**

3. Remove the plug and let the oil drain into the pan.

➡**Do not drop the plug into the drain pan.**

4. When all of the oil has drained, clean off the drain plug and put it back into the hole. Remember to tighten the plug 20 ft. lbs. (27 Nm) on gasoline engines or 30 ft. lbs. (40 Nm) for diesel engines.
5. Loosen the filter with a band wrench or special oil filter cap wrench. On most Chevrolet engines, especially the V8s, the oil filter is next to the exhaust pipes. Stay clear of these, since even a passing contact will result in a painful burn.

➡**On trucks equipped with catalytic converters stay clear of the converter. The outside temperature of a hot catalytic converter can approach 1,200°F (648°C).**

6. Cover your hand with a rag, and spin the filter off by hand.
7. Coat the rubber gasket on a new filter with a light film of clean engine oil. Screw the filter onto the mounting stud and tighten according to the directions on the filter (usually hand tight one turn past the point where the gasket contacts the mounting base). Don't overtighten the filter.
8. Refill the engine with the specified amount of clean engine oil.

9. Run the engine for several minutes, checking for leaks. Check the level of the oil and add oil if necessary.

When you have finished this job, you will notice that you now possess four or five quarts of dirty oil. The best thing to do with it is to pour it into plastic jugs, such as milk or antifreeze containers. Then, if you are on good terms with you gas station man, he might let you pour it into his used oil container for recycling. Otherwise, the only thing to do with it is to put the containers into the trash.

## Manual Transmission

### FLUID RECOMMENDATION

Where ambient temperatures are consistently above freezing, use SAE 80W-90 GL-5. For vehicles normally operated in cold climates, use SAE 80W GL-5 gear lubricant.

### FLUID LEVEL CHECK

Check the lubricant level at the interval specified in the maintenance chart.

1. With the truck parked on a level surface, remove the filler plug from the side of the transmission case. Be careful not to take out the drain plug at the bottom.

2. If lubricant begins to trickle out of the hole, there is enough. If not, carefully insert a finger (watch out for sharp threads) and check that the level is up to the edge of the hole.

3. If not, add sufficient lubricant with a funnel and tube, or a squeeze bulb to bring it to the proper level.

4. Replace the plug and check for leaks.

### DRAIN AND REFILL

No intervals are specified for changing the transmission lubricant, but it is a good idea on a used vehicle, one that has been worked hard, or one driven in deep water. The vehicle should be on a level surface and the lubricant should be at operating temperature.

1. Position the truck on a level surface.

2. Place a pan of sufficient capacity under the transmission drain plug.

3. Remove the upper (fill) plug to provide a vent opening.

4. Remove the lower (drain) plug and let the lubricant drain out. The 1976-82 Tremec top cover 3-speed is drained by removing the lower extension housing bolt.

5. Replace the drain plug.

6. Add lubricant with a suction gun or squeeze bulb.

7. Reinstall the filler plug. Run the engine and check for leaks.

## Automatic Transmission

### FLUID RECOMMENDATIONS

Use only high quality automatic transmission fluids that are identified by the name DEXRON®II or its superceding fluid type.

### LEVEL CHECK

▶ **See Figure 100**

Check the level of the fluid at the specified interval. The fluid level should be checked with the engine at normal operating temperature and running. If the truck has been running at high speed for a long period, in city traffic on a hot day, or pulling a trailer, let it cool down for about thirty minutes before checking the level.

1. Park on the level with the engine running and the shift lever in Park.

2. Remove the dipstick at the rear of the engine compartment. Cautiously feel the end of the dipstick with your fingers. Wipe it off and replace it, then pull it again and check the level of the fluid on the dipstick.

3. If the fluid felt cool, the level should be between the two dimples below ADD. If it was too hot to hold, the level should be between the ADD and FULL marks.

4. If the fluid is at or below the ADD mark, add fluid through the dipstick tube. One pint raises the level from ADD to FULL when the fluid is hot. The correct fluid to use is DEXRON®II. Be certain that the transmission is not overfilled, this will cause foaming, fluid loss, and slippage.

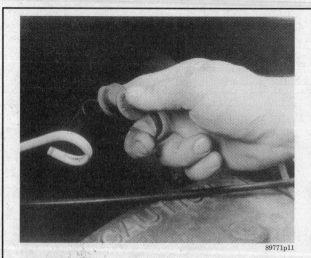

89771p11

**Fig. 100 Remove the automatic transmission dipstick to check the fluid level**

## PAN AND FILTER SERVICE

▶ **See Figures 101, 102, 103, 104, 105 and 106**

The fluid should be drained with the transmission warm. It is easier to change the fluid if the truck is raised somewhat from the ground, but this is not always easy without a lift. The transmission must be level for it to drain properly.

1. Place a shallow pan underneath to catch the transmission fluid (about 5 pints). On earlier models, the transmission pan has a drain plug. Remove this and drain the fluid. For later models, loosen all the pan bolts, then pull one corner down to drain most of the fluid. If it sticks, VERY CAREFULLY pry the pan loose. You can buy aftermarket drain plug kits that makes this operation a bit less messy, once installed.

➡ **If the fluid removed smells burnt, serious transmission troubles, probably due to overheating, should be suspected.**

Fig. 103 Unfasten the transmission filter retaining screws . . .

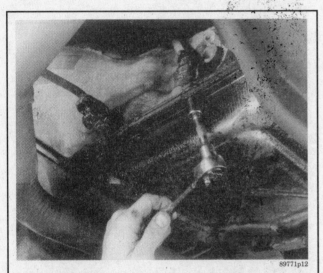

Fig. 101 Remove the transmission pan retaining screws

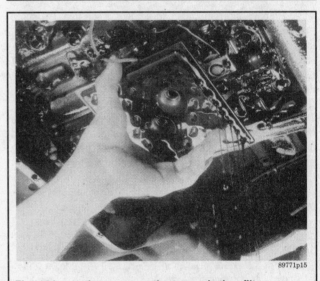

Fig. 104 . . . then remove the transmission filter

Fig. 102 Allow the fluid to drain, then lower the pan

Fig. 105 Be sure the old filter gasket is not stuck on the valve body

**Fig. 106 Remove the old pan gasket; always replace it with a new one**

2. Remove the pan bolts and empty out the pan. On some models, there may not be much room to get at the screws at the front of the pan.

3. Clean the pan with solvent and allow it to air dry. If you use a rag to wipe it out, you risk leaving bits of lint and threads in the transmission.

4. Remove the filter or strainer retaining bolts. On the Turbo Hydra-Matic 400, there are two screws securing the filter or screen to the valve body. A reusable strainer may be found on some models. The strainer may be cleaned in solvent and air dried thoroughly. The filter and gasket must be replaced.

5. Install a new gasket and filter.

6. Install a new gasket on the pan, and tighten the bolts evenly to 12 ft lbs. (16 Nm) in a criss-cross pattern.

7. Add DEXRON®II (or its superceding fluid type) transmission fluid through the dipstick tube. The correct amount is in the Capacities Chart. Do not overfill.

8. With the gearshift lever in PARK, start the engine and let it idle. Do not race the engine.

9. Move the gearshift lever through each position, holding the brakes. Return the lever to PARK, and check the fluid level with the engine idling. The level should be between the two dimples on the dipstick, about ¼ in. (6mm) below the ADD mark. Add fluid, if necessary.

10. Check the fluid level after the truck has been driven enough to thoroughly warm up the transmission. Details are given under Fluid Level Checks earlier in the section. If the transmission is overfilled, the excess must be drained off. Overfilling causes aerated fluid, resulting in transmission slippage and probable damage.

## Rear Axle Differential

### FLUID RECOMMENDATION

Rear axles use SAE 80W-90 GL-5 gear oil. Positraction® axles must use special lubricant available from dealers. If the special fluid is not used, noise, uneven operation, and damage will result. There is also a Positraction® additive used to cure

noise and slippage. Positraction axles have an identifying tag, as well as a warning sticker near the jack or on the rear wheel well.

## FLUID LEVEL CHECK

▶ **See Figures 107, 108 and 109**

Lubricant levels in the rear axle should be checked as specified in the Maintenance chart. To check the lubricant level:

1. Park on level ground.

2. Remove the filler plug from the differential housing cover.

3. If lubricant trickles out, there is enough. If not, carefully insert a finger and check that the level is up to the bottom of the hole. Front axles should be full up to the level of the hole when warm, and ½ in. (12.7mm) below when cool.

Lubricant may be added with a funnel or a squeeze bulb. Rear axles use SAE 80W-90 GL-5 gear lubricant.

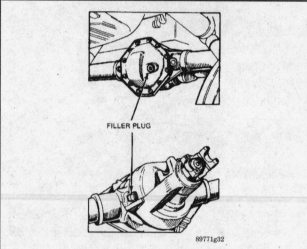

**Fig. 107 The rear axle filler plug may be in either of the two locations shown here**

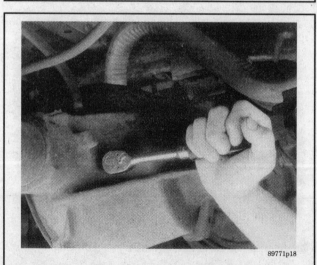

**Fig. 108 Remove the filler plug from the housing with a ratchet**

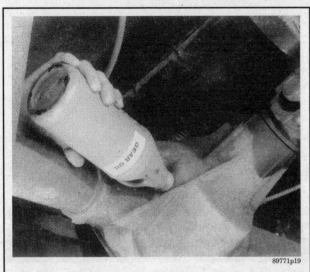

**Fig. 109 If needed, add the fluid through the filler hole**

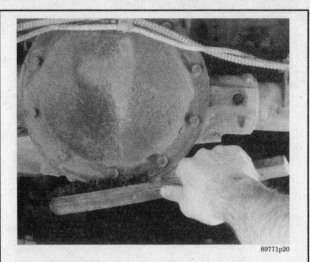

**Fig. 110 Use a wire brush to clean the dirt and rust from the differential cover**

Positraction® limited slip axles must use a special lubricant available from dealers. If the special fluid is not used, noise, uneven operation, and damage will result. There is also a Positraction® additive to cure noise and slippage. Positraction® axles have an identifying tag, as well as a warning sticker near the jack or on the rear wheel well.

## DRAIN AND REFILL

▶ **See Figures 110, 111, 112, 113 and 114**

No intervals are specified for changing axle lubricant, but it is a good idea, especially if you have driven in water over the axle vents.

1. Park the vehicle on the level with the axles at normal operating temperature.
2. Place a pan of at least 6 pints capacity under the differential housing.
3. Remove the filler plug.
4. If you have a drain plug, remove it. If not, unbolt and remove the differential cover.
5. Replace the drain plug, or differential cover. Use a new gasket if the differential cover has been removed.
6. Lubricant may be added with a suction gun or squeeze bulb. Rear axles use SAE 80W-90 gear oil. Positraction® axles must use special lubricant available from dealers. If the special fluid is not used, noise, uneven operation, and damage will result. There is also a Positraction® additive used to cure noise and slippage. Positraction axles have an identifying tag, as well as a warning sticker near the jack or on the rear wheel well. Rear axle lubricant level should be up to the bottom of the filler plug opening.

## Cooling System

The coolant level should be checked at each fuel stop, ideally, to prevent the possibility of overheating and serious engine damage. If not, it should at least be checked once each month.

The cooling system was filled at the factory with a high quality coolant solution that is good for year around operation

**Fig. 111 Unfasten the bolts from the cover**

**Fig. 112 Using a prytool, carefully separate the cover from the case to drain the fluid**

**Fig. 113 After the fluid drains, remove the cover from the case**

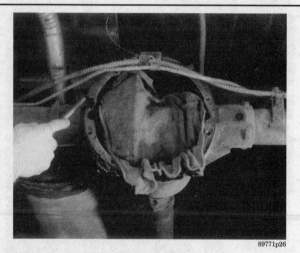

**Fig. 114 Cover the differential gears with a rag before cleaning the old gasket from the case**

and protects the system from freezing down to 20°F (29°C) (32°F/36°C in Canada). It is good for two full calendar years or 24,000 miles (38,000 km), whichever occurs first, provided that the proper concentration of coolant is maintained.

The 1973 and later cooling system differs slightly from those used on 1967-72 trucks. The 1973 and later system incorporates a plastic expansion tank connected to the radiator by a hose from the base of the radiator filler neck. The hot coolant level on 1973 and later trucks should be at the FULL HOT mark on the expansion tank and the cold coolant level should be at the FULL COLD mark on the tank. Do not remove the radiator cap to check the coolant level on 1973 and later trucks. On 1967-72 trucks, the cold coolant level should be approximately 3 in. (76mm) below the bottom of the filler neck, and the hot level should be 1-1½ in. (25.4-38.1mm) below the bottom of the filler neck.

## FLUID RECOMMENDATION

Recommended coolant mixture in these models is a 50/50 ethylene glycol and water mix for year round use. Use a good quality antifreeze with water pump lubricants, rust inhibitors and other corrosion inhibitors along with acid neutralizers.

## LEVEL CHECK

▶ **See Figures 115, 116, 117 and 118**

1. On 1973 and later models, check the level on the see-through expansion tank. On earlier models it will be necessary to CAREFULLY remove the radiator cap.

### ✳✳CAUTION

**The radiator coolant is under pressure when hot. To avoid the danger of physical harm, coolant level should be checked or replenished only when the engine is cold. To remove the radiator cap when the engine is hot, first cover the cap with a thick rag, or wear a heavy glove for protection. Press down on the cap slightly and slowly turn it counterclockwise until it reaches the first stop. Allow all the pressure to vent (indicated when the hissing sound stops). When the pressure is released, press down on the cap and continue to rotate it counterclockwise. Some radiator caps have a lever for venting the pressure, but you should still exercise extreme caution when removing the cap.**

2. Check the level and, if necessary, add coolant to the proper level. Use a 50/50 mix of ethylene glycol antifreeze and water. Alcohol or methanol base coolants are not recommended. Antifreeze solutions should be used, even in summer, to prevent rust and to take advantage of the solution's higher boiling point compared to plain water. This is imperative on air conditioned trucks; the heater core can freeze if it isn't pro-

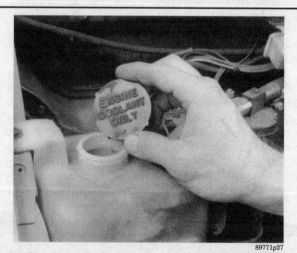

**Fig. 115 If equipped, remove the expansion tank cap . .**

**Fig. 116 . . . then add the proper mixture of fluid to bring it to the proper level**

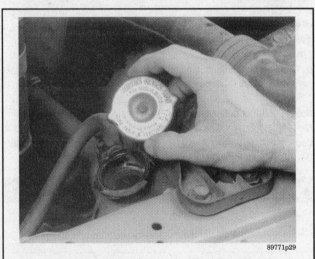

**Fig. 117 If not equipped with an expansion tank, remove the radiator cap . . .**

**Fig. 118 . . . then add the proper mixture of fluid to bring it to the proper level**

tected. On 1974 and later models, coolant should be added through the coolant recovery tank, not the radiator filler neck.

**✳✳WARNING**

**Never add large quantities of cold coolant to a hot engine. A cracked engine block may result.**

3. Replace the plug.

Each year the cooling system should be serviced as follows:

- Wash the radiator cap and filler neck with clean water.
- Check the coolant for proper level and freeze protection.
- Have the system pressure tested, it should hold 15 psi (103 kPa) of vacuum. If a replacement cap is installed, be sure that it conforms to the original specifications.
- Tighten the hose clamps and inspect all hoses. Replace hoses that are swollen, cracked or otherwise deteriorated.
- Clean the frontal area of the radiator core and the air conditioning condenser, if so equipped.

## DRAINING, FLUSHING AND TESTING THE SYSTEM

▶ **See Figures 119, 120, 121 and 122**

The cooling system in you car accumulates some internal rust and corrosion in its normal operation. A simple method of keeping the system clean is known as flushing the system. It is performed by circulating a can of radiator flush through the system, and then draining and refilling the system with the normal coolant. Radiator flush is marketed by several different manufacturers, and is available in cans at auto departments, parts stores, and many hardware stores. This operation should be performed every 30,000 miles (48,000 km) or once a year.

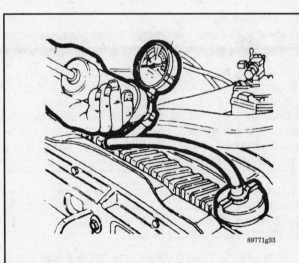

**Fig. 119 The system should be pressure tested once a year**

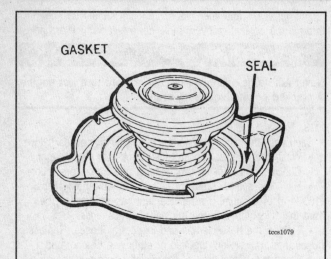

**Fig. 120 Be sure the rubber gasket on the radiator cap has a tight seal**

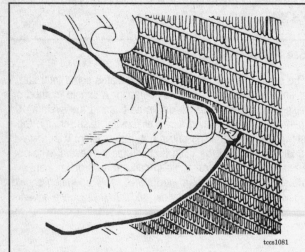

**Fig. 121 Periodically remove all debris from the radiator fins**

To flush the cooling system:

### ❊❊CAUTION

**When draining the coolant, keep in mind that cats and dogs are attracted by ethylene glycol antifreeze, and are quite likely to drink any that is left in an uncovered container or in puddles on the ground. This will prove fatal in sufficient quantity. Always drain the coolant into a sealable container. Coolant should be reused unless it is contaminated or several years old.**

1. Drain the existing antifreeze and coolant. Open the radiator and engine drain petcocks (located near the bottom of the radiator and engine block, respectively), or disconnect the bottom radiator hose at the radiator outlet.

➡Before opening the radiator petcock, spray it with some penetrating oil. Be aware that if the engine has been run up to operating temperature, the coolant emptied will be HOT.

2. Close the petcock or reconnect the lower hose and fill the system with hot water if the system has just been run.

3. Add a can of quality radiator flush to the radiator or recovery tank, following any special instructions on the can.

4. Idle the engine as long as specified on the can of flush, or until the upper radiator hose gets hot.

5. Drain the system again. There should be quite a bit of scale and rust in the drained water.

6. Repeat this process until the drained water is mostly clear.

7. Close all petcocks and connect all hoses.

8. Flush the coolant recovery reservoir with water and leave empty.

9. Determine the capacity of your car's cooling system (see Capacities specifications in this guide. Add a 50/50 mix of ethylene glycol antifreeze and water to provide the desired protection.

10. Run the engine to operating temperature, then stop the engine and check for leaks. Check the coolant level and top up if necessary.

11. Check the protection level of your antifreeze mix with an antifreeze tester (a small, inexpensive syringe type device available at any auto parts store). The tester has five or six small colored balls inside, each of which signify a certain temperature rating. Insert the tester in the recovery tank and suck just enough coolant into the syringe to float as many individual balls as you can (without sucking in too much coolant and floating all the balls at once). A table supplied with the tester will explain how many floating balls equal protection down to a certain temperature (three floating balls might mean the coolant will protect your engine down to +5°F (-15°C), for example.

## Master Cylinder

### FLUID RECOMMENDATIONS

Only high quality brake fluids, such as General Motors Supreme No. 11 Hydraulic Brake Fluid, Delco Supreme No. 11 Hydraulic Brake Fluid or fluids meeting DOT-3 specifications should be used.

### LEVEL CHECK

▶ **See Figures 123, 124 and 125**

Beginning in 1967, Chevrolet and GMC vans were equipped with a dual braking system, allowing a vehicle to be brought to a safe stop in the event of failure in either front or rear brakes. The dual master cylinder has 2 entirely separate reservoirs, one connected to the front brakes and the other connected to the rear brakes. In the event of failure in either portion, the remaining part is not affected.

On 1967-69, the master cylinder is located beneath an access in front of the driver's seat. On 1971 and later models, it is mounted to the left side of the firewall. On 1973-75 G-30 and G-3500 models with the Hydro-Boost power brake system, it is mounted transversely near the center of the firewall.

1. Clean all of the dirt from around the cover of the master cylinder.

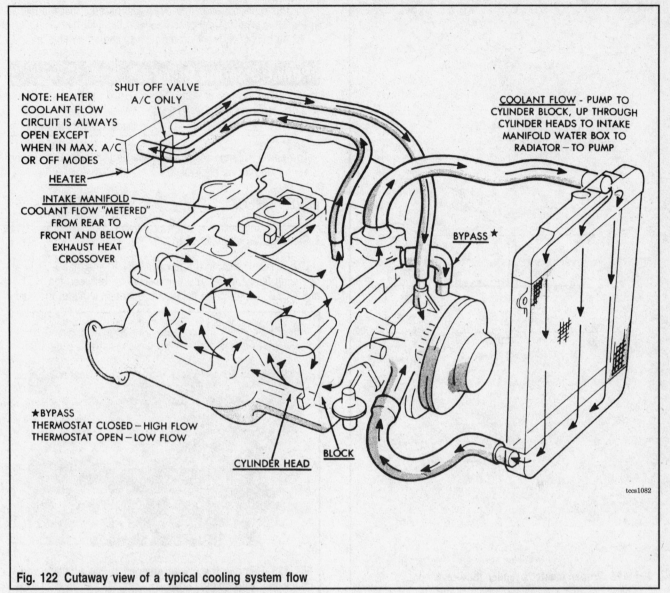

NOTE: HEATER COOLANT FLOW CIRCUIT IS ALWAYS OPEN EXCEPT WHEN IN MAX. A/C OR OFF MODES

SHUT OFF VALVE A/C ONLY

HEATER

INTAKE MANIFOLD COOLANT FLOW "METERED" FROM REAR TO FRONT AND BELOW EXHAUST HEAT CROSSOVER

COOLANT FLOW - PUMP TO CYLINDER BLOCK, UP THROUGH CYLINDER HEADS TO INTAKE MANIFOLD WATER BOX TO RADIATOR - TO PUMP

BYPASS ★

★BYPASS
THERMOSTAT CLOSED – HIGH FLOW
THERMOSTAT OPEN – LOW FLOW

CYLINDER HEAD

BLOCK

tccs1082

Fig. 122 Cutaway view of a typical cooling system flow

89771p31

Fig. 123 Remove the brake master cylinder cap

89771p32

Fig. 124 Add the proper amount and type of fresh clean brake fluid

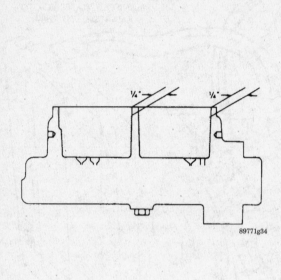

**Fig. 125 Proper master cylinder fluid level**

2. Be sure that the vehicle is resting on a level surface. If necessary, remove the floor mat and access cover.

3. Carefully pry the clip from the top of the master cylinder to release the cover.

4. The fluid level should be approximately ¼ in. (6mm) from the top of the master cylinder. If not, add fluid until the level is correct. Replacement fluid should be Delco Supreme No. 11, DOT 3, or its equivalent.

➡️It is normal for the fluid level to fall as the disc brake ads wear.

### ❄❄WARNING

**Brake fluid dissolves paint. It also absorbs moisture from the air. Never leave a container or the master cylinder uncovered any longer than necessary.**

5. Install the cover of the master cylinder. On most models there is a rubber gasket under the cover, which fits into 2 slots on the cover. Be sure that this is seated properly.

6. Push the clip back into place and be sure that it seats in the groove on the top of the cover.

7. As necessary, replace the access cover and floor mat.

## Power Steering Pump

### FLUID RECOMMENDATION

The power steering reservoir should be filled with GM Power Steering fluid, or its equivalent.

### LEVEL CHECK

▶ **See Figures 126, 127 and 128**

Check the dipstick in the pump reservoir when the fluid is at operating temperature. The fluid should be between the HOT and COLD marks. If the fluid is at room temperature, the fluid

**Fig. 126 Remove the power steering pump dipstick and check the fluid level**

**Fig. 127 If the level is low, add clean power steering fluid until the proper level is achieved**

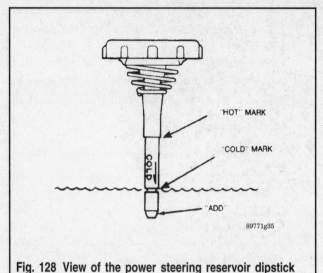

**Fig. 128 View of the power steering reservoir dipstick level marks**

should be between the ADD and COLD marks. The fluid does not require periodic changing.

On systems with a remote reservoir, the level should be maintained approximately ½-1 in. (12.7-25.4mm) from the top with the wheels in the full left turn position.

## Manual Steering Gear

### FLUID RECOMMENDATION

On 1967-69 models, the steering gear should be filled with water resistant EP Chassis Lubricant that meets General Motors Specification GM 6031M.

Beginning 1970, no lubrication is needed for the life of the gear, except in the event of seal replacement or overhaul, when the gear should be refilled with a 13 oz. (368g) container of Steering Gear Lubricant (Part No. 1051052) which meets GM Specification GM 4673M, or its equivalent.

➡**On these models do not use EP Chassis Lubricant.**

### LEVEL CHECK

▶ **See Figure 129**

#### 1967-69 Models

The steering gear is filled at the factory with a water resistant grease. Seasonal change of the lubricant is not required and the housing should not be drained. However, the lubricant should be checked and additions made, as necessary, with water resistant EP chassis lubricant. The lubricant level should be at the level of the filler plug opening on those models that have a filler plug. If not equipped with a filler plug, check and fill the steering gear as follows:

1. Remove the lower and outboard cover retaining screws.
2. Insert the filling device in the lower screw hole.
3. Inject lubricant until it appears on the other screw hole. The gear is now filled to the correct level.

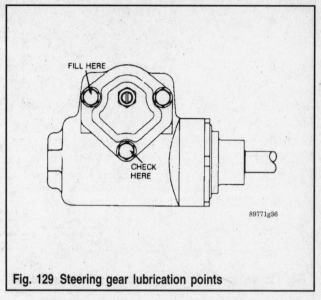

**Fig. 129 Steering gear lubrication points**

4. Replace the lower and outboard cover retaining screws.

#### 1970-86 Models

The steering gear is factory filled with a lubricant which does not require seasonal change. The housing should not be drained. No lubricant is required for the life of the gear.

The gear should be inspected for seal leakage. Look for solid grease, not an oily film. If a seal is replaced or the gear overhauled, the gear should be filled with Part No. 1051052, which is a 13 oz. (368g) container of Steering Gear lubricant which meets GM Specifications. Do not use EP Chassis Lube to lubricate the gear and do not overfill.

## Chassis Greasing

▶ **See Figures 130 and 131**

Refer to the diagrams for chassis points to be lubricated. Not all vehicles have all the fittings illustrated. Water resistant EP chassis lubricant (grease) conforming to GM specification 6031-M should be used for all chassis grease points.

## Body Lubrication

### HOOD LATCH AND HINGES

Clean the latch surfaces and apply clean engine oil to the latch pilot bolts and the spring anchor. Also lubricate the hood hinges with engine oil. Use a chassis grease to lubricate all the pivot points in the latch release mechanism.

### DOOR HINGES

The gas tank filler door and truck doors should be wiped clean and lubricated with clean engine oil once a year. The door lock cylinders and latch mechanisms should be lubricated periodically with a few drops of graphite lock lubricant or a few shots of silicone spray.

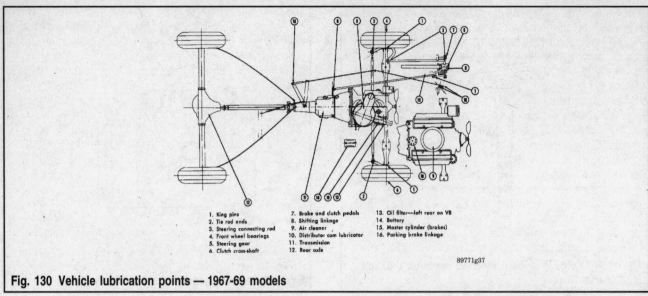

1. King pins
2. Tie rod ends
3. Steering connecting rod
4. Front wheel bearings
5. Steering gear
6. Clutch cross-shaft
7. Brake and clutch pedals
8. Shifting linkage
9. Air cleaner
10. Distributor cam lubricator
11. Transmission
12. Rear axle
13. Oil filter—left rear on V8
14. Battery
15. Master cylinder (brakes)
16. Parking brake linkage

89771g37

**Fig. 130 Vehicle lubrication points — 1967-69 models**

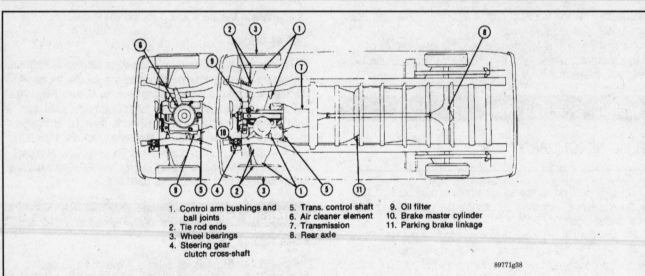

1. Control arm bushings and ball joints
2. Tie rod ends
3. Wheel bearings
4. Steering gear clutch cross-shaft
5. Trans. control shaft
6. Air cleaner element
7. Transmission
8. Rear axle
9. Oil filter
10. Brake master cylinder
11. Parking brake linkage

89771g38

**Fig. 131 Vehicle lubrication points — 1970 and later models**

## Front Wheel Bearings

Refer to Section 8 in this manual for this procedure.

## TRAILER TOWING

Chevrolet and GMC vans have long been popular as trailer towing vehicles. Their strong construction, and wide range of engine/transmission combinations make them ideal for towing campers, boat trailers and utility trailers.

Factory trailer towing packages are available on most Chevrolet and GMC vans, if you are installing a trailer hitch and wiring on your van, there are a few thing that you ought to know.

### Trailer Weight

The weight of the trailer is the most important factor. A good weight-to-horsepower ratio is about 35:1, 35 lbs. of Gross

Combined Weight (GCW) for every horsepower your engine develops. Multiply the engine's rated horsepower by 35 and subtract the weight of the vehicle passengers and luggage. The number remaining is the approximate ideal maximum weight you should tow, although a numerically higher axle ratio can help compensate for heavier weight.

### Hitch (Tongue) Weight

▶ See Figure 132

Calculate the hitch weight in order to select a proper hitch. The weight of the hitch is usually 9-11% of the trailer gross weight and should be measured with the trailer loaded. Hitches fall into various categories: those that mount on the frame and rear bumper, the bolt-on type, or the weld-on distribution type used for larger trailers. Axle mounted or clamp-on bumper hitches should never be used.

Check the gross weight rating of your trailer. Tongue weight is usually figured as 10% of gross trailer weight. Therefore, a trailer with a maximum gross weight of 2000 lbs. will have a maximum tongue weight of 200 lbs. Class I trailers fall into this category. Class II trailers are those with a gross weight rating of 2000-3000 lbs., while Class III trailers fall into the 3500-6000 lbs. category. Class IV trailers are those over 6000 lbs. and are for use with fifth wheel trucks, only.

When you've determined the hitch that you'll need, follow the manufacturer's installation instructions, exactly, especially when it comes to fastener torques. The hitch will subjected to a lot of stress and good hitches come with hardened bolts. Never substitute an inferior bolt for a hardened bolt.

## Cooling

### ENGINE

#### Overflow Tank

One of the most common, if not THE most common, problems associated with trailer towing is engine overheating. If you have a cooling system without an expansion tank, you'll definitely need to get an aftermarket expansion tank kit, preferably one with at least a 2 quart capacity. These kits are easily installed on the radiator's overflow hose, and come with a pressure cap designed for expansion tanks.

#### Flex Fan

Another helpful accessory for vehicles using a belt-driven radiator fan is a flex fan. These fans are large diameter units designed to provide more airflow at low speeds, by using fan

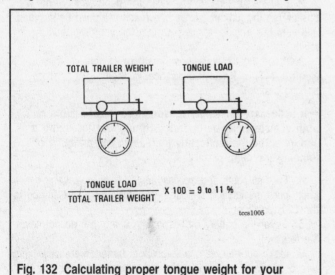

Fig. 132 Calculating proper tongue weight for your trailer

blades that have deeply cupped surfaces. The blades then flex, or flatten out, at high speed, when less cooling air is needed. These fans are far lighter in weight than stock fans, requiring less horsepower to drive them. Also, they are far quieter than stock fans. If you do decide to replace your stock fan with a flex fan, note that if your vehicle has a fan clutch, a spacer will be needed between the flex fan and water pump hub.

#### Oil Cooler

Aftermarket engine oil coolers are helpful for prolonging engine oil life and reducing overall engine temperatures. Both of these factors increase engine life. While not absolutely necessary in towing Class I and some Class II trailers, they are recommended for heavier Class II and all Class III towing. Engine oil cooler systems usually consist of an adapter, screwed on in place of the oil filter, a remote filter mounting and a multi-tube, finned heat exchanger, which is mounted in front of the radiator or air conditioning condenser.

## TRANSMISSION

An automatic transmission is usually recommended for trailer towing. Modern automatics have proven reliable and, of course, easy to operate, in trailer towing. The increased load of a trailer, however, causes an increase in the temperature of the automatic transmission fluid. Heat is the worst enemy of an automatic transmission. As the temperature of the fluid increases, the life of the fluid decreases.

It is essential, therefore, that you install an automatic transmission cooler. The cooler, which consists of a multi-tube, finned heat exchanger, is usually installed in front of the radiator or air conditioning compressor, and hooked in-line with the transmission cooler tank inlet line. Follow the cooler manufacturer's installation instructions.

Select a cooler of at least adequate capacity, based upon the combined gross weights of the vehicle and trailer.

Cooler manufacturers recommend that you use an aftermarket cooler in addition to, and not instead of, the present cooling tank in your radiator. If you do want to use it in place of the radiator cooling tank, get a cooler at least two sizes larger than normally necessary.

➡ **A transmission cooler can, sometimes, cause slow or harsh shifting in the transmission during cold weather, until the fluid has a chance to come up to normal operating temperature. Some coolers can be purchased with or retrofitted with a temperature bypass valve which will allow fluid flow through the cooler only when the fluid has reached above a certain operating temperature.**

## Handling A Trailer

Towing a trailer with ease and safety requires a certain amount of experience. It's a good idea to learn the feel of a trailer by practicing turning, stopping and backing in an open area such as an empty parking lot.

## TOWING THE VEHICLE

Chevrolet and GMC vans can be towed on all four wheels (flat towed) at speeds of less than 35 mph (56 km) for distances less than 50 miles (80 km), providing that the axle, driveline and engine/transmission are normally operable. The transmission should be in Neutral, the engine off, the steering unlocked, and the parking brake released.

The rear wheels must be raised off the ground or the driveshaft disconnected when the transmission if not operating properly, or when speeds of over 35 mph (56 km) will be used or when towing more than 50 miles (80 km).

Do not attach chains to the bumpers or bracketing. All attachments must be made to the structural members. Safety chains should be used. It should also be remembered that power steering and brake assists will not be working with the engine off.

## JUMP STARTING A DEAD BATTERY

▶ See Figure 133

Whenever a vehicle is jump started, precautions must be followed in order to prevent the possibility of personal injury. Remember that batteries contain a small amount of explosive hydrogen gas which is a by-product of battery charging. Sparks should always be avoided when working around batteries, especially when attaching jumper cables. To minimize the possibility of accidental sparks, follow the procedure carefully.

### ❋❋CAUTION

**NEVER hook the batteries up in a series circuit or the entire electrical system will go up in smoke, including the starter!**

Vehicles equipped with a diesel engine may utilize two 12 volt batteries. If so, the batteries are connected in a parallel circuit (positive terminal to positive terminal, negative terminal to negative terminal). Hooking the batteries up in parallel circuit increases battery cranking power without increasing total battery voltage output. Output remains at 12 volts. On the other hand, hooking two 12 volt batteries up in a series circuit (positive terminal to negative terminal, positive terminal to negative terminal) increases total battery output to 24 volts (12 volts plus 12 volts).

### Jump Starting Precautions

- Be sure that both batteries are of the same voltage. Vehicles covered by this manual and most vehicles on the road today utilize a 12 volt charging system.
- Be sure that both batteries are of the same polarity (have the same terminal, in most cases NEGATIVE grounded).
- Be sure that the vehicles are not touching or a short could occur.
- On serviceable batteries, be sure the vent cap holes are not obstructed.
- Do not smoke or allow sparks anywhere near the batteries.
- In cold weather, make sure the battery electrolyte is not frozen. This can occur more readily in a battery that has been in a state of discharge.
- Do not allow electrolyte to contact your skin or clothing.

### Jump Starting Procedure

1. Make sure that the voltages of the 2 batteries are the same. Most batteries and charging systems are of the 12 volt variety.

2. Pull the jumping vehicle (with the good battery) into a position so the jumper cables can reach the dead battery and that vehicle's engine. Make sure that the vehicles do NOT touch.

3. Place the transmissions/transaxles of both vehicles in **Neutral** (MT) or **P** (AT), as applicable, then firmly set their parking brakes.

➡If necessary for safety reasons, the hazard lights on both vehicles may be operated throughout the entire procedure without significantly increasing the difficulty of jumping the dead battery.

4. Turn all lights and accessories OFF on both vehicles. Make sure the ignition switches on both vehicles are turned to the **OFF** position.

5. Cover the battery cell caps with a rag, but do not cover the terminals.

6. Make sure the terminals on both batteries are clean and free of corrosion or proper electrical connection will be impeded. If necessary, clean the battery terminals before proceeding.

7. Identify the positive (+) and negative (-) terminals on both batteries.

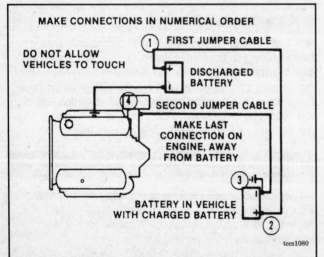

**Fig. 133 Connect the jumper cables to the batteries and engine in the order shown**

8. Connect the first jumper cable to the positive (+) terminal of the dead battery, then connect the other end of that cable to the positive (+) terminal of the booster (good) battery.

9. Connect one end of the other jumper cable to the negative (-) terminal on the booster battery and the final cable clamp to an engine bolt head, alternator bracket or other solid, metallic point on the engine with the dead battery. Try to pick a ground on the engine that is positioned away from the battery in order to minimize the possibility of the 2 clamps touching should one loosen during the procedure. DO NOT connect this clamp to the negative (-) terminal of the bad battery.

## ✳✳CAUTION

**Be very careful to keep the jumper cables away from moving parts (cooling fan, belts, etc.) on both engines.**

10. Check to make sure that the cables are routed away from any moving parts, then start the donor vehicle's engine. Run the engine at moderate speed for several minutes to allow the dead battery a chance to receive some initial charge.

11. With the donor vehicle's engine still running slightly above idle, try to start the vehicle with the dead battery. Crank the engine for no more than 10 seconds at a time and let the starter cool for at least 20 seconds between tries. If the vehicle does not start in 3 tries, it is likely that something else is also wrong or that the battery needs additional time to charge.

12. Once the vehicle is started, allow it to run at idle for a few seconds to make sure that it is operating properly.

13. Turn ON the headlights, heater blower and, if equipped, the rear defroster of both vehicles in order to reduce the severity of voltage spikes and subsequent risk of damage to the vehicles' electrical systems when the cables are disconnected. This step is especially important to any vehicle equipped with computer control modules.

14. Carefully disconnect the cables in the reverse order of connection. Start with the negative cable that is attached to the engine ground, then the negative cable on the donor battery. Disconnect the positive cable from the donor battery and finally, disconnect the positive cable from the formerly dead battery. Be careful when disconnecting the cables from the positive terminals not to allow the alligator clips to touch any metal on either vehicle or a short and sparks will occur.

## JACKING

Your vehicle was supplied with a jack for emergency road repairs. This jack is fine for changing a flat tire or other short term procedures not requiring you to go beneath the vehicle. If it is used in an emergency situation, carefully follow the instructions provided either with the jack or in your owner's manual. Do not attempt to use the jack on any portions of the vehicle other than specified by the vehicle manufacturer. Always block the diagonally opposite wheel when using a jack.

A more convenient way of jacking is the use of a garage or floor jack. You may use the floor jack at the specified points indicated under the jacking points illustration shown in this section.

Never place the jack under the radiator, engine or transmission components. Severe and expensive damage will result when the jack is raised. Additionally, never jack under the floorpan or bodywork; the metal will deform.

Whenever you plan to work under the vehicle, you must support it on jackstands or ramps. Never use cinder blocks or stacks of wood to support the vehicle, even if you're only going to be under it for a few minutes. Never crawl under the vehicle when it is supported only by the tire-changing jack or other floor jack.

➡**Always position a block of wood or small rubber pad on top of the jack or jackstand to protect the lifting point's finish when lifting or supporting the vehicle.**

Small hydraulic, screw, or scissors jacks are satisfactory for raising the vehicle. Drive-on trestles or ramps are also a handy and safe way to both raise and support the vehicle. Be careful though, some ramps may be too steep to drive your vehicle onto without scraping the front bottom panels. Never support the vehicle on any suspension member (unless specifically in-

structed to do so by a repair manual) or by an underbody panel.

## Jacking Precautions

The following safety points cannot be overemphasized:
• Always block the opposite wheel or wheels to keep the vehicle from rolling off the jack.
• When raising the front of the vehicle, firmly apply the parking brake.
• When the drive wheels are to remain on the ground, leave the vehicle in gear to help prevent it from rolling.
• Always use jackstands to support the vehicle when you are working underneath. Place the stands beneath the vehicle's jacking brackets. Before climbing underneath, rock the vehicle a bit to make sure it is firmly supported.

## Jacking Points

### 1967 MODELS

• Front: Under the axle center, near the spring seat.
• Rear: Under the rear axle housing, near the wheel to be raised

### 1968-86 MODELS

▶ **See Figures 134, 135, 136, 137 and 138**

Follow the recommended jacking points as illustrated.

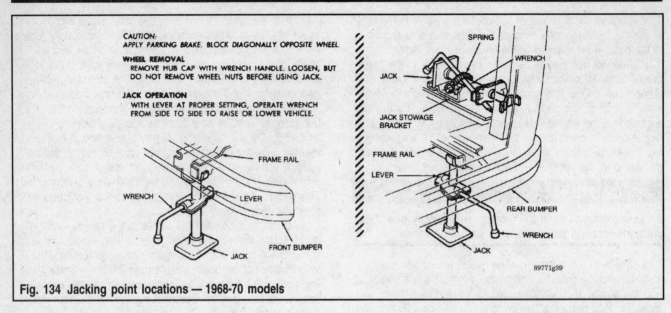

Fig. 134 Jacking point locations — 1968-70 models

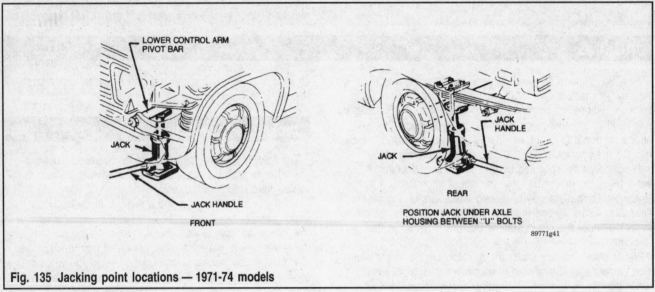

Fig. 135 Jacking point locations — 1971-74 models

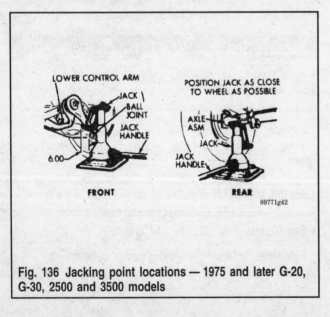

Fig. 136 Jacking point locations — 1975 and later G-20, G-30, 2500 and 3500 models

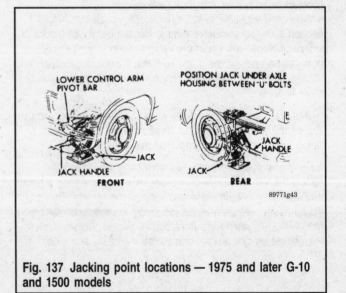

Fig. 137 Jacking point locations — 1975 and later G-10 and 1500 models

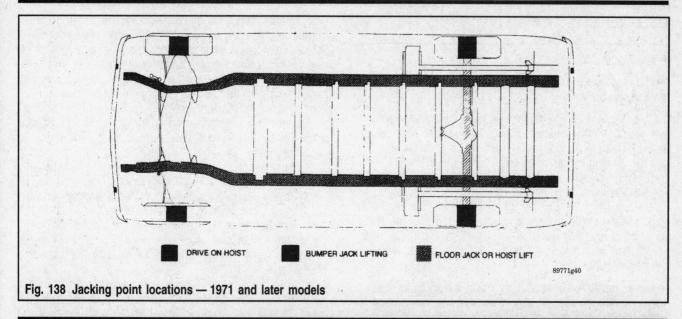

DRIVE ON HOIST     BUMPER JACK LIFTING     FLOOR JACK OR HOIST LIFT

89771g40

**Fig. 138 Jacking point locations — 1971 and later models**

## HOW TO BUY A USED VEHICLE

Many people believe that a two or three year old used car or truck is a better buy than a new vehicle. This may be true as most new vehicles suffer the heaviest depreciation in the first two years and, at three years old, a vehicle is usually not old enough to present a lot of costly repair problems. But keep in mind, when buying a non-warranted automobile, there are no guarantees. Whatever the age of the used vehicle you might want to purchase, this section and a little patience should increase your chances of selecting one that is safe and dependable.

### Tips

1. First decide what model you want, and how much you want to spend.
2. Check the used car lots and your local newspaper ads. Privately owned vehicles are usually less expensive, however, you may not get a warranty that, in many cases, comes with a used vehicle purchased from a lot. Of course, some aftermarket warranties may not be worth the extra money, so this is a point you will have to debate and consider based on your priorities.
3. Never shop at night. The glare of the lights make it easy to miss faults on the body caused by accident or rust repair.
4. Try to get the name and phone number of the previous owner. Contact him/her and ask about the vehicle. If the owner of a lot refuses this information, look for a vehicle somewhere else.

A private seller can tell you about the vehicle and maintenance. But remember, there's no law requiring honesty from private citizens selling used vehicles. There is a law that forbids tampering with or turning back the odometer mileage. This includes both the private citizen and the lot owner. The law also requires that the seller or anyone transferring ownership of the vehicle must provide the buyer with a signed statement indicating the mileage on the odometer at the time of transfer.

5. You may wish to contact the National Highway Traffic Safety Administration (NHTSA) to find out if the vehicle has ever been included in a manufacturer's recall. Write down the year, model and serial number before you buy the vehicle, then contact NHTSA (there should be a 1-800 number that your phone company's information line can supply). If the vehicle was listed for a recall, make sure the needed repairs were made.

6. Refer to the Used Vehicle Checklist in this section and check all the items on the vehicle you are considering. Some items are more important than others. Only you know how much money you can afford for repairs, and depending on the price of the vehicle, may consider performing any needed work yourself. Beware, however, of trouble in areas that will affect operation, safety or emission. Problems in the Used Vehicle Checklist break down as follows:

- Numbers 1-8: Two or more problems in these areas indicate a lack of maintenance. You should beware.
- Numbers 9-13: Problems here tend to indicate a lack of proper care, however, these can usually be corrected with a tune-up or relatively simple parts replacement.
- Numbers 14-17: Problems in the engine or transmission can be very expensive. Unless you are looking for a project, walk away from any vehicle with problems in 2 or more of these areas.

7. If you are satisfied with the apparent condition of the vehicle, take it to an independent diagnostic center or mechanic for a complete check. If you have a state inspection program, have it inspected immediately before purchase, or specify on the bill of sale that the sale is conditional on passing state inspection.

8. Road test the vehicle — refer to the Road Test Checklist in this section. If your original evaluation and the road test agree — the rest is up to you.

## USED VEHICLE CHECKLIST

▶ See Figure 139

➡**The numbers on the illustrations refer to the numbers on this checklist.**

1. Mileage: Average mileage is about 12,000-15,000 miles per year. More than average mileage may indicate hard usage or could indicate many highway miles (which could be less detrimental than half as many tough around town miles).

2. Paint: Check around the tailpipe, molding and windows for overspray indicating that the vehicle has been repainted.

3. Rust: Check fenders, doors, rocker panels, window moldings, wheelwells, floorboards, under floormats, and in the trunk for signs of rust. Any rust at all will be a problem. There is no way to permanently stop the spread of rust, except to replace the part or panel.

➡**If rust repair is suspected, try using a magnet to check for body filler. A magnet should stick to the sheet metal parts of the body, but will not adhere to areas with large amounts of filler.**

4. Body appearance: Check the moldings, bumpers, grille, vinyl roof, glass, doors, trunk lid and body panels for general overall condition. Check for misalignment, loose hold-down clips, ripples, scratches in glass, welding in the trunk, severe misalignment of body panels or ripples, any of which may indicate crash work.

5. Leaks: Get down and look under the vehicle. There are no normal leaks, other than water from the air conditioner evaporator.

6. Tires: Check the tire air pressure. One old trick is to pump the tire pressure up to make the vehicle roll easier. Check the tread wear, then open the trunk and check the spare too. Uneven wear is a clue that the front end may need an alignment.

7. Shock absorbers: Check the shock absorbers by forcing downward sharply on each corner of the vehicle. Good shocks will not allow the vehicle to bounce more than once after you let go.

8. Interior: Check the entire interior. You're looking for an interior condition that agrees with the overall condition of the vehicle. Reasonable wear is expected, but be suspicious of new seat covers on sagging seats, new pedal pads, and worn armrests. These indicate an attempt to cover up hard use. Pull back the carpets and look for evidence of water leaks or flooding. Look for missing hardware, door handles, control knobs, etc. Check lights and signal operations. Make sure all accessories (air conditioner, heater, radio, etc.) work. Check windshield wiper operation.

9. Belts and Hoses: Open the hood, then check all belts and hoses for wear, cracks or weak spots.

10. Battery: Low electrolyte level, corroded terminals and/or cracked case indicate a lack of maintenance.

11. Radiator: Look for corrosion or rust in the coolant indicating a lack of maintenance.

12. Air filter: A severely dirty air filter would indicate a lack of maintenance.

13. Ignition wires: Check the ignition wires for cracks, burned spots, or wear. Worn wires will have to be replaced.

14. Oil level: If the oil level is low, chances are the engine uses oil or leaks. Beware of water in the oil (there is probably a cracked block or bad head gasket), excessively thick oil (which is often used to quiet a noisy engine), or thin, dirty oil with a distinct gasoline smell (this may indicate internal engine problems).

15. Automatic Transmission: Pull the transmission dipstick out when the engine is running. The level should read FULL, and the fluid should be clear or bright red. Dark brown or black fluid that has distinct burnt odor, indicates a transmission in need of repair or overhaul.

16. Exhaust: Check the color of the exhaust smoke. Blue smoke indicates, among other problems, worn rings. Black smoke can indicate burnt valves or carburetor problems. Check the exhaust system for leaks; it can be expensive to replace.

17. Spark Plugs: Remove one or all of the spark plugs (the most accessible will do, though all are preferable). An engine in good condition will show plugs with a light tan or gray deposit on the firing tip.

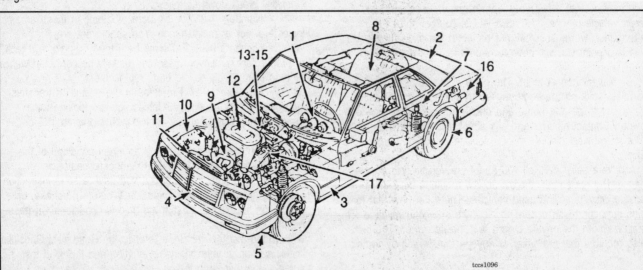

tccs1096

**Fig. 139 Each of the numbered items should be checked when purchasing a used vehicle**

## ROAD TEST CHECKLIST

1. Engine Performance: The vehicle should be peppy whether cold or warm, with adequate power and good pickup. It should respond smoothly through the gears.

2. Brakes: They should provide quick, firm stops with no noise, pulling or brake fade.

3. Steering: Sure control with no binding harshness, or looseness and no shimmy in the wheel should be expected. Noise or vibration from the steering wheel when turning the vehicle means trouble.

4. Clutch (Manual Transmission/Transaxle): Clutch action should give quick, smooth response with easy shifting. The clutch pedal should have free-play before it disengages the clutch. Start the engine, set the parking brake, put the transmission in first gear and slowly release the clutch pedal. The engine should begin to stall when the pedal is 1/2-3/4 of the way up.

5. Automatic Transmission/Transaxle: The transmission should shift rapidly and smoothly, with no noise, hesitation, or slipping.

6. Differential: No noise or thumps should be present. Differentials have no normal leaks.

7. Driveshaft/Universal Joints: Vibration and noise could mean driveshaft problems. Clicking at low speed or coast conditions means worn U-joints.

8. Suspension: Try hitting bumps at different speeds. A vehicle that bounces excessively has weak shock absorbers or struts. Clunks mean worn bushings or ball joints.

9. Frame/Body: Wet the tires and drive in a straight line. Tracks should show two straight lines, not four. Four tire tracks indicate a frame/body bent by collision damage. If the tires can't be wet for this purpose, have a friend drive along behind you and see if the vehicle appears to be traveling in a straight line.

## Capacities

| Year | Model | Engine Displacement Cu in. | Engine Crankcase (qts) With Filter | Engine Crankcase (qts) Without Filter | Transmission (pts) Manual 3-spd | Transmission (pts) Manual 4-spd | Transmission (pts) Automatic | Drive Axle (pts) | Gasoline Tank (gals) | Cooling System (qts) With Heater | Cooling System (qts) Without Heater |
|------|-------|------|------|------|------|------|------|------|------|------|------|
| 1967 | All | 6-230 | 5 | 4 | 2.5 | 3 | 4② | 3.5① | 16 | 13 | 12 |
|      |     | 6-250 | 5 | 4 | 2.5 | 3 | 4② | 3.5① | 16 | 13 | 12 |
|      |     | 8-283 | 5 | 4 | 2.5 | 3 | 4② | 3.5① | 16 | 18 | 17 |
| 1968 | All | 6-230 | 5 | 4 | 2.5 | 3 | 4② | 3.5① | 16 | 13 | 17 |
|      |     | 6-250 | 5 | 4 | 2.5 | 3 | 4② | 3.5① | 16 | 13 | 17 |
|      |     | 8-307 | 5 | 4 | 2.5 | 3 | 4② | 3.5① | 16 | 18 | 17 |
| 1969 | All | 6-230 | 5 | 4 | 2.5 | 3 | 4② | 4.5 | 24.5 | 13 | 12 |
|      |     | 6-250 | 5 | 4 | 2.5 | 3 | 4② | 4.5 | 24.5 | 13 | 12 |
|      |     | 8-307 | 5 | 4 | 2.5 | 3 | 4② | 4.5 | 24.5 | 18 | 17 |
| 1970 | All | 6-250 | 5 | 4 | 2.5 | 3 | 4② | 4.5 | 24.5③ | 13 | 12 |
|      |     | 8-307 | 5 | 4 | 2.5 | 3 | 4② | 4.5 | 24.5③ | 18 | 17 |
|      |     | 8-350 | 5 | 4 | 2.5 | 3 | 4② | 4.5 | 24.5③ | 18 | 17 |

89771c03

## Capacities (cont.)

| Year | Model | Engine Displacement Cu in. | Engine Crankcase (qts) With Filter | Without Filter | Transmission (pts) Manual 3-spd | 4-spd | Automatic | Drive Axle (pts) | Gasoline Tank (gals) | Cooling System (qts) With Heater | Without Heater |
|------|-------|------|---|---|---|---|---|---|---|---|---|
| 1971 | All | 6-250 | 5 | 4 | 2.5 | — | 4② | 4.5 | 24.5③ | 13 | 12 |
| | | 8-307 | 5 | 4 | 2.5 | — | 4② | 4.5 | 24.5③ | 18 | 17 |
| | | 8-350 | 5 | 4 | 2.5 | — | 4② | 4.5 | 24.5③ | 18 | 17 |
| 1972 | All | 6-250 | 5 | 4 | 2.5 | — | 5 | ⑤ | 24.5③ | 13 | 12 |
| | | 8-307 | 5 | 4 | 2.5 | — | 5 | ⑤ | 24.5③ | 16④ | 15④ |
| | | 8-350 | 5 | 4 | 2.5 | — | 5 | ⑤ | 24.5③ | 16④ | 15④ |
| 1973 | All | 6-250 | 5 | 4 | 2.5 | — | 5 | ⑤ | 21 | 13 | 12 |
| | | 8-307 | 5 | 4 | 2.5 | — | 5 | ⑤ | 21 | 16④⑥ | 15④⑥ |
| | | 8-350 | 5 | 4 | 2.5 | — | 5 | ⑤ | 21 | 16④⑥ | 15④⑥ |
| 1974 | All | 6-250 | 5 | 4 | 2.5 | — | 5 | ⑤ | 21 | 13 | 12 |
| | | 8-350 | 5 | 4 | 2.5 | — | 5 | ⑤ | 21 | 16④⑥ | 15④⑥ |
| 1975 | All | 6-250 | 5 | 4 | 3.2 | — | 5 | 4.3 | 21/36 | 15 | — |
| | 20, 2500 | 6-292 | 6 | 5 | 3.2 | — | 5 | 3.5 | 21/36 | 14.8 | — |
| | 30, 3500 | 6-292 | 6 | 5 | 3.2 | — | 5 | 5.4 | 21/36 | 14.8 | — |
| | All | 8-350 2 bbl | 5 | 4 | 3.2 | — | 5 | 4.3 | 21/36 | 17.5 | — |
| | 10, 1500 | 8-350 4 bbl | 5 | 4 | 3.2 | — | 5 | 4.3 | 21/36 | 18 | — |
| | 20, 2500 | 8-350 4 bbl | 5 | 4 | 4.6 | — | 5 | 3.5 | 21/36 | 18 | — |
| | 30, 3500 | 8-350 4 bbl | 5 | 4 | 4.6 | — | 5 | 5.4 | 21/36 | 18 | — |
| | 20, 2500 | 8-400 | 5 | 4 | — | — | 5 | 3.5 | 21/36 | 19.9 | — |
| | 30, 2500 | 8-400 | 5 | 4 | — | — | 5 | 5.4 | 21/36 | 19.9 | — |
| 1976 | All | 6-250 | 5 | 4 | 3.2 | — | 5 | 4.3 | 21/36 | 15 | — |
| | 20, 2500 | 6-292 | 6 | 5 | 3.2 | — | 5 | 3.5 | 21/36 | 14.8 | — |
| | 30, 3500 | 6-292 | 6 | 5 | 3.2 | — | 5 | 5.4 | 21/36 | 14.8 | — |
| | 10, 1500 | 8-350 | 5 | 4 | 4.6 | — | 5 | 4.3 | 21/36 | 18 | — |
| 1976 | 20, 2500 | 8-350 | 5 | 4 | 4.6 | — | 5 | 3.5 | 21/36 | 18 | — |
| | 30, 3500 | 8-350 | 5 | 4 | 4.6 | — | 5 | 5.4 | 21/36 | 18 | — |
| | 20, 2500 | 8-400 | 5 | 4 | — | — | 5 | 3.5 | 21/36 | 19.9 | — |
| | 30, 3500 | 8-400 | 5 | 4 | — | — | 5 | 5.4 | 21/36 | 19.9 | — |
| 1977–78 | All | 6-250 | 5 | 4 | 3.2 | — | 5 | 3.5 | 22/33 | 15 | — |
| | 20, 2500 | 6-292 | 6 | 5 | 3.2 | — | 5 | 3.5 | 22/33 | 14.8 | — |
| | 30, 3500 | 6-292 | 6 | 5 | 3.2 | — | 5 | 5.4 | 22/33 | 14.8 | — |
| | All | 8-305 | 5 | 4 | 3.2 | — | 5 | 3.5 | 22/33 | 18 | — |
| | 10, 20, 1500, 2500 | 8-350 | 5 | 4 | 4.6⑦ | — | 5 | 3.5 | 22/33 | 18 | — |
| | 30, 3500 | 8-350 | 5 | 4 | 4.6⑦ | — | 5⑧ | 5.4 | 22/33 | 18 | — |
| | 20, 2500 | 8-400 | 5 | 4 | — | — | 5 | 3.5 | 22/33 | 19.9 | — |
| | 30, 3500 | 8-400 | 5 | 4 | — | — | 5⑧ | 5.4 | 22/33 | 19.9 | — |

89771c04

## Capacities (cont.)

| Year | Model | Engine Displacement Cu in. | Engine Crankcase (qts) | | Transmission (pts) | | | Drive Axle (pts) | Gasoline Tank (gals) | Cooling System (qts) | |
| | | | With Filter | Without Filter | Manual | | Automatic | | | With Heater | Without Heater |
| | | | | | 3-spd | 4-spd | | | | | |
|---|---|---|---|---|---|---|---|---|---|---|---|
| 1979–80 | All | 6-250 | 5 | 4 | 3.2 | — | 5 | 3.5 | 22/33 | 17 | — |
| | All | 8-305 | 5 | 4 | 3.2⑦ | — | 5 | 3.5 | 22/33 | 19.5 | — |
| | 10, 20 1500, 2500 | 8-350 | 5 | 4 | 3.2⑦ | — | 5 | 3.5 | 22/33 | 20 | — |
| | 30, 3500 | 8-350 | 5 | 4 | 3.2⑦ | — | 5 | 3.5 | 22/33 | 20 | — |
| | All | 8-400 | 5 | 4 | 3.2⑦ | — | 5 | 3.5 | 22/33 | 20 | — |
| 1981–82 | All | 6-250 | 5 | 4 | 3.0 | — | 6 | ⑨ | 22/33 | 20 | — |
| | All | 8-305 | 5 | 4 | 3.0 | — | 6 | ⑨ | 22/33 | 20 | — |
| | All | 8-350LD | 5 | 4 | 3.0 | — | 6 | ⑨ | 22/23 | 22 | — |
| | All | 8-350HD | 5 | 4 | 3.0 | — | 7 | ⑨ | 22/33 | 22 | — |
| 1983–86 | All | 6-250 | 5 | 4 | 3 | 8 | ⑩ | ⑨ | 22/33 | 14.5 | — |
| | All | 6-262 | 5 | 4 | 3 | 8 | 6.3 | ⑨ | 22/33 | 17 | — |
| | All | 8-305 | 5 | 4 | 3 | 8 | ⑩ | ⑨ | 22/33 | 17 | — |
| | All | 8-350 | 5 | 4 | 3 | 8 | ⑩ | ⑨ | 22/33 | 17 | — |
| | All | 8-379 Diesel | 7 | — | 3 | 8 | ⑩ | ⑨ | 22/33 | 24 | — |

LD: Light Duty; HD: Heavy Duty

① 4.5 pts with heavy-duty differential.
② Turbo Hydra-Matic 400—7.5 pts (1967–68). Turbo Hydra-Matic 350—5 pts (1969–74).
③ 22 gallons with Evaporative Emission Canister.
④ Increase by 1 qt for G—10 models with special radiator.
⑤ G—10, G—1500 van—3.5 pts.
   G—10, G—1500 Sportvan and G—20, G—2500—5.0 pts.
   G—30 and G—3500—6.5 pts.
⑥ 18 qts with air conditioning.
⑦ 4 pts with top-cover Tremec three-speed and Saginaw three-speed
⑧ 7 pts with 10,000 lb or higher GVW.
⑨ 8½ in. ring gear—4.2 pts
   8⅞ in. ring gear (Chevrolet)—4.5 pts (3.5 pts 1977–82)
   9¾ in. ring gear (Dana) 6.0 pts.
   10½ in. ring gear (Chevrolet)—6½ pts
   10½ in. ring gear (Dana)—7.2 pts
   12½ in. ring gear (Chevrolet)—26.8 pts
⑩ Turbo Hydra-Matic 350—6 pts
   Turbo Hydra-Matic 400—7 pts
   Turbo Hydra-Matic 700R4—10 pts

89771c05

## Maintenance Intervals

See text for procedures concerning regular maintenance.

NOTE: *Heavy-duty operation (trailer towing, prolonged idling, severe stop-and-start driving) should be accompanied by a 50% increase in maintenance. Cut the interval in half for these conditions. Figures given are maintenance intervals when service should be performed.*

| Maintenance | 1967–70 | 1971–74 | 1975–86 |
|---|---|---|---|
| **Air Cleaner (Check and Clean)** | | | |
| Paper element ① | 24,000 mi (replace) | 24,000 mi (replace) | 30,000 mi (replace) ⑥ |
| **PCV Valve (Replace)** | 12 mo/12,000 mi | 12 mo/12,000 mi | 12 mo/15,000 mi ⑦ ⑧ |
| **Evaporative Canister** | | | |
| Replace filter | — | 12 mo/12,000 mi | 24 mo/30,000 mi ⑥ |
| **Engine Oil** | | | |
| Check | Each fuel stop | Each fuel stop | Each fuel stop |
| Replace | 4 mo/6,000 mi | 4 mo/6,000 mi | 6 mo/7,500 mi ⑨ ⑬ ⑭ |
| **Engine Oil Filter (Replace)** | At 1st oil change; then every 2nd | At 1st oil change; then every 2nd | At 1st oil change; then every 2nd ⑬ |
| **Fuel Filter** | | | |
| Replace ⑮ | 12,000 mi | 12,000 mi | 12 mo/15,000 mi ⑥ ⑫ |
| **Powerguide Transmission Fluid** | | | |
| Check | 6,000 mi | 6,000 mi | |
| Replace | 24,000 mi ⑥ | 24,000 mi | — |
| **Turbo Hydra-Matic Fluid & Filter** | | | |
| Check fluid | 6,000 mi | 6,000 mi | Each oil change |
| Change fluid | 24,000 mi | 24,000 mi | 30,000 mi |
| Replace filter | 24,000 mi | 24,000 mi | 30,000 ⑧ ⑩ |
| **Manual transmission (All)** | | | |
| Check lubricant | 6,000 mi | 4 mo/6,000 mi | 6 mo/7,500 mi ⑨ |
| Add lubricant | As necessary | As necessary | As necessary |
| **Battery** | | | |
| Lubricate terminal felt washer | 6,000 mi ④ | — | — |
| Clean terminal | 6,000 mi | As necessary | As necessary |
| Check electrolyte level | Twice monthly | Twice monthly | Twice monthly |
| **Coolant level** | Each fuel stop | Each fuel stop | Each fuel stop |
| **Front Wheel Bearings** | | | |
| Lubricate | 30,000 mi | 30,000 mi ③ | 30,000 mi ⑧ ⑪ |
| **Front and Rear Axle Lube** | | | |
| Check | 6,000 mi | 6,000 mi | 6 mo/7,500 mi ⑨ |
| Replace | 24,000 mi | 24,000 mi | 1st 15,000 mi w/Posi-traction |
| **Brake Fluid (Master Cylinder)** | | | |
| Check fluid level | 6,000 mi | 6,000 mi | 6 mo/7,500 mi ⑨ |
| Add fluid | As necessary | As necessary | As necessary |
| **Manual Steering Gear Lubricant** | | | |
| Check level | 36,000 mi ② | 36,000 mi ② | 30,000 mi |
| Add lubricant | As necessary ② | ② | ② |
| **Power Steering Reservoir** | | | |
| Check fluid level | At each oil change | At each oil change | 6 mo/7,500 mi |
| Add fluid | As necessary | As necessary | As necessary |

89771c01

## Maintenance Intervals (cont.)

| Maintenance | 1967–70 | 1971–74 | 1975–86 |
|---|---|---|---|
| Rotate Tires | 6,000 mi | 6,000 mi | Radial—1st 7,500 mi, then every 15,000 mi Bias Belted—every 7,500 mi |
| Chassis Lubrication | See Chassis Lubrication charts | See Chassis Lubrication charts | See Chassis Lubrication charts |
| Drive Belts<br>Check and adjust (as necessary) | 6,000 mi | 6,000 mi | 6 mo/7,500 mi |

—Not applicable
mi—Miles
mo—Months

① Paper element air cleaners should be rotated 180° each time they are checked
② From 1970 on, no lubrication of the manual steering gear is recommended. The gear should be inspected for leaks at the seal (lubricant leaks, not filmy oil leaks). Seasonal change of the lubricant is not required and the housing should not be drained.
③ 24,000 miles in 1972–72
④ May be equipped with a felt terminal washer
⑤ 20 Series—every 12,000 miles
⑥ 12,000 mi in heavy duty emissions vehicles
⑦ 24 mo/30,000 mi 1976–86
⑧ 24,000 mi in heavy duty emission vehicles
⑨ 4 mo/6,000 mi in heavy duty emission vehicles
⑩ 60,000 mi 1976–78, 100,000 mi 1979–86, light duty emissions vehicles
⑪ 12,000 mi in four wheel drive vehicles
⑫ 24 mo/24,000 mi in California 350 and 400 engines through 1977; 12,000 mi on 1979–86 heavy duty emissions vehicles
⑬ Change at 3,000 mile intervals for 350 Diesel; 6,000 miles for 1981 and later models
⑭ Change at 5,000 mile intervals for 379 (6.2L) Diesel; or every 2,500 miles when operating under extreme temperatures, extended high speed or idle conditions, or frequent trailer towing.
⑮ Figures include diesel fuel filters

89771c02

## ENGLISH TO METRIC CONVERSION: MASS (WEIGHT)

Current **mass** measurement is expressed in pounds and ounces (lbs. & ozs.). The metric unit of mass (or weight) is the kilogram (kg). Even although this table does not show conversion of masses (weights) larger than 15 lbs, it is easy to calculate larger units by following the data immediately below.

To convert ounces (oz.) to grams (g): multiply th number of ozs. by 28
To convert grams (g) to ounces (oz.): multiply the number of grams by .035

To convert pounds (lbs.) to kilograms (kg): multiply the number of lbs. by .45
To convert kilograms (kg) to pounds (lbs.): multiply the number of kilograms by 2.2

| lbs | kg | lbs | kg | oz | kg | oz | kg |
|-----|-----|-----|-----|-----|-------|-----|-------|
| 0.1 | 0.04 | 0.9 | 0.41 | 0.1 | 0.003 | 0.9 | 0.024 |
| 0.2 | 0.09 | 1 | 0.4 | 0.2 | 0.005 | 1 | 0.03 |
| 0.3 | 0.14 | 2 | 0.9 | 0.3 | 0.008 | 2 | 0.06 |
| 0.4 | 0.18 | 3 | 1.4 | 0.4 | 0.011 | 3 | 0.08 |
| 0.5 | 0.23 | 4 | 1.8 | 0.5 | 0.014 | 4 | 0.11 |
| 0.6 | 0.27 | 5 | 2.3 | 0.6 | 0.017 | 5 | 0.14 |
| 0.7 | 0.32 | 10 | 4.5 | 0.7 | 0.020 | 10 | 0.28 |
| 0.8 | 0.36 | 15 | 6.8 | 0.8 | 0.023 | 15 | 0.42 |

## ENGLISH TO METRIC CONVERSION: TEMPERATURE

To convert Fahrenheit (°F) to Celsius (°C): take number of °F and subtract 32; multiply result by 5; divide result by 9

To convert Celsius (°C) to Fahrenheit (°F): take number of °C and multiply by 9; divide result by 5; add 32 to total

| Fahrenheit (F) | | Celsius (C) | | Fahrenheit (F) | | Celsius (C) | | Fahrenheit (F) | | Celsius (C) | |
|------|-------|------|-------|------|-------|------|-------|------|-------|------|------|
| °F | °C | °C | °F | °F | °C | °C | °F | °F | °C | °C | °F |
| −40 | −40 | −38 | −36.4 | 80 | 26.7 | 18 | 64.4 | 215 | 101.7 | 80 | 176 |
| −35 | −37.2 | −36 | −32.8 | 85 | 29.4 | 20 | 68 | 220 | 104.4 | 85 | 185 |
| −30 | −34.4 | −34 | −29.2 | 90 | 32.2 | 22 | 71.6 | 225 | 107.2 | 90 | 194 |
| −25 | −31.7 | −32 | −25.6 | 95 | 35.0 | 24 | 75.2 | 230 | 110.0 | 95 | 202 |
| −20 | −28.9 | −30 | −22 | 100 | 37.8 | 26 | 78.8 | 235 | 112.8 | 100 | 212 |
| −15 | −26.1 | −28 | −18.4 | 105 | 40.6 | 28 | 82.4 | 240 | 115.6 | 105 | 221 |
| −10 | −23.3 | −26 | −14.8 | 110 | 43.3 | 30 | 86 | 245 | 118.3 | 110 | 230 |
| −5 | −20.6 | −24 | −11.2 | 115 | 46.1 | 32 | 89.6 | 250 | 121.1 | 115 | 239 |
| 0 | −17.8 | −22 | −7.6 | 120 | 48.9 | 34 | 93.2 | 255 | 123.9 | 120 | 248 |
| 1 | −17.2 | −20 | −4 | 125 | 51.7 | 36 | 96.8 | 260 | 126.6 | 125 | 257 |
| 2 | −16.7 | −18 | −0.4 | 130 | 54.4 | 38 | 100.4 | 265 | 129.4 | 130 | 266 |
| 3 | −16.1 | −16 | 3.2 | 135 | 57.2 | 40 | 104 | 270 | 132.2 | 135 | 275 |
| 4 | −15.6 | −14 | 6.8 | 140 | 60.0 | 42 | 107.6 | 275 | 135.0 | 140 | 284 |
| 5 | −15.0 | −12 | 10.4 | 145 | 62.8 | 44 | 112.2 | 280 | 137.8 | 145 | 293 |
| 10 | −12.2 | −10 | 14 | 150 | 65.6 | 46 | 114.8 | 285 | 140.6 | 150 | 302 |
| 15 | −9.4 | −8 | 17.6 | 155 | 68.3 | 48 | 118.4 | 290 | 143.3 | 155 | 311 |
| 20 | −6.7 | −6 | 21.2 | 160 | 71.1 | 50 | 122 | 295 | 146.1 | 160 | 320 |
| 25 | −3.9 | −4 | 24.8 | 165 | 73.9 | 52 | 125.6 | 300 | 148.9 | 165 | 329 |
| 30 | −1.1 | −2 | 28.4 | 170 | 76.7 | 54 | 129.2 | 305 | 151.7 | 170 | 338 |
| 35 | 1.7 | 0 | 32 | 175 | 79.4 | 56 | 132.8 | 310 | 154.4 | 175 | 347 |
| 40 | 4.4 | 2 | 35.6 | 180 | 82.2 | 58 | 136.4 | 315 | 157.2 | 180 | 356 |
| 45 | 7.2 | 4 | 39.2 | 185 | 85.0 | 60 | 140 | 320 | 160.0 | 185 | 365 |
| 50 | 10.0 | 6 | 42.8 | 190 | 87.8 | 62 | 143.6 | 325 | 162.8 | 190 | 374 |
| 55 | 12.8 | 8 | 46.4 | 195 | 90.6 | 64 | 147.2 | 330 | 165.6 | 195 | 383 |
| 60 | 15.6 | 10 | 50 | 200 | 93.3 | 66 | 150.8 | 335 | 168.3 | 200 | 392 |
| 65 | 18.3 | 12 | 53.6 | 205 | 96.1 | 68 | 154.4 | 340 | 171.1 | 205 | 401 |
| 70 | 21.1 | 14 | 57.2 | 210 | 98.9 | 70 | 158 | 345 | 173.9 | 210 | 410 |
| 75 | 23.9 | 16 | 60.8 | 212 | 100.0 | 75 | 167 | 350 | 176.7 | 215 | 414 |

tccs1c01

## ENGLISH TO METRIC CONVERSION: LENGTH

To convert inches (ins.) to millimeters (mm): multiply number of inches by 25.4

To convert millimeters (mm) to inches (ins.): multiply number of millimeters by .04

| Inches | | Decimals | Milli-meters | Inches to millimeters inches | mm | Inches | | Decimals | Milli-meters | Inches to millimeters inches | mm |
|---|---|---|---|---|---|---|---|---|---|---|---|
| | 1/64 | 0.051625 | 0.3969 | 0.0001 | 0.00254 | | 33/64 | 0.515625 | 13.0969 | 0.6 | 15.24 |
| 1/32 | | 0.03125 | 0.7937 | 0.0002 | 0.00508 | 17/32 | | 0.53125 | 13.4937 | 0.7 | 17.78 |
| | 3/64 | 0.046875 | 1.1906 | 0.0003 | 0.00762 | | 35/64 | 0.546875 | 13.8906 | 0.8 | 20.32 |
| 1/16 | | 0.0625 | 1.5875 | 0.0004 | 0.01016 | 9/16 | | 0.5625 | 14.2875 | 0.9 | 22.86 |
| | 5/64 | 0.078125 | 1.9844 | 0.0005 | 0.01270 | | 37/64 | 0.578125 | 14.6844 | 1 | 25.4 |
| 3/32 | | 0.09375 | 2.3812 | 0.0006 | 0.01524 | 19/32 | | 0.59375 | 15.0812 | 2 | 50.8 |
| | 7/64 | 0.109375 | 2.7781 | 0.0007 | 0.01778 | | 39/64 | 0.609375 | 15.4781 | 3 | 76.2 |
| 1/8 | | 0.125 | 3.1750 | 0.0008 | 0.02032 | 5/8 | | 0.625 | 15.8750 | 4 | 101.6 |
| | 9/64 | 0.140625 | 3.5719 | 0.0009 | 0.02286 | | 41/64 | 0.640625 | 16.2719 | 5 | 127.0 |
| 5/32 | | 0.15625 | 3.9687 | 0.001 | 0.0254 | 21/32 | | 0.65625 | 16.6687 | 6 | 152.4 |
| | 11/64 | 0.171875 | 4.3656 | 0.002 | 0.0508 | | 43/64 | 0.671875 | 17.0656 | 7 | 177.8 |
| 3/16 | | 0.1875 | 4.7625 | 0.003 | 0.0762 | 11/16 | | 0.6875 | 17.4625 | 8 | 203.2 |
| | 13/64 | 0.203125 | 5.1594 | 0.004 | 0.1016 | | 45/64 | 0.703125 | 17.8594 | 9 | 228.6 |
| 7/32 | | 0.21875 | 5.5562 | 0.005 | 0.1270 | 23/32 | | 0.71875 | 18.2562 | 10 | 254.0 |
| | 15/64 | 0.234375 | 5.9531 | 0.006 | 0.1524 | | 47/64 | 0.734375 | 18.6531 | 11 | 279.4 |
| 1/4 | | 0.25 | 6.3500 | 0.007 | 0.1778 | 3/4 | | 0.75 | 19.0500 | 12 | 304.8 |
| | 17/64 | 0.265625 | 6.7469 | 0.008 | 0.2032 | | 49/64 | 0.765625 | 19.4469 | 13 | 330.2 |
| 9/32 | | 0.28125 | 7.1437 | 0.009 | 0.2286 | 25/32 | | 0.78125 | 19.8437 | 14 | 355.6 |
| | 19/64 | 0.296875 | 7.5406 | 0.01 | 0.254 | | 51/64 | 0.796875 | 20.2406 | 15 | 381.0 |
| 5/16 | | 0.3125 | 7.9375 | 0.02 | 0.508 | 13/16 | | 0.8125 | 20.6375 | 16 | 406.4 |
| | 21/64 | 0.328125 | 8.3344 | 0.03 | 0.762 | | 53/64 | 0.828125 | 21.0344 | 17 | 431.8 |
| 11/32 | | 0.34375 | 8.7312 | 0.04 | 1.016 | 27/32 | | 0.84375 | 21.4312 | 18 | 457.2 |
| | 23/64 | 0.359375 | 9.1281 | 0.05 | 1.270 | | 55/64 | 0.859375 | 21.8281 | 19 | 482.6 |
| 3/8 | | 0.375 | 9.5250 | 0.06 | 1.524 | 7/8 | | 0.875 | 22.2250 | 20 | 508.0 |
| | 25/64 | 0.390625 | 9.9219 | 0.07 | 1.778 | | 57/64 | 0.890625 | 22.6219 | 21 | 533.4 |
| 13/32 | | 0.40625 | 10.3187 | 0.08 | 2.032 | 29/32 | | 0.90625 | 23.0187 | 22 | 558.8 |
| | 27/64 | 0.421875 | 10.7156 | 0.09 | 2.286 | | 59/64 | 0.921875 | 23.4156 | 23 | 584.2 |
| 7/16 | | 0.4375 | 11.1125 | 0.1 | 2.54 | 15/16 | | 0.9375 | 23.8125 | 24 | 609.6 |
| | 29/64 | 0.453125 | 11.5094 | 0.2 | 5.08 | | 61/64 | 0.953125 | 24.2094 | 25 | 635.0 |
| 15/32 | | 0.46875 | 11.9062 | 0.3 | 7.62 | 31/32 | | 0.96875 | 24.6062 | 26 | 660.4 |
| | 31/64 | 0.484375 | 12.3031 | 0.4 | 10.16 | | 63/64 | 0.984375 | 25.0031 | 27 | 690.6 |
| 1/2 | | 0.5 | 12.7000 | 0.5 | 12.70 | | | | | | |

## ENGLISH TO METRIC CONVERSION: TORQUE

To convert foot-pounds (ft. lbs.) to Newton-meters: multiply the number of ft. lbs. by 1.3

To convert inch-pounds (in. lbs.) to Newton-meters: multiply the number of in. lbs. by .11

| in lbs | N-m | in lbs | N-m | in lbs | N-m | in lbs | N-m | in lbs | N-m |
|---|---|---|---|---|---|---|---|---|---|
| 0.1 | 0.01 | 1 | 0.11 | 10 | 1.13 | 19 | 2.15 | 28 | 3.16 |
| 0.2 | 0.02 | 2 | 0.23 | 11 | 1.24 | 20 | 2.26 | 29 | 3.28 |
| 0.3 | 0.03 | 3 | 0.34 | 12 | 1.36 | 21 | 2.37 | 30 | 3.39 |
| 0.4 | 0.04 | 4 | 0.45 | 13 | 1.47 | 22 | 2.49 | 31 | 3.50 |
| 0.5 | 0.06 | 5 | 0.56 | 14 | 1.58 | 23 | 2.60 | 32 | 3.62 |
| 0.6 | 0.07 | 6 | 0.68 | 15 | 1.70 | 24 | 2.71 | 33 | 3.73 |
| 0.7 | 0.08 | 7 | 0.78 | 16 | 1.81 | 25 | 2.82 | 34 | 3.84 |
| 0.8 | 0.09 | 8 | 0.90 | 17 | 1.92 | 26 | 2.94 | 35 | 3.95 |
| 0.9 | 0.10 | 9 | 1.02 | 18 | 2.03 | 27 | 3.05 | 36 | 4.07 |

## ENGLISH TO METRIC CONVERSION: TORQUE

Torque is now expressed as either foot-pounds (ft./lbs.) or inch-pounds (in./lbs.). The metric measurement unit for torque is the Newton-meter (Nm). This unit—the Nm—will be used for all SI metric torque references, both the present ft./lbs. and in./lbs.

| ft lbs | N-m | ft lbs | N-m | ft lbs | N-m | ft lbs | N-m |
|--------|------|--------|------|--------|-------|--------|-------|
| 0.1 | 0.1 | 33 | 44.7 | 74 | 100.3 | 115 | 155.9 |
| 0.2 | 0.3 | 34 | 46.1 | 75 | 101.7 | 116 | 157.3 |
| 0.3 | 0.4 | 35 | 47.4 | 76 | 103.0 | 117 | 158.6 |
| 0.4 | 0.5 | 36 | 48.8 | 77 | 104.4 | 118 | 160.0 |
| 0.5 | 0.7 | 37 | 50.7 | 78 | 105.8 | 119 | 161.3 |
| 0.6 | 0.8 | 38 | 51.5 | 79 | 107.1 | 120 | 162.7 |
| 0.7 | 1.0 | 39 | 52.9 | 80 | 108.5 | 121 | 164.0 |
| 0.8 | 1.1 | 40 | 54.2 | 81 | 109.8 | 122 | 165.4 |
| 0.9 | 1.2 | 41 | 55.6 | 82 | 111.2 | 123 | 166.8 |
| 1 | 1.3 | 42 | 56.9 | 83 | 112.5 | 124 | 168.1 |
| 2 | 2.7 | 43 | 58.3 | 84 | 113.9 | 125 | 169.5 |
| 3 | 4.1 | 44 | 59.7 | 85 | 115.2 | 126 | 170.8 |
| 4 | 5.4 | 45 | 61.0 | 86 | 116.6 | 127 | 172.2 |
| 5 | 6.8 | 46 | 62.4 | 87 | 118.0 | 128 | 173.5 |
| 6 | 8.1 | 47 | 63.7 | 88 | 119.3 | 129 | 174.9 |
| 7 | 9.5 | 48 | 65.1 | 89 | 120.7 | 130 | 176.2 |
| 8 | 10.8 | 49 | 66.4 | 90 | 122.0 | 131 | 177.6 |
| 9 | 12.2 | 50 | 67.8 | 91 | 123.4 | 132 | 179.0 |
| 10 | 13.6 | 51 | 69.2 | 92 | 124.7 | 133 | 180.3 |
| 11 | 14.9 | 52 | 70.5 | 93 | 126.1 | 134 | 181.7 |
| 12 | 16.3 | 53 | 71.9 | 94 | 127.4 | 135 | 183.0 |
| 13 | 17.6 | 54 | 73.2 | 95 | 128.8 | 136 | 184.4 |
| 14 | 18.9 | 55 | 74.6 | 96 | 130.2 | 137 | 185.7 |
| 15 | 20.3 | 56 | 75.9 | 97 | 131.5 | 138 | 187.1 |
| 16 | 21.7 | 57 | 77.3 | 98 | 132.9 | 139 | 188.5 |
| 17 | 23.0 | 58 | 78.6 | 99 | 134.2 | 140 | 189.8 |
| 18 | 24.4 | 59 | 80.0 | 100 | 135.6 | 141 | 191.2 |
| 19 | 25.8 | 60 | 81.4 | 101 | 136.9 | 142 | 192.5 |
| 20 | 27.1 | 61 | 82.7 | 102 | 138.3 | 143 | 193.9 |
| 21 | 28.5 | 62 | 84.1 | 103 | 139.6 | 144 | 195.2 |
| 22 | 29.8 | 63 | 85.4 | 104 | 141.0 | 145 | 196.6 |
| 23 | 31.2 | 64 | 86.8 | 105 | 142.4 | 146 | 198.0 |
| 24 | 32.5 | 65 | 88.1 | 106 | 143.7 | 147 | 199.3 |
| 25 | 33.9 | 66 | 89.5 | 107 | 145.1 | 148 | 200.7 |
| 26 | 35.2 | 67 | 90.8 | 108 | 146.4 | 149 | 202.0 |
| 27 | 36.6 | 68 | 92.2 | 109 | 147.8 | 150 | 203.4 |
| 28 | 38.0 | 69 | 93.6 | 110 | 149.1 | 151 | 204.7 |
| 29 | 39.3 | 70 | 94.9 | 111 | 150.5 | 152 | 206.1 |
| 30 | 40.7 | 71 | 96.3 | 112 | 151.8 | 153 | 207.4 |
| 31 | 42.0 | 72 | 97.6 | 113 | 153.2 | 154 | 208.8 |
| 32 | 43.4 | 73 | 99.0 | 114 | 154.6 | 155 | 210.2 |

tccs1c03

## ENGLISH TO METRIC CONVERSION: FORCE

Force is presently measured in pounds (lbs.). This type of measurement is used to measure spring pressure, specifically how many pounds it takes to compress a spring. Our present force unit (the pound) will be replaced in SI metric measurements by the Newton (N). This term will eventually see use in specifications for electric motor brush spring pressures, valve spring pressures, etc.

To convert pounds (lbs.) to Newton (N): multiply the number of lbs. by 4.45

| lbs | N | lbs | N | lbs | N | oz | N |
|---|---|---|---|---|---|---|---|
| 0.01 | 0.04 | 21 | 93.4 | 59 | 262.4 | 1 | 0.3 |
| 0.02 | 0.09 | 22 | 97.9 | 60 | 266.9 | 2 | 0.6 |
| 0.03 | 0.13 | 23 | 102.3 | 61 | 271.3 | 3 | 0.8 |
| 0.04 | 0.18 | 24 | 106.8 | 62 | 275.8 | 4 | 1.1 |
| 0.05 | 0.22 | 25 | 111.2 | 63 | 280.2 | 5 | 1.4 |
| 0.06 | 0.27 | 26 | 115.6 | 64 | 284.6 | 6 | 1.7 |
| 0.07 | 0.31 | 27 | 120.1 | 65 | 289.1 | 7 | 2.0 |
| 0.08 | 0.36 | 28 | 124.6 | 66 | 293.6 | 8 | 2.2 |
| 0.09 | 0.40 | 29 | 129.0 | 67 | 298.0 | 9 | 2.5 |
| 0.1 | 0.4 | 30 | 133.4 | 68 | 302.5 | 10 | 2.8 |
| 0.2 | 0.9 | 31 | 137.9 | 69 | 306.9 | 11 | 3.1 |
| 0.3 | 1.3 | 32 | 142.3 | 70 | 311.4 | 12 | 3.3 |
| 0.4 | 1.8 | 33 | 146.8 | 71 | 315.8 | 13 | 3.6 |
| 0.5 | 2.2 | 34 | 151.2 | 72 | 320.3 | 14 | 3.9 |
| 0.6 | 2.7 | 35 | 155.7 | 73 | 324.7 | 15 | 4.2 |
| 0.7 | 3.1 | 36 | 160.1 | 74 | 329.2 | 16 | 4.4 |
| 0.8 | 3.6 | 37 | 164.6 | 75 | 333.6 | 17 | 4.7 |
| 0.9 | 4.0 | 38 | 169.0 | 76 | 338.1 | 18 | 5.0 |
| 1 | 4.4 | 39 | 173.5 | 77 | 342.5 | 19 | 5.3 |
| 2 | 8.9 | 40 | 177.9 | 78 | 347.0 | 20 | 5.6 |
| 3 | 13.4 | 41 | 182.4 | 79 | 351.4 | 21 | 5.8 |
| 4 | 17.8 | 42 | 186.8 | 80 | 355.9 | 22 | 6.1 |
| 5 | 22.2 | 43 | 191.3 | 81 | 360.3 | 23 | 6.4 |
| 6 | 26.7 | 44 | 195.7 | 82 | 364.8 | 24 | 6.7 |
| 7 | 31.1 | 45 | 200.2 | 83 | 369.2 | 25 | 7.0 |
| 8 | 35.6 | 46 | 204.6 | 84 | 373.6 | 26 | 7.2 |
| 9 | 40.0 | 47 | 209.1 | 85 | 378.1 | 27 | 7.5 |
| 10 | 44.5 | 48 | 213.5 | 86 | 382.6 | 28 | 7.8 |
| 11 | 48.9 | 49 | 218.0 | 87 | 387.0 | 29 | 8.1 |
| 12 | 53.4 | 50 | 224.4 | 88 | 391.4 | 30 | 8.3 |
| 13 | 57.8 | 51 | 226.9 | 89 | 395.9 | 31 | 8.6 |
| 14 | 62.3 | 52 | 231.3 | 90 | 400.3 | 32 | 8.9 |
| 15 | 66.7 | 53 | 235.8 | 91 | 404.8 | 33 | 9.2 |
| 16 | 71.2 | 54 | 240.2 | 92 | 409.2 | 34 | 9.4 |
| 17 | 75.6 | 55 | 244.6 | 93 | 413.7 | 35 | 9.7 |
| 18 | 80.1 | 56 | 249.1 | 94 | 418.1 | 36 | 10.0 |
| 19 | 84.5 | 57 | 253.6 | 95 | 422.6 | 37 | 10.3 |
| 20 | 89.0 | 58 | 258.0 | 96 | 427.0 | 38 | 10.6 |

tccs1c04

## ENGLISH TO METRIC CONVERSION: LIQUID CAPACITY

Liquid or fluid capacity is presently expressed as pints, quarts or gallons, or a combination of all of these. In the metric system the liter (l) will become the basic unit. Fractions of a liter would be expressed as deciliters, centiliters, or most frequently (and commonly) as milliliters.

To convert pints (pts.) to liters (l): multiply the number of pints by .47
To convert liters (l) to pints (pts.): multiply the number of liters by 2.1
To convert quarts (qts.) to liters (l): multiply the number of quarts by .95

To convert liters (l) to quarts (qts.): multiply the number of liters by 1.06
To convert gallons (gals.) to liters (l): multiply the number of gallons by 3.8
To convert liters (l) to gallons (gals.): multiply the number of liters by .26

| gals | liters | qts | liters | pts | liters |
|------|--------|-----|--------|-----|--------|
| 0.1 | 0.38 | 0.1 | 0.10 | 0.1 | 0.05 |
| 0.2 | 0.76 | 0.2 | 0.19 | 0.2 | 0.10 |
| 0.3 | 1.1 | 0.3 | 0.28 | 0.3 | 0.14 |
| 0.4 | 1.5 | 0.4 | 0.38 | 0.4 | 0.19 |
| 0.5 | 1.9 | 0.5 | 0.47 | 0.5 | 0.24 |
| 0.6 | 2.3 | 0.6 | 0.57 | 0.6 | 0.28 |
| 0.7 | 2.6 | 0.7 | 0.66 | 0.7 | 0.33 |
| 0.8 | 3.0 | 0.8 | 0.76 | 0.8 | 0.38 |
| 0.9 | 3.4 | 0.9 | 0.85 | 0.9 | 0.43 |
| 1 | 3.8 | 1 | 1.0 | 1 | 0.5 |
| 2 | 7.6 | 2 | 1.9 | 2 | 1.0 |
| 3 | 11.4 | 3 | 2.8 | 3 | 1.4 |
| 4 | 15.1 | 4 | 3.8 | 4 | 1.9 |
| 5 | 18.9 | 5 | 4.7 | 5 | 2.4 |
| 6 | 22.7 | 6 | 5.7 | 6 | 2.8 |
| 7 | 26.5 | 7 | 6.6 | 7 | 3.3 |
| 8 | 30.3 | 8 | 7.6 | 8 | 3.8 |
| 9 | 34.1 | 9 | 8.5 | 9 | 4.3 |
| 10 | 37.8 | 10 | 9.5 | 10 | 4.7 |
| 11 | 41.6 | 11 | 10.4 | 11 | 5.2 |
| 12 | 45.4 | 12 | 11.4 | 12 | 5.7 |
| 13 | 49.2 | 13 | 12.3 | 13 | 6.2 |
| 14 | 53.0 | 14 | 13.2 | 14 | 6.6 |
| 15 | 56.8 | 15 | 14.2 | 15 | 7.1 |
| 16 | 60.6 | 16 | 15.1 | 16 | 7.6 |
| 17 | 64.3 | 17 | 16.1 | 17 | 8.0 |
| 18 | 68.1 | 18 | 17.0 | 18 | 8.5 |
| 19 | 71.9 | 19 | 18.0 | 19 | 9.0 |
| 20 | 75.7 | 20 | 18.9 | 20 | 9.5 |
| 21 | 79.5 | 21 | 19.9 | 21 | 9.9 |
| 22 | 83.2 | 22 | 20.8 | 22 | 10.4 |
| 23 | 87.0 | 23 | 21.8 | 23 | 10.9 |
| 24 | 90.8 | 24 | 22.7 | 24 | 11.4 |
| 25 | 94.6 | 25 | 23.6 | 25 | 11.8 |
| 26 | 98.4 | 26 | 24.6 | 26 | 12.3 |
| 27 | 102.2 | 27 | 25.5 | 27 | 12.8 |
| 28 | 106.0 | 28 | 26.5 | 28 | 13.2 |
| 29 | 110.0 | 29 | 27.4 | 29 | 13.7 |
| 30 | 113.5 | 30 | 28.4 | 30 | 14.2 |

tccs1c05

# 2

# ENGINE
# PERFORMANCE
# AND
# TUNE-UP

## TUNE-UP PROCEDURES

Neither tune-up nor troubleshooting can be considered independently since each has a direct relationship with the other.

It is advisable to follow a definite and thorough tune-up procedure. Tune-up consists of three separate steps: Analysis, the process of determining whether normal wear is responsible for performance loss, and whether parts require replacement or service; parts replacement or service; and adjustment, where engine adjustments are performed.

The manufacturer's recommended interval for tune-ups is every 12,000 miles (19,000 km) or 12 months, whichever comes first for 1970-74, and 22,500 miles (36,200 km) or 18 months for 1975-86, except for heavy duty emission models, which use the 12 month/12,000 miles (19,000 km) schedule in all years. These intervals should be shortened if the truck is subjected to severe operating conditions such as trailer pulling, or if starting and running problems are noticed. It is assumed that the routine maintenance described in Section 1 has been kept up, as this will have an effect on the results of the tune-up. All the applicable tune-up steps should be followed, as each adjustment complements the effects of the others. If the tune-up (emission control) sticker in the engine compartment disagrees with the information presented in the Tune-up Specifications chart in this section, the sticker figures must be followed. The sticker information reflects running changes made by the manufacturer during production. The light duty sticker is usually found on the underhood sheet metal above the grille. The heavy duty sticker is usually on top of the air cleaner.

Diesel engines do not require tune-ups per say, as there is no ignition system.

Troubleshooting is a logical sequence of procedures designed to locate a particular cause of trouble. It is advisable to read the entire section before beginning a tune-up, although those who are more familiar with tune-up procedures may wish to go directly to the instructions.

## Spark Plugs

▶ See Figure 1

A typical spark plug consists of a metal shell surrounding a ceramic insulator. A metal electrode extends downward through the center of the insulator and protrudes a small distance. Located at the end of the plug and attached to the side of the outer metal shell is the side electrode. The side electrode bends in at a 90° angle so that its tip is just past and parallel to the tip of the center electrode. The distance between these two electrodes (measured in thousandths of an inch or hundredths of a millimeter) is called the spark plug gap.

The spark plug does not produce a spark but instead provides a gap across which the current can arc. The coil produces anywhere from 20,000 to 50,000 volts (depending on the type and application) which travels through the wires to the spark plugs. The current passes along the center electrode and jumps the gap to the side electrode, and in doing so, ignites the air/fuel mixture in the combustion chamber.

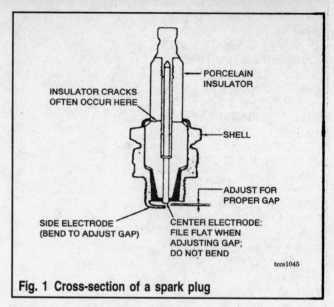

**Fig. 1 Cross-section of a spark plug**

## SPARK PLUG HEAT RANGE

▶ See Figure 2

Spark plug heat range is the ability of the plug to dissipate heat. The longer the insulator (or the farther it extends into the engine), the hotter the plug will operate; the shorter the insulator (the closer the electrode is to the block's cooling passages) the cooler it will operate. A plug that absorbs little heat and remains too cool will quickly accumulate deposits of oil and carbon since it is not hot enough to burn them off. This leads to plug fouling and consequently to misfiring. A plug that absorbs too much heat will have no deposits but, due to the excessive heat, the electrodes will burn away quickly and might possibly lead to preignition or other ignition problems. Preignition takes place when plug tips get so hot that they glow sufficiently to ignite the air/fuel mixture before the actual spark occurs. This early ignition will usually cause a pinging during low speeds and heavy loads.

The general rule of thumb for choosing the correct heat range when picking a spark plug is: if most of your driving is long distance, high speed travel, use a colder plug; if most of your driving is stop and go, use a hotter plug. Original equipment plugs are generally a good compromise between the 2 styles and most people never have the need to change their plugs from the factory-recommended heat range.

## REMOVAL & INSTALLATION

▶ See Figures 3 and 4

A set of spark plugs usually requires replacement after about 20,000-30,000 miles (32,000-48,000 km), depending on your style of driving. In normal operation plug gap increases about 0.001 in (0.025 mm) for every 2,500 miles (4000 km). As the gap increases, the plug's voltage requirement also increases. It requires a greater voltage to jump the wider gap and about two to three times as much voltage to fire the plug at high

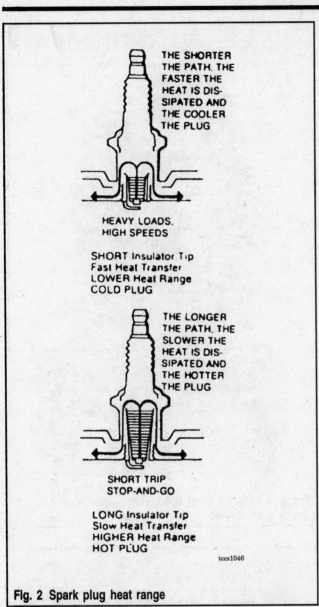

THE SHORTER
THE PATH, THE
FASTER THE
HEAT IS DIS-
SIPATED AND
THE COOLER
THE PLUG

HEAVY LOADS,
HIGH SPEEDS

SHORT Insulator Tip
Fast Heat Transfer
LOWER Heat Range
COLD PLUG

THE LONGER
THE PATH, THE
SLOWER THE
HEAT IS DIS-
SIPATED AND
THE HOTTER
THE PLUG

SHORT TRIP
STOP-AND-GO

LONG Insulator Tip
Slow Heat Transfer
HIGHER Heat Range
HOT PLUG

tccs1046

**Fig. 2 Spark plug heat range**

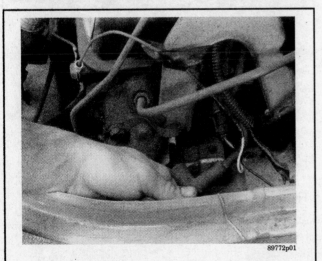

**Fig. 3 Disconnect the spark plug wire by pulling the boot**

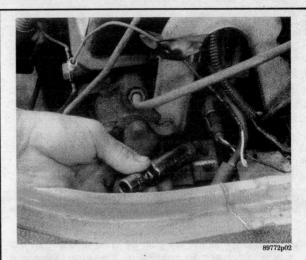

89772p02

**Fig. 4 Use a spark plug socket that is equipped with a rubber insert to properly hold the plug**

speeds than at idle. The improved air/fuel ratio control of modern fuel injection combined with the higher voltage output of modern ignition systems will often allow an engine to run significantly longer on a set of standard spark plugs, but keep in mind that efficiency will drop as the gap widdens (along with fuel economy and power).

When you're removing spark plugs, work on one at a time. Don't start by removing the plug wires all at once, because, unless you number them, they may become mixed up. Take a minute before you begin and number the wires with tape.

1. Disconnect the negative battery cable, and if the vehicle has been run recently, allow the engine to thoroughly cool.

2. Carefully twist the spark plug wire boot to loosen it, then pull upward and remove the boot from the plug. Be sure to pull on the boot and not on the wire, otherwise the connector located inside the boot may become separated.

3. Using compressed air, blow any water or debris from the spark plug well to assure that no harmful contaminants are allowed to enter the combustion chamber when the spark plug is removed. If compressed air is not available, use a rag or a brush to clean the area.

➡ **Remove the spark plugs when the engine is cold, if possible, to prevent damage to the threads. If removal of the plugs is difficult, apply a few drops of penetrating oil or silicone spray to the area around the base of the plug, and allow it a few minutes to work.**

4. Using a spark plug socket that is equipped with a rubber insert to properly hold the plug, turn the spark plug counterclockwise to loosen and remove the spark plug from the bore.

**✳✳WARNING**

**Be sure not to use a flexible extension on the socket. Use of a flexible extension may allow a shear force to be applied to the plug. A shear force could break the plug off in the cylinder head, leading to costly and frustrating repairs.**

To install:

5. Inspect the spark plug boot for tears or damage. If a damaged boot is found, the spark plug wire must be replaced.

6. Using a wire feeler gauge, check and adjust the spark plug gap. When using a gauge, the proper size should pass between the electrodes with a slight drag. The next larger size should not be able to pass while the next smaller size should pass freely.

7. Carefully thread the plug into the bore by hand. If resistance is felt before the plug is almost completely threaded, back the plug out and begin threading again. In small, hard to reach areas, an old spark plug wire and boot could be used as a threading tool. The boot will hold the plug while you twist the end of the wire and the wire is supple enough to twist before it would allow the plug to crossthread.

### ❋❋WARNING

**Do not use the spark plug socket to thread the plugs. Always carefully thread the plug by hand or using an old plug wire to prevent the possibility of crossthreading and damaging the cylinder head bore.**

8. Carefully tighten the spark plug. If the plug you are installing is equipped with a crush washer, seat the plug, then tighten about ¼ turn to crush the washer. If you are installing a tapered seat plug, tighten the plug to specifications provided by the vehicle or plug manufacturer.

9. Apply a small amount of silicone dielectric compound to the end of the spark plug lead or inside the spark plug boot to prevent sticking, then install the boot to the spark plug and push until it clicks into place. The click may be felt or heard, then gently pull back on the boot to assure proper contact.

## INSPECTION & GAPPING

▶ See Figures 5, 6, 7, 8, 9, 10, 11, 12, 13 and 14

Check the plugs for deposits and wear. If they are not going to be replaced, clean the plugs thoroughly. Remember that any kind of deposit will decrease the efficiency of the plug. Plugs can be cleaned on a spark plug cleaning machine, which can sometimes be found in service stations, or you can do an acceptable job of cleaning with a stiff brush. If the plugs are cleaned, the electrodes must be filed flat. Use an ignition points file, not an emery board or the like, which will leave deposits. The electrodes must be filed perfectly flat with sharp edges; rounded edges reduce the spark plug voltage by as much as 50%.

Check spark plug gap before installation. The ground electrode (the L-shaped one connected to the body of the plug) must be parallel to the center electrode and the specified size wire gauge (please refer to the Tune-Up Specifications chart for details) must pass between the electrodes with a slight drag.

➡NEVER adjust the gap on a used platinum type spark plug.

tccs2135

**Fig. 5 A normally worn spark plug should have light tan or gray deposits on the firing tip**

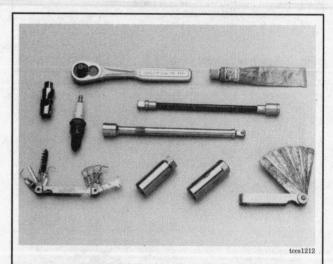

tccs1212

**Fig. 6 A variety of tools and gauges are needed for spark plug service**

Fig. 7 A carbon fouled plug, identified by soft, sooty, black deposits, may indicate an improperly tuned vehicle. Check the air cleaner, ignition components and engine control system

Fig. 9 A physically damaged spark plug may be evidence of severe detonation in that cylinder. Watch that cylinder carefully between services, as a continued detonation will not only damage the plug, but could also damage the engine

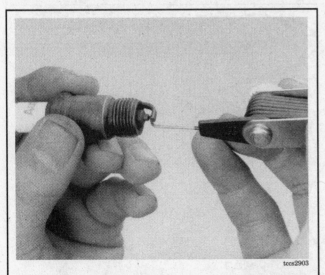

Fig. 8 Checking the spark plug gap with a feeler gauge

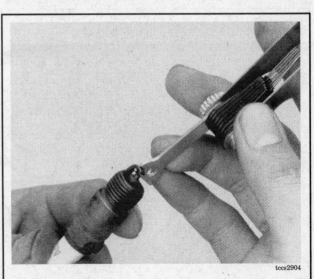

Fig. 10 Adjusting the spark plug gap

Fig. 11 An oil fouled spark plug indicates an engine with worn piston rings and/or bad valve seals allowing excessive oil to enter the chamber

Fig. 12 This spark plug has been left in the engine too long, as evidenced by the extreme gap — Plugs with such an extreme gap can cause misfiring and stumbling accompanied by a noticeable lack of power

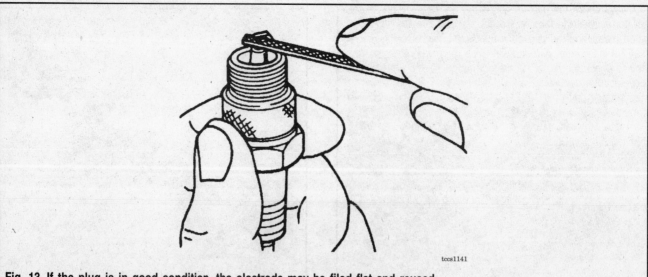

Fig. 13 If the plug is in good condition, the electrode may be filed flat and reused

tccs2140

**Fig. 14 A bridged or almost bridged spark plug, identified by a build-up between the electrodes caused by excessive carbon or oil build-up on the plug**

Always check the gap on new plugs as they are not always set correctly at the factory. Do not use a flat feeler gauge when measuring the gap on a used plug, because the reading may be inaccurate. A round-wire type gapping tool is the best way to check the gap. The correct gauge should pass through the electrode gap with a slight drag. If you're in doubt, try one size smaller and one larger. The smaller gauge should go through easily, while the larger one shouldn't go through at all. Wire gapping tools usually have a bending tool attached. Use that to adjust the side electrode until the proper distance is obtained. Absolutely never attempt to bend the center electrode. Also, be careful not to bend the side electrode too far or too often as it may weaken and break off within the engine, requiring removal of the cylinder head to retrieve it.

## Spark Plug Wires

### TESTING

▶ **See Figure 15**

At every tune-up/inspection, visually check the spark plug cables for burns cuts, or breaks in the insulation. Check the boots and the nipples on the distributor cap and/or coil. Replace any damaged wiring.

Every 50,000 miles (80,000 km) or 60 months, the resistance of the wires should be checked with an ohmmeter. Wires with excessive resistance will cause misfiring, and may make the engine difficult to start in damp weather.

To check resistance, remove the distributor cap, leaving the wires in place. Connect one lead of an ohmmeter to an electrode within the cap. Connect the other lead to the corresponding spark plug terminal (remove it from the spark plug for this test). Replace any wire which shows a resistance over 30,000 ohms. Generally speaking, however, resistance should not be over 25,000 ohms, and 30,000 ohms must be considered the outer limit of acceptability.

It should be remembered that resistance is also a function of length. The longer the wire, the greater the resistance. Thus, if the wires on your car are longer than the factory originals, the resistance will be higher, possibly outside these limits.

### REMOVAL & INSTALLATION

▶ **See Figures 16 and 17**

When installing new wires, replace them one at a time to avoid mixups. Start by replacing the longest one first. Install the boot firmly over the spark plug. Route the wire over the same path as the original. Insert the nipple firmly onto the tower on the distributor cap, then install the cap cover and latches to secure the wires.

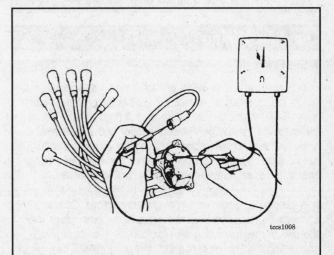

tccs1008

**Fig. 15 Checking plug wire resistance through the distributor cap with an ohmmeter**

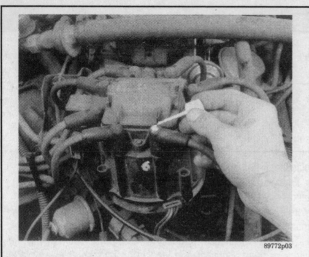

Fig. 16 Mark the wires and cap before disconnecting the wires

Fig. 17 Pull the wire from the boot, not the wire itself

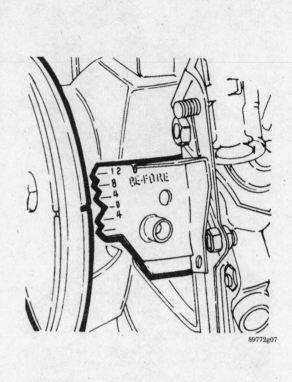

Fig. 18 Common ignition timing marks and location

## Ignition Timing

▶ See Figure 18

Timing should be checked at each tune-up and any time the points are adjusted or replaced. It isn't likely to change much with HEI. The timing marks consist of a notch on the rim of the crankshaft pulley or vibration damper and a graduated scale attached to the engine front (timing) cover. A strobo-scopic flash (dynamic) timing light must be used, as a static light is too inaccurate for emission controlled engines.

There are three basic types of timing light available. The first is a simple neon bulb with two wire connections. One wire connects to the spark plug terminal and the other plugs into the end of the spark plug wire for the No. 1 cylinder, thus connecting the light in series with the spark plug. This type of light is pretty dim and must be held very closely to the timing marks to be seen. Sometimes a dark corner has to be sought out to see the flash at all. This type of light is very inexpensive. The second type operates from the vehicle battery, two

alligator clips connect to the battery terminals, while an adapter enables a third clip to be connected between No. 1 spark plug and wire. This type is a bit more expensive, but it provides a nice bright flash that you can see even in bright sunlight. It is the type most often seen in professional shops. The third type replaces the battery power source with 100 volt current.

Some timing lights have other features built into them, such as dwell meters, or tachometers. These are convenient, in that they reduce the tangle of wires under the hood when you're working, but may duplicate the functions of tools you already have. One worthwhile feature, which is becoming more of a necessity with higher voltage ignition systems, is an inductive pickup. The inductive pickup clamps around the No. 1 spark plug wire, sensing the surges of high voltage electricity as they are sent to the plug. The advantage is that no mechanical connection is inserted between the wire and the plug. The advantage is that no mechanical connection is inserted be-tween the wire and the plug, which eliminates false signals to the timing light. A timing light with an inductive pickup should be used on HEI systems.

## CHECKING & ADJUSTMENT

1. Warm up the engine to normal operating temperature. Stop the engine and connect the timing light to the No. 1 (left front on V8, front on 6-cylinder) spark plug wire, wither at the plug or at the distributor cap. You can also use the No. 6 wire, if it is more convenient. No. 6 is the rear cylinder on a 6-cylinder, and the third cylinder back on the right bank of a V8. Numbering is illustrated earlier in this section.

➡**Do not pierce the plug wire insulation with HEI; it will cause a miss. The best method is an inductive pickup timing light.**

Clean off the timing marks and mark the pulley or damper notch and timing scale with white chalk.

2. Disconnect and plug the vacuum line at the distributor. This is done to prevent any distributor vacuum advance. Check the underhood emission sticker for any other hoses or wires which may need to be disconnected.

3. Start the engine and adjust the idle speed to that specified in the Tune-up Specifications chart. With automatic transmission, set the specified idle speed in Park. It will be too high, since it is normally (in most cases) adjusted in Drive. You can disconnect the idle solenoid, if any, to get the speed down. Otherwise, adjust the idle speed screw. This is done to prevent any centrifugal (mechanical) advance. The tachometer hookup for 1967-74 models is the same as the dwell meter hookup shown in the Troubleshooting section. On 1975 and later HEI systems, the tachometer connects to the TACH terminal on the distributor or on the coil (6-cylinder through 1977) and to a ground. Some tachometers must connect to the TACH terminal and to the positive battery terminal. Some tachometers won't work with HEI.

### ✳✳WARNING

**Never ground the HEI TACH terminal; serious system damage will result.**

4. Aim the timing light at the pointer marks. Be careful not to touch the fan, because it may appear to be standing still. If the pulley or damper notch isn't aligned with the proper timing mark (see the Tune-up Specifications chart), the timing will have to be adjusted.

➡**TDC or Top Dead Center corresponds to 0°B, or BTDC, or Before Top Dead Center may be shown as BEFORE. A, or ATDC, or After Top Dead Center may be shown as AFTER.**

5. Loosen the distributor base clamp locknut. You can buy trick wrenches which make this task a lot easier on V8s. Turn

the distributor slowly to adjust the timing, holding it by the body and not the cap. Turn the distributor in the direction of rotor rotation (found in the firing order illustrations) to retard, and against the direction of rotation to advance.

6. Tighten the locknut. Check the timing again, in case the distributor moved slightly as you tightened it.

7. Replace the distributor vacuum line. Correct the idle speed.

8. Stop the engine and disconnect the timing light.

## Diesel Injection Timing

▶ **See Figure 19**

For the engine to be properly timed, the marks on the top of the engine front cover must be aligned with the marks on the injection pump flange. The engine must be OFF when the timing is reset.

➡**On 49-state 6.2L engines, the marks are scribe lines. On California 6.2L engines, the marks are half circles.**

1. Loosen the three pump retaining nuts. If the marks are not aligned, adjustment is necessary.

2. Loosen the three pump retaining nuts.

3. Align the mark on the injection pump with the mark on the front cover. Tighten the nuts to 30 ft. lbs. (40 Nm).

➡**Use a ³⁄₄in. (19.05mm) open end wrench on the nut at the front of the injection pump to aid in rotating the pump to align the marks.**

4. Adjust the throttle linkage if necessary.

89772g08

**Fig. 19 Diesel injection timing marks, 6.2L shown. Marks shown are in alignment**

## FIRING ORDERS

➡To avoid confusion, remove and tag the spark plug wires one at a time, for replacement.

If a distributor is not keyed for installation with only one orientation, it could have been removed previously and rewired. The resultant wiring would hold the correct firing order, but could change the relative placement of the plug towers in relation to the engine. For this reason it is imperative that you label all wires before disconnecting any of them. Also, before removal, compare the current wiring with the accompanying illustrations. If the current wiring does not match, make notes in your book to reflect how your engine is wired.

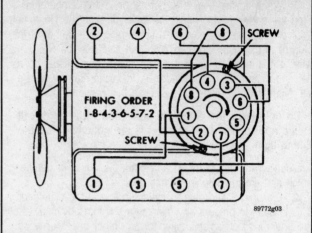

**Fig. 22 V8 engines — electronic ignition**
**Firing order: 1-8-4-3-6-5-7-2**
**Distributor rotation: clockwise**

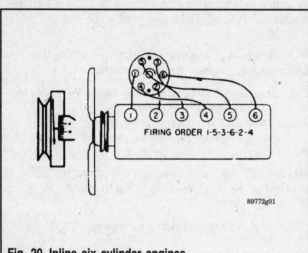

**Fig. 20 Inline six cylinder engines**
**Firing order: 1-5-3-6-2-4**
**Distributor rotation: clockwise**

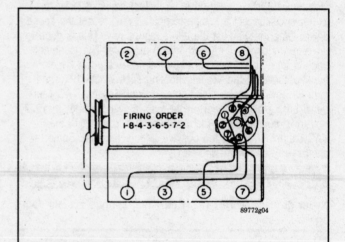

**Fig. 23 V8 engine — point type ignition**
**Firing order: 1-8-4-3-6-5-7-2**
**Distributor rotation: clockwise**

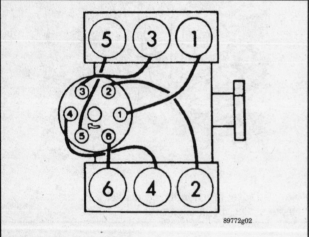

**Fig. 21 4.3L V6 engines**
**Firing order: 1-6-5-4-3-2**
**Distributor rotation: clockwise**

## POINT TYPE IGNITION SYSTEM

### Breaker Points and Condenser

#### REMOVAL & INSTALLATION

▶ See Figures 24 and 25

The usual procedure is to replace the condenser each time the point is replaced. Although this is not always necessary, it is easy to do at this time and the cost is negligible. Every time you adjust or replace the breaker points, the ignition timing must be checked and, if necessary, adjusted. No special equipment other than a feeler gauge is required for point replacement or adjustment, but a dwell meter is strongly advised.

1. Push down on the spring loaded V8 distributor cap retaining screws and give them ½ turn to release. Unscrew the cap retaining screws on the 6-cyl. Remove the cap. You might have to unclip or detach some or all of the plug wires to remove the cap.

2. Clean the cap inside and out with a clean rag. Check for cracks and carbon paths. A carbon path shows up as a dark line, usually from the cap sockets or inside terminals to a ground. Check the condition of the carbon button inside the center of the cap and the inside terminals. Replace the cap as necessary.

3. Pull the 6-cylinder rotor up and off the shaft. Remove the two screws and lift the round V8 rotor off. There is less danger of losing the screws if you just back them out all the way and lift them off with the rotor. Clean off the metal outer tip if it is burned or corroded. Don't file it. Replace the rotor as necessary or if one came with your tune-up kit.

4. Remove the radio frequency interference shield if your 1973-74 V8 distributor has one. Watch out for those little screws! The factory says that the points don't need to be replaced if they are only slightly rough or pitted. However, sad experience shows that it is more economical and reliable in the long run to replace the point set while the distributor is open, than to have to do this at a later (and possibly more inconvenient) time.

5. Pull off the two wire terminals from the point assembly. One wire comes from the condenser and the other comes from within the distributor. The terminals are usually held in place by spring tension only. There might be a clamp screw securing the terminals on some older versions. There is also available a one piece point/condenser assembly for V8s. The radio frequency interference shield isn't needed with this set. Loosen the point set hold-down screw(s). Be very careful not to drop any of these little screws inside the distributor. If this happens, the distributor will probably have to be removed to get at the screw. If the hold-down screw is lost elsewhere, it must be replaced with one that is no longer than the original to avoid interference with the distributor workings. Remove the point set, even if it is to be reused.

6. If the points are to be reused, clean them with a few strokes of a special point file. This is done with the points removed to prevent tiny metal filings getting into the distributor.

LATERAL MISALIGNMENT     PROPER LATERAL ALIGNMENT

CORRECT LATERAL MISALIGNMENT BY BENDING FIXED CONTACT SUPPORT *NEVER BEND BREAKER LEVER*

89772g05

Fig. 24 View of the improper and proper breaker point alignments

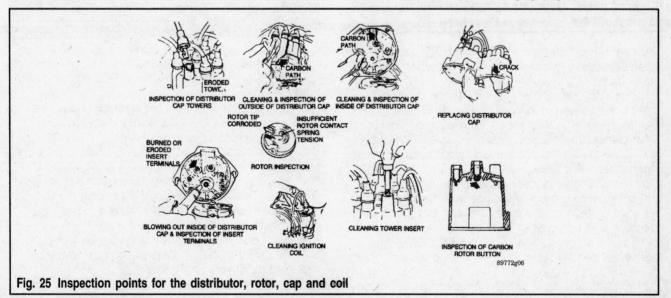

INSPECTION OF DISTRIBUTOR CAP TOWERS

CLEANING & INSPECTION OF OUTSIDE OF DISTRIBUTOR CAP

CLEANING & INSPECTION OF INSIDE OF DISTRIBUTOR CAP

REPLACING DISTRIBUTOR CAP

ROTOR TIP CORRODED

INSUFFICIENT ROTOR CONTACT SPRING TENSION

BURNED OR ERODED INSERT TERMINALS

ROTOR INSPECTION

BLOWING OUT INSIDE OF DISTRIBUTOR CAP & INSPECTION OF INSERT TERMINALS

CLEANING TOWER INSERT

CLEANING IGNITION COIL

INSPECTION OF CARBON ROTOR BUTTON

89772g06

Fig. 25 Inspection points for the distributor, rotor, cap and coil

Don't use sandpaper or emery cloth; they will cause rapid point burning.

7. Loosen the condenser hold-down screw and slide the condenser out of the clamp. This will save you a struggle with the clamp, condenser, and the tiny screw when you install the new one. If you have the type of clamp that is permanently fastened to the condenser, remove the screw and the condenser. Don't lose the screw.

8. Attend to the distributor cam lubricator. If you have the round kind, turn it around on its shaft at the first tune-up and replace it at the second. If you have the long kind, switch ends at the first tune-up and replace it at the second.

➡**Don't oil or grease the lubricator. The foam is impregnated with a special lubricant.**

If you didn't get any lubricator at all, or if it looks like someone took it off, don't worry. You don't really need it. Just rub a matchhead size dab of high melting point grease on the cam lobes. You can buy special distributor cam lube.

**To install:**

9. Install the new condenser. If you left the clamp in place, just slide the new condenser into the clamp.

10. Replace the point set and tighten the screws on a V8. Leave the screw slightly loose on a six. Replace the two wire terminals, making sure that the wires don't interfere with anything. Some V8 distributors have a ground wire that must go under one of the screws.

11. Check that the contacts meet squarely. If they don't, bend the tab supporting the fixed contact.

➡**If you are installing preset points on a V8, go ahead to Step 16. If they are preset, it will say so on the package. It would be a good idea to make a quick check on point gap, anyway. Sometimes those preset points aren't.**

12. Turn the engine until a high point on the cam that opens the points contacts the rubbing block on the point arm. You can turn the engine by hand if you can get a wrench on the crankshaft pulley nut, or you can grasp the fan belt and turn the engine with the spark plugs removed.

### ✳✳CAUTION

**If you try turning the engine by hand, be very careful not to get your fingers pinched in the pulleys.**

On a stick shift you can push it forward in High gear. Another alternative is to bump the starter switch or use a remote starter switch.

13. On a six, there is a screwdriver slot near the contact. Insert a screwdriver and lever the points open or closed until they appear to be at about the gap specified in the Tune-up Specifications. On a V8, simply insert a ⅛ in. (.125mm) allen wrench into the adjustment screw and turn. The wrench sometimes comes with a tune-up kit.

Insert the correct size feeler gauge and adjust the gap until you can push the gauge in and out between the contacts with a slight drag, but without disturbing the point arm. This operation takes a bit of experience to obtain the correct feel. Check by trying the gauges 0.001-0.002 in. (0.025-0.050mm) larger and smaller than the setting size. The larger one should dis-

turb the point arm, while the smaller one should not drag at all. Tighten the 6-cylinder point set hold-down screw. Recheck the gap, because it often changes when the screw is tightened.

14. After all the point adjustments are complete, pull a white business card through (between) the contacts to remove any traces of oil. Oil will cause rapid contact burning.

➡**You can adjust 6-cylinder dwell at this point, if you wish. Refer to Step 18.**

15. Replace the 1973-74 V8 radio frequency interference shield, if any. You don't need it if you are installing the one piece point/condenser set. Push the rotor firmly down into place. It will only go one way. Tighten the V8 rotor screws. If the rotor is not installed properly, it will probably break when the starter is operated.

16. Replace the distributor cap.

17. If a dwell meter is available, check the dwell. The dwell meter hookup is shown in the Troubleshooting section.

## DWELL ADJUSTMENT

➡**This hookup may not apply to electronic, capacitive discharge, or other special ignition systems. Some dwell meters won't work at all with such systems.**

Dwell can be checked with the engine running or cranking. Decrease dwell by increasing the point gap; increase by decreasing the gap. Dwell angle is simply the number of degrees of distributor shaft rotation during which the points stay closed. Theoretically, if the point gap is correct, the dwell should also be correct or nearly so. Adjustment with a dwell meter produces more exact, consistent results since it is a dynamic adjustment. If dwell varies more than 3° from idle speed to 1,750 engine rpm, the distributor is worn.

1. To adjust dwell on a 6-cylinder, trial and error point adjustments are required. On a V8, simply open the metal window on the distributor and insert a ⅛ in. (3.17mm) allen wrench. Turn until the meter shows the correct reading. Be sure to snap the window closed.

2. An approximate dwell adjustment can be made without a meter on a V8. Turn the adjusting screw clockwise until the engine begins to misfire, then turn it out ½ turn.

If the engine won't start, check:
- That all the spark plug wires are in place.
- That the rotor has been installed.
- That the two (of three) wires inside the distributor are connected.
- That the points open and close when the engine turns.
- That the gap is correct and the hold-down screw (on a 6-cylinder) is tight.

3. After the first 200 miles (321 km) or so on a new set of points, the point gap often closes up due to initial rubbing block wear. For best performance, recheck the dwell (or gap) at this time. This quick initial wear is the reason why the factory recommends 0.003 in. (.076mm) more gap on new points.

4. Since changing the gap affects the ignition timing, the timing should be checked and adjusted as necessary after each point replacement or adjustment.

## HIGH ENERGY IGNITION (HEI) SYSTEM

### General Information

The General Motors HEI system is a pulse-triggered, transistorized controlled, inductive discharge ignition system. Except on early inline 6-cylinder models, the entire HEI system is contained within the distributor cap. Inline 6-cylinder engines through 1977 have an external coil. Otherwise, the systems are the same.

The distributor, in addition to housing the mechanical and vacuum advance mechanisms, contains the ignition coil (except on 1975-77 inline 6-cylinder engines), the electronic control module, and the magnetic triggering device. The magnetic pick-up assembly contains a permanent magnet, a pole piece with internal teeth, and a pick-up coil (not to be confused with the ignition coil).

In the HEI system, as in other electronic ignition systems, the breaker points have been replaced with an electronic switch-a transistor-which is located within the control module. This switching transistor performs the same function the points did in a conventional ignition system. It simply turns coil primary current on and off at the correct time. Essentially then, electronic and conventional ignition systems operate on the same principle.

The module which houses the switching transistor is controlled (turned on and off) by a magnetically generated impulse induced in the pick-up coil. When the teeth of the rotating timer align with the teeth of the pole piece, the induced voltage in the pick-up coil signals the electronic module to open the coil primary circuit. The primary current then decreases, and a high voltage is induced in the ignition coil secondary windings which is then directed through the rotor and high voltage leads (spark plug wires) to fire the spark plugs.

In essence then, the pick-up coil module system simply replaces the conventional breaker points and condenser. The condenser found within the distributor is for radio suppression purposes only and had nothing to do with the ignition process. The module automatically controls the dwell period, increasing it with increasing engine speed. Since dwell is automatically controlled, it cannot be adjusted. The module itself is non-adjustable and non-repairable and must be replaced if found defective.

## PRECAUTIONS

Before going on to troubleshooting, it might be a good idea to take note of the following precautions:

### Timing Light Use

Inductive pick-up timing lights are the best kind to use if your van is equipped with HEI. Timing lights which connect between the spark plug and the spark plug wire occasionally (not always) give false readings.

### Spark Plug Wires

The plug wires used with HEI systems are of a different construction than conventional wires. When replacing them, make sure you get the correct wires, since conventional wires won't carry the voltage. Also, handle them carefully to avoid cracking or splitting them and never pierce them.

### Tachometer Use

Not all tachometers will operate or indicate correctly when used on a HEI system. While some tachometers may give a reading, this does not necessarily mean the reading is correct. In addition, some tachometers hook up differently from others. If you can't figure out whether or not your tachometer will work on your car, check with the tachometer manufacturer. Dwell readings, of course, have no significance at all.

### HEI Systems Testers

Instruments designed specifically for testing HEI systems are available from several tool manufacturers. Some of these will even test the module itself. However, the tests given in the following section will require only a ohmmeter and a voltmeter.

## TROUBLESHOOTING

The symptoms of a defective component within the HEI system are exactly the same as those you would encounter in a conventional system. Some of these symptoms are:
- Hard or no starting
- Rough idle
- Poor fuel economy
- Engine misses under load or while accelerating.

If you suspect a problem in your ignition system, there are certain preliminary checks which you should carry out before you begin to check the electronic portions of the system. First, it is extremely important to make sure the vehicle battery is in a good state of charge. A defective or poorly charged battery will cause the various components of the ignition system to read incorrectly when they are being tested. Second, make sure all wiring connections are clean and tight, not only at the battery, but also at the distributor cap, ignition coil, and at the electronic control module.

Since the only change between electronic and conventional ignition systems is in the distributor component area, it is imperative to check the secondary ignition circuit first. If the secondary circuit checks out properly, then the engine condition is probably not the fault of the ignition system. To check the secondary ignition system, perform a simple spark test. Remove one of the plug wires and insert some sort of extension in the plug socket. An old spark plug with the ground electrode removed makes a good extension. Hold the wire and extension about 1/4 in. (6mm) away from the block and crank the engine. If a normal spark occurs, then the problem is most likely not in the ignition system. Check for fuel system problems, or fouled spark plugs.

If, however, there is no spark or a weak spark, then further ignition system testing will have to be done. Troubleshooting techniques fall into two categories, depending on the nature of the problem. The categories are (1) Engine cranks, but won't start or (2) Engine runs, but runs rough or cuts out.

### Engine Fails to Start

If the engine won't start, perform a spark test as described earlier. If no spark occurs, check for the presence of normal battery voltage at the battery (BAT) terminal in the distributor cap. The ignition system must be in the ON position for this test. Either a voltmeter or a test light may be used for this test. Connect the test light wire to ground and the probe end to the BAT terminal at the distributor. If the light comes on, you have voltage on the distributor. If the light fails to come on, this indicates an open circuit in the ignition primary wiring leading to the distributor. In this case, you will have to check wiring continuity back to the ignition switch using a test light. If there is battery voltage at the BAT terminal, but no spark at the plugs, then the problem lies within the distributor assembly. Go on to the distributor components test section.

### Engine Runs, But Rough or Cuts Out

1. Make sure the plug wires are in good shape first. There should be no obvious cracks or breaks. You can check the plug wires with an ohmmeter, but do not pierce the wires with a probe. Check the chart for the correct plug wire resistance.

2. If the plug wires are OK, remove the cap assembly, and check for moisture, cracks, chips, or carbon tracks, or any other high voltage leaks or failures. Replace the cap if you find any defects. Make sure the timer wheel rotates when the engine is cranked. If everything is all right so far, go on to the distributor components test section.

## COMPONENT TESTING

▶ **See Figures 26 and 27**

If the trouble has been narrowed down to the units within the distributor, the following tests can help pinpoint the defective component. An ohmmeter with both high and low ranges should be used. These tests are made with the cap assembly removed and the battery wire disconnected.

1. Connect an ohmmeter between the TACH and BAT terminals in the distributor cap. The primary coil resistance should be 1 ohm; (zero or nearly zero).

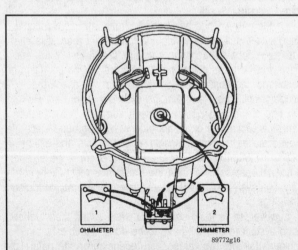

**Fig. 26 When connected as shown, ohmmeter 1 shows the primary coil resistance. Ohmmeter 2 shows the secondary coil resistance**

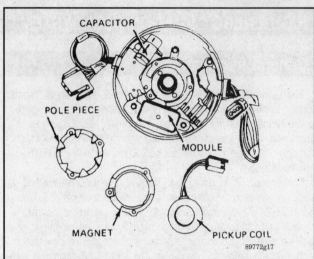

**Fig. 27 Exploded view of the pickup coil assembly and related components**

2. To check the coil secondary resistance, connect an ohmmeter between the rotor button and the BAT terminal. Then connect the ohmmeter between the ground terminal and the rotor button. The resistance in both cases should be between 6,000 and 30,000 ohms.

3. Replace the coil only if the readings in step one and two are infinite.

➡ **These resistance checks will not disclose shorted coil windings. This condition can be detected only with scope analysis or a suitably designed coil tester. If these instruments are unavailable, replace the coil with a known good coil as a final coil test.**

4. To test the pick-up coil, first disconnect the white and green module leads. Set the ohmmeter on the high scale and connect it between a ground and either the white or green lead. Any resistance measurement less than infinity requires replacement of the pick-up coil.

5. Pick-up coil continuity is tested by connecting the ohmmeter (on low range) between the white and green leads. Normal resistance is between 650 and 850 ohms, or 500 and 1,500 ohms; on 1977 and later models. Move the vacuum advance arm while performing this test. This will detect any break in coil continuity. Such a condition can cause intermittent misfiring. Replace the pick-up coil if the reading is outside the specified limits.

6. If no defects have been found at this time, and you still have a problem, then the module will have to be checked. If you do not have access to a module tester, the only possible alternative is a substitution test. If the module fails the substitution test, replace it.

## REMOVAL & INSTALLATION

### Integral Ignition Coil

1. Disconnect the feed and module wire terminal connectors from the distributor cap.

2. Remove the ignition set retainer.

3. Remove the 4 coil cover-to-distributor cap screws and coil cover.

4. Remove the 4 coil-to-distributor cap screws.

5. Using a blunt drift, press the coil wire spade terminals up out of the distributor cap.

6. Lift the coil up out of the distributor cap.

7. Remove and clean the coil spring, rubber seal washer and coil cavity of the distributor cap.

8. Coat the rubber seal with a dielectric lubricant furnished in the replacement ignition coil package.

9. Reverse the above procedures to install.

## Distributor Cap

▶ **See Figures 28, 29 and 30**

1. Remove the feed and module wire terminal connectors from the distributor cap.

2. Remove the retainer and spark plug wires from the cap.

3. Depress and release the 4 distributor cap-to-housing retainers and lift off the cap assembly.

4. Remove the 4 coil cover screws and cover.

5. Using a finger or a blunt drift, push the spade terminals up out of the distributor cap.

6. Remove all 4 coil screws and lift the coil, coil spring and rubber seal washer out of the cap coil cavity.

7. Using a new distributor cap, reverse the above procedures to assemble, being sure to clean and lubricate the rubber seal washer with dielectric lubricant.

## Rotor

▶ **See Figures 31 and 32**

1. Disconnect the feed and module wire connectors from the distributor.

2. Depress and release the 4 distributor cap-to-housing retainers and lift off the cap assembly.

3. Remove the two rotor attaching screws and rotor.

4. Reverse the above procedure to install.

## Vacuum Advance

1. Remove the distributor cap and rotor as previously described.

2. Disconnect the vacuum hose from the vacuum advance unit.

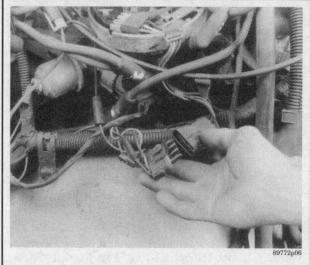

Fig. 29 . . . and the module harness

Fig. 30 After unfastening the spark plug wires and retaining screws, remove the distributor cap

Fig. 28 Disengage the feed wires . . .

Fig. 31 Unfasten the rotor retaining screws . . .

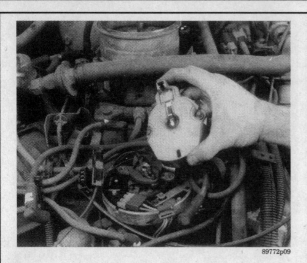

Fig. 32 . . . then remove the rotor from the distributor housing

89772p09

3. Remove the two vacuum advance retaining screws, pull the advance unit outward, rotate and disengage the operating rod from its tang.

4. Reverse the above procedure to install.

**Module**

1. Remove the distributor cap and rotor as previously described.

2. Disconnect the harness connector and pick-up coil spade connectors from the module. Be careful not to damage the wires when removing the connector.

3. Remove the two screws and module from the distributor housing.

4. Coat the bottom of the new module with dielectric lubricant supplied with the new module. Reverse the above procedure to install.

## IDLE SPEED AND MIXTURE ADJUSTMENTS

### Carbureted Engines

In most cases, the mixture screws have limiter caps, but in later years the mixture screws are concealed under staked-in plugs. Idle mixture is adjustable only during carburetor overhaul, and requires the addition of propane as an artificial mixture enrichener. For these reasons, mixture adjustments are not covered here for affected models.

See the emission control label in the engine compartment for procedures and specifications not supplied here.

➡See Carburetor Identification in Section 5 for carburetor I.D. specifics.

### ADJUSTMENT

These procedures require the use of a tachometer. In some cases, the degree of accuracy required is greater than that available on a hand-held unit; a shop tachometer would be required to follow the instructions exactly. If the idle speed screws have plastic limiter caps (1971-82), it is not recommended that they be removed unless a satisfactory idle cannot be obtained with them in place. If the caps are removed, exhaust emissions may go beyond the specified legal limits. This can be checked on an exhaust gas analyzer.

➡Most 1973 and later 4-bbl carburetors have an internal fuel passage restriction. Beyond a certain limited point, turning the idle mixture screws out has no further richening effect.

Idle speed and mixture are set with the engine at normal running temperature. The automatic transmission should be in Drive, except when specified otherwise. The air conditioner should be off for adjusting mixture and off unless otherwise

specified in the text or specifications chart for setting idle speed.

### ❊❊CAUTION

**Block the wheels, set the parking brake, and don't stand in front of the truck.**

**1967 Models**

Turn the idle screw(s) slightly in to seat, and then back them out 2 turns (3 when equipped with air pump). Do not turn the idle mixture screws tightly against their seats or you could damage them. With the engine idling at operating temperature (air cleaner on and choke valve wide open), adjust the idle speed to the specified rpm (automatic transmission in Drive; manual in Neutral.

Adjust the mixture screw to obtain the highest steady idle speed, then adjust the idle speed screw to the specified rpm. Adjust the mixture screw in to obtain a 20 rpm drop, then back the screw out 1/4 turn. Repeat this operation on the second mixture screw, if so equipped. Readjust the idle speed screw as necessary until the specified rpm is reached.

**1968-69 Models**

Turn the idle mixture screw(s) in to seat and then back them out 3 turns. Don't turn the screws in tightly or you will damage them. Bring the engine to its operating temperature (air cleaner installed and choke valve open), and adjust the idle speed screw to obtain the specified rpm (automatic transmission in Drive, manual transmission in Neutral).

➡On air conditioned models, turn the air conditioner off except on 6-cylinder engines with automatic transmission. On these models idle speed is set with the air conditioning on.

Set the idle mixture screw(s) to give the highest steady idle speed. Adjust the idle speed to the specified rpm. Set the idle speed for engines with idle solenoids as follows: set the idle speed to 500 rpm by turning the idle solenoid hex bolt. Disconnect the solenoid wire and check the idle speed. De-energizing the solenoid will allow the throttle lever to seat against the carburetor idle screw. Turn the carburetor idle screw to obtain 400 rpm.

Turn the mixture screw(s) in to get a 20 rpm drop. Turn the mixture screw out ¼ turn. Repeat for the second mixture screw, if so equipped. Readjust the idle speed screw, as necessary, to obtain the specified idle rpm.

## 1970-71 Models

On all vehicles, disconnect the FUEL TANK line from the vapor canister. Remember to reconnect the line after setting the idle speed and mixture. The engine should be at operating temperature with the choke valve and air cleaner damper door fully open, air conditioning OFF and parking brake ON.

On 6-cylinder engines, 10 Series: Turn the mixture screw in until it lightly contacts the seat, then back out 4 turns. Adjust the solenoid screw to obtain 800 rpm with manual transmission in Neutral or 630 rpm with automatic transmission in Drive. Adjust the mixture screw to obtain 750 rpm with manual transmission in Neutral or automatic in Drive. Electrically disconnect the solenoid and set the carburetor idle speed screw to obtain 400 rpm and connect the solenoid. Reconnect the vacuum line.

On 6-cylinder engines, 20 and 30 Series: Disconnect and plug the distributor vacuum line. Turn the mixture screws in until they lightly contact the seats and back the screw(s) out 4 turns. On manual transmission models, adjust the carburetor idle speed screw to obtain 600 rpm in Neutral. Then adjust the mixture screw to obtain 550 rpm in Neutral. On automatic transmission models, adjust the solenoid screw to obtain 550 rpm with transmission in Drive. Adjust the mixture screw to obtain 500 rpm with transmission in Drive. Disconnect the solenoid and set the carburetor idle speed screw to obtain 400 rpm and connect the solenoid. Reconnect the distributor vacuum line on all models.

On V8-307 engines, 10 Series: Disconnect and plug the distributor vacuum line. Turn the mixture screws in until they lightly contact the seats then back them out 4 turns. Adjust the carburetor idle speed screw to obtain 800 rpm with manual transmission in Neutral. Adjust the mixture screw to obtain 630 rpm with automatic transmission in Drive. Adjust the mixture screws in equally to obtain 700 rpm with manual transmission in Neutral or 600 rpm with automatic transmission in Drive. Disconnect the solenoid and set the carburetor idle speed screw to obtain 450 rpm and reconnect the solenoid. Reconnect the vacuum line.

On 1970 V8-307, 20 & 30 Series: Set the mixture screws for maximum idle rpm and adjust the idle speed screw to obtain 700 rpm with manual transmission in Neutral or 600 rpm with automatic transmission in Drive. Adjust the mixture screws equally to obtain a 20 rpm drop, then back the idle screw on manual transmission models to obtain 700 rpm with the transmission in Neutral. On automatic transmission models, adjust the solenoid screw to obtain 600 rpm with the transmission in Drive. Disconnect the solenoid electrically and set the carburetor idle screw to obtain 450 rpm and reconnect the solenoid. Reconnect the vacuum line.

On 1970-71 V8-350, 20 & 30 Series: Disconnect and plug the distributor vacuum line. Turn the mixture screws in until they lightly contact the seats and back them out 4 turns. Adjust the carburetor idle speed screw to obtain 775 rpm (manual transmission in Neutral) or 630 rpm (automatic transmission in Drive). Adjust the mixture screws equally to obtain 700 rpm (manual transmission in Neutral) or 600 rpm (automatic transmission in Drive). Reconnect the vacuum line.

The engine should be at normal operating temperature with the choke valve fully open, parking brake ON and the drive wheels blocked. All carburetors are equipped with idle mixture limiter caps, which provide for only a small adjustment range. Normally, if they are removed, the CO content of the exhaust should be checked to be sure that it meets Federal Emission Control limits.

On 6 cyl-250 engines: Disconnect the FUEL TANK line from the vapor canister. Remember to reconnect it after making the adjustment. Disconnect and plug the vacuum line. Adjust the idle stop solenoid to obtain 700 rpm with manual transmission in Neutral or 600 rpm with automatic transmission in Drive. Do not adjust the CEC solenoid screw.

### ✳✳CAUTION

**If the CEC solenoid screw is adjusted out of limits, a decrease in engine braking may result.**

Reconnect the vacuum line.

On V8-307 engines: Disconnect the FUEL TANK line from the vapor canister and remove and plug the vacuum line. With the air conditioner OFF, adjust the idle stop solenoid screw to obtain 900 rpm with manual transmission in Neutral or 600 rpm with automatic transmission in Drive. With transmission in Park or Neutral, adjust the fast idle speed to obtain 1850 rpm. Reconnect the FUEL TANK line and the vacuum line.

On V8-350 engines: Disconnect the FUEL TANK line and disconnect and plug the vacuum line. On vehicles with TCS (transmission controlled spark), turn the air conditioner OFF and adjust the idle solenoid screw to obtain 800 rpm with manual transmission in Neutral or 600 rpm with automatic transmission in Drive. On vehicles without TCS, adjust the carburetor speed screw to obtain 600 rpm with transmission in Neutral. Place the fast idle cam follower on the 2nd step of the fast idle cam, turn the air conditioner OFF and adjust the fast idle to 1350 rpm with manual transmission in Neutral or automatic transmission in Drive. Reconnect the FUEL TANK and vacuum lines.

## 1973-74 Models

All adjustments should be made with the engine at operating temperature, choke valve fully open, air conditioning OFF, parking brake ON and drive wheels blocked.

On 6 cyl-250 engines: Disconnect the FUEL TANK line and the distributor vacuum line. Plug the vacuum line. Adjust the idle stop solenoid by turning the hex nut to obtain:
- 700 rpm (1973) or 850 rpm (1974) on manual transmission in Neutral
- 600 rpm (1973 74) on automatic transmission in Drive

Do not adjust the CEC solenoid on 1973 vehicles or a decrease in engine braking may result. Place automatic transmission in Neutral and adjust the fast idle to 1800 rpm, on the top step of the fast idle cam. Reconnect the FUEL TANK and vacuum lines.

On 1973 V8-307 engines: On light duty vehicles, disconnect the FUEL TANK line from the vapor canister and plug the distributor vacuum line. Adjust the idle stop solenoid to obtain 600 rpm with automatic transmission in Drive or 900 rpm with manual transmission in Neutral. Disconnect the idle stop solenoid and adjust the low idle screw located inside the solenoid hex nut, to obtain 450 rpm. Reconnect the idle stop solenoid, the FUEL TANK line, and the vacuum line.

On 8-350 engines: On the light duty vehicles, disconnect the FUEL TANK line from the vapor canister. Disconnect and plug the distributor vacuum line. On heavy duty vehicles, adjust the carburetor idle speed screw to obtain 600 rpm with automatic transmission in Park or manual transmission in Neutral. On light duty vehicles, adjust the idle stop solenoid screw to obtain 600 rpm with automatic transmission in Drive or 900 rpm with manual transmission in Neutral. On light duty vehicles with automatic transmission, reconnect the vacuum line and adjust the fast idle to 1600 rpm on the top step of the fast idle cam. On light duty vehicles with manual transmission, adjust the fast idle screw to obtain 1300 rpm with the screw on the top step of the fast idle cam and the distributor vacuum line disconnected. Reconnect the FUEL TANK line and the vacuum line.

## 1975 Models

On 6-cylinder engines: Do not disconnect the distributor vacuum line. Disconnect the vapor canister FUEL TANK hose. With automatic transmission in Drive and manual in Neutral, adjust the solenoid to get the specified idle speed. Use a 1/8 in. (3.17mm) allen wrench in the end of the solenoid body to set the low idle speed to 450 rpm with the solenoid wire disconnected. Reset the idle speed with the air conditioning on, except on the 250 engine.

On V8 engines with the 2-bbl carburetor: Disconnect the vapor canister FUEL TANK hose. Leave the distributor vacuum advance hose in place. Adjust the idle speed screw to get the specified idle speed with automatic in Drive and manual in Neutral.

On light duty V8 engines with the 4-bbl carburetor: Disconnect the vapor canister FUEL TANK hose. Leave the distributor vacuum advance hose in place. Disconnect the solenoid wire. Place automatic in Drive and manual in Neutral. Turn the low idle speed screw on the carburetor to get about 450 rpm. Connect the solenoid wire and open the throttle slightly, so that the solenoid plunger can extend. Turn the plunger screw to get the specified idle speed.

On heavy duty V8 engines with the 4-bbl carburetor: This adjustment is the same as for 1974. Reset the idle speed with the air conditioner on.

## 1976 Models

On 6-cylinder engines: Disconnect and plug the CARBURETOR and PCV vapor canister hoses on the 250. Disconnect the canister FUEL TANK hose on the 292. If the engine has a vacuum advance hose running directly from the vacuum source to the distributor vacuum advance unit, disconnect and plug it. Turn the air conditioner on, only on the 292. Set the manual transmission in Neutral. Set the 250 automatic in Drive and the 292 in Neutral. Turn the solenoid to get the specified idle speed. Disconnect the solenoid wire and turn off

the air conditioner. Use a allen 1/8 in. (3.17mm) wrench in the end of the solenoid body to set the low idle speed to 450 rpm.

On V8 engines with the two barrel carburetor: This procedure is the same as 1975, except that the canister hose can be left in place.

On light duty V8 engines with the 4-bbl carburetor: Place the automatic in Drive and manual in Neutral. Set the idle speed screw on the carburetor to obtain the specified rpm.

On heavy duty V8 engines with the 4-bbl carburetor: Disconnect the vapor canister FUEL TANK hose on California models. Leave the vacuum advance hose in place. Turn the air conditioner on. Set the automatic in Park and manual in Neutral. Set the idle speed screw on the carburetor to obtain the specified rpm.

## 1977 Models

▶ **See Figures 33, 34, 35 and 36**

See the underhood emission sticker for any hoses or wires that may need to be disconnected.

On 1 bbl equipped models: Start the engine and allow it to run until it reaches normal operating temperature. Be sure the choke is fully open and the cam follower is off the steps of the cam. Turn the nut on the end of the solenoid to obtain the specified rpm. See the Tune-up chart. Disconnect the wire from the solenoid and turn the 1/8 in. (3.17mm) allen head screw in the end of the solenoid to set the base idle to specification. Refer to the Tune-up chart or the underhood emission sticker. Reconnect the wire.

On 2 and 4 bbl equipped models: Be sure the ignition timing is correct. Refer to the underhood emission sticker in order to prepare the vehicle for adjustment.

On carburetors without a solenoid: Be sure the idle speed screw is on the low step of the fast idle cam. Turn the screw to obtain the idle specified in the Tune-Up chart.

On carburetors with a solenoid: Turn the idle screw to obtain the idle speed specified in the Tune-Up chart. Disconnect the electrical lead from between the solenoid and the A/C compressor at the compressor and turn the A/C On. Place the automatic transmission in Drive. Open the throttle momentarily to fully extend the solenoid plunger. Turn the solenoid screw to obtain the base idle speed as specified in the Tune-Up chart

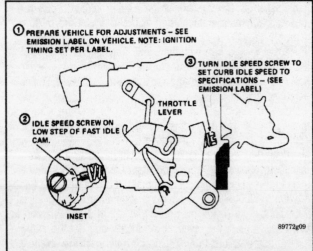

**Fig. 33 1977-78 2bbl idle speed adjustment — without solenoid**

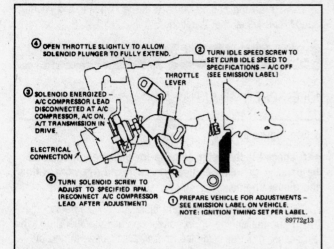

**Fig. 34  1977-78 2bbl idle speed adjustment — with solenoid**

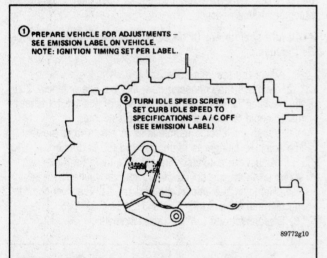

**Fig. 35  1977 and later 4bbl idle speed adjustment — without solenoid**

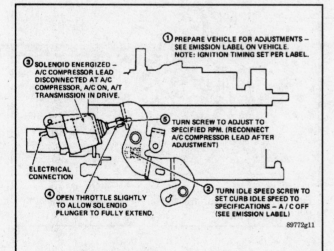

**Fig. 36  1977 and later 4bbl and 1979 and later 2 bbl (V8 only) idle speed adjustment — with solenoid**

or on the emission sticker. Reconnect the electrical lead at the compressor.

### 1978 Models

▶ See Figure 37

On 1-bbl equipped models: The idle speed adjusting procedure is the same as 1977. Refer to the Tune-Up chart for the correct idle speed.

On 2-bbl equipped models: Be sure the ignition timing is correct. Refer to the underhood emission sticker in order to prepare the vehicle for adjustment.

On carburetors without a solenoid: This procedure is the same as 1977. See the Tune-Up chart for the correct idle speed.

On models with a solenoid and without air conditioning: Rev the engine momentarily to fully extend the solenoid plunger. Turn the solenoid screw to obtain the curb idle speed listed in the Tune-Up chart. Disconnect the wire from the solenoid. Turn the idle speed screw to obtain the solenoid idle speed listed on the underhood emission sticker. Reconnect the wire at the solenoid.

On models with air conditioning: Turn the idle speed screw to obtain the idle speed listed in the Tune-Up chart. Disconnect the wire at the A/C compressor and turn the A/C On. Rev the engine momentarily to fully extend the solenoid plunger. Turn the solenoid screw to obtain the solenoid idle speed listed on the underhood emission sticker. Reconnect the wire at the compressor.

On 4-bbl equipped models: Refer to the underhood emission sticker and prepare the vehicle for adjustment as specified on the sticker.

On models without a solenoid, turn the idle speed to obtain the idle speed listed in the Tune-Up chart.

On models with a solenoid, turn the idle speed screw to obtain the idle speed listed in the Tune-Up chart. Disconnect the wire at the A/C compressor and turn the A/C On. Rev the engine momentarily to fully extend the solenoid plunger. Turn the solenoid screw to obtain the solenoid idle speed listed on the underhood emission sticker. Reconnect the A/C wire at the compressor.

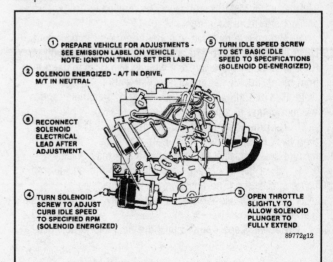

**Fig. 37  1978 and later idle speed adjustment — six cylinder engine**

### 1979 and Later Idle Speed Adjustment

Idle mixture is not adjustable in these years, except for the heavy duty emission V8s engines equipped with the 4-bbl M4MC carburetors.

All adjustments should be made with the engine at normal operating temperature, air cleaner on, choke open, and air conditioning off, unless otherwise noted. Set the parking brake and block the rear wheels. Automatic transmissions should be set in Drive, manuals in Neutral, unless otherwise noted in the procedures or on the emission control label.

• On 6-cyl-250 engines: Check the emission control label for any special instructions. Open the throttle slightly to allow the solenoid plunger to extend. Turn the solenoid screw to adjust the curb idle to the figure given in the Tune-Up Specifications chart or on the emission control label. Disconnect the electrical connector from the solenoid. The idle speed will drop. Adjust the idle to the basic idle speed figure given on the emission control label by means of the idle speed screw. Connect the solenoid lead and shut off the engine.

• On 6 cyl-262 engines and V8-305 engines: Check the emission control label in the engine compartment to determine which hoses, if any, must be disconnected. Make sure the idle speed screw is on the low (L) step of the fast idle cam. Turn the idle speed screw to adjust the idle speed to the figure given in the Tune-Up Specifications chart or on the emission control label.

On carburetors equipped with a solenoid (air conditioned trucks): turn the idle speed screw to set the idle to specifications, as in the previous paragraph. Then, disconnect the air compressor electrical lead at the compressor. Turn the air conditioning on. Open the throttle slightly to allow the solenoid plunger to fully extend. Turn the solenoid screw and adjust to 700 rpm with manual transmission (Neutral), or 600 rpm with automatic transmission (Drive). Reconnect the air conditioner electrical lead.

• On V8-350 engines: The idle speed procedure is the same as given for 1977-78 models. Check the emission control label and the Tune-Up Specifications chart to determine the proper idle speeds.

Mixture is adjustable on heavy duty emissions V8 engines with the 4-bbl M4MC carburetor. This procedure will not work on light duty emissions trucks.

1. The engine must be at normal operating temperature, choke open, parking brake applied, and the transmission in Park or Neutral. Block the rear wheels and do not stand in from of the truck when making adjustments.

2. Remove the air cleaner. Connect a tachometer and a vacuum gauge to the engine.

3. Turn the idle mixture screws in lightly until they seat, then back them out two turns. Be careful not to tighten the mixture screw against its seat, or damage may result.

4. Adjust the idle speed screw to obtain the engine rpm figure specified on the emission control label.

5. Adjust the idle mixture screws equally to obtain the highest engine speed.

6. Repeat Steps 4 and 5 until the best idle is obtained.

7. Shut off the engine, remove the tachometer and vacuum gauge, and install the air cleaner.

## Diesel Engines

### IDLE SPEED ADJUSTMENT

♦ See Figure 38

➡A special tachometer suitable for diesel engines must be used. A gasoline engine type tach will not work with the diesel engine.

1. Set the parking brake and block the drive wheels.

2. Run the engine up to normal operating temperature. The air cleaner must be mounted and all accessories turned off.

3. Install the diesel tachometer as per the manufacturer's instructions.

4. Adjust the low idle speed screw on the fuel injection pump to 650 rpm in Neutral or Park for both manual and automatic transmissions.

➡All idle speeds are to be set within 25 rpm of the specified values.

5. Adjust the fast idle speed as follows:

a. Remove the connector from the fast idle solenoid. Use an insulated jumper wire from the battery positive terminal to the solenoid terminal to energize the solenoid.

b. Open the throttle momentarily to ensure that the fast idle solenoid plunger is energized and fully extended.

c. Adjust the extended plunger by turning the hex-head screw to an engine speed of 800 rpm in Neutral.

d. Remove the jumper wire and reinstall the connector to the fast idle solenoid.

6. Disconnect and remove the tachometer.

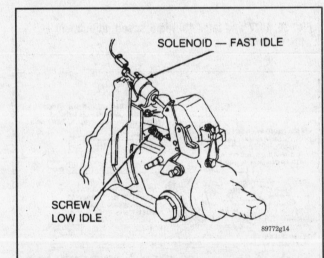

SOLENOID — FAST IDLE

SCREW LOW IDLE

89772g14

**Fig. 38 6.2L (379 cu. in.) diesel injection pump showing idle adjustments**

## Diesel Tune-Up Specifications ⑧

| Year | Engine No. Cyl Displacement (cu in.) | Fuel Pump Pressure (psi) | Compression (lbs.) | Intake Valve Opens (deg) | Idle Speed (rpm) ● |
|---|---|---|---|---|---|
| 1983–86 | 8-379 | 5.5–6.5 ① | 275 min. | NA | 575/550 ② |

NOTE: The underhood specifications sticker often reflects tune-up specifications changes made in production. Sticker figures must be used if they disagree with those in this chart.

● Where two idle speed figures appear separately by a slash, the first is for manual trans, the second is for auto trans.

① Transfer pump pressure given—injector opening pressure for used injector—1500 psi

② '83–'84 slow idle: 650 rpm; fast idle: 800 rpm

NA—Not available

89772c01

## Tune-Up Specifications 1967–81

When analyzing compression results, look for uniformity among cylinders rather than specific pressures.

| Year | Engine Cu in. Displacement | Spark Plugs Orig Type | Gap (in.) | Distributor Point Dwell (deg) | Point Gap (in.) | Ignition Timing* (deg) ▲ MT | AT | Intake Valve Opens (deg) | Fuel Pump Pressure (psi) | (See Text) Curb Idle Speed (rpm)* MT | AT | Solenoid or Base Idle Speed (rpm)* MT | AT |
|---|---|---|---|---|---|---|---|---|---|---|---|---|---|
| 1967 | 6-230 | 46N | .035 | 31–34 | 0.019 | 4B | 4B | 48 | 3–4.5 | 700 | 500 | See Text | See Text |
| | 6-250 | 46N | .035 | 31–34 | 0.019 | 4B | 4B | 62 | 3–4.5 | 700 | 500 | See Text | See Text |
| | 8-283 | 44 | .035 | 28–32 | 0.019 | 6A② | 4B | 36 | 5–6.5 | 700 | 600③ | See Text | See Text |
| 1968 | 6-230 | 46N | .035 | 31–34 | 0.019 | TDC② | 4B | 48 | 3–4.5 | 700 | 500 | See Text | See Text |
| | 6-250 | 46N | .035 | 31–34 | 0.019 | TDC② | 4B | 16 | 3–4.5 | 700 | 500 | See Text | See Text |
| | 8-307 | 44S | .035 | 28–32 | 0.019 | 2B | 2B | 28 | 5–6.5 | 700 | 600③ | See Text | See Text |
| 1969 | 6-230 | R46N | .035 | 31–34 | 0.019 | TDC | 4B | 16 | 3–4.5 | 700 | 550 | See Text | See Text |
| | 6-250 | R46N | .035 | 31–34 | 0.019 | TDC | 4B | 16 | 3–4.5 | 700 | 550 | See Text | See Text |
| | 8-307 | R44 | .035 | 28–32 | 0.019 | 2B | 2B | 28 | 5–6.5 | 700 | 600 | See Text | See Text |
| 1970 | 6-250 | R46T | .035 | 31–34 | 0.019 | TDC | 4B | 16 | 3.5–4.5 | See Text | See Text | See Text | See Text |
| | 8-307 | R45 | .035 | 28–32 | 0.019 | 2B | 8B | 28 | 5–6.5 | See Text | See Text | See Text | See Text |
| | 8-350 | R44 | .035 | 28–32 | 0.019 | TDC | 4B | 28 | 7–8.5 | See Text | See Text | See Text | See Text |
| 1971 | 6-250 | R46TS | .035 | 31–34 | 0.019 | TDC | 4B | 16 | 3.5–4.5 | See Text | See Text | See Text | See Text |
| | 8-307 | R45TS | .035 | 28–32 | 0.019 | 2B | 2B | 28 | 5–6.5 | See Text | See Text | See Text | See Text |
| | 8-350 | R44TS | .035 | 28–32 | 0.019 | 4B | 4B | 28 | 7–8.5 | See Text | See Text | See Text | See Text |
| 1972 | 6-250 | R46T | .035 | 31–34 | 0.019 | 4B | 4B | 16 | 3.5–4.5 | See Text | See Text | See Text | See Text |
| | 8-307 | R44T | .035 | 28–32 | 0.019 | 4B | 8B | 28 | 5–6.5 | See Text | See Text | See Text | See Text |
| | 8-350 | R44T | .035 | 28–32 | 0.019 | 4B | 8B | 28 | 7–8.5 | See Text | See Text | See Text | See Text |
| 1973 | 6-250LD | R46T | .035 | 31–34 | 0.019 | 6B | 6B | 16 | 3.5–4.5 | See Text | See Text | See Text | See Text |
| | 8-307 LD | R44T | .035 | 28–32 | 0.019 | 4B | 8B | 28 | 5–6.5 | See Text | See Text | See Text | See Text |
| | 8-350 LD | R44T | .035 | 28–32 | 0.019 | 8B | 12B | 28 | 7–8.5 | See Text | See Text | See Text | See Text |
| | 6-250 HD | R46T | .035 | 31–34 | 0.019 | 4B | 4B | 16 | 3.5–4.5 | See Text | See Text | See Text | See Text |
| 1973 | 8-307 HD | R44T | .035 | 28–32 | 0.019 | TDC | TDC | 28 | 5–6.5 | See Text | See Text | See Text | See Text |
| | 8-350 HD | R44T | .035 | 28–32 | 0.019 | 4B | 4B | 28 | 7–8.5 | See Text | See Text | See Text | See Text |

89772c02

## Tune-Up Specifications 1967–81 (cont.)

When analyzing compression results, look for uniformity among cylinders rather than specific pressures.

| Year | Engine Cu In. Displacement | Spark Plugs Orig Type | Gap (in.) | Distributor Point Dwell (deg) | Point Gap (in.) | Ignition Timing* (deg) ▲ MT | AT | Intake Valve Opens (deg) | Fuel Pump Pressure (psi) | (See Text) Curb Idle Speed (rpm)* MT | AT | Solenoid or Base Idle Speed (rpm)* MT | AT |
|---|---|---|---|---|---|---|---|---|---|---|---|---|---|
| 1974 | 6-250 | R46T | .035 | 31–34 | 0.019 | 8B | 8B | 16 | 3.5–4.5 | See Text | See Text | See Text | See Text |
| | 8-350 (2-bbl) | R44T | .035 | 29–31 | 0.019 | TDC | 8B | 28 | 7–8.5 | See Text | See Text | See Text | See Text |
| | 8-350 (4-bbl) LD | R44T | .035 | 29–31 | 0.019 | 8B | 8B | 44 | 7–8.5 | See Text | See Text | See Text | See Text |
| | 8-350 (4-bbl) HD | R44T | .035 | 29–31 | 0.019 | 8B | 12B | 44 | 7–8.5 | See Text | See Text | See Text | See Text |
| 1975 | 6-250 | R46TX | .060 | Electronic | | 10B | 10B | 16 | 3.5–4.5 | 900 | 550 | See Text | See Text |
| | 6-292 | R44TX | .060 | Electronic | | 8B | 8B | 33 | 3.5–4.5 | 600 | 600 | See Text | See Text |
| | 8-350 (2-bbl) | R44TX | .060 | Electronic | | ① | 6B | 28 | 7–8.5 | ① | 600 | See Text | See Text |
| | 8-350 (4-bbl) LD | R44TX | .060 | Electronic | | 6B | 6B | 28 | 7–8.5 | 800 | 600 | See Text | See Text |
| | 8-350 (4-bbl) HD | R44TX | .060 | Electronic | | 8B(2B) | 8B(2B) | 28 | 7–8.5 | 600(700) | 600(700) | See Text | See Text |
| | 8-400 | R44TX | .060 | Electronic | | — | 4B(8B) | 28 | 7–8.5 | — | 700 | See Text | See Text |
| 1976 | 6-250 | R46TS | .035 | Electronic | | 6B | 10B | 16 | 3.5–4.5 | 900(1000) ④ | 550(600) ④ | See Text | See Text |
| | 6-292 | R44T | .035 | Electronic | | 8B | 8B | 33 | 3.5–4.5 | 600 | 600 N | See Text | See Text |
| | 8-350 (2-bbl) | R45TS | .045 | Electronic | | 2B | 6B | 28 | 7–8.5 | 800 | 600 | See Text | See Text |
| | 8-350 (4-bbl) LD | R45TS | .045 | Electronic | | 8B(6B) | 8B(6B) | 28 | 7–8.5 | 800 | 600 | See Text | See Text |
| | 8-350 (4-bbl) HD | R44TX | .060 | Electronic | | 8B(2B) | 8B(2B) | 28 | 7–8.5 | 600(700) | 600(700) N | See Text | See Text |
| | 8-400 | R44TX | .060 | Electronic | | — | 4B | 28 | 7–8.5 | — | 700 N | See Text | See Text |
| 1977 | 6-250 | R46TS | .035 | Electronic | | 8B(6B) | 12B(10B) | 16 | 3.5–4.5 | 750(850) ④ | 600 ④ | 425 | 425D |
| | 6-292 | R44T | .035 | Electronic | | 8B | 8B | 33 | 3.5–4.5 | 600 | 600 N | 450 | 450 N |
| | 8-305 | R45TS | .045 | Electronic | | 8B | 8B | 28 | 7–8.5 | 600 | 500 | 700 | 650 N |
| | 8-350 LD | R45TS | .045 | Electronic | | 8B(6B) | 8B(6B) | 28 | 7–8.5 | 700 | 500 | — | 650 D |
| | 8-350 HD | R44T (R44TX) | .045 (.060) | Electronic | | 8B(2B) | 8B(2B) | 28 | 7–8.5 | 700 | 700 N | — | — |
| | 8-400 | R44T | .045 | Electronic | | — | 4B(2B) | 28 | 7–8.5 | — | 700 N | — | — |
| 1978 | 6-250 | R46TS | .035 | Electronic | | 8B | 8B(10B) ⑥ | 16 | 4.5–6 | 750 | 600 ⑤ | 425 | 425D |
| | 6-292 | R44T | .035 | Electronic | | 8B | 8B | 33 | 4.5–6 | 600 | 600 | 450 | 450 N |
| | 8-305 | R45TS | .045 | Electronic | | 4B | 4B | 28 | 7.5–9 | 600 | 500 | — | — |
| | 8-350 LD | R45TS | .045 | Electronic | | 8B | 8B | 28 | 7.5–9 | 600(700) | 500 | — | 600 D |
| | 8-350 HD | R44T (R44TX) | .045 (.060) | Electronic | | 8B(2B) | 8B(2B) | 28 | 7.5–9 | 700 | 700 | — | — |

89772c03

## Tune-Up Specifications 1967–81 (cont.)

When analyzing compression results, look for uniformity among cylinders rather than specific pressures.

| Year | Engine Cu in. Displacement | Spark Plugs Orig Type | Spark Plugs Gap (in.) | Distributor Point Dwell (deg) | Distributor Point Gap (in.) | Ignition Timing* (deg) ▲ MT | Ignition Timing* (deg) ▲ AT | Intake Valve Opens (deg) | Fuel Pump Pressure (psi) | (See Text) Curb Idle Speed (rpm)* MT | (See Text) Curb Idle Speed (rpm)* AT | Solenoid or Base Idle Speed (rpm)* MT | Solenoid or Base Idle Speed (rpm)* AT |
|---|---|---|---|---|---|---|---|---|---|---|---|---|---|
| | 8-400 LD ⑦ | R45TS | .045 | Electronic | | — | 4B | 28 | 7.5–9 | — | 500 | — | 600 D |
| | 8-400 HD | R44T | .045 | Electronic | | — | 4B(2B) | 28 | 7.5–9 | — | 700 | — | — |
| 1979 | 6-250 | R46TS | .035 | Electronic | | 10B ⑨ | 10B ⑨ | 16 | 4.5–6 | 750 | 600 | 425 | 425 D |
| | 8-305 | R45TS | .045 | Electronic | | 6B | 6B | 28 | 7.5–9 | 700 | 600 | 600 | 500 D |
| | 8-350 ⑩ | R45TS | .045 | Electronic | | 8B | 8B | 28 | 7.5–9 | 700 | 500 | — | 600 D |
| | 8-400 ⑩ | R45TS | .045 | Electronic | | — | 4B | 28 | 7.5–9 | — | 500 | — | 600 D |
| 1980–81 | 6-250 | R46TS | .035 | Electronic | | 10B | 8B ⑪ | — | 4–6 | 750 | 650 (D) | — | — |
| | 8-305 (2-bbl) | R45TS | .045 | Electronic | | 8B | 8B | — | 7–9 | 700 | 600 (D) | — | — |
| | 8-305 (4-bbl) | R45TS | .045 | Electronic | | 6B | 4B | — | 7–9 | 700 | 500 (D) | — | — |
| | 8-350 | R45TS | .045 | Electronic | | 8B ⑫ | 8B ⑬ | — | 7–9 | 700 | 500 (D) ⑭ | — | — |

*Figures in parentheses are for California and high altitude and are given only if they differ from the 49 state specification. Automatic transmission idle speeds are set in Drive, unless specified otherwise.

▲At idle speed with vacuum advance hose disconnected and plugged, unless specified otherwise in the text
① See the underhood specifications sticker
② Without air pump system—4B
③ Without air pump system—500 rpm
④ Air conditioner on
⑤ 49 state without A/C—550
⑥ High alt.—12B
⑦ California only
⑧ G—20, G—30, 2500, 3500 series in Calif.—6B
⑨ G—20, G—30, 2500, 3500 series in Calif.—8B
⑩ Some G—30/3500 series vans differ. Check the underhood emission sticker.
⑪ High Alt.: 10B
⑫ Fed. 1 ton models: 4B
  Calif. ¾ & 1 ton models: 6B
⑬ 1 ton models: 6B
⑭ 1 ton models: 700 (N)
  Calif. ½ & ¾ ton models: 550 (D)
N—Transmission in Neutral
D—Transmission in Drive
HD (Heavy Duty) 1971 G—30, 3500; 1972–73 G—30, 3500 except passenger models; 1974–78 G—20, 2500, 30, 3500
LD (Light Duty) All 1967–69; 1979–71 G—10, 1500, 20, 2500; 1972–73 G—10, 1500, 20, 2500; 1972–73 G—30, 3500 passenger models; 1974–78 G—10, 1500
NOTE: The underhood specifications sticker often reflects tune-up specifications changes made in production. Sticker figures must be used if they disagree with those in this chart.
Part numbers in this chart are not recommendations by Chilton for any product by brand name.

89772c04

## Tune-Up Specifications 1982–86

When analyzing compression results, look for uniformity among cylinders rather than specific pressures.

| Year | Engine Cu In. Displacement | Spark Plugs | | Distributor | Ignition Timing● (deg)▲ | | Fuel Pump Pressure (psi) | Curb Idle Speed (rpm)● | |
|------|------|------|------|------|------|------|------|------|------|
| | | Orig Type | Gap (in.) | | MT | AT | | MT | AT |
| 1982 | 6-250 | R45TS | .045 | Electronic | ① | ① | 4–6 | ① | ① |
| | 8-305 | R45TS | .045 | Electronic | ① | ① | 7–9 | ① | ① |
| | 8-350 | R45TS | .045 | Electronic | ① | ① | 7–9 | ① | ① |
| 1983 | 6-250 | R45TS | .045 | Electronic | ① | ① | 4–6 | ① | ① |
| | 8-305 | R45TS | .045 | Electronic | ① | ① | 7–9 | ① | ① |
| | 8-350 | R45TS | .045 | Electronic | ① | ① | 7–9 | ① | ① |
| | 8-379 | Diesel | — | — | ① | ① | — | ① | ① |
| 1984 | 6-250 | R45TS | .045 | Electronic | ① | ① | 4–6 | ① | ① |
| | 8-305 | R45TS | .045 | Electronic | ① | ① | 7–9 | ① | ① |
| | 8-350 | R45TS | .045 | Electronic | ① | ① | 7–9 | ① | ① |
| | 8-379 | Diesel | — | — | ① | ① | — | ① | ① |
| 1985–86 | 6-252 | R43CTS | ① | Electronic | ① | ① | 4–6.5 | ③ | ③ |
| | 8-305 | R45TS | ① | Electronic | ① | ① | 4–6.5 | ③ | ③ |
| | 8-350 | R45TS | ② | Electronic | ① | ① | 4–6.5 | ③ | ③ |
| | 8-379 | — | — | Diesel | — | — | 6.5–9 | 650 | 650 ④ |

NOTE: The underhood specifications sticker often reflects tune-up changes made in production. Sticker figures must be used if they disagree with those in this chart.

NOTE: Part numbers in this chart are not recommendations by Chilton for any product by brand name.

NOTE: All engines use hydraulic valve lifters.

● Figures in parentheses are for California, and are given only if they differ from the 49 state specification. Automatic transmission idle speeds are set in Drive, unless specified otherwise.

▲ At idle speed with vacuum advance hose disconnected and plugged, unless specified otherwise in the text.

N—Transmission in Neutral

D—Transmission in Drive

HD—Heavy Duty

LD—Light Duty

① See the underhood specifications sticker

② Vehicles w/HD emissions use R44T

③ If equipped w/ECM, no adjustment required

④ Adjust w/AT in Park

⑤ California only

⑥ G-20, G-30, 2500, 3500 series in Calif.—6B

⑦ G-20, G-30, 2500, 3500 series in Calif.—8B

⑧ Some G-30/3500 series vans differ. Check the underhood emission sticker.

⑨ High Alt.—10B

⑩ Fed 1 ton models—4B
   Calif ¾ and 1 ton models—6B

⑪ 1 ton models—6B

⑫ 1 ton models—700(N)
   Calif. ½ and ⅓ ton models—550 (D)

89772c05

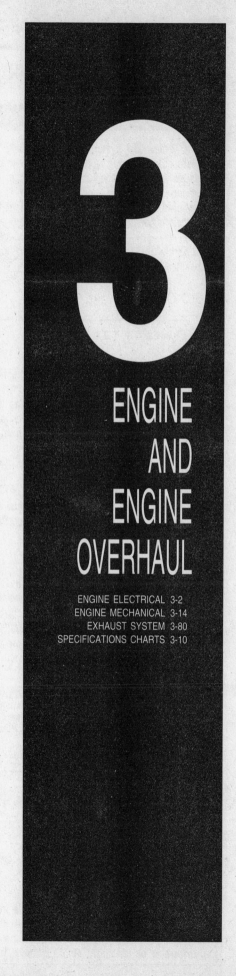

# 3

# ENGINE AND ENGINE OVERHAUL

## ENGINE ELECTRICAL

## Understanding Electricity

For any electrical system to operate, there must be a complete circuit. This simply means that the power flow from the battery must make a full circle. When an electrical component is operating, power flows from the battery to the components, passes through the component (load) causing it to function, and returns to the battery through the ground path of the circuit. This ground may be either another wire or a metal part of the vehicle (depending upon how the component is designed).

## BASIC CIRCUITS

▶ **See Figures 1 and 2**

Perhaps the easiest way to visualize a circuit is to think of connecting a light bulb (with two wires attached to it) to the battery. If one of the two wires was attached to the negative post (-) of the battery and the other wire to the positive post (+), the circuit would be complete and the light bulb would illuminate. Electricity could follow a path from the battery to the bulb and back to the battery. It's not hard to see that with longer wires on our light bulb, it could be mounted anywhere on the vehicle. Further, one wire could be fitted with a switch so that the light could be turned on and off. Various other items could be added to our primitive circuit to make the light flash, become brighter or dimmer under certain conditions, or advise the user that it's burned out.

### Ground

Some automotive components are grounded through their mounting points. The electrical current runs through the chassis of the vehicle and returns to the battery through the ground (-) cable; if you look, you'll see that the battery ground cable connects between the battery and the body of the vehicle.

### Load

Every complete circuit must include a "load" (something to use the electricity coming from the source). If you were to connect a wire between the two terminals of the battery (DON'T do this, but take our word for it) without the light bulb, the battery would attempt to deliver its entire power supply from one pole to another almost instantly. This is a short circuit. The electricity is taking a short cut to get to ground and is not being used by any load in the circuit. This sudden and uncontrolled electrical flow can cause great damage to other components in the circuit and can develop a tremendous amount of heat. A short in an automotive wiring harness can develop sufficient heat to melt the insulation on all the surrounding wires and reduce a multiple wire cable to one sad lump of plastic and copper. Two common causes of shorts are broken insulation (thereby exposing the wire to contact with surrounding metal surfaces or other wires) or a failed switch (the pins inside the switch come out of place and touch each other).

### Switches and Relays

Some electrical components which require a large amount of current to operate also have a relay in their circuit. Since these circuits carry a large amount of current (amperage or amps), the thickness of the wire in the circuit (wire gauge) is also greater. If this large wire were connected from the load to the control switch on the dash, the switch would have to carry the high amperage load and the dash would be twice as large to accommodate wiring harnesses as thick as your wrist. To prevent these problems, a relay is used. The large wires in the circuit are connected from the battery to one side of the relay and from the opposite side of the relay to the load. The relay is normally open, preventing current from passing through the circuit. An additional, smaller wire is connected from the relay to the control switch for the circuit. When the control switch is turned on, it grounds the smaller wire to the relay and completes its circuit. The main switch inside the relay closes, sending power to the component without routing the main

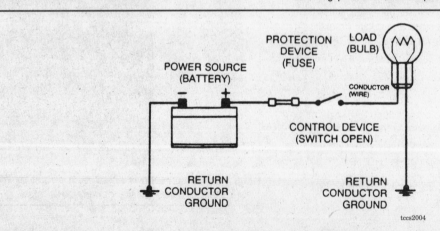

tccs2004

**Fig. 1 Here is an example of a simple automotive circuit. When the switch is closed, power from the positive battery terminal flows through the fuse, the switch and then the load (light bulb). The light illuminates and the circuit is completed through the return conductor and the vehicle ground. If the light did not work, the tests could be made with a voltmeter or test light at the battery, fuse, switch or bulb socket**

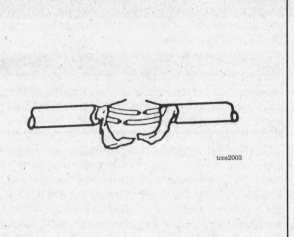

**Fig. 2 Damaged insulation can allow wires to break (causing an open circuit) or touch (causing a short circuit)**

power through the inside of the vehicle. Some common circuits which may use relays are the horn, headlights, starter and rear window defogger systems.

### Protective Devices

It is possible for larger surges of current to pass through the electrical system of your vehicle. If this surge of current were to reach the load in the circuit, it could burn it out or severely damage it. To prevent this, fuses, circuit breakers and/or fusible links are connected into the supply wires of the electrical system. These items are nothing more than a built-in weak spot in the system. It's much easier to go to a known location (the fusebox) to see why a circuit is inoperative than to dissect 15 feet of wiring under the dashboard, looking for what happened.

When an electrical current of excessive power passes through the fuse, the fuse blows (the conductor melts) and breaks the circuit, preventing the passage of current and protecting the components.

A circuit breaker is basically a self repairing fuse. It will open the circuit in the same fashion as a fuse, but when either the short is removed or the surge subsides, the circuit breaker resets itself and does not need replacement.

A fuse link (fusible link or main link) is a wire that acts as a fuse. One of these is normally connected between the starter relay and the main wiring harness under the hood. Since the starter is usually the highest electrical draw on the vehicle, an internal short during starting could direct about 130 amps into the wrong places. Consider the damage potential of introducing this current into a system whose wiring is rated at 15 amps and you'll understand the need for protection. Since this link is very early in the electrical path, it's the first place to look if nothing on the vehicle works, but the battery seems to be charged and is properly connected.

## TROUBLESHOOTING

♦ **See Figures 3, 4 and 5**

Electrical problems generally fall into one of three areas:
• The component that is not functioning is not receiving current.
• The component is receiving power but is not using it or is using it incorrectly (component failure).
• The component is improperly grounded.

The circuit can be can be checked with a test light and a jumper wire. The test light is a device that looks like a pointed screwdriver with a wire on one end and a bulb in its handle. A jumper wire is simply a piece of wire with alligator clips or special terminals on each end. If a component is not working,

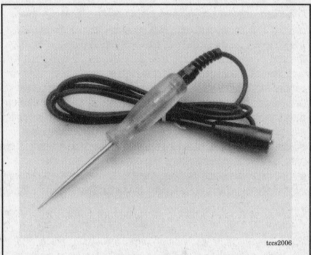

**Fig. 3 A 12 volt test light is useful when checking parts of a circuit for power**

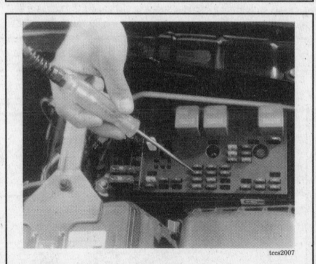

**Fig. 4 Here, someone is checking a circuit by making sure there is power to the component's fuse**

you must follow a systematic plan to determine which of the three causes is the villain.

1. Turn ON the switch that controls the item not working.

➡Some items only work when the ignition switch is turned ON.

2. Disconnect the power supply wire from the component.
3. Attach the ground wire of a test light or a voltmeter to a good metal ground.
4. Touch the end probe of the test light (or the positive lead of the voltmeter) to the power wire; if there is current in the wire, the light in the test light will come on (or the voltmeter will indicate the amount of voltage). You have now established that current is getting to the component.
5. Turn the ignition or dash switch OFF and reconnect the wire to the component.

If there was no power, then the problem is between the battery and the component. This includes all the switches, fuses, relays and the battery itself. The next place to look is the fusebox; check carefully either by eye or by using the test light across the fuse clips. The easiest way to check is to simply replace the fuse. If the fuse is blown, and upon replacement, immediately blows again, there is a short between the fuse and the component. This is generally (not always) a sign of an internal short in the component. Disconnect the power wire at the component again and replace the fuse; if the fuse holds, the component is the problem.

### ✳✳WARNING

DO NOT test a component by running a jumper wire from the battery UNLESS you are certain that it operates on 12 volts. Many electronic components are designed to operate with less voltage and connecting them to 12 volts could destroy them. Jumper wires are best used to bypass a portion of the circuit (such as a stretch of wire or a switch) that DOES NOT contain a resistor and is suspected to be bad.

If all the fuses are good and the component is not receiving power, find the switch for the circuit. Bypass the switch with the jumper wire. This is done by connecting one end of the jumper to the power wire coming into the switch and the other end to the wire leaving the switch. If the component comes to life, the switch has failed.

### ✳✳WARNING

Never substitute the jumper for the component. The circuit needs the electrical load of the component. If you bypass it, you will cause a short circuit.

Checking the ground for any circuit can mean tracing wires to the body, cleaning connections or tightening mounting bolts for the component itself. If the jumper wire can be connected to the case of the component or the ground connector, you can ground the other end to a piece of clean, solid metal on the vehicle. Again, if the component starts working, you've found the problem.

A systematic search through the fuse, connectors, switches and the component itself will almost always yield an answer. Loose and/or corroded connectors, particularly in ground circuits, are becoming a larger problem in modern vehicles. The computers and on-board electronic (solid state) systems are highly sensitive to improper grounds and will change their function drastically if one occurs.

Remember that for any electrical circuit to work, ALL the connections must be clean and tight.

➡For more information on Understanding and Troubleshooting Electrical Systems, please refer to Section 6 of this manual.

## Battery, Starting and Charging Systems

### BASIC OPERATING PRINCIPLES

**Battery**

The battery is the first link in the chain of mechanisms which work together to provide cranking of the automobile engine. In most modern vehicles, the battery is a lead/acid electrochemical device consisting of six 2v subsections (cells) connected in series so the unit is capable of producing approximately 12v of electrical pressure. Each subsection consists of a series of positive and negative plates held a short distance apart in a solution of sulfuric acid and water.

The two types of plates are of dissimilar metals. This sets-up a chemical reaction, and it is this reaction which produces current flow from the battery when its positive and negative terminals are connected to an electrical accessory such as a lamp or motor. The continued transfer of electrons would eventually convert the sulfuric acid to water, and make the two plates identical in chemical composition. As electrical energy is removed from the battery, its voltage output tends to drop. Thus, measuring battery voltage and battery electrolyte composition are two ways of checking the ability of the unit to supply power. During engine cranking, electrical energy is removed from the battery. However, if the charging circuit is in good condition and the operating conditions are normal, the power removed from the battery will be replaced by the alternator which will force electrons back through the battery, reversing

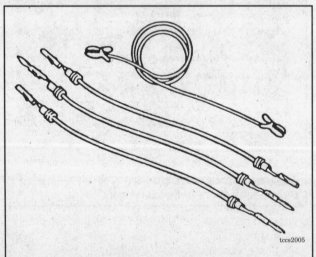

Fig. 5 Jumper wires with various connectors are handy for quick electrical testing

tccs2005

the normal flow, and restoring the battery to its original chemical state.

## Starting System

The battery and starting motor are linked by very heavy electrical cables designed to minimize resistance to the flow of current. Generally, the major power supply cable that leaves the battery goes directly to the starter, while other electrical system needs are supplied by a smaller cable. During starter operation, power flows from the battery to the starter and is grounded through the vehicle's frame/body or engine and the battery's negative ground strap.

The starter is a specially designed, direct current electric motor capable of producing a great amount of power for its size. One thing that allows the motor to produce a great deal of power is its tremendous rotating speed. It drives the engine through a tiny pinion gear (attached to the starter's armature), which drives the very large flywheel ring gear at a greatly reduced speed. Another factor allowing it to produce so much power is that only intermittent operation is required of it. Thus, little allowance for air circulation is necessary, and the windings can be built into a very small space.

The starter solenoid is a magnetic device which employs the small current supplied by the start circuit of the ignition switch. This magnetic action moves a plunger which mechanically engages the starter and closes the heavy switch connecting it to the battery. The starting switch circuit usually consists of the starting switch contained within the ignition switch, a neutral safety switch or clutch pedal switch, and the wiring necessary to connect these in series with the starter solenoid or relay.

The pinion, a small gear, is mounted to a one way drive clutch. This clutch is splined to the starter armature shaft. When the ignition switch is moved to the **START** position, the solenoid plunger slides the pinion toward the flywheel ring gear via a collar and spring. If the teeth on the pinion and flywheel match properly, the pinion will engage the flywheel immediately. If the gear teeth butt one another, the spring will be compressed and will force the gears to mesh as soon as the starter turns far enough to allow them to do so. As the solenoid plunger reaches the end of its travel, it closes the contacts that connect the battery and starter, then the engine is cranked.

As soon as the engine starts, the flywheel ring gear begins turning fast enough to drive the pinion at an extremely high rate of speed. At this point, the one-way clutch begins allowing the pinion to spin faster than the starter shaft so that the starter will not operate at excessive speed. When the ignition switch is released from the starter position, the solenoid is de-energized, and a spring pulls the gear out of mesh interrupting the current flow to the starter.

Some starters employ a separate relay, mounted away from the starter, to switch the motor and solenoid current on and off. The relay replaces the solenoid electrical switch, but does not eliminate the need for a solenoid mounted on the starter used to mechanically engage the starter drive gears. The relay is used to reduce the amount of current the starting switch must carry.

## Charging System

The automobile charging system provides electrical power for operation of the vehicle's ignition system, starting system and all electrical accessories. The battery serves as an electrical surge or storage tank, storing (in chemical form) the energy originally produced by the engine driven generator. The system also provides a means of regulating output to protect the battery from being overcharged and to avoid excessive voltage to the accessories.

The storage battery is a chemical device incorporating parallel lead plates in a tank containing a sulfuric acid/water solution. Adjacent plates are slightly dissimilar, and the chemical reaction of the two dissimilar plates produces electrical energy when the battery is connected to a load such as the starter motor. The chemical reaction is reversible, so that when the generator is producing a voltage (electrical pressure) greater than that produced by the battery, electricity is forced into the battery, and the battery is returned to its fully charged state.

Newer automobiles use alternating current generators or alternators, because they are more efficient, can be rotated at higher speeds, and have fewer brush problems. In an alternator, the field usually rotates while all the current produced passes only through the stator winding. The brushes bear against continuous slip rings. This causes the current produced to periodically reverse the direction of its flow. Diodes (electrical one way valves) block the flow of current from traveling in the wrong direction. A series of diodes is wired together to permit the alternating flow of the stator to be rectified back to 12 volts DC for use by the vehicle's electrical system.

The voltage regulating function is performed by a regulator. The regulator is often built in to the alternator; this system is termed an integrated or internal regulator.

## Ignition Coil

## TESTING

▶ **See Figures 6 and 7**

1. A six cylinder EST distributor with coil-in-cap is illustrated, the 8-cyl EST distributor is similar.
2. Detach the wiring connector from the distributor cap.
3. Turn the four latches and remove the cap and coil assembly from the lower housing.
4. Connect ohmmeter. Test 1.
5. Reading should be zero, or nearly zero. If not replace coil.
6. Connect ohmmeter both ways. Test 2. Use the high scale. Replace coil only if both readings are infinite.
7. If coil is good, go to step 13.
8. Remove coil cover attaching screws and lift off cover.
9. Remove ignition coil attaching screws and lift coil with leads from cap.
10. Remove ignition coil arc seal.
11. Clean with soft cloth and inspect cap for defects. Replace if necessary.
12. Assemble the new coil and cover to cap.
13. .On all distributors, including distributors with Hall Effect Switch identified in step 27, remove rotor and pick-up coil leads from module.
14. Connect ohmmeter Test 1 and then test 2.
15. If vacuum unit is used, connect a vacuum source to the vacuum unit. Replace the vacuum unit if inoperative. Observe

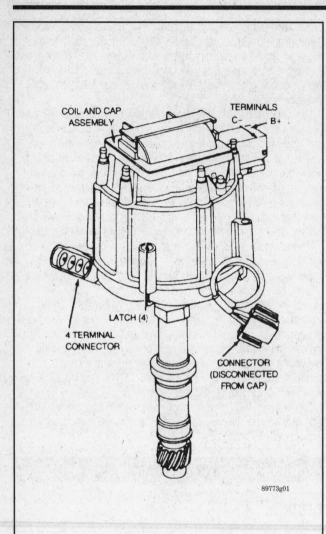

**Fig. 6 View of the "coil in cap" distributor and related components**

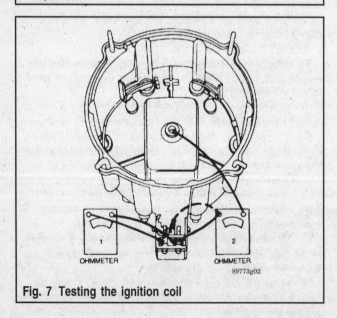

**Fig. 7 Testing the ignition coil**

the ohmmeter throughout vacuum range: flex leads by hand without vacuum to check for intermittent opens.

16. Test 1 should read infinite at all times. Test 2 should read steady at one value within 500-1,500 ohms range.

➡ **Ohmmeter may deflect if operating vacuum unit causes teeth to align. This is not a defect.**

17. If pickup coil is defective go to step 18. If coil is okay, go to step 23.

18. Mark distributor shaft and gear so they can be reassembled in the same position.

19. Drive out poll pin.

20. Remove gear and pull shaft assembly from distributor.

21. Remove three attaching screws and remove the magnetic shield.

22. Remove retaining ring and remove pickup coil, magnet and pole piece.

23. Remove two module attaching screws, and the capacitor attaching screw. Lift module, capacitor and harness assembly from base.

24. Disconnect wiring harness from module.

25. Check the module with an approved module tester.

26. Install module, wiring harness, and capacitor assembly. Use silicone lubricant on housing under module.

27. The procedures previously covered, Steps 1-26, also apply to distributors with Hall Effect Switches.

## REMOVAL & INSTALLATION

▶ **See Figure 8**

1. Detach the wiring connector from the distributor cap.

2. Turn the four latches and remove the cap and coil assembly from the lower housing.

3. Remove coil cover attaching screws and lift off cover.

4. Remove ignition coil attaching screws and lift coil with leads from cap.

5. Remove ignition coil arc seal.

6. Clean with soft cloth and inspect cap for defects. Replace if necessary.

7. Assemble the new coil and cover to cap.

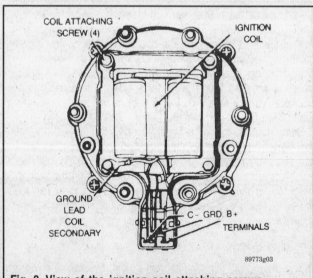

**Fig. 8 View of the ignition coil attaching screws**

## Ignition Module

### REMOVAL & INSTALLATION

▶ See Figure 9

1. Remove distributor cap and rotor.
2. Remove two module attaching screws, and capacitor attaching screw. Lift module, capacitor and harness assembly from base.
3. Disconnect wiring harness from module.
4. Check module with approved module tester.
5. Install module, wiring harness, and capacitor assembly. Use silicone lubricant on housing under module.

## Distributor

### REMOVAL & INSTALLATION

**1967-74 Models**

▶ See Figure 10

1. Remove the distributor cap and position it out of the way.
2. Disconnect the primary coil wire (the thin wire) and the vacuum advance hose.
3. Scribe a mark on the distributor body and the engine block showing their relationship. Mark the distributor housing to show the direction in which the rotor is pointing. Note the positioning of the vacuum advance unit.
4. Remove the hold-down bolt and clamp and remove the distributor.
   **To install the distributor with the engine undisturbed:**
5. Reinsert the distributor into its opening, aligning the previously made marks on the housing and the engine block.
6. The rotor may have to be turned either way a slight amount before inserting the distributor to align the rotor-to-housing marks.

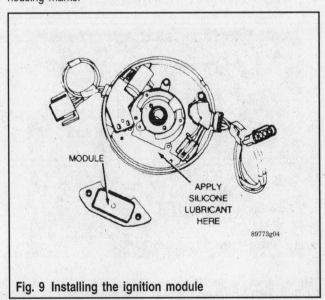

**Fig. 9 Installing the ignition module**

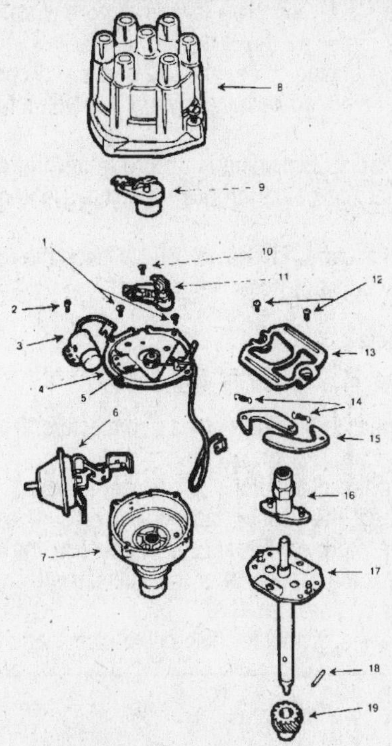

1. Breaker plate attaching screws
2. Condenser screw
3. Condenser
4. Breaker plate assembly
5. Cam lubricator
6. Vacuum control assembly
7. Housing
8. Distributor cap
9. Rotor
10. Contact point attaching screw
11. Contact point assembly
12. Weight cover attaching screws
13. Weight cover
14. Weight springs
15. Advance weights
16. Cam assembly
17. Mainshaft assembly
18. Roll pin
19. Drive gear

89773g05

**Fig. 10 Exploded view of a six cylinder point type distributor**

7. Install the retaining clamp and bolt. Install the distributor cap, primary wire, and the vacuum hose.
8. Start the engine and check the ignition timing.
   **To install the distributor with the engine disturbed (the engine was turned while the distributor was out) or to install a new distributor:**
9. Turn the engine to bring the No. 1 piston to the top of its compression stroke. This may be determined by covering the No. 1 spark plug hole with your thumb and slowly turning the engine over. When the timing mark on the crankshaft pulley aligns with the 0 on the timing scale and your thumb is pushed out by compression, No. 1 piston is at top dead center (TDC). If you don't feel compression, you've got No. 6 at TDC.
10. Install the distributor to the engine block so that the vacuum advance unit points in the correct direction.
11. Turn the rotor so that it will point to the No. 1 terminal in the cap. Some distributors have a punch mark on the gear facing the same way as the rotor tip.
12. Install the distributor into the engine block. It may be necessary to turn the rotor a little in either direction in order to engage the gears.

13. Tap the starter switch a few times to ensure that the oil pump shaft is mated to the distributor shaft.

14. Bring the engine to No. 1 TDC again and check to see that the rotor is indeed pointing toward the No. 1 terminal of the cap.

15. After correct positioning is assured, turn the distributor housing so that the points are just opening. Tighten the retaining clamp.

16. Install the cap and primary wire. Check the ignition timing. Install the vacuum hose.

### 1975-86 Models

▶ See Figures 11, 12, 13, 14 and 15

1. Disconnect the wiring harness connectors at the side of the distributor cap.

2. Remove the distributor cap and set it aside.

3. Disconnect the vacuum advance line.

4. Scribe a mark on the engine in line with the rotor and note the approximate position of the vacuum advance unit in relation to the engine.

5. Remove the distributor hold-down clamp and nut.

Fig. 12 Remove the distributor cap

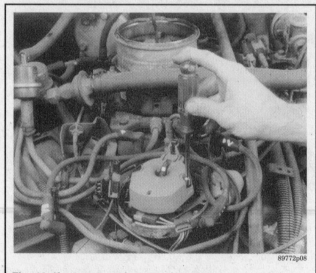

Fig. 13 If necessary, remove the rotor

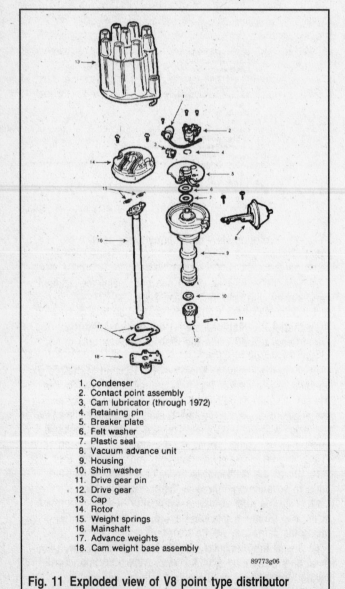

1. Condenser
2. Contact point assembly
3. Cam lubricator (through 1972)
4. Retaining pin
5. Breaker plate
6. Felt washer
7. Plastic seal
8. Vacuum advance unit
9. Housing
10. Shim washer
11. Drive gear pin
12. Drive gear
13. Cap
14. Rotor
15. Weight springs
16. Mainshaft
17. Advance weights
18. Cam weight base assembly

Fig. 11 Exploded view of V8 point type distributor

Fig. 14 Using a distributor wrench, unfasten the hold-down bolt and clamp

**Fig. 15 Remove the distributor from the engine**

6. Lift the distributor from the engine.
7. Installation is the same as for the standard (1967-74) distributor.

## Alternator

Three basic alternators are used: the 5.5 in. (140mm) Series 1D Delcotron, the 6.2 in. (158mm) Series 150 Delcotron and the integral regulator 10 SI Delcotron.

### ALTERNATOR PRECAUTIONS

1. When installing a battery, ensure that the ground polarity of the battery and the ground polarity of the alternator and the regulator are the same.
2. When connecting a jumper battery, be certain that the correct terminals are connected.
3. When charging, connect the correct charger leads to the battery terminals.
4. Never operate the alternator on an open circuit. Be sure that all connections in the charging circuit are tight.
5. Do not short across or ground any of the terminals on the alternator or regulator.
6. Never polarize an AC system.

### PRELIMINARY CHARGING SYSTEM TESTS

1. If you suspect a defect in your charging system, first perform these general checks before going on to more specific tests.
2. Check the condition of the alternator belt and tighten it if necessary.
3. Clean the battery cable connections at the battery. Make sure the connections between the battery wires and the battery clamps are good. Reconnect the negative terminal only and proceed to the next step.
4. With the key off, insert a test light between the positive terminal on the battery and the disconnected positive battery terminal clamp. If the test light comes on, there is a short in the electrical system of the van. The short must be repaired before proceeding. If the light does not come on, proceed to the next step.

➡ **If the van is equipped with an electric shock, the clock must be disconnected.**

5. Check the charging system wiring for any obvious breaks or shorts.
6. Check the battery to make sure it is fully charged and in good condition.

### CHARGING SYSTEM OPERATIONAL TEST

➡ **You will need a current indicator to perform this test. If the current indicator is to give an accurate reading, the battery cables must be the same gauge and length as the original equipment.**

1. With the engine running and all electrical systems turned off, place a current indicator over the positive battery cable.
2. If a charge of roughly five amps is recorded, the charging system is working. If a draw of about five amps is recorded, the system is not working. The needle moves toward the battery when a charge condition is indicated, and away from the battery when a draw condition is indicated.
3. If a draw is indicated, proceed with further testing. If an excessive charge (10-15 amps) is indicated, the regulator may be at fault.

### ALTERNATOR OUTPUT TEST

**With External Regulator**

1. You will need a tachometer and a voltmeter for this test. You will also need a jumper wire.
2. Connect the tachometer to the engine.
3. Disconnect the wiring harness at the voltage regulator. With a jumper wire, connect the **F** wire to the number **3** wire in the wire harness plug.
4. Connect a voltmeter across the battery terminals, the positive voltmeter lead to the positive battery terminal and the negative lead to the negative terminal. Note the reading.
5. Start the engine and let it idle.
6. Gradually raise the engine speed to 1,500-2,000 rpm. The reading on the voltmeter should increase 1.0-2.0v over the initial reading. If there is no increase in the reading, the alternator is defective and must be repaired. If the increase is greater than 2v, then the regulator is defective and must be adjusted or replaced. (See voltage adjustment in the regulator section.)

**With Integral Regulator**

1. You will need an ammeter for this test.
2. Disconnect the battery ground cable.
3. Disconnect the wire from the battery terminal on the alternator.
4. Connect the ammeter negative lead to the battery terminal wire removed in step three, and connect the ammeter positive lead to the battery terminal on the alternator.

5. Reconnect the battery ground cable and turn on all electrical accessories. If the battery is fully charged, disconnect the coil wire and bump the starter a few times to partially discharge it.

6. Start the engine and run it until you obtain a maximum current reading on the ammeter.

7. If the current is not within ten amps of the rated output of the alternator, the alternator is working properly. If the current is not within ten amps, insert a screwdriver in the test hole in the end frame of the alternator and ground the tab in the test hole against the side of the hole.

8. If the current is now within ten amps of the rated output, remove the alternator and have the voltage regulator replaced. If it is still below ten amps of rated output, have the alternator repaired.

## REMOVAL & INSTALLATION

▶ **See Figures 16 and 17**

1. Disconnect the battery ground cable to prevent diode damage.

2. Disconnect and tag all wiring to the alternator.

3. Remove the alternator brace bolt.

4. Remove the drive belt.

5. Support the alternator and remove the mounting bolts. Remove the alternator.

6. Install the unit using the reverse procedure of removal. Adjust the belt to have ½ in. (12.7mm) depression under thumb pressure on its longest run.

## Alternator and Regulator Specifications

| Year | Alternator Part No. or Manufacturer | Field Current @ 12V | Output (amps) | Part No. or Manufacturer | Field Relay Air Gap (in.) | Point Gap (in.) | Volts to Close | Regulator Air Gap (in.) | Point Gap (in.) | Volts at 85° F |
|---|---|---|---|---|---|---|---|---|---|---|
| 1967 | 1100695 | 2.2–2.6 | 32 | 1119515 | 0.015 | 0.030 | 2.3–3.7 | 0.067 | 0.014 | 13.8–14.8 |
| | 1100696 | 2.2–2.6 | 42 | 1119515 | 0.015 | 0.030 | 2.3–3.7 | 0.067 | 0.014 | 13.8–14.8 |
| | 1100750 | 2.2–2.6 | 61 | 1119515 | 0.015 | 0.030 | 2.3–3.7 | 0.067 | 0.014 | 13.8–14.8 |
| | 1100754 | 3.7–4.4 | 62 | 1116378 | 0.011–0.018 | 0.020–0.030 | 2.5–3.5 | NA | NA | 13.7–14.8 |
| 1968 | — | 2.2–2.6 | 37 | — | 0.015 | 0.030 | 2.3–3.7 | 0.067 | 0.014 | 13.8–14.8 |
| | — | 2.2–2.6 | 42 | — | 0.015 | 0.030 | 2.3–3.7 | 0.067 | 0.014 | 13.8–14.8 |
| | — | 2.2–2.6 | 61 | — | 0.015 | 0.030 | 2.3–3.7 | 0.067 | 0.014 | 13.8–14.8 |
| | — | 3.7–4.4 | 62 | — | 0.011–0.018 | 0.020–0.030 | 2.5–3.5 | NA | NA | 13.8–14.8 |
| 1969–70 | 1100834, 38 | 2.2–2.6 | 37 | 1119515 | 0.015 | 0.030 | 2.3–2.7 | 0.067 | 0.014 | 13.8–14.8 |
| | 1100839, 41, 42 | 2.2–2.6 | 42 | 1119515 | 0.015 | 0.030 | 2.3–2.7 | 0.067 | 0.014 | 13.8–14.8 |
| | 1100843, 49 | 2.2–2.6 | 61 | 1119515 | 0.015 | 0.030 | 2.3–2.7 | 0.067 | 0.014 | 13.8–14.8 |
| | — | 3.7–4.4 | 62 | 1116378 | 0.011–0.018 | 0.020–0.030 | 2.5–3.5 | NA | NA | 13.8–14.8 |
| | 1100825 | 22–2.6 | 61 | 1119515 | 0.015 | 0.030 | 2.3–2.7 | 0.067 | 0.014 | 13.8–14.8 |
| | 1100833 ① | 2.2–2.6 | 61 | Integral with alternator | | | | | | |
| 1971–72 | 1100834 | 2.2–2.6 | 37 | 1119515 | 0.015 | 0.030 | 2.3–2.7 | 0.067 | 0.014 | 13.8–14.8 |
| | 1100839 | 2.2–2.6 | 42 | 1119515 | 0.015 | 0.030 | 2.3–2.7 | 0.067 | 0.014 | 13.8–14.8 |
| | 1100849 | 2.2–2.6 | 61 | 1119515 | 0.015 | 0.030 | 2.3–2.7 | 0.067 | 0.014 | 13.8–14.8 |
| 1973–86 | See Casing Stamp | | | Integral with alternator | | | | | | |

—Not available
NA Not Applicable
① 10 SI Integral Alternator

89773c01

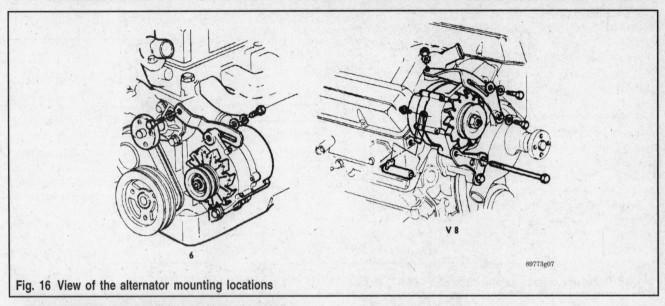

Fig. 16 View of the alternator mounting locations

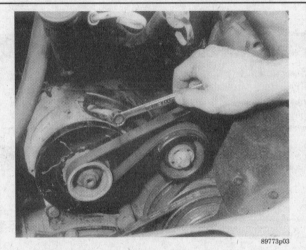

Fig. 17 Loosen the alternator pivot bolts to remove the drive belt

## Regulator

### REMOVAL & INSTALLATION

#### 1967-72 Models

▶ See Figure 18

1. Disconnect the ground cable from the battery.
2. Disconnect the wiring harness from the regulator.
3. Remove the mounting screws and remove the regulator.
4. Make sure that the regulator base gasket is in place before installation.
5. Clean the attaching area for proper grounding.
6. Install the regulator. Do not overtighten the mounting screws, as this will cancel the cushioning effect of the rubber grommets.

#### 1973 and Later Models

The regulator on these models is an integral part of the alternator. Alternator disassembly is required to replace it.

### VOLTAGE ADJUSTMENT

#### 1967-72 Models

The standard voltage regulator from 1967-72 is a conventional double contact unit, although an optional double contact unit, although an optional transistorized regulator was available. Voltage adjustment procedures are the same for both types except for the point of adjustment. The double contact adjusting screw is located under the cover and the transistorized regulator is adjusted externally after removing an allen screw from the adjustment hole.

1. Insert a 0.25 ohm, 25 watt fixed resistor into the charging circuit at the horn relay junction block, between both leads and the terminal. Use a 0.50 ohm, 25 watt resistor for 1971-72.
2. Install a voltmeter as shown.
3. Warm the engine by running it for several minutes at 1,500 rpm or more.
4. Cycle the voltage regulator by disconnecting and reconnecting the regulator connector.
5. Read the voltage on the voltmeter. If it is between 13.5 and 15.2, the regulator does not need adjustment or replacement. If the voltage is not within these limits, leave the engine running at 1,500 rpm.
6. Disconnect the 4-terminal connector and remove the regulator cover (except on transistorized regulators). Reconnect the 4-terminal connector and adjust the voltage to between 14.2 and 14.6 volts by turning the adjusting screw while observing the voltmeter.
7. Disconnect the terminal, install the cover, then reconnect the terminal.
8. Continue running the engine at 1,500 rpm to re-establish the regulator internal temperature.

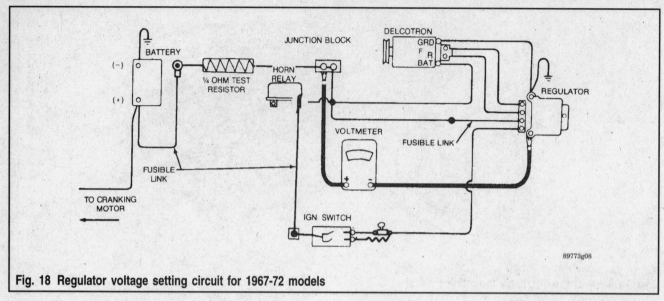

**Fig. 18 Regulator voltage setting circuit for 1967-72 models**

9. Cycle the regulator by disconnecting/reconnecting the regulator connector. Check the voltage. If the voltage is between 13.5 and 15.2, the regulator is good.

### ❋❋WARNING

**Always disconnect the regulator before removing or installing the cover in order to prevent damage by short circuiting.**

#### 1973 and Later Models

On 1973 and later models, the 10 SI Delcotron is used which is equipped with an integral regulator that cannot be adjusted.

### Battery

Please refer to Section 1 for additional information on the battery.

### REMOVAL & INSTALLATION

1. Disconnect the negative (ground) cable terminal and then the positive cable terminal. Special pullers are available to remove clamp type battery terminals.

➡**To avoid sparks, always disconnect the battery ground cable first, and connect it last.**

2. Remove the hold-down clamp.
3. Remove the battery, being careful not to spill the acid.

➡**Spilled acid can be neutralized with a backing soda/water solution. If you somehow get acid in your eyes, flush with lots of water and visit a doctor.**

4. Clean the cable terminals of any corrosion, using a wire brush tool or an old jackknife inside and out.
5. Install the battery. Replace the hold down clamp.
6. Connect the positive and then the negative cable terminal. Do not hammer them in place. The terminals should be

coated lightly (externally) with grease or petroleum jelly to prevent corrosion.

### ❋❋WARNING

**Make absolutely sure that the battery is connected properly before you start the engine. Reversed polarity can destroy your alternator and regulator in a matter of seconds.**

### Starter

### REMOVAL & INSTALLATION

▶ **See Figures 19, 20, 21, 22 and 23**

The following is a general procedure for all vans, and may vary slightly depending on model and series.
1. Disconnect the battery ground cable at the battery.
2. Raise and support the vehicle.

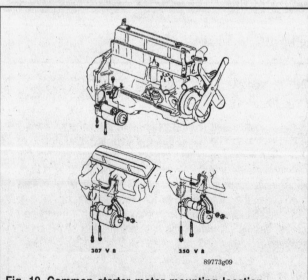

**Fig. 19 Common starter motor mounting location**

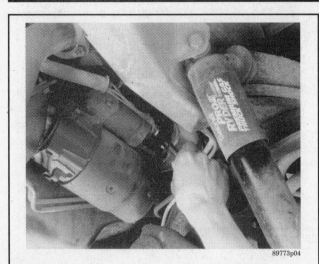

Fig. 20 Disengage the starter solenoid electrical connections

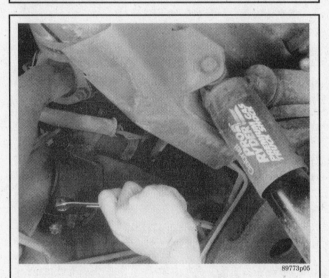

Fig. 21 Unfasten the starter retaining bolts

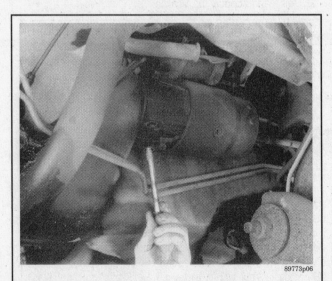

Fig. 22 Remove the starter retaining bolts

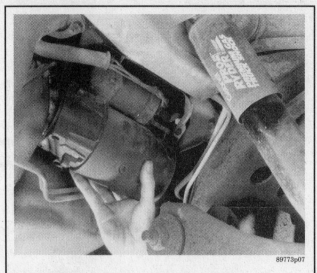

Fig. 23 Remove the starter from the vehicle

3. Disconnect and tag all wires at the solenoid terminal.

➡1975 and later starters do not require the R terminal. The High Energy Ignition System does not need a cable from solenoid to ignition coil.

4. Reinstall all nuts as soon as they are removed, since the thread sizes are different.

5. Remove the front bracket from the starter and the two mounting bolts. On engines with a solenoid heat shield, remove the front bracket upper bolt and detach the bracket from the starter.

6. Remove the front bracket bolt or nut. Lower the starter front end first, and then remove the unit from the van.

7. Reverse the removal procedures to install the starter. Torque the two mounting bolts to 25-35 ft. lbs. (33-47 Nm).

## OVERHAUL

### Brush Replacement

1. Disconnect the field coil connectors from the starter motor solenoid terminal.

2. Remove the through-bolts.

3. Remove the end frame and the field frame from the drive housing.

4. Disassemble the brush assembly from the field frame by releasing the spring and removing the supporting pin. Pull the brushes and the brush holders out and disconnect the wiring.

5. Install the new brushes into the holders.

6. Assemble the brush holder using the spring and position the unit on the supporting pin.

7. Install the unit in the starter motor and attach the wiring.

8. Position the field frame over the armature.

9. Install the through-bolts.

10. Connect the field coil connectors to the solenoid.

### Starter Drive Replacement

1. Remove the starter motor as previously outlined.

2. Disconnect the field coil connections from the solenoid terminal.

3. Remove the through-bolts.

4. Remove the commutator end frame, the field frame assembly and the armature assembly from the housing.

5. Remove the armature assembly from the housing. On some models it may be necessary to remove the solenoid and the shift lever assembly from the housing first.

6. Slide a small piece of ½ in. (12.7mm) pipe over the end of the shaft so the end of the pipe butts against the edge of

the retainer. Carefully tap the end of the pipe with a hammer, driving the retainer towards the armature end of the snapring.

7. Remove the snapring from the groove.

8. Slide the retainer and clutch off the shaft.

9. To assemble the drive mechanism, slide the drive assembly onto the armature shaft after lubricating it with silicone.

## Starter Specifications

| Year | Identification | Starter ③ | | |
|---|---|---|---|---|
| | | Volts | No Load Test | |
| | | | Amps ① | rpm |
| 1967–69 | 1107372 ① | 10.6 | 55–95 | 3800–6000 |
| 1970–75 | 1108744 1108788 ② | 9 | 50–80 | 5500–10,500 |
| | 1108747 1108780 ② | 9 | 50–80 | 3500–6000 |
| | 1108748 1108781 ② | 9 | 65–90 | 7500–10,500 |
| | 1108748 1108781 ② | 9 | 65–90 | 7500–10,500 |
| 1976 | 1108778 ② | 9 | 50–80 | 5500–10,500 |
| | 1108780 ② | 9 | 50–80 | 3500–6000 |
| | 1108781 ② | 9 | 65–90 | 7500–10,500 |
| | 1108781 ② | 9 | 65–90 | 7500–10,500 |
| 1977–82 | 1108778 ② | 9 | 50–80 | 5500–10,500 |
| | 1187780 ② | 9 | 50–80 | 3500–6000 |
| | 1109056 ② | 9 | 50–80 | 5500–10,500 |
| | 1109052 ② | 9 | 65–95 | 7500–10,500 |
| | 1108776 ② | 9 | 65–95 | 7500–10,500 |
| | 1108776 ② | 9 | 65–95 | 7500–10,500 |
| 1983–86 | 1109561 | 9 | 50–75 | 6000–11,900 |
| | 1109535 | 9 | 45–70 | 7000–11,900 |
| | 1998241 | 10 | 65–95 | 7500–10,500 |
| | 1998244 | 10 | 60–85 | 6800–10,500 |
| | 1998211 | 10 | 65–95 | 7500–10,500 |
| | 1998396 | 10 | 70–110 | 6500–10,700 |
| | 1998397 | 10 | 70–110 | 6500–10,700 |
| | 1109563 | 10 | 120–210 | 9000–13,400 |

① Solenoid included
② "R" terminal removed
③ Brush spring tension is 35 oz. for all starters. Lock test is not recommended.

89773C02

# ENGINE MECHANICAL

## Design

All Chevrolet and GMC van engines are water cooled, overhead valve powerplants, using cast iron cylinder blocks and heads.

The 230 and 250 cu in., inline six cylinder engine crankshaft has seven main bearings, with the thrust taken by No. 7. This results in a very rigid crankshaft assembly. The camshaft is low in the block and driven by gears rather than the usual

chains and sprockets. Fairly long pushrods actuate the valves through ball mounted rocker arms. This engine has changed very little over the years, giving a great interchangeability of parts. A major change was introduced in 1975. This is an integral cylinder head and intake manifold casting. The integral design results in better emission control and more power and economy. The 292 six, introduced in 1975, is similar to the 250 in design but with a longer stroke. It has special valves with rotators, aluminum bearings, a larger oil capacity, larger crankpins, longer connecting rods, and a number of other heavy duty features derived from its years of use in heavier trucks.

The 4.3 Liter engines are 90° V6 type, over head valve, water cooled, with cast iron block and heads. The crankshaft is supported by four precision insert main bearings, with crankshaft thrust taken at the number 4 (rear) bearing. The camshaft is supported by four plain bearings and is chain driven. Motion from the camshaft is transmitted to the valves by hydraulic lifters, pushrods, and ball type rocker arms. The valve guides are integral in the cylinder head. The connecting rods are forged steel, with precision insert type crankpin bearings. The piston pins are a press fit in the connecting rods. The pistons are cast aluminum alloy and the piston pins are a floating fit in the piston.

The small block family of V8 engines, 283, 305, 307, 350 and 400 cu in., are all derived from the innovative design of the original 1955 265 cu in. Chevrolet V8. This engine introduced the ball mounted rocker arm design, replacing the once standard shaft mounted rocker arms. There is extensive interchangeability of components among these engines, extending to the several other small block displacement sizes available in passenger cars. The 400 cu in. version differs in block design; it does not have cooling passages between the cylinders, as on the smaller V8s.

➡**Don't confuse the Chevrolet/GMC van 400 with the big block engine used in passenger cars, identified variously as 396, 400, or 402 cu in. The small block engine can quickly be identified by the placement of the distributor at the rear.**

A new V8 diesel of 6.2L (379 cu in.) was introduced for the vans in 1983. This engine is built by Chevrolet; GM's Detroit Diesel Division aided in much of the engine's design. The 379 is even stronger, component by component, than the 350 diesel. Designed "from the block up" as a diesel, it utilizes robust features such as four-bolt main bearing caps.

## Engine Overhaul Tips

Most engine overhaul procedures are fairly standard. In addition to specific parts replacement procedures and specifications for your individual engine, this section is also a guide to acceptable rebuilding procedures. Examples of standard rebuilding practice are given and should be used along with specific details concerning your particular engine.

Competent and accurate machine shop services will ensure maximum performance, reliability and engine life. In most instances it is more profitable for the do-it-yourself mechanic to remove, clean and inspect the component, buy the necessary parts and deliver these to a shop for actual machine work.

On the other hand, much of the rebuilding work (crankshaft, block, bearings, piston rods, and other components) is well within the scope of the do-it-yourself mechanic's tools and abilities. You will have to decide for yourself the depth of involvement you desire in an engine repair or rebuild.

## TOOLS

The tools required for an engine overhaul or parts replacement will depend on the depth of your involvement. With a few exceptions, they will be the tools found in a mechanic's tool kit (see Section 1 of this manual). More in-depth work will require some or all of the following:
- A dial indicator (reading in thousandths) mounted on a universal base
- Micrometers and telescope gauges
- Jaw and screw-type pullers
- Scraper
- Valve spring compressor
- Ring groove cleaner
- Piston ring expander and compressor
- Ridge reamer
- Cylinder hone or glaze breaker
- Plastigage®
- Engine stand

The use of most of these tools is illustrated in this section. Many can be rented for a one-time use from a local parts jobber or tool supply house specializing in automotive work.

Occasionally, the use of special tools is called for. See the information on Special Tools and the Safety Notice in the front of this book before substituting another tool.

## INSPECTION TECHNIQUES

Procedures and specifications are given in this section for inspecting, cleaning and assessing the wear limits of most major components. Other procedures such as Magnaflux® and Zyglo® can be used to locate material flaws and stress cracks. Magnaflux® is a magnetic process applicable only to ferrous materials. The Zyglo® process coats the material with a fluorescent dye penetrant and can be used on any material.

Checking for suspected surface cracks can be more readily made using spot check dye. The dye is sprayed onto the suspected area, wiped off and the area sprayed with a developer. Cracks will show up brightly.

## OVERHAUL TIPS

Aluminum has become extremely popular for use in engines, due to its low weight. Observe the following precautions when handling aluminum parts:
- Never hot tank aluminum parts (the caustic hot tank solution will eat the aluminum.
- Remove all aluminum parts (identification tag, etc.) from engine parts prior to the tanking.
- Always coat threads lightly with engine oil or anti-seize compounds before installation, to prevent seizure.
- Never overtorque bolts or spark plugs especially in aluminum threads.

Stripped threads in any component can be repaired using any of several commercial repair kits (Heli-Coil®, Microdot®, Keenserts®, etc.).

When assembling the engine, any parts that will be exposed to frictional contact must be prelubed to provide lubrication at

initial start-up. Any product specifically formulated for this purpose can be used, but engine oil is not recommended as a
prelube in most cases.

When semi-permanent (locked, but removable) installation of
bolts or nuts is desired, threads should be cleaned and coated
with Loctite® or another similar, commercial non-hardening
sealant.

## REPAIRING DAMAGED THREADS

▶ **See Figures 24, 25, 26, 27 and 28**

Several methods of repairing damaged threads are available.
Heli-Coil® (shown here), Keenserts® and Microdot® are
among the most widely used. All involve basically the same
principle — drilling out stripped threads, tapping the hole and
installing a prewound insert — making welding, plugging and
oversize fasteners unnecessary.

Two types of thread repair inserts are usually supplied: a
standard type for most inch coarse, inch fine, metric course

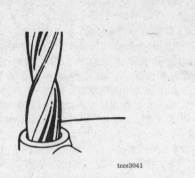

Fig. 26 Drill out the damaged threads with the specified
size bit. Be sure to drill completely through the hole or
to the bottom of a blind hole

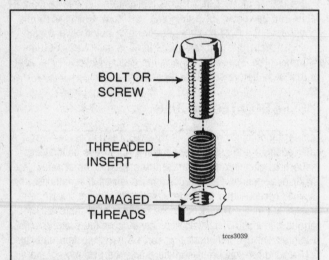

Fig. 24 Damaged bolt hole threads can be replaced with
thread repair inserts

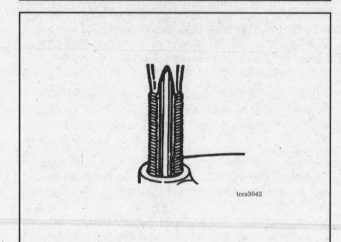

Fig. 27 Using the kit, tap the hole in order to receive
the thread insert. Keep the tap well oiled and back it
out frequently to avoid clogging the threads

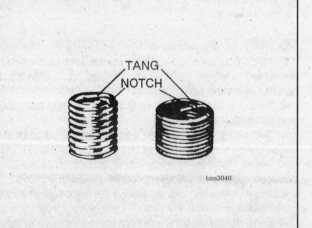

Fig. 25 Standard thread repair insert (left), and spark
plug thread insert

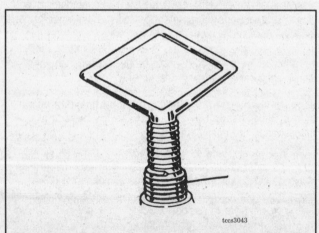

Fig. 28 Screw the insert onto the installer tool until the
tang engages the slot. Thread the insert into the hole
until it is $\frac{1}{4}$-$\frac{1}{2}$ turn below the top surface, then remove
the tool and break off the tang using a punch

and metric fine thread sizes and a spark lug type to fit most spark plug port sizes. Consult the individual tool manufacturer's catalog to determine exact applications. Typical thread repair kits will contain a selection of prewound threaded inserts, a tap (corresponding to the outside diameter threads of the insert) and an installation tool. Spark plug inserts usually differ because they require a tap equipped with pilot threads and a combined reamer/tap section. Most manufacturers also supply blister-packed thread repair inserts separately in addition to a master kit containing a variety of taps and inserts plus installation tools.

Before attempting to repair a threaded hole, remove any snapped, broken or damaged bolts or studs. Penetrating oil can be used to free frozen threads. The offending item can usually be removed with locking pliers or using a screw/stud extractor. After the hole is clear, the thread can be repaired, as shown in the series of accompanying illustrations and in the kit manufacturer's instructions.

## Checking Engine Compression

A noticeable lack of engine power, excessive oil consumption and/or poor fuel mileage measured over an extended period are all indicators of internal engine war. Worn piston rings, scored or worn cylinder bores, blown head gaskets, sticking or burnt valves and worn valve seats are all possible culprits here. A check of each cylinder's compression will help you locate the problems.

A screw-in type compression gauge is more accurate that the type you simply hold against the spark plug hole, although it takes slightly longer to use. It's worth it to obtain a more accurate reading. Follow the procedures below for gasoline and diesel engine trucks.

### GASOLINE ENGINES

▶ See Figure 29

1. Warm up the engine to normal operating temperature.
2. Remove all spark plugs.
3. Disconnect the high tension lead from the ignition coil.
4. On fully open the throttle either by operating the carburetor throttle linkage by hand or by having an assistant floor the accelerator pedal.
5. Screw the compression gauge into the no.1 spark plug hole until the fitting is snug.

➡**Be careful not to crossthread the plug hole. On aluminum cylinder heads use extra care, as the threads in these heads are easily ruined.**

6. Ask an assistant to depress the accelerator pedal fully on both carbureted and fuel injected trucks. Then, while you read the compression gauge, ask the assistant to crank the engine two or three times in short bursts using the ignition switch.
7. Read the compression gauge at the end of each series of cranks, and record the highest of these readings. Repeat

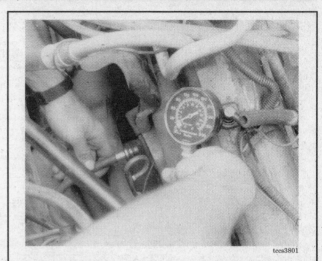

tccs3801

**Fig. 29 A screw-in type compression gauge is more accurate and easier to use without an assistant**

this procedure for each of the engine's cylinders. Compare the highest reading of each cylinder to the compression pressure specification in the Tune-Up Specifications chart in Section 2. The specs in this chart are maximum values.

A cylinder's compression pressure is usually acceptable if it is not less than 80% of maximum. The difference between each cylinder should be no more than 12-14 pounds.

8. If a cylinder is unusually low, pour a tablespoon of clean engine oil into the cylinder through the spark plug hole and repeat the compression test. If the compression comes up after adding the oil, it appears that the cylinder's piston rings or bore are damaged or worn. If the pressure remains low, the valves may not be seating properly (a valve job is needed), or the head gasket may be blown near that cylinder. If compression in any two adjacent cylinders is low, and if the addition of oil doesn't help the compression, there is leakage past the head gasket. Oil and coolant water in the combustion chamber can result from this problem. There may be evidence of water droplets on the engine dipstick when a head gasket has blown.

### DIESEL ENGINES

Checking cylinder compression on diesel engines is basically the same procedure as on gasoline engines except for the following:

1. A special compression gauge adaptor suitable for diesel engines (because these engines have much greater compression pressures) must be used.
2. Remove the injector tubes and remove the injectors from each cylinder.
3. When fitting the compression gauge adaptor to the cylinder head, make sure the bleeder of the gauge (if equipped) is closed.
4. When reinstalling the injector assemblies, install new washers underneath each injector.

## General Engine Specifications

| Year | Engine Cu in. Displacement | Carburetor Type | Horsepower @ rpm ■ | Torque @ rpm (ft. lbs.) ■ | Bore and Stroke (in.) | Compression Ratio | Oil Pressure @ 2000 rpm |
|---|---|---|---|---|---|---|---|
| 1967 | 6-230 | 1 bbl | 140 @ 4400 | 220 @ 1600 | 3.875 x 3.250 | 8.5:1 | 38 |
| | 6-250 | 1 bbl | 155 @ 4200 | 235 @ 1600 | 3.875 x 3.530 | 8.5:1 | 38 ① |
| | 8-283 | 2 bbl | 175 @ 4400 | 275 @ 2400 | 3.875 x 3.000 | 9.1:1 | 38 ① |
| 1968 | 6-230 | 1 bbl | 140 @ 4400 | 220 @ 1600 | 3.875 x 3.250 | 8.5:1 | 58 |
| | 6-250 | 1 bbl | 155 @ 4200 | 235 @ 1600 | 3.875 x 3.530 | 8.5:1 | 58 |
| | 8-307 | 2 bbl | 200 @ 4600 | 300 @ 2400 | 3.875 x 3.250 | 9.0:1 | 58 |
| 1969 | 6-230 | 1 bbl | 140 @ 4400 | 220 @ 1600 | 3.875 x 3.250 | 8.5:1 | 58 |
| | 6-250 | 1 bbl | 155 @ 4200 | 235 @ 1600 | 3.875 x 3.530 | 8.5:1 | 58 |
| | 8-307 | 2 bbl | 200 @ 4600 | 300 @ 2400 | 3.875 x 3.250 | 9.0:1 | 58 |
| 1970 | 6-250 | 1 bbl | 155 @ 4200 | 235 @ 1600 | 3.875 x 3.530 | 8.5:1 | 40 |
| | 8-307 | 2 bbl | 200 @ 4600 | 300 @ 2400 | 3.875 x 3.250 | 9.0:1 | 40 |
| | 8-350 | 2 bbl | 255 @ 4600 | 355 @ 3000 | 4.000 x 3.480 | 9.0:1 | 40 |
| 1971 | 6-250 | 1 bbl | 145 @ 4200 | 235 @ 1600 | 3.875 x 3.530 | 8.5:1 | 40 |
| | 8-307 | 2 bbl | 200 @ 4600 | 300 @ 2400 | 3.875 x 3.250 | 8.5:1 | 40 |
| | 8-350 | 2 bbl | 255 @ 4600 | 355 @ 3000 | 4.000 x 3.480 | 9.0:1 | 40 |
| 1972 | 6-250 | 1 bbl | 110 @ 3800 | 185 @ 1600 | 3.875 x 3.530 | 8.5:1 | 40 |
| | 8-307 | 2 bbl | 130 @ 4000 | 230 @ 2400 | 3.875 x 3.250 | 8.5:1 | 40 |
| | 8-350 | 2 bbl | 175 @ 4000 | 290 @ 2400 | 4.000 x 3.480 | 8.5:1 | 40 |
| 1973 | 6-250 | 1 bbl | 100 @ 3800 | 175 @ 2000 | 3.875 x 3.530 | 8.25:1 | 40 |
| | 8-307 | 2 bbl | 115 @ 3600 | 225 @ 2000 | 3.875 x 3.250 | 8.5:1 | 40 |
| | 8-350 | 2 bbl | 155 @ 4000 | 255 @ 2400 | 4.000 x 3.480 | 8.5:1 | 40 |
| | 8-350 | 4 bbl | 175 @ 4400 | 270 @ 2400 | 4.000 x 3.480 | 8.5:1 | 40 |
| 1974 | 6-250 | 1 bbl | 100 @ 3600 | 175 @ 1800 | 3.875 x 3.530 | 8.25:1 | 40 |
| | 8-350 | 2 bbl | 145 @ 3600 | 250 @ 2200 | 4.000 x 3.480 | 8.5:1 | 40 |
| | 8-350 | 4 bbl | 160 @ 3800 | 255 @ 2400 | 4.000 x 3.480 | 8.5:1 | 40 |
| 1975 | 6-250 | 1 bbl | 105 @ 3800 | 185 @ 1200 | 3.875 x 3.530 | 8.25:1 | 40 |
| | 6-292 | 1 bbl | 120 @ 3600 | 215 @ 2000 | 3.875 x 4.120 | 8.0:1 | 40 |
| | 8-350 | 2 bbl | 145 @ 3800 | 250 @ 2200 | 4.000 x 3.480 | 8.5:1 | 40 |
| | 8-350 | 4 bbl | 160 @ 3800 | 250 @ 2400 | 4.000 x 3.480 | 8.5:1 | 40 |
| | 8-400 | 4 bbl | 175 @ 3600 | 290 @ 2800 | 4.125 x 3.750 | 8.5:1 | 40 |
| 1976 | 6-250 | 1 bbl | 105 @ 3800 | 185 @ 1200 | 3.875 x 3.530 | 8.25:1 | 40 |
| | 6-292 | 1 bbl | 120 @ 3600 | 215 @ 2000 | 3.875 x 4.120 | 8.0:1 | 40 |
| | 8-350 | 2 bbl | 145 @ 3800 | 250 @ 2200 | 4.000 x 3.480 | 8.5:1 | 40 |
| | 8-350 LD | 4 bbl | 165 @ 3800 | 260 @ 2400 | 4.000 x 3.480 | 8.5:1 | 40 |
| | 8-350 HD | 4 bbl | 165 @ 3800 | 255 @ 2800 | 4.000 x 3.480 | 8.5:1 | 40 |
| | 8-400 | 4 bbl | 175 @ 3600 | 290 @ 2800 | 4.125 x 3.750 | 8.5:1 | 40 |
| 1977 | 6-250 | 1 bbl | 110 @ 3800 | 195 @ 1600 | 3.875 x 3.530 | 8.25:1 | 40 |
| | 6-292 | 1 bbl | 120 @ 3600 | 215 @ 2000 | 3.875 x 4.120 | 8.0:1 | 40 |
| | 8-305 | 2 bbl | 145 @ 3800 | 245 @ 2400 | 3.736 x 3.480 | 8.5:1 | 40 |

89773c03

## General Engine Specifications (cont.)

| Year | Engine Cu in. Displacement | Carburetor Type | Horsepower @ rpm ■ | Torque @ rpm (ft. lbs.) ■ | Bore and Stroke (in.) | Compression Ratio | Oil Pressure @ 2000 rpm |
|------|------|------|------|------|------|------|------|
| 1977 | 8-350 LD | 4 bbl | 165 @ 3800 | 260 @ 2400 | 4.000 x 3.480 | 8.5:1 | 40 |
|  | 8-350 HD | 4 bbl | 165 @ 3800 | 255 @ 2800 | 4.000 x 3.480 | 8.5:1 | 40 |
|  | 8-400 | 4 bbl | 175 @ 3600 | 290 @ 2800 | 4.125 x 3.750 | 8.5:1 | 40 |
| 1978 | 6-250 | 1 bbl | 110 @ 3800 | 195 @ 1600 | 3.876 x 3.530 | 8.3:1 | 40 |
|  | 6-292 | 1 bbl | 120 @ 3600 | 215 @ 2000 | 3.876 x 4.120 | 8.0:1 | 40 |
|  | 8-305 | 2 bbl | 145 @ 3800 | 245 @ 2400 | 3.736 x 3.480 | 8.5:1 | 40 |
|  | 8-350 LD | 4 bbl | 165 @ 3800 | 260 @ 2400 | 4.000 x 3.480 | 8.5:1 | 40 |
|  | 8-350 HD | 4 bbl | 165 @ 3800 | 255 @ 2800 | 4.000 x 3.480 | 8.5:1 | 40 |
|  | 8-400 | 4 bbl | 175 @ 3600 | 290 @ 2800 | 4.125 x 3.750 | 8.5:1 | 40 |
| 1979–80 | 6-250 | 2 bbl | 130 @ 3500 | 210 @ 2400 | 3.876 x 3.530 | 8.3:1 | 40 |
|  | 8-305 | 2 bbl | 140 @ 4000 | 240 @ 2000 | 3.736 x 3.480 | 8.4:1 | 45 |
|  | 8-350 Fed. | 4 bbl | 165 @ 3800 | 270 @ 2000 | 4.000 x 3.480 | 8.2:1 | 45 |
|  | 8-350 Cal. | 4 bbl | 155 @ 3800 | 260 @ 2000 | 4.000 x 3.480 | 8.2:1 | 45 |
|  | 8-400 Fed. | 4 bbl | 175 @ 3600 | 290 @ 2800 | 4.125 x 3.750 | 8.5:1 | 40 |
|  | 8-400 Cal. | 4 bbl | 165 @ 3600 | 290 @ 2000 | 4.125 x 3.750 | 8.5:1 | 40 |
| 1981 | 6-250 | 2 bbl | 130 @ 4000 | 210 @ 2000 | 3.870 x 3.530 | 8.3:1 | 40–60 |
|  | 8-305 | 2 bbl | 135 @ 4200 | 235 @ 2400 | 3.740 x 3.480 | 8.5:1 | 45 |
|  | 8-305 | 4 bbl | 155 @ 4400 | 252 @ 2400 | 3.740 x 3.480 | 9.2:1 | 45 |
|  | 8-350 | 4 bbl | 165 @ 3800 | 275 @ 2000 | 4.000 x 3.480 | 8.2:1 | 45 |
| 1982 | 6-250 | 2 bbl | 130 @ 4000 | 210 @ 2000 | 3.870 x 3.530 | 8.3:1 | 40–60 |
|  | 8-305 | 4 bbl | 140 @ 4200 | 240 @ 2400 | 3.740 x 3.480 | 8.5:1 | 45 |
|  | 8-350 | 4 bbl | 175 @ 4000 | 275 @ 2000 | 4.000 x 3.480 | 8.2:1 | 45 |
| 1983–86 | 6-250 | 2 bbl | 120 @ 4000 | 205 @ 2000 | 3.870 x 3.530 | 8.3:1 | 40–60 |
|  | 6-262 | 4 bbl | 150 @ 4000 | 225 @ 2400 | 4.000 x 3.480 | 9.3:1 | 40–60 |
|  | 8-305 ② | 4 bbl | 160 @ 4400 | 235 @ 2000 | 3.740 x 3.480 | 8.5:1 | 45 |
|  | 8-305 ③ | 4 bbl | 155 @ 4000 | 245 @ 1600 | 3.740 x 3.480 | 9.2:1 | 45 |
|  | 8-350 ② | 4 bbl | 165 @ 3800 | 275 @ 1600 | 4.000 x 3.480 | 8.2:1 | 45 |
|  | 8-350 ③ | 4 bbl | 155 @ 4000 | 240 @ 2800 | 4.000 x 3.480 | 8.2:1 | 45 |
|  | 8-379 | Diesel | 140 @ 3600 | 240 @ 2000 | 3.980 x 3.800 | 21.5:1 | 45 |

■Starting 1972, horsepower and torque are SAE net figures. They are measured at the rear of the transmission with all accessories installed and operating. Since the figures vary when a given engine is installed in different models, some are representative rather than exact.

① Oil pressure at 1500 rpm
② 49-states
③ Calif
HD Heavy Duty Emissions
LD Light Duty Emissions
Fed.—All states except California
Cal.—California

## Valve Specifications

| Year | Engine No. Cyl Displacement (cu in.) | Seat Angle (deg) | Face Angle (deg) | Spring Test Pressure (lbs @ in.) | Spring Installed Height (in.) ① | Stem to Guide Clearance (in.) | | Stem Diameter (in.) | |
|---|---|---|---|---|---|---|---|---|---|
| | | | | | | Intake | Exhaust | Intake | Exhaust |
| 1967 | 6-230 | 46 | 45 | 60 @ 1.66 | 1²¹⁄₃₂ | .0010–.0027 | .0015–.0032 | .3414 | .3414 |
| | 6-250 | 46 | 45 | 60 @ 1.66 | 1²¹⁄₃₂ | .0010–.0027 | .0015–.0032 | .3414 | .3414 |
| | 8-283 | 46 | 45 | 82 @ 1.66 | 1²¹⁄₃₂ | .0010–.0027 | .0010–.0027 | .3414 | .3414 |
| 1968 | 6-230 | 46 | 45 | 60 @ 1.66 | 1²¹⁄₃₂ | .0010–.0027 | .0015–.0032 | .3414 | .3414 |
| | 6-250 | 46 | 45 | 60 @ 1.66 | 1²¹⁄₃₂ | .0010–.0027 | .0015–.0032 | .3414 | .3414 |
| | 8-307 | 46 | 45 | 82 @ 1.66 | 1²¹⁄₃₂ | .0010–.0027 | .0010–.0027 | .3414 | .3414 |
| 1969 | 6-230 | 46 | 45 | 60 @ 1.66 | 1²¹⁄₃₂ | .0010–.0027 | .0015–.0032 | .3414 | .3414 |
| | 6-250 | 46 | 45 | 60 @ 1.66 | 1²¹⁄₃₂ | .0010–.0027 | .0015–.0032 | .3414 | .3414 |
| | 8-307 | 46 | 45 | 60 @ 1.66 | 1²¹⁄₃₂ | .0010–.0027 | .0010–.0027 | .3414 | .3414 |
| 1970 | 6-250 | 46 | 45 | 60 @ 1.66 | 1²¹⁄₃₂ | .0010–.0032 | .0015–.0032 | .3414 | .3414 |
| | 8-307 | 46 | 45 | 80 @ 1.70 | 1²³⁄₃₂ | .0010–.0027 | .0010–.0027 | .3414 | .3414 |
| | 8-350 | 46 | 45 | 80 @ 1.70 | 1²³⁄₃₂ | .0010–.0027 | .0010–.0027 | .3414 | .3414 |
| 1971 | 6-250 | 46 | 45 | 60 @ 1.66 | 1²¹⁄₃₂ | .0010–.0027 | .0015–.0032 | .3414 | .3414 |
| | 8-307 | 46 | 45 | 80 @ 1.70 | 1²³⁄₃₂ | .0010–.0027 | .0010–.0027 | .3414 | .3414 |
| | 8-350 | 46 | 45 | 80 @ 1.70 | 1²³⁄₃₂ | .0010–.0027 | .0010–.0027 | .3414 | .3414 |
| 1972 | 6-250 | 46 | 45 | 60 @ 1.66 | 1²¹⁄₃₂ | .0010–.0027 | .0015–.0032 | .3414 | .3414 |
| | 8-307 | 46 | 45 | 80 @ 1.70 | 1²³⁄₃₂ | .0010–.0027 | .0010–.0027 | .3414 | .3414 |
| | 8-350 | 46 | 45 | 80 @ 1.70 | 1²³⁄₃₂ | .0010–.0027 | .0010–.0027 | .3414 | .3414 |
| 1973 | 6-250 | 46 | 45 | 60 @ 1.66 | 1²¹⁄₃₂ | .0010–.0027 | .0015–.0032 | .3414 | .3414 |
| | 8-307 | 46 | 45 | 80 @ 1.70 ② | 1⁵⁄₈ | .0010–.0027 | .0010–.0027 | .3414 | .3414 |
| | 8-350 | 46 | 45 | 80 @ 1.70 ② | 1²³⁄₃₂ | .0010–.0027 | .0010–.0027 | .3414 | .3414 |
| 1974 | 6-250 | 46 | 45 | 60 @ 1.66 | 1²¹⁄₃₂ | .0010–.0027 | .0015–.0032 | .3414 | .3414 |
| | 8-350 | 46 | 45 | 80 @ 1.70 ② | 1²³⁄₃₂ | .0010–.0027 | .0010–.0027 | .3414 | .3414 |
| 1975–77 | 6-250 | 46 | 45 | 60 @ 1.66 | 1²¹⁄₃₂ | .0010–.0027 | .0015–.0032 | .3414 | .3414 |

89773C05

## Valve Specifications (cont.)

| Year | Engine No. Cyl Displacement (cu in.) | Seat Angle (deg) | Face Angle (deg) | Spring Test Pressure (lbs @ in.) | Spring Installed Height (in.) ① | Stem to Guide Clearance (in.) | | Stem Diameter (in.) | |
|---|---|---|---|---|---|---|---|---|---|
| | | | | | | Intake | Exhaust | Intake | Exhaust |
| 1975–77 | 6-292 | 46 | 45 | 89 @ 1.69 | 1⅝ | .0010–.0027 | .0010–.0027 | .3414 | .3414 |
| | 8-305 | 46 | 45 | 80 @ 1.70 ② | 1²³⁄₃₂ ③ | .0010–.0027 | .0010–.0027 | .3414 | .3414 |
| | 8-350 | 46 | 45 | 80 @ 1.70 ② | 1²³⁄₃₂ ③ | .0010–.0027 | .0010–.0027 | .3414 | .3414 |
| | 8-400 | 46 | 45 | 80 @ 1.70 ② | 1²³⁄₃₂ ③ | .0012–.0029 | .0012–.0029 | .3414 | .3414 |
| 1978–82 | 6-250 | 46 | 45 | 60 @ 1.66 | 1²¹⁄₃₂ | .0010–.0027 | .0015–.0032 | .3414 | .3414 |
| | 6-292 | 46 | 46 | 82 @ 1.66 | 1²¹⁄₃₂ | .0010–.0027 | .0015–.0032 | .3414 | .3414 |
| | 8-305 | 46 | 45 | 80 @ 1.70 ② | 1²¹⁄₃₂ ③ | .0010–.0027 | .0010–.0027 | .3414 | .3414 |
| | 8-350 | 46 | 45 | 80 @ 1.70 ② | 1²³⁄₃₂ | .0010–.0027 | .0010–.0027 | .3414 | .3414 |
| | 8-400 | 46 | 45 | 80 @ 1.70 ② | 1²³⁄₃₂ ③ | .0010–.0027 | .0012–.0029 | .3414 | .3414 |
| 1983–86 | 6-250 | 46 | 45 | 175 @ 1.26 | 1.66 | .0010–.0027 | .0015–.0032 | .3414 | .3414 |
| | 6-262 | 46 | 45 | 194–206 @ 1.25 | 1²³⁄₃₂ | .0010–.0027 | .0015–.0032 | .3414 | .3414 |
| | 8-305 | 46 | 45 | 200 @ 1.25 ④ | 1²¹⁄₃₂ ③ | .0010–.0027 | .0010–.0027 | .3414 | .3414 |
| | 8-350 | 46 | 45 | 200 @ 1.25 ④ | 1²³⁄₃₂ ③ | .0010–.0027 | .0010–.0027 | .3414 | .3414 |
| | 8-379 Diesel | 46 | 45 | 740 @ 1.40 | 1¹³⁄₁₆ | .0010–.0027 | .0010–.0027 | — | — |

① ± ¹⁄₃₂ in.
② Exhaust—80 @ 1.61 in.
③ Exhaust—1¹⁹⁄₃₂ starting 1977, 1⅝ earlier
④ Exhaust—200 @ 1.16

89773C06

## Crankshaft and Connecting Rod Specifications

All measurements are given in in.

| Year | Engine Displacement (cu. in.) | Crankshaft | | | | Connecting Rod | | |
|------|------|------|------|------|------|------|------|------|
| | | Main Brg Journal Dia | Main Brg Oil Clearance | Shaft End-Play | Thrust on No. | Journal Diameter | Oil Clearance | Side Clearance |
| 1967 | 6-230 | 2.2983– 2.2993 | .0003– .0029 | .002– .006 | 7 | 1.999– 2.000 | .0007– .0027 | .009– .014 |
| | 6-250 | 2.2983– 2.2993 | .0003– .0029 | .002– .006 | 7 | 1.999– 2.000 | .0007– .0027 | .009– .014 |
| | 8-283 | ① | ③ | .003– .011 | 5 | 1.999– 2.000 | .0007– .0027 | .009– .013 |
| 1968 | 6-230 | 2.2983– 2.2993 | .0003– .0029 | .002– .006 | 7 | 1.9999– 2.000 | .0007– .0027 | .009– .014 |
| | 6-250 | 2.2983– 2.2993 | .0003– .0029 | .002– .006 | 7 | 1.999– 2.000 | .0007– .0027 | .009– .014 |
| | 8-307 | 2.4484– 2.4493 ② | .0008– .0020 ④ | .003– .011 | 5 | 2.099– 2.100 | .0007– .0027 | .009– .013 |
| 1969 | 6-230 | 2.2983– 2.2993 | .0003– .0029 | .002– .006 | 7 | 1.999– 2.000 | .0007– .0027 | .009– .014 |
| | 6-250 | 2.2983– 2.2993 | .0003– .0029 | .002– .006 | 7 | 1.999– 2.000 | .0007– .0027 | .009– .014 |
| | 8-307 | 2.4484– 2.4493 ② | .0008– .0020 ④ | .003– .011 | 5 | 2.099– 2.100 | .0007– .0028 | .009– .013 |
| 1970 | 6-250 | 2.2983– 2.2993 | .0003– .0029 | .002– .006 | 7 | 1.999– 2.000 | .0007– .0027 | .009– .014 |
| | 8-307, 350 | 2.4484– 2.4493 ② | .0003– .0015 ⑤ | .002– .006 | 5 | 2.099– 2.100 | .0007– .0028 | .008– .014 |
| 1971 | 6-250 | 2.2983– 2.2993 | .0003– .0029 | .002– .006 | 7 | 1.999– 2.000 | .0007– .0027 | .009– .014 |
| | 8-307, 350 | 2.4484– 2.4493 ② | .0008– .0015 ⑤ | .002– .006 | 5 | 2.099– 2.100 | .0007– .0028 | .008– .014 |
| 1972 | 6-250 | 2.2983– 2.2993 | .0003– .0029 | .002– .006 | 7 | 1.999– 2.000 | .0007– .0027 | .009– .014 |
| | 8-307, 350 | 2.4484– 2.4493 ② | .0008– .0015 ⑤ | .002– .006 | 5 | 2.099– 2.100 | .0007– .0028 | .008– .014 |
| 1973–74 | 6-250 | 2.2983– 2.2993 | .0003– .0029 | .002– .006 | 7 | 1.999– 2.000 | .0007– .0027 | .006– .014 |
| | 8-307, 350 | 2.4484– 2.4493 ② | .0008– .0015 ⑤ | .002– .006 | 5 | 2.099– 2.100 | .0013– .0035 | .008– .014 |
| 1975–76 | 6-250 | 2.2983– 2.2993 | .0003– .0029 | .002– .006 | 7 | 1.999– 2.000 | .0007– .0027 | .006– .017 |
| | 6-292 | 2.2983– 2.2993 | .0008– .0034 | .002– .006 | 7 | 2.099– 2.100 | .0007– .0027 | .006– .017 |
| | 8-350 | 2.4484– 2.4493 ② | .0011– .0023 ⑥ | .002– .006 | 5 | 2.199– 2.200 | .0013– .0035 | .008– .014 |
| | 8-400 | 2.6484– 2.6493 ⑦ | .0011– .0023 ⑥ | .002– .006 | 5 | 2.199– 2.200 | .0013– .0035 | .008– .014 |
| 1977 | 6-250 | 2.2983– 2.2993 | .0003– .0029 | .002– .006 | 7 | 1.999– 2.000 | .0007– .0027 | .006– .017 |
| | 6-292 | 2.2983– 2.2993 | .0008– .0034 | .002– .006 | 7 | 2.099– 2.100 | .0007– .0027 | .006– .017 |

89773C07

## Crankshaft and Connecting Rod Specifications (cont.)

All measurements are given in in.

| Year | Engine Displacement (cu. in.) | Crankshaft | | | | Connecting Rod | | |
|------|------|------|------|------|------|------|------|------|
| | | Main Brg Journal Dia | Main Brg Oil Clearance | Shaft End-Play | Thrust on No. | Journal Diameter | Oil Clearance | Side Clearance |
| 1977 | 8-305 | 2.4481–2.4490 ⑧ | .0011–.0023 ⑥ | .002–.006 | 5 | 2.199–2.200 | .0013–.0035 | .008–.014 |
| | 8-350 | 2.4481–2.4490 ⑧ | .0011–.0023 ⑥ | .002–.006 | 5 | 2.199–2.200 | .0013–.0035 | .008–.014 |
| | 8-400 | 2.6484–2.6493 ⑦ | .0011–.0023 ⑥ | .002–.006 | 5 | 2.199–2.200 | .0013–.0035 | .008–.014 |
| 1978 | 6-250 | 2.2983–2.2993 | .0003–.0029 | .002–.006 | 7 | 1.999–2.000 | .0007–.0027 | .006–.017 |
| | 6-292 | 2.2983–2.2993 | .0008–.0034 | .002–.006 | 5 | 2.099–2.100 | .0007–.0027 | .006–.017 |
| | 8-305, 350 | 2.4481–2.4490 ⑧ | .0011–.0023 ⑥ | .002–.006 | 5 | 2.0988–2.0998 | .0013–.0035 | .008–.014 |
| | 8-400 | 2.6484–2.6493 ⑦ | .0011–.0023 ⑥ | .002–.006 | 5 | 2.0988–2.0998 | .0013–.0035 | .008–.014 |
| 1979–82 | 6-250 | 2.2979–2.2994 | .0010–.0024 ⑨ | .002–.006 | 7 | 1.999–2.000 | .0010–.0030 | .006–.017 |
| | 8-305, 350 | 2.4481–2.4490 ⑧ | .0011–.0023 ⑥ | .002–.006 | 5 | 2.0988–2.0998 | .0013–.0035 | .008–.014 |
| | 8-400 | 2.6484–2.6493 ⑦ | .0011–.0023 ⑥ | .002–.006 | 5 | 2.0988–2.0998 | .0013–.0035 | .008–.014 |
| 1983–86 | 6-250 | 2.2979–2.2994 | .0010–.0024 ⑨ | .002–.006 | 7 | 1.999–2.000 | .0010–.0026 | .006–.017 |
| | 6-262 | ⑫ | ⑬ | .002–.006 | Rear | 2.2497–2.2487 | 0.010–0.0032 | 0.007–0.015 |
| | 8-305, 350 | 2.4481–2.4490 ⑧ | .0011–.0023 ⑥ | .002–.006 | 5 | 2.0988–2.0998 | .0013–.0035 | .008–.014 |
| | 8-379 Diesel | 2.9494–2.9504 ⑩ | .0018–.0032 ⑪ | .002–.007 | 5 | 2.398–2.399 | — | .007–.024 |

① No. 1—2.2987–2.2997  
  Nos. 2–4—2.2978–2.2988  
  No. 5—2.2978–2.2988  
② No. 5—2.4479–2.4488  
③ No. 1—.0008–.0020  
  Nos. 2–4—.0018–.0020  
  No. 5—.0010–.0032  
④ No. 5—.0010–.0026  

⑤ Nos. 2–4—.0006–.0018  
  No. 5—.0008–.0023  
⑥ No. 1—.0008–.0020  
  No. 5—.0017–.0033  
⑦ No. 5—2.6479–2.6488  
⑧ No. 1—2.4484–2.4493  
  No. 5—2.4479–2.4488  
⑨ No. 7—.0016–.0035  

⑩ No. 5—2.9492–2.9502  
⑪ No. 5—.0022–.0037  
⑫ Front—2.4484–2.4493  
  Int—2.4481–2.4990  
  Rear—2.4479–2.4488  
⑬ Front—.0008–.0020  
  Int—.0011–.0023  
  Rear—.0017–.0032  

89773C08

## Piston Clearance

| Year | Engine No. Cyl Displacement (cu in.) | Piston to Bore Clearance (in.) |
|------|--------------------------------------|--------------------------------|
| '67-'68 | 6-230 | .0005-.0011 |
| '69 | 6-230 | .0005-.0014 |
| '67-'68 | 6-250 | .0005-.0011 |
| '69 | 6-250 | .0005-.0014 |
| '70-'77 | 6-250 | .0005-.0015 |
| '78-'86 | 6-250 | .0010-.0020 |
| '85-'86 | 6-262 | .0007-.0017 |
| '75-'78 | 6-292 | .0026-.0036 |
| '67 | 8-283 | .0005-.0011 |
| '86 | 8-305 | .0007-.0017 |
| '68-'70 | 8-307 | .0005-.0011 |
| '71-'73 | 8-307 | .0012-.0018 |
| '70 | 8-350 | .0012-.0022 |
| '71-'76 | 8-350 | .0007-.0013 |
| '77-'86 | 8-350 | .0007-.0017 |
| '75-'80 | 8-400 | .0014-.0024 |
| '83-'86 | 8-379 Diesel | .0040-.0050 |

89773C09

## Ring Side Clearance
(in.)

| Year | Engine No. Cyl Displacement (cu in.) | Top Compression | Bottom Compression | Oil Control |
|------|--------------------------------------|-----------------|--------------------|-------------|
| '67-'69 | 6-230 | .0012-.0027 | .0012-.0027 | .005 max |
| '67-'86 | 6-250 | .0012-.0027 | .0012-.0032 | .005 max |
| '85-'86 | 6-262 | .0012-.0032 | .0012-.0032 | .002-.007 |
| '75-'78 | 6-292 | .0020-.0040 | .0020-.0040 | .005-.0055 |
| '67 | 8-283 | .0012-.0027 | .0012-.0032 | .005 max |
| '68-'73 | 8-307 | .0007-.0027 | .0012-.0032 | .005 max |
| '70-'86 | 8-305, 350, 400 | .0012-.0032 | .0012-.0032 | .002-.007 |
| '83-'86 | 8-379 Diesel | .0030-.0070 | .0015-.0031 | .0016-.0038 |

89773C10

## Ring Gap
(in.)

| Year | Engine No. Cyl Displacement (cu in.) | Top Compression | Bottom Compression | Oil Control |
|---|---|---|---|---|
| '67–'86 | 6-250, 292 | .010–.020 | .010–.020 | .015–.055 |
| '85–'86 | 6-262 | .010–.020 | .010–.025 | .015–.055 |
| '67 | 8-283 | .0010–.0020 | .0010–.0020 | .015–.055 |
| '68–'73 | 8-307 | .010–.020 | .010–.020 | .015–.055 |
| '69–'76 | 8-350, 400 | .010–.020 | .013–.025 | .015–.055 |
| '77–'86 | 8-305, 350, 400 | .010–.020 | .010–.025 | .015–.055 |
| '83–'86 | 8-379 Diesel | .0012–.022 | .030–.040 | .0098–.0200 |

89773C11

## Torque Specifications
(ft. lb.)

| Year | Engine No. Cyl Displacement (cu in.) | Cylinder Head Bolts | Rod Bearing Bolts | Main Bearing Bolts | Crankshaft Bolt | Flywheel to Crankshaft bolts | Manifold Intake | Manifold Exhaust |
|---|---|---|---|---|---|---|---|---|
| '67–'71 | 6-230, 250 | 95 | 35 | 65 | — | 60 | 30 ① | 25 ② |
| '72 | 6-250 | 95 | 35 | 65 | — | 60 | 30 | 25 ② |
| '73–'74 | 6-250 | 95 | 35 | 65 | — | 60 | 35 | 30 ② |
| '75–'86 | 6-250 | 95 ⑤ | 36 | 65 | — | 60 | — | 30 ③ |
| '75–'78 | 6-292 | 95 | 40 | 65 | — | 110 | 35 | 30 ② |
| '67 | 8-283 | 65 | 35 | 80 | — | 60 | 30 | 20 |
| '68 | 8-307 | 65 | 35 | 80 | — | 60 | 30 | 20 ④ |
| '69–'73 | 8-307, 350 | 65 | 45 | 70 | — | 60 | 30 | 20 ④ |
| '74–'86 | 6-262, 8-305, 350, 400 | 65 | 45 | 70 | 60 | 60 | 30 | 20 ④ |
| '83–'86 | 8-379 Diesel | 100 | 48 | ⑥ | 150 | — | 31 | 22 |

① End bolts—20
② Exhaust to intake
③ 20 on four end bolts with intake manifold integral with head.
④ Inside bolts on 307 and 350—30
⑤ Left-hand front bolt: 85 ft. lbs.
⑥ Inner: 111—Outer: 100

89773C12

## Engine

### REMOVAL & INSTALLATION

In the process of removing the engine, you will come across a number of steps which call for the removal of a separate component or system, such as "disconnect the exhaust system" or "remove the radiator." In most instances, a detailed removal procedure can be found elsewhere in this manual.

It is virtually impossible to list each individual wire and hose which must be disconnected, simply because so many different model and engine combinations have been manufactured. Careful observation and common sense are the best possible additions to any repair procedure. Be absolutely sure to tag any wire or hose before it is disconnected, so that you can be assured of proper reconnection during installation.

**1967-70 Models**

▶ **See Figure 30**

The engine and transmission are removed as a unit from below the vehicle.
1. Disconnect the battery cables.
2. Drain the cooling system. Remove the air cleaner.

### ❉❉CAUTION

**When draining the coolant, keep in mind that cats and dogs are attracted by ethylene glycol antifreeze, and are quite likely to drink any that is left in an uncovered container or in puddles on the ground. This will prove fatal in sufficient quantity. Always drain the coolant into a sealable container. Coolant should be reused unless it is contaminated or several years old.**

3. Remove the engine splash shield(s).
4. Disconnect the neutral safety switch wire from the automatic transmission.
5. Disconnect the upper and lower radiator hoses from the radiator.

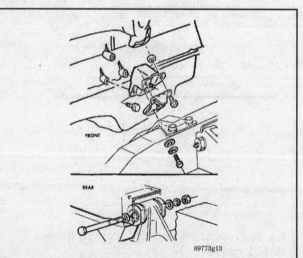

FRONT

REAR

89773g13

**Fig. 30 Engine mount and bolt locations — 1967-70 models**

6. Disconnect the wires from the starter solenoid, alternator, temperature switch, oil pressure switch and ignition coil.
7. Disconnect the following components:
   a. Accelerator linkage at the bellcrank on the manifold.
   b. Choke cable at the carburetor.
   c. Fuel line from the fuel pump.
   d. Heater hoses at the engine.
   e. Oil pressure gauge line (if used).
   f. All vacuum lines at the engine.
   g. Power steering lines at the pump.
   h. Engine ground straps; and the exhaust pipes at the manifold. Hang the exhaust pipes out of the way from the frame.
8. Disconnect the A/C compressor mounting bracket and position the compressor out of the way. Also remove the condenser from in front of the radiator. Position it out of the way. DO NOT DISCONNECT ANY OF THE REFRIGERANT LINES.
9. Remove the fan and pulley.
10. Remove the clutch cross-shaft.
11. Remove the driveshaft. If the plug for the driveshaft opening in the transmission is not easily accessible, drain the transmission.
12. Disconnect the speedometer cable at the transmission.
13. Disconnect the shift linkage at the transmission.
14. Disconnect the clutch linkage.
15. Remove the bolt which holds the starter wire harness clip and the engine ground strap from the flywheel housing.
16. Disconnect the automatic transmission cooler lines at both ends and remove the cooler lines. Plug the openings.
17. Place a jack under the engine and transmission and install safety chains. Take the weight off the engine mounts.
18. Remove the engine mount bolts and the engine mount crossmember. Check to be sure that all necessary components are removed or disconnected.
19. Slowly lower the engine/transmission assembly, pulling it to the rear to clear the front axle.
20. Depending on the service required, separate the engine/transmission and mount the engine on a stand.
21. Installation is the reverse of removal. Be sure to check all fluid capacities and check for leaks.

**1971-73 Models**

▶ **See Figures 31, 32, 33 and 34**

On these vehicles, the engine is removed as a unit with the front suspension.
1. Remove the engine cover.
2. Disconnect the battery ground strap from the engine, and at the battery.
3. Drain the cooling system and disconnect the heater hoses at the engine. Disconnect the radiator hoses at the radiator.

### ❉❉CAUTION

**When draining the coolant, keep in mind that cats and dogs are attracted by ethylene glycol antifreeze, and are quite likely to drink any that is left in an uncovered container or in puddles on the ground. This will prove fatal in sufficient quantity. Always drain the coolant into a sealable container. Coolant should be reused unless it is contaminated or several years old.**

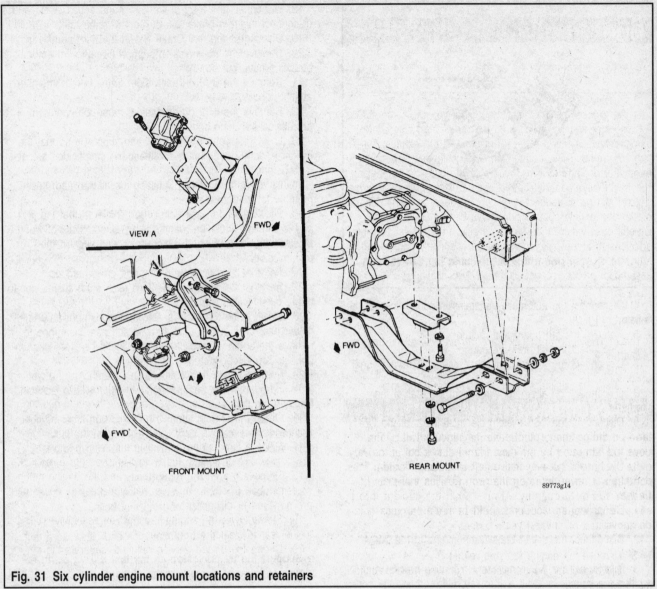

Fig. 31 Six cylinder engine mount locations and retainers

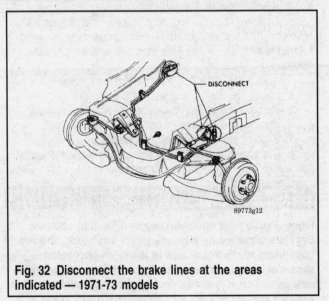

Fig. 32 Disconnect the brake lines at the areas indicated — 1971-73 models

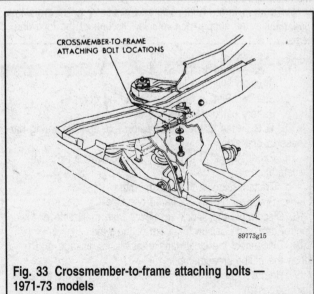

Fig. 33 Crossmember-to-frame attaching bolts — 1971-73 models

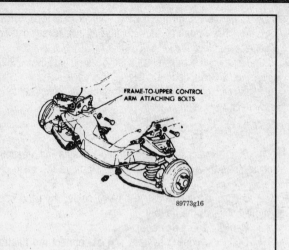

FRAME-TO-UPPER CONTROL
ARM ATTACHING BOLTS

89773g16

**Fig. 34 Suspension-to-frame attaching bolts — 1971-73 models**

4. Disconnect the automatic transmission cooler lines at the radiator.

5. Remove the fan guard and radiator.

6. Disconnect the oil pressure gauge.

7. Disconnect the engine wiring harness at the dash panel junction block.

8. Disconnect the alternator wires from the rear of the alternator.

9. Disconnect the TCS system electrical leads at the CEC valve on the carburetor and at the temperature switch. Remove the harness from the clips and position it out of the way.

10. Disconnect the evaporative emission control system lines at the rocker cover and the carburetor. Position these out of the way.

11. Disconnect the accelerator linkage at the bellcrank on the firewall.

12. Disconnect the power brake vacuum line at the intake manifold.

13. Disconnect the A/C compressor mounting bracket and position the compressor out of the way. Also remove the condenser from in front of the radiator. Position it out of the way.

14. Raise and support the vehicle. Disconnect the following items:

   a. Fuel line at the fuel pump.

   b. Engine ground straps.

   c. Steering idler arm at the frame.

   d. Steering Pitman arm at the steering gear.

   e. Battery cable from the starter.

   f. TCS switch at the transmission (position the wiring harness to one side).

   g. Exhaust pipe at the manifold (remove the exhaust system).

   h. Transmission at the crossmember.

   i. Stabilizer bar at the frame brackets.

15. Disconnect the shock absorbers from the frame or lower control arm and position them out of the way.

16. Disconnect the clutch and transmission linkage and remove the clutch crossmember.

17. Remove the driveshaft and install a plug in the transmission extension.

18. Disconnect the front brake line at the equalizer 'T" and disconnect the rear brake line at the left frame rail.

19. Disconnect the rear brake line at the right frame rail.

20. Remove the transmission support frame-to-crossmember attaching nuts, but do not remove the bolts.

21. Remove the 6 (3 on each side) frame-to-crossmember attaching bolts.

22. Remove the 4 (2 on each side) frame-to-upper control arm inside attaching bolts.

23. Lower the vehicle on a jack and support it so that the weight is on supports but the wheels and suspension are at curb height.

24. Install wooden blocks between the oil pan and crossmember to stabilize the engine.

25. Position a floor jack under the vehicle so that the jack pad is aligning under the transmission. Use a block of wood between the jack pad and transmission and support the transmission.

26. Remove the transmission support crossmember.

27. Remove the remaining 4 (2 on each side) suspension-to-frame outside retaining bolts.

28. Slowly raise the vehicle, leaving the suspension and power train on the floor until there is sufficient clearance to remove the engine. Check to be sure that all necessary components are disconnected.

29. Roll the power train/suspension assembly to the work area and support the transmission extension with a jackstand. Remove the floor jack.

30. Place a floor jack under the suspension crossmember and raise the assembly until the weight is on the jack.

31. Attach a hoist to the engine at the lifting brackets.

32. Remove the engine mount throughbolts and remove the engine assembly from the crossmember.

33. Remove the manual transmission and clutch as follows:

   a. Remove the clutch housing rear bolts.

   b. Remove the bolts attaching the clutch housing to the engine and remove the transmission and clutch as a unit.

➡**Support the transmission as the last bolt is being removed to prevent damaging the clutch.**

   c. Remove the starter and clutch housing rear cover.

   d. Loosen the clutch mounting bolts a little at a time to prevent distorting the disc until spring pressure is released. Remove all of the bolts, the clutch disc and the pressure plate.

34. Remove the automatic transmission as follows:

   a. Lower the engine and support it on blocks.

   b. Remove the starter and converter housing underpan.

   c. Remove the flywheel-to-converter attaching bolts.

   d. Support the transmission on blocks.

   e. Disconnect the throttle linkage and vacuum modulator on the Powerglide. Disconnect the detent cable on the Turbo Hydra-Matic.

   f. Remove the transmission-to-engine mounting bolts.

   g. Remove the blocks from the engine only and glide the engine away from the transmission.

35. Mount the engine a on a stand.

36. Installation is the reverse of removal. Bleed the front and rear brakes, check all fluid levels, start the engine and check for leaks.

## 1974-76 Models

The engines on these vehicles are removed through the front of the vehicle. A portable boom type hoist is necessary for this job.

1. Remove the grille. It is attached with screws.
2. Drain the cooling system and disconnect the heater hoses at the engine. Disconnect the radiator hoses at the engine.

### ✳✳CAUTION

**When draining the coolant, keep in mind that cats and dogs are attracted by ethylene glycol antifreeze, and are quite likely to drink any that is left in an uncovered container or in puddles on the ground. This will prove fatal in sufficient quantity. Always drain the coolant into a sealable container. Coolant should be reused unless it is contaminated or several years old.**

3. Disconnect the A/C compressor mounting bracket and position the compressor out of the way. Also remove the condenser from in front of the radiator. Position it out of the way. DO NOT DISCONNECT ANY OF THE REFRIGERANT LINES.
4. Disconnect the automatic transmission cooler lines at the radiator. Remove the fan guard and radiator.
5. Remove the radiator upper tie bar and radiator support.
6. Disconnect the battery cables at the battery and at the radiator support baffle.
7. Disconnect the engine wiring harness at the junction block on the firewall.
8. Disconnect the oil pressure gauge if equipped.
9. Raise and support the van. Disconnect the following items:
   a. Fuel line at the fuel pump.
   b. Engine ground straps.
   c. Battery cables at the frame mounted clip.
   d. Speedometer cable at the transmission.
   e. Exhaust pipes from the manifolds (remove the exhaust system).
   f. Transmission at the crossmember.
10. Disconnect the clutch linkage or the transmission linkage and remove the clutch cross-shaft.
11. Remove the driveshaft. Plug the opening in the extension housing of the transmission.
12. Remove the engine mount through-bolts.
13. Remove the crossmember-to-engine mount bracket (right side only) attaching bolts, but do not remove the bracket.
14. Lower the vehicle and support it approximately 12 in. (305mm) from the floor.
15. Remove the engine access cover.
16. Remove the air cleaner.
17. Disconnect the carburetor throttle linkage. Disconnect and plug the fuel line from the carburetor and remove the carburetor.
18. Disconnect the spark plug wires from the spark plugs and position them out of the way.
19. Remove the ignition coil and rear lifting bracket.
20. Securely attach a boom hoist to the engine.
21. With the aid of an assistant, slowly raise the engine to take the weight off the engine mounts. Remove the right mount frame bracket and mount.

22. Continue raising the engine and move it forward out of the van. Check often to be sure that all necessary components are disconnected.
23. Remove the transmission as outlined in Steps 33 or 34 of the 1971-73 procedure.
24. Installation is the reverse of removal. Check all fluids and check for leaks.

## 1977-78 Models

1. Scribe matchmarks on the hood hinges for reassembly and remove the hood and the grille. Remove the grille cross brace.
2. Disconnect the negative battery cable, then the positive battery cable, at the battery.
3. Remove the air cleaner.
4. Drain the cooling system and disconnect the heater hoses and radiator hoses at the radiator.

### ✳✳CAUTION

**When draining the coolant, keep in mind that cats and dogs are attracted by ethylene glycol antifreeze, and are quite likely to drink any that is left in an uncovered container or in puddles on the ground. This will prove fatal in sufficient quantity. Always drain the coolant into a sealable container. Coolant should be reused unless it is contaminated or several years old.**

5. Disconnect the A/C compressor mounting bracket and position the compressor out of the way. Also remove the condenser from in front of the radiator. Position it our of the way. DO NOT DISCONNECT ANY OF THE REFRIGERANT LINES.
6. Remove the radiator and the fan shroud.
7. Disconnect and label the wiring at the starter solenoid, alternator, temperature sending switch, oil pressure switch and the coil. Disconnect the engine ground strap.
8. Disconnect:
   a. the accelerator at the intake manifold.
   b. the fuel line from the tank at the fuel pump (plug the line).
   c. the hoses at the fuel vapor storage canister (if so equipped).
   d. the vacuum line to the power brake booster at the manifold (if so equipped).
9. Remove the power steering pump mounting bolts and lay the pump aside. Do not disconnect any of the lines.
10. Raise the van on a hoist and drain the crankcase.
11. Disconnect the exhaust pipe at the manifold. If equipped with a catalytic converter, disconnect the converter bracket at the rear transmission mount.
12. Remove the starter motor.
13. Remove the flywheel splash shield or the converter cover, as applicable.
14. On vans with automatic transmissions, remove the converter-to-flywheel attaching bolts.
15. Remove the engine mount through-bolts.
16. Remove the bell housing bolts.
17. Lower the van.
18. Using a floor jack, raise the transmission.
19. Attach a boom hoist to the engine and raise the engine slightly.
20. Remove the engine mount-to-engine brackets.

21. Remove the engine.
22. Reverse the removal procedure to install.

**1979-86 Models**

1. Have the air conditioning system discharged at a repair facility utilizing a recovery/recycling machine.
2. Disconnect the negative battery cable, then the positive battery cable, at the battery. On the V6 remove the glove box.
3. Drain the cooling system.

### ✳✳CAUTION

**When draining the coolant, keep in mind that cats and dogs are attracted by ethylene glycol antifreeze, and are quite likely to drink any that is left in an uncovered container or in puddles on the ground. This will prove fatal in sufficient quantity. Always drain the coolant into a sealable container. Coolant should be reused unless it is contaminated or several years old.**

4. Remove the engine cover.
5. Remove the air cleaner. On the V8 remove the air stove pipe. On the V6 remove the outside air duct.
6. On the V6 remove the head light bezels and the grille. On inline six cylinder, remove the grille cross brace and the grille. On the V8, remove the upper radiator support the grille and the lower grille valance.
7. Disconnect the radiator hoses at the radiator.
8. On the V8, remove the radiator coolant reservoir bottle. On the V6, remove the power steering reservoir and the hood release cable.
9. If the van is equipped with an automatic transmission, remove the fluid cooler lines from the radiator.
10. Remove the A/C vacuum reservoir. On the V8, remove the A/C condenser from in front of the radiator. On the six cylinder, remove the A/C compressor.
11. Remove the windshield wiper jar and bracket.
12. Disconnect the accelerator linkage at the carburetor and remove the carburetor.
13. Remove the radiator support bracket and remove the radiator and the shroud.
14. On all six cylinders, remove the A/C compressor mounting bracket and position the compressor out of the way.
15. On the V6 and V8, disconnect the engine wiring harness from the firewall connection. On the inline six cylinder, disconnect the wiring at the alternator, distributor, oil pressure and temperature sending switches and the starter motor.
16. On the V6 and V8:
   a. Disconnect the heater hoses at the engine.
   b. Remove the thermostat housing.
   c. Remove the oil filler pipe and the engine dipstick tube.
   d. Remove the cruise control servo, servo bracket and transducer.
   e. Remove the distributor cap.
   f. Remove the diverter valve.
   g. Remove the coolant hose at the intake manifold and the PCV valve.
   h. Remove the transmission dipstick tube and the accelerator cable at the tube.
   i. Remove the air conditioning idler pulley.
   j. Remove the lower fan shroud and filler panel.

   k. Remove the hood latch support.
   l. Remove the condenser.
17. Raise the vehicle and drain the engine oil.
18. Remove the fuel line from the fuel tank and at the fuel pump.
19. Disconnect the exhaust pipe at the manifold.
20. On the V6 only:
   a. Remove the strut rods at the torque converter or flywheel underpan.
   b. Remove the torque converter or flywheel cover.
   c. Remove the starter.
   d. Remove the flex plate to torque converter bolts (automatic transmissions).
   e. Remove the bell housing to engine bolts.
   f. Remove the engine mounting through-bolts.
   Lower the van, support the transmission and remove the engine
21. Remove the driveshaft and plug the end of the transmission.
22. Disconnect the transmission shift linkage and the speedometer cable.
23. Remove the transmission mounting bolts.
24. On the inline six cylinder with manual transmission, disconnect the clutch linkage and remove the clutch cross shaft.
25. On the V8, remove the engine mount bracket-to-frame bolts.
26. Remove the engine mount through-bolts.
27. On the inline six cylinder:
   a. Lower the van and attach a lifting device to the engine.
   b. Raise the engine slightly and remove the right hand mount from the engine.
28. On the V8: Raise the engine slightly and remove the engine mounts. Support the engine with wood between the oil pan and the crossmember.
29. Remove the engine and transmission as one unit (except the V6). Refer to Steps 33 or 34 of the 1971-73 procedure to remove the transmission.
30. Reverse the removal procedure to install.

## Valve Cover(s)

### REMOVAL & INSTALLATION

**All Engines**
▶ **See Figures 35, 36, 37 and 38**

1. Remove air cleaner.
2. Disconnect and reposition as necessary any vacuum or PCV hoses that obstruct the valve covers.
3. Disconnect electrical wire(s) (spark plug, etc.) from the valve cover slips.
4. Unbolt and remove the valve cover(s).

➡**Do not pry the covers off if they seem stuck. Instead, gently tap around each cover with a rubber mallet until the old gasket or sealer breaks loose.**

5. To install, use a new valve cover gasket or RTV (or any equivalent) sealer. If using sealer, follow directions on the tube. Install valve cover and tighten cover bolts to 3 ft. lbs. (4 Nm).

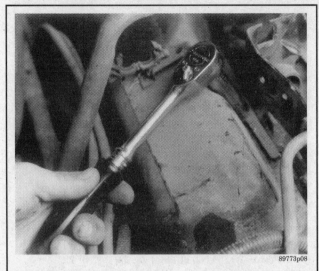

**Fig. 35 Unfasten the valve cover retainers**

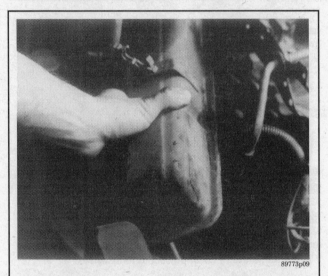

**Fig. 36 Remove the valve cover from the engine**

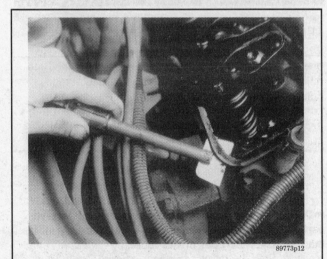

**Fig. 37 Using a gasket scraper, remove the old valve cover gasket from the cylinder head**

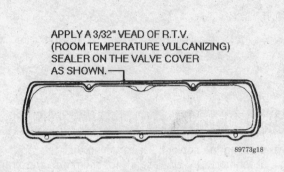

APPLY A 3/32" VEAD OF R.T.V.
(ROOM TEMPERATURE VULCANIZING)
SEALER ON THE VALVE COVER
AS SHOWN.

**Fig. 38 Apply sealer to the valve covers as shown. Always run the sealer bead on the inside edge of the bolt holes on the cover flange**

6. Connect and reposition all vacuum and PCV hoses, and reconnect electrical and/or spark plug wires at the cover clips. Install the air cleaner.

## Rocker Arms

### REMOVAL & INSTALLATION

**Gasoline Engines**
▶ See Figures 39, 40 and 41

1. Remove the valve cover.
2. Remove the rocker arm flanged bolts, and remove the rocker pivots.
3. Remove the rocker arms (and the balls on the V6).

➡Remove each set of rocker arms/balls (one set per cylinder) as a unit. Only the V6 engines have rocker balls.

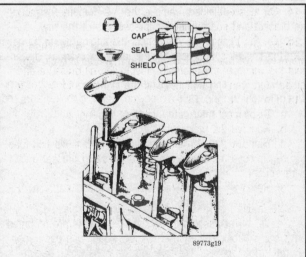

LOCKS
CAP
SEAL
SHIELD

**Fig. 39 Six cylinder rocker arm components — all gasoline V8 engines are similar**

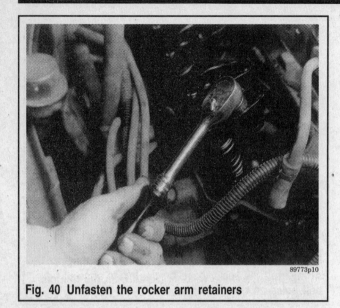

Fig. 40 Unfasten the rocker arm retainers

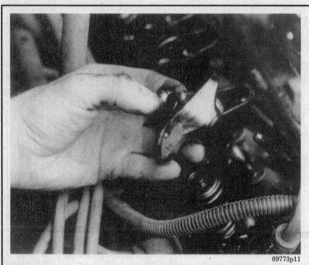

Fig. 41 Remove the rocker arms from the cylinder head

4. To install, position a set of rocker arms, and balls if you have the V6, (for one cylinder) in the proper location.

➡Install the rocker arms for each cylinder only when the lifters are off the cam lobe and both valves are closed.

5. Coat the replacement rocker arm/ball with Molycoat® or its equivalent, on the 1986 V6 engine, and the rocker arm and pivot with SAE 90 gear oil on all other engines, and install the pivots.

6. Install the flanges bolts and tighten alternately.

### 6.2L Diesel Engine

▶ See Figure 42

1. Remove the valve cover as previously explained.

2. The rocker assemblies on the 6.2L engine are mounted on two short rocker shafts per cylinder head, with each shaft operating four rockers. Remove the two bolts which secure each rocker shaft assembly, and remove the shaft.

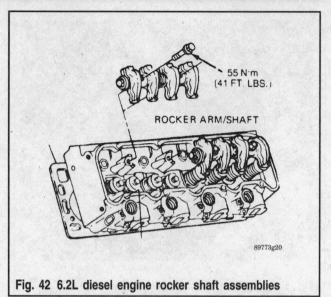

Fig. 42 6.2L diesel engine rocker shaft assemblies

3. The rocker arms can be removed from the shaft by removing the cotter pin on the end of each shaft. The rocker arms and springs slide off.

4. To install, make sure first that the rocker arms and springs go back on the shafts in the exact order in which they were removed.

➡Always install new cotter pins on the rocker shaft ends.

5. Install the rocker shaft assemblies, torquing the bolts to 41 ft. lbs. (55 Nm).

## Thermostat

### REMOVAL & INSTALLATION

▶ See Figures 43, 44, 45, 46, 47, 48, 49, 50 and 51

1. Drain the radiator until the level is below the thermostat level (below the level of the intake manifold).

### ✳✳CAUTION

When draining the coolant, keep in mind that cats and dogs are attracted by ethylene glycol antifreeze, and are quite likely to drink any that is left in an uncovered container or in puddles on the ground. This will prove fatal in sufficient quantity. Always drain the coolant into a sealable container. Coolant should be reused unless it is contaminated or several years old.

2. Remove the water outlet elbow assembly from the engine. Remove the thermostat from inside the elbow.

3. Install new thermostat in the reverse order of removal, making sue the spring side is inserted into the elbow. Clean the gasket surfaces on the water outlet elbow and the intake manifold. Use a new gasket when installing the elbow to the manifold. Refill the radiator to approximately 2 ½ in. (64mm) below the filler neck.

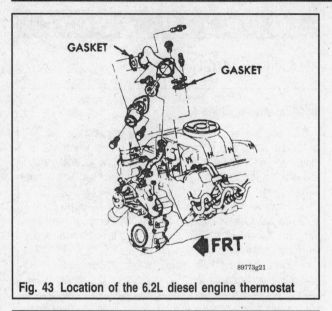

Fig. 43 Location of the 6.2L diesel engine thermostat

Fig. 46 Disengage the vacuum hoses from the thermal vacuum valve

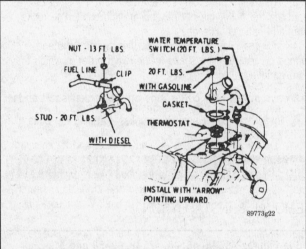

Fig. 44 Common gasoline V8 engine thermostat installation

Fig. 47 Unfasten the thermostat cover retainers

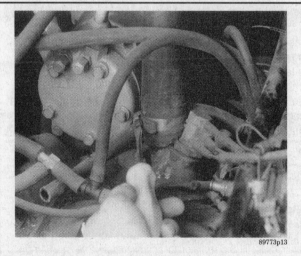

Fig. 45 Unfasten the radiator hose clamp and remove the hose from the thermostat cover

Fig. 48 If equipped, remove the bracket bolts from the air conditioning compressor and thermostat cover

Fig. 49 Remove the bracket

Fig. 50 Remove the thermostat cover . . .

Fig. 51 . . . then remove the thermostat

## Intake Manifold

### REMOVAL & INSTALLATION

#### Inline 6-Cylinder Engines

1974 and earlier 250 and 292 six cylinder engines use a combined intake and exhaust manifold, both of which are removed together. 1976 and later engines have an intake manifold which is cast integrally with the cylinder head and cannot be removed.

1. Remove the air cleaner assembly and air ducts.
2. Tag and disconnect the throttle linkage at the carburetor. Tag and disconnect the fuel line, vacuum lines, hoses, and electrical connections.
3. Disconnect the transmission downshift linkage (if equipped), and remove the PCV valve from the rocker cover. On models equipped with air injection, disconnect the air supply hose from the check valve on the air injection manifold.
4. Remove the carburetor, with spacer and heat shield (if equipped).
5. Spray the nuts and bolts connecting the exhaust manifold to the exhaust pipe with a rust penetrant, as these are usually quite difficult to remove. Unbolt the exhaust manifold from the pipe.

➡**It may be necessary to remove the generator rear bracket and/or A/C bracket on some models.**

6. Unbolt the manifold bolts and clamps, and remove the manifold assembly.
7. If you intend to separate the manifolds, remove the single bolt and two nuts at the center of the manifold assembly.
8. Installation is the reverse of removal. When assembling the manifolds, install the connecting bolts loosely first. Place the manifolds on a straight, flat surface and hold them securely during the tightening, this assures the proper mating of surfaces when the manifold assembly is fastened to the head. Stress cracking could occur if the manifolds are not assembled first in this manner. On all manifolds, always use new gaskets between the manifolds and cylinder head.

#### V6 and V8 Engines

*EXCEPT DIESEL ENGINES*

▶ **See Figures 52, 53, 54, 55, 56, 57, 58, 59 and 60**

1. Drain the cooling system.

### ✳✳CAUTION

**When draining the coolant, keep in mind that cats and dogs are attracted by ethylene glycol antifreeze, and are quite likely to drink any that is left in an uncovered container or in puddles on the ground. This will prove fatal in sufficient quantity. Always drain the coolant into a sealable container. Coolant should be reused unless it is contaminated or several years old.**

2. Remove the air cleaner assembly.

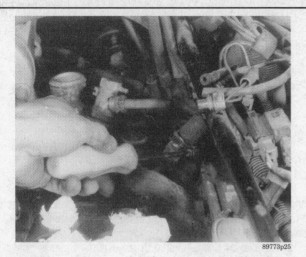

Fig. 52 Remove the water hoses from the intake manifold

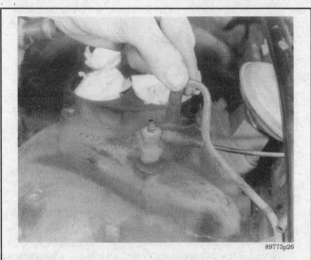

Fig. 53 Disengage all vacuum hoses from the intake manifold

Fig. 54 Unfasten the intake manifold retaining bolts

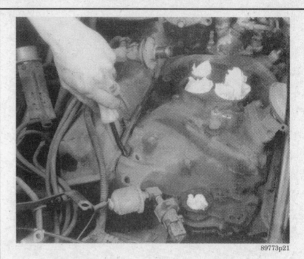

Fig. 55 Use a prytool to separate the intake manifold from the cylinder heads . . .

Fig. 56 . . . then remove the manifold from the engine

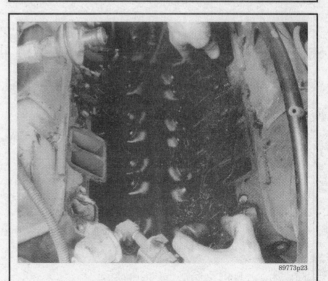

Fig. 57 Remove the old gasket from the engine

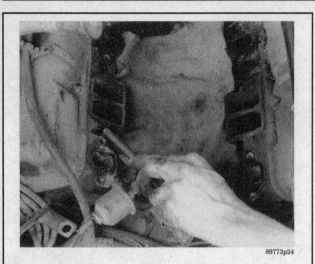

Fig. 58 Using a gasket scraper, remove any old gasket residue and dirt

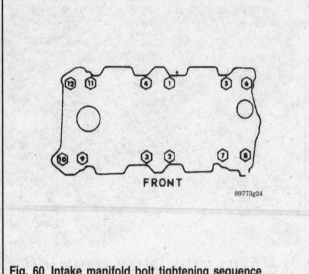

Fig. 60 Intake manifold bolt tightening sequence

3. Remove the thermostat housing and the bypass hose. It is not necessary to remove the top radiator hose from the thermostat housing.

4. Disconnect the heater hose at the rear of the manifold.

5. Disconnect all electrical connections and vacuum lines from the manifold. Remove the EGR valve if necessary.

6. On vehicles equipped with power brakes remove the vacuum line from the vacuum booster to the manifold.

7. Remove the distributor (if necessary).

8. Remove the fuel line to the carburetor.

9. Remove the carburetor linkage.

10. Remove the carburetor.

11. Remove the intake manifold bolts. Remove the manifold and the gaskets. Remember to reinstall the O-ring between the intake manifold and timing chain cover during assembly, if so equipped.

12. Installation is the reverse of removal. Use plastic gasket retainers to prevent the manifold gasket from slipping out of place, if so equipped. On the small block V8s, place a ³/₁₆ in. (4.8mm) bead of RTV type silicone sealer on the front and rear ridges of the cylinder block-to-manifold mating surfaces. Extend the bead ½ in. (12.7mm) up each cylinder head to seal and retain the manifold side gaskets.

➡Before installing the intake manifold, be sure that the gasket surfaces are thoroughly clean.

### DIESEL ENGINES

◗ See Figure 61

1. Disconnect both batteries.

2. Remove the air cleaner assembly.

3. Remove the crankcase ventilator tubes, and disconnect the secondary fuel filter lines. Remove the secondary filter and adaptor.

4. Loosen the vacuum pump hold-down clamp and rotate the pump to gain access to the nearest manifold bolt.

5. Remove the EPR/EGR valve bracket, if equipped.

6. Remove the rear air conditioning bracket, if equipped.

7. Remove the intake manifold bolts. The injection line clips are retained by these bolts.

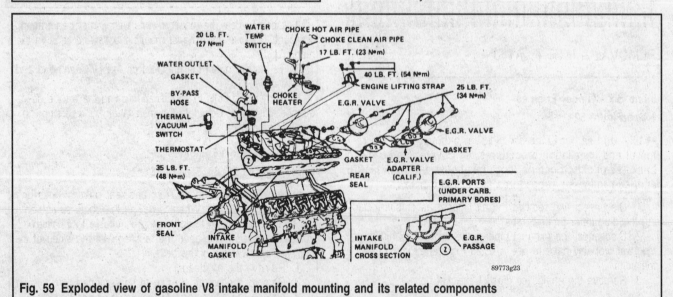

Fig. 59 Exploded view of gasoline V8 intake manifold mounting and its related components

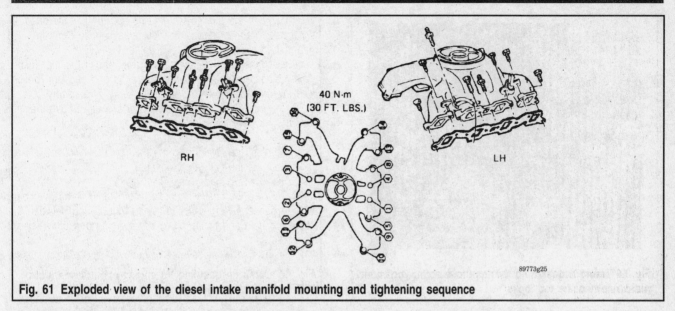

**Fig. 61 Exploded view of the diesel intake manifold mounting and tightening sequence**

8. Remove the intake manifold.

> ※※**WARNING**

**If the engine is to be further serviced with the manifold removed, install protective covers over the intake ports.**

9. Clean the manifold gasket surfaces on the cylinder heads and install new gaskets before installing the manifold.

➡**The gaskets have an opening for the EGR valve on light duty installations. An insert covers this opening on heavy duty installations.**

10. Install the manifold. Torque the bolts in the sequence illustrated.
11. The secondary filter must be filled with clean diesel fuel before it is reinstalled.
12. Reverse the remaining removal procedures to complete the installation.

## Exhaust Manifold

### REMOVAL & INSTALLATION

#### Inline Six Cylinder Engines
▶ See Figure 62

➡**1974 and earlier inline six cylinder exhaust manifold removal and installation procedures are covered under the Intake Manifold procedure (both manifolds are a unit). 1975 and later inline six procedures are covered below.**

1. Disconnect and remove the air cleaner assembly, including the carburetor preheat tube.
2. Disconnect the exhaust pipe at the exhaust manifold. You will probably have to use a liquid rust penetrant to free the bolts.
3. Remove the engine oil dipstick bracket bolt.

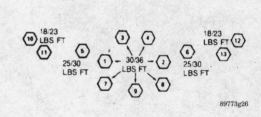

**Fig. 62 Exhaust manifold tightening sequence on 1975 and later inline 6 cylinder engines**

4. Liberally coat the manifold nuts with a rust penetrating lubricant. Remove the exhaust manifold bolts and remove the manifold.
5. To install, mount the manifold on the cylinder head and start all bolts.
6. Torque the bolts to specification using the torque sequence illustrated. Complete the installation by reversing the removal procedure.

#### Gasoline V6 and V8 Engines
▶ See Figures 63, 64, 65 and 66

Tab locks are used on the front and rear pairs of bolts on each exhaust manifold. When removing the bolts, straighten the tabs from beneath the car using a suitable tool. When installing the tab locks, bend the tabs against the sides of the bolt, not over the top of the bolt.

1. Remove the air cleaner.
2. Remove the hot air shroud, (if so equipped).
3. Loosen the alternator and remove its lower bracket.

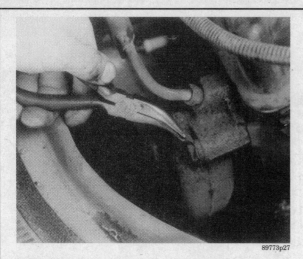

**Fig. 63 Before unfastening the manifold bolts, you must first straighten the tab locks**

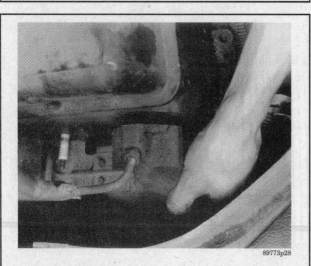

**Fig. 64 After unfastening the manifold bolts, remove the manifold**

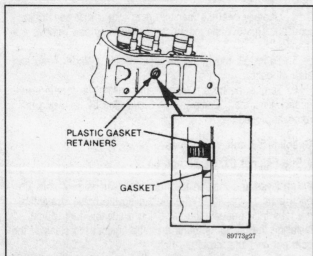

**Fig. 65 View of the plastic manifold retainers — gasoline V8 engines**

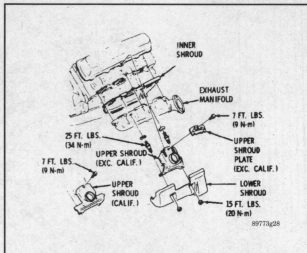

**Fig. 66 Common gasoline V8 engine exhaust manifold with exhaust shrouds**

4. Jack up your van and support it with jackstands.
5. Disconnect the crossover pipe from both manifolds.

➡**On models with air conditioning it may be necessary to remove the compressor, and tie it out of the way. Do not disconnect the compressor lines.**

6. Remove the manifold bolts and remove the manifold(s). Some models have lock tabs on the front and rear manifold bolts which must be removed before removing the bolts. These tabs can be bent with a drift pin.
7. Installation is the reverse of removal.

### 6.2L Diesel Engines

#### RIGHT SIDE

1. Disconnect the batteries.
2. Jack up the truck and safely support it with jackstands.
3. Disconnect the exhaust pipe from the manifold flange and lower the truck.
4. Disconnect the glow plug wires.
5. Remove the air cleaner duct bracket.
6. Remove the glow plug wires.
7. Remove the manifold bolts and remove the manifold.
8. To install, reverse the above procedure and torque the bolts to 25 ft. lbs. (33 Nm).

#### LEFT SIDE

1. Disconnect the batteries.
2. Remove the dipstick tube nut, and remove the dipstick tube.
3. Disconnect the glow plug wires.
4. Jack up the truck and safely support it with jackstands.
5. Disconnect the exhaust pipe at the manifold flange.
6. Remove the manifold bolts. Remove the manifold from underneath the truck.
7. Reverse the above procedure to install. Start the manifold bolts while the truck is jacked up first. Torque the bolts to 25 ft. lbs. (33 Nm).

## Air Conditioning Compressor

### REMOVAL & INSTALLATION

### ❋❋CAUTION

Discharging the air conditioning refrigerant should only be attempted by those who have the proper tools and training to do so, as serious personal injury may result. The refrigerant will instantly freeze any surface it comes in contact with, including your eyes.

1. Have the refrigerant discharged at a repair facility utilizing a recovery/recycling machine.
2. Disconnect the negative battery cable.
3. Disconnect the compressor clutch connector.
4. Remove the belt by releasing the belt tension at the idler pulley.

➡On some models it will be necessary to remove the crankshaft pulley to remove the belt.

5. Remove the engine cover (if necessary).
6. Remove the air cleaner.
7. Remove the fitting and muffler assembly. Cap and plug all open connections.
8. Remove the compressor bracket.
9. Remove the engine oil tube support bracket bolt and nut.
10. Disconnect the clutch ground lead.
11. Remove the compressor.
12. Drain and measure the oil in the compressor and check for contamination.
13. Replace with fresh oil and reinstall the compressor.
14. Installation is the reverse of the removal procedure.

## Radiator

### REMOVAL & INSTALLATION

◆ See Figures 67, 68, 69, 70, 71, 72, 73, 74 and 75

1. Drain the cooling system.

### ❋❋CAUTION

When draining the coolant, keep in mind that cats and dogs are attracted by ethylene glycol antifreeze, and are quite likely to drink any that is left in an uncovered container or in puddles on the ground. This will prove fatal in sufficient quantity. Always drain the coolant into a sealable container. Coolant should be reused unless it is contaminated or several years old.

2. Disconnect the radiator upper and lower hoses and, if applicable, the transmission coolant lines. Remove the coolant recovery system line, if so equipped.
3. Remove the radiator upper panel if so equipped.

Fig. 67 Remove the air cleaner snorkel attaching bolts and move it aside

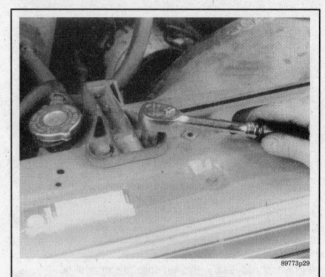

Fig. 68 Unfasten the shroud bracket retainers . . .

Fig. 69 . . . then push the shroud back and let in hang on the fan

Fig. 70 After unfastening the radiator hoses, transmission lines and retainers, remove the radiator

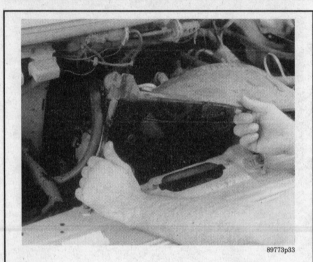

Fig. 71 If necessary, the fan shroud can now be removed

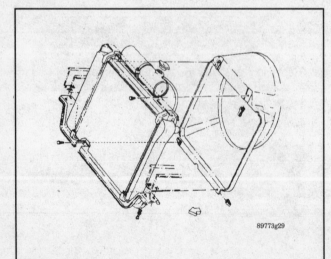

Fig. 72 Radiator and shroud mounting — 1967-70 six cylinder engine

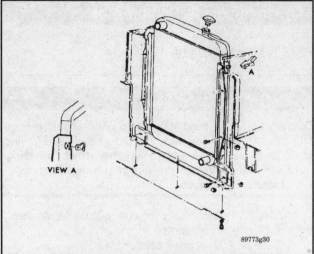

Fig. 73 Radiator and shroud mounting — 1967-70 V8 engine

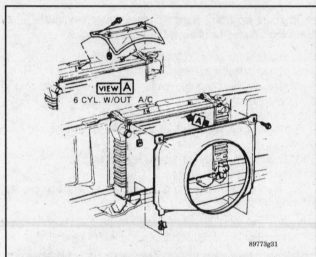

Fig. 74 Radiator and shroud mounting — 1971 and later models

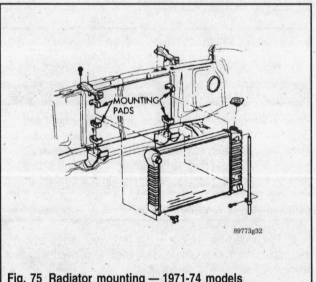

Fig. 75 Radiator mounting — 1971-74 models

4. If there is a radiator shroud in front of the radiator, the radiator and shroud are removed as an assembly.

5. If there is a fan shroud, remove the shroud attaching screws and let the shroud hang on the fan.

6. Remove the radiator attaching bolts and remove the radiator.

7. Installation is the reverse of the removal procedure.

## Water Pump

### REMOVAL & INSTALLATION

**Except 6.2L Diesel Engines**
▶ See Figures 76, 77, 78, 79 and 80

1. Disconnect the battery.

Fig. 76 Unfasten the fan retainers . . .

Fig. 77 . . . then remove the fan

2. Drain the radiator.

### ✳✳CAUTION

**When draining the coolant, keep in mind that cats and dogs are attracted by ethylene glycol antifreeze, and are quite likely to drink any that is left in an uncovered container or in puddles on the ground. This will prove fatal in sufficient quantity. Always drain the coolant into a sealable container. Coolant should be reused unless it is contaminated or several years old.**

3. Loosen the alternator and other accessories at their adjusting points, and remove the fan belts from the fan pulley.

4. Remove the fan and pulley.

5. Remove any accessory brackets that might interfere with water pump removal.

6. Disconnect the hose from the water pump inlet and the heater hose from the nipple on the pump. Remove the bolts, pump assembly and old gasket from the timing chain cover.

7. Check the pump shaft bearings for end-play or roughness in operation. Water pump bearings usually emit a squealing sound with the engine running when the bearings need to be replaced. Replace the pump if the bearings are not in good shape or have been noisy.

8. To install, make sure the gasket surfaces on the pump and timing chain cover are clean. Install the pump assembly with a new gasket. Tighten the bolts uniformly.

9. The remainder of installation is the reverse of removal. Fill the cooling system and check for leaks at the pump and hose joints. Make sure all of the accessory belts are properly tensioned.

**6.2L Diesel Engine**
▶ See Figure 81

1. Disconnect the batteries.
2. Remove the fan and fan shroud.
3. Drain the radiator.

### ✳✳CAUTION

**When draining the coolant, keep in mind that cats and dogs are attracted by ethylene glycol antifreeze, and are quite likely to drink any that is left in an uncovered container or in puddles on the ground. This will prove fatal in sufficient quantity. Always drain the coolant into a sealable container. Coolant should be reused unless it is contaminated or several years old.**

4. If the truck is equipped with air conditioning, remove the A/C hose bracket nuts.

5. Remove the oil filler tube.

6. Remove the generator pivot bolt and remove the generator belt.

7. Remove the generator lower bracket.

8. Remove the power steering belt and secure it out of the way.

9. Remove the air conditioning belt if equipped.

10. Disconnect the by-pass hose and the lower radiator hose.

11. Remove the water pump bolts. Remove the water pump plate and gasket and water pump. If the pump gasket is to be

**Fig. 78 After removing the belt, remove the pulley**

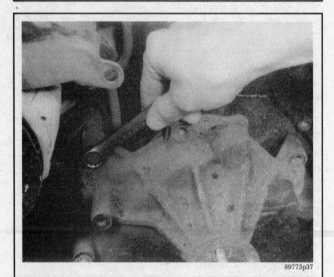

**Fig. 79 Unfasten the water pump retaining bolts**

**Fig. 80 Remove the water pump from the vehicle**

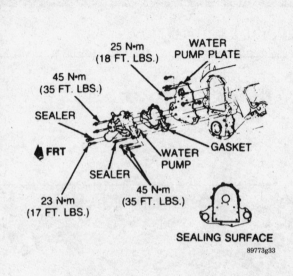

**Fig. 81 6.2L diesel engine water pump assembly. Note the sealer application surface**

replaced, remove the plate attaching bolts to the water pump and remove (and replace) the gasket.

12. When installing the pump, the flanges must be free of oil. Apply an anaerobic sealer (GM part #1052357 or equivalent) as shown in the accompanying illustration.

➡ **The sealer must be wet to the touch when the bolts are torqued.**

13. Attach the water pump and plate assembly. Torque the bolts to specifications.

14. Assemble the remaining components in the reverse order of removal. Fill the cooling system, start the engine and check for leaks.

## Cylinder Head

### REMOVAL & INSTALLATION

**Inline Six Cylinder Engine**
▶ See Figure 82

1. Drain the cooling system and remove the air cleaner. Disconnect the PCV hose. If equipped, disconnect the air injection hose.

### ✱✱CAUTION

**When draining the coolant, keep in mind that cats and dogs are attracted by ethylene glycol antifreeze, and are quite likely to drink any that is left in an uncovered container or in puddles on the ground. This will prove fatal in sufficient quantity. Always drain the coolant into a sealable container. Coolant should be reused unless it is contaminated or several years old.**

2. Disconnect the accelerator pedal rod at the bellcrank on the manifold, and the fuel and vacuum lines at the carburetor.

3. Disconnect the exhaust pipe at the manifold flange, then remove the manifold bolts and clamps and remove the manifolds and carburetor as an assembly. On those 1975 and later engines with the intake manifold integral with the head, remove the carburetor and the exhaust manifold.

4. Remove the fuel and vacuum line retaining clip from the water outlet. Then disconnect the wire harness from the heat sending unit and coil, leaving the harness clear of clips on the rocker arm cover.

5. Disconnect the radiator hose at the water outlet housing and the battery ground strap at the cylinder head.

6. Disconnect the wires and remove the spark plugs. Disconnect the coil-to-distributor primary wire lead at the coil and remove the coil on models without HEI.

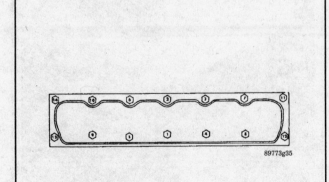

**Fig. 82 Inline six cylinder engine cylinder head tightening sequence**

7. Remove the rocker arm cover. Back off the rocker arm nuts, pivot the rocker arms to clear the pushrods and remove the pushrods.

8. Remove the cylinder head bolts, cylinder head and gasket.

**To install:**

9. Place a new cylinder head gasket over the dowel pins in the cylinder block with the bed up. Do not use sealer on composition steel/asbestos gaskets.

10. Guide and lower the cylinder head into place over the dowels and gasket.

11. Use sealant on the cylinder head bolts, install and tighten them down slightly.

12. Tighten the cylinder head bolts a little at a time with a torque wrench in the correct sequence. Final torque should be as specified.

13. Install the valve pushrods down through the cylinder head openings and seat them in their lifter sockets.

14. Install the rocker arms, balls and nuts and tighten the rocker arm nuts until all pushrod play is taken up.

15. Install the thermostat, the thermostat housing and the water outlet using new gaskets. Then connect the radiator hose.

16. Install the temperature sending switch.

17. Install the spark plugs.

18. Use new plug gaskets (if required) and torque to specifications.

19. Install the coil then connect the heat sending unit and the coil primary wires, and the battery ground cable at the cylinder head.

20. Clean the surfaces and install a new gasket over the manifold studs. Install the manifold. Install the bolts and clamps and torque as specified.

21. Connect the throttle linkage.

22. Connect the PCV fuel and vacuum lines and secure the lines in the clip at the water outlet. Connect the air injection line.

23. Fill the cooling system and check for leaks.

24. Adjust the valve lash as explained later.

25. Install the rocker arm cover and position the wiring harness in the clips.

26. Clean and install the air cleaner.

### V6 Engines
▶ See Figure 83

1. Disconnect the negative battery cable.

2. Remove the engine cover.

3. Remove the intake manifold as described later.

4. Remove the exhaust manifold as describer later.

5. Remove the air pipe at the rear of the head (right cylinder head).

6. Remove the generator mounting bolt at the cylinder head (right cylinder head).

7. Remove the power steering pump and brackets from the cylinder head, and lay them aside (left cylinder head).

8. Remove the air conditioner compressor, and lay it aside (left cylinder head).

9. Remove the rocker arm cover as outlined previously.

10. Remove the spark plugs.

11. Remove the pushrods, as outlined previously.

12. Remove the cylinder head bolts.

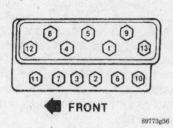

Fig. 83 V6 engine cylinder head tightening sequence

13. Remove the cylinder head.

14. Clean all gasket mating surfaces, install a new gasket and reinstall the cylinder head.

15. Install the cylinder heads using new gaskets. Install the gaskets with the head up.

➡Coat a steel gasket on both sides with sealer. If a composition gasket is used, do not use sealer.

16. Clean the bolts, apply sealer to the threads, and install them hand tight.

17. Tighten the head bolts a little at a time in the sequence shown. Head bolt torque is listed in the Torque Specifications chart.

18. Install the intake and exhaust manifolds.

19. Torque the cylinder head bolts to 65 ft. lbs. (88 Nm) and adjust the rocker arms.

20. Install the remaining components in the reverse of the removal procedure.

### Gasoline V8 Engines

▶ See Figures 84, 85, 86, 87 and 88

1. Remove the intake manifold as described later.

2. Remove the exhaust manifolds as described later and tie out of the way.

3. If the van is equipped with air conditioning, remove the A/C compressor and the forward mounting bracket and lay the compressor aside. Do not disconnect any of the refrigerant lines.

4. Back off the rocker arm nuts and pivot the rocker arms out of the way so that the pushrods can be removed. Identify the pushrods so that they can be installed in their original positions.

5. Remove the cylinder head bolts and remove the heads.

6. Install the cylinder heads using new gaskets. Install the gaskets with the head up.

➡Coat a steel gasket on both sides with sealer. If a composition gasket is used, do not use sealer.

7. Clean the bolts, apply sealer to the threads, and install them hand tight.

Fig. 84 Use a breaker bar to remove the cylinder head bolts

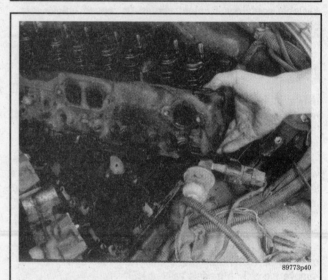

Fig. 85 Remove the cylinder head . . .

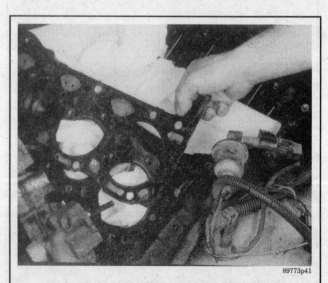

Fig. 86 . . . then remove the cylinder head gasket

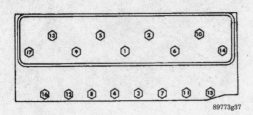

Fig. 87 V8 engine cylinder head tightening sequence

Fig. 88 Always use a torque wrench to tighten the bolts to the proper specification

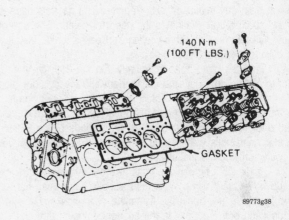

Fig. 89 Exploded view of the 6.2L diesel cylinder head mounting

8. Tighten the head bolts a little at a time in the sequence shown. Head bolt torque is listed in the Torque Specifications chart.

9. Install the intake and exhaust manifolds.

10. Adjust the rocker arms as explained later.

**Diesel Engines**

▶ **See Figures 89 and 90**

1. Remove the intake manifold, using the procedure outlined above.

2. Remove the rocker arm cover(s), after removing any accessory brackets which interfere with cover removal.

3. Disconnect and label the glow plug wiring.

4. If the right cylinder head is being removed, remove the ground strap from the head.

5. On the 350, remove the rocker arms bolts, the bridged pivots, the rocker arms, and the pushrods, keeping all the parts in order so that they can be returned to their original positions. On the 379, remove the rocker shaft assemblies. It

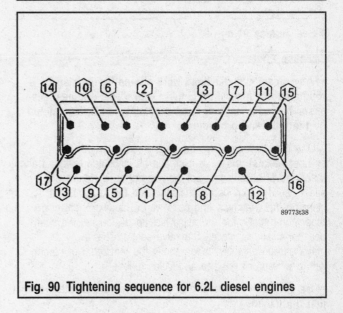

Fig. 90 Tightening sequence for 6.2L diesel engines

is a good practice to number or mark the parts to avoid interchanging them.

6. Remove the fuel return lines from the nozzles.

7. Remove the exhaust manifold(s), using the procedure outlined earlier in this section.

8. On the 350, remove the engine block drain plug on the side of the engine from which the cylinder head is being removed.

9. Remove the head bolts. Remove the cylinder head.

10. To install, first clean the mating surfaces thoroughly. Install new head gaskets on the engine block. Do not coat the gaskets with any sealer on either engine. The gaskets have a special coating that eliminates the need for sealer. The use of sealer will interfere with this coating and cause leaks. Install the cylinder head onto the block.

11. Clean the head bolts thoroughly. On the 350, dip the bolts in clean engine oil and install them into the cylinder block until the heads of the bolts lightly contact the cylinder head. On the 379, the left rear head bolt must be installed into the head prior to head installation. Coat the threads of the 379 cylinder head bolts with sealing compound (GM part #1052080 or equivalent) before installation.

12. On the 350, tighten the bolts in the illustrated sequence to 100 ft. lbs. (135 Nm). When all the bolts have been tightened to this figure, begin the tightening sequence again, and torque each bolt gradually in the sequence shown until the final torque specified is met.

13. Install the engine block drain plugs on the 350, the exhaust manifolds, the fuel return lines, the glow plug wiring, and the ground strap for the right cylinder head.

14. Install the valve train assembly. Refer to the Diesel Engine Rocker Arm Replacement in this section for the valve lifter bleeding procedures.

15. Install the intake manifold.

16. Install the valve covers. These are sealed with RTV type silicone sealer instead of a gasket. See the Valve Cover procedure for proper sealer application. Install the cover to the head within 10 minutes, while the sealer is still wet.

## CLEANING & INSPECTION

▶ **See Figures 91 and 92**

**Gasoline Engines**

➡**Any diesel cylinder head work should be handled by a reputable machine shop familiar with diesel engines. Disassembly, valve lapping, and assembly can be completed by the following procedures.**

One the complete valve train has been removed from the cylinder head(s), the head itself can be inspected, cleaned and machined (if necessary). Set the head(s) on a clean work space, so the combustion chambers are facing up. Begin cleaning the chambers and ports with a hardwood chisel or other non-metallic tool (to avoid nicking or gouging the chamber, ports, and especially the valve seats). Chip away the major carbon deposits, then remove the remainder of carbon with a wire brush fitted to an electric drill.

➡**Be sure that the carbon is actually removed, rather than just burnished.**

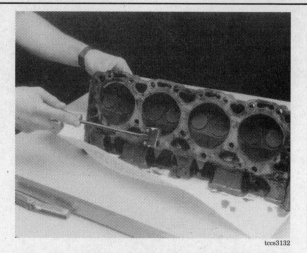

tccs3132

**Fig. 91 Use a gasket scraper to remove the bulk of the old head gasket from the mating surface**

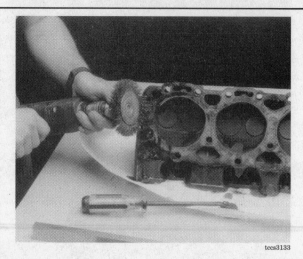

tccs3133

**Fig. 92 An electric drill equipped with a wire wheel will expedite complete gasket removal**

After decarbonizing is completed, take the head(s) to a machine shop and have the head hot tanked. In this process, the head is lowered into a hot chemical bath that very effectively cleans all grease, corrosion, and scale from all internal and external head surfaces. Also have the machinist check the valve seats and recut them if necessary. When you bring the clean head(s) home, place them on a clean surface. Completely clean the entire valve train with solvent.

## CHECKING FOR HEAD WARPAGE

▶ **See Figures 93 and 94**

Lay the head down with the combustion chambers facing up. Place a straight edge across the gasket surface of the head, both diagonally and straight across the center. Using a flat feeler gauge, determine the clearance at the center of the straight edge. If warpage exceeds 0.003 in. (0.0762mm) in a 6 in. (152mm) span, or 0.006 in. (0.152mm) over the total length, the cylinder head must be resurfaced (which is akin to

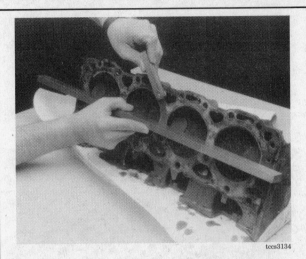

**Fig. 93 Check the cylinder head for warpage along the center using a straightedge and a feeler gauge**

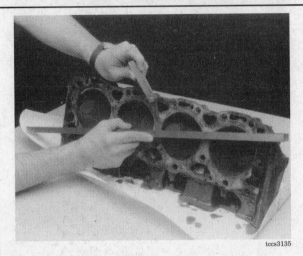

**Fig. 94 Be sure to check for warpage across the cylinder head at both diagonals**

planing a piece of wood). Resurfacing can be performed at most machine shops.

➡When resurfacing the cylinder head(s) of V type engines, the intake manifold mounting position is altered, and must be corrected by machining a proportionate amount from the intake manifold flange.

## RESURFACING

Cylinder head resurfacing should be done by a qualified machine shop.

## Valves

### REMOVAL & INSTALLATION

◗ **See Figures 95, 96, 97, 98, 99, 100 and 101**

1. Remove the head(s), and place on a clean surface.
2. Using a suitable spring compressor (for pushrod type overhead valve engines), compress the valve spring and remove the valve spring cap key. Release the spring compressor and remove the valve spring and cap (and valve rotator on some engines).

➡**Use care in removing the keys. They are easily lost.**

3. Remove the valve seals from the intake valve guides. Throw these old seals away, as you'll be installing new seals during reassembly.
4. Slide the valves out of the head from the combustion chamber side.
5. Make a holder for the valves out of a piece of wood or cardboard. Make sure you number each hole in the cardboard to keep the valves in proper order. Slide the valves out of the head from the combustion chamber side. They MUST be installed as they were removed.

New valve seals must be installed when the valve train is put back together. Certain seals slip over the valve stem and guide boss, while others require that the boss be machined. Teflon® guide seals are available. Check with a machinist and/or automotive parts store for a suggestion on the proper seals to use.

➡**Remember that when installing valve seals, a small amount of oil must be able to pass the seal to lubricate the valve guides; otherwise, excessive wear will result.**

To install:

6. Lubricate the valve stems with clean engine oil.
7. Install the valves in the cylinder head, one at a time, as numbered.
8. Lubricate and position the seals and valve springs, again a valve at a time.

**Fig. 95 Use a valve spring compressor tool to relieve spring tension from the valve caps**

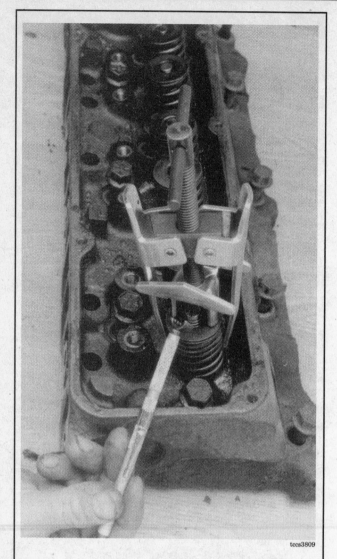

Fig. 96 A magnet may be helpful in removing the valve keepers

Fig. 98 Remove the spring from the valve stem in order to access the seal

Fig. 97 Be careful not to lose the valve keepers

Fig. 99 Once the spring has been removed, the O-ring may be removed from the valve stem

9. Install the spring retainers, and compress the springs.

10. With the valve key groove exposed above the compressed valve spring, wipe some wheel bearing grease around the groove. This will retain the keys as you release the spring compressor.

11. Using needlenose pliers (or your fingers), place the keys in the key grooves. The grease should hold the keys in place. Slowly release the spring compressor. The valve cap or rotator will raise up as the compressor is released, retaining the keys.

12. Install the rocker assembly, and install the cylinder head(s).

## INSPECTION

▶ **See Figures 102, 103, 104, 105 and 106**

Inspect the valve faces and seats (in the head) for pits, burned spots and other evidence of poor seating. If a valve face is in such bad shape that the head of the valve must be ground in order to true up the face, discard the valve because

**Fig. 100 Remove the valve stem seal from the cylinder head**

**Fig. 101 Invert the cylinder head and withdraw the valve from the cylinder head bore**

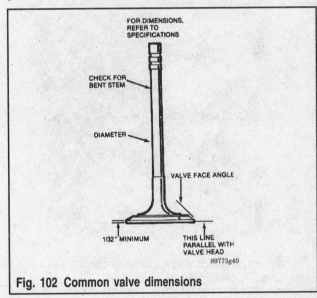

**Fig. 102 Common valve dimensions**

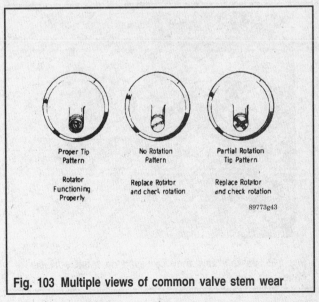

**Fig. 103 Multiple views of common valve stem wear**

the sharp edge will run too hot. The correct angle for valve faces is 45°. We recommend the refacing be done at a reputable machine shop.

Check the valve stem for scoring and burned spots. If not noticeably scored or damaged, clean the valve stem with solvent to remove all gum and varnish. Clean the valve guides using solvent an an expanding wire type valve guide cleaner. If you have access to a dial indicator for measuring valve stem-to-guide clearance, mount it so that the stem of the indicator is at 90° to the valve stem, and as close to the valve guide as possible. Move the valve off its seat, and measure the valve guide-to-stem clearance by rocking the stem back and forth to actuate the dial indicator. Measure the valve stems using a micrometer, and compare to specifications to determine whether stem or guide wear is responsible for the excess clearance. If a dial indicator and micrometer are not available to you, take your cylinder head and valves to a reputable machine shop for inspection.

Some of the engines covered in this guide are equipped with valve rotators, which double as valve spring caps. In normal operation the rotators put a certain degree of wear on the tip of the valve stem. This wear appears as concentric rings on the stem tip. However, if the rotator is not working properly, the wear may appear as straight notches or **X** patterns across the valve stem tip. Whenever the valves are removed from the cylinder head, the tips should be inspected for improper pattern, which could indicate valve rotator problems. Valve stem tips will have to be ground flat if rotator patterns are severe.

## REFACING

Valve refacing should only be handled by a reputable machine shop, as the experience and equipment needed to do the job are beyond that of the average owner/mechanic. During the course of a normal valve job, refacing is necessary when simply lapping the valves into their seats will not correct the seat and face wear. When the valves are reground (resurfaced), the valve seats must also be recut, again requiring special equipment and experience.

## VALVE LAPPING

▶ **See Figures 107 and 108**

After machine work has been performed on the valves, it may be necessary to lap the valve to assure proper contact. For this, you should first contact your machine shop to determine if lapping is necessary. Some machine shops will perform this for you as part of the service, but the precision machining which is available today often makes lapping unnecessary. Additionally, the hardened valves/seats used in modern automobiles may make lapping difficult or impossible. If your machine shop recommends that you lap the valves, proceed as follows:

1. Set the cylinder head on the workbench, combustion chamber side up. Rest the head on wooden blocks on either end, so there are two or three inches between the tops of the valve guides and the bench.

2. Lightly lube the valve stem with clean engine oil. Coat the valve seat completely with valve grinding compound. Use

tccs3142

**Fig. 104 A dial gauge may be used to check valve stem-to-guide clearance**

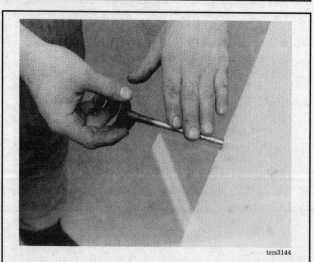
tccs3144

**Fig. 105 Valve stems may be rolled on a flat surface to check for bends**

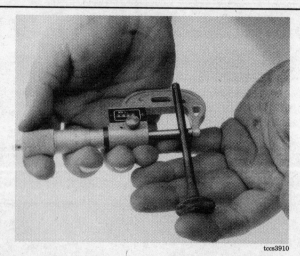
tccs3910

**Fig. 106 Use a micrometer to check the valve stem diameter**

Fig. 107 Lapping the valves by hand

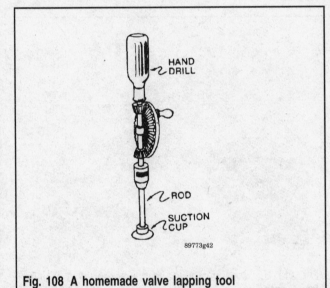

Fig. 108 A homemade valve lapping tool

just enough compound that the full width and circumference of the seat are covered.

3. Install the valve in its proper location in the head. Attach the suction cup end of the valve lapping tool to the valve head. It usually helps to put a small amount of saliva into the suction cup to aid it sticking to the valve.

4. Rotate the tool between the palms, changing position and lifting the tool often to prevent grooving. Lap the valve in until a smooth, evenly polished seat and valve face are evident.

5. Remove the valve from the head. Wipe away all traces of grinding compound from the valve face and seat. Wipe out the port with a solvent soaked rag, and swab out the valve guide with a piece of solvent soaked rag to make sure there are no traces of compound grit inside the guide. This cleaning is important.

6. Proceed through the remaining valves, one at a time. Make sure the valve faces, seats, cylinder ports and valve guides are clean before reassembling the valve train.

## Valve Stem Seals

### REMOVAL & INSTALLATION

**Cylinder Head Removed**
▶ **See Figures 109 and 110**

1. Remove the head(s), and place on a clean surface.

2. Using a suitable spring compressor (for pushrod type overhead valve engines), compress the valve spring and remove the valve spring cap key. Release the spring compressor and remove the valve spring and cap (and valve rotator on some engines).

➡ **Use care in removing the keys. They are easily lost.**

3. Remove the valve seals from the intake valve guides. Throw these old seals away, as you'll be installing new seals during reassembly.

Fig. 109 Use a valve spring compressor to remove the valve springs

Fig. 110 With the valve spring out of the way, the valve stem seals may now be replaced

New valve seals must be installed when the valve train is put back together. Certain seals slip over the valve stem and guide boss, while others require that the boss be machined. Teflon® guide seals are available. Check with a machinist and/or automotive parts store for a suggestion on the proper seals to use.

→Remember that when installing valve seals, a small amount of oil must be able to pass the seal to lubricate the valve guides; otherwise, excessive wear will result.

To install:

4. Lubricate the valve stems with clean engine oil.

5. Lubricate and position the seals and valve springs, again a valve at a time.

6. Install the spring retainers, and compress the springs.

7. With the valve key groove exposed above the compressed valve spring, wipe some wheel bearing grease around the groove. This will retain the keys as you release the spring compressor.

8. Using needlenose pliers (or your fingers), place the keys in the key grooves. The grease should hold the keys in place. Slowly release the spring compressor. The valve cap or rotator will raise up as the compressor is released, retaining the keys.

9. Install the rocker assembly, and install the cylinder head(s).

### Cylinder Head Installed

→Special tool J-23590, or its equivalent air line adaptor, will be necessary for this job.

It is often not necessary to remove the cylinder head(s) in order to service the valve train. Such is the case when valve seals need to be replaced. Valve seals can be easily replaced with the head(s) on the engine. The only special equipment needed for this job are an air line adapter (sold in most auto parts stores), which screws a compressed air line into the spark plug hole of the cylinder on which you are working, and a valve spring compressor. A source of compressed air is needed, of course.

1. Remove the cylinder head cover.

2. Remove the spark plug, rocker arm and pushrod on the cylinder(s) to be serviced.

3. Position the engine so that both valves are closed.

4. Install air line adapter (GM tool No. J-23590 or equivalent) into the spark plug hole. Turn on the air compressor to apply compressed air into the cylinder. This keeps the valves up in place.

→Set the regulator of the air compressor at least 50 psi (344 kPa) to ensure adequate pressure.

5. Using the valve spring compressor, compress the valve spring and remove the valve keys and keepers, the valve spring and damper.

6. Remove the valve stem seal.

7. To reassemble, oil the valve stem and new seal. Install a new seal over the valve stem. Set the spring, damper and keeper in place. Compress the spring. Coat the keys with grease to hold them onto the valve stem and install the keys, making sure they are seated fully in the keeper. Reinstall the cylinder head cover after adjusting the valves, as outlined in this section.

## Valve Springs

### REMOVAL & INSTALLATION

Please refer to the procedure for valve removal and installation.

### INSPECTION

▶ See Figures 111, 112, 113 and 114

Valve spring squareness, length and tension should be checked while the valve train is disassembled. Place each valve spring on a flat surface next to a steel square. Measure the length of the spring, and rotate it against the edge of the square to measure distortion. If spring length varies (by com-

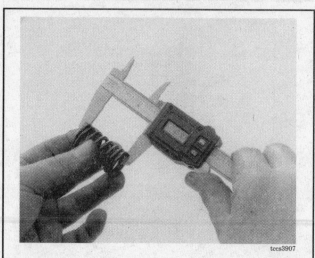

Fig. 111 Use a caliper gauge to check the valve spring free-length

Fig. 112 Check the valve spring for squareness on a flat service; a carpenter's square can be used

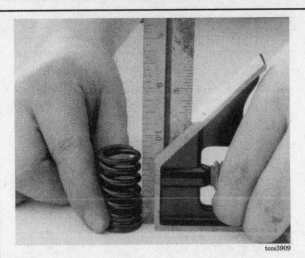

**Fig. 113 The valve spring should be straight up and down when placed like this**

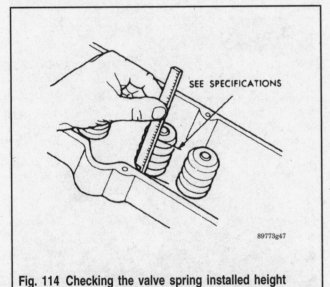

**Fig. 114 Checking the valve spring installed height**

parison) by more than 0.06 in. (1.6mm) or if distortion exceeds 0.06 in. (1.6mm), replace the spring.

Spring tension must be checked on a spring tester. Springs used on most engines should be within one pound of each other when tested at their specified installed heights.

## Valve Seats

### REMOVAL & INSTALLATION

▶ **See Figure 115**

The valve seats in these engines are not removable. Refer all servicing of the valve seats to a qualified machine shop.

**Fig. 115 Have the valve seat concentricity checked at a machine shop**

## Valve Guides

### REMOVAL & INSTALLATION

The engines covered in this guide use integral valve guides. That is, they are a part of the cylinder head and cannot be replaced. The guides can, however, be reamed oversize if they are found to be worn past an acceptable limit. Occasionally, a valve guide bore will be oversize as manufactured. These are marked on the inboard side of the cylinder heads on the machined surface just above the intake manifold.

If the guides must be reamed (this service is available at most machine shops), then valves with oversize stems must be fitted. Valves are usually available in 0.001 in. (0.0254mm), 0.003 in. (0.0762mm) and 0.005 in. (0.127mm) stem oversizes. Valve guides which are not excessively worn or distorted may, in some cases, be knurled rather than reamed. Knurling is a process in which the metal on the valve guide bore is displaced and raised, thereby reducing clearance. Knurling also provides excellent oil control. The option of knurling rather than reaming valve guides should be discussed with a reputable machinist or engine specialist.

## Valve Lifters

### REMOVAL & INSTALLATION

**Inline Six Cylinder Engines**
▶ **See Figure 116**

1. Remove the rocker arm cover.
2. Loosen the rocker arm until you can rotate it away from the pushrod, giving clearance to the top of the pushrod.
3. Remove the pushrod. If you are replacing all of the lifters, it is wise to make a pushrod holder as mentioned under Cylinder Head Removal. This will help keep the pushrods in order, as they MUST go back in their original positions.

**Fig. 116 Exploded view of the valve lifter**

**Fig. 117 A magnet is useful in removing lifters from their bores**

4. Remove the pushrod covers on the side of the block.

5. Remove the lifter(s). A Hydraulic lifter removal tool (GM part #J-3049 or equivalent) is available at dealers and most parts stores, and is quite handy for this procedure.

6. Before installing new lifters, all sealer coating must be removed from the inside. This can be done with kerosene or carburetor cleaning solvent. Also, the new lifters must be primed before installation, as dry lifters will seize when the engine is started. Submerge the lifters in clean engine oil and work the lifter plunger up and down.

7. Install the lifter(s) and pushrod(s) into the cylinder block in their original positions.

8. Pivot the rocker arm back into its original position. With the lifter on the base circle of the camshaft (valve closed), tighten the rocker arm nut to 20 ft. lbs. (27 Nm). Do not over torque. You will have to rotate the crankshaft to do the individual valves.

9. Replace the pushrod covers using new gaskets. Replace the rocker arm cover, using a new gasket or sealer.

**Gasoline V6 and V8 Engines**

▶ **See Figures 117 and 118**

➡Valve lifters and pushrods should be kept in order so they can be reinstalled in their original position. Some engines will have both standard size and 0.010 in. (0.254mm) oversize valve lifters as original equipment. The oversize lifters are etched with an O on their sides. The cylinder block will also be marked with an O if the over-size lifter is used.

1. Remove the intake manifold and gasket.

2. Remove the valve covers, rocker arm assemblies and pushrods.

3. If the lifters are coated with varnish, apply carburetor cleaning solvent to the lifter body. The solvent should dissolve the varnish in about 10 minutes.

4. Remove the lifters. Remove the lifter retainer guide bolts, and remove the guides. A special tool for removing lifters is available, and is helpful for this procedure.

5. New lifter MUST be primed before installation, as dry lifters will seize when the engine is started. Submerge the

**Fig. 118 Stuck lifters must be freed using a slide hammer type lifter removal tool**

lifters in clean engine oil and work the lifter plunger up and down.

6. Install the lifters and pushrods into the cylinder block in their original order. Install the lifter retainer guide.

7. Install the intake manifold gaskets and manifold.

8. Position the rocker arms, (rocker arms and balls on the V6) pivots and bolts on the cylinder head.

9. Install the valve covers, connect the spark plug wires and install the air cleaner.

### 6.2L Diesel Engine

▶ **See Figures 119 and 120**

1. Remove the valve covers as previously detailed.
2. Remove the rocker shaft assemblies.
3. Remove the cylinder head(s).
4. Remove the guide clamps and guide plates. It may be necessary to use mechanical fingers to remove the guide plates.

5. Using GM tool #J-29834 or another suitable lifter removal tool and a magnet, remove the lifter(s) through the access in the block.

6. Coat the lifters with clean engine oil before installation. If installing new lifters, they bust be primed first by working the lifter plunger while the lifter is submerged in clean kerosene or diesel fuel. Lifters that have not been primed will seize when the engine is started.

7. Install the lifters in their original positions in the block. A lifter installation tool can be fabricated out of welding rod or similar gauge wire and may help.

8. Install the lifter guide plate and guide plate clamp. The crankshaft must be turned 2 full rotations (720°) after assembly of the lifter guide plate clamp to insure free movement of the lifters in the guide plates.

9. Install the remainder of components in the reverse order of removal.

➡**The pushrods must be installed with their painted ends facing UP.**

## VALVE LASH ADJUSTMENT

▶ **See Figures 121, 122 and 123**

All engines described in this book use hydraulic lifters, which require no periodic adjustment. In the event of cylinder head removal or any operation that requires disturbing the rocker arms, the rocker arms will need a preliminary adjustment.

### 1967-71 Models

Normalize the engine temperature by running it for several minutes. Shut the engine off and remove the valve cover(s). After valve cover removal, torque the cylinder heads to specification. The use if oil stopper clips, readily available on the market is recommended to prevent oil splatter when adjusting

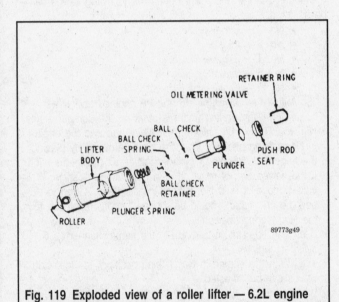

**Fig. 119 Exploded view of a roller lifter — 6.2L engine**

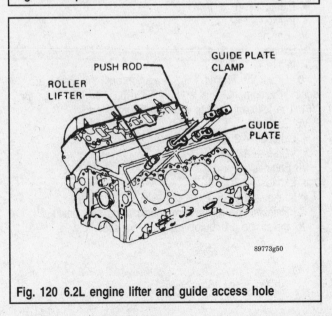

**Fig. 120 6.2L engine lifter and guide access hole**

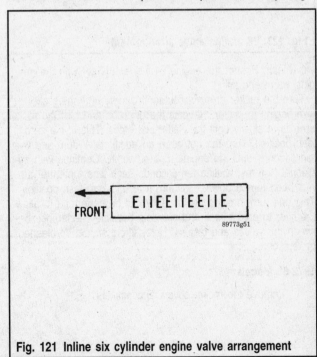

**Fig. 121 Inline six cylinder engine valve arrangement**

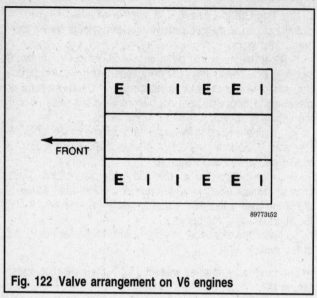

**Fig. 122 Valve arrangement on V6 engines**

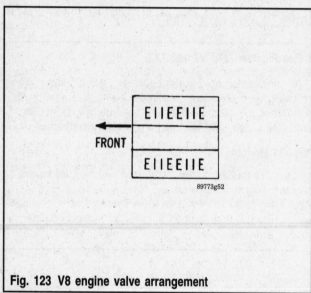

**Fig. 123 V8 engine valve arrangement**

valve lash. Restart the engine. Valve lash is set with the engine warm and idling.

Turn the rocker arm nut counterclockwise until the rocker arm begins to clatter. Reverse the direction and turn the rocker arm down slowly until the clatter just stops. This is the zero lash position. Turn the nut down an additional ¼ turn and wait ten seconds until the engine runs smoothly. Continue with additional ¼ turns, waiting ten seconds each time, until the nut has been turned down 1 full turn from the zero lash position. This one turn, preload adjustment must be performed to allow the lifter to adjust itself and prevents possible interference between the valves and pistons. Noisy lifters should be cleaned or replaced.

### 1972-86 Models

1. Remove the rocker covers and gaskets.

2. Adjust the valves on the inline six cylinder engines as follows:

a. Mark the distributor housing with a piece of chalk at No. 1 and 6 plug wire positions. Remove the distributor cap with the plug wires attached.

b. Crank the engine until the distributor rotor points to No. 1 cylinder and the points are open. At this point, adjust the following valves:
- No. 1 — Exhaust and Intake
- No. 2 — Intake
- No. 3 — Exhaust
- No. 4 — Intake
- No. 5 — Exhaust

3. Back out the adjusting nut until lash is felt at the pushrod, then turn the adjusting nut in until all lash is removed. This can be determined by checking pushrod end-play while turning the adjusting nut. When all play has been removed, turn the adjusting nut in 1 full turn.

4. Crank the engine until the distributor rotor points to No. 6 cylinder and the points are open. The following valves can be adjusted:
- No. 2 — Exhaust
- No. 3 — Intake
- No. 4 — Exhaust
- No. 5 — Intake
- No. 6 — Intake and Exhaust

5. Adjust the valves on V6 and V8 engines as follows:

a. Crank the engine until the mark on the damper aligns with the TDC or 0° mark on the timing tab and the engine is in No. 1 firing position. This can be determined by placing the fingers on the No. 1 cylinder valves as the marks align. If the valves do not move, it is in No. 1 firing position. If the valves move, it is in No. 6 firing position (No. 4 on the V6) and the crankshaft should be rotated 1 more revolution to the No. 1 firing position.

b. The adjustment is made in the same manner as 6 cylinder engines.

c. With the engine in No. 1 firing position, the following valves can be adjusted:

V6 Engines
- Exhaust — 1, 5, 6
- Intake — 1, 2, 3

V8 Engines
- Exhaust — 1, 3, 4, 8
- Intake — 1, 2, 5, 7

6. Crank the engine 1 full revolution until the marks are again in alignment. This is No. 6 firing position (No. 4 on the V6). The following valves can now be adjusted:

V6 Engines
- Exhaust — 2, 3, 4
- Intake — 4, 5, 6

V8 Engines
- Exhaust — 2, 5, 6, 7
- Intake — 3, 4, 6, 8

7. Reinstall the rocker arm covers using new gaskets.

8. Install the distributor cap and wire assembly.

## Oil Pan

### REMOVAL & INSTALLATION

**Inline Six Cylinder Engine**

#### 1967-69 MODELS

1. Disconnect the negative battery terminal.
2. Remove the fan and pulley.
3. Remove the engine splash shields if equipped.
4. On vehicles with automatic transmissions, disconnect and plug the cooler lines.
5. Drain the radiator and disconnect the lower radiator hose at the radiator.

### ✳✳CAUTION

**When draining the coolant, keep in mind that cats and dogs are attracted by ethylene glycol antifreeze, and are quite likely to drink any that is left in an uncovered container or in puddles on the ground. This will prove fatal in sufficient quantity. Always drain the coolant into a sealable container. Coolant should be reused unless it is contaminated or several years old.**

6. If equipped, remove the accessory drive pulley and shroud.
7. Install a support under the damper.
8. Place a jack under the support on the damper and jack the engine to clear the front mounts.
9. Remove the crossmember to frame bolts and lower the crossmember to rest on the front springs.
10. Drain the oil and remove the oil pan. Discard the gaskets and seals.
11. Installation is the reverse of removal. Use new gaskets and a new seal in the rear main bearing cap and crankcase front cover. Do not use sealer. Fill the engine with coolant and oil. Start the engine and check for leaks.

#### 1970-75 MODELS

1. Disconnect the negative battery terminal.
2. Raise and support the vehicle. Disconnect the starter leaving the wires attached and swing it out of the way.
3. If there is not enough clearance, remove the bolts securing the engine mounts to the crossmember and raise the engine high enough to insert a 2 in. x 4 in. (51mm x 102mm) piece of wood between the engine mounts and the crossmember brackets.
4. Drain the engine oil.
5. Remove the flywheel and converter cover.
6. Remove the oil pan.
7. Clean all gasket surfaces and install a new seal in the rear main bearing groove and a new seal in the crankcase front cover. Installation is the reverse of removal. Install new side gaskets on the block, but do not use sealer. Fill the engine with oil and run the engine, checking for leaks.

#### 1976-77 MODELS

1. Disconnect the battery ground cable.
2. Drain the oil.

3. Remove the starter.
4. Remove the manual transmission flywheel splash shield or the automatic transmission converter housing underpan.
5. Support the front of the engine. Remove the engine mount through-bolts.
6. Raise the front of the engine enough to replace the through-bolts in the engine half of the mounts.
7. Lower the engine and remove the pan bolts.
8. Clean all gasket surfaces and install a new seal in the rear main bearing cap and on the crankcase front cover. Install new side gaskets to the block, using sealer.
9. Replace the pan.
10. Raise the engine and replace the mount through-bolts. Fill the engine with oil and run it, watching for leaks.

#### 1978 AND LATER MODELS

1. Disconnect the negative battery cable and remove the engine cover.
2. Remove the air cleaner and studs.
3. Remove the fan finger guard.
4. Remove the radiator upper supporting brackets.
5. Raise the van on a hoist.
6. On vans with manual transmissions:
   a. Disconnect the clutch cross shaft from the left front mounting bracket.
   b. Remove the transmission-to-bell housing upper bolt.
   c. Remove the transmission rear mounting bolts and install two 7/16 in. x 3 in. (11mm x 76mm) bolts.
   d. Raise the transmission and place small pieces of 2 in. x 4 in. wooden blocks in between the mount and the crossmember.
7. Remove the starter motor.
8. Drain the engine oil.
9. Remove the engine mount through-bolts.
10. Raise the engine slightly and place small 2 in. x 4 in. wooden blocks in between the mount and the block.
11. Remove the flywheel splash shield or the converter cover, as applicable.
12. Remove the oil pan attaching bolts and remove the oil pan.
13. Clean the gasket surface thoroughly and use a new gasket on installation.
14. Reverse the procedure to install.

### 4.3 Liter V6 Engines

A one piece type oil pan gasket is used.
1. Disconnect the negative battery cable. Raise the vehicle, support it safely, and drain the engine oil.
2. Remove the exhaust crossover pipe.
3. Remove the torque converter cover (on models with automatic transmission).
4. Remove the strut rods at the flywheel cover.
5. Remove the strut rod brackets at the front engine mountings.
6. Remove the starter.
7. Remove the oil pan bolts, nuts and reinforcements.
8. Remove the oil pan and gaskets.
9. Thoroughly clean all gasket surfaces and install a new gasket, using only a small amount of sealer at the front and rear corners of the oil pan.
10. Installation is the reverse of the removal procedure.

### Gasoline V8 Engines

1. Drain the engine oil.
2. Remove the oil dipstick and tube.
3. If necessary remove the exhaust pipe crossover.
4. If equipped with automatic transmission, remove the converter housing pan.
5. Remove the starter brace and bolt and swing the starter aside.
6. Remove the oil pan and discard the gaskets.
7. Installation is the reverse of removal. Clean all gasket surfaces and use new gaskets to assemble. Use gasket sealer to retain side gaskets to the cylinder block. Install a new oil pan rear seal in the rear main bearing cap slot with the ends butting the side gaskets. Install a new front seal in the crankcase front cover with the ends butting the side gaskets. Fill the engine with oil and check for leaks.

### Diesel Engines

1. Remove the vacuum pump and drive (with A/C or the oil pump drive (without A/C).
2. Disconnect the batteries and remove the dipstick.
3. Remove the upper radiator support and fan shroud.
4. Raise and support the car. Drain the oil.
5. Remove the flywheel cover.
6. Disconnect the exhaust and crossover pipes.
7. Remove the oil cooler lines at the filter base.
8. Remove the starter assembly. Support the engine with a jack.
9. Remove the engine mounts from the block.
10. Raise the front of the engine and remove the oil pan.
11. Installation is the reverse of removal.

## Oil Pump

## REMOVAL & INSTALLATION

### Inline Six Cylinder Engines

▶ **See Figures 124 and 125**

1. Drain the oil and remove the oil pan.
2. Remove the 2 flanged mounting bolts and remove the pickup pipe bolt.
3. Remove the pump and screen as an assembly.
4. If the pump has been disassembled, is being replaced, or for any reason oil has been removed from it, it must be primed. It can either be filled with oil before installing the cover plate (and oil kept within the pump during handling), or the entire pump cavity can be filled with petroleum jelly. IF THE PUMP IS NOT PRIMED, THE ENGINE COULD BE DAMAGED BEFORE IT RECEIVES ADEQUATE LUBRICATION WHEN YOU START IT.
5. To install, align the oil pump driveshafts with the distributor tang and install the oil pump. Position the flange over the distributor lower bushing, using no gasket. The oil pump should slide easily into place. If not, remove it and reposition the slot to align with the distributor tang.
6. Reinstall the oil pan and fill the engine with oil.

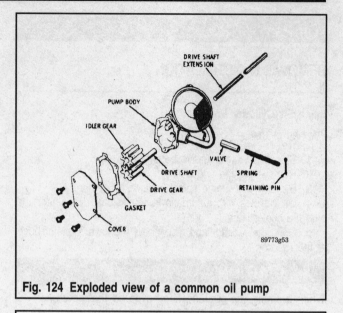

**Fig. 124 Exploded view of a common oil pump**

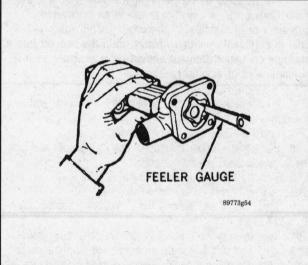

**Fig. 125 Measuring the oil pump side clearance**

### 4.3L V6 Engines

1. Remove the oil pan.
2. Remove the bolt attaching the pump to the rear main bearing cap. Remove the pump and the extension shaft, which will come out behind it.
3. If the pump has been disassembled, is being replaced, or for any reason oil has been removed from it, it must be primed. It can either be filled with oil before installing the cover plate (and oil kept within the pump during handling), or the entire pump cavity can be filled with petroleum jelly. IF THE PUMP IS NOT PRIMED, THE ENGINE COULD BE DAMAGED BEFORE IT RECEIVES ADEQUATE LUBRICATION WHEN YOU START IT.
4. Engage the extension shaft with the oil pump shaft. Align the slot on the top of the extension shaft with the drive tang on the lower end of the distributor driveshaft, and then position the pump at the rear main bearing cap so the mounting bolt can be installed. Install the bolt and tighten to 65 ft. lbs. (88 Nm).
5. Install the oil pan.

### V8 and Diesel Engines

1. Drain the oil and remove the oil pan.
2. Remove the bolt (two bolts on diesels) holding the pump to the rear main bearing cap. Remove the pump and extension shaft.
3. If the pump has been disassembled, is being replaced, or for any reason oil has been removed from it, it must be primed. It can either be filled with oil before installing the cover plate (and oil kept within the pump during handling), or the entire pump cavity can be filled with petroleum jelly. IF THE PUMP IS NOT PRIMED, THE ENGINE COULD BE DAMAGED BEFORE IT RECEIVES ADEQUATE LUBRICATION WHEN YOU START IT.
4. To install, assemble the pump and extension shaft to the rear main bearing cap aligning the slot on the top of the extension shaft with the drive tang on the distributor driveshaft. The installed position of the oil pump screen is with the bottom edge parallel to the oil pan rails. Further installation is the reverse of removal.

## OVERHAUL

### Inline Six Cylinder Engines

1. With the pump removed from the block, remove the four cover attaching screws, the cover, idler gear and drive gear and shaft.
2. Remove the pressure regulator valve and other related valve parts.

### ✳✳WARNING

**Do not disturb the oil pickup pipe on the screen or body.**

3. Inspect the pump body for excessive wear or cracks, and inspect the pump gears for excessive wear, cracks or damage. Check the shaft for looseness in the housing. It should not be a sloppy fit. Check the inside of the cover for wear that would permit oil to leak past the ends of the gears. Remove any debris from the surface of the screen, and check the screen for damage. Check the pressure regulator valve plunger for fit in the body.
4. Assembly is the reverse of the disassembly procedure. Tighten the cover screws to 8 ft. lbs. (10 Nm).

### V6 and V8 Engines

1. Remove the oil pump driveshaft extension.
2. Remove the cotter pin, spring and the pressure regulator valve.

➡**Place your thumb over the pressure regulator bore before removing the cotter pin, as the spring is under pressure.**

3. Remove the oil pump cover attaching screws and remove the oil pump cover and gasket. Clean the pump in solvent or kerosene, and wash out the pickup screen.
4. Remove the drive gear and the idler gear from the pump body.
5. Check the gears for scoring and other damage. Install the gears if in good condition or replace them if damaged.

Check gear end clearance by placing a straight edge over the gears and measuring the clearance between the straight edge and the gasket surface with a feeler gauge. End clearance for the gasoline V6 and V8 is 0.002 in. (0.051mm) to 0.0065 in. (0.165mm). If end clearance is excessive, check for scores in the cover that would bring the total clearance over the specs.

6. Check the gear side clearance by inserting the feeler gauge between the gear teeth and the side of the pump body. Clearance should be between 0.002 in. (0.051mm) and 0.005 in. (0.127mm).
7. Pack the inside of the pump completely with petroleum jelly. DO NOT USE ENGINE OIL. The pump MUST be primed this way or it will not produce any oil pressure when the engine is started.
8. Install the cover screws and tighten alternately and evenly to 8 ft. lbs. (10 Nm).
9. Position the pressure valve into the pump cover, closed end first, then install the spring and retaining pin.

➡**When assembling the driveshaft extension into the driveshaft, the end of the extension nearest the washers must be inserted into the driveshaft.**

10. Insert the driveshaft extension through the opening in the main bearing cap and block until the shaft mates into the distributor drive gear.
11. Install the pump onto the rear main bearing cap and install the attaching bolts. Torque the bolts to 35 ft. lbs. (47 Nm).
12. Install the pan.

## Crankshaft Damper

## REMOVAL & INSTALLATION

▶ **See Figures 126, 127, 128, 129 and 130**

Torsional damper puller tool # J-23523-E is required to perform this procedure.

1. Remove the fan belts, fan and pulley.
2. Remove the fan shroud assembly.

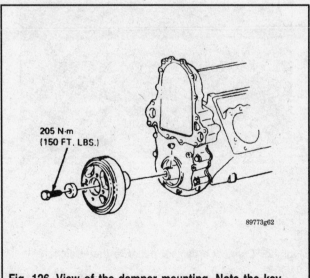

205 N·m
(150 FT. LBS.)

89773g62

**Fig. 126 View of the damper mounting. Note the key**

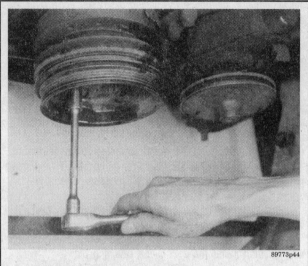

Fig. 127 Unfasten the crankshaft pulley bolt . . .

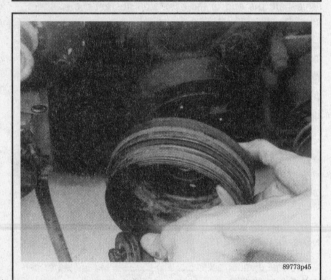

Fig. 128 . . . then remove the pulley and bolt

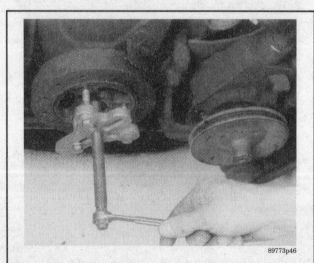

Fig. 129 Connect a damper puller to the torsional damper . . .

Fig. 130 . . . then remove the damper

3. Remove the accessory drive pulley.
4. Remove the torsional damper bolt.
5. Remove the torsional damper using tool # J-23523-E.

➡Make sure you do not loose the crankshaft key, if it has been removed.

6. Installation is the reverse of the removal procedure.

## Timing Chain Cover and Front Oil Seal

### REMOVAL & INSTALLATION

**Inline Six Cylinder Engine**

◆ See Figures 131 and 132

1. Drain the engine coolant, remove the radiator hoses, and remove the radiator.

### ❋❋CAUTION

When draining the coolant, keep in mind that cats and dogs are attracted by ethylene glycol antifreeze, and are quite likely to drink any that is left in an uncovered container or in puddles on the ground. This will prove fatal in sufficient quantity. Always drain the coolant into a sealable container. Coolant should be reused unless it is contaminated or several years old.

2. Remove the fan belt and any accessory belts. Remove the fan pulley.
3. A harmonic balancer puller is necessary to pull the balancer. Install the puller and remove the balancer.
4. Remove the two screws which attach the oil pan to the front cover. Remove the screws which attach the front cover to the block. Do not remove the cover yet.
5. Before the front cover is removed, it is necessary to cut the oil fan front seal. Pull the cover forward slightly.
6. Using a sharp knife or razor knife, cut the oil pan front seal flush with the cylinder block on both sides of the cover.

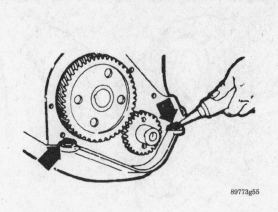

**Fig. 131 Applying sealer to the front cover on the 250 inline six engine**

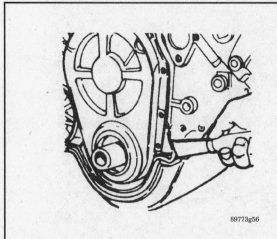

**Fig. 132 Cut the oil pan seal flush with the front of the block**

7. Remove the front cover and the attached portion of oil pan seal. Remove the front cover gasket from the block.

8. Install the front cover, first obtain an oil pan front seal. Cut the tabs from the new seal.

9. Install the seal in the front cover, pressing the tips into the holes provided in the cover. Coat the mating area of the front cover with a room temperature vulcanizing (RTV) sealer first.

10. Coat the new front cover gasket with sealer and install it on the cover.

11. Apply a ⅛ in. (3mm) bead of RTV sealer to the joint formed at the oil pan and cylinder block.

12. Install the front cover.

13. Install the harmonic balancer. Make sure the front cover seal is positioned evenly around the balancer. If you so not have access to a balancer installation tool (and you probably don't), you can either fabricate one using the illustration as a guide, or you can tap the balancer on using a brass or plastic mallet. If you use the last method, make sure the balancer goes on evenly.

14. The rest of the installation is in the reverse order of removal.

**Gasoline V6 and V8 Engines**
♦ See Figures 133, 134, 135, 136, 137, 138 and 139

1. Drain the cooling system.

### ✳✳CAUTION

**When draining the coolant, keep in mind that cats and dogs are attracted by ethylene glycol antifreeze, and are quite likely to drink any that is left in an uncovered container or in puddles on the ground. This will prove fatal in sufficient quantity. Always drain the coolant into a sealable container. Coolant should be reused unless it is contaminated or several years old.**

2. Remove the crankshaft pulley and damper. Remove the water pump. Remove the screws holding the timing case cover to the block and remove the cover and gaskets.

**Fig. 133 Remove the timing cover bolts**

**Fig. 134 Use a prytool to separate the cover from the engine**

89773p50

**Fig. 135 Remove the cover from the engine**

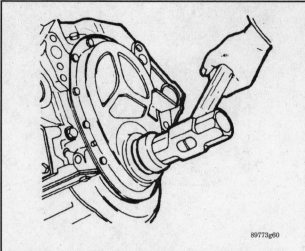

89773g60

**Fig. 138 View of the seal installation with the cover installed**

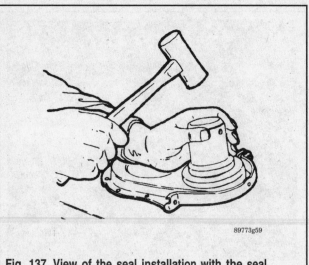

89773g59

**Fig. 137 View of the seal installation with the seal removed**

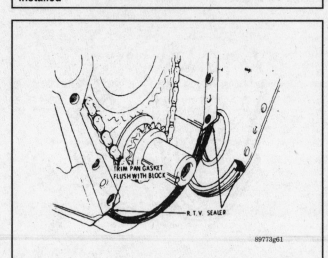

TRIM PAN GASKET FLUSH WITH BLOCK

R.T.V. SEALER

89773g61

**Fig. 139 View of the sealer application — gasoline V8 engines**

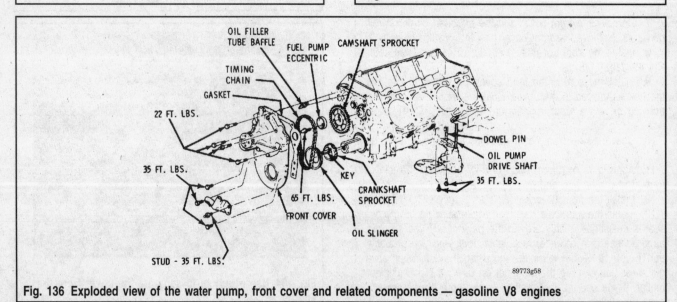

OIL FILLER TUBE BAFFLE

FUEL PUMP ECCENTRIC

CAMSHAFT SPROCKET

TIMING CHAIN

GASKET

22 FT. LBS.

35 FT. LBS.

65 FT. LBS.

FRONT COVER

KEY

CRANKSHAFT SPROCKET

OIL SLINGER

DOWEL PIN

OIL PUMP DRIVE SHAFT

35 FT. LBS.

STUD - 35 FT. LBS.

89773g58

**Fig. 136 Exploded view of the water pump, front cover and related components — gasoline V8 engines**

3. Use a suitable tool to pry the old seal out of the front face of the cover.

4. Install the new seal so that the open end is toward the inside of the cover.

➡Coat the lip of the new seal with oil prior to installation.

5. Check that the timing chain oil slinger is in place against the crankshaft sprocket.

6. Apply sealer to the front cover as shown in the accompanying illustration. Install the cover carefully onto the locating dowels.

7. Tighten the attaching screws to 6-8 ft. lbs. (8-10 Nm).

**Diesel Engine**

▶ See Figures 140 and 141

1. Drain the cooling system.

### ✳✳CAUTION

**When draining the coolant, keep in mind that cats and dogs are attracted by ethylene glycol antifreeze, and are quite likely to drink any that is left in an uncovered container or in puddles on the ground. This will prove fatal in sufficient quantity. Always drain the coolant into a sealable container. Coolant should be reused unless it is contaminated or several years old.**

2. Remove the water pump.

3. Rotate the crankshaft to align the marks on the injection pump driven gear and the camshaft gear as shown in the illustration.

4. Scribe a mark aligning the injection pump flange and the front cover.

5. Remove the crankshaft pulley and torsional damper.

6. Remove the front cover-to-oil pan bolts (4).

7. Remove the two fuel return line clips.

8. Remove the injection pump retaining nuts from the front cover.

9. Remove the baffle. Remove the remaining cover bolts, and remove the front cover.

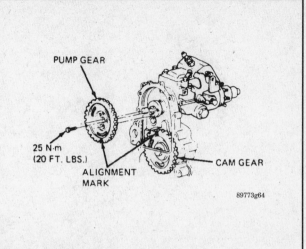

Fig. 141 Injection pump and cam gear alignment — 6.2L diesel engines

10. If the front cover oil seal is to be replaced, it can now be pried out of the cover with a suitable prying tool. Press the new seal into the cover evenly.

➡The oil seal can also be replaced with the front cover installed. Remove the torsional damper first, then pry the old seal out of the cover using a suitable prying tool. Use care not to damage the surface of the crankshaft. Install the new seal evenly into the cover and install the damper.

11. To install the front cover, first clean both sealing surfaces until all traces of old sealer are gone. Apply a 0.07 in. (2mm) bead of sealant (GM sealant #1052357 or equivalent) to the sealing surface as shown in the illustration. Apply a bead of RTV type sealer to the bottom portion of the front cover which attached to the oil pan. Install the front cover.

12. Install the baffle.

13. Install the injection pump, making sure the scribe marks on the pump and front cover are aligned.

14. Install the injection pump driven gear, making sure the marks on the cam gear and pump are aligned. Be sure the dowel pin and the three holes on the pump flange are also aligned.

15. Install the fuel line clips, the front cover-to-oil bolts, and the torsional damper and crankshaft pulley. Torque the pan bolts to 4-7 ft. lbs. (5-9 Nm), and the damper bolt to 140-162 ft. lbs. (189-219 Nm).

## Timing Gears

### REMOVAL & INSTALLATION

**Inline Six Engines**

▶ See Figure 142

The camshaft in these engines is gear driven, unlike the chain driven cams in V8s. The removal of the timing gear requires removal of the camshaft.

1. After the cam is removed, place the camshaft and gear in an arbor press and remove the gear from the cam. Many

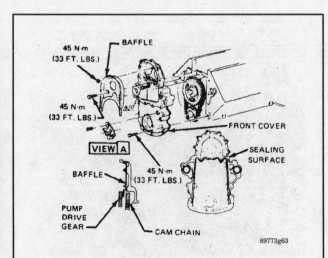

Fig. 140 Exploded view of the front cover assembly showing sealer application — 6.2L diesel engines

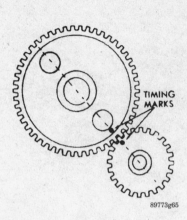

**Fig. 142 Inline six cylinder engine timing gear alignment**

**Fig. 143 Make sure the timing gears aligned before removal; this will aid in installation**

well equipped machine shops have this type of equipment if you need the gear pressed off.

2. Installation is in the reverse order of removal. The clearance between the camshaft and the thrust plate should be 0.001-0.005 in. (0.0254-0.127mm) on both engines. If less than 0.005 in. (0.127mm) clearance exists, the spacer ring should be replaced. If more than 0.005 in. (0.127mm) clearance, the thrust plate should be replaced.

### ✳✳WARNING

**The thrust plate must be positioned so that the Woodruff key in the shaft does not damage it when the shaft is pressed out of the gear. Support the hub of the gear or the gear will be seriously damaged.**

➡The 6-cylinder crankshaft gear may be removed with a gear puller while in place on the block.

## Timing Chain

### REMOVAL & INSTALLATION

#### Gasoline V6 and V8 Engines

▶ See Figures 143, 144, 145, 146 and 147

To replace the chain, remove the radiator core, water pump, the harmonic balancer and the crankcase front cover. This will allow access to the timing chain. Crank the engine until the timing marks on both sprockets are nearest each other and in line between the shaft centers. Then take out the three bolts that hold the camshaft gear to the camshaft. This gear is a light press fit on the camshaft and will come off easily. It is located by a dowel.

The chain comes off with the camshaft gear.

A gear puller will be required to remove the crankshaft gear.

Without disturbing the position of the engine, mount the new crankshaft gear on the shaft, and mount the chain over the camshaft gear. Arrange the camshaft gear in such a way that the timing marks will line up between the shaft centers and the

**Fig. 144 Unfasten the camshaft gear retaining bolts . . .**

**Fig. 145 . . . then remove the camshaft gear and the chain**

Fig. 146 Using a puller, remove the crankshaft gear

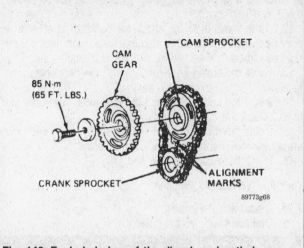

Fig. 148 Exploded view of the diesel engine timing chain assembly and alignment marks

5. Rotate the crankshaft 360° so that the camshaft gear and the injection pump gear are aligned.

6. Install the front cover as previously detailed. The injection pump must be retimed since the timing chain assembly was removed. See Section 2 for this procedure.

## Camshaft

### REMOVAL & INSTALLATION

#### Inline Six Cylinder Engines

1. Remove the grille. Remove the radiator hoses and remove the radiator.
2. Remove the timing gear cover.
3. Remove the valve cover and gasket, loosen all the rocker arm nuts, and pivot the rocker arms clear of the pushrods.
4. Remove the distributor and the fuel pump.
5. Remove the pushrods. Remove the coil and then remove the side cover. Remove the valve lifters.
6. Remove the two camshaft thrust plate retaining screws by working through the holes in the camshaft gear.
7. Remove the camshaft and gear assembly by pulling it out through the front of the block.
8. If either the camshaft or the camshaft gear is being renewed, the gear must be pressed off the camshaft. The replacement parts must be assembled in the same way. When placing the gear on the camshaft, press the gear onto the shaft until it bottoms against the gear spacer ring. The end clearance of the thrust plate should be 0.001-0.005 in. (0.0254-0.127mm).
9. Prelube the camshaft lobes with clean engine oil and then install the camshaft assembly in the engine. Be careful not to damage the bearings.
10. Turn the crankshaft and the camshaft gears so that the timing marks align. Push the camshaft into position and install and torque the thrust plate bolts to 7 ft. lbs. (9 Nm).
11. Check camshaft and crankshaft gear runout with a dial indicator. Camshaft gear runout should not exceed 0.004 in.

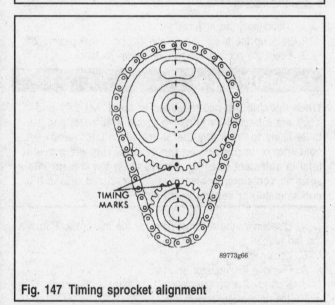

Fig. 147 Timing sprocket alignment

camshaft locating dowel will enter the dowel hole in the cam sprocket.

Place the cam sprocket, with its chain mounted over it, in position on the front of the car and pull up with the three bolts that hold it to the camshaft.

After the gears are in place, turn the engine two full revolutions to make certain that the timing marks are in correct alignment between the shaft centers.

End-play of the camshaft is zero.

#### 6.2L Diesel Engine

▶ See Figure 148

1. Remove the front cover as previously detailed.
2. Remove the bolt and washer attaching the camshaft gear. Remove the injection pump gear.
3. Remove the camshaft sprocket, timing chain and crankshaft sprocket as a unit.
4. To install, the cam sprocket, timing chain and crankshaft sprocket as a unit, aligning the timing marks on the sprockets as shown in the illustration.

(0.1016mm) and crankshaft gear runout should not be above 0.003 in. (0.0762mm).

12. Using a dial indicator, check the backlash at several points between the camshaft and crankshaft gear teeth. Backlash should be 0.004-0.006 in. (0.1016 0.152mm).

13. Install the timing gear cover. Install the harmonic balancer.

14. Install the valve lifters and the pushrods. Install the side cover. Install the coil and the fuel pump.

15. Install the distributor and set the timing. Pivot the rocker arms over the pushrods and adjust the valves.

16. Install the radiator, hoses and grille.

### Gasoline V6 and V8 Engines

1. Disconnect the battery.
2. Drain and remove the radiator.

### ✳✳CAUTION

**When draining the coolant, keep in mind that cats and dogs are attracted by ethylene glycol antifreeze, and are quite likely to drink any that is left in an uncovered container or in puddles on the ground. This will prove fatal in sufficient quantity. Always drain the coolant into a sealable container. Coolant should be reused unless it is contaminated or several years old.**

3. Disconnect the fuel line at the fuel pump. Remove the pump on 1978 and later models.

4. Disconnect the throttle cable and the air cleaner.

5. Remove the alternator belt, loosen the alternator bolts and move the alternator to one side.

6. Remove the power steering pump from its brackets and move it out of the way.

7. Remove the air conditioning compressor from its brackets and move the compressor out of the way without disconnecting the lines.

8. Disconnect the hoses from the water pump.

9. Disconnect the electrical and vacuum connections.

10. Mark the distributor as to location in the block. Remove the distributor.

11. Raise the car and drain the oil pan.

12. Remove the exhaust crossover pipe and starter motor.

13. Disconnect the exhaust pipe at the manifold.

14. Remove the harmonic balancer and pulley.

15. Support the engine and remove the front motor mounts.

16. Remove the flywheel inspection cover.

17. Remove the engine oil pan.

18. Support the engine by placing wooden blocks between the exhaust manifolds and the front crossmember.

19. Remove the engine front cover.

20. Remove the valve covers.

21. Remove the intake manifold, oil filler pipe, and temperature sending switch.

22. Mark the lifters, pushrods, and rocker arms as to location so that they may be installed in the same position. Remove these parts.

23. If the car is equipped with air conditioning, discharge the A/C system and remove the condenser.

24. Remove the fuel pump eccentric, camshaft gear, oil slinger, and timing chain. Remove the camshaft thrust plate (on front of camshaft) if equipped.

25. Carefully remove the camshaft from the engine.

26. Inspect the shaft for signs of excessive wear or damage.

27. Liberally coat camshaft and bearing with heavy engine oil or engine assembly lubricant and insert the cam into the engine.

28. Align the timing marks on the camshaft and crankshaft gears. See Timing Chain Replacement for details.

29. Install the distributor using the locating marks made during removal. If any problems are encountered, see Distributor Installation.

30. To install, reverse the removal procedure but pay attention to the following points:

 a. Install the timing indicator before installing the power steering pump bracket.

 b. Install the flywheel inspection cover after installing the starter.

 c. Replace the engine oil and radiator coolant.

### 6.2L Diesel Engines

◗ See Figure 149

1. Disconnect the battery.
2. Jack up the truck and safely support it with jackstands.
3. Drain the cooling system, including the block.

### ✳✳CAUTION

**When draining the coolant, keep in mind that cats and dogs are attracted by ethylene glycol antifreeze, and are quite likely to drink any that is left in an uncovered container or in puddles on the ground. This will prove fatal in sufficient quantity. Always drain the coolant into a sealable container. Coolant should be reused unless it is contaminated or several years old.**

4. Disconnect the exhaust pipes at the manifolds. Remove the fan shroud.

5. Lower the truck.

6. Remove the radiator and fan.

7. Remove the vacuum pump, and remove the intake manifolds as previously detailed.

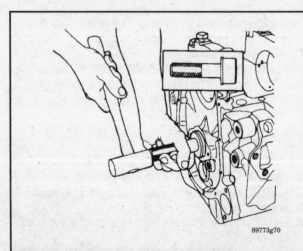

89773g70

**Fig. 149 Installing the front cam bearing on a diesel engine using a common tool (which is illustrated inset). The method is similar on most engines**

8. Remove the injection pump and lines as outlined in Section 5.

Make sure you cap all injection lines to prevent dirt from entering the system, and tag the lines for later installation

9. Remove the water pump.

10. Remove the injection pump drive gear.

11. Scribe a mark aligning the line on the injection pump flange to the front cover.

12. Remove the injection pump from the cover.

13. Remove the power steering pump and the generator and lay them aside.

14. If the truck is equipped with air conditioning, remove the compressor (with the lines attached) and position it out of the way.

## ✳✳CAUTION

**DO NOT disconnect the air conditioning lines.**

15. Remove the valve covers.

16. Remove the rocker shaft assemblies and pushrods. Place the pushrods in order in a rack (easily by punching holes in a piece of heavy cardboard and numbering the holes) so that they can be installed in correct order.

17. Remove the thermostat housing and the crossover from the cylinder heads.

18. Remove the cylinder heads as previously detailed, with the exhaust manifolds attached.

19. Remove the valve lifter clamps, guide plates and valve lifters. Place these parts in a rack so they can be installed in the correct order.

20. Remove the front cover.

21. Remove the timing chain assembly.

22. Remove the fuel pump.

23. Remove the camshaft retainer plate.

24. If the truck is equipped with air conditioning, remove the A/C condenser mounting bolts. Have an assistant help in lifting the condenser out of the way.

25. Remove the camshaft by carefully sliding it out of the block.

Whenever a new camshaft installed, GM recommends replacing all the valve lifters, as well as the oil filter. The engine oil must be changed. These measures will help ensure proper wear characteristics of the new camshaft.

26. Coat the camshaft lobes with Molykote® or an equivalent lube. Liberally tube the camshaft journals with clean engine oil and install the camshaft carefully.

27. Install the camshaft retainer plate and torque the bolts to 20 ft. lbs. (27 Nm).

28. Install the fuel pump.

29. Install the timing chain assembly as previously detailed.

30. Install the front cover as previously detailed.

31. Install the valve lifters, guide plates and clamps, and rotate the crankshaft as previously outlined so that the lifters are free to travel.

32. Install the cylinder heads.

33. Install the pushrods in their original order. Install the rocker shaft assemblies, then install the valve covers.

34. Install the injection pump to the front cover, making sure the lines on the pump and the scribe line on the front cover are aligned.

35. Install the injection pump driven gear, making sure the gears are aligned. Retime the injection pump.

36. Install the remaining engine components in the reverse order of removal. Make the necessary adjustments (drive belts, etc.) and refill the cooling system.

## CAMSHAFT INSPECTION

Completely clean the camshaft with solvent, paying special attention to cleaning the oil holes. Visually inspect the cam lobes and bearing journals for excessive wear. If a lobe is questionable, have the cam checked at a reputable machine shop. If a journal or lobe is worn, the camshaft must be reground or replaced. Also have the camshaft checked for straightness on a dial indicator.

➡If a cam journal is worn, there is a good chance that the bushings are worn.

## Camshaft Bearings

### REMOVAL & INSTALLATION

▶ **See Figures 150 and 151**

If excessive camshaft wear is found, or if the engine is completely rebuilt, the camshaft bearings should be replaced.

➡The front and rear bearings should be removed last, and installed first. Those bearings act as guides for the other bearings and pilot.

1. Drive the camshaft rear plug from the block.

2. Assemble the removal puller with its shoulder on the bearing to be removed. Gradually tighten the puller nut until the bearing is removed.

3. Remove the remaining bearings, leaving the front and rear for last. To remove these, reverse the position of the puller, so as to pull the bearings towards the center of the

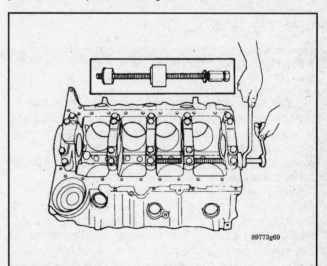

89773g69

**Fig. 150 View of a camshaft bearing removal and installation tool**

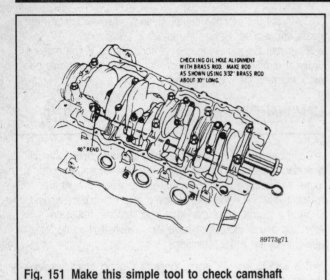

Fig. 151 Make this simple tool to check camshaft bearing oil hole alignment

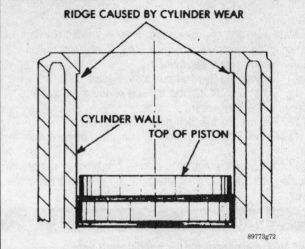

Fig. 152 View of the ridge formed by the piston rings at the top of their travel

Fig. 153 Place rubber hose over the connecting rod studs to protect the crank and bores from damage

block. Leave the tool in this position, pilot the new front and rear bearings on the installer, and pull them into position.

4. Return the puller to its original position and pull the remaining bearings into position.

➡You must make sure that the oil holes of the bearings and block align when installing the bearings. If they don't align, the camshaft will not get proper lubrication and may seize or at least be seriously damaged. To check for correct oil hole alignment, use a piece of brass rod with a 90° bend in the end as shown in the illustration. Check all oil hole openings. The wire must enter each hole, or the hole is not properly aligned.

5. Replace the camshaft rear plug, and stake it into position. On the 6.2L diesel, coat the outer diameter of the new plug with GM sealant #1052080 or equivalent, and install it flush to 1/32 in. (0.794mm) deep.

## Pistons and Connecting Rods

### REMOVAL & INSTALLATION

▶ See Figures 152, 153, 154, 155, 156, 157, 158, 159, 160 and 161

Before removing the pistons, the top of the cylinder bore must be examined for a ridge. A ridge at the top of the bore is the result of normal cylinder wear, caused by the piston rings only traveling so far up the bore in the course of the piston stroke. The ridge can be felt by hand. It must be removed before the pistons are removed.

A ridge reamer is necessary for this operation. Place the piston at the bottom of its stroke, and cover it with a rag. Cut the ridge away with the ridge reamer, using extreme care to avoid cutting too deeply. Remove the rag, and remove the cuttings that remain on the piston with a magnet and a rag soaked in clean oil. Make sure the piston top and cylinder bore are absolutely clean before moving the piston.

1. Remove intake manifold and cylinder head or heads.

2. Remove oil pan.

3. Remove oil pump assembly if necessary.

4. Matchmark the connecting rod cap to the connecting rod with a scribe. Each cap must be reinstalled on its proper rod in the proper direction. Remove the connecting rod bearing cap and the rod bearing. Number the top of each piston with silver paint or a felt tip pen for later assembly.

5. Cut lengths of 3/8 in. (9.53mm) diameter hose to use as rod bolt guides. Install the hose over the threads of the rod bolts, to prevent the bolt threads from damaging the crankshaft journals and cylinder walls when the piston is removed.

6. Squirt some clean engine oil onto the cylinder wall from above, until the wall is coated. Carefully push the piston and rod assembly up and out of the cylinder by tapping on the bottom of the connecting rod with a wooden hammer hand

Place the rod bearing and cap back on the connecting rod, and install the nuts temporarily. Using a number stamp or punch, stamp the cylinder number on the side of the connect-

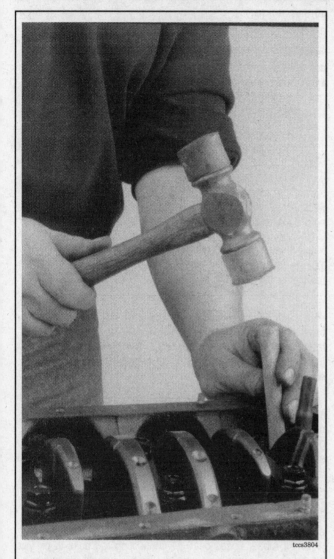

Fig. 154 Carefully tap the piston out of the bore using a wooden dowel

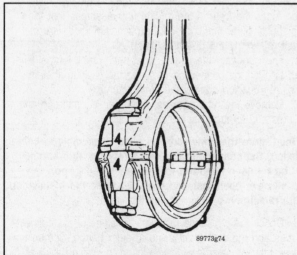

Fig. 155 Match the connecting rods to their cylinders and caps with a number stamp

Fig. 156 Most pistons are marked to indicate positioning in the engine

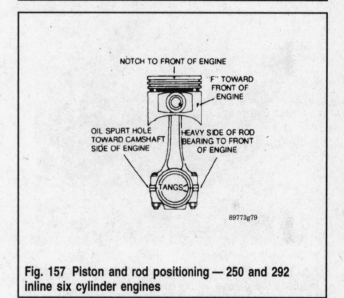

Fig. 157 Piston and rod positioning — 250 and 292 inline six cylinder engines

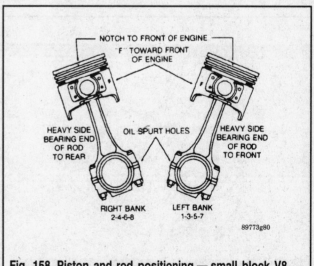

Fig. 158 Piston and rod positioning — small block V8 engine

Fig. 159 Installing the piston into the block using a ring compressor and the handle of a hammer

Fig. 160 The notch on the the side of the bearing cap matches the groove on the bearing insert

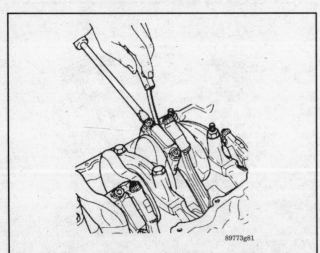

Fig. 161 Use a prytool to spread the connecting rods, then use a feeler gauge to check the connecting rod side clearance

ing rod and cap. This will help keep the proper piston and rod assembly on the proper cylinder.

➡On all V8s, starting at the front the right bank cylinders are 2-4-6-8 and the left bank 1-3-5-7. On the V6 engine even number cylinders 2-4-6 are in the right bank, odd number cylinders 1-3-5 are in the left bank, when viewed from the rear of the engine.

7. Remove remaining pistons in similar manner.

On all gasoline engines, the notch on the piston will face the front of the engine for assembly. The chamfered corners of the bearing caps should face toward the front of the left bank and toward the rear of the right bank, and the boss on the connecting rod should face toward the front of the engine for the right bank and to the rear of the engine on the left bank.

On various engines, the piston compression rings are marked with a dimple, a letter **T**, a letter **O**, **GM** or the word **TOP** to identify the side of the ring which must face toward the top of the piston.

**To install:**

➡In 1985 GM introduced engines with silicone coated pistons. If your engine has these pistons, if replaced, they must be replaced with silicone coated pistons. Substituting another type of piston could reduce the life of the engine.

Install the connecting rod to the piston, making sure piston installation notches and any marks on the rod are in proper relation to one another. Lubricate the wrist pin with clean engine oil, and install the pin into the rod and piston assembly, either by hand or by using a wrist pin press as required. Install snaprings if equipped, and rotate them in their grooves to make sure they are seated. To install the piston and connecting rod assembly:

8. Make sure connecting rod big end bearings (including end cap) are of the correct size and properly installed.

9. Fit rubber hoses over the connecting rod bolts to protect the crankshaft journals, as in the Piston Removal procedure. Coat the rod bearings with clean oil.

10. Using the proper ring compressor, insert the piston assembly into the cylinder so that the notch in the top of the piston faces the front of the engine (this assumes that the dimple(s) or other markings on the connecting rods are in correct relation to the piston notch(s).

11. From beneath the engine, coat each crank journal with clean oil. Pull the connecting rod, with the bearing shell in place, into position against the crank journal.

12. Remove the rubber hoses. Install the bearing cap and cap nuts and torque to specification.

➡When more than one rod and piston assembly is being installed, the connecting rod cap attaching nuts should only be tightened enough to keep each rod in position until all have been installed. This will ease the installation of the remaining piston assemblies.

13. Check the clearance between the sides of the connecting rods and the crankshaft using a feeler gauge. Spread the rods slightly with a screwdriver to insert the gauge. If clearance is below the minimum tolerance, the rod may be machined to provide adequate clearance. If clearance is excessive, substitute an unworn rod, and recheck. If clearance is still

outside specifications, the crankshaft must be welded and reground or replaced.

14. Replace the oil pump if removed and the oil pan.
15. Install the cylinder head(s) and intake manifold.

## Piston Ring and Wrist Pin

### REMOVAL

▶ See Figures 162, 163, 164, 165, 166, 167 and 168

Some of the engines covered in this guide utilize pistons with pressed in wrist pins. These must be removed by a special press designed for this purpose. Other pistons have their wrist pins secured by snaprings, which are easily removed with snapring pliers. Separate the piston from the connecting rod.

A piston ring expander is necessary for removing piston rings without damaging them. Any other method (screwdriver blades, pliers. etc.) usually results in the rings being bent,

Fig. 164 You can use a piece of an old ring to clean the piston grooves, BUT be careful, the ring is sharp

Fig. 162 Use a ring expander tool to remove the piston rings

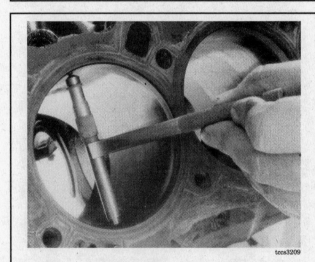
Fig. 165 A telescoping gauge may be used to measure the cylinder bore diameter

Fig. 163 Clean the piston grooves using a ring groove cleaner

Fig. 166 Measure the piston's outer diameter using a micrometer

Fig. 167 Removing cylinder glazing using a flexible hone

Fig. 168 A properly cross-hatched cylinder bore

scratched or distorted, or the piston itself being damaged. When the rings are removed, clean the ring grooves using an appropriate ring groove cleaning tool, using care not to cut too deeply. Thoroughly clean all carbon and varnish from the piston with solvent.

**✳✳CAUTION**

Do not use a wire brush or caustic solvent (acids, etc.) on pistons.

Inspect the pistons for scuffing, scoring, cracks, pitting, or excessive ring groove wear. If these are evident, the piston must be replaced.

The piston should also be checked in relation to the cylinder diameter. Using a telescoping gauge and micrometer, or a dial gauge, measure the cylinder bore diameter perpendicular (90°) to the piston pin, 2 ½ in. (63.5mm) below the cylinder block deck (surface where the block mates with the heads). Then,

with the micrometer, measure the piston perpendicular to its wrist pin on the shirt. The difference between the two measurements is the piston clearance. If the clearance is within specifications or slightly below (after the cylinders have been bored or honed), finish honing is all that is necessary. If the clearance is excessive, try to obtain a slightly larger piston to bring clearance to within specifications. If this is not possible, obtain the first oversize piston and hone (if necessary, bore) the cylinder to size. Generally, if the cylinder bore is tapered 0.005 in. (0.127mm) or more or is out-of-round 0.003 in. (0.0762mm) or more, it is advisable to rebore for the smallest possible oversize piston and rings.

After measuring, mark pistons with a felt tip pen for reference and for assembly.

➡Cylinder honing and/or boring should be performed by a reputable, professional mechanic with the proper equipment. In some cases, cleanup honing can be done with the cylinder block in the car, but most excessive honing and all cylinder boring must be done with the block stripped and removed from the car.

## PISTON RING END-GAP

▶ See Figure 169

Piston ring end-gap should be checked while the rings are removed from the pistons. Incorrect end-gap indicates that the wrong size rings are being used; ring breakage could occur.

Compress the piston rings to be used in a cylinder, one at a time, into that cylinder. Squirt clean oil into the cylinder, so that the rings and the top 2 in. (51mm) of cylinder wall are coated. Using an inverted piston, press the rings approximately 1 in. (25.4mm) below the deck of the block (on diesels, measure ring gap clearance with the ring positioned at the bottom of ring travel in the bore). Measure the ring end-gap with a feeler gauge, and compare to the Ring Gap chart. Carefully pull the ring out of the cylinder and file the ends squarely with a fine file to obtain the proper clearance.

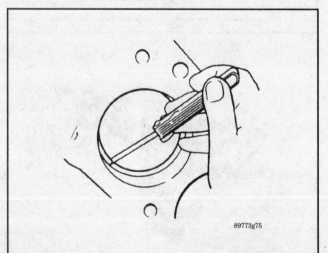

Fig. 169 Checking piston ring end-gap with a feeler gauge

## PISTON RING SIDE CLEARANCE CHECK AND INSTALLATION

▶ See Figures 170, 171, 172 and 173

Check the piston to see that the ring grooves and oil return holes have been properly cleaned. Slide a piston ring into its groove, and check the side clearance with a feeler gauge. On gasoline engines, make sure you insert the gauge between the ring and its lower land (lower edge of the groove), because any wear that occurs forms a step at the inner portion of the lower land. On diesels, insert the gauge between the ring and the upper land. If the piston grooves have worn to the extent that relatively high steps exist on the lower land, the piston should be replaced, because these will interfere with the operation of the new rings and ring clearances will be excessive. Pistons rings are not furnished in oversize widths to compensate for ring groove wear.

Install the rings on the piston, lowest ring first, using a piston ring expander. There is a high risk of breaking or distorting the rings, or scratching the piston, if the rings are installed by hand or other means.

Position the rings on the piston as illustrated. Spacing of the various piston ring gaps is crucial to proper oil retention and even cylinder wear. When installing new rings, refer to the illustration diagram furnished with the new parts.

## Connecting Rod Bearings

Connecting rod bearings for the engine covered in this guide consist of two halves or shells which are interchangable in the rod and cap. When the shells are placed in position, the ends extend slightly beyond the rod and cap surfaces so that when the rod bolts are torqued the shells will be capped tightly in place to insure positive seating and to prevent turning. A tang holds the shells in place.

➡ The ends of the bearing shell must never be filed flush with the mating surface of the rod and cap.

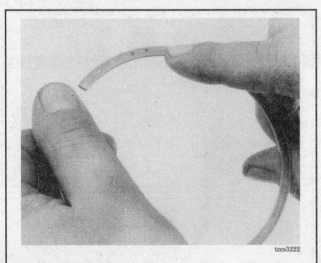

Fig. 170 Most rings are marked to show which side should face upward

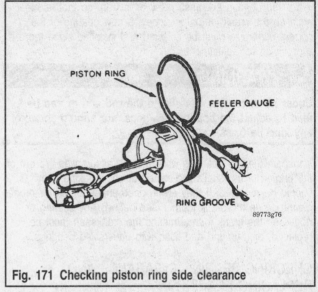

Fig. 171 Checking piston ring side clearance

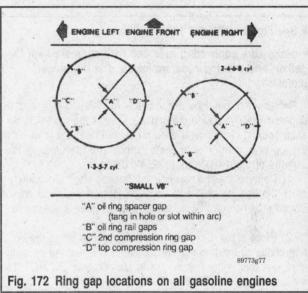

"A" oil ring spacer gap
    (tang in hole or slot within arc)
"B" oil ring rail gaps
"C" 2nd compression ring gap
"D" top compression ring gap

Fig. 172 Ring gap locations on all gasoline engines

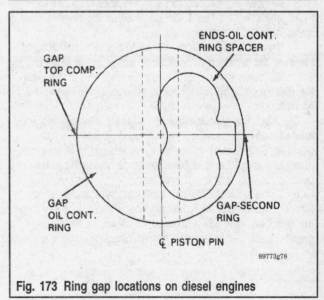

Fig. 173 Ring gap locations on diesel engines

If a rod bearing becomes noisy or is worn so that its clearance on the crank journal is sloppy, a new bearing of the correct undersize must be selected and installed since there is a provision for adjustment.

### ✳✳WARNING

**Under no circumstances should the rod end or cap be filed to adjust the bearing clearance, nor should shims of any kind be used.**

Inspect the rod bearings while the rod assemblies are out of the engine. If the shells are scored or show flaking, they should be replaced. If they are in good shape check for proper clearance on the crank journal (see below). Any scoring or ridges on the crank journal means the crankshaft must be replaced, or reground and fitted with undersized bearings.

## CHECKING BEARING CLEARANCE AND REPLACING BEARINGS

◗ **See Figures 174 and 175**

➡**Make sure connecting rods and their caps are kept together, and that the caps are installed in the proper direction.**

Replacement bearings are available in standard size, and in undersizes for reground crankshafts. Connecting rod-to-crankshaft bearing clearance is checked using Plastigage® at either the top or bottom of each crank journal. The Plastigage® has a range of 0.001-0.003 in. (0.0254-0.0762mm).

1. Remove the rod cap with the bearing shell. Completely clean the bearing shell and the crank journal, and blow any oil from the oil hole in the crankshaft; Plastigage® is soluble in oil.

2. Place a piece of Plastigage® lengthwise along the bottom center of the lower bearing shell, then install the cap with shell and torque the bolt or nuts to specification. DO NOT turn the crankshaft with Plastigage® in the bearing.

3. Remove the bearing cap with the shell. The flattened Plastigage® will be found sticking to either the bearing shell or crank journal. Do not remove it yet.

4. Use the scale printed on the Plastigage® envelope to measure the flattened material at its widest point. The number within the scale which most closely corresponds to the width of the Plastigage® indicates bearing clearance in thousandths of an inch.

5. Check the specifications chart for the desired clearance. It is advisable to install a new bearing if clearance exceeds 0.003 in. (0.0762mm). However, if the bearing is in good condition and is not being checked because of bearing noise, bearing replacement is not necessary.

6. If you are installing new bearings, try a standard size, then each undersize in order until one is found that is within the specified limits when checked for clearance with Plastigage®. Each undersize shell has its size stamped on it.

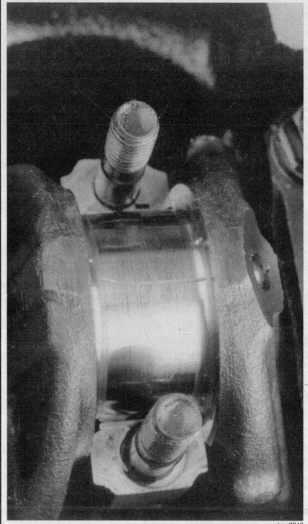

tccs3243

**Fig. 174 Apply a strip of gauging material to the bearing journal, then install and torque the cap**

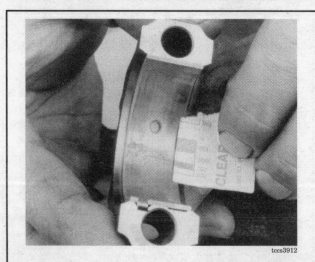

tccs3912

**Fig. 175 After the cap is removed again, use the scale supplied with the gauge material to check clearances**

7. When the proper size shell is found, clean off the Plasti-gage®, oil the bearing thoroughly, reinstall the cap with its shell and torque the rod bolt nuts to specification.

➡With the proper bearing selected and the nuts torqued, it should be possible to move the connecting rod back and forth freely on the crank journal as allowed by the specified connecting rod and clearance. If the rod cannot be moved, either the rod bearing is too far undersize or the rod is misaligned.

## Rear Main Oil Seal

### REMOVAL & INSTALLATION

#### Gasoline Engines

▶ See Figures 176, 177, 178, 179, 180, 181 and 182

Both halves of the rear main oil seal can be replaced without removing the crankshaft. Always replace the upper and lower seal together. The lip should face the front of the engine. Be very careful that you do not break the sealing bead in the channel on the outside portion of the seal while installing it. An installation tool can be fabricated to protect the seal bead.

1. Remove the oil pan, oil pump and rear main bearing cap.

2. Remove the oil seal from the bearing cap by prying it out with a suitable tool.

3. Remove the upper half of the seal with a small punch. Drive it around far enough to be gripped with pliers.

4. Clean the crankshaft and bearing cap.

5. Coat the lips and bead of the seal with light engine oil, keeping oil from the ends of the seal.

6. Position the fabricated tool between the crankshaft and seal seat.

7. Position the seal between the crankshaft and tip of the tool so that the seal bead contacts the tip of the tool. The oil seal lip should face forward.

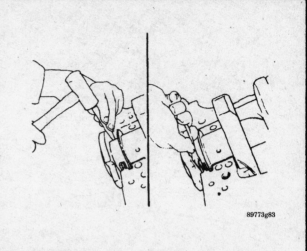

Fig. 177 Removing the upper half of the seal from the block

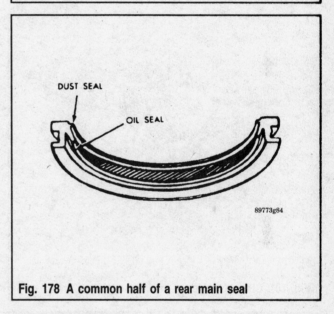

Fig. 178 A common half of a rear main seal

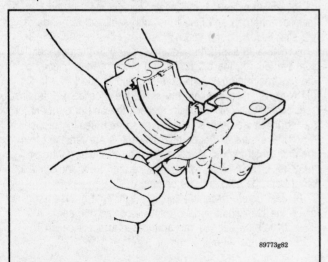

Fig. 176 Remove the seal half from the bearing cap without scratching the cap

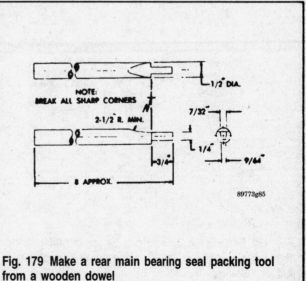

Fig. 179 Make a rear main bearing seal packing tool from a wooden dowel

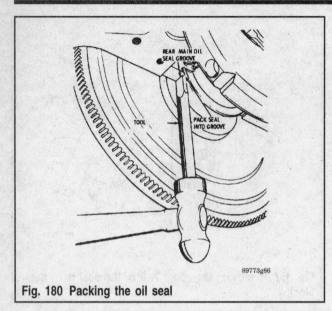

**Fig. 180 Packing the oil seal**

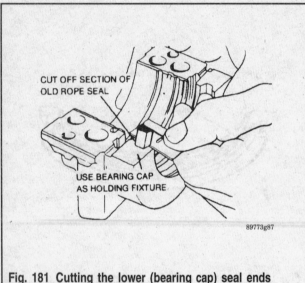

**Fig. 181 Cutting the lower (bearing cap) seal ends**

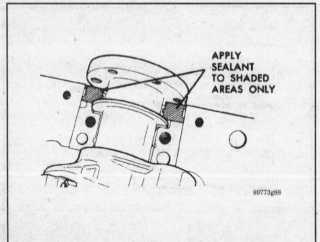

**Fig. 182 Sealing the bearing cap before the final tightening. Apply a bit of oil to the crank journal just before installing the cap**

8. Roll the seal around the crankshaft using the tool to protect the seal bead from the sharp corners of the crankcase.

9. The installation tool should be left installed until the seal is properly positioned with both ends flush with the block.

10. Remove the tool.

11. Install the other half of the seal in the bearing cap using the tool in the same manner as before. Light thumb pressure should install the seal.

12. Install the bearing cap with sealant applied to the mating areas of the cap and block. Keep sealant from the ends of the seal.

13. Torque the main bearing cap retaining bolts to 10-12 ft. lbs. (13-16 Nm). Tap the end of the crankshaft first rearward, then forward with a lead hammer. This will line up the rear main bearing and the crankshaft thrust surfaces. Tighten the main bearing cap to specification.

14. Further installation is the reverse of removal.

**Diesel Engines**

The crankshaft need not be removed to replace the rear main bearing upper oil seal. The lower seal is installed in the bearing cap.

1. Drain the crankcase oil and remove the oil pan and rear main bearing cap.

2. Using a special main seal tool or a tool that can be made from a dowel (see illustration), drive the upper seal into its groove on each side until it is tightly packed. This is usually $\frac{1}{4}$-$\frac{3}{4}$ in. (6.35-19.05mm).

3. Measure the amount the seal was driven up on one side. Add $\frac{1}{16}$ in. (1.5875mm) and cut another length from the old seal. Use the main bearing cap as a holding fixture when cutting the seal as illustrated. Carefully trim protruding seal.

4. Work these two pieces of seal up into the cylinder block on each side with two nailsets or small screwdrivers. Using the packing tool again, pack these pieces into the block, then trim the flush with a razor blade or hobby knife as shown. Do not scratch the bearing surface with the razor.

➡️It may help to use a bit of oil on the short pieces of the rope seal when packing it into the block.

5. Apply Loctite® # 496 sealer or equivalent to the rear main bearing cap and install the rope seal. Cut the ends of the seal flush with the cap.

6. Check to see if the rear main cap with the new seal will seat properly on the block. Place a piece of Plastigage® on the rear main journal, install the cap and torque to 70 ft. lbs. (94 Nm). Remove the cap and check the Plastigage® against specifications. If out of specs, recheck the end of the seal for fraying that may be preventing the cap from seating properly.

7. Make sure all traces of Plastigage® are removed from the crankshaft journal. Apply a thin film of sealer (GM part # 1052357 or equivalent) to the bearing cap. Keep the sealant off of both the seal and the bearing.

8. Just before assembly, apply a light coat of clean engine oil on the crankshaft surface that will contact the seal.

9. Install the bearing cap and torque to specification.

10. Install the oil pump and oil pan.

## Crankshaft and Main Bearings

### REMOVAL

▶ See Figure 183

1. Drain the engine oil and remove the engine from the car. Mount the engine on a work stand in a suitable working area. Invert the engine, so the oil pan is facing up.
2. Remove the engine front (timing) cover.
3. Remove the timing chain and gars.
4. Remove the oil pan.
5. Remove the oil pump.
6. Stamp the cylinder number on the machined surfaces of the bolt bosses of the connecting rods and caps for identification when reinstalling. If the pistons are to be removed eventually from the connecting rod, mark the cylinder number on the pistons with silver paint or felt tip pen for proper cylinder identification and cap-to-rod location.
7. Remove the connecting rod caps. Install lengths of rubber hose on each of the connecting rod bolts, to protect the crank journals when the crank is removed.
8. Mark the main bearing caps with a number punch or punch so that they can be reinstalled in their original positions.
9. Remove all main bearing caps.
10. Note the position of the keyway in the crankshaft so it can be installed in the same position.
11. Install rubber bands between a bolt on each connecting rod and oil pan bolts that have been reinstalled in the block (see illustration). This will keep the rods from banging on the block when the crank is removed.
12. Carefully lift the crankshaft out of the block. The rods will pivot to the center of the engine when the crank is removed.

### CHECKING CLEARANCE

Like connecting rod big end bearings, the crankshaft main bearings are shell type inserts that do not utilize shims and

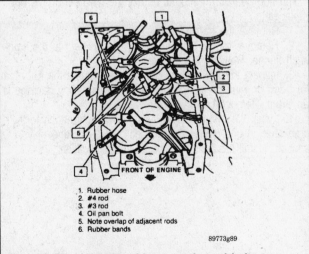

1. Rubber hose
2. #4 rod
3. #3 rod
4. Oil pan bolt
5. Note overlap of adjacent rods
6. Rubber bands

89773g89

**Fig. 183 Place lengths of hose on the rod bolts to protect the crankshaft**

cannot be adjusted. The bearings are available in various standard and undersizes. If main bearing clearance is found to be too sloppy, a new bearing (both upper and lower halves) is required.

➡**Factory undersized crankshafts are marked, sometimes with a 9 and/or a large spot of light green paint. The bearing caps also will have the paint on each side of the undersized journal.**

Generally, the lower half of the bearing shell (except No. 1 bearing) shows greater wear and fatigue. If the lower half only shows the effects of normal wear (no heavy scoring or discoloration), it can usually be assumed that the upper half is also in good shape. Conversely, if the lower half is heavily worn or damaged, both halves should be replaced. Never replace one bearing half without replacing the other.

Main bearing clearance can be checked both with the crankshaft in the car and with the engine out of the car. If the engine block is still in the car, the crankshaft should be supported both front and rear (by the damper and to remove clearance from the upper bearing. Total clearance can then be measured between the lower bearing and journal. If the block has been removed from the car, and is inverted, the crank will rest on the upper bearings and the total clearance can be measured between the lower bearing and journal. Clearance is checked in the same manner as the connecting rod bearings, with Plastigage®.

➡**Crankshaft bearing caps and bearing shells should NEVER be filed flush with the cap-to-block mating surface to adjust for wear in the old bearings. Always install new bearings.**

1. If the crankshaft has been removed, install it (block removed from car). If the block is still in the car, remove the oil pan and oil pump. Starting with the rear bearing cap, remove the cap and wipe all oil from the crank journal and bearing cap.
2. Place a strip of Plastigage® the full width of the bearing, (parallel to the crankshaft), on the journal.

➡**Do not rotate the crankshaft while the gaging material is between the bearing and the journal.**

3. Install the bearing cap and evenly torque the cap bolts to specification.
4. Remove the bearing cap. The flattened Plastigage® will be sticking to either the bearing shell or the crank journal.
5. Use the graduated scale on the Plastigage® envelope to measure the material at its widest point.

➡**If the flattened Plastigage® tapers toward the middle or ends, there is a difference in clearance indicating the bearing or journal has a taper, low spot or other irregularity. If this is indicated, measure the crank journal with a micrometer.**

6. If bearing clearance is within specifications, the bearing insert is in good shape. Replace the insert if the clearance is not within specifications. Always replace both upper and lower inserts as a unit.
7. Standard, 0.001 in. (0.0254mm) or 0.002 in. (0.051mm) undersize bearings should produce the proper clearance. If these sizes still produce too sloppy a fit, the crankshaft must

be reground for use with the next undersize bearing. Recheck all clearances after installing new bearings.

8. Replace the rest of the bearings in the same manner. After all bearings have been checked, rotate the crankshaft to make sure there is no excessive drag. When checking the No. 1 main bearing, loosen the accessory drive belts (engine in car) to prevent a tapered reading with the Plastigage®.

## MAIN BEARING REPLACEMENT

### Engine Out of Vehicle

1. Remove and inspect the crankshaft.
2. Remove the main bearings from the bearing saddles in the cylinder block and main bearing caps.
3. Coat the bearing surfaces of the new, correct size main bearings with clean engine oil and install them in the bearing saddles in the block and in the main bearing caps.
4. Install the crankshaft. See Crankshaft Installation.

### Engine In Vehicle

▶ See Figure 184

1. With the oil pan, oil pump and spark plugs removed, remove the cap from the main bearing needing replacement and remove the bearing from the cap.
2. Make a bearing roll out pin, using a bent cotter pin as shown in the illustration. Install the end of the pin in the oil hole in the crankshaft journal.
3. Rotate the crankshaft clockwise as viewed from the front of the engine. This will roll the upper bearing out of the block.
4. Lube the new upper bearing with clean engine oil and insert the plain (unnotched) end between the crankshaft and

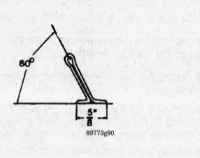

89773g90

Fig. 184 Homemade bearing roll out pin

the indented or notched side of the block. Roll the bearing into place, making sure that the oil holes are aligned. Remove the roll pin from the oil hole.

5. Lube the new lower bearing and install the main bearing cap. Install the main bearing cap, making sure it is positioned in proper direction with the matchmarks in alignment.

6. Torque the main bearing cap bolts to specification.

➡See Crankshaft Installation for thrust bearing alignment.

## CRANKSHAFT END-PLAY AND INSTALLATION

▶ See Figures 185, 186, 187, 188 and 189

When main bearing clearance has been checked, bearings examined and/or replaced, the crankshaft can be installed. Thoroughly clean the upper and lower bearing surfaces, and lube them with clean engine oil. Install the crankshaft and main bearing caps.

Dip all main bearing cap bolts in clean oil, and torque all main bearing caps, excluding the thrust bearing cap, to specifications (see the Crankshaft and Connecting Rod chart to determine which bearing is the thrust bearing). Tighten the thrust bearing bolts finger tight. To align the thrust bearing, pry the crankshaft the extent of its axial travel several times, holding the last movement toward the front of the engine. Add thrust washers if required for proper alignment. Torque the thrust bearing cap to specifications.

To check crankshaft end-play, pry the crankshaft to the extreme rear of its axial travel, then to the extreme front of its travel. Using a feeler gauge, measure the end plat at the front of the rear main bearing. End-play may also be measured at the thrust bearing. Install a new rear main bearing oil seal in the cylinder block and main bearing cap. Continue to reassemble the engine.

## Flywheel and Ring Gear

## REMOVAL & INSTALLATION

The ring gear is an integral part of the flywheel and is not replaceable.

1. Remove the transmission.
2. Remove the six bolts attaching the flywheel to the crankshaft flange. Remove the flywheel.
3. Inspect the flywheel for cracks, and inspect the ring gear for burrs or worn teeth. Replace the flywheel if any damage is apparent. Remove burrs with a mill file.
4. Install the flywheel. The flywheel will only attach to the crankshaft in one position, as the bolt holes are unevenly spaced. Install the bolts and torque to specification.

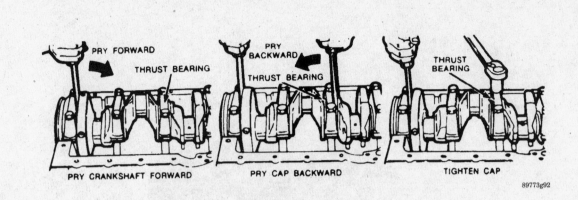

Fig. 185 Aligning the crankshaft thrust bearing

Fig. 186 A dial gauge may be used to check crankshaft end-play

Fig. 187 Carefully pry the shaft back and forth while reading the dial gauge for play

Fig. 188 Mounting a dial gauge to read crankshaft run-out

Fig. 189 Turn the crankshaft slowly by hand while checking the gauge

# EXHAUST SYSTEM

## General Information

➡Safety glasses should be worn at all times when working on or near the exhaust system. Older exhaust systems will almost always be covered with loose rust particles, which will shower you when disturbed. These particles are more than a nuisance and could injure your eye.

Whenever working on the exhaust system always keep the following in mind:
• Check the complete exhaust system for open seams, holes loose connections, or other deterioration which could permit exhaust fumes to seep into the passenger compartment.
• The exhaust system is usually supported by free-hanging rubber mountings which permit some movement of the exhaust system, but does not permit transfer of noise and vibration into the passenger compartment. Do not replace the rubber mounts with solid ones.
• Before removing any component of the exhaust system, ALWAYS squirt a liquid rust dissolving agent onto the fasteners for ease of removal. A lot of knuckle skin will be saved by following this rule. It may even be wise to spray the fasteners and allow them to sit overnight.

### ✳✳CAUTION

Allow the exhaust system to cool sufficiently before spraying a solvent on exhaust fasteners. Some solvents are highly flammable and could ignite when sprayed on hot exhaust components.

• Annoying rattles and noise vibrations in the exhaust system are usually caused by misalignment of the parts. When aligning the system, leave all bolts and nuts loose until all parts are properly aligned, then tighten, working from front to rear.
• When installing exhaust system parts, make sure there is enough clearance between the hot exhaust parts and pipes and hoses that would be adversely affected by excessive heat. Also make sure there is adequate clearance from the floor pan to avoid possible overheating of the floor.

## SPECIAL TOOLS

A number of special exhaust system tools can be rented from auto supply houses or local stores that rent special equipment. A common one is a tail pipe expander, designed to enable you to join pipes of identical diameter.
It may also be quite helpful to use solvents designed to loosen rusted bolts or flanges. Soaking rusted parts the night before you do the job can speed the work of freeing rusted parts considerably. Remember that these solvents are are often flammable. Apply only to parts after they are cool!

## Crossover Pipe

### REMOVAL & INSTALLATION

The crossover pipe (used on V-type engines only) is typically connected to the manifolds by flanged connections or collars. In some cases, bolts that are unthreaded for part of their length are used in conjunction with springs. Make sure you install the springs and that they are in good mechanical condition (no broken coils) when installing the new pipe. Replace ring type seals, also.

## Headpipe

### REMOVAL & INSTALLATION

The headpipe is typically attached to the rear of one exhaust manifold with a flange or collar type connector and flagged to the front of the catalytic converter. Remove nuts and bolts and, if springs are used to maintain the seal, the springs. The pipe may then be separated from the rest of the system at both flanges.

Replace ring seals; inspect springs and replace them if any coils are broken.

## Catalytic Converter

### REMOVAL & INSTALLATION

▶ **See Figure 190**

### ☀☀CAUTION

**Be very careful when working on or near the converter. External temperatures can reach +1,500°F (+816°C) and more, causing severe burns. Removal or installation should only be performed on a cold exhaust system.**

Remove bolts at the flange at the rear end. Then, loosen nuts and remove U-clamp to remove the catalyst. Slide the catalyst out of the outlet pipe. Replace all ring seals. In some cases, you'll have to disconnect an air line coming from the engine compartment before catalyst removal. In some cases, a hanger supports the converter via one of the flange bolts. Make sure the hanger gets properly reconnected. Also, be careful to retain all parts used to heat shield the converter and reinstall them. Make sure the converter is replaced for proper direction of flow and air supply connections.

## Muffler and Tailpipes

### REMOVAL & INSTALLATION

▶ **See Figure 191**

These units are typically connected by flanges at the rear of the converter and at either end of mufflers either by an original

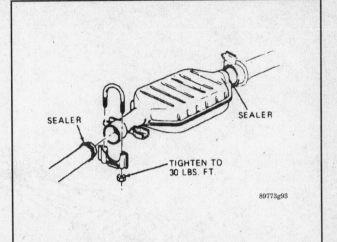

**Fig. 190 View of a catalytic converter mounting — G series**

weld or by U-clamps working over a pipe connection in which one side of the connection is slightly larger than the other. You may have to cut the original connection and use the pipe expander to allow the original equipment exhaust pipe to be fitted over the new muffler. In this case, you'll have to purchase new U-clamps to fasten the joints. GM recommends that whenever you replace a muffler, all parts to the rear of the muffler in the exhaust system must be replaced. Also, all slip joints rearward of the converter should be coated with sealer before they are assembled.

Be careful to connect all U-clamps or other hanger arrangements so the exhaust system will not flex. Assemble all parts loosely and rotate parts inside one another or clamps on the pipes to ensure proper routing of all exhaust system parts to avoid excessive heating of the floorpan, fuel lines and tank, etc. Also, make sure there is clearance to prevent the system from rattling against spring shackles, the differential, etc. You may be able to bend long pipes slightly by hand to help get enough clearance, if necessary.

While disassembling the system, keep your eye open for any leaks or for excessively close clearance to any brake system parts. Inspect the brake system for any sort of heat damage and repair as necessary.

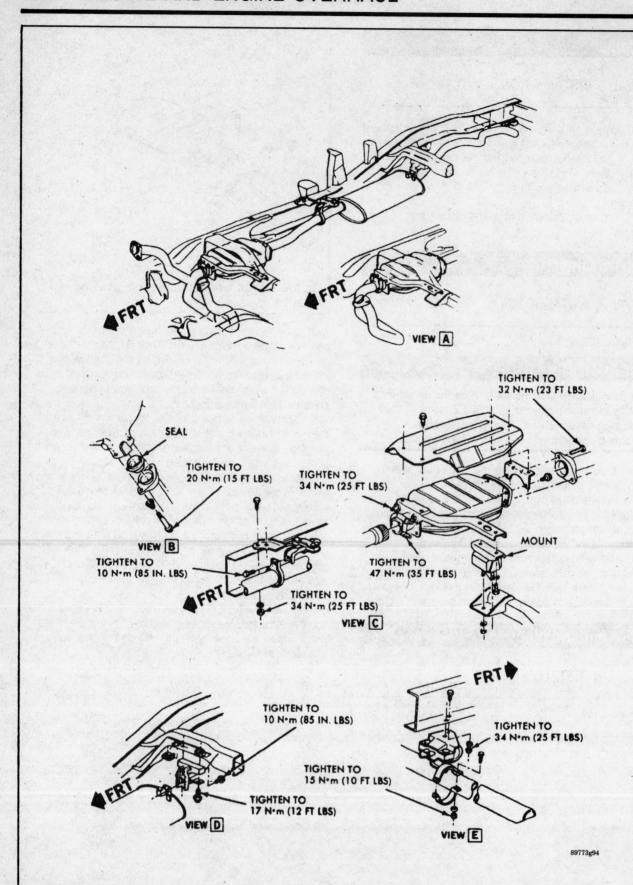

**Fig. 191 Views of the engine exhaust system components**

## USING A VACUUM GAUGE

**White needle = steady needle**  **Dark needle = drifting needle**

The vacuum gauge is one of the most useful and easy-to-use diagnostic tools. It is inexpensive, easy to hook up, and provides valuable information about the condition of your engine.

*Indication: Normal engine in good condition*

Gauge reading: Steady, from 17–22 in./Hg.

*Indication: Sticking valve or ignition miss*

Gauge reading: Needle fluctuates from 15–20 in./Hg. at idle

*Indication: Late ignition or valve timing, low compression, stuck throttle valve, leaking carburetor or manifold gasket.*

Gauge reading: Low (15–20 in./Hg.) but steady

*Indication: Improper carburetor adjustment, or minor intake leak at carburetor or manifold*

*NOTE: Bad fuel injector O-rings may also cause this reading.*

Gauge reading: Drifting needle

*Indication: Weak valve springs, worn valve stem guides, or leaky cylinder head gasket (vibrating excessively at all speeds).*

*NOTE: A plugged catalytic converter may also cause this reading.*

Gauge reading: Needle fluctuates as engine speed increases

*Indication: Burnt valve or improper valve clearance. The needle will drop when the defective valve operates.*

Gauge reading: Steady needle, but drops regularly

*Indication: Choked muffler or obstruction in system. Speed up the engine. Choked muffler will exhibit a slow drop of vacuum to zero.*

Gauge reading: Gradual drop in reading at idle

*Indication: Worn valve guides*

Gauge reading: Needle vibrates excessively at idle, but steadies as engine speed increases

tccs3c01

## Troubleshooting Engine Mechanical Problems

| Problem | Cause | Solution |
|---|---|---|
| External oil leaks | • Cylinder head cover RTV sealant broken or improperly seated | • Replace sealant; inspect cylinder head cover sealant flange and cylinder head sealant surface for distortion and cracks |
| | • Oil filler cap leaking or missing | • Replace cap |
| | • Oil filter gasket broken or improperly seated | • Replace oil filter |
| | • Oil pan side gasket broken, improperly seated or opening in RTV sealant | • Replace gasket or repair opening in sealant; inspect oil pan gasket flange for distortion |
| | • Oil pan front oil seal broken or improperly seated | • Replace seal; inspect timing case cover and oil pan seal flange for distortion |
| | • Oil pan rear oil seal broken or improperly seated | • Replace seal; inspect oil pan rear oil seal flange; inspect rear main bearing cap for cracks, plugged oil return channels, or distortion in seal groove |
| | • Timing case cover oil seal broken or improperly seated | • Replace seal |
| | • Excess oil pressure because of restricted PCV valve | • Replace PCV valve |
| | • Oil pan drain plug loose or has stripped threads | • Repair as necessary and tighten |
| | • Rear oil gallery plug loose | • Use appropriate sealant on gallery plug and tighten |
| | • Rear camshaft plug loose or improperly seated | • Seat camshaft plug or replace and seal, as necessary |
| Excessive oil consumption | • Oil level too high | • Drain oil to specified level |
| | • Oil with wrong viscosity being used | • Replace with specified oil |
| | • PCV valve stuck closed | • Replace PCV valve |
| | • Valve stem oil deflectors (or seals) are damaged, missing, or incorrect type | • Replace valve stem oil deflectors |
| | • Valve stems or valve guides worn | • Measure stem-to-guide clearance and repair as necessary |
| | • Poorly fitted or missing valve cover baffles | • Replace valve cover |
| | • Piston rings broken or missing | • Replace broken or missing rings |
| | • Scuffed piston | • Replace piston |
| | • Incorrect piston ring gap | • Measure ring gap, repair as necessary |
| | • Piston rings sticking or excessively loose in grooves | • Measure ring side clearance, repair as necessary |
| | • Compression rings installed upside down | • Repair as necessary |
| | • Cylinder walls worn, scored, or glazed | • Repair as necessary |

tccs3c02

## Troubleshooting Engine Mechanical Problems

| Problem | Cause | Solution |
|---|---|---|
| Excessive oil consumption (cont.) | • Piston ring gaps not properly staggered | • Repair as necessary |
| | • Excessive main or connecting rod bearing clearance | • Measure bearing clearance, repair as necessary |
| No oil pressure | • Low oil level | • Add oil to correct level |
| | • Oil pressure gauge, warning lamp or sending unit inaccurate | • Replace oil pressure gauge or warning lamp |
| | • Oil pump malfunction | • Replace oil pump |
| | • Oil pressure relief valve sticking | • Remove and inspect oil pressure relief valve assembly |
| | • Oil passages on pressure side of pump obstructed | • Inspect oil passages for obstruction |
| | • Oil pickup screen or tube obstructed | • Inspect oil pickup for obstruction |
| | • Loose oil inlet tube | • Tighten or seal inlet tube |
| Low oil pressure | • Low oil level | • Add oil to correct level |
| | • Inaccurate gauge, warning lamp or sending unit | • Replace oil pressure gauge or warning lamp |
| | • Oil excessively thin because of dilution, poor quality, or improper grade | • Drain and refill crankcase with recommended oil |
| | • Excessive oil temperature | • Correct cause of overheating engine |
| | • Oil pressure relief spring weak or sticking | • Remove and inspect oil pressure relief valve assembly |
| | • Oil inlet tube and screen assembly has restriction or air leak | • Remove and inspect oil inlet tube and screen assembly. (Fill inlet tube with lacquer thinner to locate leaks.) |
| | • Excessive oil pump clearance | • Measure clearances |
| | • Excessive main, rod, or camshaft bearing clearance | • Measure bearing clearances, repair as necessary |
| High oil pressure | • Improper oil viscosity | • Drain and refill crankcase with correct viscosity oil |
| | • Oil pressure gauge or sending unit inaccurate | • Replace oil pressure gauge |
| | • Oil pressure relief valve sticking closed | • Remove and inspect oil pressure relief valve assembly |
| Main bearing noise | • Insufficient oil supply | • Inspect for low oil level and low oil pressure |
| | • Main bearing clearance excessive | • Measure main bearing clearance, repair as necessary |
| | • Bearing insert missing | • Replace missing insert |
| | • Crankshaft end-play excessive | • Measure end-play, repair as necessary |
| | • Improperly tightened main bearing cap bolts | • Tighten bolts with specified torque |
| | • Loose flywheel or drive plate | • Tighten flywheel or drive plate attaching bolts |
| | • Loose or damaged vibration damper | • Repair as necessary |

tccs3c03

## Troubleshooting Engine Mechanical Problems

| Problem | Cause | Solution |
|---|---|---|
| Connecting rod bearing noise | • Insufficient oil supply | • Inspect for low oil level and low oil pressure |
| | • Carbon build-up on piston | • Remove carbon from piston crown |
| | • Bearing clearance excessive or bearing missing | • Measure clearance, repair as necessary |
| | • Crankshaft connecting rod journal out-of-round | • Measure journal dimensions, repair or replace as necessary |
| | • Misaligned connecting rod or cap | • Repair as necessary |
| | • Connecting rod bolts tightened improperly | • Tighten bolts with specified torque |
| Piston noise | • Piston-to-cylinder wall clearance excessive (scuffed piston) | • Measure clearance and examine piston |
| | • Cylinder walls excessively tapered or out-of-round | • Measure cylinder wall dimensions, rebore cylinder |
| | • Piston ring broken | • Replace all rings on piston |
| | • Loose or seized piston pin | • Measure piston-to-pin clearance, repair as necessary |
| | • Connecting rods misaligned | • Measure rod alignment, straighten or replace |
| | • Piston ring side clearance excessively loose or tight | • Measure ring side clearance, repair as necessary |
| | • Carbon build-up on piston is excessive | • Remove carbon from piston |
| Valve actuating component noise | • Insufficient oil supply | • Check for:<br>(a) Low oil level<br>(b) Low oil pressure<br>(c) Wrong hydraulic tappets<br>(d) Restricted oil gallery<br>(e) Excessive tappet to bore clearance |
| | • Rocker arms or pivots worn | • Replace worn rocker arms or pivots |
| | • Foreign objects or chips in hydraulic tappets | • Clean tappets |
| | • Excessive tappet leak-down | • Replace valve tappet |
| | • Tappet face worn | • Replace tappet; inspect corresponding cam lobe for wear |
| | • Broken or cocked valve springs | • Properly seat cocked springs; replace broken springs |
| | • Stem-to-guide clearance excessive | • Measure stem-to-guide clearance, repair as required |
| | • Valve bent | • Replace valve |
| | • Loose rocker arms | • Check and repair as necessary |
| | • Valve seat runout excessive | • Regrind valve seat/valves |
| | • Missing valve lock | • Install valve lock |
| | • Excessive engine oil | • Correct oil level |

tccs3c04

## Troubleshooting Engine Performance

| Problem | Cause | Solution |
| --- | --- | --- |
| Hard starting (engine cranks normally) | • Faulty engine control system component | • Repair or replace as necessary |
| | • Faulty fuel pump | • Replace fuel pump |
| | • Faulty fuel system component | • Repair or replace as necessary |
| | • Faulty ignition coil | • Test and replace as necessary |
| | • Improper spark plug gap | • Adjust gap |
| | • Incorrect ignition timing | • Adjust timing |
| | • Incorrect valve timing | • Check valve timing; repair as necessary |
| Rough idle or stalling | • Incorrect curb or fast idle speed | • Adjust curb or fast idle speed (If possible) |
| | • Incorrect ignition timing | • Adjust timing to specification |
| | • Improper feedback system operation | • Refer to Chapter 4 |
| | • Faulty EGR valve operation | • Test EGR system and replace as necessary |
| | • Faulty PCV valve air flow | • Test PCV valve and replace as necessary |
| | • Faulty TAC vacuum motor or valve | • Repair as necessary |
| | • Air leak into manifold vacuum | • Inspect manifold vacuum connections and repair as necessary |
| | • Faulty distributor rotor or cap | • Replace rotor or cap (Distributor systems only) |
| | • Improperly seated valves | • Test cylinder compression, repair as necessary |
| | • Incorrect ignition wiring | • Inspect wiring and correct as necessary |
| | • Faulty ignition coil | • Test coil and replace as necessary |
| | • Restricted air vent or idle passages | • Clean passages |
| | • Restricted air cleaner | • Clean or replace air cleaner filter element |
| Faulty low-speed operation | • Restricted idle air vents and passages | • Clean air vents and passages |
| | • Restricted air cleaner | • Clean or replace air cleaner filter element |
| | • Faulty spark plugs | • Clean or replace spark plugs |
| | • Dirty, corroded, or loose ignition secondary circuit wire connections | • Clean or tighten secondary circuit wire connections |
| | • Improper feedback system operation | • Refer to Chapter 4 |
| | • Faulty ignition coil high voltage wire | • Replace ignition coil high voltage wire (Distributor systems only) |
| | • Faulty distributor cap | • Replace cap (Distributor systems only) |
| Faulty acceleration | • Incorrect ignition timing | • Adjust timing |
| | • Faulty fuel system component | • Repair or replace as necessary |
| | • Faulty spark plug(s) | • Clean or replace spark plug(s) |
| | • Improperly seated valves | • Test cylinder compression, repair as necessary |
| | • Faulty ignition coil | • Test coil and replace as necessary |

tccs3c05

## Troubleshooting Engine Performance

| Problem | Cause | Solution |
| --- | --- | --- |
| Faulty acceleration (cont.) | • Improper feedback system operation | • Refer to Chapter 4 |
| Faulty high speed operation | • Incorrect ignition timing<br>• Faulty advance mechanism | • Adjust timing (if possible)<br>• Check advance mechanism and repair as necessary (Distributor systems only) |
| | • Low fuel pump volume<br>• Wrong spark plug air gap or wrong plug | • Replace fuel pump<br>• Adjust air gap or install correct plug |
| | • Partially restricted exhaust manifold, exhaust pipe, catalytic converter, muffler, or tailpipe | • Eliminate restriction |
| | • Restricted vacuum passages<br>• Restricted air cleaner | • Clean passages<br>• Cleaner or replace filter element as necessary |
| | • Faulty distributor rotor or cap | • Replace rotor or cap (Distributor systems only) |
| | • Faulty ignition coil<br>• Improperly seated valve(s) | • Test coil and replace as necessary<br>• Test cylinder compression, repair as necessary |
| | • Faulty valve spring(s) | • Inspect and test valve spring tension, replace as necessary |
| | • Incorrect valve timing | • Check valve timing and repair as necessary |
| | • Intake manifold restricted | • Remove restriction or replace manifold |
| | • Worn distributor shaft | • Replace shaft (Distributor systems only) |
| | • Improper feedback system operation | • Refer to Chapter 4 |
| Misfire at all speeds | • Faulty spark plug(s)<br>• Faulty spark plug wire(s)<br>• Faulty distributor cap or rotor | • Clean or relace spark plug(s)<br>• Replace as necessary<br>• Replace cap or rotor (Distributor systems only) |
| | • Faulty ignition coil<br>• Primary ignition circuit shorted or open intermittently<br>• Improperly seated valve(s) | • Test coil and replace as necessary<br>• Troubleshoot primary circuit and repair as necessary<br>• Test cylinder compression, repair as necessary |
| | • Faulty hydraulic tappet(s)<br>• Improper feedback system operation | • Clean or replace tappet(s)<br>• Refer to Chapter 4 |
| | • Faulty valve spring(s) | • Inspect and test valve spring tension, repair as necessary |
| | • Worn camshaft lobes<br>• Air leak into manifold | • Replace camshaft<br>• Check manifold vacuum and repair as necessary |
| | • Fuel pump volume or pressure low<br>• Blown cylinder head gasket<br>• Intake or exhaust manifold passage(s) restricted | • Replace fuel pump<br>• Replace gasket<br>• Pass chain through passage(s) and repair as necessary |
| Power not up to normal | • Incorrect ignition timing<br>• Faulty distributor rotor | • Adjust timing<br>• Replace rotor (Distributor systems only) |

## Troubleshooting Engine Performance

| Problem | Cause | Solution |
|---|---|---|
| Power not up to normal (cont.) | • Incorrect spark plug gap | • Adjust gap |
| | • Faulty fuel pump | • Replace fuel pump |
| | • Faulty fuel pump | • Replace fuel pump |
| | • Incorrect valve timing | • Check valve timing and repair as necessary |
| | • Faulty ignition coil | • Test coil and replace as necessary |
| | • Faulty ignition wires | • Test wires and replace as necessary |
| | • Improperly seated valves | • Test cylinder compression and repair as necessary |
| | • Blown cylinder head gasket | • Replace gasket |
| | • Leaking piston rings | • Test compression and repair as necessary |
| | • Improper feedback system operation | • Refer to Chapter 4 |
| Intake backfire | • Improper ignition timing | • Adjust timing |
| | • Defective EGR component | • Repair as necessary |
| | • Defective TAC vacuum motor or valve | • Repair as necessary |
| Exhaust backfire | • Air leak into manifold vacuum | • Check manifold vacuum and repair as necessary |
| | • Faulty air injection diverter valve | • Test diverter valve and replace as necessary |
| | • Exhaust leak | • Locate and eliminate leak |
| Ping or spark knock | • Incorrect ignition timing | • Adjust timing |
| | • Distributor advance malfunction | • Inspect advance mechanism and repair as necessary (Distributor systems only) |
| | • Excessive combustion chamber deposits | • Remove with combustion chamber cleaner |
| | • Air leak into manifold vacuum | • Check manifold vacuum and repair as necessary |
| | • Excessively high compression | • Test compression and repair as necessary |
| | • Fuel octane rating excessively low | • Try alternate fuel source |
| | • Sharp edges in combustion chamber | • Grind smooth |
| | • EGR valve not functioning properly | • Test EGR system and replace as necessary |
| Surging (at cruising to top speeds) | • Low fuel pump pressure or volume | • Replace fuel pump |
| | • Improper PCV valve air flow | • Test PCV valve and replace as necessary |
| | • Air leak into manifold vacuum | • Check manifold vacuum and repair as necessary |
| | • Incorrect spark advance | • Test and replace as necessary |
| | • Restricted fuel filter | • Replace fuel filter |
| | • Restricted air cleaner | • Clean or replace air cleaner filter element |
| | • EGR valve not functioning properly | • Test EGR system and replace as necessary |
| | • Improper feedback system operation | • Refer to Chapter 4 |

## Troubleshooting the Serpentine Drive Belt

| Problem | Cause | Solution |
|---|---|---|
| Tension sheeting fabric failure (woven fabric on outside circumference of belt has cracked or separated from body of belt) | • Grooved or backside idler pulley diameters are less than minimum recommended<br>• Tension sheeting contacting (rubbing) stationary object<br>• Excessive heat causing woven fabric to age<br>• Tension sheeting splice has fractured | • Replace pulley(s) not conforming to specification<br>• Correct rubbing condition<br>• Replace belt<br>• Replace belt |
| Noise (objectional squeal, squeak, or rumble is heard or felt while drive belt is in operation) | • Belt slippage<br>• Bearing noise<br>• Belt misalignment<br>• Belt-to-pulley mismatch<br>• Driven component inducing vibration<br>• System resonant frequency inducing vibration | • Adjust belt<br>• Locate and repair<br>• Align belt/pulley(s)<br>• Install correct belt<br>• Locate defective driven component and repair<br>• Vary belt tension within specifications. Replace belt. |
| Rib chunking (one or more ribs has separated from belt body) | • Foreign objects imbedded in pulley grooves<br>• Installation damage<br>• Drive loads in excess of design specifications<br>• Insufficient internal belt adhesion | • Remove foreign objects from pulley grooves<br>• Replace belt<br>• Adjust belt tension<br>• Replace belt |
| Rib or belt wear (belt ribs contact bottom of pulley grooves) | • Pulley(s) misaligned<br>• Mismatch of belt and pulley groove widths<br>• Abrasive environment<br>• Rusted pulley(s)<br>• Sharp or jagged pulley groove tips<br>• Rubber deteriorated | • Align pulley(s)<br>• Replace belt<br>• Replace belt<br>• Clean rust from pulley(s)<br>• Replace pulley<br>• Replace belt |
| Longitudinal belt cracking (cracks between two ribs) | • Belt has mistracked from pulley groove<br>• Pulley groove tip has worn away rubber-to-tensile member | • Replace belt<br>• Replace belt |
| Belt slips | • Belt slipping because of insufficient tension<br>• Belt or pulley subjected to substance (belt dressing, oil, ethylene glycol) that has reduced friction<br>• Driven component bearing failure<br>• Belt glazed and hardened from heat and excessive slippage | • Adjust tension<br>• Replace belt and clean pulleys<br>• Replace faulty component bearing<br>• Replace belt |
| "Groove jumping" (belt does not maintain correct position on pulley, or turns over and/or runs off pulleys) | • Insufficient belt tension<br>• Pulley(s) not within design tolerance<br>• Foreign object(s) in grooves | • Adjust belt tension<br>• Replace pulley(s)<br>• Remove foreign objects from grooves |

## Troubleshooting the Cooling System

| Problem | Cause | Solution |
|---|---|---|
| High temperature gauge indication— overheating | • Coolant level low<br>• Improper fan operation<br>• Radiator hose(s) collapsed<br>• Radiator airflow blocked<br><br>• Faulty pressure cap<br>• Ignition timing incorrect<br>• Air trapped in cooling system<br>• Heavy traffic driving<br><br>• Incorrect cooling system component(s) installed<br>• Faulty thermostat<br>• Water pump shaft broken or impeller loose<br>• Radiator tubes clogged<br>• Cooling system clogged<br>• Casting flash in cooling passages<br><br>• Brakes dragging<br>• Excessive engine friction<br>• Antifreeze concentration over 68%<br><br>• Missing air seals<br>• Faulty gauge or sending unit<br><br>• Loss of coolant flow caused by leakage or foaming<br>• Viscous fan drive failed | • Replenish coolant<br>• Repair or replace as necessary<br>• Replace hose(s)<br>• Remove restriction (bug screen, fog lamps, etc.)<br>• Replace pressure cap<br>• Adjust ignition timing<br>• Purge air<br>• Operate at fast idle in neutral intermittently to cool engine<br>• Install proper component(s)<br><br>• Replace thermostat<br>• Replace water pump<br><br>• Flush radiator<br>• Flush system<br>• Repair or replace as necessary. Flash may be visible by removing cooling system components or removing core plugs.<br>• Repair brakes<br>• Repair engine<br>• Lower antifreeze concentration percentage<br>• Replace air seals<br>• Repair or replace faulty component<br>• Repair or replace leaking component, replace coolant<br>• Replace unit |
| Low temperature indication— undercooling | • Thermostat stuck open<br>• Faulty gauge or sending unit | • Replace thermostat<br>• Repair or replace faulty component |
| Coolant loss—boilover | • Overfilled cooling system<br>• Quick shutdown after hard (hot) run<br>• Air in system resulting in occasional "burping" of coolant<br>• Insufficient antifreeze allowing coolant boiling point to be too low<br>• Antifreeze deteriorated because of age or contamination<br>• Leaks due to loose hose clamps, loose nuts, bolts, drain plugs, faulty hoses, or defective radiator | • Reduce coolant level to proper specification<br>• Allow engine to run at fast idle prior to shutdown<br>• Purge system<br>• Add antifreeze to raise boiling point<br>• Replace coolant<br>• Pressure test system to locate source of leak(s) then repair as necessary |

tccs3c11

## Troubleshooting the Cooling System (cont.)

| Problem | Cause | Solution |
|---|---|---|
| Coolant loss—boilover | • Faulty head gasket<br>• Cracked head, manifold, or block<br>• Faulty radiator cap | • Replace head gasket<br>• Replace as necessary<br>• Replace cap |
| Coolant entry into crankcase or cylinder(s) | • Faulty head gasket<br>• Crack in head, manifold or block | • Replace head gasket<br>• Replace as necessary |
| Coolant recovery system inoperative | • Coolant level low<br>• Leak in system<br><br>• Pressure cap not tight or seal missing, or leaking<br>• Pressure cap defective<br>• Overflow tube clogged or leaking<br>• Recovery bottle vent restricted | • Replenish coolant to FULL mark<br>• Pressure test to isolate leak and repair as necessary<br>• Repair as necessary<br><br>• Replace cap<br>• Repair as necessary<br>• Remove restriction |
| Noise | • Fan contacting shroud<br><br><br>• Loose water pump impeller<br>• Glazed fan belt<br>• Loose fan belt<br>• Rough surface on drive pulley<br>• Water pump bearing worn<br><br>• Belt alignment | • Reposition shroud and inspect engine mounts (on electric fans inspect assembly)<br>• Replace pump<br>• Apply silicone or replace belt<br>• Adjust fan belt tension<br>• Replace pulley<br>• Remove belt to isolate. Replace pump.<br>• Check pulley alignment. Repair as necessary. |
| No coolant flow through heater core | • Restricted return inlet in water pump<br>• Heater hose collapsed or restricted<br>• Restricted heater core<br>• Restricted outlet in thermostat housing<br>• Intake manifold bypass hole in cylinder head restricted<br>• Faulty heater control valve<br>• Intake manifold coolant passage restricted | • Remove restriction<br><br>• Remove restriction or replace hose<br>• Remove restriction or replace core<br>• Remove flash or restriction<br><br>• Remove restriction<br><br>• Replace valve<br>• Remove restriction or replace intake manifold |

NOTE: *Immediately after shutdown, the engine enters a condition known as heat soak. This is caused by the cooling system being inoperative while engine temperature is still high. If coolant temperature rises above boiling point, expansion and pressure may push some coolant out of the radiator overflow tube. If this does not occur frequently it is considered normal.*

tccs3c12

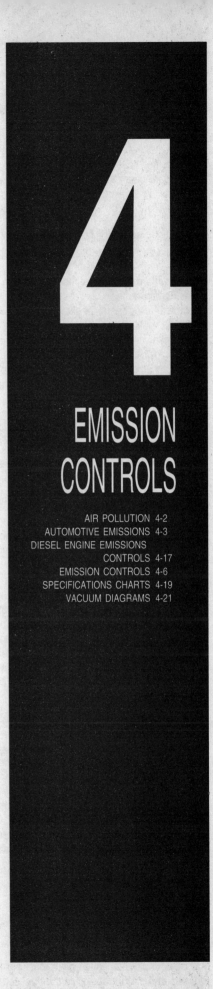

# 4

# EMISSION
# CONTROLS

## AIR POLLUTION

The earth's atmosphere, at or near sea level, consists approximately of 78 percent nitrogen, 21 percent oxygen and 1 percent other gases. If it were possible to remain in this state, 100 percent clean air would result. However, many varied sources allow other gases and particulates to mix with the clean air, causing our atmosphere to become unclean or polluted.

Some of these pollutants are visible while others are invisible, with each having the capability of causing distress to the eyes, ears, throat, skin and respiratory system. Should these pollutants become concentrated in a specific area and under certain conditions, death could result due to the displacement or chemical change of the oxygen content in the air. These pollutants can also cause great damage to the environment and to the many man made objects that are exposed to the elements.

To better understand the causes of air pollution, the pollutants can be categorized into 3 separate types, natural, industrial and automotive.

### Natural Pollutants

Natural pollution has been present on earth since before man appeared and continues to be a factor when discussing air pollution, although it causes only a small percentage of the overall pollution problem. It is the direct result of decaying organic matter, wind born smoke and particulates from such natural events as plain and forest fires (ignited by heat or lightning), volcanic ash, sand and dust which can spread over a large area of the countryside.

Such a phenomenon of natural pollution has been seen in the form of volcanic eruptions, with the resulting plume of smoke, steam and volcanic ash blotting out the sun's rays as it spreads and rises higher into the atmosphere. As it travels into the atmosphere the upper air currents catch and carry the smoke and ash, while condensing the steam back into water vapor. As the water vapor, smoke and ash travel on their journey, the smoke dissipates into the atmosphere while the ash and moisture settle back to earth in a trail hundreds of miles long. In some cases, lives are lost and millions of dollars of property damage result.

### Industrial Pollutants

Industrial pollution is caused primarily by industrial processes, the burning of coal, oil and natural gas, which in turn produce smoke and fumes. Because the burning fuels contain large amounts of sulfur, the principal ingredients of smoke and fumes are sulfur dioxide and particulate matter. This type of pollutant occurs most severely during still, damp and cool weather, such as at night. Even in its less severe form, this pollutant is not confined to just cities. Because of air movements, the pollutants move for miles over the surrounding countryside, leaving in its path a barren and unhealthy environment for all living things.

Working with Federal, State and Local mandated regulations and by carefully monitoring emissions, big business has greatly reduced the amount of pollutant introduced from its industrial sources, striving to obtain an acceptable level. Because of the mandated industrial emission clean up, many land areas and streams in and around the cities that were formerly barren of vegetation and life, have now begun to move back in the direction of nature's intended balance.

### Automotive Pollutants

The third major source of air pollution is automotive emissions. The emissions from the internal combustion engines were not an appreciable problem years ago because of the small number of registered vehicles and the nation's small highway system. However, during the early 1950's, the trend of the American people was to move from the cities to the surrounding suburbs. This caused an immediate problem in transportation because the majority of suburbs were not afforded mass transit conveniences. This lack of transportation created an attractive market for the automobile manufacturers, which resulted in a dramatic increase in the number of vehicles produced and sold, along with a marked increase in highway construction between cities and the suburbs. Multi-vehicle families emerged with a growing emphasis placed on an individual vehicle per family member. As the increase in vehicle ownership and usage occurred, so did pollutant levels in and around the cities, as suburbanites drove daily to their businesses and employment, returning at the end of the day to their homes in the suburbs.

It was noted that a smoke and fog type haze was being formed and at times, remained in suspension over the cities, taking time to dissipate. At first this "smog," derived from the words "smoke" and "fog," was thought to result from industrial pollution but it was determined that automobile emissions shared the blame. It was discovered that when normal automobile emissions were exposed to sunlight for a period of time, complex chemical reactions would take place.

It is now known that smog is a photo chemical layer which develops when certain oxides of nitrogen (NOx) and unburned hydrocarbons (HC) from automobile emissions are exposed to sunlight. Pollution was more severe when smog would become stagnant over an area in which a warm layer of air settled over the top of the cooler air mass, trapping and holding the cooler mass at ground level. The trapped cooler air would keep the emissions from being dispersed and diluted through normal air flows. This type of air stagnation was given the name "Temperature Inversion."

## TEMPERATURE INVERSION

In normal weather situations, surface air is warmed by heat radiating from the earth's surface and the sun's rays. This causes it to rise upward, into the atmosphere. Upon rising it will cool through a convection type heat exchange with the cooler upper air. As warm air rises, the surface pollutants are carried upward and dissipated into the atmosphere.

When a temperature inversion occurs, we find the higher air is no longer cooler, but is warmer than the surface air, causing the cooler surface air to become trapped. This warm air blanket can extend from above ground level to a few hundred or even a few thousand feet into the air. As the surface air is trapped, so are the pollutants, causing a severe smog condition. Should this stagnant air mass extend to a few thousand feet high, enough air movement with the inversion takes place to allow the smog layer to rise above ground level but the pollutants still cannot dissipate. This inversion can remain for days over an area, with the smog level only rising or lowering from ground level to a few hundred feet high. Meanwhile, the pollutant levels increase, causing eye irritation, respiratory problems, reduced visibility, plant damage and in some cases, even disease.

This inversion phenomenon was first noted in the Los Angeles, California area. The city lies in terrain resembling a basin and with certain weather conditions, a cold air mass is held in the basin while a warmer air mass covers it like a lid.

Because this type of condition was first documented as prevalent in the Los Angeles area, this type of trapped pollution was named Los Angeles Smog, although it occurs in other areas where a large concentration of automobiles are used and the air remains stagnant for any length of time.

## HEAT TRANSFER

Consider the internal combustion engine as a machine in which raw materials must be placed so a finished product comes out. As in any machine operation, a certain amount of wasted material is formed. When we relate this to the internal combustion engine, we find that through the input of air and fuel, we obtain power during the combustion process to drive the vehicle. The by-product or waste of this power is, in part, heat and exhaust gases with which we must dispose.

The heat from the combustion process can rise to over 4000°F (2204°C). The dissipation of this heat is controlled by a ram air effect, the use of cooling fans to cause air flow and a liquid coolant solution surrounding the combustion area to transfer the heat of combustion through the cylinder walls and into the coolant. The coolant is then directed to a thin-finned, multi-tubed radiator, from which the excess heat is transferred to the atmosphere by 1 of the 3 heat transfer methods, conduction, convection or radiation.

The cooling of the combustion area is an important part in the control of exhaust emissions. To understand the behavior of the combustion and transfer of its heat, consider the air/fuel charge. It is ignited and the flame front burns progressively across the combustion chamber until the burning charge reaches the cylinder walls. Some of the fuel in contact with the walls is not hot enough to burn, thereby snuffing out or quenching the combustion process. This leaves unburned fuel in the combustion chamber. This unburned fuel is then forced out of the cylinder and into the exhaust system, along with the exhaust gases.

Many attempts have been made to minimize the amount of unburned fuel in the combustion chambers due to quenching, by increasing the coolant temperature and lessening the contact area of the coolant around the combustion area. However, design limitations within the combustion chambers prevent the complete burning of the air/fuel charge, so a certain amount of the unburned fuel is still expelled into the exhaust system, regardless of modifications to the engine.

## AUTOMOTIVE EMISSIONS

Before emission controls were mandated on internal combustion engines, other sources of engine pollutants were discovered along with the exhaust emissions. It was determined that engine combustion exhaust produced approximately 60 percent of the total emission pollutants, fuel evaporation from the fuel tank and carburetor vents produced 20 percent, with the final 20 percent being produced through the crankcase as a by-product of the combustion process.

### Exhaust Gases

The exhaust gases emitted into the atmosphere are a combination of burned and unburned fuel. To understand the exhaust emission and its composition, we must review some basic chemistry.

When the air/fuel mixture is introduced into the engine, we are mixing air, composed of nitrogen (78 percent), oxygen (21 percent) and other gases (1 percent) with the fuel, which is 100 percent hydrocarbons (HC), in a semi-controlled ratio. As the combustion process is accomplished, power is produced to move the vehicle while the heat of combustion is transferred to the cooling system. The exhaust gases are then composed of nitrogen, a diatomic gas ($N_2$), the same as was introduced in the engine, carbon dioxide ($CO_2$), the same gas that is used in beverage carbonation, and water vapor ($H_2O$). The nitrogen ($N_2$), for the most part, passes through the engine unchanged, while the oxygen ($O_2$) reacts (burns) with the hydrocarbons (HC) and produces the carbon dioxide ($CO_2$) and the water vapors ($H_2O$). If this chemical process would be the only process to take place, the exhaust emissions would be harmless. However, during the combustion process, other compounds are formed which are considered dangerous. These pollutants are hydrocarbons (HC), carbon monoxide (CO), oxides of nitrogen (NOx) oxides of sulfur (SOx) and engine particulates.

## HYDROCARBONS

Hydrocarbons (HC) are essentially fuel which was not burned during the combustion process or which has escaped into the atmosphere through fuel evaporation. The main sources of incomplete combustion are rich air/fuel mixtures, low engine temperatures and improper spark timing. The main sources of hydrocarbon emission through fuel evaporation on most vehicles used to be the vehicle's fuel tank and carburetor float bowl.

To reduce combustion hydrocarbon emission, engine modifications were made to minimize dead space and surface area in the combustion chamber. In addition, the air/fuel mixture was made more lean through the improved control which feedback carburetion and fuel injection offers and by the addition of external controls to aid in further combustion of the hydrocarbons outside the engine. Two such methods were the addition of air injection systems, to inject fresh air into the exhaust manifolds and the installation of catalytic converters, units that are able to burn traces of hydrocarbons without affecting the internal combustion process or fuel economy.

To control hydrocarbon emissions through fuel evaporation, modifications were made to the fuel tank to allow storage of the fuel vapors during periods of engine shut-down. Modifications were also made to the air intake system so that at specific times during engine operation, these vapors may be purged and burned by blending them with the air/fuel mixture.

## CARBON MONOXIDE

Carbon monoxide is formed when not enough oxygen is present during the combustion process to convert carbon (C) to carbon dioxide ($CO_2$). An increase in the carbon monoxide (CO) emission is normally accompanied by an increase in the hydrocarbon (HC) emission because of the lack of oxygen to completely burn all of the fuel mixture.

Carbon monoxide (CO) also increases the rate at which the photo chemical smog is formed by speeding up the conversion of nitric oxide (NO) to nitrogen dioxide ($NO_2$). To accomplish this, carbon monoxide (CO) combines with oxygen ($O_2$) and nitric oxide (NO) to produce carbon dioxide ($CO_2$) and nitrogen dioxide ($NO_2$). ($CO + O_2 + NO = CO_2 + NO_2$).

The dangers of carbon monoxide, which is an odorless and colorless toxic gas are many. When carbon monoxide is inhaled into the lungs and passed into the blood stream, oxygen is replaced by the carbon monoxide in the red blood cells, causing a reduction in the amount of oxygen supplied to the many parts of the body. This lack of oxygen causes headaches, lack of coordination, reduced mental alertness and, should the carbon monoxide concentration be high enough, death could result.

## NITROGEN

Normally, nitrogen is an inert gas. When heated to approximately 2500°F (1371°C) through the combustion process, this gas becomes active and causes an increase in the nitric oxide (NO) emission.

Oxides of nitrogen (NOx) are composed of approximately 97-98 percent nitric oxide (NO). Nitric oxide is a colorless gas but when it is passed into the atmosphere, it combines with oxygen and forms nitrogen dioxide ($NO_2$). The nitrogen dioxide then combines with chemically active hydrocarbons (HC) and when in the presence of sunlight, causes the formation of photo-chemical smog.

### Ozone

To further complicate matters, some of the nitrogen dioxide ($NO_2$) is broken apart by the sunlight to form nitric oxide and oxygen. ($NO_2 + sunlight = NO + O$). This single atom of oxygen then combines with diatomic (meaning 2 atoms) oxygen ($O_2$) to form ozone ($O_3$). Ozone is one of the smells associated with smog. It has a pungent and offensive odor, irritates the eyes and lung tissues, affects the growth of plant life and causes rapid deterioration of rubber products. Ozone

can be formed by sunlight as well as electrical discharge into the air.

The most common discharge area on the automobile engine is the secondary ignition electrical system, especially when inferior quality spark plug cables are used. As the surge of high voltage is routed through the secondary cable, the circuit builds up an electrical field around the wire, which acts upon the oxygen in the surrounding air to form the ozone. The faint glow along the cable with the engine running that may be visible on a dark night, is called the "corona discharge." It is the result of the electrical field passing from a high along the cable, to a low in the surrounding air, which forms the ozone gas. The combination of corona and ozone has been a major cause of cable deterioration. Recently, different and better quality insulating materials have lengthened the life of the electrical cables.

Although ozone at ground level can be harmful, ozone is beneficial to the earth's inhabitants. By having a concentrated ozone layer called the "ozonosphere," between 10 and 20 miles (16-32 km) up in the atmosphere, much of the ultra violet radiation from the sun's rays are absorbed and screened. If this ozone layer were not present, much of the earth's surface would be burned, dried and unfit for human life.

## OXIDES OF SULFUR

Oxides of sulfur (SOx) were initially ignored in the exhaust system emissions, since the sulfur content of gasoline as a fuel is less than $\frac{1}{10}$ of 1 percent. Because of this small amount, it was felt that it contributed very little to the overall pollution problem. However, because of the difficulty in solving the sulfur emissions in industrial pollutions and the introduction of catalytic converter to the automobile exhaust systems, a change was mandated. The automobile exhaust system, when equipped with a catalytic converter, changes the sulfur dioxide ($SO_2$) into sulfur trioxide ($SO_3$).

When this combines with water vapors ($H_2O$), a sulfuric acid mist ($H_2SO_4$) is formed and is a very difficult pollutant to handle since it is extremely corrosive. This sulfuric acid mist that is formed, is the same mist that rises from the vents of an automobile battery when an active chemical reaction takes place within the battery cells.

When a large concentration of vehicles equipped with catalytic converters are operating in an area, this acid mist may rise and be distributed over a large ground area causing land, plant, crop, paint and building damage.

## PARTICULATE MATTER

A certain amount of particulate matter is present in the burning of any fuel, with carbon constituting the largest percentage of the particulates. In gasoline, the remaining particulates are the burned remains of the various other compounds used in its manufacture. When a gasoline engine is in good internal condition, the particulate emissions are low but as the engine wears internally, the particulate emissions increase. By visually inspecting the tail pipe emissions, a determination can be made as to where an engine defect may exist. An engine with light gray or blue smoke emitting from the tail pipe normally indicates an increase in the oil consumption through burning due to internal engine wear. Black smoke would indicate a defective fuel delivery system, causing the engine to operate in a rich mode. Regardless of the color of the smoke, the internal part of the engine or the fuel delivery system should be repaired to prevent excess particulate emissions.

Diesel and turbine engines emit a darkened plume of smoke from the exhaust system because of the type of fuel used. Emission control regulations are mandated for this type of emission and more stringent measures are being used to prevent excess emission of the particulate matter. Electronic components are being introduced to control the injection of the fuel at precisely the proper time of piston travel, to achieve the optimum in fuel ignition and fuel usage. Other particulate after-burning components are being tested to achieve a cleaner emission.

Good grades of engine lubricating oils should be used, which meet the manufacturers specification. Cut-rate oils can contribute to the particulate emission problem because of their low flash or ignition temperature point. Such oils burn prematurely during the combustion process causing emission of particulate matter.

The cooling system is an important factor in the reduction of particulate matter. The optimum combustion will occur, with the cooling system operating at a temperature specified by the manufacturer. The cooling system must be maintained in the same manner as the engine oiling system, as each system is required to perform properly in order for the engine to operate efficiently for a long time.

## Crankcase Emissions

Crankcase emissions are made up of water, acids, unburned fuel, oil fumes and particulates. These emissions are classified as hydrocarbons (HC) and are formed by the small amount of unburned, compressed air/fuel mixture entering the crankcase from the combustion area (between the cylinder walls and piston rings) during the compression and power strokes. The head of the compression and combustion help to form the remaining crankcase emissions.

Since the first engines, crankcase emissions were allowed into the atmosphere through a road draft tube, mounted on the lower side of the engine block. Fresh air came in through an open oil filler cap or breather. The air passed through the crankcase mixing with blow-by gases. The motion of the vehicle and the air blowing past the open end of the road draft tube caused a low pressure area (vacuum) at the end of the tube. Crankcase emissions were simply drawn out of the road draft tube into the air.

To control the crankcase emission, the road draft tube was deleted. A hose and/or tubing was routed from the crankcase to the intake manifold so the blow-by emission could be burned with the air/fuel mixture. However, it was found that intake manifold vacuum, used to draw the crankcase emissions into the manifold, would vary in strength at the wrong time and not allow the proper emission flow. A regulating valve was needed to control the flow of air through the crankcase.

Testing, showed the removal of the blow-by gases from the crankcase as quickly as possible, was most important to the longevity of the engine. Should large accumulations of blow-by gases remain and condense, dilution of the engine oil would occur to form water, soots, resins, acids and lead salts, resulting in the formation of sludge and varnishes. This condensation of the blow-by gases occurs more frequently on vehicles used in numerous starting and stopping conditions, excessive idling and when the engine is not allowed to attain normal operating temperature through short runs.

## Evaporative Emissions

Gasoline fuel is a major source of pollution, before and after it is burned in the automobile engine. From the time the fuel is refined, stored, pumped and transported, again stored until it is pumped into the fuel tank of the vehicle, the gasoline gives off unburned hydrocarbons (HC) into the atmosphere. Through the redesign of storage areas and venting systems, the pollution factor was diminished, but not eliminated, from the refinery standpoint. However, the automobile still remained the primary source of vaporized, unburned hydrocarbon (HC) emissions.

Fuel pumped from an underground storage tank is cool but when exposed to a warmer ambient temperature, will expand. Before controls were mandated, an owner might fill the fuel tank with fuel from an underground storage tank and park the vehicle for some time in warm area, such as a parking lot. As the fuel would warm, it would expand and should no provisions or area be provided for the expansion, the fuel would spill out of the filler neck and onto the ground, causing hydrocarbon (HC) pollution and creating a severe fire hazard. To correct this condition, the vehicle manufacturers added overflow plumbing and/or gasoline tanks with built in expansion areas or domes.

However, this did not control the fuel vapor emission from the fuel tank. It was determined that most of the fuel evaporation occurred when the vehicle was stationary and the engine not operating. Most vehicles carry 5-25 gallons (19-95 liters) of gasoline. Should a large concentration of vehicles be parked in one area, such as a large parking lot, excessive fuel vapor emissions would take place, increasing as the temperature increases.

To prevent the vapor emission from escaping into the atmosphere, the fuel systems were designed to trap the vapors while the vehicle is stationary, by sealing the system from the atmosphere. A storage system is used to collect and hold the fuel vapors from the carburetor (if equipped) and the fuel tank when the engine is not operating. When the engine is started, the storage system is then purged of the fuel vapors, which are drawn into the engine and burned with the air/fuel mixture.

## EMISSION CONTROLS

### General Information

The emission control devices required on these vans are determined by the weight classification. Light duty models use the same emission controls as passenger cars:

- All 1967-69 models
- 1970-71 G-10, 1500, 20, 2500 models
- 1972-73 G-10, 1500, 20, 2500 models
- 1972-73 G-30, 3500 passenger models
- 1974-78 G-10, 1500 models
- All 1979 and later models

Heavy duty models operate under less stringent rules and use less emission control devices. These include:

- 1971 G-30, 3500 models
- 1972-73 G-30, 3500 models (except passenger vans)
- 1974-78 G-20, 2500, 30, 3500 models

Positive Crankcase Ventilation (PCV) was the earliest form of automotive emission control, dating back to 1955 on Chevrolet vehicles. Still in use today, it routes cylinder blow-by gases from the crankcase through a PCV valve and back into the combustion chamber for reburning.

In 1966, the Air Injection Reactor (AIR) system was introduced to satisfy the California emission requirements. This system pumps oxygen to the exhaust gases as they exit from the cylinder, where they are ignited and burned more completely to further reduce hydrocarbon and carbon monoxide exhaust emission.

Chevrolet introduced the Controlled Combustion System (CCS) in 1968, which uses various components and design calibrations to further reduce pollutants.

The Combined Emission Control (CEC) and Transmission Controlled Spark (TCS) have been used since 1970 and basically do not allow distributor vacuum advance in Low gear.

In 1973, the Exhaust Gas Recirculation (EGR) system was developed in response to more stringent Federal exhaust emission standards regarding oxides of nitrogen (Nox). Oxides of nitrogen are formed at higher combustion chamber temperatures and increase with higher temperatures. The EGR system is designed to reduce combustion temperature thereby reducing the formation of NOx.

The Evaporative Control System (ECS) is designed to control fuel vapors that escape from the fuel tank and carburetor through evaporation. This system seals the fuel tank to retain vapors in a charcoal canister. The stored vapors are burned during engine operation.

### Positive Crankcase Ventilation

#### OPERATION

PCV is the earliest form of emission control. Prior to its use, crankcase vapors were vented into the atmosphere through a road draft tube or crankcase breather. The PCV system first appeared in 1955. Beginning 1961, the PCV system was used on all California models and in 1963 the system became standard on all models.

This system draws crankcase vapors that are formed through normal combustion into the intake manifold and subsequently into the combustion chambers to be burned. Fresh air is introduced to the crankcase by way of a hose connected to the carburetor air cleaner or a vented oil filler cap or older models. Manifold vacuum is used to draw the vapors from the crankcase through a PCV valve and into the intake manifold. Vented and nonvented filler caps were used on various models until 1968, after which only nonvented caps were used.

#### SERVICE

Other than checking and replacing the PCV valve and associated hoses, there is no other service required. Engine operating conditions that would direct suspicion to the PCV system are rough idle, oil present in the air cleaner, oil leaks and excessive oil sludging or dilution. If any of the above conditions exist, remove the PCV valve and shake it. A clicking sound indicates that the valve is free. If no clicking sound is heard, replace the valve. Inspect the PCV breather in the air cleaner. Replace the breather if it is so dirty that it will not allow gases to pass through. Check all the PCV hoses for condition and tight connections. Replace any hoses that have deteriorated.

#### TESTING

▶ See Figure 1

With the engine running, remove the PCV from the valve cover and place your thumb over the end of the valve. Check if vacuum is present at the valve. If vacuum is not present, check for plugged hoses, blockage of the manifold port at the throttle body/carburetor unit or a faulty PCV valve. Replace as necessary. With the engine not running, remove the PCV valve from the vehicle. Shake the valve and listen for the rattle of the check valve needle. If no rattle is heard the valve is defective and must be replaced.

#### REMOVAL & INSTALLATION

Refer to Section 1 of this manual for this procedure.

### Air Injector Reactor (AIR) System

This system was first introduced on California vans in 1966. The AIR system injects compressed air into the exhaust system, near enough to the exhaust valves to continue the burning of the normally unburned segment of the exhaust gases. To do this it employs an air injection pump and a system of hoses, valves, tubes, etc., necessary to carry the compressed air from the pump to the exhaust manifolds.

A diverter valve is used to prevent backfiring. The valve senses sudden increases in manifold vacuum and ceases the injection of air during dual rich periods. During coasting, this

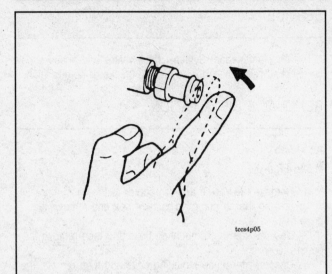

**Fig. 1 Check the PCV valve for vacuum at idle**

valve diverts the entire air flow through a muffler and during high engine speeds, expels it through a relief valve. Check valves in the system prevent exhaust gases from entering the pump.

## TESTING

### Check Valve

To test the check valve, disconnect the hose at the diverter valve. Blow into the hose and suck on it. Air should flow only into the engine.

### Diverter Valve

Pull off the vacuum line to the top of the valve with the engine running. There should be vacuum in the line. Replace the line. No air should be escaping with the engine running at a steady idle. Open and quickly close the throttle. A blast of air should come out of the valve muffler for at least one second.

### Air Pump

Disconnect the hose from the diverter valve. Start the engine and accelerate it to about 1,500 rpm. The air flow should increase as the engine is accelerated. If no air flow is noted or it remains constant, check the following:
1. Drive belt tension.
2. Listen for a leaking pressure relief valve. If it is defective, replace the whole relief/diverter valve.
3. Foreign matter in pump filter openings. If the pump is defective or excessively noisy, it must be replaced.

## SERVICE

All hoses and fittings should be inspected for condition and tightness of connections. Check the drive belt for wear and tension periodically.

➡**The AIR system is not completely silent under normal conditions. Noises will rise in pitch as engine speed increases. If the noise is excessive, eliminate the air pump itself by disconnecting the drive belt. If the noise disappears, the air pump is not at fault.**

## REMOVAL & INSTALLATION

1. Disconnect the output hose.
2. Hold the pump from turning by squeezing the drive belt.
3. Loosen the pulley bolts.
4. Loosen the alternator so the belt can be removed.
5. Remove the pulley.
6. Remove the pump mounting bolts and the pump.
**To install:**
7. Install the pump with the mounting bolts loose.
8. Install the pulley and tighten the bolts finger tight.
9. Install and adjust the drive belt.
10. Squeeze the drive belt to prevent the pump from turning.
11. Torque the pulley bolts to 25 ft. lbs. (33 Nm). Tighten the pump mountings.
12. Check and adjust the belt tension again, if necessary.
13. Connect the hose.
14. If any hose leaks are suspected, pour soapy water over the suspected area with the engine running. Bubbles will form wherever air is escaping.

## FILTER REPLACEMENT

1. Disconnect the air and vacuum hoses from the diverter valve.
2. Loosen the pump pivot and adjusting bolts and remove the drive belt.
3. Remove the pivot and adjusting bolts from the pump. Remove the pump and the diverter valve as an assembly.

### ✳✳WARNING

**Do not clamp the pump in a vise or use a hammer or prybar on the pump housing.**

4. To change the filter, break the plastic fan from the hub. It is seldom possible to remove the fan without breaking it.
5. Remove the remaining portion of the fan filter from the pump hub. Be careful that filter fragments do not enter the air intake hole.
6. Position the new centrifugal fan filter on the pump hub. Place the pump pulley against the fan filter and install the securing screws. Torque the screws alternately to 95 in. lbs. (10 Nm) and the fan filter will be pressed onto the pump hub.
7. Install the pump on the engine and adjust its drive belt.

## Air Management System

### OPERATION

The Air Management System is used on 1981 and later computer controlled engines to provide additional oxygen to continue the combustion process after the exhaust gases leave the combustion chamber; much the same as the AIR system described earlier. Air is injected into either the exhaust port(s), the exhaust manifold(s) or the catalytic converter by an engine driven air pump. The system is in operating at all times and will bypass air only momentarily during deceleration and at high speeds. The bypass function is performed by the Air Management Valve, which the check valve protects the air pump by preventing any backflow of exhaust gases.

The AIR system helps to reduce HC and CO content in the exhaust gases by injecting air into the exhaust ports during cold engine operation. This air injection also helps the catalytic converter to reach the proper temperature quicker during warm-up. When the engine warm (closed loop), the AIR system injects air into the beds of a 3-way converter to lower the HC and CO content in the exhaust.

The Air Management System utilizes the following components:

1. An engine driven air pump.
2. Air management valves (Air Control and Air Switching).
3. Air flow and control hoses.
4. Check valves.
5. A dual bed, 3-way catalytic converter.

The belt driven, vane type air pump is located at the front of the engine and supplies clean air to the system for purposes already stated. When the engine is cold, the Electronic Control Module (ECM) energizes an air control solenoid. This allows air to flow to the air switching valve. The air switching valve is then energized to direct air into the exhaust ports.

When the engine is warm, the ECM de-energizes the air switching valve, thus directing the air between the beds of the catalytic converter. This then provides additional oxygen for the oxidizing catalyst in the second bed to decrease HC and CO levels, while at the same time keeping oxygen levels low in the first bed, enabling the reducing catalyst to effectively decrease the levels of NOx.

If the air control valve detects a rapid increase in manifold vacuum (deceleration), certain operating modes (wide open throttle, etc.) or if the ECM self diagnostic system detects any problems in the system, air is diverted to the air cleaner or directly into the atmosphere.

The primary purpose of the ECM's divert mode is to prevent backfiring. Throttle closure at the beginning of deceleration will temporarily create air/fuel mixtures which are too rich to burn completely. These mixtures will be come burnable when they reach the exhaust if they are combined with injection air. The next firing of the engine will ignite the mixture causing an exhaust backfire. Momentary diverting of the injection air from the exhaust prevents this.

### SERVICE

The Air Management System check valves and hoses should be checked periodically for any leaks, cracks or deterioration.

### REMOVAL & INSTALLATION

**Air Pump**

▶ **See Figure 2**

1. Remove the valves and/or adapter at the air pump.
2. Loosen the air pump adjustment bolt and remove the drive belt.
3. Unscrew the three mounting bolts and then remove the pump pulley.
4. Unscrew the pump mounting bolts and then remove the pump.
5. Installation is in the reverse order of removal. Be sure to adjust the drive belt tension after installing it.

**Check Valve**

1. Release the clamp and disconnect the air hoses from the valve.
2. Unscrew the check valve from the air injection pipe.
3. Installation is in the reverse order of removal.

**Air Management Valve**

1. Disconnect the negative battery cable.
2. Remove the air cleaner.
3. Tag and disconnect the vacuum hose from the valve.
4. Tag and disconnect the air outlet hoses from the valve.
5. Bend back the lock tabs and then remove the bolts holding the elbow to the valve.
6. Tag and disconnect any electrical connections at the valve and then remove the valve from the elbow.
7. Installation is in the reverse order of removal.

Fig. 2 Be sure to properly tension the drive belt

## Pulse Air Injection Reactor (PAIR) System

### OPERATION

This system consists of four air valves which inject fresh air into the exhaust system in order to further the combustion process of the exhaust gases. The firing of the engine creates a pulsating flow of exhaust gases, which are of either positive or negative pressure. Negative pressure at the pulse air valve will result in air being injected into the exhaust system. Positive pressure will force the check valve closed and no exhaust gases will flow into the fresh air supply.

### SERVICE

Regularly inspect the pulse air valves, pipes, grommets and hose for cracks and leaks. Replace the necessary part if any are found. If a check valve fails, exhaust gases will get into the carburetor through the air cleaner and cause the engine to surge and perform poorly.

If exhaust gases pass through a pulse air valve, the paint will be burned off the rocker arm cover plenum as a result of the excessive heat. The rubber grommets and hose will also deteriorate. Failure of the pulse air valve can also be indicated by a hissing sound.

### REMOVAL & INSTALLATION

▶ **See Figure 3**

1. Remove the air cleaner. Disconnect the rubber hose from the plenum connecting pipe.
2. Disconnect the four check valve fittings at the cylinder head and remove the check valve pipes from the plenum grommets.

3. Disconnect the check valve from the check valve pipe.
4. Assemble the replacement check valve to the check valve pipe.
5. Attach the check valve assembly to the cylinder head as illustrated. Hand tighten the fittings.
6. Using a 1 in. (25mm) open end wrench as a lever, align the check valve on pipe **A** with the plenum grommet. Using the palm of your left hand, press the check valve into the grommet. Using a silicone lubricant on the grommet will make thing a little easier. Repeat this procedure for pipe **B** using your left hand for the tool and your right hand for installing the valve in the grommet.

## Controlled Combustion System

### DESCRIPTION

The CCS system is a combination of systems and calibrations. Many of these are not visible or serviceable, but are designed into the engine. Originally, in 1968-69, the system was comprised of special carburetion and distributor settings, higher engine operating temperatures and a thermostatically controlled air cleaner. In later years, the thermostatically controlled air cleaner (CHA) was used independently of the other settings on some engines. Likewise, some engines used the special settings without CHA. In 1970, the TCS system was incorporated and the entire system was renamed CEC in 1971. The name reverted to TCS in 1972. In 1973, EGR was also added to the system.

The various systems, CHA, TCS, CEC and EGR are all part of the Controlled Combustion System.

### SERVICE

Refer to the appropriate component section for maintenance and service (if applicable).

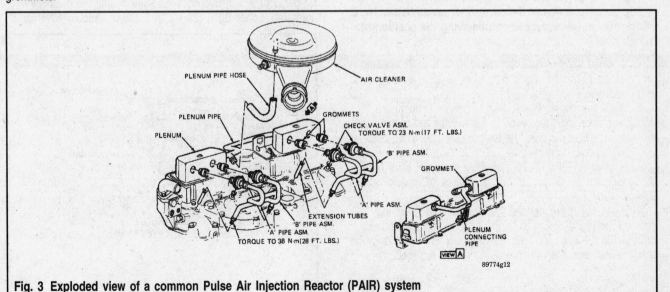

**Fig. 3 Exploded view of a common Pulse Air Injection Reactor (PAIR) system**

89774g12

## Thermostatic Air Cleaner

### DESCRIPTION

The use of carburetor heated air dates back to 1960 when it was first used on heavy trucks.

This system is designed to warm the air entering the carburetor when underhood temperatures are low. This allows more precise calibration of the carburetor.

The thermostatically controlled air cleaner is composed of the air cleaner body, a filter, sensor unit, vacuum diaphragm, damper door and associated hoses and connections. Heat radiating from the exhaust manifold is trapped by a heat stove and is ducted to the air cleaner to supply heated air to the carburetor. A movable door in the air cleaner snorkel allows air to be drawn in from the heat stove (cold operation) or from the underhood air (warm operation). Periods of extended idling, climbing a grade or high speed operation are followed by a considerable increase in engine compartment temperature. Excessive fuel vapors enter the intake manifold causing an over-rich mixture, resulting in a rough idle. To overcome this, some engines may be equipped with a hot idle compensator.

### TESTING

#### System

1. Either start with a cold engine or remove the air cleaner from the engine for at least half an hour. While cooling the air cleaner, leave the engine compartment hood open.

2. Tape a thermometer, of known accuracy, to the inside of the air cleaner so that it is near the temperature sensor unit. Install the air cleaner on the engine but do not fasten its securing nut.

3. Start the engine. With the engine cold and the outside temperature less than 90°F (32°C), the door should be in the heat on position (closed to outside air).

➡ Due to the position of the air cleaner on some trucks, a mirror may be necessary when observing the position of the air door.

4. Operate the throttle lever rapidly to 1/2-3/4 of its opening and release it. The air door should open to allow outside air to enter and then close again.

5. Allow the engine to warm up to normal temperature. Watch the door. When it opens to the outside air, remove the cover from the air cleaner. The temperature should be over 90°F (32°C) and no more than 130°F (54°C). Normal temperature is about 115°F (46°C). If the door does not work within these temperature ranges, or fails to work at all, check for linkage or door binding.

If binding is not present and the air door is not working, proceed with the vacuum tests, given below. If these indicate no faults in the vacuum motor and the door is not working, the temperature sensor is defective and must be replaced.

#### Vacuum Motor

➡ Be sure that the vacuum hose which runs between the temperature switch and the vacuum motor is not pinched by the retaining clip under the air cleaner. This could prevent the air door from closing.

1. Check all of the vacuum lines and fittings for leaks. Correct any leaks. If none are found, proceed with the test.

2. Remove the hose which runs from the sensor to the vacuum motor. Run a hose directly from the manifold vacuum source to the vacuum motor.

3. If the motor closes the air door, it is functioning properly and the temperature sensor is defective.

4. If the motor does not close the door and no binding is present in its operation, the vacuum motor is defective and must be replaced.

➡ If an alternate vacuum source is applied to the motor, insert a vacuum gauge in the line by using a T-fitting. Apply at least 9 in.Hg (62 kPa) of vacuum in order to operate the motor.

## Transmission Controlled Spark (TCS)

### OPERATION

▶ See Figure 4

Introduced in 1970, this system controls exhaust emissions by eliminating vacuum advance in the lower forward gears.

The 1970 system consists of a transmission switch, solenoid vacuum switch, time delay relay, and a thermostatic water temperature switch. The solenoid vacuum switch is de-energized in the lower gears via the transmission switch and closes off distributor vacuum. The 2-way transmission switch is activated by the shifter shaft on manual transmissions, and by fluid pressure on automatic transmissions. The switch energizes the solenoid in High gear, the plunger extends and uncovers the vacuum port, and the distributor receives full vacuum. The temperature switch overrides the system until the engine temperature reaches 82°F (28°C). This allows vacuum advance in

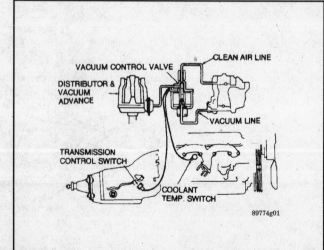

Fig. 4 View of the TCS system components

all gears, thereby preventing stalling after starting. A time delay relay opens fifteen seconds after the ignition is switched on. Full vacuum advance during this delay eliminates the possibility of stalling.

The 1971 system is similar, except that the vacuum solenoid (now called a Combination Emissions Control solenoid) serves two functions. One function is to control distributor vacuum; the added function is to act as a deceleration throttle stop in High gear. This cuts down on emissions when the vehicle is coming to stop in High gear. Two throttle settings are necessary; one for curb idle and one for emission control on coast.

The 1972 six cylinder system is similar to that used in 1971, except that an idle stop solenoid has been added to the system and the name was changed back to TCS. In the energized position, the solenoid maintains engine speed at the predetermined fast idle. When de-energized the solenoid allows the throttle plates to close beyond the normal idle position, thus cutting off the air supply and preventing engine run-on. The six is the only 1972 engine with a CEC valve, which serves the same deceleration function as in 1971. The time delay relay delays full vacuum twenty seconds after the transmission is shifted into High gear. 1972 V8 engines use a vacuum advance solenoid similar to that used in 1970. The solenoid controls distributor vacuum advance and performs no throttle positioning function. The idle stop solenoid used on V8s operates in the same manner as the one on sixes. All air conditioned models have an additional anti-diesel (run-on) solenoid which engages the compressor clutch for 3 seconds after the ignition is switched off. The 1973 TCS system on the six is identical to that on 1972 six, except for recalibration of the temperature switch. The system used on 1973 engines changed slightly from 1972. In place of the CEC solenoid on the six, the V8 continues to use a vacuum advance solenoid. The other differences are: The upshift delay relay, previously located under the instrument panel has been done away with; a 20 second time delay relay identical to the one on sixes is now used; V8s use manifold vacuum with TCS and ported vacuum (above the throttle plates) without TCS.

The six cylinder TCS system was revised for 1974 by replacing the CEC solenoid with a vacuum advance solenoid. Otherwise the system remains the same as 1973.

## TESTING

### System Check

If there is a TCS system malfunction, first connect a vacuum gauge in the hose between the solenoid valve and the distributor vacuum unit. Drive the vehicle or raise it on a frame lift and observe the vacuum gauge.

If full vacuum is available in all gears, check for the following:
- Blown fuse
- Disconnected wire at solenoid operated vacuum valve
- Disconnected wire at transmission switch.
- Temperature override switch energized due to low engine temperature
- Solenoid failure

If no vacuum is available in any gear, check the following:
- Solenoid valve vacuum lines switched
- Clogged solenoid vacuum valve
- Distributor or manifold vacuum lines leaking or disconnected
- Transmission switch or wire grounded

### Idle Stop Solenoid

This unit may be checked simply by observing it while an assistant switches the ignition on and off. It should extend further with the current switched on. The unit is not repairable.

### Solenoid Vacuum Valve

Check that proper manifold vacuum is available. Connect the vacuum gauge in the line between the solenoid valve and the distributor. Apply 12 volts to the solenoid. If vacuum is still not available, the valve is defective, either mechanically or electrically. The unit is not repairable. If the valve is satisfactory, check the relay next.

### Relay

1. With the engine at normal operating temperature and the ignition on, ground the solenoid vacuum valve terminal with the black lead. The solenoid should energize (no vacuum) if the relay is satisfactory.

2. With the solenoid energized as in Step 1, connect a jumper from the relay terminal with the green/white stripe lead to ground. The solenoid should de-energize (vacuum available) if the relay is satisfactory.

3. If the relay worked properly in Steps 1 and 2, check the temperature switch. The relay unit is not repairable.

### Temperature Switch

The vacuum valve solenoid should be de-energized (vacuum available) with the engine cold. If it is not, ground the green/white stripe wire from the switch. If the solenoid now de-energizes, replace the switch. If the switch was satisfactory, check the transmission switch.

### Transmission Switch

With the engine at normal operating temperature and the transmission in one of the no vacuum gears, the vacuum valve solenoid should be energized (no vacuum). If not, remove and ground the switch electrical lead. If the solenoid energizes, replace the switch.

## Exhaust Gas Recirculation (EGR)

### DESCRIPTION

The EGR system and valve were introduced in 1973. Its purpose is to control oxides of nitrogen which are formed during the peak combustion temperatures. The end products of combustion are relatively inert gases derived from the exhaust gases which are directed into the EGR valve to help lower peak combustion temperatures.

The EGR valve contains a vacuum diaphragm operated by manifold vacuum. The vacuum signal port is located in the carburetor body and is exposed to engine vacuum in the off/idle and part throttle operation. In 1974, a thermal delay switch was added to delay operation of the valve during engine warmup, when NOx levels are already at a minimum.

On inline sixes, the EGR valve is located on the intake manifold adjacent to the carburetor. On V6 and V8 engines, the valve is located on the right rear side of the intake manifold adjacent to the rocker arm cover.

## TESTING

▶ See Figure 5

The EGR valve is not serviceable, except for replacement. To check the valve, proceed as follows:
1. Connect a tachometer to the engine.
2. With the engine running at normal operating temperature, with the choke valve fully open, set the engine rpm at 2000. The transmission should be in Park (automatic) or Neutral (manual) with the parking brake On and the wheels blocked.
3. Disconnect the vacuum hose at the valve. Make sure that vacuum is available at the valve and look at the tachometer to see if the engine speed increases. If it does, the system is OK.
4. If necessary, replace the valve.

## REMOVAL & INSTALLATION

▶ See Figures 6, 7, 8, 9 and 10

1. Disconnect the negative battery cable.
2. Remove the air cleaner assembly from the engine.
3. Remove the EGR valve vacuum tube from the valve.
4. Remove the EGR bolts and/or nuts and remove the EGR valve and gasket.
   **To install:**
5. Install a new gasket to the EGR valve and install the EGR valve to the manifold.
6. Install the nuts and/or bolts. Tighten the bolts to 17 ft. lbs. (24 Nm) and the nuts to 15 ft. lbs. (20 Nm).

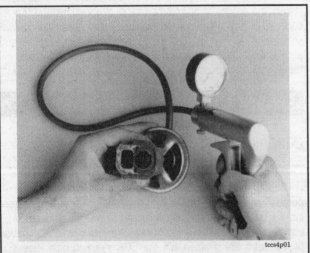
Fig. 5 Some EGR valves may be tested using a vacuum pump by watching for diaphragm movement

Fig. 6 Remove the air cleaner assembly from the vehicle

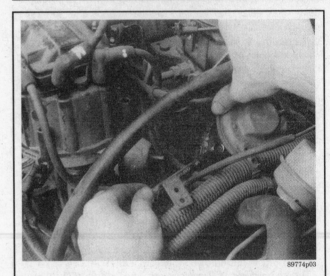
Fig. 7 Unfasten the EGR valve retaining bolts . . .

Fig. 8 . . . then remove the EGR valve and gasket

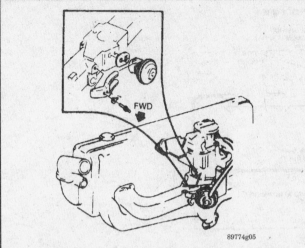

**Fig. 9 Common location and mounting of the EGR valve on the inline six cylinder engine**

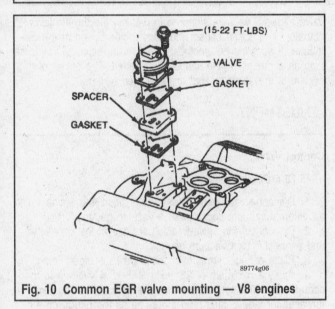

**Fig. 10 Common EGR valve mounting — V8 engines**

7. Connect the vacuum tube to the EGR valve.

8. Install the air cleaner and connect the negative battery cable.

## Evaporation Control System

### OPERATION

Introduced on California vehicles in 1970, and nationwide in 1971, this system reduces the amount of escaping gasoline vapors. Float bowl emissions are controlled by internal carburetor modifications. Redesigned bowl vents, reduced bowl capacity, heat shields, and improved intake manifold-to-carburetor insulation serve to reduce vapor loss into the atmosphere. The venting of fuel tank vapors into the air has been stopped. Fuel vapors are now directed through lines to a canister containing an activated charcoal filter. Unburned vapors are trapped here until the engine is started. When the engine is running, the canister is purged by air drawn in by manifold vacuum. The air and fuel vapors are directed into the engine to be burned.

### SERVICE

Replace the filter in the engine compartment canister at the intervals shown in the Maintenance Intervals Chart in Section 1. If the fuel tank cap requires replacement, ensure that the new cap is the correct part for your truck.

## Early Fuel Evaporation (EFE) System

### OPERATION

This system is used on 1975 and later light duty models. The six cylinder system consists of an EFE valve mount at the flange of the exhaust manifold, an actuator, a thermal vacuum switch (TVS), and a vacuum solenoid. The TVS is on the right side of the engine forward of the oil pressure switch. The TVS is normally closed and sensitive to oil temperature.

The V6 and V8 EFE system consists of an EFE valve at the flange of the exhaust manifold, an actuator, and a thermal vacuum switch. The TVS is located in the coolant outlet housing and directly controls vacuum.

In both systems, manifold vacuum is applied to the actuator, which in turn, closes the EFE valve. This routes hot exhaust gases to the base of the carburetor. When coolant (V6/V8) or oil (six cylinder) temperatures reach a set limit, vacuum is denied to the actuator allowing an internal spring to return the actuator to its normal position, opening the EFE valve.

## Throttle Return Control (TRC)

### OPERATION

▶ **See Figures 11, 12 and 13**

Two different Throttle Return Control (TRC) systems are used. The first is used from 1975 to 1978. It consists of a control valve and a throttle lever actuator. When the truck is coasting against the engine, the control valve is open to allow vacuum to operate the throttle lever actuator. The throttle lever actuator then pushes the throttle lever slightly open reducing the HC (hydrocarbon) emission level during coasting. When manifold vacuum drops below a predetermined level, the control valve closes, the throttle lever retracts, and the throttle lever closes to the idler position.

The second TRC system is used in 1979 and later. It consists of a throttle lever actuator, a solenoid vacuum control valve, and an electronic speed sensor. The throttle lever actuator, mounted on the carburetor, opens the primary throttle plates a present amount, above normal engine idle speed, in response to a signal from the solenoid vacuum control valve. The valve, mounted at the left rear of the engine above the intake manifold on the six cylinder, or on the thermostat housing mounting stud on the V6 or V8, is held open in response to a signal from the electronic speed sensor. When open, the

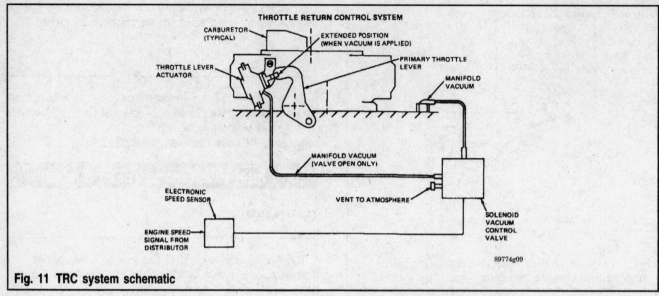

Fig. 11 TRC system schematic

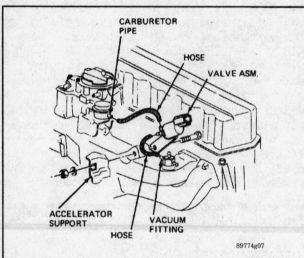

Fig. 12 View of the TRC components — inline six engines

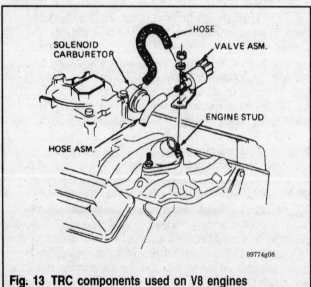

Fig. 13 TRC components used on V8 engines

valve allows a vacuum signal to be sent to the throttle lever actuator. The speed sensor monitors engine speed at the distributor. It supplies an electrical signal to the solenoid valve, as long as a preset engine speed is exceeded. The object of this system is the same as that of the earlier system.

## ADJUSTMENT

### Control Valve

#### 1975-76 MODELS

1. Disconnect the valve-to-carburetor hose and connect it to an external vacuum source with a vacuum gauge.

2. Disconnect the valve-to-actuator hose at the connector and connect it to a vacuum gauge.

3. Place a finger firmly over the end of the bleed fitting.

4. Apply a minimum of 23 in.Hg (158 kPa) vacuum to the control valve and seal off the vacuum source. The gauge on the actuator side should read the same as the gauge on the source side. If not, the valve needs adjustment. If vacuum drops off on either side (with the finger still on the bleed fitting), the valve is defective and should be replaced.

5. With a minimum of 23 in.Hg (158 kPa) vacuum in the valve, remove the finger from the bleed fitting. The vacuum level in the actuator side will drop to zero and the reading on the source side will drop to a value that will be the value set point. If the value is not within ½ in.Hg vacuum of the specified valve set point, adjust the valve.

6. Gently pry off the plastic cover.

7. Turn the adjusting screw in (clockwise) to raise the set point or out (counterclockwise) to lower the set point.

8. Recheck the valve set point.

9. If necessary, repeat the adjustment until the valve set point is attained between 22.5 in.Hg and 23.5 in.Hg vacuum.

#### 1977-78 MODELS

1. Disconnect the valve-to-carburetor hose at the carburetor. Connect the hose to an external vacuum source, with an accurate vacuum gauge connected into the line near the valve.

2. Apply a minimum of 25 in.Hg (172 kPa) of vacuum to the control valve vacuum supply fitting while sealing off the vacuum supply between the gauge and the vacuum source. The vacuum gauge will indicate the set point value of the valve.

3. If the gauge reading is not within 0.5 in.Hg (3.4 kPa) of the specified value (see the chart), the valve must be adjusted. If the trapped vacuum drops off faster than 0.1 in.Hg (0.68 kPa) per second, the valve is leaking and must be replaced.

4. To adjust the valve set point, follow Steps 6-9 of the 1975-76 adjustment procedure.

### Throttle Valve

1. Disconnect the valve-to-actuator hose at the valve and connect it to an external vacuum source.

2. Apply 20 in.Hg (137 kPa) vacuum to the actuator and seal the vacuum source. If the vacuum gauge reading drops, the valve is leaking and should be replaced.

3. Check the throttle lever, shaft, and linkage for freedom of operation.

4. Start the engine and warm it to operating temperature.

5. Note the idle rpm.

6. Apply 20 in.Hg (137 kPa) vacuum to the actuator and manually operate the throttle. Allow it to close against the extended actuator plunger. Note the engine rpm.

7. Release and reapply 20 in.Hg (137 kPa) vacuum to the actuator and note the rpm at which the engine speed increases (do not assist the actuator).

8. If the engine speed obtained in Step 7 is not within 150 rpm of that obtained in Step 6, then the actuator may be binding. If the binding cannot be corrected, replace the actuator.

9. Release the vacuum from the actuator and the engine speed should return to within 50 rpm of the speed noted in Steps 4 and 5.

10. To adjust the actuator, turn the screw on the actuator plunger until the specified TRC speed range is obtained.

## TESTING

▶ See Figures 14 and 15

➡This procedure applies to 1979 and later models only.

1. Connect a tachometer to the distributor TACH terminal. Start the engine and raise the engine speed to 1890 rpm. The throttle lever actuator on the carburetor should extend.

2. Reduce the engine speed to 1700 rpm. The lever actuator should retract.

3. If the actuator operates outside of the speed limits, the speed switch is faulty and must be replaced. It cannot be adjusted.

4. If the actuator does not operate at all:

a. Check the voltage at the vacuum solenoid and the speed switch with a voltmeter. Connect the negative probe of the voltmeter to the engine ground and the positive probe to the voltage source wire on the component. The positive probe can be inserted on the connector body at the wire side; it is not necessary to unplug the connector. Voltage should be 12 to 14 volts in both cases.

b. If the correct voltage is present at one component but not the other, the engine wiring harness is faulty.

### Fig. 14

**TRS Control Valve Set Points**

| Engine | Set Point (in. Hg) |
|---|---|
| 292 | 22.5 |
| 305 | 22.5 |
| 350 | 21.5 |

89774g03

Fig. 14 TRS control valve set points

### Fig. 15

**TRC Speed**

| Engine | Setting (rpm) |
|---|---|
| 292 | 1600 |
| 305 | 1600 |
| 350 | 1500 |

89774g04

Fig. 15 TRC speed settings

c. If the voltage is not present at all, check the engine harness connections at the distributor and the bulkhead connector and repair as necessary.

d. If the correct voltage is present at both components, check the solenoid operation: ground the solenoid-to-speed switch connecting wire terminal at the solenoid connector with a jumper wire. This should cause the throttle lever actuator to extend, with the engine running.

e. If the lever actuator does not extend, remove the hose from the solenoid side port which connects the actuator hose. Check the port for obstructions or blockage. If the port is not plugged, replace the solenoid.

f. If the actuator extends in Step d, ground the solenoid-to-speed switch wire terminal at the switch. If the actuator does not extend, the wire between the speed switch and the solenoid is open and must be repaired. If the actuator does extend, check the speed switch ground wire for a ground; it should read zero volts with the engine running. Check the speed switch-to-distributor wire for a proper connection. If the ground and distributor wires are properly connected and the actuator still does not extend when the engine speed is above 1890 rpm, replace the speed switch.

5. If the actuator is extended at all speeds:

a. Remove the connector from the vacuum solenoid.

b. If the actuator remains extended, check the solenoid side port orifice for blockage. If plugged, clear and reconnect the system and recheck. If the actuator is still extended, remove the solenoid connector; if the actuator does not retreat, replace the vacuum solenoid.

c. If the actuator retracts with the solenoid connector off, reconnect it and remove the speed switch connector. If the actuator retracts, the problem is in the speed switch, which should be replaced. If the actuator does not retract, the solenoid-to-speed switch wire is shorted to ground in the wiring harness. Repair the short.

## Oxygen Sensor

### OPERATION

▸ **See Figure 16**

The oxygen sensor is a spark plug shaped device that is screwed into the exhaust manifold on V8s and into the exhaust pipe on inline sixes. It monitors the oxygen content of the exhaust gases and sends a voltage signal to the Electronic Control Module (ECM). The ECM monitors this voltage and, depending on the value of the received signal, issues a command to the mixture control solenoid on the carburetor to adjust for rich or lean conditions.

The proper operation of the oxygen sensor depends upon four basic conditions:

1. Good electrical connections. Since the sensor generates low currents, good clean electrical connections at the sensor are a must.

2. Outside air supply. Air must circulate to the internal portion of the sensor. When servicing the sensor, do not restrict the air passages.

3. Proper operating temperatures. The ECM will not recognize the sensor's signals until the sensor reaches approximately 600°F (316°C).

4. Non-leaded fuel. The use of leaded gasoline will damage the sensor very quickly.

### TESTING

1. Start the engine and bring it to normal operating temperature, then run the engine above 1200 rpm for two minutes.

2. Backprobe with a high impedance averaging voltmeter (set to the DC voltage scale) between the Oxygen Sensor (02S) and battery ground.

3. Verify that the 02S voltage fluctuates rapidly between 0.40-0.60 volts.

4. If the 02S voltage is stabilized at the middle of the specified range (approximately 0.45-0.55 volts) or if the 02S voltage fluctuates very slowly between the specified range (02S signal crosses 0.5 volts less than 5 times in ten seconds), the 02S may be faulty.

5. If the 02S voltage stabilizes at either end of the specified range, the ECM is probably not able to compensate for a mechanical problem such as a vacuum leak or a high float level. These types of mechanical problems will cause the 02S to sense a constant lean or constant rich mixture. The mechanical problem will first have to be repaired and then the 02S test repeated.

6. Pull a vacuum hose located after the throttle plate. Voltage should drop to approximately 0.12 volts (while still fluctuating rapidly). This tests the ability of the 02S to detect a lean mixture condition. Reattach the vacuum hose.

7. Richen the mixture using a propane enrichment tool. Voltage should rise to approximately 0.90 volts (while still fluctuating rapidly). This tests the ability of the 02S to detect a rich mixture condition.

8. If the 02S voltage is above or below the specified range, the 02S and/or the 02S wiring may be faulty. Check the wiring for any breaks, repair as necessary and repeat the test.

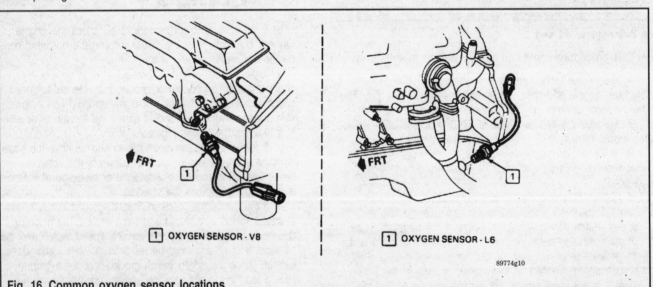

1 OXYGEN SENSOR - V8

1 OXYGEN SENSOR - L6

89774g10

**Fig. 16 Common oxygen sensor locations**

## REMOVAL & INSTALLATION

### ✳✳WARNING

**The sensor uses a permanently attached pigtail and connector. This pigtail should not be removed from the sensor. Damage or removal of the pigtail or connector could affect the proper operation of the sensor. Keep the electrical connector and louvered end of the sensor clean and free of grease. NEVER use cleaning solvents of any type on the sensor. The oxygen sensor may be difficult to remove when the temperature of the engine is below 120°F (49°C). Excessive force may damage the threads in the exhaust manifold or exhaust pipe.**

1. Disconnect the electrical connector and any attaching hardware.
2. Remove the sensor.
3. Coat the threads of the sensor with a GM anti-seize compound # 5613695 or equivalent before installation. New sensors are precoated with this compound.

➡The GM anti-seize compound is NOT a conventional anti-seize paste. The use of a regular paste may electrically insulate the sensor, rendering it useless. The threads MUST be coated with the proper electrically conductive anti-seize compound.

4. Install the sensor and torque to 30 ft. lbs. (40 Nm). Use care in making sure the silicone boot is in the correct position to avoid melting it during operation.
5. Connect the electrical connector and attaching hardware if used.

## Oxidizing Catalytic Converter

### DESCRIPTION

◗ See Figure 17

An underfloor oxidizing catalytic converter is used to control hydrocarbon and carbon monoxide emissions on many 1975 and later models. Control is accomplished by placing a catalyst in the exhaust system to enable all exhaust gas flow to pass through it and undergo a chemical reaction before passing into the atmosphere. The chemical reaction involved is the oxidizing of hydrocarbons and carbon monoxide into water vapor and carbon dioxide.

Fig. 17 The catalytic convertor is mounted forward of the muffler

## DIESEL ENGINE EMISSIONS CONTROLS

## Crankcase Ventilation System

### OPERATION

◗ See Figure 18

A Crankcase Depression Regulator Valve (CDRV) is used to regulate (meter) the flow of crankcase gases back into the engine to be burned. The CDRV is designed to limit vacuum in the crankcase as the gases are drawn from the valve covers through the CDRV and into the intake manifold (air crossover).

Fresh air enters the engine through the combination filter, check valve and oil fill cap. The fresh air mixes with blow-by gases and enters both valve covers. The gases pass through a filter installed on the valve covers and are drawn into connecting tubing.

Intake manifold vacuum acts against a spring loaded diaphragm to control the flow of crankcase gases. Higher intake vacuum levels pull the diaphragm closer to the top of the outlet tube. This reduces the amount of gases being drawn from the crankcase and decreases the vacuum level in the crankcase. As the intake vacuum decreases, the spring pushes the diaphragm away from the top of the outlet tube allowing more gases to flow to the intake manifold.

### ✳✳WARNING

**Do not allow any solvent to come in contact with the diaphragm of the Crankcase Depression Regulator Valve. The diaphragm will fail.**

### TESTING

Do not attempt to test the valve. If you suspect problems with the system, clean the filter and vent pipes with solvent. Be sure to dry the components before installing them.

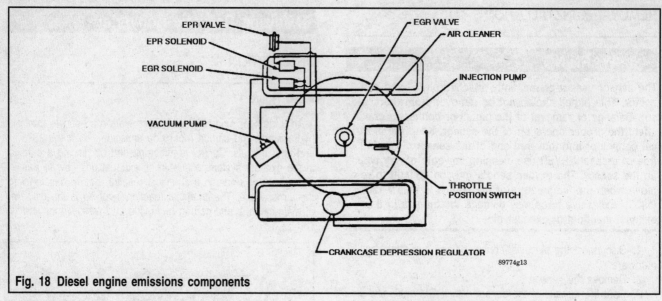

**Fig. 18 Diesel engine emissions components**

## REMOVAL & INSTALLATION

▶ See Figure 19

The components of this system can be removed by disconnecting the hoses and pulling the component from its mounting grommet. Be careful not to damage the grommet; replace if necessary.

## Vacuum Pump

### DESCRIPTION

Since the air crossover and intake manifold in a diesel engine is unrestricted (unlike a gasoline engine which has throttle plates creating a venturi effect) there is no vacuum source. To provide vacuum, a vacuum pump is mounted in the location occupied by the distributor in a gasoline engine. This pump supplies the air conditioning servos, the cruise control servos, and the transmission vacuum modulator where required.

The pump is a diaphragm type which needs no maintenance. It is driven by a drive gear on its lower end which meshes with gear teeth on the end of the engine's camshaft.

## REMOVAL & INSTALLATION

### 6.2L Diesel Engine
▶ See Figure 20

1. Disconnect the batteries.
2. Remove the air cleaner, and cover the intake manifold.
3. Remove the vacuum pump clamp, disconnect the vacuum line and remove the pump.
4. Install a new gasket. Install the pump and reverse the removal procedures for installation.

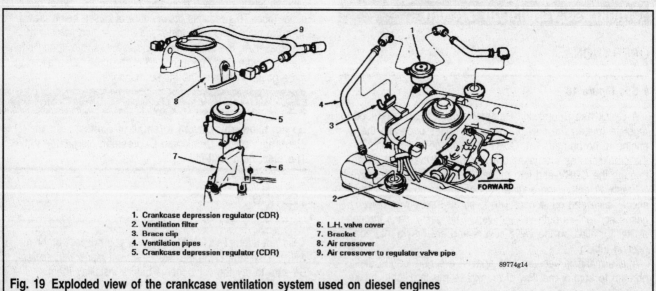

1. Crankcase depression regulator (CDR)
2. Ventilation filter
3. Brace clip
4. Ventilation pipes
5. Crankcase depression regulator (CDR)
6. L.H. valve cover
7. Bracket
8. Air crossover
9. Air crossover to regulator valve pipe

**Fig. 19 Exploded view of the crankcase ventilation system used on diesel engines**

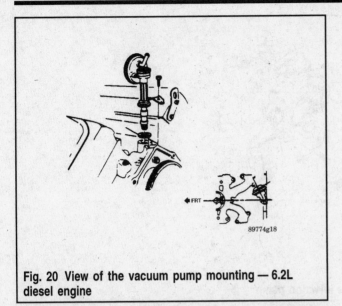

**Fig. 20 View of the vacuum pump mounting — 6.2L diesel engine**

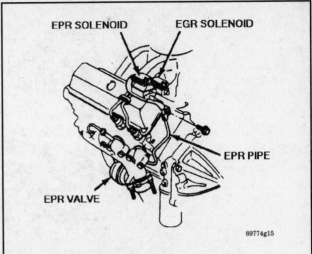

**Fig. 21 Exhaust pressure regulator valve and solenoid — 6.2L diesel engine**

## Exhaust Gas Recirculation (EGR)

### OPERATION

◗ **See Figure 21**

To lower the formation of nitrogen oxides (NOx) in the exhaust, it is necessary to reduce combustion temperatures. This is done in the diesel, as in the gasoline engine, by introducing exhaust gases into the cylinders through the EGR valve.

On the 379 diesel, and Exhaust Pressure Regulator (EPR) valve and solenoid operate in conjunction with the EGR valve. The EPR valve's job is to increase exhaust backpressure in order to increase EGR flow (to reduce nitrous oxide emissions). The EPR valve is usually open, and the solenoid is normally closed. When energized by the B+ wire from the Throttle Position Switch (TPS), the solenoid opens, allowing vacuum to the EPR valve, closing it. This occurs at idle. As the throttle is opened, at a calibrated throttle angle, the TPS de-energizes the EPR solenoid, cutting off vacuum to the EPR valve, closing the valve.

### TESTING

#### Vacuum Regulator Valve (VRV)

◗ **See Figure 22**

The Vacuum Regulator Valve is attached to the side of the injection pump and regulates vacuum in proportion to throttle angle. Vacuum from the vacuum pump is supplied to port A and vacuum at port B is reduced as the throttle is opened. At closed throttle, the vacuum is 15 in. Hg. (103 kPa) at half throttle, 6 in. Hg. (41 kPa) at wide open throttle there is zero vacuum.

#### Exhaust Gas Recirculation (EGR) Valve

◗ **See Figure 23**

Apply vacuum to the vacuum port. The valve should be fully open at 10.5 in. Hg. (72 kPa) and closed below 6 in. Hg. (41 kPa).

#### Response Vacuum Reducer (RVR)

Connect a vacuum gauge to the ports marked to EGR valve and to T.C.C. solenoid. Connect a hand operated vacuum pump to the VRV port. Draw a 15 in.Hg (50.66 kPa) vacuum on the pump and the reading on the vacuum gauge should be lower than the vacuum pump reading as follows:

- 0.75 in.Hg (5 kPa) — except high altitude
- 2.50 in.Hg (17 kPa) — high altitude

#### Torque Converter Clutch Operated Solenoid

When the torque converter clutch is engaged, an electrical signal energizes the solenoid allowing ports 1 and 2 to be interconnected. When the solenoid is not energized, port 1 is closed and ports 2 and 3 are interconnected.

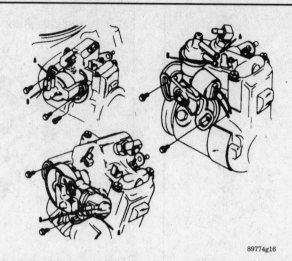

89774g16

**Fig. 22 Diesel Vacuum Regulator Valve (VRV), mounted to the injection pump**

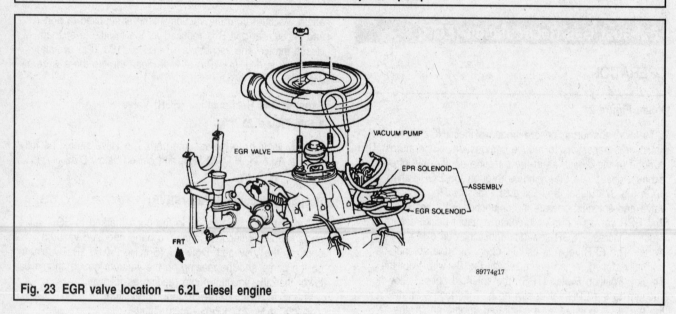

VACUUM PUMP

EGR VALVE

EPR SOLENOID

ASSEMBLY

EGR SOLENOID

FRT

89774g17

**Fig. 23 EGR valve location — 6.2L diesel engine**

## EGR System Diagnosis—Diesel Engine

| Condition | Possible Causes | Correction |
| --- | --- | --- |
| EGR valve will not open. Engine stalls on deceleration. Engine runs rough on light throttle. | Binding or stuck EGR valve. No vacuum to EGR valve. Control valve blocked or air flow restricted. | Replace EGR valve. Replace EGR valve. Check VRV, RVR, solenoid, T.C.C. Operation, Vacuum Pump and connecting hoses. |
| EGR valve will not close.. (Heavy smoke on acceleration). | Binding or stuck EGR valve. Constant high vacuum to EGR valve. | Replace EGR valve. Check VRV, RVR, solenoid, and connecting hoses. |
| EGR valve opens partially. | Binding EGR valve. Low vacuum at EGR valve. | Replace EGR valve. Check VRV, RVR, solenoid, vacuum pump, and connecting hoses. |

89774e01

## VACUUM DIAGRAMS

Following are vacuum diagrams for most of the engine and emissions package combinations covered by this manual. Because vacuum circuits will vary based on various engine and vehicle options, always refer first to the vehicle emission control information label, if present. Should the label be missing, or should vehicle be equipped with a different engine from the vehicle's original equipment, refer to the diagrams below for the same or similar configuration.

If you wish to obtain a replacement emissions label, most manufacturers make the labels available for purchase. The labels can usually be ordered from a local dealer.

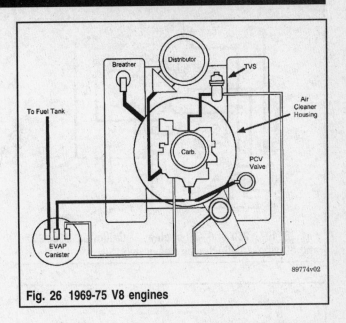

Fig. 26  1969-75 V8 engines

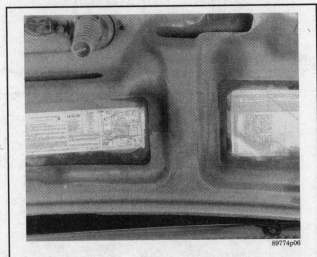

Fig. 24 Most vehicle emission control information labels may be found under the hood of the vehicle

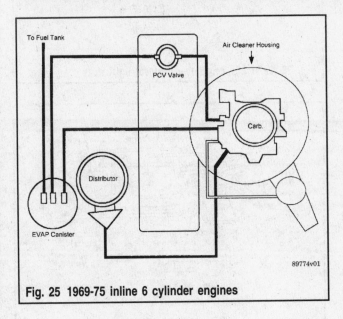

Fig. 25  1969-75 inline 6 cylinder engines

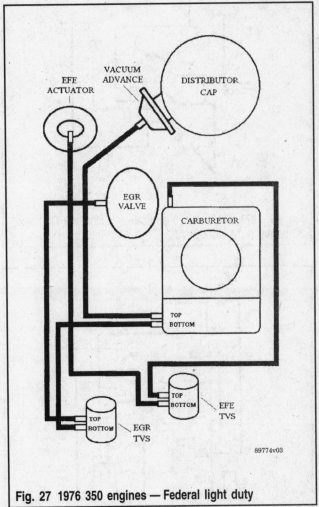

Fig. 27  1976 350 engines — Federal light duty

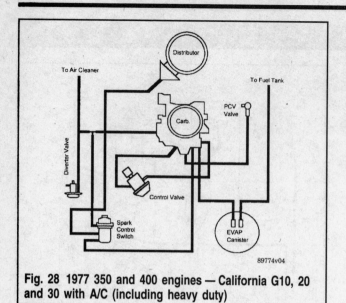

**Fig. 28 1977 350 and 400 engines — California G10, 20 and 30 with A/C (including heavy duty)**

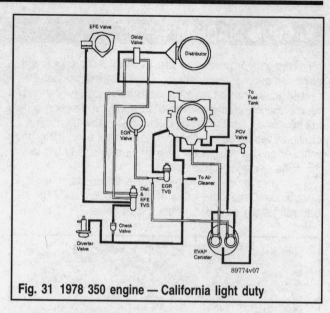

**Fig. 31 1978 350 engine — California light duty**

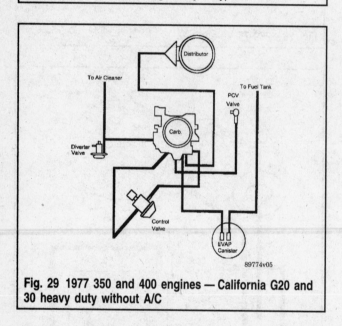

**Fig. 29 1977 350 and 400 engines — California G20 and 30 heavy duty without A/C**

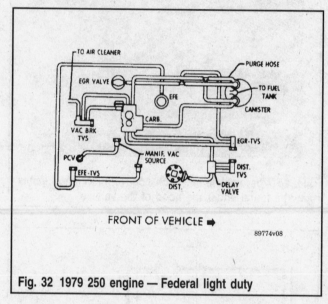

**Fig. 32 1979 250 engine — Federal light duty**

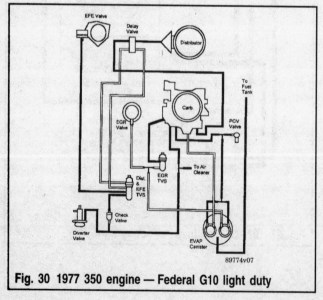

**Fig. 30 1977 350 engine — Federal G10 light duty**

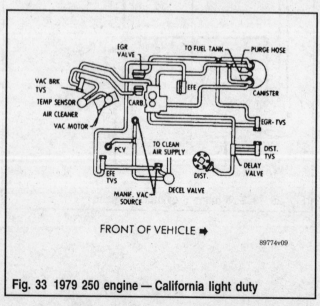

**Fig. 33 1979 250 engine — California light duty**

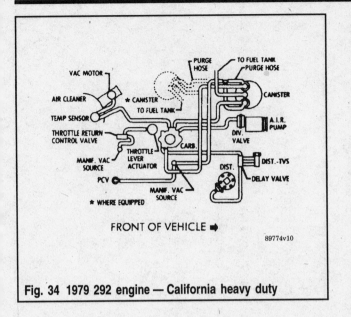

Fig. 34 1979 292 engine — California heavy duty

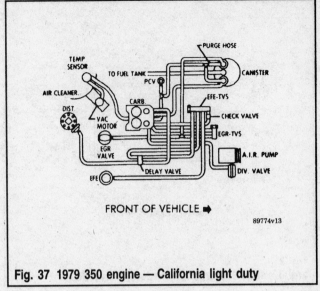

Fig. 37 1979 350 engine — California light duty

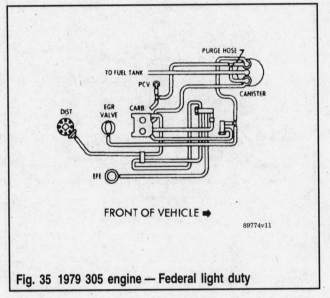

Fig. 35 1979 305 engine — Federal light duty

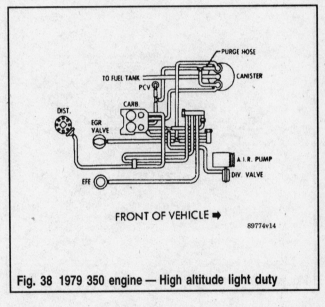

Fig. 38 1979 350 engine — High altitude light duty

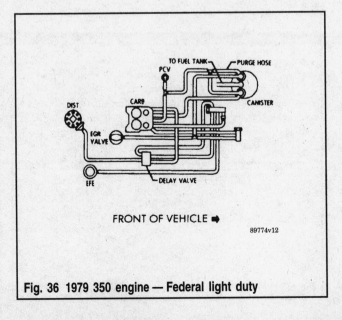

Fig. 36 1979 350 engine — Federal light duty

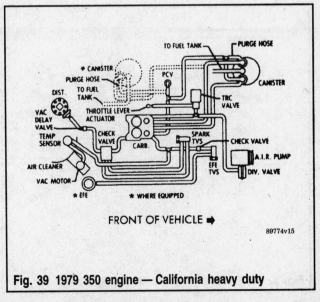

Fig. 39 1979 350 engine — California heavy duty

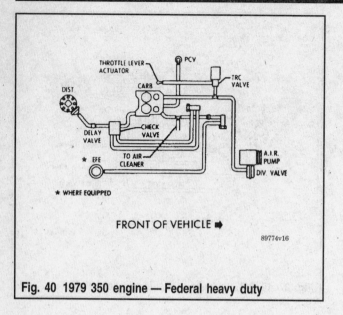

**Fig. 40 1979 350 engine — Federal heavy duty**

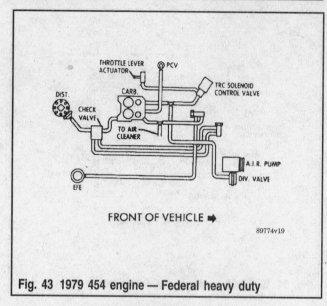

**Fig. 43 1979 454 engine — Federal heavy duty**

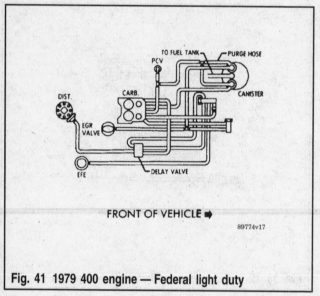

**Fig. 41 1979 400 engine — Federal light duty**

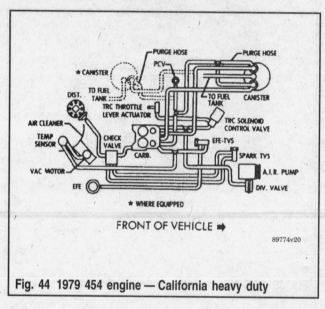

**Fig. 44 1979 454 engine — California heavy duty**

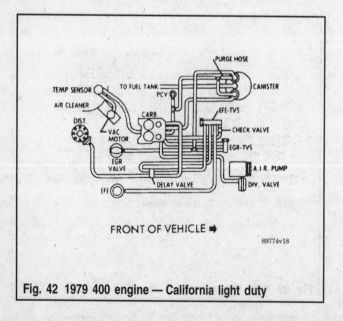

**Fig. 42 1979 400 engine — California light duty**

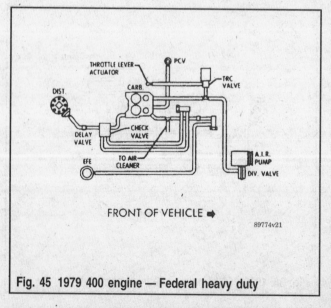

**Fig. 45 1979 400 engine — Federal heavy duty**

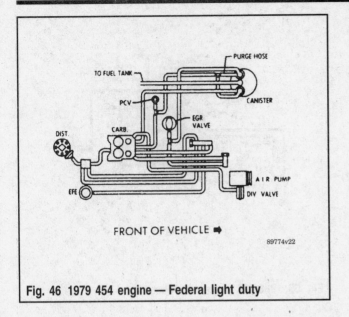

**Fig. 46 1979 454 engine — Federal light duty**

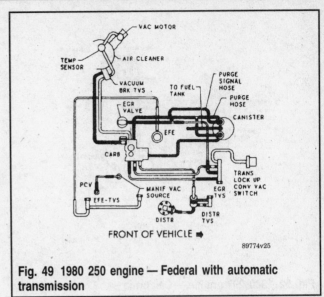

**Fig. 49 1980 250 engine — Federal with automatic transmission**

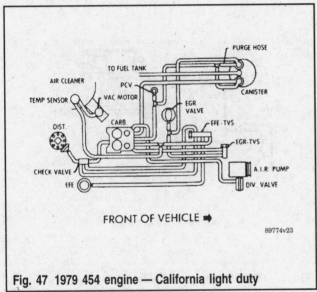

**Fig. 47 1979 454 engine — California light duty**

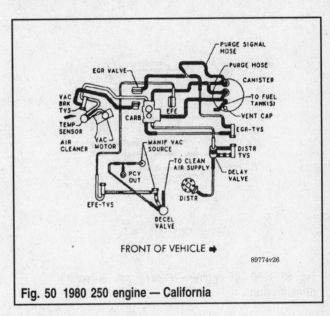

**Fig. 50 1980 250 engine — California**

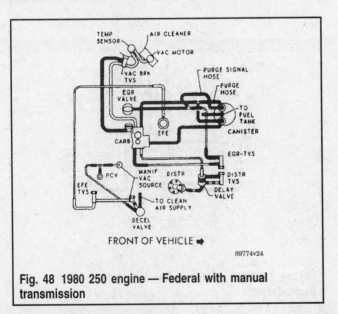

**Fig. 48 1980 250 engine — Federal with manual transmission**

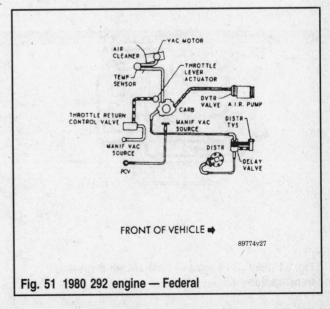

**Fig. 51 1980 292 engine — Federal**

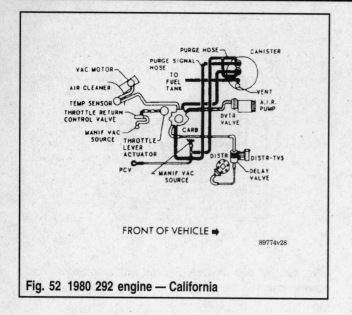

Fig. 52 1980 292 engine — California

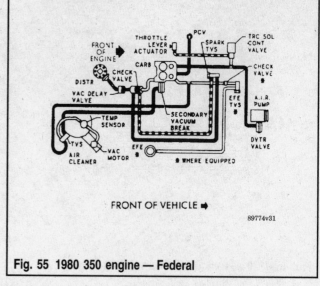

Fig. 55 1980 350 engine — Federal

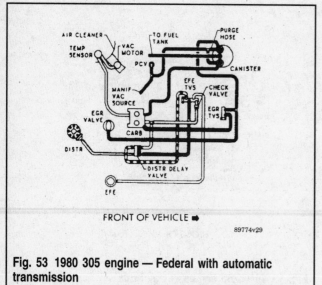

Fig. 53 1980 305 engine — Federal with automatic transmission

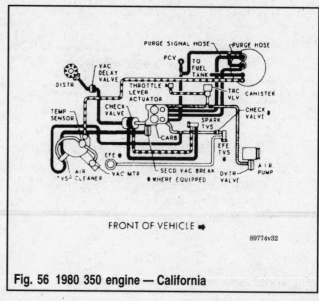

Fig. 56 1980 350 engine — California

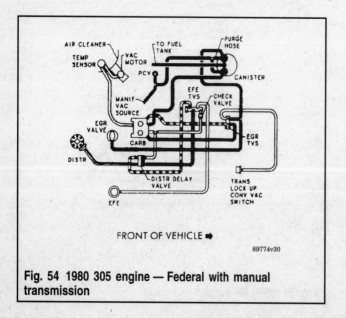

Fig. 54 1980 305 engine — Federal with manual transmission

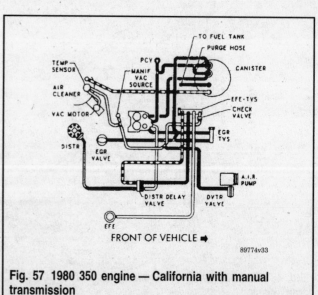

Fig. 57 1980 350 engine — California with manual transmission

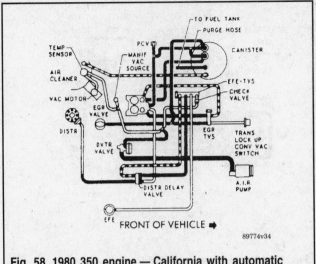

**Fig. 58 1980 350 engine — California with automatic transmission and inline diverter valve**

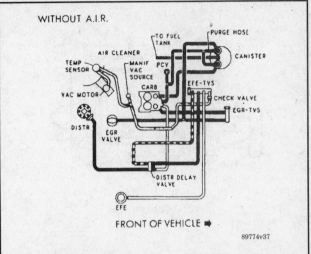

**Fig. 61 1980 350 engine — Federal manual transmission without AIR**

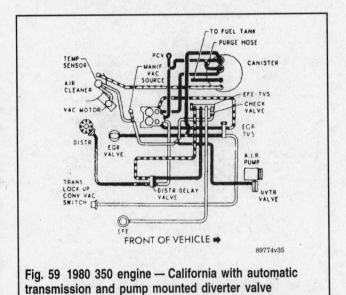

**Fig. 59 1980 350 engine — California with automatic transmission and pump mounted diverter valve**

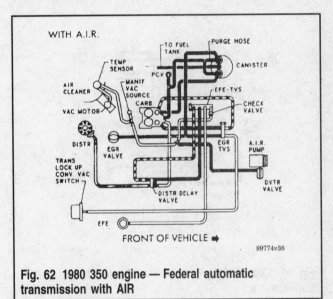

**Fig. 62 1980 350 engine — Federal automatic transmission with AIR**

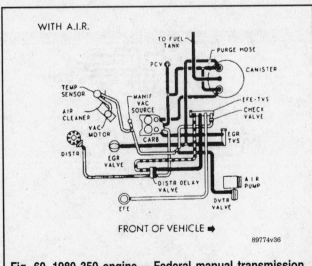

**Fig. 60 1980 350 engine — Federal manual transmission with AIR**

**Fig. 63 1980 350 engine — Federal automatic transmission without AIR**

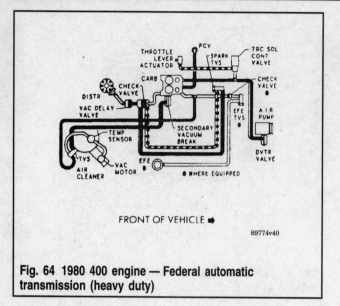

**Fig. 64  1980 400 engine — Federal automatic transmission (heavy duty)**

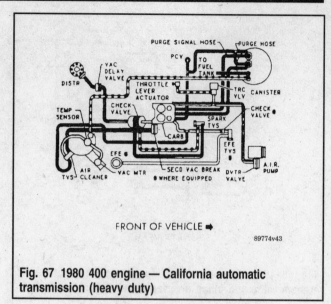

**Fig. 67  1980 400 engine — California automatic transmission (heavy duty)**

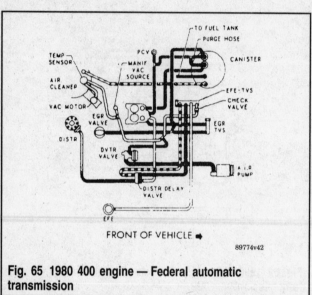

**Fig. 65  1980 400 engine — Federal automatic transmission**

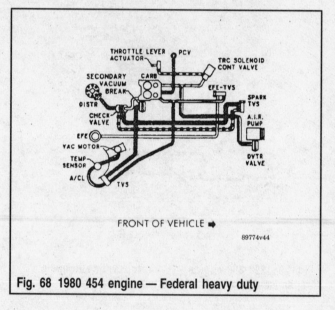

**Fig. 68  1980 454 engine — Federal heavy duty**

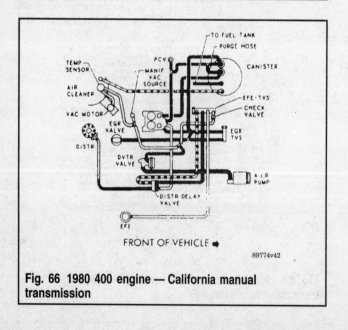

**Fig. 66  1980 400 engine — California manual transmission**

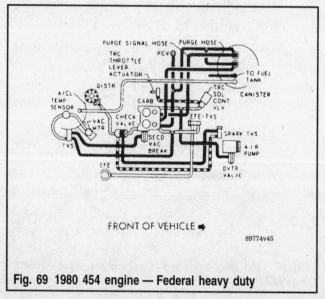

**Fig. 69  1980 454 engine — Federal heavy duty**

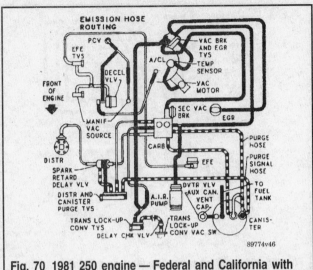

**Fig. 70 1981 250 engine — Federal and California with automatic transmission and auxiliary tank**

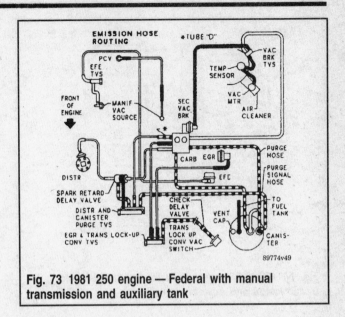

**Fig. 73 1981 250 engine — Federal with manual transmission and auxiliary tank**

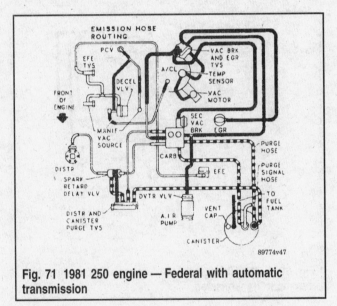

**Fig. 71 1981 250 engine — Federal with automatic transmission**

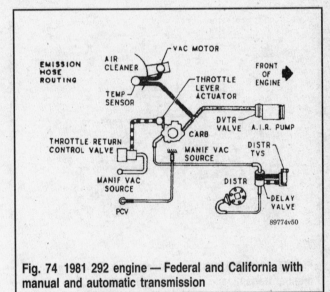

**Fig. 74 1981 292 engine — Federal and California with manual and automatic transmission**

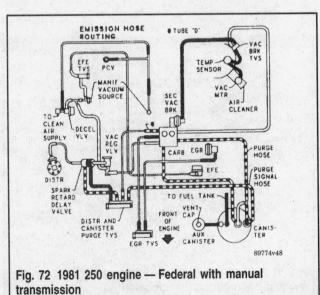

**Fig. 72 1981 250 engine — Federal with manual transmission**

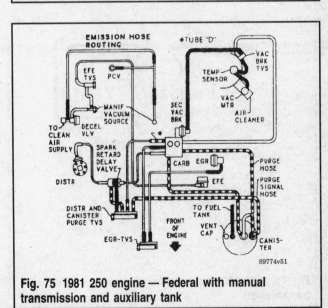

**Fig. 75 1981 250 engine — Federal with manual transmission and auxiliary tank**

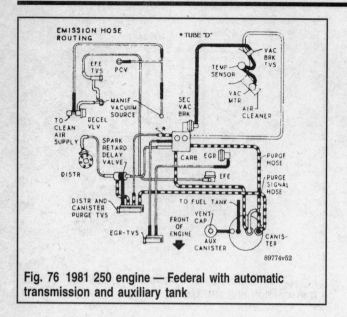

Fig. 76 1981 250 engine — Federal with automatic transmission and auxiliary tank

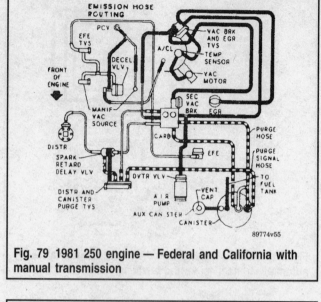

Fig. 79 1981 250 engine — Federal and California with manual transmission

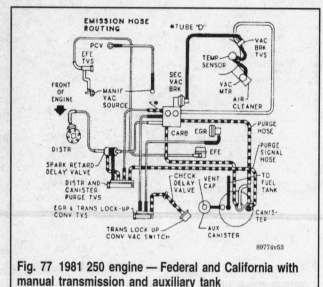

Fig. 77 1981 250 engine — Federal and California with manual transmission and auxiliary tank

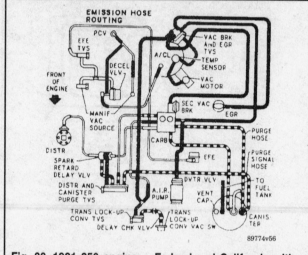

Fig. 80 1981 250 engine — Federal and California with automatic transmission

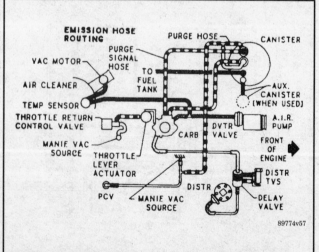

Fig. 78 1981 250 engine — Federal with manual transmission

Fig. 81 1981 292 engine — Federal and California with automatic and manual transmission

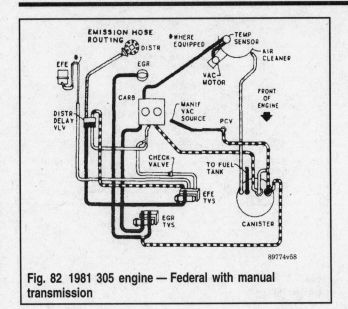

**Fig. 82 1981 305 engine — Federal with manual transmission**

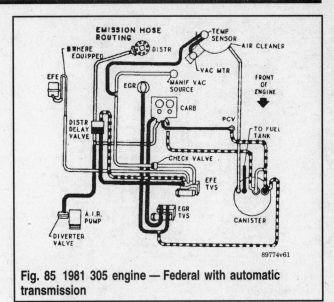

**Fig. 85 1981 305 engine — Federal with automatic transmission**

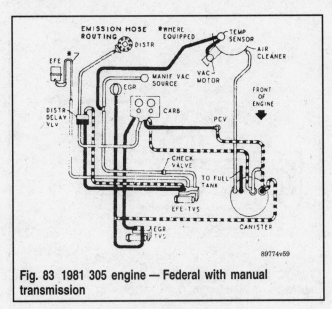

**Fig. 83 1981 305 engine — Federal with manual transmission**

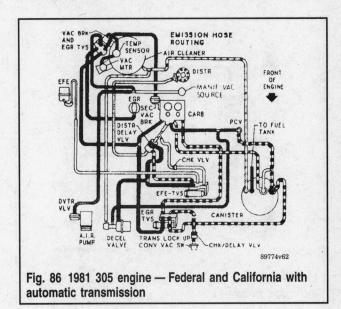

**Fig. 86 1981 305 engine — Federal and California with automatic transmission**

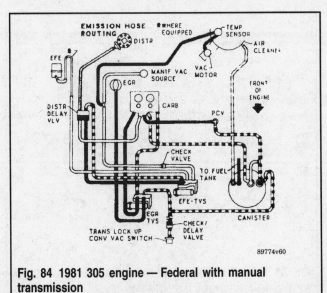

**Fig. 84 1981 305 engine — Federal with manual transmission**

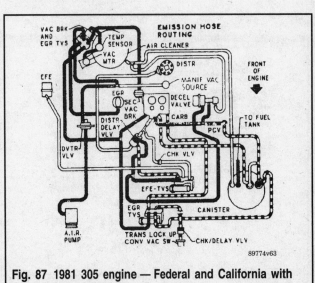

**Fig. 87 1981 305 engine — Federal and California with automatic transmission**

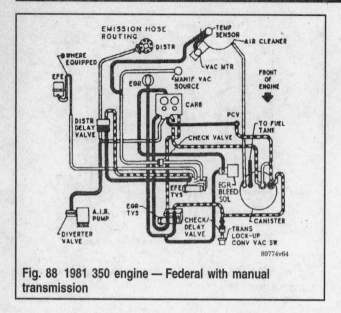

Fig. 88 1981 350 engine — Federal with manual transmission

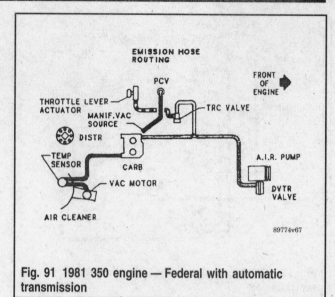

Fig. 91 1981 350 engine — Federal with automatic transmission

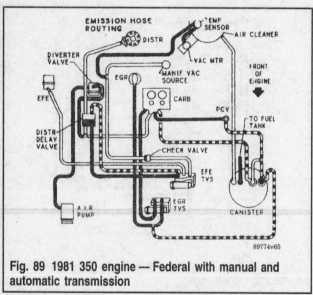

Fig. 89 1981 350 engine — Federal with manual and automatic transmission

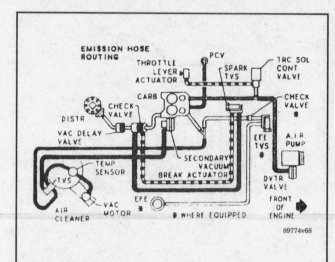

Fig. 92 1981 350 engine — Federal with manual and automatic transmission

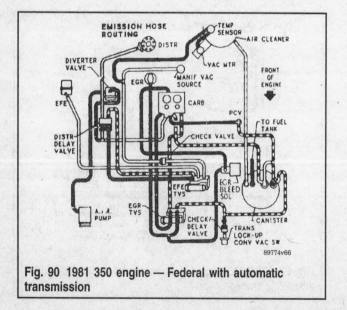

Fig. 90 1981 350 engine — Federal with automatic transmission

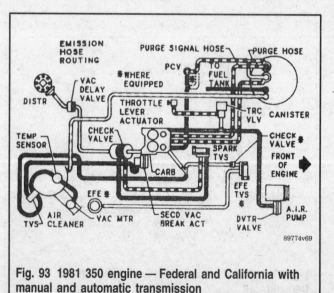

Fig. 93 1981 350 engine — Federal and California with manual and automatic transmission

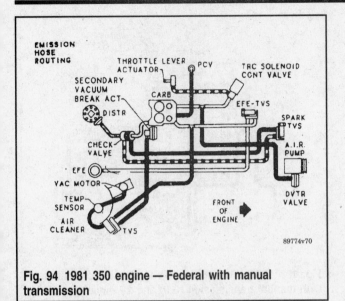

Fig. 94 1981 350 engine — Federal with manual transmission

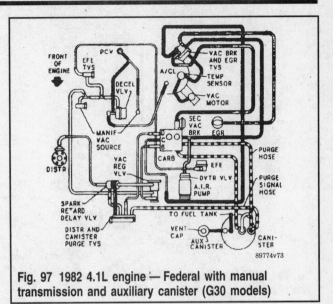

Fig. 97 1982 4.1L engine — Federal with manual transmission and auxiliary canister (G30 models)

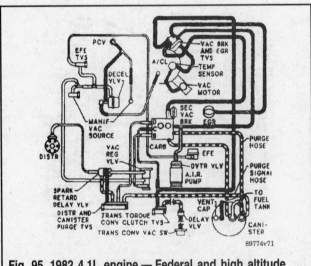
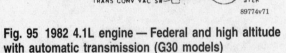

Fig. 95 1982 4.1L engine — Federal and high altitude with automatic transmission (G30 models)

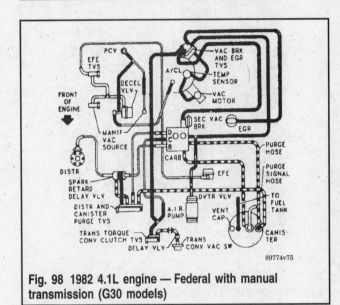

Fig. 98 1982 4.1L engine — Federal with manual transmission (G30 models)

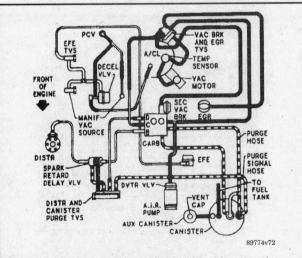

Fig. 96 1982 4.1L engine — California with manual transmission and auxiliary canister (G10 and 20 models)

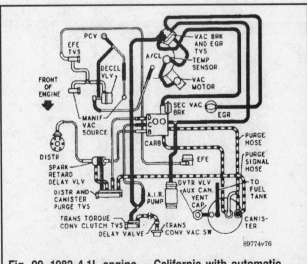

Fig. 99 1982 4.1L engine — California with automatic transmission (G10 and 20 models)

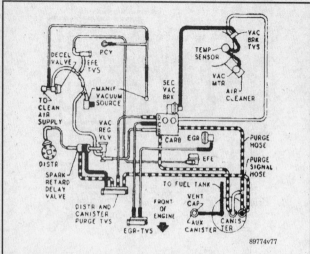

Fig. 100 1982 4.1L engine — Federal with manual transmission (G10 and 20 models)

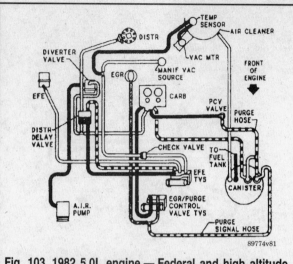

Fig. 103 1982 5.0L engine — Federal and high altitude with manual transmission (G10 and 20 models)

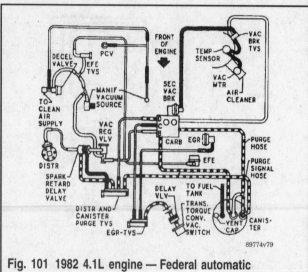

Fig. 101 1982 4.1L engine — Federal automatic transmission (G10 and 20 models)

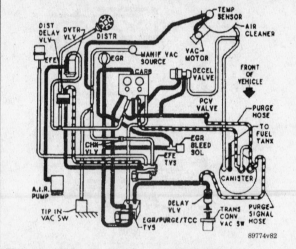

Fig. 104 1982 5.0L engine — High altitude with automatic transmission (G10 and 20 models)

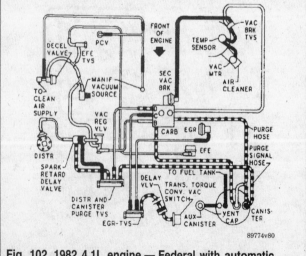

Fig. 102 1982 4.1L engine — Federal with automatic transmission (G10 and 20 models)

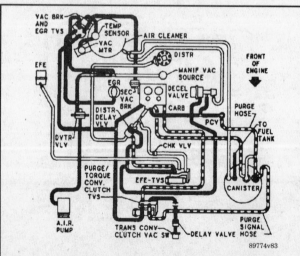

Fig. 105 1982 5.0L engine — Automatic transmission G10 and 20 models

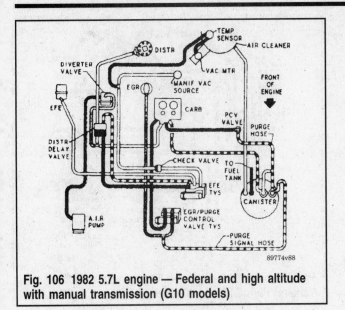

**Fig. 106 1982 5.7L engine — Federal and high altitude with manual transmission (G10 models)**

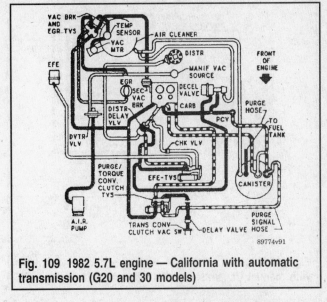

**Fig. 109 1982 5.7L engine — California with automatic transmission (G20 and 30 models)**

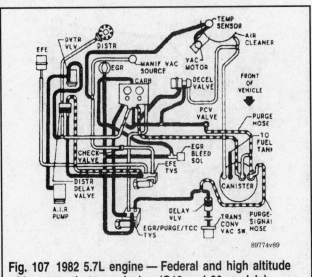

**Fig. 107 1982 5.7L engine — Federal and high altitude with automatic transmission (G10 and 20 models)**

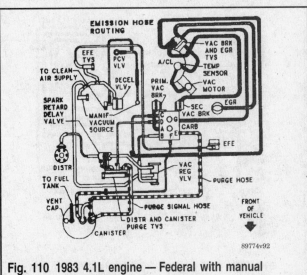

**Fig. 110 1983 4.1L engine — Federal with manual transmission (G10, 20 and 30 models)**

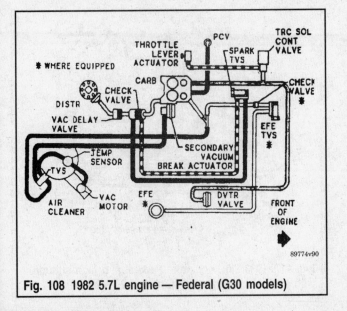

**Fig. 108 1982 5.7L engine — Federal (G30 models)**

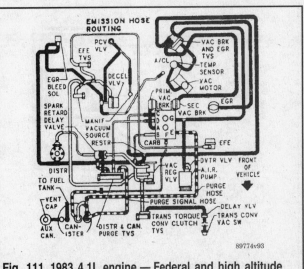

**Fig. 111 1983 4.1L engine — Federal and high altitude with automatic transmission (G10, 20 and 30 models)**

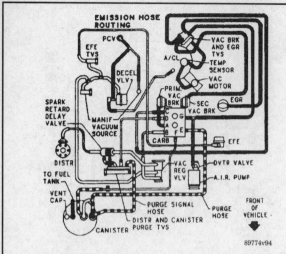

Fig. 112 1983 4.1L engine — Federal and high altitude with manual transmission (G10, 20 and 30 models)

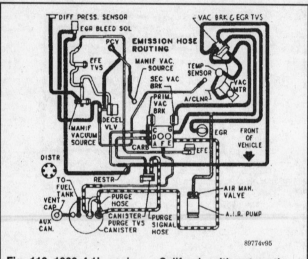

Fig. 113 1983 4.1L engine — California with automatic transmission (G10, 20 and 30 models)

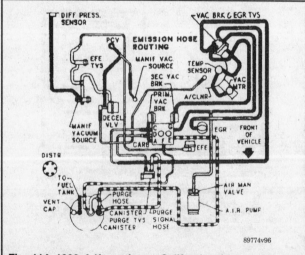

Fig. 114 1983 4.1L engine — California with manual transmission (G10, 20 and 30 models)

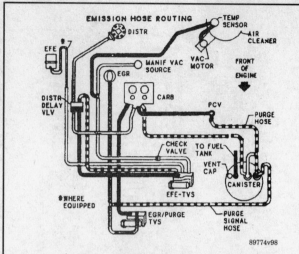

Fig. 115 1983 5.0L engine — Federal with manual transmission (G10 and 20 models)

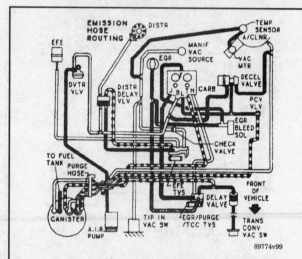

Fig. 116 1983 5.0L engine — Federal and high altitude with automatic transmission (G10 and 20 models)

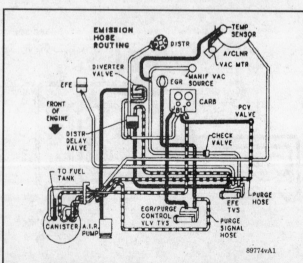

Fig. 117 1983 5.0L engine — Federal and high altitude with manual transmission (G10 and 20 models)

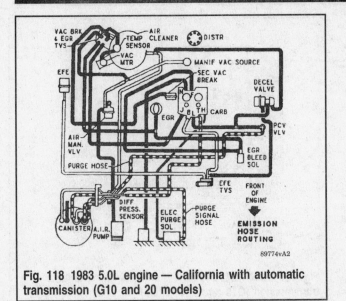

Fig. 118 1983 5.0L engine — California with automatic transmission (G10 and 20 models)

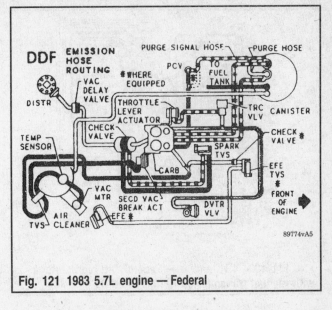

Fig. 121 1983 5.7L engine — Federal

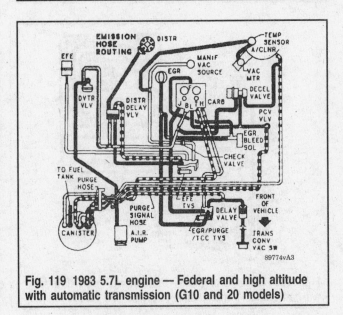

Fig. 119 1983 5.7L engine — Federal and high altitude with automatic transmission (G10 and 20 models)

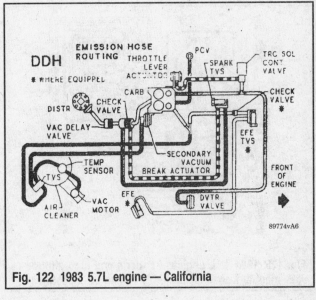

Fig. 122 1983 5.7L engine — California

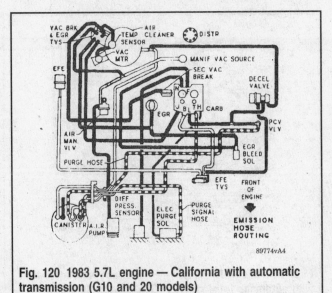

Fig. 120 1983 5.7L engine — California with automatic transmission (G10 and 20 models)

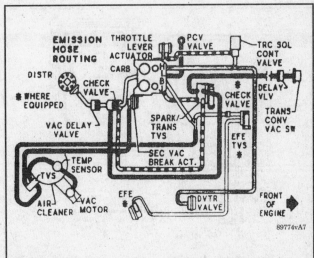

Fig. 123 1983 5.7L engine — California with automatic transmission

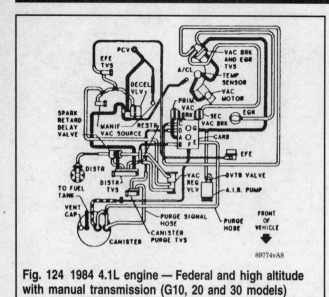

**Fig. 124 1984 4.1L engine — Federal and high altitude with manual transmission (G10, 20 and 30 models)**

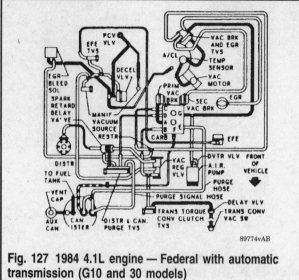

**Fig. 127 1984 4.1L engine — Federal with automatic transmission (G10 and 30 models)**

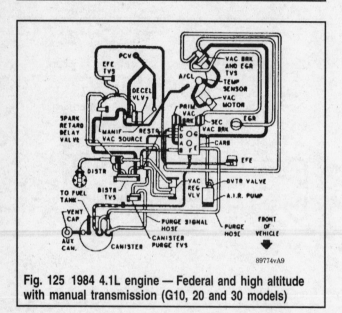

**Fig. 125 1984 4.1L engine — Federal and high altitude with manual transmission (G10, 20 and 30 models)**

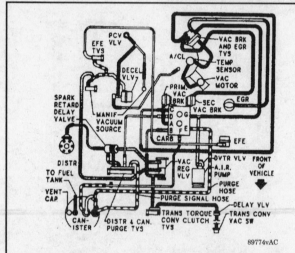

**Fig. 128 1984 4.1L engine — Federal and high altitude with automatic transmission (G10, 20 and 30 models)**

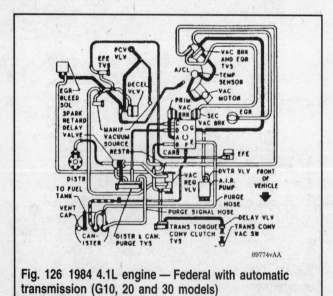

**Fig. 126 1984 4.1L engine — Federal with automatic transmission (G10, 20 and 30 models)**

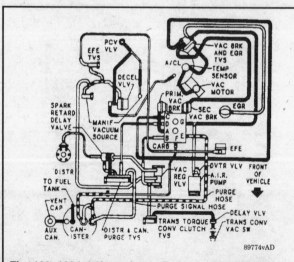

**Fig. 129 1984 4.1L engine — Federal and high altitude with automatic transmission (G10, 20 and 30 models)**

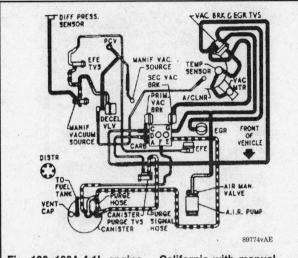

Fig. 130 1984 4.1L engine — California with manual transmission (G10 and 20 models)

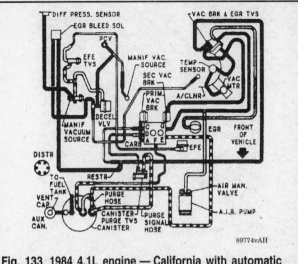

Fig. 133 1984 4.1L engine — California with automatic transmission (G10 and 20 models)

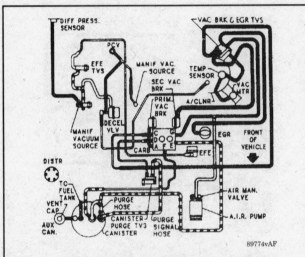

Fig. 131 1984 4.1L engine — California with manual transmission (G10 and 20 models)

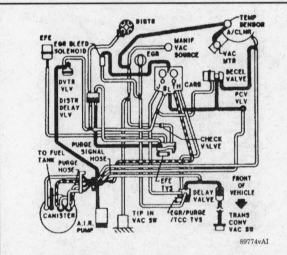

Fig. 134 1984 5.0L engine — Federal with automatic transmission (G10 and 20 models)

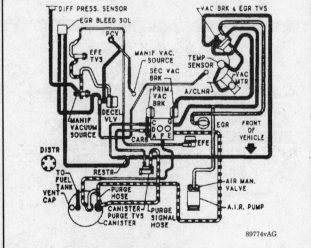

Fig. 132 1984 4.1L engine — California with automatic transmission (G10 and 20 models)

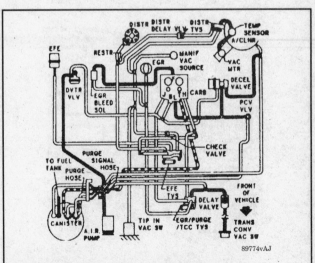

Fig. 135 1984 5.0L engine — High altitude with automatic transmission (G10 and 20 models)

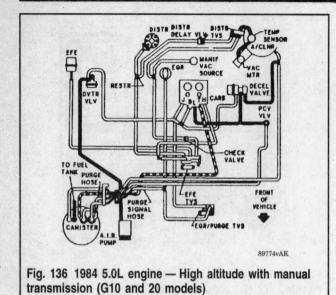

Fig. 136 1984 5.0L engine — High altitude with manual transmission (G10 and 20 models)

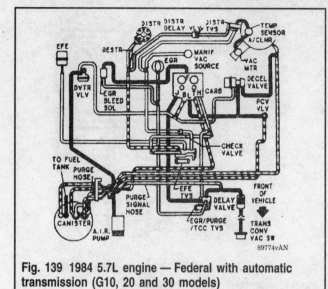

Fig. 139 1984 5.7L engine — Federal with automatic transmission (G10, 20 and 30 models)

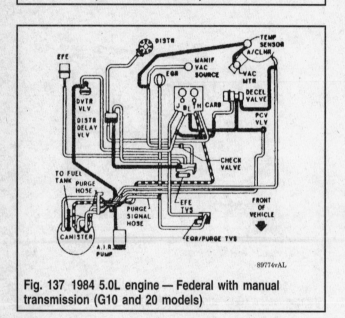

Fig. 137 1984 5.0L engine — Federal with manual transmission (G10 and 20 models)

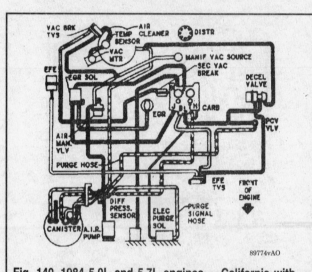

Fig. 140 1984 5.0L and 5.7L engines — California with automatic transmission (G10, 20 and 30 models)

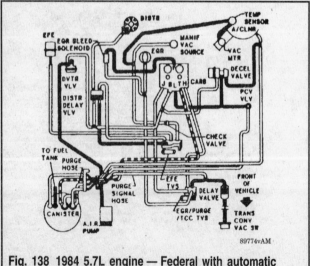

Fig. 138 1984 5.7L engine — Federal with automatic transmission (G10, 20 and 30 models)

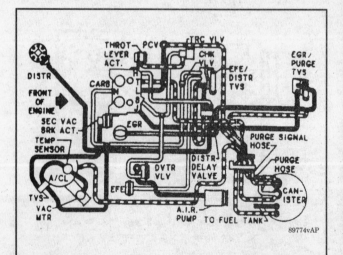

Fig. 141 1984 5.7L engine — California with automatic transmission (G30 heavy duty models)

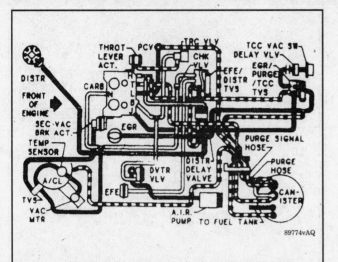

Fig. 142  1984 5.7L engine — California with automatic transmission (G30 heavy duty models)

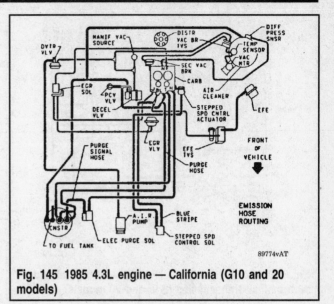

Fig. 145  1985 4.3L engine — California (G10 and 20 models)

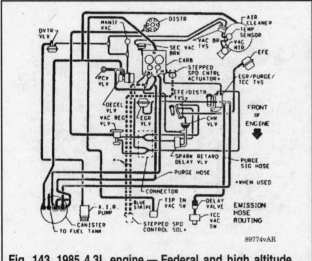

Fig. 143  1985 4.3L engine — Federal and high altitude with automatic transmission (G10, 20 and 30 models)

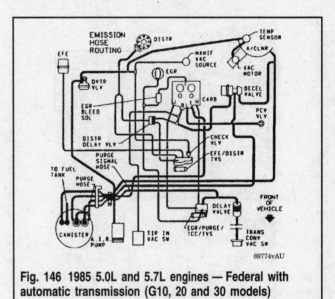

Fig. 146  1985 5.0L and 5.7L engines — Federal with automatic transmission (G10, 20 and 30 models)

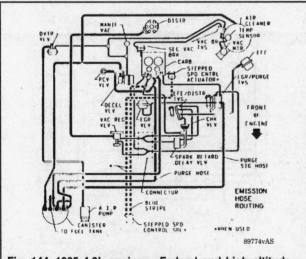

Fig. 144  1985 4.3L engine — Federal and high altitude with manual transmission (G10, 20 and 30 models)

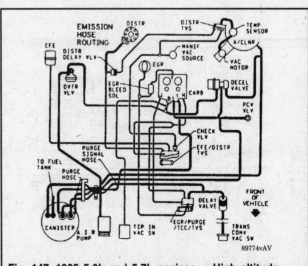

Fig. 147  1985 5.0L and 5.7L engines — High altitude with automatic transmission (G10, 20 and 30 models)

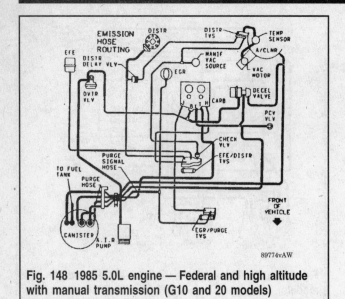

Fig. 148 1985 5.0L engine — Federal and high altitude with manual transmission (G10 and 20 models)

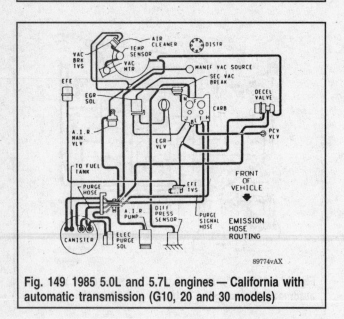

Fig. 149 1985 5.0L and 5.7L engines — California with automatic transmission (G10, 20 and 30 models)

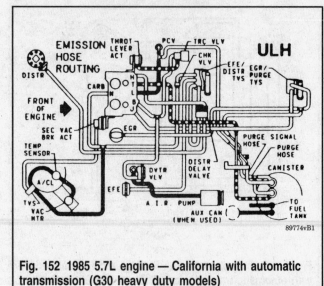

Fig. 151 1985 5.7L engine — California with automatic transmission (G30 heavy duty models)

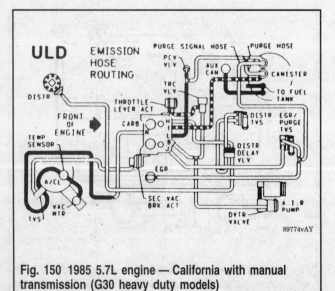

Fig. 150 1985 5.7L engine — California with manual transmission (G30 heavy duty models)

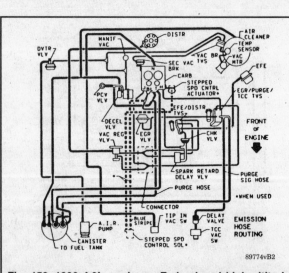

Fig. 152 1985 5.7L engine — California with automatic transmission (G30 heavy duty models)

Fig. 153 1986 4.3L engine — Federal and high altitude with automatic transmission (G10, 20 and 30 models)

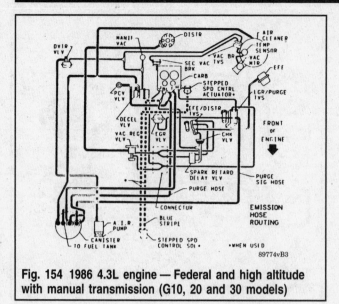

Fig. 154  1986 4.3L engine — Federal and high altitude with manual transmission (G10, 20 and 30 models)

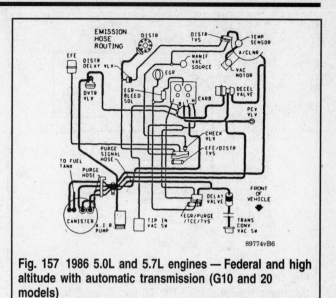

Fig. 157  1986 5.0L and 5.7L engines — Federal and high altitude with automatic transmission (G10 and 20 models)

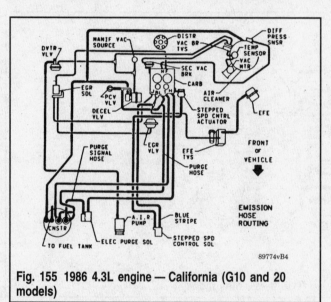

Fig. 155  1986 4.3L engine — California (G10 and 20 models)

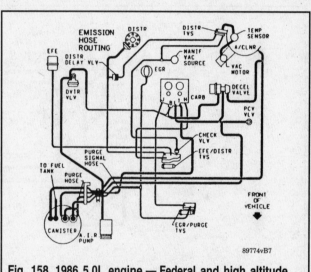

Fig. 158  1986 5.0L engine — Federal and high altitude with manual transmission (G10 and 20 models)

Fig. 156  1986 5.0L engine — Federal with automatic transmission (G10 and 20 models)

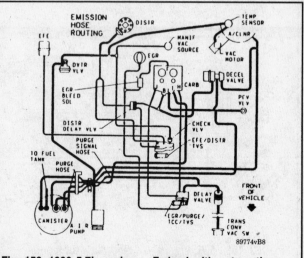

Fig. 159  1986 5.7L engine — Federal with automatic transmission (G10, 20 and 30 models)

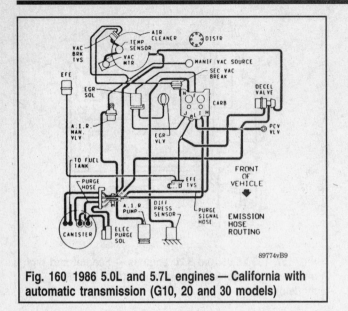

Fig. 160 1986 5.0L and 5.7L engines — California with automatic transmission (G10, 20 and 30 models)

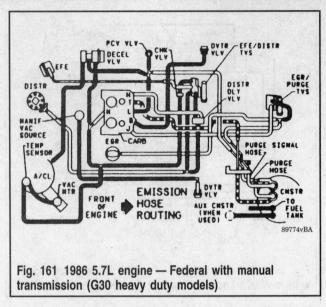

Fig. 161 1986 5.7L engine — Federal with manual transmission (G30 heavy duty models)

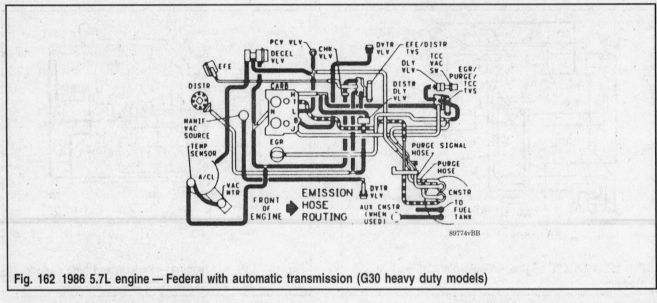

Fig. 162 1986 5.7L engine — Federal with automatic transmission (G30 heavy duty models)

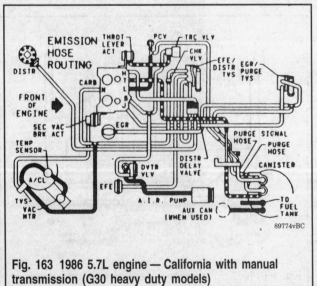

Fig. 163 1986 5.7L engine — California with manual transmission (G30 heavy duty models)

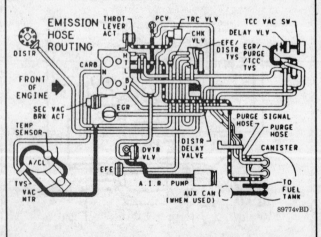

Fig. 164 1986 5.7L engine — California with automatic transmission G30 (heavy duty models)

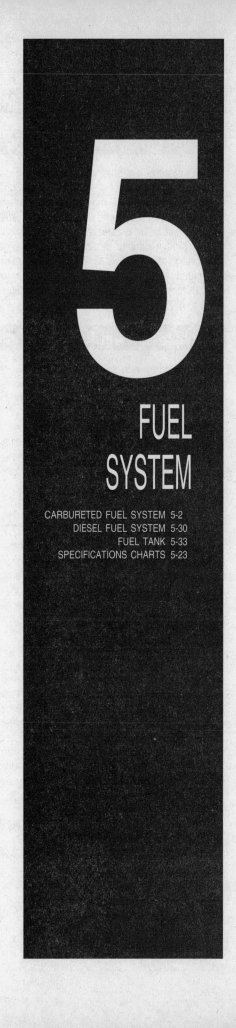

# 5

# FUEL SYSTEM

## CARBURETED FUEL SYSTEM

### Basic Fuel System Diagnosis

When there is a problem starting or driving a vehicle, two of the most important checks involve the ignition and the fuel systems. The questions most mechanics attempt to answer first, "is there spark?" and "is there fuel?" will often lead to solving most basic problems. For ignition system diagnosis and testing, please refer to the information on engine electrical components and ignition systems found earlier in this manual. If the ignition system checks out (there is spark), then you must determine if the fuel system is operating properly (is there fuel?).

### Mechanical Fuel Pump

The fuel pump is a single action AC diaphragm type. All fuel pumps used on inline and V8 engines in vans are diaphragm type and because of design are serviced by replacement only. No adjustments or repairs are possible.

The pump is operated by an eccentric on the camshaft. On six cylinder engines, the eccentric acts directly on the pump rocker arm. On V8 engines, a pushrod between the camshaft eccentric and the fuel pump operates the pump rocker arm.

### TESTING

Fuel pumps should always be tested on the vehicle. The larger line between the pump and tank is the suction side of the system and the smaller line, between the pump and carburetor, is the pressure side. A leak in the pressure side would be apparent because of dripping fuel. A leak in the suction side is usually only apparent because of a reduced volume of fuel delivered to the pressure side.

1. Tighten any loose line connections and look for any kinks or restrictions.
2. Disconnect the fuel line at the carburetor. Disconnect the distributor-to-coil primary wire. Place a container at the end of the fuel line and crank the engine a few revolutions. If little or no gasoline flows from the line, either the fuel pump is inoperative or the line is plugged. Disconnect the line at the pump and the tank; blow through the line with compressed air and try again. Reconnect the line. If the problem is traced to the tank, the tank and gauge unit must be removed to check the condition of the inlet filter screen. See Section 10 for tank removal.
3. If fuel flows in good volume, check the fuel pump pressure to be sure.
4. Attach a pressure gauge to the pressure side of the fuel line.
5. Run the engine and note the reading on the gauge. Stop the engine and compare the reading with the specifications listed in the Tune-Up Specifications chart. If the pump is operating properly, the pressure will be as specified and will be constant at idle speed. If pressure varies or is too high or low, the pump should be replaced.
6. Remove the pressure gauge.

### REMOVAL & INSTALLATION

▶ See Figure 1

### ✳✳CAUTION

**Never smoke when working around gasoline! Avoid all sources of sparks or ignition. Gasoline vapors are EXTREMELY volatile!**

➡**When you connect the fuel pump outlet fitting, always use 2 wrenches to avoid damaging the pump.**

1. Disconnect the fuel intake and outlet lines at the pump and plug the pump intake line.
2. On V6 and V8 engines, you can remove the upper bolt from the right front engine mounting boss (on the front of the block) and insert a long bolt to hold the fuel pump pushrod.
3. Remove the two pump mounting bolts and lockwashers; remove the pump and its gasket.
4. If the rocker arm pushrod is to be removed from the V6s and V8s, remove the two adapter bolts and lockwashers and remove the adapter and its gasket.
5. Install the fuel pump with a new gasket reversing the removal procedure. Heavy grease can be used to hold the fuel pump pushrod up when installing the pump, if you didn't install the long bolt in Step 2. Coat the mating surfaces with sealer.
6. Connect the fuel lines an check for leaks.

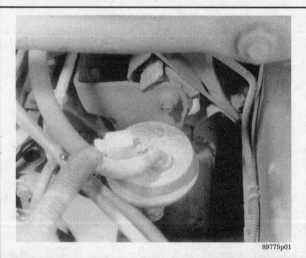

89775p01

**Fig. 1 Common mechanical fuel pump used on GM full-size vans**

## Carburetor

### PRELIMINARY CHECKS

#### All Models

The following should be observed before attempting any adjustments.

1. Thoroughly warm the engine. If the engine is cold, be sure that it reaches operating temperature.

2. Check the torque of all carburetor mounting nuts. Also check the intake manifold-to-cylinder head bolts. If air is leaking at any of these points, any attempts at adjustment will inevitably lead to frustration.

3. Check the manifold heat control valve (if used) to be sure that it is free.

4. Check and adjust the choke as necessary.

5. Adjust the idle speed and mixture. If any adjustments are performed that might possibly change the idle speed or mixture, adjust the idle and mixture again when you are finished.

### ADJUSTMENTS

These adjustment are arranged by carburetor model. Most of these vans use General Motors Rochester carburetors. The first number of the carburetor model number indicates the number of barrels, while the last letter indicates the type of choke used. These are V for the manifold mounted choke coil, C for the choke coil mounted on the carburetor, and E for electric choke.

➡**Most of these adjustments require that measurements be made to thousandths of an inch, using some sort of gauge. Drill bits are ideal for this purpose.**

#### Rochester B Carburetor — 1967 Models

##### FLOAT LEVEL AND FLOAT DROP

▶ **See Figures 2 and 3**

The air horn must be removed to make this adjustment. The carburetor need not be removed from the manifold.

1. Remove the air cleaner and the air horn.

2. Hold the air horn (with the gasket in place) so that the floats hang free.

3. Measure the distance from the gasket surface to the bottom of the float with a T-scale. The distance should be as specified. If not, bend the tang until the floats are parallel and the specified distance from the gasket. The floats should also be aligned to avoid interference with the bowl.

4. Turn the air horn over so that the float arm closes the needle valve. Bend the tang until the distance is as specified.

5. Reinstall the air horn and adjust the idle speed and mixture.

##### IDLE VENT

1. Open the throttle and insert the specified gauge between the throttle valve and the bore opposite the idle needle.

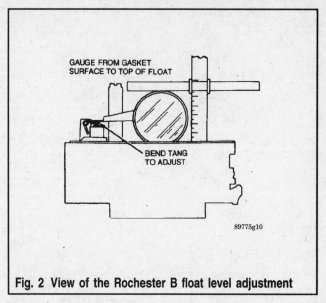

**Fig. 2 View of the Rochester B float level adjustment**

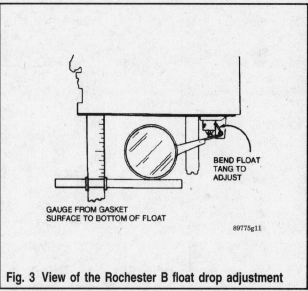

**Fig. 3 View of the Rochester B float drop adjustment**

2. Adjust by turning the valve on top of the air horn until the vent is just opening.

#### Carter YF Carburetor — 1967 Models

▶ **See Figure 4**

##### IDLE VENT

1. With choke open, back out the idle speed screw until free to close the throttle valve.

2. Insert feeler gauge between the air horn and vent valve. Adjust to get 0.065 in. (1.651mm) clearance.

##### FAST IDLE AND CHOKE VALVE

1. Hold the choke valve closed.

2. Close the throttle and mark the position of the throttle lever tang on the fast idle cam.

3. The mark on the fast idle cam should align with the upper edge of the tang on the throttle lever. If not, bend the choke rod as necessary.

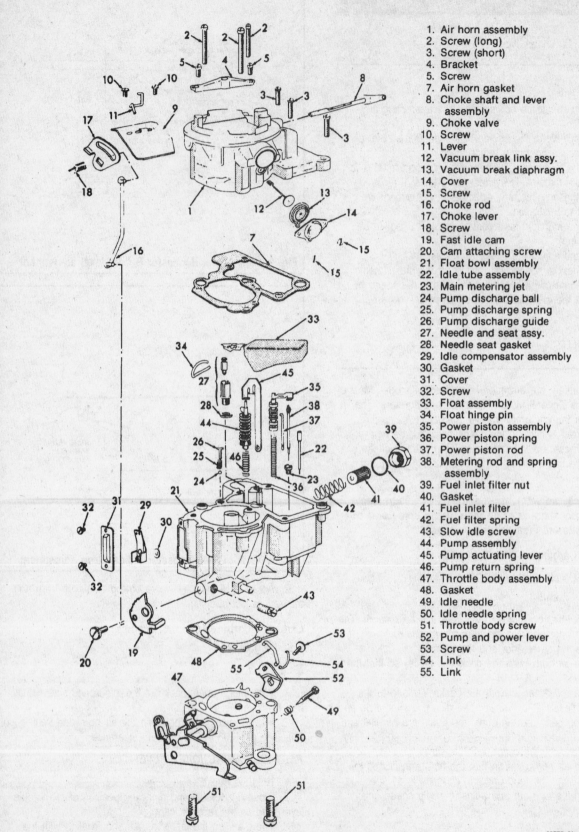

1. Air horn assembly
2. Screw (long)
3. Screw (short)
4. Bracket
5. Screw
7. Air horn gasket
8. Choke shaft and lever assembly
9. Choke valve
10. Screw
11. Lever
12. Vacuum break link assy.
13. Vacuum break diaphragm
14. Cover
15. Screw
16. Choke rod
17. Choke lever
18. Screw
19. Fast idle cam
20. Cam attaching screw
21. Float bowl assembly
22. Idle tube assembly
23. Main metering jet
24. Pump discharge ball
25. Pump discharge spring
26. Pump discharge guide
27. Needle and seat assy.
28. Needle seat gasket
29. Idle compensator assembly
30. Gasket
31. Cover
32. Screw
33. Float assembly
34. Float hinge pin
35. Power piston assembly
36. Power piston spring
37. Power piston rod
38. Metering rod and spring assembly
39. Fuel inlet filter nut
40. Gasket
41. Fuel inlet filter
42. Fuel filter spring
43. Slow idle screw
44. Pump assembly
45. Pump actuating lever
46. Pump return spring
47. Throttle body assembly
48. Gasket
49. Idle needle
50. Idle needle spring
51. Throttle body screw
52. Pump and power lever
53. Screw
54. Link
55. Link

89775g01

**Fig. 4 Exploded view of a Carter YF carburetor**

### CHOKE UNLOADER

1. Open the throttle to the wide open position.
2. Using a rubber band, hold the choke valve closed.
3. Bend the unloader tang on the throttle lever to get the proper clearance between the lower edge of the choke valve and the air horn wall.

### VACUUM BREAK

1. Hold the vacuum break arm against its stop and hold the choke closed with a rubber band.
2. Bend the vacuum bread link to get the specified distance between the lower edge of the choke valve and the air horn wall.

### FLOAT LEVEL

1. Turn the bowl cover upside down and measure the float level by measuring the distance between the float (free end) and the cover. The distance should be $7/32$ in. (5.5mm); if not bend the lip of the float, not the float arm.
2. Hold the cover in proper position (not upside down) and measure the amount of float drop from the cover to the float bottom at the end opposite the hinge. This distance should be specified.
3. Make the adjustment by the stop tab on the float arm.

### ACCELERATOR PUMP

1. Seat the throttle valve by backing off the idle speed screw.
2. Hold the throttle valve closed.
3. Fully depress the diaphragm shaft and check the contact between lower retainer and the lifter link.
4. This retainer (upper pump spring) should just contact the pump lifter link buy do not compress the spring.
5. To adjust bend the pump connector link at its U-bend.

### METERING ROD

1. Insert the metering rod through the metering jet and close the throttle valve. Press down on the upper pump spring until the pump bottoms.
2. Metering rod arm must rest on the pump lifter link and the rod eye should just slide over the arm pin.
3. To adjust, bend the metering rod arm.

**Rochester M and MV Carburetors — 1968-74 Models**

### FAST IDLE SPEED

➡The fast idle adjustment must be made with the transmission in Neutral.

1. Position the fast idle lever on the high step of the fast idle cam.
2. Be sure that the choke is properly adjusted and in the wide open position with the engine warm.
3. Bend the fast idle lever until the specified speed is obtained.

### CHOKE ROD (FAST IDLE CAM)

➡Adjust the fast idle before making choke rod adjustments.

1. Place the fast idle cam follower on the second step of the fast idle cam and hold it firmly against the rise to the high step.
2. Rotate the choke valve in the direction of a closed choke by applying force to the choke coil lever.
3. Bend the choke rod, at the lower angle, to give the specified opening between the lower edge of the choke valve and the inside air horn wall.

➡Measurement must be made at the center of the choke valve.

### CHOKE VACUUM BREAK

The adjustment of the vacuum break diaphragm unit insures correct choke valve opening after engine starting.
1. Remove the air cleaner on vehicles with Therm/AC air cleaner; plug the sensor's vacuum take off port.
2. Using an external vacuum source, apply vacuum to the vacuum break diaphragm until the plunger is seated, push the choke valve toward the closed position. The vacuum break rod should be in the end of the slot.
3. Holding the choke valve in this position, place the specified gauge between the lower edge of the choke valve and the air horn wall.
4. If the measurement is not correct, bend the vacuum break rod at the angle.

### CHOKE UNLOADER

1. Apply pressure to the choke valve and hold it in the closed position.
2. Open the throttle valve to the wide open position.
3. Check the dimension between the lower edge of the choke plate and the air horn wall; if adjustment is needed, bend the unloader tang on the throttle lever to adjust to specification.

### AUTOMATIC CHOKE COIL ROD

1. Disconnect the coil rod from the upper choke lever and hold the choke valve closed.
2. Push down on the coil rod to the end of its travel.
3. The top of the rod should be even with the bottom hole in the choke lever.
4. To make adjustments, bend the rod at the center.

### FLOAT LEVEL

1. Remove the carburetor top. Hold the float retainer in place and the float arm against the top of the float needle by pushing down on the flat arm at the outer end toward the flat bowl casting.
2. Using an adjustable T scale, measure the distance from the tow of the float to the float bowl gasket surface.

➡The float bowl gasket should be removed and the gauge held on the index point on the float for accurate measurement.

3. Adjust the float level by bending the float arm up or down at the float arm junction.

### METERING ROD

1. Hold the throttle valve wide-open and push down on the metering rod against spring tension, then remove the rod from the main metering jet.

2. In order to check adjustment, the slow idle screw must be backed out and the fast idle cam rotated so that the fast idle cam follower does not contact the steps on the cam.

3. With the throttle valve closed, push down on the power piston until it contacts its stop.

4. With the power piston depressed, swing the metering rod holder over the flat surface of the bowl casting next to the carburetor bore.

5. Insert a specified size drill between the bowl casting sealing beak and the lower surface of the metering rod holder. The drill should slide smoothly between both surfaces.

6. If adjustment is needed, carefully bend the metering rod holder up or down at the point shown. After adjustment, reinstall the metering rod.

### IDLE VENT — 1968-69 MODELS

1. The engine idle must be set at the specified rpm and the choke valve held wide-open so that the fast idle cam follower is not contacting the cam.

➡**If the carburetor is off the car, a preliminary idle setting can be made by turning the idle speed screw in 1½ turns from the closed throttle valve position.**

2. With the throttle stop screw held against the idle stop screw, the idle vent valve should be open 0.050 in. (1.27mm). To check, a drill of specified size may be inserted between the top of the air horn casting and the bottom surface of the valve.

3. If adjustment is necessary, turn the slotted vent valve head with a screwdriver. Turning the head clockwise increases the clearance.

➡**On models equipped with an idle stop solenoid, the solenoid must be activated when checking and adjusting the valve.**

### COMBINED EMISSION CONTROL (CEC) SOLENOID — 1971-73 MODELS

➡**Do not use the CEC valve to set idle rpm.**

1. With the engine running, and transmission in Neutral (manual) or Drive (automatic), air conditioner OFF, distributor vacuum hose removed and plugged, and fuel tank vapor hose disconnected, manually extend the CEC valve plunger to contact the throttle lever.

2. Adjust the plunger length to obtain the CEC valve rpm.

3. Reconnect the vapor hose and vacuum hose.

### Model 1MV and 1ME Carburetors — 1975-78 Models

### FAST IDLE SPEED

▸ **See Figure 5**

1. Check and adjust the idle speed.

2. With the engine at normal operating temperature, air cleaner ON, EGR valve signal line disconnected and plugged and the air conditioning OFF, connect a tachometer.

3. Disconnect the vacuum advance hose at the distributor and plug the line.

4. With the transmission in Neutral (park on automatic), start the engine and set the fast idle cam follower on the high step of the cam.

5. Bend the tang in or out to obtain the fast idle speed.

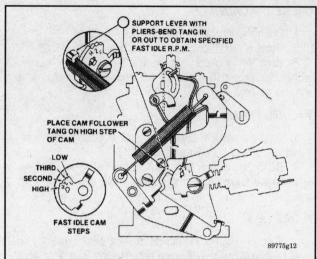

Fig. 5 Location of the cam follower and the tang for the fast idle adjustment — 1MV and 1ME carburetors

### FAST IDLE CAM (CHOKE ROD)

1. Check and adjust the fast idle speed.

2. Set the fast idle cam follower on the second step of the cam.

3. Apply force to the choke coil rod to hold the choke valve toward the closed position.

4. Measure the clearance between the upper edge (lower 1975) of the choke valve and the inside of the air horn wall.

5. Bend the rod at the lower angle to adjust.

### CHOKE UNLOADER

1. Hold the choke valve down by applying light force to the choke coil lever.

2. Open the throttle valve to wide open.

3. Measure the clearance between the upper edge of the choke valve and the air horn wall.

4. If adjustment is necessary, bend the tang on the throttle lever.

### FLOAT LEVEL

The adjustment is the same as that for the Model MV carburetor, which appears earlier in this section.

### AUTOMATIC CHOKE COIL ROD — 1975 MODELS

1. Detach the top of the rod. Pull the rod up to the end of its travel. Completely close the choke valve.

2. The bottom of the rod should be even with the top of the lever.

3. If adjustment is necessary, bend the rod.

### AUTOMATIC CHOKE COIL ROD — 1976 MODELS

1. Detach the top of the rod. Completely close the choke valve. Push the rod down to the end of its travel.

2. The top of the rod should be even with the bottom of the hole in the choke lever.

3. Bend the rod to adjust.

### ELECTRIC CHOKE ADJUSTMENT — 1977-78 1ME MODELS

1. Place the cam follower on the highest step of the fast idle cam.

2. Hold the choke valve completely closed.

3. Insert a 0.120 in. (3mm) drill bit through the hole in the end of the choke coil housing lever. It should go into the hole in the casting at about the 11 o'clock position.

4. Bend the choke coil rod to adjust.

5. Loosen the three retaining screws and set the choke coil pointer to the center index mark.

➡**Failure of the electric choke heater circuit will cause the oil pressure light to go on.**

### PRIMARY VACUUM BREAK — 1975 MODELS

1. With an outside vacuum source, apply vacuum to the primary vacuum break diaphragm until the plunger is fully seated. The primary diaphragm is the one on the opposite side from the idle speed solenoid.

2. Measure the clearance between the lower edge of the choke valve and the air horn wall.

3. Bend the vacuum break rod to adjust the clearance. Be sure there is no binding or interference.

### PRIMARY VACUUM BREAK — 1976-77 MODELS

1. Place the cam follower on the highest step of the fast idle cam.

2. Tape over the diaphragm housing bleed hole.

3. Apply vacuum until the plunger seats.

4. Push up on the choke coil lever rod in the end of the slot.

5. Measure between the upper end of the choke valve and the air horn. Bend the rod to adjust.

### AUXILIARY VACUUM BREAK — 1975 MODELS

1. With the outside vacuum source, apply vacuum to the auxiliary vacuum break diaphragm (on the same side of the carburetor as the idle speed solenoid) until the plunger seats.

2. Place the cam follower on the high step of the fast idle cam.

3. Measure the clearance between the upper edge of the choke valve and the air horn wall. Bend the link between the vacuum break and the choke valve to adjust.

### Rochester 2G and 2GV Carburetors — 1967-74 Models

These procedures are for both the 1¼ in. (31.75mm) and 1½ in. (38.1mm) models. Where there are differences these are noted. The 1¼ in. model has larger throttle bores and an additional fuel feed circuit to make it suitable for use on the 350 V8.

### FAST IDLE CAM (CHOKE ROD)

1. Turn the idle screw onto the second step of the fast idle cam, abutting against the top step.

2. Hold the choke valve toward the closed position and check the clearance between the upper edge of the choke valve and the air horn wall.

3. If this measurement varies from specifications, bend the tang on the choke lever.

### CHOKE VACUUM BREAK

1. Apply vacuum to the diaphragm to fully seat the plunger.

2. Push the choke valve in toward the closed position and hold it there.

3. Check the distance between the lower edge of the choke valve and the air horn wall.

4. If this dimension is not within specifications, bend the vacuum break rod to adjust.

### CHOKE UNLOADER

1. Hold the throttle valves wide-open and use a rubber band to hold the choke valve toward the closed position.

2. Measure the distance between the upper edge of the choke valve and the air horn wall.

3. If this measurement is not within specifications, bend the unloader tang on the throttle lever to correct it.

### AUTOMATIC CHOKE COIL ROD

1. Hold the choke valve completely open.

2. With the choke coil rod disconnected from the upper level, push downward on the end of the rod to the end of its travel.

3. With the rod pushed fully downward, the bottom of the rod should be even with the bottom of the slotted hole in the lever.

4. To adjust the lever, bend it by using a screwdriver in the smaller slot.

### ACCELERATOR PUMP ROD

1. Back the idle stop screw out and close the throttle valves in their bores.

2. Measure the distance from the top of the air horn to the top of the pump rod.

3. Bend the pump rod at a lower angle to correct this dimension.

### FLOAT LEVEL

Invert the air horn, and with the gasket in place and the needle seated, measure the level as follows:
• On nitrophyl floats, measure from the air horn gasket to the lip on the toe of the float.
• On brass floats, measure from the air horn gasket to the lower edge of the float seam.
Bend the float tang to adjust the level.

### FLOAT DROP

Holding the air horn right side up, measure float drop as follows:
• On nitrophyl floats, measure from the air horn gasket to the lip at the toe of the float.
• On brass floats, measure from the air horn gasket to the bottom of the float.
Bend the float tang to adjust either type floats.

### Model 2GC Carburetor — 1975-78 Models

### ACCELERATOR PUMP ROD

1. Back out the idle speed adjusting screw.

2. Hold the throttle valve completely closed.

3. Measure the distance from the top of the air horn ring to the top of the pump rod.

4. If necessary, bend the pump rod to adjust.

### FAST IDLE CAM

1. Place the idle speed screw on the second step of the fast idle cam against the highest step.
2. Measure the clearance between the upper edge of the choke valve and the air horn wall.
3. Bend the choke lever tang to adjust.

### CHOKE UNLOADER

1. With the throttle valves wide open, place the choke valve in the closed position.
2. Measure the clearance between the upper edge of the choke valve and the air horn casting.
3. Bend the throttle lever tang to adjust.

### INTERMEDIATE CHOKE ROD

1. Remove the thermostatic cover coil, gasket, and inside baffle plate.
2. Place the idle screw on the high step of the fast idle cam.
3. Close the choke valve by pushing up on the intermediate choke lever.
4. Insert a 0.120 in. (3mm) drill bit into the hole inside the choke housing (at about the 11 o'clock position). The edge of the choke lever must align with the edge of the bit.
5. Bend the intermediate choke rod between the two upper bends to adjust.

### AUTOMATIC CHOKE COIL

1. Place the idle screw on the high step of the fast idle cam.
2. Loosen the thermostatic choke coil cover retaining screws.
3. Rotate the choke cover against coil tension until the choke valve begins to close. Continue rotating it until the index mark aligns with the specified point on the choke housing. This point is centered (index), except for 1975-76 automatic, which is one notch rich.
4. Tighten the choke cover retaining screws.

### CHOKE VACUUM BREAK

1. Disconnect the vacuum hose. Using an outside vacuum source, seat the vacuum diaphragm.
2. Cover the vacuum break bleed hole with a small piece of tape so that the diaphragm will be hold inward.
3. Place the idle speed screw on the high step of the fast idle cam.
4. Hold the choke coil lever inside the choke housing toward the closed choke position.
5. Measure the clearance between the upper edge of the choke valve and the air horn wall.
6. Bend the vacuum break rod to adjust.
7. After adjustment, remove the piece of tape and reconnect the vacuum hose.

### FLOAT LEVEL AND FLOAT DROP

These procedures are the same as for the model 2GV, covered earlier.

## Rochester 2SE Carburetor — 1979-84 Models
♦ See Figures 6 and 7

### FLOAT ADJUSTMENT

1. Hold the float retainer in place with you hand and push the float down against the needle.
2. Place a 1/8 in. (3mm) gauge at the toe of the float, as illustrated.
3. Remove the float and bend the arm as necessary to adjust the level.

### FAST IDLE ADJUSTMENT

1. Refer to the underhood emissions sticker. Disconnect and plug any hoses indicted on the sticker.
2. Adjust the curb idle speed as outlined in Section 2.
3. Place the fast idle screw on the high step of the fast idle cam.
4. Turn the screw in or out to adjust the fast idle speed.

### CHOKE COIL LEVER ADJUSTMENT

Refer to the illustration for this adjustment.

### ELECTRIC CHOKE SETTING

1. Loosen the three choke coil retaining screws.
2. Place the fast idle screw on the high step of the fast idle adjusting cam.
3. Set the line on the choke 1 notch counterclockwise from the center mark.

### AIR VALVE ROD ADJUSTMENT

1. Fully seat the diaphragm using an outside vacuum source.
2. Be sure the air valve is completely closed.
3. Place a 0.040 in. (1mm) gauge between the rod and the end of the slot in the lever.
4. Bend the rod to obtain 0.040 in. (1mm) clearance.

### FAST IDLE CAM CHOKE ROD ADJUSTMENT

1. The choke coil lever and the fast idle adjustments must be correct before performing this adjustment.
2. Install a special choke valve measuring gauge (no. J-26701) on the carburetor.
3. Rotate the degree scale until the zero mark is opposite the pointer.
4. With the choke valve completely open, place the magnet directly on top of the choke valve.
5. Rotate the bubble until it is centered.
6. Rotate the scale to place the 17° mark opposite the pointer.
7. Place the fast idle screw on the second highest step of the fast idle cam.
8. Close the choke by pushing on the intermediate choke lever.
9. Push on the vacuum break lever toward the open choke lever until the lever is against the rear tang on the choke lever.
10. Bend the fast idle cam rod until the bubble on the gauge is centered. Remove the gauge.

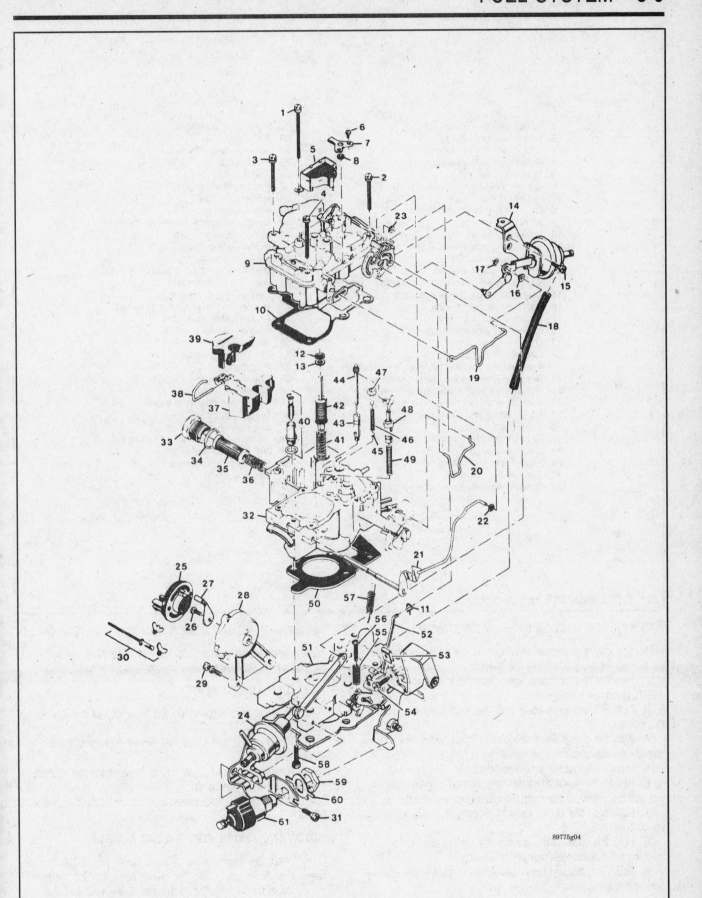

**Fig. 6 Exploded view of the Rochester 2SE carburetor (key list appears on next page)**

89775g04

1. Screw—air horn (long) (2)
2. Screw—air horn (large)
3. Screw—air horn (short) (3)
4. Screw—air horn (medium)
5. Vent stack assembly
6. Screw—hot idle compensator (2)
7. Hot idle compensator
8. Gasket—hot idle compensator
9. Air horn assembly
10. Gasket—air horn
11. Retainer—pump link
12. Seal—pump stem
13. Retainer—stem seal
14. Vacuum break and bracket assembly—primary
15. Screw—vacuum break attaching
16. Bushing—air valve—link
17. Retainer—air valve link
18. Hose—vacuum break—primary
19. Link—air valve
20. Link—fast idle cam
21. Intermediate choke shaft/lever/link assembly
22. Bushing—intermediate choke shaft link
23. Retainer—intermediate choke shaft link
24. Vacuum break and bracket assembly—secondary
25. Choke cover and coil assembly
26. Screw—choke lever
27. Choke lever and contact assembly
28. Choke housing
29. Screw—choke housing (2)
30. Stat cover retainer kit
31. Screw—vacuum break attaching (2)

32. Float bowl assembly
33. Nut—fuel inlet
34. Gasket—fuel inlet nut
35. Filter—fuel inlet
36. Spring—fuel filter
37. Float assembly
38. Hinge pin—float
39. Insert—float bowl
40. Needle and seat assembly
41. Spring—pump return
42. Pump—assembly
43. Jet—main metering
44. Rod—main metering assembly
45. Ball—pump discharge
46. Spring—pump discharge
47. Retainer—pump discharge spring
48. Power piston assembly
49. Spring—power piston
50. Gasket—throttle body
51. Throttle body assembly
52. Pump rod
53. Clip—cam screw
54. Screw—cam
55. Spring—throttle stop screw
56. Screw—throttle stop
57. Idle needle and spring
58. Screw—throttle body attaching (4)
59. Nut—idle solenoid
60. Retainer—idle solenoid
61. Idle solenoid

89775g05

**Fig. 7 Rochester 2SE carburetor key list**

### PRIMARY SIDE VACUUM BREAK ADJUSTMENT

1. The choke coil lever and the fast idle adjustments must be correct before performing this adjustment.

2. Install a special choke valve measuring gauge (no. J-26701) on the carburetor.

3. Rotate the degree scale until the zero mark is opposite the pointer.

4. With the choke valve completely open, place the magnet directly on top of the choke valve.

5. Rotate the bubble until it is centered.

6. Rotate the scale to place the specified degree opposite the pointer. Refer to the carburetor specification chart.

7. Fully seat the choke vacuum diaphragm using an outside vacuum source.

8. Hold the choke valve toward the closed position by pushing on the intermediate choke lever.

9. Bend the vacuum break rod until the bubble is centered and remove the gauge.

### Rochester M2MC and M2ME Carburetors — 1979-81 Models

All adjustments for this carburetor are the same as for the Rochester M4MC/M4ME, with the exception of the following:

### FAST IDLE ADJUSTMENT

1. Hold the cam follower on the high step of the fast idle cam.

2. Turn the fast idle screw out until the primary throttle valves are closed.

3. Turn the fast idle screw out to contact the lever, then turn the screw in two turns.

4. Check the fast idle speed and adjust by turning the screw.

### AUTOMATIC CHOKE COIL — M2MC MODELS

1. Install the thermostatic coil and cover with a gasket between the choke cover and the choke housing. The thermostatic coil must be installed in the slot in the inside of the choke coil lever pick-up arm.

2. Place the fast idle cam follower on the high step of the fast idle cam.

3. Rotate the cover and coil assembly counterclockwise until the choke valve just opens.

4. Align the index point on the cover with the specified mark on the choke housing. The setting is 1 notch lean.

5. Tighten the retaining screws.

### CHOKE COIL LEVER ADJUSTMENT — M2ME MODELS

1. Drill out and remove the cover rivets.

2. Remove the cover and coil.

3. Place the fast idle cam follower on the high step of the cam.

4. Push clockwise upward on the thermostatic coil tang until the choke valve is closed.

5. Insert a 0.12 in. (3mm) gauge rod into the hole in the choke housing.

6. The lower edge of the lever should just touch the gauge rod.

7. Bend the choke rod at its mid-point to adjust.

### Rochester 4MV (Quadrajet) Carburetor — 1970-78 Models

### FAST IDLE SPEED

▶ See Figure 8

1. Position the fast idle lever on the high step of the fast idle cam.

2. Be sure that the choke is wide open and the engine warm. On 1973-74 manual transmission models, disconnect the distributor vacuum advance hose.

3. Turn the fast idle screw to gain the proper fast idle rpm.

### CHOKE ROD (FAST IDLE CAM)

1. Place the cam follower on the second step of the fast idle cam.

2. Close the choke valve by exerting counterclockwise pressure on the external choke lever.

3. Insert a gauge of the proper size between the lower edge (upper, starting with 1975 models) of the choke valve and the inside air horn wall.

4. To adjust, bend the choke rod.

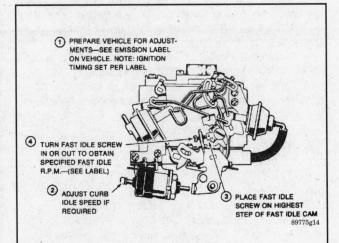

① PREPARE VEHICLE FOR ADJUSTMENTS—SEE EMISSION LABEL ON VEHICLE. NOTE: IGNITION TIMING SET PER LABEL

④ TURN FAST IDLE SCREW IN OR OUT TO OBTAIN SPECIFIED FAST IDLE R.P.M.—(SEE LABEL)

② ADJUST CURB IDLE SPEED IF REQUIRED

③ PLACE FAST IDLE SCREW ON HIGHEST STEP OF FAST IDLE CAM

89775g14

Fig. 8 View of the fast idle adjustment — Rochester 4MV carburetor

### VACUUM BREAK

1. Fully seat the vacuum break diaphragm using an outside vacuum source.

2. Open the throttle valve enough to allow the fast idle cam follower to clear the fast idle cam. Starting with 1975 models, place the cam follower on the high step.

3. The end of the vacuum break rod should be at the outer end of the slot in the vacuum break diaphragm plunger.

4. The specified clearance should register from the lower end of the choke valve to the inside air horn wall.

5. If the clearance is not correct, bend the vacuum break link.

### CHOKE UNLOADER

1. Push up on the vacuum break lever and fully open the throttle valves.

2. Measure the distance from the lower edge (upper, starting with 1975 models) of the choke valve to the air horn wall.

3. To adjust, bend the tang on the fast idle lever.

### AUTOMATIC CHOKE COIL ROD

1. Close the choke valve by rotating the choke coil lever counterclockwise.

2. Disconnect the thermostatic coil rod from the upper lever.

3. Push down on the rod until it contacts the bracket of the coil.

4. The rod must fit in the notch of the upper lever.

5. If it does not, it must be bent on the curved portion just below the upper lever.

➡1976 models that hesitate or stall on acceleration during warm-up may be cured by installation of a new choke coil no. 460110.

### SECONDARY CLOSING

This adjustment assures proper closing of the secondary throttle plates.

1. Set the slow idle as per instructions in Section 2. Make sure that the fast idle cam follower is not resting on the fast idle cam.

2. There should be 0.020 in. (0.5mm) clearance between the secondary throttle actuating rod and the front of the slot on the secondary throttle lever with the closing tang on the throttle lever resting against the actuating lever.

3. Bend the tang on the primary throttle actuating rod to adjust.

### SECONDARY OPENING

1. Open the primary throttle valves until the actuating link contacts the upper tang on the secondary lever.

2. The bottom of the link should be in the center of the secondary lever slot.

3. Bend the upper tang on the secondary lever to adjust as necessary.

### FLOAT LEVEL

▶ See Figure 9

1. Push the float down lightly against the needle, and measure the distance from the air horn gasket surface (gasket removed) to the top of the float at the toe. Measure at a point

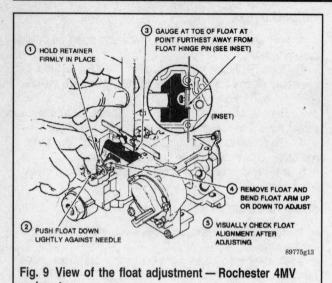

① HOLD RETAINER FIRMLY IN PLACE
③ GAUGE AT TOE OF FLOAT AT POINT FURTHEST AWAY FROM FLOAT HINGE PIN (SEE INSET)
(INSET)
④ REMOVE FLOAT AND BEND FLOAT ARM UP OR DOWN TO ADJUST
② PUSH FLOAT DOWN LIGHTLY AGAINST NEEDLE
⑤ VISUALLY CHECK FLOAT ALIGNMENT AFTER ADJUSTING

89775g13

**Fig. 9 View of the float adjustment — Rochester 4MV carburetor**

3/16 in. (4.76mm) back from the toe for all models except for 1973-76, which should be measured at a point 1/16 in. (1.58mm) back.

➡ **Make sure that the retaining pin is firmly hold in place and that the tang of the float is firmly against the needle and seat assembly.**

2. If necessary, remove the float and bend the float arm up or down to adjust to specifications.
3. Check the float alignment after adjusting.

### ACCELERATOR PUMP

1. Close the primary throttle valves by backing out the slow idle screw and making sure that the fast idle cam follower is off the steps of the fast idle cam.
2. Bend the secondary throttle closing tang away from the primary throttle lever.
3. With the pump in the inner hole (unless specified otherwise in the carburetor chart) in the pump lever, measure from the top of the choke valve wall to the top of the pump stem.
4. To adjust, bend the pump lever.
5. After adjusting, readjust the secondary throttle tang and the slow idle screw.

### AIR VALVE SPRING

To adjust the air valve spring windup, loosen the allen head lockscrew and turn the adjusting screw counterclockwise to remove all spring tension. With the air valve closed, turn the adjusting screw clockwise the specified number of turns after the torsion spring contacts the pin on the shaft. Hold the adjusting screw in this position and tighten the lockscrew.

### Model M4MC and M4ME Carburetors — 1975-86 Models
▶ See Figures 10, 11, 12 and 13

### ACCELERATOR PUMP ROD

1. Take the fast idle cam follower off the fast idle cam steps.
2. Back out the idle speed screw until the throttle valves are completely closed.

3. Be sure that the secondary actuating rod is not preventing the throttle from closing completely. If the primary throttle valves do not close completely, bend the secondary closing tang out of the position, then readjust later.
4. Place the pump rod in the inner hole in the lever, unless specified otherwise in the carburetor chart.
5. Measure the clearance from the top of the choke valve wall, next to the vent stack, and the top of the pump stem.
6. To adjust the dimension, support the pump lever and bend the pump lever.
7. Adjust the idle speed.
8. If necessary, readjust the secondary actuating rod.

### FAST IDLE SPEED

1. Hold the cam follower on the high step of the fast idle cam.
2. Turn the fast idle screw out until the primary throttle valves are closed.
3. Turn the fast idle screw in to contact the lever, then turn the screw in 3 turns.
4. Check the fast idle speed, adjust by turning the screw.

### AUTOMATIC CHOKE COIL LEVER

➡ **For M4ME carburetor adjustments, refer to the M2MC/M2ME carburetor adjustment section.**

1. Loosen the three retaining screws and remove the cover and coil assembly from the choke housing.
2. Place the cam follower on the high step of the fast idle cam.
3. Push up on the thermostatic coil tang (counterclockwise) until the choke valve closes.
4. Insert a 0.120 in. (3mm) drill bit into the hole (at about the 4 o'clock position) in the choke housing.
5. The lower edge of the choke coil lever should just contact the side of the bit.
6. Bend the choke rod to adjust.

### CHOKE ROD (FAST IDLE CAM)
▶ See Figure 14

1. Adjust the fast idle.
2. Place the cam follower on the second step of the fast idle cam firmly against the ride of the high step.
3. Close the choke valve by pushing up on the choke coil lever inside the choke housing.
4. Measure the clearance between the upper edge of the choke valve and the inside of the air horn wall.
5. Bend the tang on the fast idle cam to adjust the clearance. Be sure that the tang lies against the cam after bending it.
6. Recheck the fast idle speed.

### AIR VALVE DASHPOT

1. Seat the front vacuum diaphragm using an outside vacuum source.
2. The air valves must be completely closed.
3. Measure the clearance between the air valve dashpot and the end of the slot in the air valve lever. It should be 0.015 in. (0.38mm).
4. Bend the air valve dashpot to adjust the clearance.

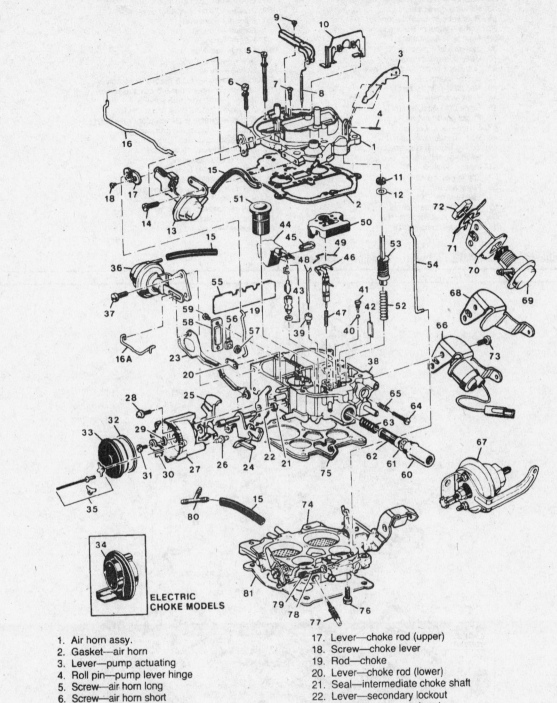

ELECTRIC CHOKE MODELS

1. Air horn assy.
2. Gasket—air horn
3. Lever—pump actuating
4. Roll pin—pump lever hinge
5. Screw—air horn long
6. Screw—air horn short
7. Screw—air horn countersunk
8. Metering rod—secondary
9. Holder and screw—secondary metering rod
10. Baffle—secondary air
11. Seal—pump plunger
12. Retainer—pump seal
13. Vac. break control & bracket—front
14. Screw—control attaching
15. Hose—vacuum
16. Rod—air valve
16A. Rod—air valve (truck)

17. Lever—choke rod (upper)
18. Screw—choke lever
19. Rod—choke
20. Lever—choke rod (lower)
21. Seal—intermediate choke shaft
22. Lever—secondary lockout
23. Link—rear vacuum break
24. Int. choke shaft & lever
25. Cam—fast idle
26. Seal—choke housing to bowl (hot air choke)
27. Kit—choke housing
28. Screw—choke housing to bowl
29. Seal—intermediate choke shaft (hot air choke)
30. Lever—choke coil
31. Screw—choke coil lever
32. Gasket—stat cover (hot air choke)
33. Stat cover & coil assy. (hot air choke)

89775g06

Fig. 10 Exploded view of the Rochester M4MC/M4ME carburetor (key list continues on next page)

34. Stat cover & coil assy. (electric choke)
35. Kit—stat cover attaching
36. Rear vacuum break assembly
37. Screw—vacuum break attaching (2)
38. Float bowl assembly
39. Jet—primary metering (2)
40. Ball—pump discharge
41. Retainer—pump discharge ball
42. Baffle—pump well
43. Needle & seat assembly
44. Float assembly
45. Hinge pin—float assembly
46. Power piston assembly
47. Spring—power piston
48. Rod—primary metering (2)
49. Spring—metering rod retainer
50. Insert—float bowl
51. Insert—bowl cavity
52. Spring—pump return
53. Pump assembly
54. Rod—pump
55. Baffle—secondary bores
56. Idle compensator assembly
57. Seal—idle compensator

58. Cover—idle compensator
59. Screw—idle compensator cover (2)
60. Filter nut—fuel inlet
61. Gasket—filter nut
62. Filter—fuel inlet
63. Spring—fuel filter
64. Screw—idle stop
65. Spring—idle stop screw
66. Idle speed solenoid & bracket assembly
67. Idle load compensator & bracket assembly
68. Bracket—throttle return spring
69. Actuator—throttle lever (truck only)
70. Bracket—throttle lever actuator (truck only)
71. Washer—actuator nut (truck only)
72. Nut—actuator attaching (truck only)
73. Screw—bracket attaching (2)
74. Throttle body assembly
75. Gasket—throttle body
76. Screw—throttle body (3)
77. Idle mixture needle & spring assy. (2)
78. Screw—fast idle adjusting
79. Spring—fast idle screw
80. Tee—vacuum hose
81. Gasket—flange

89775g07

**Fig. 11 Rochester M4MC/M4ME carburetor key list (continued)**

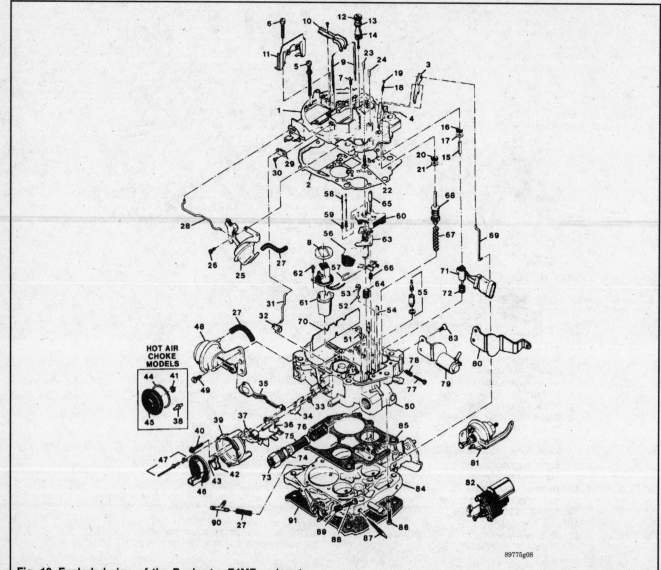

HOT AIR CHOKE MODELS

89775g08

**Fig. 12 Exploded view of the Rochester E4ME carburetor**

1. Air horn assembly
2. Gasket—air horn
3. Lever—pump actuating
4. Roll pin—pump lever hinge
5. Screw—air horn, long (2)
6. Screw—air horn, short
7. Screw—air horn, countersunk (2)
8. Gasket—solenoid connector to air horn
9. Metering rod—secondary (2)
10. Holder & screw—secondary metering rod
11. Baffle—secondary air
12. Valve—idle air bleed
13. "O" ring (thick)—idle air bleed valve
14. "O" ring (thin)—idle air bleed valve
15. Plunger—TPS actuator
16. Seal—TPS plunger
17. Retainer—TPS seal
18. Screw—TPS adjusting
19. Plug—TPS screw
20. Seal—pump plunger
21. Retainer—pump seal
22. Screw—solenoid plunger stop (rich mixture stop)
23. Plug—plunger stop screw (rich mixture stop)
24. Plug—solenoid adjusting screw (lean mixture)
25. Vacuum break & bracket—front
26. Screw—vacuum break attaching (2)
27. Hose—vacuum
28. Rod—air valve
29. Lever—choke rod (upper)
30. Screw—choke lever
31. Rod—choke
32. Lever—choke rod (lower)
33. Seal—intermediate choke shaft
34. Lever—secondary lockout
35. Link—rear vacuum break
36. Intermediate choke shaft & lever
37. Cam—fast idle
38. Seal—choke housing to bowl (hot air choke)
39. Choke housing
40. Screw—choke housing to bowl
41. Seal—intermediate choke shaft (hot air choke)
42. Lever—choke coil
43. Screw—choke coil lever
44. Gasket—stat cover (hot air choke)
45. Stat cover & coil assembly (hot air choke)
46. Stat cover & coil assembly (electric choke)
47. Kit—stat cover attaching
48. Vacuum break assembly—rear
49. Screw—vacuum break attaching (2)
50. Float bowl assembly
51. Jet—primary metering (2)
52. Ball—pump discharge
53. Retainer—pump discharge ball
54. Baffle—pump well
55. Needle & seat assembly
56. Float assembly
57. Hinge pin—float assembly
58. Rod—primary metering (2)
59. Spring—pimary metering rod (2)
60. Insert—float bowl
61. Insert—bowl cavity
62. Screw—connector attaching
63. Mixture control (M/C) solenoid & plunger assembly
64. Spring—solenoid tension
65. Screw—solenoid adjusting (lean mixture)
66. Spring—solenoid adjusting screw
67. Spring—pump return
68. Pump assembly
69. Link—pump
70. Baffle—secondary bores
71. Throttle position sensor (TPS)
72. Spring—TPS tension
73. Filter nut—fuel inlet
74. Gasket—filter nut
75. Filter—fuel inlet
76. Spring—fuel filter
77. Screw—idle stop
78. Spring—idle stop screw
79. Idle speed solenoid & bracket assembly
80. Bracket—throttle return spring
81. Idle load compensator & bracket assembly
82. Idle speed control & bracket assembly
83. Screw—bracket attaching
84. Throttle body assembly
85. Gasket—throttle body
86. Screw—throttle body
87. Idle needle & spring assembly (2)
88. Screw—fast idle adjusting
89. Spring—fast idle screw
90. Tee—vacuum hose
91. Gasket—flange

89775g09

**Fig. 13 Rochester E4ME carburetor key list**

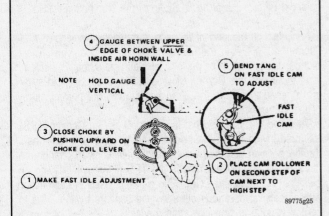

**Fig. 14 View of the E4ME/MC carburetor fast idle cam adjustment**

## FRONT VACUUM BREAK

▶ See Figure 15

1. Remove the thermostatic cover and coil assembly from the choke housing.

2. Place the cam follower on the high step of the fast idle cam.

3. Seat the front vacuum diaphragm using an outside vacuum source.

4. Push up on the inside choke coil lever until the tang on the vacuum break lever contacts the tang on the vacuum break plunger.

5. Measure the clearance between the upper edge of the choke valve and the air horn wall.

6. Turn the adjusting screw on the vacuum break plunger lever to adjust.

7. Reconnect the vacuum hose after adjustment.

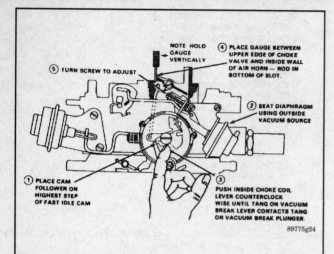

**Fig. 15 View of the E4ME/MC carburetor front vacuum adjustment**

### REAR VACUUM BREAK

▶ See Figure 16

1. Remove the thermostatic cover and coil assembly from the choke housing.

2. Place the cam follower on the high step of the fast idle cam.

3. Plug the bleed hose in the vacuum break unit cover with tape.

4. Seat the rear vacuum diaphragm using an outside vacuum source.

5. Push up the choke coil lever inside the choke housing toward the closed position.

6. With the choke rod in the bottom slot of the choke lever, measure the clearance between the upper edge of the choke valve and air horn wall.

7. Bend the vacuum break rod if necessary to adjust.

8. After adjustment, remove the tape and install the vacuum hose.

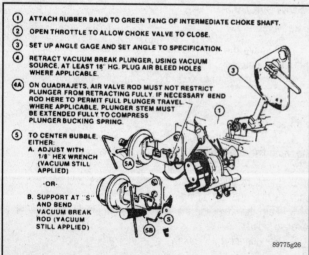

**Fig. 16 View of the E4ME/MC carburetor rear vacuum break adjustment**

### CHOKE UNLOADER

1. Install the thermostatic coil and cover with a gasket between the choke cover and the choke housing. The thermostatic coil must be installed in the slot in the inside of the choke coil lever pick-up arm.

2. Hold the throttle valves wide open with the choke valve completely closed. On a warm engine, close the choke valve by pushing up on the tang of the intermediate choke lever which contact the fast idle cam. A rubber band will hold it in position.

3. Measure the distance between the upper edge of the choke valve and the air horn wall.

4. Bend the tang on the fast idle lever to adjust the clearance. Check to be sure that the tang on the fast idle cam lever is contacting the center of the fast idle cam after adjustment.

### AIR VALVE SPRING

1. Remove the front vacuum break diaphragm and the air valve dashpot rod.

2. Loosen the lockscrew.

3. Turn the tension adjusting screw counterclockwise until the air valve opens part way.

4. Turn the tension adjusting screw clockwise while tapping lightly on the casting with the handle of a screwdriver.

5. When the air valve just closes, turn the tension adjusting screw clockwise the specified number of turns after the spring contacts the pin.

6. Tighten the lockscrew and reinstall the diaphragm and dashpot rod.

### FLOAT LEVEL

Use the procedure given earlier for the model 4MV, measuring at a point 3/16 in. (4.76mm) from the toe of the float.

### Rochester E2SE 2-Bbl. Carburetor

▶ See Figures 17 and 18

The model E2SE carburetor, introduced on Chevrolet trucks in 1983, is designed as a part of the GM Computer Command Control (C3) system. An electrically operated mixture control solenoid differentiates the E2SE from the conventional 2SE series.

A plunger in the end of the above mentioned solenoid is submerged in fuel in the fuel chamber of the float bowl. The plunger is controlled, or pulsed, by electrical signals received from the Electronic Control Module (ECM). The solenoid system is used to control the air/fuel mixture in the primary bore of the carburetor.

The model E2SE also has a Throttle Position Sensor (TPS) mounted in the float bowl and is used to signal the ECM as throttle position changes occur. As throttle position changes, a tang on the pump lever moves the TPS plunger, modifying an electrical signal to the ECM. This signal is used in conjunction with signals from various other engine sensors by the ECM to control various engine operating modes.

### FLOAT ADJUSTMENT

▶ See Figure 19

1. Remove the air horn from the throttle body.

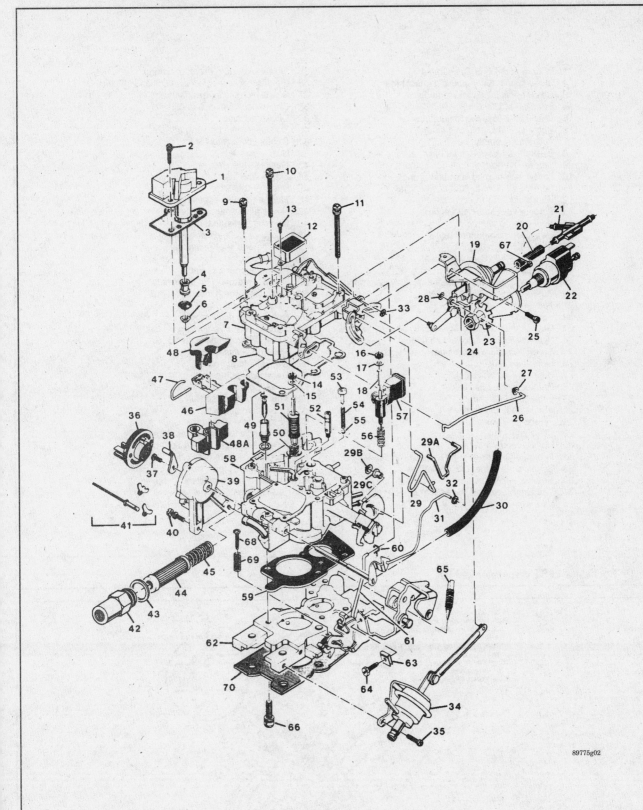

Fig. 17 Exploded view of the Rochester E2SE carburetor (key list appears on next page)

89775g02

1. Mixture control (M/C) solenoid
2. Screw assembly—solenoid attaching
3. Gasket—M/C solenoid to air horn
4. Spacer—M/C solenoid
5. Seal—M/C solenoid to float bowl
6. Retainer—M/C solenoid seal
7. Air horn assembly
8. Gasket—air horn to float bowl
9. Screw—air horn to float bowl (short)
10. Screw—air horn to float bowl (long)
11. Screw—air horn to float bowl (large)
12. Vent stack and screen assembly
13. Screw—vent stack attaching
14. Seal—pump stem
15. Retainer—pump stem seal
16. Seal—T.P.S. plunger
17. Retainer—T.P.S. plunger seal
18. Plunger—T.P.S. actuator
19. Vacuum break and bracket assembly—primary
20. Hose—vacuum break primary
21. Tee—vacuum break
22. Solenoid—idle speed
23. Retainer—idle speed solenoid
24. Nut—idle speed solenoid attaching
25. Screw—vacuum break bracket attaching
26. Link—air valve
27. Bushing—air valve link
28. Retainer—air valve link
29. Link—fast idle cam
29A. Link—fast idle cam
29B. Retainer—link
29C. Bushing—link
30. Hose—vacuum break
31. Intermediate choke shaft/lever/link assembly
32. Bushing—intermediate choke link
33. Retainer—intermediate choke link
34. Vacuum break and link assembly—secondary
35. Screw—vacuum break attaching
36. Electric choke—cover and coil assembly
37. Screw—choke lever attaching
38. Choke coil lever assembly
39. Choke housing
40. Screw—choke housing attaching
41. Choke cover retainer kit
42. Nut—fuel inlet
43. Gasket—fuel inlet nut
44. Filter—fuel inlet
45. Spring—fuel filter
46. Float and lever assembly
47. Hinge pin—float
48. Upper insert—float bowl
48A. Lower insert—float bowl
49. Needle and seat assembly
50. Spring—pump return
51. Pump plunger assembly
52. Primary metering jet assembly
53. Retainer—pump discharge ball
54. Spring—pump discharge
55. Ball—pump discharge
56. Spring—T.P.S. adjusting
57. Sensor—throttle position T.P.S.
58. Float bowl assembly
59. Gasket—float bowl
60. Retainer—pump link
61. Link—pump
62. Throttle body assembly
63. Clip—cam screw
64. Screw—fast idle cam
65. Idle needle and spring assembly
66. Screw—throttle body to float bowl
67. Screw—vacuum break bracket attaching
68. Screw—idle stop
69. Spring—idle stop screw
70. Gasket—insulator flange

89775g03

**Fig. 18 Rochester E2SE carburetor key list**

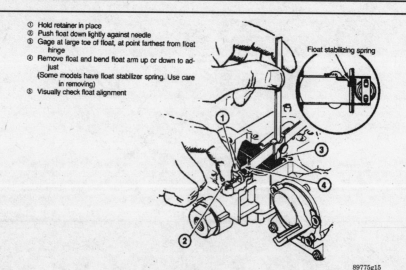

① Hold retainer in place
② Push float down lightly against needle
③ Gage at large toe of float, at point farthest from float hinge
④ Remove float and bend float arm up or down to adjust
   (Some models have float stabilizer spring. Use care in removing)
⑤ Visually check float alignment

Float stabilizing spring

89775g15

**Fig. 19 View of the E2SE 2-bbl. carburetor float adjustment**

2. Use your fingers to hold the retainer in place, and to push the float down into light contact with the needle.

3. Measure the distance from the tow of the float (furthest from the hinge) to the top of the carburetor (gasket removed).

4. To adjust, remove the float and gently bend the arm to specification. After adjustment, check the float alignment in the chamber.

## PUMP ADJUSTMENT
▶ See Figure 20

1. With the throttle closed and the fast idle screw off the steps of the fast idle cam, measure the distance from the air horn casting to the top of the pump stem.

2. To adjust, remove the retaining screw and washer and remove the pump lever. Bend the end of the lever to correct the stem height. Do not twist the lever or bend it sideways.

3. Install the lever, washer and screw and check the adjustment. When correct, open and close the throttle a few times to check the linkage movement and alignment.

➡No pump adjustment is required on 1981 and later models.

## FAST IDLE ADJUSTMENT
▶ See Figure 21

1. Set the ignition timing and curb idle speed, and disconnect the plug hoses as directed on the emission control decal.

2. Place the fast idle screw on the highest step of the cam.

3. Start the engine and adjust the engine speed to specification with the fast idle screw.

## CHOKE COIL LEVER ADJUSTMENT
▶ See Figure 22

1. Remove the three retaining screws and remove the choke cover and coil. On models with a riveted choke cover, drill out the three rivets and remove the cover and choke coil.

➡A choke stat cover retainer kit is required for reassembly.

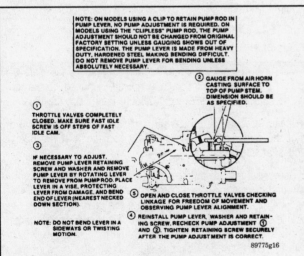

Fig. 20 View of the E2SE 2-bbl. carburetor pump adjustment

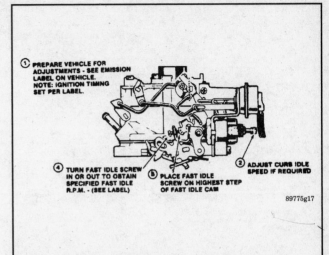

Fig. 21 View of the E2SE 2-bbl. carburetor fast idle adjustment

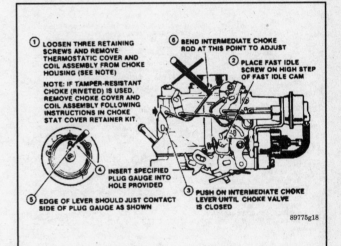

Fig. 22 View of the E2SE 2-bbl. carburetor choke coil lever adjustment

2. Place the fast idle screw on the high step of the cam.

3. Close the choke by pushing in on the intermediate choke lever. On front wheel drive models, the intermediate choke lever is behind the choke vacuum diaphragm.

4. Insert a drill or gauge of the specified size into the hole in the choke housing. The choke lever in the housing should be up against the side of the gauge.

5. If the lever does not just touch the gauge, bend the intermediate choke rod to adjust.

## AIR VALVE ROD ADJUSTMENT
▶ See Figure 23

Refer to the accompanying illustration for this procedure.

## PRIMARY SIDE VACUUM BREAK ADJUSTMENT
▶ See Figure 24

Refer to the accompanying illustration for this procedure.

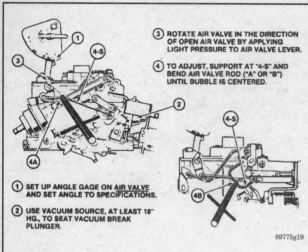

**Fig. 23 View of the E2SE 2-bbl. carburetor air valve rod adjustment**

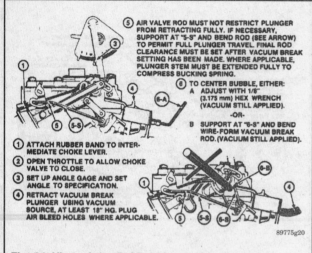

**Fig. 24 View of the E2SE 2-bbl. carburetor primary vacuum break adjustment**

## ELECTRIC CHOKE SETTING

This procedure is only for those carburetors with choke covers retained by screws. Riveted choke covers are preset and nonadjustable.

1. Loosen the three retaining screws.
2. Place the fast idle screw on the high step of the cam.
3. Rotate the choke cover to align the cover mark with the specified housing mark.

## CHOKE UNLOADER ADJUSTMENT

♦ See Figure 25

Refer to the accompanying illustration for this procedure.

### Rochester E4ME and E4MC Quadrajet 4-Bbl. Carburetor

These 4-bbl. carburetors feature an electrically operated mixture control solenoid, and are designed as part of the GM Computer Command Control (C3) system. As with the E2SE 2-bbl. the electric mixture control solenoid is mounted in the float bowl, and is used to control the air/fuel mixture in the

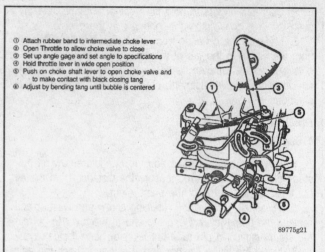

**Fig. 25 View of the E2SE 2-bbl. carburetor choke unloader adjustment**

primary bores of the carburetor. The plunger in the solenoid is controlled, or pulsed, by electrical signals received from the Electronic Control Module.

An Idle Speed Control (ISC) assembly, monitored by the ECM, controls engine idle speed. The curb (base) idle is programmed into the ECM and is not adjustable. When the throttle lever is resting against the ISC plunger, the ISC acts as a dashpot on throttle closing. An Idle Speed Solenoid or Idle Load Compensator is used on some models to position the primary throttle valve, providing engine idle speed requirements.

On E4MC models, the Idle Load Compensator (ILC) mounted on the float bowl is used to control curb idle speeds. The ILC uses manifold vacuum to sense changes in engine load (the A/C compressor clutch engaged, for example) and compensates by adjusting throttle angle for the curb idle speed. The ILC uses an spring loaded vacuum sensitive diaphragm whose plunger either extends (vacuum decrease) or retracts (vacuum increase) to adjust throttle angle for curb idle speeds. Both the ISC and ILC are factory adjusted.

## FLOAT LEVEL

♦ See Figure 26

With the air horn assembly removed, measure the distance from the air horn gasket surface (gasket removed) to the top of the float at the toe 1/16 in. (1.58mm) back from the toe).

➡ **Make sure the retaining pin is firmly held in place and that the tang of the float is lightly held against the needle and seat assembly.**

Remove the float and bend the float arm to adjust except on carburetors used with the computer controlled systems (E4MC and E4ME). For those carburetors, if the float level is too high, hold the retainer firmly in place and push down on the center of the float to adjust. If the float level is too low on models with the computer controlled system, lift out the metering rods. Remove the solenoid connector screw. Turn the lean mixture solenoid screw in clockwise, counting and recording the exact number of turns until the screw is lightly bottomed in the bowl. Then turn the screw out clockwise and remove. Lift out the solenoid and connector. Remove the float and bend the arm

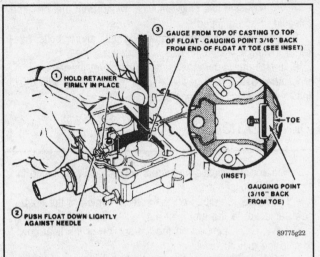

Fig. 26 View of the E4ME/MC carburetor float level adjustment

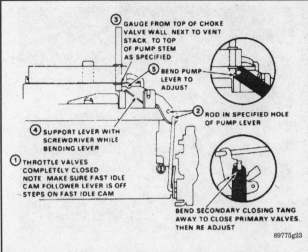

Fig. 27 View of the E4ME/MC carburetor accelerator pump adjustment

up to adjust. Install the parts, turning the mixture solenoid screw in until it is lightly bottomed, then unscrewing it the exact number of turns counted earlier.

### ACCELERATOR PUMP
▶ See Figure 27

The accelerator pump is not adjustable on computer controlled carburetors (E4MC and E4ME).

1. Close the primary throttle valves by backing out the slow idle screw and making sure that the fast idle cam follower is off the steps of the fast idle cam.
2. Bend the secondary throttle closing tang away from the primary throttle lever, if necessary, to insure that the primary throttle valves are fully closed.
3. With the pump in the appropriate hole in the pump lever, measure from the top of the choke valve wall to the top of the pump stem.
4. To adjust, bend the pump lever.
5. After adjusting, readjust the secondary throttle tang and the slow idle screw.

## REMOVAL & INSTALLATION

▶ See Figures 28, 29, 30, 31 and 32

### ❊❊CAUTION

Never smoke when working around gasoline! Avoid all sources of sparks or ignition. Gasoline vapors are EXTREMELY volatile!

1. Remove the air cleaner and its gasket.
2. Disconnect the fuel and vacuum lines from the carburetor.
3. Disconnect the choke coil rod or heated air line tube.
4. Disconnect the throttle linkage.
5. On automatic transmission cars, disconnect the throttle valve linkage.
6. Remove the CEC valve vacuum hose and electrical connector.

Fig. 28 Tag and disengage all the vacuum lines

Fig. 29 Tag and disengage any electrical connections that will impede the carburetor removal

**Fig. 30 When disconnecting the fuel lines, make sure to use a backup line wrench**

**Fig. 31 Unfasten the carburetor retaining bolts**

**Fig. 32 After all the linkages have been tagged and disengaged, remove the carburetor from the vehicle**

7. Remove the idle stop electrical wiring from the idle stop solenoid, if so equipped.

8. Remove the carburetor attaching nuts and/or bolts, gasket or insulator, and remove the carburetor.

9. Install the carburetor using a reverse of the removal procedure. Use a new gasket and fill the float bowl with gasoline to ease starting the engine.

## IDENTIFICATION

Carburetor identification numbers will generally be found in the following locations:
• 1 MV, ME: Stamped on the vertical portion of the float bowl, adjacent to the fuel inlet nut.
• 2 GV, GC: Stamped on the flat section of the float bowl next to the fuel inlet nut.
• E2SE, 2SE: Stamped on the vertical surface of the float bowl adjacent to the vacuum tube.
• M2MC: Stamped on the vertical surface of the left rear corner of the float bowl.
• E4ME, 4 MV, M4MC, M4ME: Stamped on the vertical section of the float bowl, near the secondary throttle lever.

## OVERHAUL

Efficient carburetion depends greatly on careful cleaning and inspection during overhaul, since dirt, gum, water, or varnish in or on the carburetor parts are often responsible for poor performance.

Overhaul you carburetor in a clean, dust free area. Carefully disassembly the carburetor, referring often to the exploded views and directions packaged with the rebuilding kit. Keep all similar and look alike parts segregated during disassembly and cleaning to avoid accidental interchange during assembly. Make a note of all jet sizes.

When the carburetor is disassembled, wash all parts (except diaphragms, electric choke units, pump plunger, and any other plastic, leather, fiber, or rubber parts) in clean carburetor solvent. Do not leave parts in the solvent any longer than is necessary to sufficiently loosen the deposits. Excessive cleaning may remove the special finish from the float bowl and choke valve bodies, leaving these parts unfit for service. Soak all parts in clean solvent and blow them dry with compressed air or allow them to air dry. Wipe clean all cork, plastic, leather, and fiber parts with a clean, lint free cloth.

Blow out all passages and jets with compressed air and be sure that there are no restrictions or blockages. Never use wire or similar tools to clean jets, fuel passages, or air bleeds. Clean all jets and valves separately to avoid accidental interchange.

Check all parts for wear or damage. If wear or damage is found, replace the defective parts.

Especially check the following:
1. Check the float needle and seat for wear. If wear is found, replace the complete assembly.
2. Check the float hinge pin for wear and the float(s) for dents or distortion. Replace the float if fuel has leaked into it.
3. Check the throttle and choke shaft bores for wear or an out-of-round condition. Damage or wear to the throttle arm,

shaft, or shaft bore will often require replacement of the throttle body. These parts require a close tolerance of fit; wear may allow air leakage, which could affect starting and idling.

➡️**Throttle shafts and bushings are not included in overhaul kits. They can be purchased separately.**

4. Inspect the idle mixture adjusting needles for burrs or grooves. Any such condition requires replacement of the needle, since you will not be able to obtain a satisfactory idle.

5. Test the accelerator pump check valves. They should pass air one way but not the other. Test for proper seating by blowing and sucking on the valve. Replace the valve as necessary. If the valve is satisfactory, wash the valve again to remove breath moisture.

6. Check the bowl cover for warped surfaces with a straightedge.

7. Closely inspect the valves and seats for wear and damage, replacing as necessary.

8. After the carburetor is assembled, check the choke valve for freedom of operation.

Carburetor overhaul kits are recommended for each overhaul. These kits contain all gaskets and new parts to replace those which deteriorate most rapidly. Failure to replace all parts supplied with the kit (especially gaskets) can result in poor performance later.

Some carburetor manufacturers supply overhaul kits of three basic types: minor repair; major repair; and gasket kits.

After cleaning and checking all components, reassemble the carburetor, using new parts and referring to the exploded view. When reassembling, make sure that all screws and jets are tight in their seats, buy do not overtighten as the tips will be distorted. Tighten all screws gradually, in rotation. Do not tighten needle valves into their seats; uneven jetting will result. Always use new gaskets. Be sure to adjust the float level when reassembling.

## Carburetor Applications

| Year | Engine | Carburetor | Year | Engine | Carburetor |
|---|---|---|---|---|---|
| 1967 | 6-230 | Rochester B | 1976 | 6-250 | Rochester 1MV |
| | | Carter YF | | 6-292 | Rochester 1MV |
| | 6-250 | Rochester B | | 8-350 | Rochester 2GC |
| | | Carter YF | | 8-350 LD | Rochester M4MC |
| | V8-283 | Rochester 2G | | 8-350 HD | Rochester 4MV |
| 1968 | 6-230 | Rochester M | | 8-400 | Rochester 4MV |
| | 6-250 | Rochester M | 1977 | 6-250 | Rochester 1ME |
| | V8-307 | Rochester 2G | | 6-292 | Rochester 1ME |
| 1969 | 6-230 | Rochester M | | 8-305 | Rochester 2GC |
| | 6-250 | Rochester M | | 8-350 LD | Rochester M4MC |
| | | Rochester MV | | 8-350 HD | Rochester 4MV |
| | V8-307 | Rochester 2G (1¼ in.) | | 8-400 | Rochester 4MV |
| | | Rochester 2GV (1¼ in.) | 1978 | 6-250 | Rochester 1ME |
| 1970 | 6-250 | Rochester M | | 6-292 | Rochester 1ME |
| | | Rochester MV | | 8-305 | Rochester 2GC |
| | V8-307 | Rochester 2GV (1¼ in.) | | 8-350 LD | Rochester M4MC |
| | V8-350 | Rochester 2G (1¼ in.) | | 8-350 HD | Rochester 4MV/M4MC |
| | | Rochester 4MV | | 8-400 | Rochester 4MV/M4MC |
| | | (Quadrajet) | 1979–80 | 6-250 | Rochester 2SE |
| 1971 | 6-250 | Rochester MV | | 8-305 | Rochester M2MC |
| | V8-307 | Rochester 2GV | | 8-350 | Rochester M4MC |
| | V8-350 | Rochester 4MV | | 8-400 | Rochester M4MC |
| | | (Quadrajet) | 1981 | 6-250 | Rochester 2SE |
| 1972–73 | 6-250 | Rochester MV | | 8-305 | Rochester M2ME |
| | V8-307, 350 | Rochester 2GV | | 8-305 | Rochester M4MC/M4ME |
| | V8-350 | Rochester 4MV | | 8-350 | Rochester M4MC/M4ME |
| | | (Quadrajet) | 1982 | 6-250 | Rochester 2SE |
| 1974 | 6-250 | Rochester MV | | 8-305 | Rochester M4MC/M4ME |
| | 8-350 | Rochester 2GV | | 8-350 | Rochester M4MC/M4ME |
| | 8-350 | Rochester 4MV | 1983–86 | 6-250 | Rochester 2SE |
| 1975 | 6-250 | Rochester 1MV | | | Rochester E2SE |
| | 6-292 | Rochester 1MV | | 6-262, 8-305 | Rochester M4MC/M4ME |
| | 8-350 | Rochester 2GC | | | Rochester E4ME |
| | 8-350 LD | Rochester M4MC | | 8-350 | Rochester M4MC/M4ME |
| | 8-350 HD | Rochester 4MV | | | Rochester E4ME |
| | 8-400 | Rochester 4MV | | | |

LD, HD See the beginning of the Chapter for explanation.

89775c01

## Carburetor Specifications

| Year | Carburetor Model | Float Level (in.) | Float Drop (in.) | Idle Vent (in.) | Accelerator Pump (in.) | Fast Idle Speed (rpm) | Fast Idle Cam Choke Rod (in.) | Primary or Front Choke Vacuum Break (in.) | Choke Unloader (in.) | Metering Rod (in.) | Rear or Auxiliary Vacuum Break (in.) | Air Valve Spring (turns) |
|---|---|---|---|---|---|---|---|---|---|---|---|---|
| 1967 | Carter YF | 7/32 | 1 3/16 | 0.065 | — | — | — | — | — | — | — | — |
| | Rochester B | 1 9/32 | 1 3/4 | 0.066 | — | — | — | — | — | — | — | — |
| | Rochester 2G | 3/4 ① | 1 29/32 | — | 1 1/8 | — | — | — | — | — | — | — |
| 1968 | Rochester M | 11/32 | — | 0.050 | — | 2400 | 0.150 | — | — | 0.070 | — | — |
| | Rochester 2G | 3/4 | 1 3/4 | 1.000 | 1 1/8 | 1800–2000 | — | — | — | — | — | — |
| 1969 | Rochester M | 1/4 | — | 0.050 | — | 2400 | 0.150 | — | — | 0.070 | — | — |
| | Rochester MV | 1/4 | — | 0.050 | — | 2400 | 0.180 | 2.260 | 0.350 | 0.070 | — | — |
| | Rochester 2G | 27/32 | 1 3/4 | 0.020 | 1 1/8 | 1800–2400 | 0.095 | 0.130 | 0.215 | — | — | — |
| 1970–71 | Rochester MV | 1/4 | — | — | — | 2400 | 0.190 ② | 0.230 ③ | 0.350 | 0.070 | — | — |
| | Rochester 2GV | 23/32 ④ | 1 3/4 | 0.027 | 1 3/8 | 2200–2400 | 0.060 | 0.140 ⑤ | 0.215 | — | — | — |
| | Rochester 2G | 23/32 | 1 3/4 | 0.020 | 1 17/32 | 2200–2400 | — | — | — | — | — | — |
| | Rochester 4MV | 1/4 | — | 3/8 | 5/16 | 2400 | 0.100 | 0.245 ⑦ | 0.450 | — | — | 7/16 |
| 1972 | Rochester MV | 1/4 | — | — | — | 2400 | — | ⑧ | 0.500 | 0.080 | — | — |
| | Rochester 2 GV | 21/32 | 1 9/32 | — | — | ⑨ | — | 0.110 ⑩ | 0.210 | — | — | — |
| | Rochester 4MV | 3/16 | — | — | — | ⑪ | — | 0.215 | 0.450 | — | — | 1/2 |
| 1973 | Rochester MV | 1/4 | — | — | — | 2400 | ⑫ | 0.430 ⑬ | 0.600 ⑭ | 0.080 | — | — |
| | Rochester 2GV | 21/32 ⑮ | 1 9/32 | — | — | 1600 | 0.150 ⑯ | 0.080 ⑰ | 0.215 ⑱ | — | — | — |
| | Rochester 4MV | 7/32 ⑳ | — | — | — | 1600 ⑲ | 0.430 | 0.215 | 0.450 | — | — | 1/2 |
| 1974 | Rochester MV 7044021 | 0.295 | — | — | — | 1800 | 0.275 | 0.350 | 0.500 | 0.080 | — | — |
| | 7044022 | 0.295 | — | — | — | 1800 | 0.245 | 0.300 | 0.500 | 0.080 | — | — |
| | 7044025 | 0.250 | — | — | — | 1800 | 0.245 | 0.300 | 0.521 | 0.070 | — | — |
| | 7044321 | 0.295 | — | — | — | 2400 | 0.300 | 0.375 | 0.500 | 0.080 | — | — |
| | Rochester 2GV 7044123 | 19/32 | 1 9/32 | — | 1 9/32 | 1600 | 0.200 | 0.140 | 0.250 | — | — | — |
| | 7044124 | 19/32 | 1 9/32 | — | 1 3/16 | 1600 | 0.245 | 0.130 | 0.325 | — | — | — |
| | Rochester 4MV 7044214, 7044514 | 11/32 | — | — | 13/32 | 1600 | 0.430 | 0.215 | 0.450 | — | — | 7/8 |
| | 7044218, 7044518 | 1/4 | — | — | 13/32 | 1600 | 0.430 | 0.215 | 0.450 | — | — | 7/8 |
| | 7044219, 7044519 | 1/4 | — | — | 13/32 | 1600 | 0.430 | 0.215 | 0.450 | — | — | 7/8 |
| | 7044224 | 11/32 | — | — | 13/32 | 1600 | 0.430 | 0.215 | 0.450 | — | — | 7/8 |
| 1975 | Rochester 1MV 7045004 | 11/32 | — | — | — | 1800 | 0.245 | 0.300 | 0.325 | 0.080 | 0.150 | — |
| | 7045005 | 11/32 | — | — | — | 1800 | 0.275 | 0.350 | 0.325 | 0.080 | 0.290 | — |
| | 7045304 | 11/32 | — | — | — | 1800 | 0.245 | 0.300 | 0.325 | 0.080 | 0.290 | — |
| | 7045305 | 11/32 | — | — | — | 1800 | 0.275 | 0.350 | 0.325 | 0.080 | 0.290 | — |
| | Rochester 2GC 7045123, 7045124 | 21/32 | 31/32 | — | 1 5/8 | — | 0.400 | 0.130 | 0.350 | — | — | — |
| | Rochester M4MC 7045218, 7045219 | 15/32 | — | — | 0.275 | 1600 | 0.325 | 0.180 | 0.325 | — | 0.170 | 3/4 |
| | Rochester 4MV 7045214, 7045584 | 11/32 | — | — | 0.275 | 1600 | 0.430 | 0.215 | 0.450 | — | — | 7/8 |
| | 7045588 | 11/32 | — | — | 0.275 | 1600 | 0.430 | 0.230 | 0.450 | — | — | 3/4 |

## Carburetor Specifications (cont.)

| Year | Carburetor Model | Float Level (in.) | Float Drop (in.) | Idle Vent (in.) | Accelerator Pump (in.) | Fast Idle Speed (rpm) | Fast Idle Cam Choke Rod (in.) | Primary or Front Choke Vacuum Break (in.) | Choke Unloader (in.) | Metering Rod (in.) | Rear or Auxiliary Vacuum Break (in.) | Air Valve Spring (turns) |
|---|---|---|---|---|---|---|---|---|---|---|---|---|
| 1976 | Rochester 1MV 17056002 | 11/32 | — | — | — | 2100 | 0.130 | 0.165 | 0.335 | 0.080 | 0.265 | — |
| | 17056003 | 11/32 | — | — | — | 2100 | 0.145 | 0.180 | 0.335 | 0.080 | WO | — |
| | 17056008, 17056009 | 1/4 | — | — | — | 2400 | 0.150 | 0.190 | 0.275 | 0.070 | — | — |
| | 17056302 | 11/32 | — | — | — | 2100 | 0.155 | 0.190 | 0.325 | 0.080 | WO | — |
| | 17056303 | 11/32 | — | — | — | 2100 | 0.180 | 0.225 | 0.325 | 0.080 | WO | — |
| | 17056308, 17056309 | 1/4 | — | — | — | 2400 | 0.150 | 0.190 | 0.275 | 0.070 | — | — |
| | Rochester 2GC 17056123, 17056124 | 21/32 | 19/32 | — | 111/16 | — | 0.260 | 0.130 | 0.325 | — | — | — |
| | Rochester M4MC 17056218, 17056219, 17056518, 17056519 | 5/16 | — | — | 9/32 | 1600 | 0.325 | 0.185 | 0.325 | — | — | 7/8 |
| | Rochester 4MV 7045214 | 11/32 | — | — | 9/32 | 1600 | 0.290 | 0.145 | 0.295 | — | — | 7/8 |
| | 7045225 | 11/32 | — | — | 9/32 | 1600 | 0.290 | 0.138 | 0.295 | — | — | 3/4 |
| | 7045584 | 11/32 | — | — | 9/32 | 1600 | 0.290 | 0.155 | 0.295 | — | — | 7/8 |
| | 7045589 | 11/32 | — | — | 9/32 | 1600 | 0.290 | 0.155 | 0.295 | — | — | 3/4 |
| 1977 | Rochester 1ME 17057001 | 3/8 | — | — | — | 2100 | 0.125 | 0.150 | 0.325 | 0.080 | — | — |
| | 17057002 | 3/8 | — | — | — | 2100 | 0.110 | 0.135 | 0.325 | 0.080 | — | — |
| | 17057004 | 3/8 | — | — | — | 2100 | 0.110 | 0.135 | 0.325 | 0.080 | — | — |
| | 17057005 | 3/8 | — | — | — | 2100 | 0.125 | 0.180 | 0.325 | 0.080 | — | — |
| | 17057010 | 3/8 | — | — | — | 2100 | 0.110 | 0.135 | 0.325 | 0.080 | — | — |
| | 17057302 | 3/8 | — | — | — | 2100 | 0.110 | 0.135 | 0.325 | 0.080 | — | — |
| | 17057303 | 3/8 | — | — | — | 2100 | 0.125 | 0.150 | 0.325 | 0.090 | — | — |
| | 17057008, 17057009, 17057308, 17057309 | 5/16 | — | — | — | 2400 | 0.150 | 0.180 | 0.275 | 0.065 | — | — |
| | Rochester 2GC 17057108, 17057110, 17057113, 17057123 | 19/32 | 19/32 | — | 121/32 | — | 0.260 | 0.160 | 0.325 | — | — | — |
| | Rochester M4MC 17057218 | 7/16 | — | — | 9/32 | 1600 | 0.325 | 0.160 | 0.280 | — | — | 7/8 |
| | 17057219 | 7/16 | — | — | 9/32 | 1300 | 0.325 | 0.165 | 0.280 | — | — | 7/8 |
| | 17057222 | 7/16 | — | — | 9/32 | 1600 | 0.325 | 0.160 | 0.280 | — | — | 7/8 |
| | 17057518 | 7/16 | — | — | 9/32 | 1600 | 0.325 | 0.165 | 0.280 | — | — | 7/8 |
| | 17057519 | 7/16 | — | — | 9/32 | 1300 | 0.325 | 0.165 | 0.280 | — | — | 7/8 |
| | 17057522 | 7/16 | — | — | 9/32 | 1600 | 0.325 | 0.165 | 0.280 | — | — | 7/8 |
| | 17057586 | 7/16 | — | — | 3/8 ㉒ | 1600 | 0.325 | 0.180 | 0.280 | — | — | 7/8 |
| | 17057588 | 7/16 | — | — | 3/8 ㉒ | 1600 | 0.325 | 0.180 | 0.280 | — | — | 7/8 |
| | Rochester 4MV 17057213 | 11/32 | — | — | 9/32 | 1600 | 0.220 | 0.115 | 0.205 | — | — | 7/8 |
| | 17057229 | 11/32 | — | — | 9/32 | 1600 | 0.220 | 0.110 | 0.205 | — | — | 7/8 |
| | 17057514 | 11/32 | — | — | 9/32 | 1600 | 0.220 | 0.120 | 0.225 | — | — | 7/8 |
| | 17057525 | 11/32 | — | — | 9/32 | 1600 | 0.220 | 0.120 | 0.225 | — | — | 3/4 |

## Carburetor Specifications (cont.)

| Year | Carburetor Model | Float Level (in.) | Float Drop (in.) | Idle Vent (in.) | Accelerator Pump (in.) | Fast Idle Speed (rpm) | Fast Idle Cam Choke Rod (in.) | Primary or Front Choke Vacuum Break (in.) | Choke Unloader (in.) | Metering Rod (in.) | Rear or Auxiliary Vacuum Break (in.) | Air Valve Spring (turns) |
|---|---|---|---|---|---|---|---|---|---|---|---|---|
| 1978 | **Rochester 1ME** | | | | | | | | | | | |
| | 17058008, 17058009 | 5/16 | — | — | — | 2400 | 0.275 | 0.275 | 0.520 | 0.065 | — | — |
| | 17058017, 17058312 | 5/16 | — | — | — | 2100 | 0.190 | 0.250 | 0.600 | 0.080 | — | — |
| | 17058313 | 5/16 | — | — | — | 2100 | 0.190 | 0.250 | 0.600 | 0.100 | — | — |
| | 17058081, 17058082, 17058084 | 5/16 | — | — | — | 2000 | 0.200 | 0.250 | 0.450 | 0.080 | — | — |
| | **Rochester 2GC** | | | | | | | | | | | |
| | All | 19/32 | 1 9/32 | — | 1 21/32 | [21] | 0.260 | 0.190 | 0.355 | — | — | — |
| | **Rochester M4MC/4MV** | | | | | | | | | | | |
| | 17058213, 17058229 | 15/32 | — | — | 9/32 | 1700 | 0.277 | 0.123 | 0.260 | — | — | 7/8 |
| | 17058218, 17058222 | 7/16 | — | — | 9/32 | 1600 | 0.314 | 0.157 | 0.277 | — | — | 7/8 |
| | 17058219 | 7/16 | — | — | 9/32 | 1300 | 0.314 | 0.168 | 0.277 | — | — | 7/8 |
| | 17058514 | 15/32 | — | — | 9/32 | 1600 | 0.277 | 0.153 | 0.287 | — | — | 7/8 |
| | 17058518, 17058522, 17058523, 17058524, 17058586, 17058588 | 15/32 | — | — | 9/32 | 1600 | 0.314 | 0.179 | 0.277 | — | — | 7/8 |
| | 17058519 | 15/32 | — | — | 9/32 | 1300 | 0.314 | 0.179 | 0.277 | — | — | 7/8 |
| | 17058525 | 7/16 | — | — | 9/32 | 1600 | 0.277 | 0.153 | 0.277 | — | — | 3/4 |
| 1979 | **Rochester 2SE** | | | | | | | | | | | |
| | 17059640, 17059642, 17059740 | 1/8 | — | — | 9/16 | 2000 | 17° | 20° | 49° | — | 37° | — |
| | 17059641 | 1/8 | — | — | 9/16 | 1800 | 17° | 23.5° | 49° | — | ;37° | — |
| | 17059741, 17059764 | 1/8 | — | — | 9/16 | 2100 | 17° | 20° | 49° | — | 37° | — |
| | 17059765, 17059767 | 1/8 | — | — | 9/16 | 2100 | 17° | 23.5° | 49° | — | 37° | — |
| | **Rochester M2MC** | | | | | | | | | | | |
| | 17059142, 17059144 | 15/32 | — | — | 13/32 | 1600 | 0.243 | 0.171 | 0.243 | — | — | — |
| | 17059143, 17059145 | 15/32 | — | — | 13/32 | 1300 | 0.243 | 0.171 | 0.243 | — | — | — |
| | **Rochester M4MC** | | | | | | | | | | | |
| | 17059061, 17059201 | 15/32 | — | — | 13/32 | 1300 | 0.314 | — | 0.277 | — | 0.129 | 7/8 |
| | 17059213, 17059215 | 15/32 | — | — | 9/32 | 1900 | 0.234 | 0.129 | 0.260 | — | — | 1 |
| | 17059229, 17059513, 17059515, 17059529, 17059527, 17059528 | 15/32 | — | — | 9/32 [22] | 1600 | 0.314 | — | 0.277 | — | 0.149 | 7/8 |
| | All Others | 15/32 | — | — | 13/32 | 1600 | 0.314 | — | 0.277 | — | 0.129 | 7/8 |
| 1980–81 | Rochester 2SE | 3/16 | — | — | 5/8 | 2000 | 0.077 | 0.149 [23] | 0.243 [24] | — | 0.149 | 1 |
| | Rochester M2ME | 13/32 | — | — | 5/16 | 1600 | 0.243 | 0.142 | — | 0.243 | — | — |
| | Rochester M4ME,C | [25] | — | — | 9/32 [26] | 1800 | 0.314 | 0.136 | 0.277 [28] | — | — | — |
| 1982 | Rochester 2SE | 3/16 | — | — | 9/16 | [21] | 0.077 | 0.149 [29] | 0.277 | — | 0.243 [30] | 1 |
| | Rochester M4ME,C | 3/8 [31] | — | — | 9/32 [32] | [21] | 0.314 [33] | 0.129 [34] | 0.277 [35] | — | 0.179 [36] | 7/8 [37] |
| 1983 | Rochester 2SE | 3/16 | — | — | Fixed | [21] | 0.077 | 0.149 [38] | 0.277 | — | 0.243 | — |
| | Rochester E2SE | 11/32 | — | — | Fixed | [21] | 0.077 | 0.149 | 0.277 | — | 0.243 | 1 |
| | Rochester M4ME,C | 13/32 [39] | — | — | 9/16 | [21] | 0.314 [40] | [41] | 0.251 [42] | — | 0.136 [43] | 7/8 [44] |
| | Rochester E4ME,C | 11/32 [45] | — | — | 9/16 | [21] | 0.110 [46] | [47] | 0.243 [48] | — | 0.157 [49] | 7/8 |
| 1984 | Rochester 2SE | 11/32 [49] | — | — | — | [21] | 0.123 [50] | 0.179 [51] | 0.260 [52] | — | 0.195 [53] | 1 [54] |
| | Rochester E2SE | 9/32 [55] | — | — | — | [21] | 0.164 [56] | 0.142 [57] | 0.304 [58] | — | 0.220 [59] | 1/2 [60] |
| | Rochester M4ME,C | 13/32 [61] | — | — | 9/32 | [21] | 0.314 [62] | [63] | 0.251 [64] | — | 0.149 [65] | 7/8 [66] |
| | Rochester E4ME,C | 11/32 [67] | — | — | — | [21] | 0.110 [68] | 0.157 [69] | 0.243 [70] | — | [70] | 7/8 [71] |

① #7026113—⅝ in.
② 20 & 30 Series—0.180 in.
③ 20 & 30 Series—0.260 in.
④ 1970 20 & 30 Series—²⁷⁄₃₂ in.
⑤ 20 & 30 Series—0.130 in.
⑥ Bottom of rod should be even with top of hole
⑦ 1970 10 Series w/man. trans.—0.275 in.
⑧ Man. Trans.—0.225 in.
  Auto Trans.—0.190 in.
  All Trans. (H/D)—0.260 in.
⑨ 1850 rpm (1¼)
  2200 rpm (1½)
⑩ Auto trans.—0.080 in.
⑪ Auto—1500 rpm
  Man.—1350 rpm
⑫ Auto Trans. (Carb #7043022)—0.245 in.
  Man. Trans. (Carb #7043021)—0.275 in.
  Carb #7043025—0.350 in.
  Carb #7043026 & all California cars—0.375 in.
⑬ Man. Trans.—0.300 in.
  Auto Trans.—0.350 in.
⑭ Auto only and Man. only—0.500 in.
⑮ Carb #7043108—²⁵⁄₃₂ in.
⑯ Carb #7043108—0.200 in.
⑰ Carb #7043108—0.140 in.
⑱ Carb #7043108—0.250 in.
⑲ L.D. Man. Trans.—1300 rpm w/o vacuum advance
  H.D. Man. Trans.—1600 rpm w/vacuum advance
⑳ Carb #'s 7043028, 215—⁵⁄₁₆ in.
  Carb #'s 7043200, 216—¼ in.
㉑ See the underhood emission sticker
㉒ Outer hole
㉓ #17081629:0.136
  17081720, 1708121,
  17081725, 17081726,
  17081727:0.179
㉔ 17081629, 17081720,
  17081725, 17081726,
  17081727:0.269
㉕ M4MC:⅜"
  M4ME:¹⁵⁄₃₂"
㉖ #17081524, 17081526:⁵⁄₁₆"
㉗ 17080213, 17080215,
  17080298, 17080507,
  17080513:0.234
㉘ 17080212, 17080213,
  17080215, 17080298,
  17080507, 17080512,
  17080513:0.251
  17081506, 17081508:0.227
  17081524, 17081526:0.243
㉙ 17082341, 17082342,
  17082344, 17082345: 0.179 in.
  17082431, 17082433: 0.136 in.
  17082482: 0.129 in.
  17082486, 17082487,
  17082488, 17082489: 0.164 in.
㉚ 17082341, 17082342,
  17082344, 17082345: 0.234 in.
㉛ 17081200, 17081205,
  17081206, 17081220,
  17081226, 17081227: ¹⁵⁄₃₂ in.
  17081290, 17081291,
  17081292, 17081506,
  17081508, 17081524,
  17081526: ¹³⁄₃₂ in.
㉜ 17081524, 1708526: ⁵⁄₁₆ in.
㉝ 17080213, 1708215,
  17080298, 1708507,
  17080513, 0.234 in.
㉞ 17080212, 17080512,
  17081200, 17081226,
  17081227: 0.136 in.
  17081524, 17081526: 0.142 in.
㉟ 17080212, 17080213,
  17080215, 17080298,
  17080507, 17080512,
  17080513: 0.260 in.
  17081506, 17081508: 0.227 in.
  17081524, 17081526: 0.243 in.

㊱ 17081200, 17081201,
  17081205, 17081206,
  17081220, 17081226,
  17081227: 0.129 in.
  17081290, 17081291,
  17081292: 0.136 in.
  17081506, 17081508,
  17081524, 17081526: 0.227 in.
㊲ 17080212, 17080512,
  17080513: ¾ turn
  17080213, 17080215,
  17080298, 17080507: 1 turn
㊳ 17083410, 17083412,
  17083414, 17083416: 0.129 in.
  17083423, 17083429,
  17083560, 17083562,
  17083565, 17083569: 0.164 in.
㊴ 17080213, 17080298,
  17080507, 17080513,
  17083298, 17083507: ⅜ in.
  17082213: ⁹⁄₃₂ in.
  17080201, 17080205,
  17080206, 17080290,
  17080291, 17080292: ¹⁵⁄₃₂ in.
㊵ 17080213, 17080298,
  17080507, 17080513,
  17082213, 17083298,
  17083507: 0.234 in.
㊶ 17080213, 17080298,
  17080507, 17080513,
  17082213, 17083298,
  17083507: 0.129 in.
㊷ 17080201, 17080205,
  17080206, 17080290,
  17080291, 17080292: 0.277 in.
  17080213, 17080298,
  17080507, 17080513,
  17082213, 17083298,
  17083507: 0.260 in.
㊸ 17080201, 17080205,
  17080206: 0.129 in.
  17080213, 17080298,
  17080507, 17080513,
  17082213, 17083298,
  17083507, 0.179 in.
㊹ 17080213, 17080298,
  17080507, 17080513,
  17082213, 17083298,
  17083507: 1 turn
㊺ 17083506, 17083508,
  17083524, 17083526: ⁷⁄₁₆ in.
㊻ 17083203, 17083207: 0.243 in.
㊼ 17083506, 17083508: 0.157 in.
  17083524, 17083526: 0.142 in.
㊽ 17083506, 17083508,
  17083524, 17083526: 0.227 in.
㊾ 17084360, 17084362,
  17084364, 17084366: ⁵⁄₃₂ in.
  17084390, 17084391,
  17084392, 17084393: ⁷⁄₁₆ in.
㊿ 17084390, 17084391,
  17084392, 17084393: 0.164 in.
  17084410, 17084412,
  17084425, 17084427,
  17084560, 17084562,
  17084569: 0.077 in.
51 17084410, 17084412: 0.129 in.
  17084425, 17084427: 0.149 in.
  17084560, 17084562,
  17084569: 0.136 in.
52 17084410, 17084412: 0.277 in.
  17084390, 17084391,
  17084392, 17084393,
  17084560, 17084562,
  17084569: 0.243 in.

53 17084352, 17084353,
  17084354, 17084355,
  17084364, 17084366: 0.220 in.
  17084390, 17084391,
  17084392, 17084393,
  17084410, 17084412: 0.243 in.
  17084425, 17084427: 0.227 in.
  17084560, 17084562,
  17084569: 0.211 in.
54 17084390, 17084391,
  17084392, 17084393: 1½ turns
  17084410, 17084412,
  17084425, 17084427,
  17084560, 17084562,
  17084569, Not Adjustable
55 17084368, 17084370,
  17084542: ⁴⁄₃₂ in.
  17084430, 17084431,
  17084434, 17084435: ¹¹⁄₃₂ in.
  17084534, 17084535,
  17084537, 17084538,
  17084540: ⁵⁄₃₂ in.
56 17084356, 17084357,
  17084358, 17084359,
  17084369, 17084370: 0.123 in.
  17084430, 17084431,
  17084434, 17084435: 0.077 in.
57 17084430, 17084431,
  17084434, 17084435: 0.149 in.
58 17084356, 17084357,
  17084358, 17084359,
  17084369, 17084370: 0.179 in.
  17084430, 17084431,
  17084434, 17084435: 0.277 in.
59 17084356, 17084357,
  17084358, 17084359,
  17084369, 17084370: 0.179 in.
  17084430, 17084431,
  17084434, 17084435: 0.243 in.
60 17084356, 17084357,
  17084358, 17084359,
  17084369, 17084370: ¾ turn
  17084430, 17084431,
  17084434, 17084435: 1 turn
  Idle mixture screw: 4 turns
  Lean mixture screw: 2½ turns
61 17080212, 17080213,
  17080298, 17082213,
  17083298, 17084500,
  17084501, 17084502: ⅜ in.
62 17080213, 17080298,
  17082213, 17083298,
  17084500, 17084501: 0.234 in.
63 17080212, 17084502: 0.136 in.
  17080213, 17080298,
  17082213, 17083298,
  17084500, 17084501: 0.129 in.
64 17080212, 17084502,
  17080213, 17080298,
  17082213, 17083298,
  17084500, 17084501: 0.260 in.
65 17080212, 17084502,
  17080213, 17080298,
  17082213, 17083298,
  17084500, 17084501: 0.179 in.
  17084226, 17084227,
  17084290, 17084292: 0.136 in.
66 17080213, 17080298,
  17082213, 17083298,
  17084500, 17084501: 1 turn
  17080212, 17084502: ⅞ turn
67 17084507, 17084509,
  17084525, 17084527: ¹⁴⁄₃₂ in.
68 17084205, 17084209: 0.243 in.
69 17084525, 17084527: 0.142 in.
70 17084507, 17084509,
  17084525, 17084527: 0.227 in.
71 17084507, 17084509,
  17084525, 17084527: 1 turn

## Model 1ME/1M/1MEF

(All measurements in inches)

| Year | Carburetor Number | Float Level | Choke Unloader Setting | Choke Setting | Fast Idle Speed (rpm) | Metering Rod Setting | Fast Idle Cam 2nd Step | Choke Vacuum Break |
|------|-------------------|-------------|------------------------|---------------|-----------------------|---------------------|------------------------|---------------------|
| 1984–86 | 17081009 | 11/32 | .520 | ① | ② | .090 | .275 | .400 |
| | 17084329 | 11/32 | .520 | ① | ② | .090 | .275 | .400 |
| | 17085009 | 11/32 | .520 | ① | ② | .090 | .275 | .400 |
| | 17085036 | 11/32 | .520 | ① | ② | .090 | .275 | .400 |
| | 17085044 | 11/32 | .520 | ① | ② | .090 | .275 | .400 |
| | 17085045 | 11/32 | .520 | ① | ② | .090 | .275 | .400 |
| | 17086096 | 11/32 | .520 | ① | ② | .090 | .275 | .400 |
| | 17086101 | 11/32 | .520 | ① | ② | .090 | .275 | .400 |
| | 17086102 | 11/32 | .520 | ① | ② | .090 | .275 | .400 |

① Not adjustable
② See emission label under hood

89775C10

## Model E2SE

(All measurements in inches or degrees)

| Year | Carburetor Number | Float Level | Choke Coil Lever | Choke Rod ① | Primary Vacuum Break | Secondary Vacuum Break | Air Valve Rod | Choke Unloader |
|------|-------------------|-------------|------------------|-------------|----------------------|------------------------|---------------|----------------|
| 1985–86 | 17084636 | 9/32 | .085 | 28° | 25° | 35° | 1° | 45° |
| | 17085356 | 4/32 | .085 | 22° | 25° | 30° | 1° | 30° |
| | 17085357 | 9/32 | .085 | 22° | 25° | 30° | 1° | 30° |
| | 17085358 | 4/32 | .085 | 22° | 25° | 30° | 1° | 30° |
| | 17085359 | 9/32 | .085 | 22° | 25° | 30° | 1° | 30° |
| | 17085368 | 4/32 | .085 | 22° | 25° | 30° | 1° | 30° |
| | 17085369 | 9/32 | .085 | 22° | 25° | 30° | 1° | 30° |
| | 17085370 | 4/32 | .085 | 22° | 25° | 30° | 1° | 30° |
| | 17085371 | 9/32 | .085 | 22° | 25° | 30° | 1° | 30° |
| | 17085452 | 5/32 | .085 | 28° | 25° | 35° | 1° | 45° |
| | 17085453 | 5/32 | .085 | 28° | 25° | 35° | 1° | 45° |
| | 17085458 | 5/32 | .085 | 28° | 25° | 35° | 1° | 45° |

Note: Specified angle for use with angle degree tool
① All models: Lean mixture screw–2½ turns
Idle mixture screw–4 turns

89775C11

## Model M4MC/M4ME Quadrajet
(All measurements in inches or degrees)

| Year | Carburetor Number | Float Level | Pump Rod Hole | Pump Rod Setting | Choke Rod ① Setting | Air Valve Rod | Vacuum Break Front | Vacuum Break Rear | Air Valve Turns | Choke Unloader | Propane Enrichment (rpm) |
|---|---|---|---|---|---|---|---|---|---|---|---|
| 1985–86 | 17084500 | 12/32 | inner | 9/32 | 37° | .025 | 23° | 30° | 1 | 40° | ② |
| | 17084501 | 12/32 | inner | 9/32 | 37° | .025 | 23° | 30° | 1 | 40° | ② |
| | 17084502 | 12/32 | inner | 9/32 | 46° | .025 | 24° | 30° | 7/8 | 40° | ② |
| | 17085000 | 12/32 | inner | 9/32 | 46° | .025 | 24° | 30° | 7/8 | 40° | ② |
| | 17085001 | 12/32 | inner | 9/32 | 46° | .025 | 23° | 30° | 1 | 40° | ② |
| | 17085003 | 12/32 | inner | 9/32 | 46° | .025 | 23° | — | 7/8 | 35° | ② |
| | 17085004 | 12/32 | inner | 9/32 | 46° | .025 | 23° | — | 7/8 | 35° | ② |
| | 17085205 | 13/32 | inner | 9/32 | 20° | .025 | 26° | 38° | 7/8 | 39° | ② |
| | 17085206 | 13/32 | inner | 9/32 | 46° | .025 | — | 26° | 7/8 | 39° | 20 |
| | 17085208 | 13/32 | inner | 9/32 | 20° | .025 | 26° | 38° | 7/8 | 39° | 10 |
| | 17085209 | 13/32 | outer | 3/8 | 20° | .025 | 26° | 36° | 7/8 | 39° | 50 |
| | 17085210 | 13/32 | inner | 9/32 | 20° | .025 | 26° | 38° | 7/8 | 39° | 10 |
| | 17085211 | 13/32 | outer | 3/8 | 20° | .025 | 26° | 36° | 7/8 | 39° | 50 |
| | 17085212 | 13/32 | inner | 9/32 | 46° | .025 | 23° | — | 7/8 | 35° | ② |
| | 17085213 | 13/32 | inner | 9/32 | 46° | .025 | 23° | — | 7/8 | 35° | ② |
| | 17085215 | 13/32 | inner | 9/32 | 46° | .025 | — | 26° | 7/8 | 32° | ② |
| | 17085216 | 13/32 | inner | 9/32 | 20° | .025 | 26° | 38° | 7/8 | 39° | ② |
| | 17085217 | 13/32 | inner | 9/32 | 20° | .025 | 26° | 36° | 1/2 | 39° | ② |
| | 17085219 | 13/32 | inner | 9/32 | 20° | .025 | 26° | 36° | 1/2 | 39° | ② |
| | 17085220 | 13/32 | outer | 3/8 | 20° | .025 | — | 26° | 7/8 | 32° | 75 |
| | 17085221 | 13/32 | outer | 3/8 | 20° | .025 | — | 26° | 7/8 | 32° | 75 |
| | 17085222 | 13/32 | inner | 9/32 | 20° | .025 | 26° | 36° | 1/2 | 39° | 20 |
| | 17085223 | 13/32 | outer | 3/8 | 20° | .025 | 26° | 36° | 1/2 | 39° | 50 |
| | 17085224 | 13/32 | inner | 9/32 | 20° | .025 | 26° | 36° | 1/2 | 39° | 20 |
| | 17085225 | 13/32 | outer | 3/8 | 20° | .025 | 26° | 36° | 1/2 | 39° | 50 |
| | 17085226 | 13/32 | inner | 9/32 | 20° | .025 | — | 24° | 7/8 | 32° | 20 |
| | 17085227 | 13/32 | inner | 9/32 | 20° | .025 | — | 24° | 7/8 | 32° | 20 |
| | 17085228 | 13/32 | inner | 9/32 | 46° | .025 | — | 24° | 7/8 | 39° | 30 |
| | 17085229 | 13/32 | inner | 9/32 | 46° | .025 | — | 24° | 7/8 | 39° | 30 |
| | 17085230 | 13/32 | inner | 9/32 | 20° | .025 | — | 26° | 7/8 | 32° | 20 |
| | 17085231 | 13/32 | inner | 9/32 | 20° | .025 | — | 26° | 7/8 | 32° | 40 |
| | 17085235 | 13/32 | inner | 9/32 | 46° | .025 | — | 26° | 7/8 | 39° | 80 |
| | 17085238 | 13/32 | outer | 3/8 | 20° | .025 | — | 26° | 7/8 | 32° | 75 |
| | 17085239 | 13/32 | outer | 3/8 | 20° | .025 | — | 26° | 7/8 | 32° | 75 |
| | 17085290 | 13/32 | inner | 9/32 | 46° | .025 | — | 24° | 7/8 | 39° | 30 |
| | 17085291 | 13/32 | outer | 3/8 | 46° | .025 | — | 26° | 7/8 | 39° | 100 |
| | 17085292 | 13/32 | inner | 9/32 | 46° | .025 | — | 24° | 7/8 | 39° | 30 |
| | 17085293 | 13/32 | outer | 3/8 | 46° | .025 | — | 26° | 7/8 | 39° | 100 |
| | 17085294 | 13/32 | inner | 9/32 | 46° | .025 | — | 26° | 7/8 | 39° | ② |
| | 17085298 | 13/32 | inner | 9/32 | 46° | .025 | — | 26° | 7/8 | 39° | ② |

Note: Specified angle for use with angle degree tool. Choke coil lever setting is .120 in. for all carburetors.
① Second step of fast idle cam
② See Underhood Specifications sticker

89775C12

## Angle Degree to Decimal Conversion
### Model M2MC, M2ME and M4MC Carburetor

| Angle Degrees | Decimal Equiv. Top of Valve | Angle Degrees | Decimal Equiv. Top of Valve |
|---|---|---|---|
| 5 | .023 | 33 | .203 |
| 6 | .028 | 34 | .211 |
| 7 | .033 | 35 | .220 |
| 8 | .038 | 36 | .227 |
| 9 | .043 | 37 | .234 |
| 10 | .049 | 38 | .243 |
| 11 | .054 | 39 | .251 |
| 12 | .060 | 40 | .260 |
| 13 | .066 | 41 | .269 |
| 14 | .071 | 42 | .277 |
| 15 | .077 | 43 | .287 |
| 16 | .083 | 44 | .295 |
| 17 | .090 | 45 | .304 |
| 18 | .096 | 46 | .314 |
| 19 | .103 | 47 | .322 |

89775C13

# DIESEL FUEL SYSTEM

## Fuel Supply Pump

### REMOVAL & INSTALLATION

The diesel fuel supply pump is serviced in the same manner as the fuel pump on the gasoline engines.

## Fuel Filter

Refer to the Diesel Fuel Filter coverage in Section 1 for service procedures.

### WATER IN FUEL (DIESEL)

Water is the worst enemy of the diesel fuel injection system. The injection pump, which is designed and constructed to extremely close tolerances, and the injectors can be easily damaged if enough water if forced through them in the fuel. Engine performance will also be drastically affected, and engine damage can occur.

Diesel fuel is much more susceptible than gasoline to water contamination. Diesel engine trucks are equipped with an indicator lamp system that turns on an instrument panel lamp if water (1 to 2½ gallons) is detected in the fuel tank. The lamp will come on for 2 to 5 seconds each time the ignition is turned on, assuring the driver the lamp is working. If there is water in the fuel, the light will come back on after a 15 to 20 second off delay, and then remain on.

## PURGING THE FUEL TANK

### 6.2L Engine

The 6.2L diesel equipped trucks also have a water-in-fuel warning system. The fuel tank is equipped with a filter which screens out the water and lets it lay in the bottom of the tank below the fuel pickup. When the water level reaches a point where it could be drawn into the system, a warning light flashes in the cab. A built-in siphoning system starting at the fuel tank and going to the rear spring hanger on some models, and at the midway point of the right frame rail on other models permits you to attach a hose at the shut-off and siphon out the water.

If it becomes necessary to drain water from the fuel tank, also check the primary fuel filter for water. This procedure is covered under the Diesel Fuel Filter portion of Section 1.

## Fuel Injection Pump

### REMOVAL & INSTALLATION

### 6.2L Engine
▶ See Figures 33, 34, 35 and 36

1. Disconnect both batteries.
2. Remove the fan and fan shroud.
3. Remove the intake manifold as described in Section 3.
4. Remove the fuel lines as described in this section.
5. Disconnect the alternator cable at the injection pump, and the detent cable (see illustration) where applicable.
6. Tag and disconnect the necessary wires and hoses at the injection pump.
7. Disconnect the fuel return line at the top of the injection pump.
8. Disconnect the fuel feed line at the injection pump.

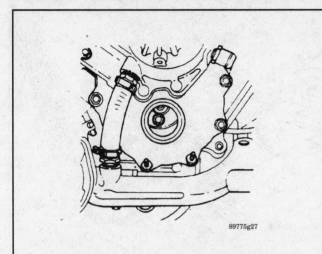

**Fig. 33 Rotate the crankshaft so the injection pump drive gear bolts become accessible through the hole**

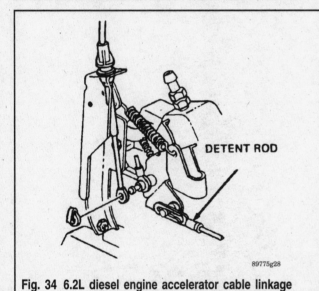

**Fig. 34 6.2L diesel engine accelerator cable linkage**

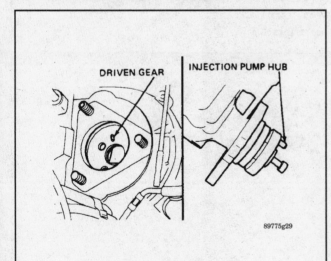

**Fig. 35 6.2L diesel engine injection pump locating pin**

9. Remove the air conditioning hose retainer bracket if equipped with A/C.

10. Remove the oil fill tube, including the crankcase depression valve vent hose assembly.

11. Remove the grommet.

12. Scribe or paint a matchmark on the front cover and on the injection pump flange.

13. The crankshaft must be rotated in order to gain access to the injection pump drive gear bolts through the oil filler neck hole.

14. Remove the injection pump-to-front cover attaching nuts. Remove the pump and cap all open lines and nozzles.

**To install:**

15. Replace the gasket. This is important.

16. Align the locating pin on the pump hub with the slot in the injection pump driven gear. At the same time, align the timing marks.

17. Attach the injection pump to the front cover, aligning the timing marks before torquing the nuts to 30 ft. lbs.

18. Install the drive gear to injection pump bolts, torquing the bolts to 20 ft. lbs. (27 Nm).

19. Install the remaining components in the reverse order of removal. Torque the fuel feed line at the injection pump to 20 ft. lbs. (27 Nm). Start the engine and check for leaks.

## Injection Pump Fuel Lines

### REMOVAL & INSTALLATION

**6.2L Engine**

▶ **See Figure 37**

➡ **When the fuel lines are to be removed, clean all fuel line fittings thoroughly before loosening. Immediately cap the lines, nozzles and pump fittings to maintain cleanliness.**

1. Disconnect both batteries.

2. Disconnect the air cleaner bracket at the valve cover.

3. Remove the crankcase ventilator bracket and move it aside.

4. Disconnect the secondary filter lines.

5. Remove the secondary filter adapter.

6. Loosen the vacuum pump hold-down clamp and rotate the pump in order to gain access to the intake manifold bolt. Remove the intake manifold bolts. The injection line clips are retained by the same bolts.

7. Remove the intake manifold. Install a protective cover (GM part J-29664-1 or equivalent) so no foreign material falls into the engine.

8. Remove the injection line clips at the loom brackets.

9. Remove the injection lines at the nozzles and cover the nozzles with protective caps.

10. Remove the injection lines at the pump and tag the lines for later installation.

11. Remove the fuel line from the injection pump.

12. Install all components in the reverse order of removal. Follow the illustrations for injection line connection.

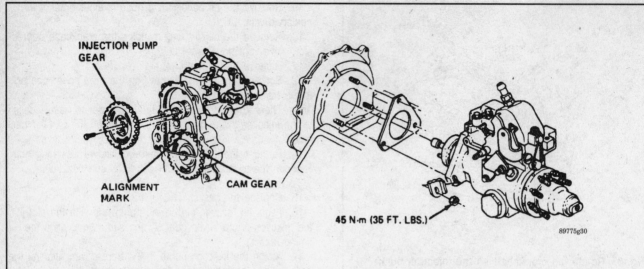

**Fig. 36 6.2L diesel engine injection pump mounting**

INJECTION PUMP GEAR

ALIGNMENT MARK

CAM GEAR

45 N·m (35 FT. LBS.)

89775g30

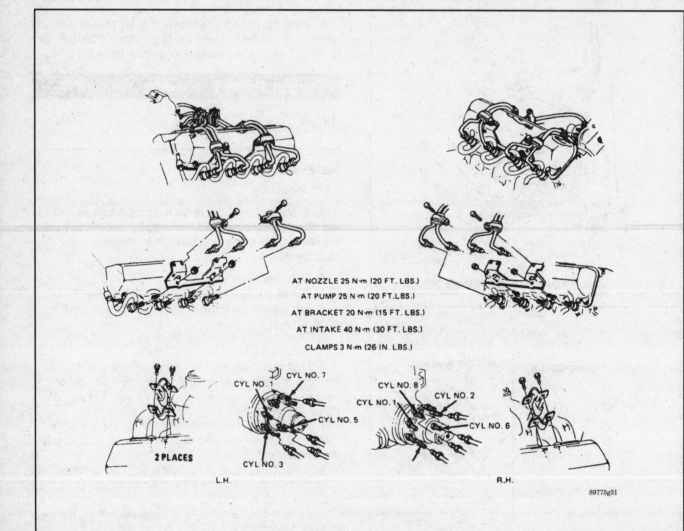

AT NOZZLE 25 N·m (20 FT. LBS.)

AT PUMP 25 N·m (20 FT. LBS.)

AT BRACKET 20 N·m (15 FT. LBS.)

AT INTAKE 40 N·m (30 FT. LBS.)

CLAMPS 3 N·m (26 IN. LBS.)

2 PLACES

CYL NO. 7

CYL NO. 1

CYL NO. 5

CYL NO. 3

CYL NO. 8

CYL NO. 1

CYL NO. 2

CYL NO. 6

L.H.

R.H.

89775g31

**Fig. 37 Fuel line routing and tightening specifications — 6.2L diesel engines**

## Fuel Injectors

### REMOVAL & INSTALLATION

**6.2L Engine**

▶ **See Figure 38**

1. Disconnect the truck's batteries.

2. Disconnect the fuel line clip, and remove the fuel return hose.

3. Remove the fuel injection line as previously detailed.

4. Using GM special tool J-29873, remove the injector. Always remove the injector by turning the 30mm hex portion of the injector; turning the round portion will damage the injector. Always cap the injector and fuel lines when disconnected, to prevent contamination.

5. Install the injector with new gasket and torque to 50 ft. lbs. (67 Nm). Connect the injection line and torque the nut to 20 ft. lbs. (27 Nm). Install the fuel return hose, fuel line clips, and connect the batteries.

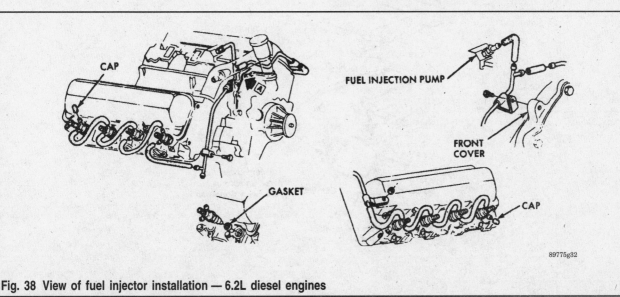

**Fig. 38 View of fuel injector installation — 6.2L diesel engines**

## FUEL TANK

### Tank Assembly

### DRAINING

### ✳✳CAUTION

**Disconnect the battery before beginning the draining operation.**

If the vehicle is not equipped with a drain plug, use the following procedure to remove the gasoline.

1. Using a 10 ft. piece of ⅜ in. (9.525mm) hose cut a flap slit 18 in. (457mm) from one end.

2. Install a pipe nipple, of slightly larger diameter than the hose, into the opposite end of the hose.

3. Install the nipple end of the hose into the fuel tank with the natural curve of the hose pointing downward. Keep feeding the hose in until the nipple hits the bottom of the tank.

4. Place the other end of the hose in a suitable container and insert a air hose pointing it in the downward direction of the slit and inject air into the line.

➡**If the vehicle is to be stored, always drain the gasoline from the complete fuel system including the carburetor, fuel pump, fuel lines, and tank.**

### REMOVAL & INSTALLATION

▶ **See Figure 39**

1. Drain the tank.

2. Jack up your vehicle and support it with jackstands.

3. Remove the clamp on the filler neck and the vent tube hose.

4. Remove the gauge hose which is attached to the frame.

5. While supporting the tank securely, remove the support straps.

6. Lower the tank until the gauge wiring can be removed.

7. Remove the tank.

8. Install the unit by reversing the removal procedure. Make certain that the anti-squeak material is replaced during installation.

9. Lower the vehicle.

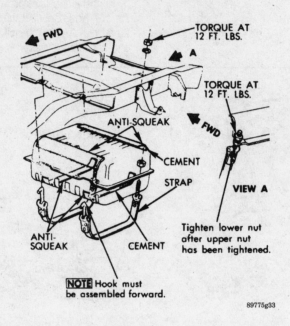

FWD

TORQUE AT
12 FT. LBS.

A

TORQUE AT
12 FT. LBS.

ANTI-SQUEAK

CEMENT

FWD

STRAP

VIEW A

ANTI-
SQUEAK

CEMENT

Tighten lower nut
after upper nut
has been tightened.

NOTE Hook must
be assembled forward.

89775g33

**Fig. 39 Common fuel tank installation on models covered in this manual**

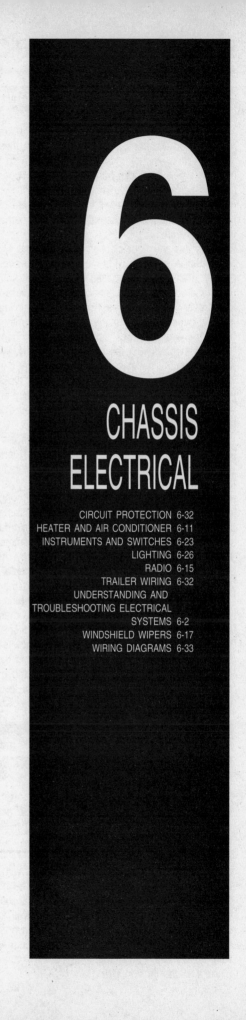

# 6

## CHASSIS ELECTRICAL

## UNDERSTANDING AND TROUBLESHOOTING ELECTRICAL SYSTEMS

Over the years import and domestic manufacturers have incorporated electronic control systems into their production lines. In fact, electronic control systems are so prevalent that all new cars and trucks built today are equipped with at least one on-board computer. These electronic components (with no moving parts) should theoretically last the life of the vehicle, provided that nothing external happens to damage the circuits or memory chips.

While it is true that electronic components should never wear out, in the real world malfunctions do occur. It is also true that any computer-based system is extremely sensitive to electrical voltages and cannot tolerate careless or haphazard testing/service procedures. An inexperienced individual can literally cause major damage looking for a minor problem by using the wrong kind of test equipment or connecting test leads/connectors with the ignition switch **ON**. When selecting test equipment, make sure the manufacturer's instructions state that the tester is compatible with whatever type of system is being serviced. Read all instructions carefully and double check all test points before installing probes or making any test connections.

The following section outlines basic diagnosis techniques for dealing with automotive electrical systems. Along with a general explanation of the various types of test equipment available to aid in servicing modern automotive systems, basic repair techniques for wiring harnesses and connectors are also given. Read the basic information before attempting any repairs or testing. This will provide the background of information necessary to avoid the most common and obvious mistakes that can cost both time and money. Although the replacement and testing procedures are simple in themselves, the systems are not, and unless one has a thorough understanding of all components and their function within a particular system, the logical test sequence these systems demand cannot be followed. Minor malfunctions can make a big difference, so it is important to know how each component affects the operation of the overall system in order to find the ultimate cause of a problem without replacing good components unnecessarily. It is not enough to use the correct test equipment; the test equipment must be used correctly.

## Safety Precautions

### ✷✷CAUTION

**Whenever working on or around any electrical or electronic systems, always observe these general precautions to prevent the possibility of personal injury or damage to electronic components.**

• Never install or remove battery cables with the key **ON** or the engine running. Jumper cables should be connected with the key **OFF** to avoid power surges that can damage electronic control units. Engines equipped with computer controlled systems should avoid both giving and getting jump starts due to the possibility of serious damage to components from arcing in the engine compartment if connections are made with the ignition **ON**.

• Always remove the battery cables before charging the battery. Never use a high output charger on an installed battery or attempt to use any type of "hot shot" (24 volt) starting aid.

• Exercise care when inserting test probes into connectors to insure good contact without damaging the connector or spreading the pins. Always probe connectors from the rear (wire) side, NOT the pin side, to avoid accidental shorting of terminals during test procedures.

• Never remove or attach wiring harness connectors with the ignition switch **ON**, especially to an electronic control unit.

• Do not drop any components during service procedures and never apply 12 volts directly to any component (like a solenoid or relay) unless instructed specifically to do so. Some component electrical windings are designed to safely handle only 4 or 5 volts and can be destroyed in seconds if 12 volts are applied directly to the connector.

• Remove the electronic control unit if the vehicle is to be placed in an environment where temperatures exceed approximately 176°F (80°C), such as a paint spray booth or when arc/gas welding near the control unit location.

## Understanding Basic Electricity

Understanding the basic theory of electricity makes electrical troubleshooting much easier. Several gauges are used in electrical troubleshooting to see inside the circuit being tested. Without a basic understanding, it will be difficult to understand testing procedures.

### THE WATER ANALOGY

Electricity is the flow of electrons — hypothetical particles thought to constitute the basic stuff of electricity. Many people have been taught electrical theory using an analogy with water. In a comparison with water flowing in a pipe, the electrons would be the water. As the flow of water can be measured, the flow of electricity can be measured. The unit of measurement is amperes, frequently abbreviated amps. An ammeter will measure the actual amount of current flowing in the circuit.

Just as the water pressure is measured in units such as pounds per square inch, electrical pressure is measured in volts. When a voltmeter's two probes are placed on two live portions of an electrical circuit with different electrical pressures, current will flow through the voltmeter and produce a reading which indicates the difference in electrical pressure between the two parts of the circuit.

While increasing the voltage in a circuit will increase the flow of current, the actual flow depends not only on voltage, but on the resistance of the circuit. The standard unit for measuring circuit resistance is an ohm, measured by an ohmmeter. The ohmmeter is somewhat similar to an ammeter, but incorporates its own source of power so that a standard voltage is always present.

## CIRCUITS

An actual electric circuit consists of four basic parts. These are: the power source, such as a generator or battery; a hot wire, which conducts the electricity under a relatively high voltage to the component supplied by the circuit; the load, such as a lamp, motor, resistor or relay coil; and the ground wire, which carries the current back to the source under very low voltage. In such a circuit the bulk of the resistance exists between the point where the hot wire is connected to the load, and the point where the load is grounded. In an automobile, the vehicle's frame or body, which is made of steel, is used as a part of the ground circuit for many of the electrical devices.

Remember that, in electrical testing, the voltmeter is connected in parallel with the circuit being tested (without disconnecting any wires) and measures the difference in voltage between the locations of the two probes; that the ammeter is connected in series with the load (the circuit is separated at one point and the ammeter inserted so it becomes a part of the circuit); and the ohmmeter is self-powered, so that all the power in the circuit should be off and the portion of the circuit to be measured contacted at either end by one of the probes of the meter.

For any electrical system to operate, it must make a complete circuit. This simply means that the power flow from the battery must make a complete circle. When an electrical component is operating, power flows from the battery to the component, passes through the component causing it to perform it to function (such as lighting a light bulb) and then returns to the battery through the ground of the circuit. This ground is usually (but not always) the metal part of the vehicle on which the electrical component is mounted.

Perhaps the easiest way to visualize this is to think of connecting a light bulb with two wires attached to it to your vehicle's battery. The battery in your vehicle has two posts (negative and positive). If one of the two wires attached to the light bulb was attached to the negative post of the battery and the other wire was attached to the positive post of the battery, you would have a complete circuit. Current from the battery would flow out one post, through the wire attached to it and then to the light bulb, where it would pass through causing it to light. It would then leave the light bulb, travel through the other wire, and return to the other post of the battery.

## AUTOMOTIVE CIRCUITS

The normal automotive circuit differs from this simple example in two ways. First, instead of having a return wire from the bulb to the battery, the light bulb return the current to the battery through the chassis of the vehicle. Since the negative battery cable is attached to the chassis and the chassis is made of electrically conductive metal, the chassis of the vehicle can serve as a ground wire to complete the circuit. Secondly, most automotive circuits contain switches to turn components on and off.

Some electrical components which require a large amount of current to operate also have a relay in their circuit. Since these circuits carry a large amount of current, the thickness of the wire in the circuit (gauge size) is also greater. If this large wire were connected from the component to the control switch on the instrument panel, and then back to the component, a voltage drop would occur in the circuit. To prevent this potential drop in voltage, an electromagnetic switch (relay) is used. The large wires in the circuit are connected from the vehicle battery to one side of the relay, and from the opposite side of the relay to the component. The relay is normally open, preventing current from passing through the circuit. An additional, smaller wire is connected from the relay to the control switch for the circuit. When the control switch is turned on, it grounds the smaller wire from the relay and completes the circuit.

## SHORT CIRCUITS

If you were to disconnect the light bulb (from the previous example of a light-bulb being connected to the battery by two wires) from the wires and touch the two wires together (please take our word for this; don't try it), the result will be a shower of sparks. A similar thing happens (on a smaller scale) when the power supply wire to a component or the electrical component itself becomes grounded before the normal ground connection for the circuit. To prevent damage to the system, the fuse for the circuit blows to interrupt the circuit — protecting the components from damage. Because grounding a wire from a power source makes a complete circuit — less the required component to use the power — the phenomenon is called a short circuit. The most common causes of short circuits are: the rubber insulation on a wire breaking or rubbing through to expose the current carrying core of the wire to a metal part of the car, or a shorted switch.

Some electrical systems on the vehicle are protected by a circuit breaker which is, basically, a self-repairing fuse. When either of the described events takes place in a system which is protected by a circuit breaker, the circuit breaker opens the circuit the same way a fuse does. However, when either the short is removed from the circuit or the surge subsides, the circuit breaker resets itself and does not have to be replaced as a fuse does.

## Troubleshooting

When diagnosing a specific problem, organized troubleshooting is a must. The complexity of a modern automobile demands that you approach any problem in a logical, organized manner. There are certain troubleshooting techniques that are standard:

1. Establish when the problem occurs. Does the problem appear only under certain conditions? Were there any noises, odors, or other unusual symptoms?

2. Isolate the problem area. To do this, make some simple tests and observations; then eliminate the systems that are working properly. Check for obvious problems such as broken wires, dirty connections or split/disconnected vacuum hoses. Always check the obvious before assuming something complicated is the cause.

3. Test for problems systematically to determine the cause once the problem area is isolated. Are all the components functioning properly? Is there power going to electrical switches and motors? Is there vacuum at vacuum switches and/or actuators? Is there a mechanical problem such as bent linkage

or loose mounting screws? Performing careful, systematic checks will often turn up most causes on the first inspection without wasting time checking components that have little or no relationship to the problem.

4. Test all repairs after the work is done to make sure that the problem is fixed. Some causes can be traced to more than one component, so a careful verification of repair work is important in order to pick up additional malfunctions that may cause a problem to reappear or a different problem to arise. A blown fuse, for example, is a simple problem that may require more than another fuse to repair. If you don't look for a problem that caused a fuse to blow, a shorted wire (for example) may go undetected.

Experience has shown that most problems tend to be the result of a fairly simple and obvious cause, such as loose or corroded connectors or air leaks in the intake system. This makes careful inspection of components during testing essential to quick and accurate troubleshooting.

## BASIC TROUBLESHOOTING THEORY

Electrical problems generally fall into one of three areas:
• The component that is not functioning is not receiving current.
• The component itself is not functioning.
• The component is not properly grounded.

Problems that fall into the first category are by far the most complicated. It is the current supply system to the component which contains all the switches, relay, fuses, etc.

The electrical system can be checked with a test light and a jumper wire. A test light is a device that looks like a pointed screwdriver with a wire attached to it. It has a light bulb in its handle. A jumper wire is a piece of insulated wire with an alligator clip attached to each end.

If a light bulb is not working, you must follow a systematic plan to determine which of the three causes is the villain.

1. Turn on the switch that controls the inoperable bulb.
2. Disconnect the power supply wire from the bulb.
3. Attach the ground wire to the test light to a good metal ground.
4. Touch the probe end of the test light to the end of the power supply wire that was disconnected from the bulb. If the bulb is receiving current, the test light will go on.

➡**If the bulb is one which works only when the ignition key is turned on (turn signal), make sure the key is turned on.**

If the test light does not go on, then the problem is in the circuit between the battery and the bulb. As mentioned before, this includes all the switches, fuses, and relays in the system. Turn to a wiring diagram and find the bulb on the diagram. Follow the wire that runs back to the battery. The problem is an open circuit between the battery and the bulb. If the fuse is blown and, when replaced, immediately blows again, there is a short circuit in the system which must be located and repaired. If there is a switch in the system, bypass it with a jumper wire. This is done by connecting one end of the jumper wire to the power supply wire into the switch and the other end of the jumper wire to the wire coming out of the switch. If the test

light illuminates with the jumper wire installed, the switch or whatever was bypassed is defective.

➡**Never substitute the jumper wire for the bulb, as the bulb is the component required to use the power from the power source.**

5. If the bulb in the test light goes on, then the current is getting to the bulb that is not working in the car. This eliminates the first of the three possible causes. Connect the power supply wire and connect a jumper wire from the bulb to a good metal ground. Do this with the switch which controls the bulb works with jumper wire installed, then it has a bad ground. This is usually caused by the metal area on which the bulb mounts to the vehicle being coated with some type of foreign matter.

6. If neither test located the source of the trouble, then the light bulb itself is defective.

The above test procedure can be applied to any of the components of the chassis electrical system by substituting the component that is not working for the light bulb. Remember that for any electrical system to work, all connections must be clean and tight.

## TEST EQUIPMENT

➡**Pinpointing the exact cause of trouble in an electrical system can sometimes only be accomplished by the use of special test equipment. The following describes different types of commonly used test equipment and explains how to use them in diagnosis. In addition to the information covered below, the tool manufacturer's instructions booklet (provided with the tester) should be read and clearly understood before attempting any test procedures.**

### Jumper Wires

Jumper wires are simple, yet extremely valuable, pieces of test equipment. They are basically test wires which are used to bypass sections of a circuit. The simplest type of jumper wire is a length of multi-strand wire with an alligator clip at each end. Jumper wires are usually fabricated from lengths of standard automotive wire and whatever type of connector (alligator clip, spade connector or pin connector) that is required for the particular vehicle being tested. The well equipped tool box will have several different styles of jumper wires in several different lengths. Some jumper wires are made with three or more terminals coming from a common splice for special purpose testing. In cramped, hard-to-reach areas it is advisable to have insulated boots over the jumper wire terminals in order to prevent accidental grounding, sparks, and possible fire, especially when testing fuel system components.

Jumper wires are used primarily to locate open electrical circuits, on either the ground (-) side of the circuit or on the hot (+) side. If an electrical component fails to operate, connect the jumper wire between the component and a good ground. If the component operates only with the jumper installed, the ground circuit is open. If the ground circuit is good, but the component does not operate, the circuit between the power feed and component may be open. By moving the jumper wire successively back from the lamp toward the power source, you can isolate the area of the circuit where the open is located. When the component stops functioning, or the power is cut off, the open is in the segment of wire between the jumper and the point previously tested.

You can sometimes connect the jumper wire directly from the battery to the hot terminal of the component, but first make sure the component uses 12 volts in operation. Some electrical components, such as fuel injectors, are designed to operate on about 4 volts and running 12 volts directly to the injector terminals can cause damage.

By inserting an in-line fuse holder between a set of test leads, a fused jumper wire can be used for bypassing open circuits. Use a 5 amp fuse to provide protection against voltage spikes. When in doubt, use a voltmeter to check the voltage input to the component and measure how much voltage is normally being applied.

### ✱✱CAUTION

**Never use jumpers made from wire that is of lighter gauge than that which is used in the circuit under test. If the jumper wire is of too small a gauge, it may overheat and possibly melt. Never use jumpers to bypass high resistance loads in a circuit. Bypassing resistances, in effect, creates a short circuit. This may, in turn, cause damage and fire. Jumper wires should only be used to bypass lengths of wire.**

### Unpowered Test Lights

The 12 volt test light is used to check circuits and components while electrical current is flowing through them. It is used for voltage and ground tests. Twelve volt test lights come in different styles but all have three main parts; a ground clip, a probe, and a light. The most commonly used 12 volt test lights have pick-type probes. To use a 12 volt test light, connect the ground clip to a good ground and probe wherever necessary with the pick. The pick should be sharp so that it can be probed into tight spaces.

### ✱✱WARNING

**Do not use a test light to probe electronic ignition spark plug or coil wires. Never use a pick-type test light to probe wiring on computer controlled systems unless specifically instructed to do so. Any wire insulation that is pierced by the test light probe should be taped and sealed with silicone after testing.**

Like the jumper wire, the 12 volt test light is used to isolate opens in circuits. But, whereas the jumper wire is used to bypass the open to operate the load, the 12 volt test light is used to locate the presence of voltage in a circuit. If the test light glows, you know that there is power up to that point; if the 12 volt test light does not glow when its probe is inserted into the wire or connector, you know that there is an open circuit (no power). Move the test light in successive steps back toward the power source until the light in the handle does

glow. When it glows, the open is between the probe and point which was probed previously.

➡**The test light does not detect that 12 volts (or any particular amount of voltage) is present; it only detects that some voltage is present. It is advisable before using the test light to touch its terminals across the battery posts to make sure the light is operating properly.**

### Self-Powered Test Lights

The self-powered test light usually contains a 1.5 volt penlight battery. One type of self-powered test light is similar in design to the 12 volt unit. This type has both the battery and the light in the handle, along with a pick-type probe tip. The second type has the light toward the open tip, so that the light illuminates the contact point. The self-powered test light is a dual purpose piece of test equipment. It can be used to test for either open or short circuits when power is isolated from the circuit (continuity test). A powered test light should not be used on any computer controlled system or component unless specifically instructed to do so. Many engine sensors can be destroyed by even this small amount of voltage applied directly to the terminals.

### Voltmeters

A voltmeter is used to measure voltage at any point in a circuit, or to measure the voltage drop across any part of a circuit. It can also be used to check continuity in a wire or circuit by indicating current flow from one end to the other. Analog voltmeters usually have various scales on the meter dial and a selector switch to allow the selection of different voltages. The voltmeter has a positive and a negative lead. To avoid damage to the meter, always connect the negative lead to the negative (-) side of the circuit (to ground or nearest the ground side of the circuit) and connect the positive lead to the positive (+) side of the circuit (to the power source or the nearest power source). Note that the negative voltmeter lead will always be black and that the positive voltmeter will always be some color other than black (usually red).

Depending on how the voltmeter is connected into the circuit, it has several uses. A voltmeter can be connected either in parallel or in series with a circuit and it has a very high resistance to current flow. When connected in parallel, only a small amount of current will flow through the voltmeter current path; the rest will flow through the normal circuit current path and the circuit will work normally. When the voltmeter is connected in series with a circuit, only a small amount of current can flow through the circuit. The circuit will not work properly, but the voltmeter reading will show if the circuit is complete or not.

### Ohmmeters

The ohmmeter is designed to read resistance (which is measured in ohms or $\Omega$) in a circuit or component. Although there are several different styles of ohmmeters, all analog meters will usually have a selector switch which permits the measurement of different ranges of resistance (usually the selector switch allows the multiplication of the meter reading by 10, 100, 1000, and 10,000). A calibration knob allows the meter to be set at zero for accurate measurement. Since all ohmmeters are powered by an internal battery, the ohmmeter can be used as a self-powered test light. When the ohmmeter is connected, current from the ohmmeter flows through the circuit or component being tested. Since the ohmmeter's internal resistance and voltage are known values, the amount of current flow through the meter depends on the resistance of the circuit or component being tested.

The ohmmeter can be used to perform a continuity test for opens or shorts (either by observation of the meter needle or as a self-powered test light), and to read actual resistance in a circuit. It should be noted that the ohmmeter is used to check the resistance of a component or wire while there is no voltage applied to the circuit. Current flow from an outside voltage source (such as the vehicle battery) can damage the ohmmeter, so the circuit or component should be isolated from the vehicle electrical system before any testing is done. Since the ohmmeter uses its own voltage source, either lead can be connected to any test point.

➡**When checking diodes or other solid state components, the ohmmeter leads can only be connected one way in order to measure current flow in a single direction. Make sure the positive (+) and negative (-) terminal connections are as described in the test procedures to verify the one-way diode operation.**

In using the meter for making continuity checks, do not be concerned with the actual resistance readings. Zero resistance, or any ohm reading, indicates continuity in the circuit. Infinite resistance indicates an open in the circuit. A high resistance reading where there should be none indicates a problem in the circuit. Checks for short circuits are made in the same manner as checks for open circuits except that the circuit must be isolated from both power and normal ground. Infinite resistance indicates no continuity to ground, while zero resistance indicates a dead short to ground.

### Ammeters

An ammeter measures the amount of current flowing through a circuit in units called amperes or amps. Amperes are units of electron flow which indicate how fast the electrons are flowing through the circuit. Since Ohms Law dictates that current flow in a circuit is equal to the circuit voltage divided by the total circuit resistance, increasing voltage also increases the current level (amps). Likewise, any decrease in resistance will increase the amount of amps in a circuit. At normal operating voltage, most circuits have a characteristic amount of amperes, called "current draw" which can be measured using an ammeter. By referring to a specified current draw rating, measuring the amperes, and comparing the two values, one can determine what is happening within the circuit to aid in diagnosis. An open circuit, for example, will not allow any current to flow so the ammeter reading will be zero. More current flows through a heavily loaded circuit or when the charging system is operating.

An ammeter is always connected in series with the circuit being tested. All of the current that normally flows through the circuit must also flow through the ammeter; if there is any other path for the current to follow, the ammeter reading will not be accurate. The ammeter itself has very little resistance to current flow and therefore will not affect the circuit, but it will measure current draw only when the circuit is closed and electricity is flowing. Excessive current draw can blow fuses

and drain the battery, while a reduced current draw can cause motors to run slowly, lights to dim and other components to not operate properly. The ammeter can help diagnose these conditions by locating the cause of the high or low reading.

### Multimeters

Different combinations of test meters can be built into a single unit designed for specific tests. Some of the more common combination test devices are known as Volt/Amp testers, Tach/Dwell meters, or Digital Multimeters. The Volt/Amp tester is used for charging system, starting system or battery tests and consists of a voltmeter, an ammeter and a variable resistance carbon pile. The voltmeter will usually have at least two ranges for use with 6, 12 and/or 24 volt systems. The ammeter also has more than one range for testing various levels of battery loads and starter current draw. The carbon pile can be adjusted to offer different amounts of resistance. The Volt/Amp tester has heavy leads to carry large amounts of current and many later models have an inductive ammeter pickup that clamps around the wire to simplify test connections. On some models, the ammeter also has a zero-center scale to allow testing of charging and starting systems without switching leads or polarity. A digital multimeter is a voltmeter, ammeter and ohmmeter combined in an instrument which gives a digital readout. These are often used when testing solid state circuits because of their high input impedance (usually 10 megohms or more).

The tach/dwell meter that combines a tachometer and a dwell (cam angle) meter is a specialized kind of voltmeter. The tachometer scale is marked to show engine speed in rpm and the dwell scale is marked to show degrees of distributor shaft rotation. In most electronic ignition systems, dwell is determined by the control unit, but the dwell meter can also be used to check the duty cycle (operation) of some electronic engine control systems. Some tach/dwell meters are powered by an internal battery, while others take their power from the vehicle battery in use. The battery powered testers usually require calibration (much like an ohmmeter) before testing.

## TESTING

### Open Circuits

To use the self-powered test light or a multimeter to check for open circuits, first isolate the circuit from the vehicle's 12 volt power source by disconnecting the battery or wiring harness connector. Connect the test light or ohmmeter ground clip to a good ground and probe sections of the circuit sequentially with the test light. (start from either end of the circuit). If the light is out/or there is infinite resistance, the open is between the probe and the circuit ground. If the light is on/or the meter shows continuity, the open is between the probe and end of the circuit toward the power source.

### Short Circuits

By isolating the circuit both from power and from ground, and using a self-powered test light or multimeter, you can check for shorts to ground in the circuit. Isolate the circuit from power and ground. Connect the test light or ohmmeter ground clip to a good ground and probe any easy-to-reach test point in the circuit. If the light comes on or there is continuity, there is a short somewhere in the circuit. To isolate the short, probe a test point at either end of the isolated circuit (the light should be on/there should be continuity). Leave the test light probe engaged and open connectors, switches, remove parts, etc., sequentially, until the light goes out/continuity is broken. When the light goes out, the short is between the last circuit component opened and the previous circuit opened.

➡**The battery in the test light and does not provide much current. A weak battery may not provide enough power to illuminate the test light even when a complete circuit is made (especially if there are high resistances in the circuit). Always make sure that the test battery is strong. To check the battery, briefly touch the ground clip to the probe; if the light glows brightly the battery is strong enough for testing. Never use a self-powered test light to perform checks for opens or shorts when power is applied to the electrical system under test. The 12 volt vehicle power will quickly burn out the light bulb in the test light.**

### Available Voltage Measurement

Set the voltmeter selector switch to the 20V position and connect the meter negative lead to the negative post of the battery. Connect the positive meter lead to the positive post of the battery and turn the ignition switch **ON** to provide a load. Read the voltage on the meter or digital display. A well charged battery should register over 12 volts. If the meter reads below 11.5 volts, the battery power may be insufficient to operate the electrical system properly. This test determines voltage available from the battery and should be the first step in any electrical trouble diagnosis procedure. Many electrical problems, especially on computer controlled systems, can be caused by a low state of charge in the battery. Excessive corrosion at the battery cable terminals can cause a poor contact that will prevent proper charging and full battery current flow.

Normal battery voltage is 12 volts when fully charged. When the battery is supplying current to one or more circuits it is said to be "under load." When everything is off the electrical system is under a "no-load" condition. A fully charged battery may show about 12.5 volts at no load; will drop to 12 volts under medium load; and will drop even lower under heavy load. If the battery is partially discharged the voltage decrease under heavy load may be excessive, even though the battery shows 12 volts or more at no load. When allowed to discharge further, the battery's available voltage under load will decrease more severely. For this reason, it is important that the battery be fully charged during all testing procedures to avoid errors in diagnosis and incorrect test results.

### Voltage Drop

When current flows through a resistance, the voltage beyond the resistance is reduced (the larger the current, the greater the reduction in voltage). When no current is flowing, there is no voltage drop because there is no current flow. All points in the circuit which are connected to the power source are at the same voltage as the power source. The total voltage drop always equals the total source voltage. In a long circuit with many connectors, a series of small, unwanted voltage drops

due to corrosion at the connectors can add up to a total loss of voltage which impairs the operation of the normal loads in the circuit. The maximum allowable voltage drop under load is critical, especially if there is more than one high resistance problem in a circuit because all voltage drops are cumulative. A small drop is normal due to the resistance of the conductors.

### INDIRECT COMPUTATION OF VOLTAGE DROPS

1. Set the voltmeter selector switch to the 20 volt position.
2. Connect the meter negative lead to a good ground.
3. While operating the circuit, probe all loads in the circuit with the positive meter lead and observe the voltage readings. A drop should be noticed after the first load. But, there should be little or no voltage drop before the first load.

### DIRECT MEASUREMENT OF VOLTAGE DROPS

1. Set the voltmeter switch to the 20 volt position.
2. Connect the voltmeter negative lead to the ground side of the load to be measured.
3. Connect the positive lead to the positive side of the resistance or load to be measured.
4. Read the voltage drop directly on the 20 volt scale.

Too high a voltage indicates too high a resistance. If, for example, a blower motor runs too slowly, you can determine if perhaps there is too high a resistance in the resistor pack. By taking voltage drop readings in all parts of the circuit, you can isolate the problem. Too low a voltage drop indicates too low a resistance. Take the blower motor for example again. If a blower motor runs too fast in the MED and/or LOW position, the problem might be isolated in the resistor pack by taking voltage drop readings in all parts of the circuit to locate a possibly shorted resistor.

### HIGH RESISTANCE TESTING

1. Set the voltmeter selector switch to the 4 volt position.
2. Connect the voltmeter positive lead to the positive post of the battery.
3. Turn on the headlights and heater blower to provide a load.
4. Probe various points in the circuit with the negative voltmeter lead.
5. Read the voltage drop on the 4 volt scale. Some average maximum allowable voltage drops are:
   - FUSE PANEL: 0.7 volts
   - IGNITION SWITCH: 0.5 volts
   - HEADLIGHT SWITCH: 0.7 volts
   - IGNITION COIL (+): 0.5 volts
   - ANY OTHER LOAD: 1.3 volts

➡**Voltage drops are all measured while a load is operating; without current flow, there will be no voltage drop.**

### Resistance Measurement

The batteries in an ohmmeter will weaken with age and temperature, so the ohmmeter must be calibrated or "zeroed" before taking measurements. To zero the meter, place the selector switch in its lowest range and touch the two ohmmeter leads together. Turn the calibration knob until the meter needle is exactly on zero.

➡All analog (needle) type ohmmeters must be zeroed before use, but some digital ohmmeter models are automatically calibrated when the switch is turned on. Self-calibrating digital ohmmeters do not have an adjusting knob, but its a good idea to check for a zero readout before use by touching the leads together. All computer controlled systems require the use of a digital ohmmeter with at least 10 megohms impedance for testing. Before any test procedures are attempted, make sure the ohmmeter used is compatible with the electrical system or damage to the on-board computer could result.

To measure resistance, first isolate the circuit from the vehicle power source by disconnecting the battery cables or the harness connector. Make sure the key is **OFF** when disconnecting any components or the battery. Where necessary, also isolate at least one side of the circuit to be checked in order to avoid reading parallel resistances. Parallel circuit resistances will always give a lower reading than the actual resistance of either of the branches. When measuring the resistance of parallel circuits, the total resistance will always be lower than the smallest resistance in the circuit. Connect the meter leads to both sides of the circuit (wire or component) and read the actual measured ohms on the meter scale. Make sure the selector switch is set to the proper ohm scale for the circuit being tested to avoid misreading the ohmmeter test value.

### ❊❊WARNING

Never use an ohmmeter with power applied to the circuit. Like the self-powered test light, the ohmmeter is designed to operate on its own power supply. The normal 12 volt automotive electrical system current could damage the meter!

### Wiring Harnesses

The average automobile contains about ½ mile of wiring, with hundreds of individual connections. To protect the many wires from damage and to keep them from becoming a confusing tangle, they are organized into bundles, enclosed in plastic or taped together and called wiring harnesses. Different harnesses serve different parts of the vehicle. Individual wires are color coded to help trace them through a harness where sections are hidden from view.

Automotive wiring or circuit conductors can be in any one of three forms:
1. Single strand wire
2. Multi-strand wire
3. Printed circuitry

Single strand wire has a solid metal core and is usually used inside such components as alternators, motors, relays and other devices. Multi-strand wire has a core made of many small strands of wire twisted together into a single conductor. Most of the wiring in an automotive electrical system is made up of multi-strand wire, either as a single conductor or grouped together in a harness. All wiring is color coded on the insulator, either as a solid color or as a colored wire with an identification stripe. A printed circuit is a thin film of copper or other conductor that is printed on an insulator backing. Occasionally, a printed circuit is sandwiched between two sheets of plastic for more protection and flexibility. A complete printed circuit, consisting of conductors, insulating material and connectors for lamps or other components is called a printed circuit board. Printed circuitry is used in place of individual wires or harnesses in places where space is limited, such as behind instrument panels.

Since automotive electrical systems are very sensitive to changes in resistance, the selection of properly sized wires is critical when systems are repaired. A loose or corroded connection or a replacement wire that is too small for the circuit will add extra resistance and an additional voltage drop to the circuit. A ten percent voltage drop can result in slow or erratic motor operation, for example, even though the circuit is complete. The wire gauge number is an expression of the cross-section area of the conductor. The most common system for expressing wire size is the American Wire Gauge (AWG) system.

Gauge numbers are assigned to conductors of various cross-section areas. As gauge number increases, area decreases and the conductor becomes smaller. A 5 gauge conductor is smaller than a 1 gauge conductor and a 10 gauge is smaller than a 5 gauge. As the cross-section area of a conductor decreases, resistance increases and so does the gauge number. A conductor with a higher gauge number will carry less current than a conductor with a lower gauge number.

➡Gauge wire size refers to the size of the conductor, not the size of the complete wire. It is possible to have two wires of the same gauge with different diameters because one may have thicker insulation than the other.

12 volt automotive electrical systems generally use 10, 12, 14, 16 and 18 gauge wire. Main power distribution circuits and larger accessories usually use 10 and 12 gauge wire. Battery cables are usually 4 or 6 gauge, although 1 and 2 gauge wires are occasionally used. Wire length must also be considered when making repairs to a circuit. As conductor length increases, so does resistance. An 18 gauge wire, for example, can carry a 10 amp load for 10 feet without excessive voltage drop; however if a 15 foot wire is required for the same 10 amp load, it must be a 16 gauge wire.

An electrical schematic shows the electrical current paths when a circuit is operating properly. It is essential to understand how a circuit works before trying to figure out why it doesn't. Schematics break the entire electrical system down into individual circuits and show only one particular circuit. In a schematic, no attempt is made to represent wiring and components as they physically appear on the vehicle; switches and other components are shown as simply as possible. Face views of harness connectors show the cavity or terminal locations in all multi-pin connectors to help locate test points.

If you need to backprobe a connector while it is on the component, the order of the terminals must be mentally reversed. The wire color code can help in this situation, as well as a keyway, lock tab or other reference mark.

## WIRING REPAIR

Soldering is a quick, efficient method of joining metals permanently. Everyone who has the occasion to make wiring repairs should know how to solder. Electrical connections that are soldered are far less likely to come apart and will conduct electricity much better than connections that are only "pig-tailed" together. The most popular (and preferred) method of soldering is with an electrical soldering gun. Soldering irons are available in many sizes and wattage ratings. Irons with higher wattage ratings deliver higher temperatures and recover lost heat faster. A small soldering iron rated for no more than 50 watts is recommended, especially on electrical systems where excess heat can damage the components being soldered.

There are three ingredients necessary for successful soldering; proper flux, good solder and sufficient heat. A soldering flux is necessary to clean the metal of tarnish, prepare it for soldering and to enable the solder to spread into tiny crevices. When soldering, always use a rosin core solder which is non-corrosive and will not attract moisture once the job is finished. Other types of flux (acid core) will leave a residue that will attract moisture and cause the wires to corrode. Tin is a unique metal with a low melting point. In a molten state, it dissolves and alloys easily with many metals. Solder is made by mixing tin with lead. The most common proportions are 40/60, 50/50 and 60/40, with the percentage of tin listed first. Low priced solders usually contain less tin, making them very difficult for a beginner to use because more heat is required to melt the solder. A common solder is 40/60 which is well suited for all-around general use, but 60/40 melts easier and is preferred for electrical work.

### Soldering Techniques

Successful soldering requires that the metals to be joined be heated to a temperature that will melt the solder, usually 360-460°F (182-238°C). Contrary to popular belief, the purpose of the soldering iron is not to melt the solder itself, but to heat the parts being soldered to a temperature high enough to melt the solder when it is touched to the work. Melting flux-cored solder on the soldering iron will usually destroy the effectiveness of the flux.

➡**Soldering tips are made of copper for good heat conductivity, but must be "tinned" regularly for quick transference of heat to the project and to prevent the solder from sticking to the iron. To "tin" the iron, simply heat it and touch the flux-cored solder to the tip; the solder will flow over the hot tip. Wipe the excess off with a clean rag, but be careful as the iron will be hot.**

After some use, the tip may become pitted. If so, simply dress the tip smooth with a smooth file and "tin" the tip again. Flux-cored solder will remove oxides but rust, bits of insulation and oil or grease must be removed with a wire brush or emery cloth. For maximum strength in soldered parts, the joint must start off clean and tight. Weak joints will result in gaps too wide for the solder to bridge.

If a separate soldering flux is used, it should be brushed or swabbed on only those areas that are to be soldered. Most solders contain a core of flux and separate fluxing is unnecessary. Hold the work to be soldered firmly. It is best to solder on a wooden board, because a metal vise will only rob the piece to be soldered of heat and make it difficult to melt the solder. Hold the soldering tip with the broadest face against the work to be soldered. Apply solder under the tip close to the work, using enough solder to give a heavy film between the iron and the piece being soldered, while moving slowly and making sure the solder melts properly. Keep the work level or the solder will run to the lowest part and favor the thicker parts, because these require more heat to melt the solder. If the soldering tip overheats (the solder coating on the face of the tip burns up), it should be retinned. Once the soldering is completed, let the soldered joint stand until cool. Tape and seal all soldered wire splices after the repair has cooled.

### Wire Harness Connectors

Most connectors in the engine compartment or that are otherwise exposed to the elements are protected against moisture and dirt which could create oxidation and deposits on the terminals.

These special connectors are weather-proof. All repairs require the use of a special terminal and the tool required to service it. This tool is used to remove the pin and sleeve terminals. If removal is attempted with an ordinary pick, there is a good chance that the terminal will be bent or deformed. Unlike standard blade type terminals, these weather-proof terminals cannot be straightened once they are bent. Make certain that the connectors are properly seated and all of the sealing rings are in place when connecting leads. On some models, a hinge-type flap provides a backup or secondary locking feature for the terminals. Most secondary locks are used to improve connector reliability by retaining the terminals if the small terminal lock tangs are not positioned properly.

Molded-on connectors require complete replacement of the connection. This means splicing a new connector assembly into the harness. All splices should be soldered to insure proper contact. Use care when probing the connections or replacing terminals in them as it is possible to short between opposite terminals. If this happens to the wrong terminal pair, it is possible to damage certain components. Always use jumper wires between connectors for circuit checking and never probe through weatherproof seals.

Open circuits are often difficult to locate by sight because corrosion or terminal misalignment are hidden by the connectors. Merely wiggling a connector on a sensor or in the wiring harness may correct the open circuit condition. This should always be considered when an open circuit or a failed sensor is indicated. Intermittent problems may also be caused by oxidized or loose connections. When using a circuit tester for diagnosis, always probe connections from the wire side. Be careful not to damage sealed connectors with test probes.

All wiring harnesses should be replaced with identical parts, using the same gauge wire and connectors. When signal wires are spliced into a harness, use wire with high temperature insulation only. It is seldom necessary to replace a complete harness. If replacement is necessary, pay close attention to insure proper harness routing. Secure the harness with suitable plastic wire clamps to prevent vibrations from causing the harness to wear in spots or contact any hot components.

➡**Weatherproof connectors cannot be replaced with standard connectors. Instructions are provided with replacement connector and terminal packages. Some wire harnesses have mounting indicators (usually pieces of colored tape) to mark where the harness is to be secured.**

In making wiring repairs, its important that you always replace damaged wires with wiring of the same gauge as the wire being replaced. The heavier the wire, the smaller the gauge number. Wires are color-coded to aid in identification and whenever possible the same color coded wire should be used for replacement. A wire stripping and crimping tool is necessary to install solderless terminal connectors. Test all crimps by pulling on the wires; it should not be possible to pull the wires out of a good crimp.

Wires which are open, exposed or otherwise damaged are repaired by simple splicing. Where possible, if the wiring harness is accessible and the damaged place in the wire can be located, it is best to open the harness and check for all possible damage. In an inaccessible harness, the wire must be bypassed with a new insert, usually taped to the outside of the old harness.

When replacing fusible links, be sure to use fusible link wire, NOT ordinary automotive wire. Make sure the fusible segment is of the same gauge and construction as the one being replaced and double the stripped end when crimping the terminal connector for a good contact. The melted (open) fusible link segment of the wiring harness should be cut off as close to the harness as possible, then a new segment spliced in as described. In the case of a damaged fusible link that feeds two harness wires, the harness connections should be replaced with two fusible link wires so that each circuit will have its own separate protection.

➡**Most of the problems caused in the wiring harness are due to bad ground connections. Always check all vehicle ground connections for corrosion or looseness before performing any power feed checks to eliminate the chance of a bad ground affecting the circuit.**

### Hard-Shell Connectors

Unlike molded connectors, the terminal contacts in hard-shell connectors can be replaced. Weatherproof hard-shell connectors with the leads molded into the shell have non-replaceable terminal ends. Replacement usually involves the use of a special terminal removal tool that depresses the locking tangs (barbs) on the connector terminal and allows the connector to be removed from the rear of the shell. The connector shell should be replaced if it shows any evidence of burning, melting, cracks, or breaks. Replace individual terminals that are burnt, corroded, distorted or loose.

➡**The insulation crimp must be tight to prevent the insulation from sliding back on the wire when the wire is pulled. The insulation must be visibly compressed under the crimp tabs, and the ends of the crimp should be turned in for a firm grip on the insulation.**

The wire crimp must be made with all wire strands inside the crimp. The terminal must be fully compressed on the wire strands with the ends of the crimp tabs turned in to make a firm grip on the wire. Check all connections with an ohmmeter to insure a good contact. There should be no measurable resistance between the wire and the terminal when connected.

### Fusible Links

The fuse link is a short length of special, Hypalon (high temperature) insulated wire, integral with the engine compartment wiring harness and should not be confused with standard wire. It is several wire gauges smaller than the circuit which it protects. Under no circumstances should a fuse link replacement repair be made using a length of standard wire cut from bulk stock or from another wiring harness.

To repair any blown fuse link use the following procedure:

1. Determine which circuit is damaged, its location and the cause of the open fuse link. If the damaged fuse link is one of three fed by a common No. 10 or 12 gauge feed wire, determine the specific affected circuit.

2. Disconnect the negative battery cable.

3. Cut the damaged fuse link from the wiring harness and discard it. If the fuse link is one of three circuits fed by a single feed wire, cut it out of the harness at each splice end and discard it.

4. Identify and procure the proper fuse link with butt connectors for attaching the fuse link to the harness.

➡**Heat shrink tubing must be slipped over the wire before crimping and soldering the connection.**

5. To repair any fuse link in a 3-link group with one feed:

a. After cutting the open link out of the harness, cut each of the remaining undamaged fuse links close to the feed wire weld.

b. Strip approximately ½ in. (13mm) of insulation from the detached ends of the two good fuse links. Insert two wire ends into one end of a butt connector, then carefully push one stripped end of the replacement fuse link into the same end of the butt connector and crimp all three firmly together.

➡**Care must be taken when fitting the three fuse links into the butt connector as the internal diameter is a snug fit for three wires. Make sure to use a proper crimping tool. Pliers, side cutters, etc. will not apply the proper crimp to retain the wires and withstand a pull test.**

c. After crimping the butt connector to the three fuse links, cut the weld portion from the feed wire and strip approximately ½ in. (13mm) of insulation from the cut end. Insert the stripped end into the open end of the butt connector and crimp very firmly.

d. To attach the remaining end of the replacement fuse link, strip approximately ½ in. (13mm) of insulation from the wire end of the circuit from which the blown fuse link was removed, and firmly crimp a butt connector or equivalent to the stripped wire. Then, insert the end of the replacement link into the other end of the butt connector and crimp firmly.

e. Using rosin core solder with a consistency of 60 percent tin and 40 percent lead, solder the connectors and the wires at the repairs then insulate with electrical tape or heat shrink tubing.

6. To replace any fuse link on a single circuit in a harness, cut out the damaged portion, strip approximately ½ in. (13mm) of insulation from the two wire ends and attach the appropriate replacement fuse link to the stripped wire ends with two proper

size butt connectors. Solder the connectors and wires, then insulate.

7. To repair any fuse link which has an eyelet terminal on one end such as the charging circuit, cut off the open fuse link behind the weld, strip approximately ½ in. (13mm) of insulation from the cut end and attach the appropriate new eyelet fuse link to the cut stripped wire with an appropriate size butt connector. Solder the connectors and wires at the repair, then insulate.

8. Connect the negative battery cable to the battery and test the system for proper operation.

➡️**Do not mistake a resistor wire for a fuse link. The resistor wire is generally longer and has print stating, "Resistor-don't cut or splice."**

When attaching a single No. 16, 17, 18 or 20 gauge fuse link to a heavy gauge wire, always double the stripped wire end of the fuse link before inserting and crimping it into the butt connector for positive wire retention.

## Add-On Electrical Equipment

The electrical system in your vehicle is designed to perform under reasonable operating conditions without interference between components. Before any additional electrical equipment is installed, it is recommended that you consult your dealer or a reputable repair facility that is familiar with the vehicle and its systems.

If the vehicle is equipped with mobile radio equipment and/or mobile telephone, it may have an effect upon the operation of any on-board computer control modules. Radio Frequency Interference (RFI) from the communications system can be picked up by the vehicle's wiring harnesses and conducted into the control module, giving it the wrong messages at the wrong time. Although well shielded against RFI, the computer should be further protected by taking the following measures:

• Install the antenna as far as possible from the control module. For instance, if the module is located behind the center console area, then the antenna should be mounted at the rear of the vehicle.

• Keep the antenna wiring a minimum of eight inches away from any wiring running to control modules and from the module itself. NEVER wind the antenna wire around any other wiring.

• Mount the equipment as far from the control module as possible. Be very careful during installation not to drill through any wires or short a wire harness with a mounting screw.

• Insure that the electrical feed wire(s) to the equipment are properly and tightly connected. Loose connectors can cause interference.

• Make certain that the equipment is properly grounded to the vehicle. Poor grounding can damage expensive equipment.

# HEATER AND AIR CONDITIONER

## Blower Motor

### REMOVAL & INSTALLATION

▶ See Figures 1, 2, 3, 4 and 5

1. Disconnect the battery cables. On 1971-86 models, remove the battery.
2. Unclip the blower motor lead wire.
3. On 1967-69 models, scribe the location of the motor flange in relation to the blower case.
4. Remove the blower attaching screws.
5. Remove the blower assembly. It may be necessary to pry gently on the blower flange. Sometimes the sealer acts as an adhesive.
6. If the motor is being replaced, remove the nut attaching the blower wheel to the blower motor shaft and separate the two.
7. Assembly the blower wheel to the motor with the open end away from the motor.
8. If the sealer has hardened or it otherwise useless, apply a new bead of sealer to the mounting flange.

89776p01

**Fig. 1 Disengage the blower motor electrical connections**

9. Installation of the blower motor and wheel is the reverse of removal. Connect the lead wires and the battery cables and check the operation of the motor.

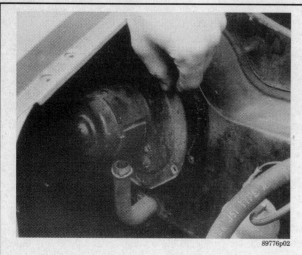

**Fig. 2 Unfasten the retainers and remove the blower motor from its housing**

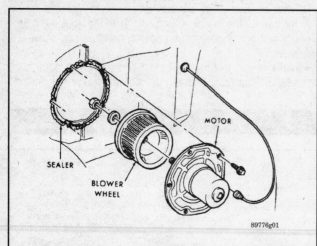

**Fig. 3 Exploded view of the blower motor assembly — 1970-73 models**

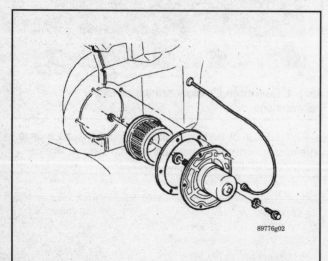

**Fig. 4 Exploded view of the blower motor assembly — 1974-82 models**

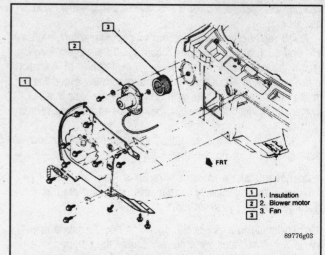

**Fig. 5 Exploded view of the blower motor assembly — 1983-86 models**

## Heater Core

### REMOVAL & INSTALLATION

**1967-70 Models**
▶ See Figures 6 and 7

1. Disconnect the battery ground cable.
2. Drain the radiator.

**✲✲CAUTION**

When draining the coolant, keep in mind that cats and dogs are attracted by ethylene glycol antifreeze, and are quite likely to drink any that is left in an uncovered container or in puddles on the ground. This will prove fatal in sufficient quantity. Always drain the coolant into a sealable container. Coolant should be reused unless it is contaminated or several years old.

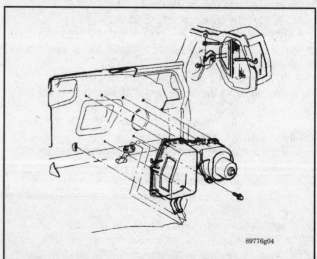

**Fig. 6 Exploded view of the heater assembly — 1967-70 models**

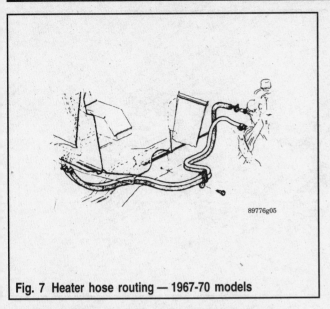

**Fig. 7 Heater hose routing — 1967-70 models**

3. Disconnect the heater hoses below the toe pan.
4. Remove the glove compartment.
5. Unclip the blower motor wire at the terminal.
6. Disconnect the defroster and air door cables at the distributor duct.
7. Remove the distributor duct mounting screws.
8. Remove the defroster hoses from the distributor duct.
9. Remove the core tube grommet from the floor pan and slide the grommet up the core tube.
10. Remove the screw holding the heater case to the toe pan.
11. Pull the case away from the toe pan and slide the core tubes down through the floor pan. When it is clear, pull the assembly out and withdraw the core tubes from the floor pan.
12. Remove the temperature door cable.
13. Remove the core from the case.
14. Installation is the reverse of removal. Fill the cooling system.

### All 1971-73 Models; 1974-77 Models Without Air Conditioning

▶ See Figure 8

This procedure applies to models without air conditioning and to those with the floor mounted air conditioner.
1. Disconnect the battery ground cable.
2. Place a pan under the van and disconnect the heater intake and outlet hoses. Quickly, remove and plug the heater hoses and support them in an upright position. Drain the coolant from the heater core into the pan.

### ✳✳CAUTION

When draining the coolant, keep in mind that cats and dogs are attracted by ethylene glycol antifreeze, and are quite likely to drink any that is left in an uncovered container or in puddles on the ground. This will prove fatal in sufficient quantity. Always drain the coolant into a sealable container. Coolant should be reused unless it is contaminated or several years old.

3. Disconnect the right hand air distributor hose from the heater case and put it aide.
4. Pry the eyelet clip from the temperature door cable and remove the Bowden cable attaching screw.
5. Remove the distributor duct and pull it rearward from the retainer.
6. Remove the heater case and core as an assembly.
7. Remove the core from the case. To install a new core, never the above steps.

### 1974-77 Models With Air Conditioning

These models have the air conditioning equipment mounted under the right side of the instrument panel.
1. Remove the battery.
2. Remove the engine cover.
3. Remove the evaporator/blower shield and bracket.
4. Remove the left floor outlet deflector and bracket.
5. Loosen the steering column to instrument panel reinforcement screws. Remove one screw.
6. Disconnect the speedometer cable at the instrument.
7. Remove the instrument panel to lower reinforcement screws. Move the instrument panel back and detach the radio antenna and wires. Disconnect the brake switch electrical connector.
8. Detach the blower/evaporator support bracket from the door pillar and the engine housing. Move it back for access.
9. Detach the heater hoses at the core (from under the hood). Plug the hoses to prevent spillage.
10. Remove the air inlet valve assembly from the kick panel. Remove the temperature door control cable at the heater case.
11. Remove the heater assembly. Remove the core from the assembly.
12. Reverse the procedure for installation. Tighten the column screw to 22 ft. lbs. (29 Nm). Refill the cooling system as necessary.

### 1978 Models Without Air Conditioning

1. Disconnect the negative battery cable.
2. Place a pan under the van and disconnect the heater intake and outlet hoses. Quickly remove and plug the hoses and support them in an upright position. Drain the coolant from the heater core into the pan.

### ✳✳CAUTION

When draining the coolant, keep in mind that cats and dogs are attracted by ethylene glycol antifreeze, and are quite likely to drink any that is left in an uncovered container or in puddles on the ground. This will prove fatal in sufficient quantity. Always drain the coolant into a sealable container. Coolant should be reused unless it is contaminated or several years old.

3. Remove the heater distributor duct-to-case attaching screws and the duct-to-engine cover screw. Remove the duct.
4. Remove the screw attaching the defroster duct to the distributor case.
5. Disconnect the temperature door cable. Carefully fold the cable back and out of the way.
6. Remove the three nuts from the engine compartment side of the distributor case and the screw from the passenger compartment side.

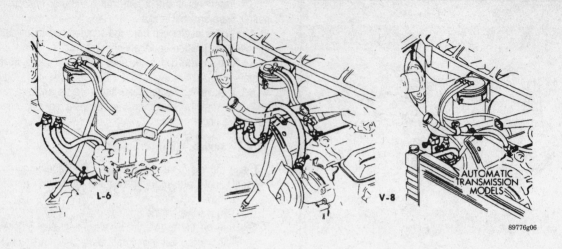

Fig. 8 Heater hose routing — 1971 and later models

7. Remove the heater case and core assembly.

8. Remove the core retaining straps and remove the core.

9. Reverse to install.

### 1979-86 Models Without Air Conditioning

1. Disconnect the negative battery cable.

2. Place a pan under the van and disconnect the heater intake and outlet hoses. Quickly remove and plug the hoses and support them in an upright position. Drain the coolant from the heater core into the pan.

### ✳✳CAUTION

**When draining the coolant, keep in mind that cats and dogs are attracted by ethylene glycol antifreeze, and are quite likely to drink any that is left in an uncovered container or in puddles on the ground. This will prove fatal in sufficient quantity. Always drain the coolant into a sealable container. Coolant should be reused unless it is contaminated or several years old.**

3. Remove the heater distributor duct-to-case attaching screws and the duct-to-engine cover screw. Remove the duct.

4. Remove the engine cover.

5. Remove all the instrument panel attaching screws.

6. Carefully lower the steering column. Raise and support the right side of the instrument panel.

7. Remove the defroster duct-to-case attaching screws and the two screws attaching the distributor to the heater case.

8. Disconnect the temperature door cable. Carefully fold the cable back and out of the way.

9. Remove the three nuts from the engine compartment side of the distributor case and the screw from the passenger compartment side.

10. Remove the heater case and core assembly.

11. Remove the core retaining straps and remove the core.

12. Reverse to install.

### 1978-86 Models With Air Conditioning

1. Disconnect the battery ground cable.

2. Remove the engine cover.

3. Remove the steering column to instrument panel bolts. Lower the column carefully.

4. Remove the upper and lower instrument panel attaching screws. Remove the radio support bracket screw.

5. Raise and support the right side of the instrument panel.

6. Remove the lower right instrument panel bracket.

7. Remove the vacuum actuator from the kick panel.

8. Disconnect the temperature cable and vacuum hoses at the case. Remove the heater distributor duct from over the engine hump.

9. Remove the two defroster duct to firewall attaching screws below the windshield.

10. Under the hood, disconnect and plug the heater hoses at the firewall.

11. Remove the three nuts and one screw (inside) holding the heater case to the firewall.

12. Remove the case from the truck. Remove the gasket for access to the screws holding the case together. Remove the temperature cable support bracket. Remove the screws and separate the case. Remove the heater core.

13. Reverse the procedure for installation. Refill the cooling system as necessary.

## Control Head

### REMOVAL & INSTALLATION

1. Disconnect the negative battery cable.

2. Remove the headlamp switch control knob.

3. Remove the instrument panel bezel.

4. Remove the control screws.

5. Disconnect the temperature cable eyelet clip and retainer.

6. Remove the control lower right mounting tab through the dash opening.

7. Remove the upper tab and the lower right tab.

8. Disconnect the electrical harness.

9. Disconnect the vacuum harness.

10. Remove the control assembly.

11. Installation is the reverse of the removal procedure.

## Evaporative Core

### REMOVAL & INSTALLATION

1. Disconnect the negative battery cable.
2. Purge the system of refrigerant.
3. Remove the coolant recovery tank and bracket.
4. Disconnect the electrical connectors from the core case assembly.

## RADIO

### Radio Receiver

### REMOVAL & INSTALLATION

#### 1967-70 Models

1. Disconnect the battery ground cable.
2. Remove the knobs, washers, and nuts from the radio shafts.
3. Detach any support brackets.
4. Lower the radio and detach the wiring for power, speaker, and antenna.
5. Remove the radio. Reverse the procedure for installation.

5. Remove the bracket at the evaporator case.
6. Remove the right marker lamp for access.
7. Disconnect the accumulator inlet and outlet lines, and the two brackets that attach the accumulator to the case.
8. Disconnect the evaporator inlet line.
9. Remove the three nuts and one screw that attaching the module to the dash panel.
10. Remove the core case assembly from the vehicle.
11. Remove the screws, separate the case sections and remove the evaporator core.
12. Installation is the reverse of the removal procedure.

➡**Add 3 ounces of 525 viscosity refrigerant oil to the condenser if a new one is installed.**

#### 1971-86 Models
▶ **See Figures 9, 10 and 11**

1. Disconnect the ground cable from the battery.
2. Remove the engine cover.
3. Remove the air cleaner from the carburetor.
4. On models through 1977, remove the stud in the carburetor which holds the air cleaner.
5. Cover the carburetor with a clean rag.
6. Remove the knobs, washers and nuts from the front of the radio.
7. Remove the rear bracket screw and bracket from the radio.
8. Remove the radio through the engine access area. Lower the radio far enough to detach the wiring.
9. Remove the radio.
10. Installation is the reverse of removal.

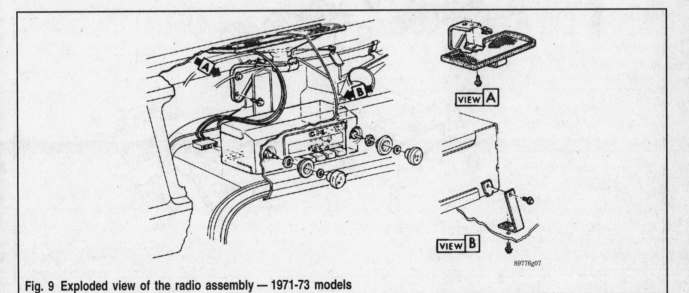

Fig. 9 Exploded view of the radio assembly — 1971-73 models

89776g07

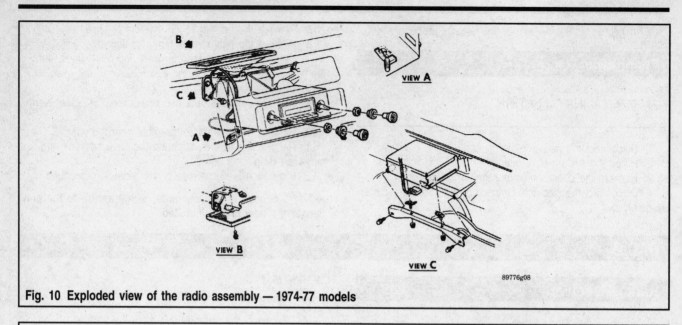

Fig. 10 Exploded view of the radio assembly — 1974-77 models

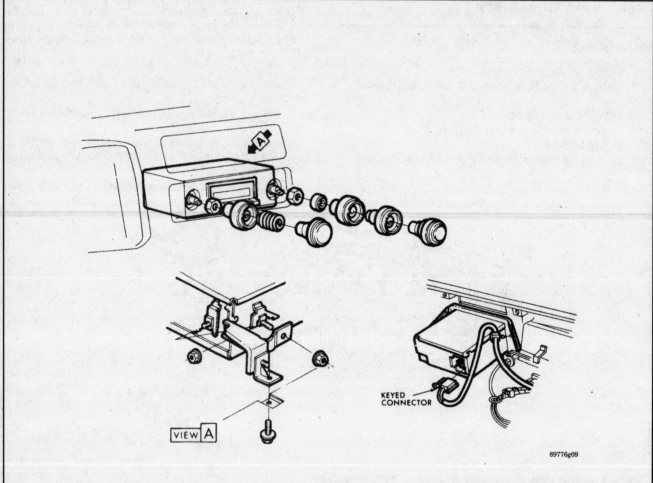

Fig. 11 Exploded view of the radio assembly — 1978-86 models

## WINDSHIELD WIPERS

### Windshield Wiper Blade and Arm

#### REMOVAL & INSTALLATION

▶ See Figure 12

1. Pull the wiper arms away from the glass and release the clip underneath. The wiper arms are splined to the shafts and can be pulled off.
2. To remove the arm, pry underneath it with a screwdriver or similar tool. Be careful not to scratch the paint.
3. To install, position the arm over the shaft and press down. Make sure you install the arms in the same position on the windshield as they were when they were removed.

#### ELEMENT (REFILL) CARE AND REPLACEMENT

▶ See Figures 13, 14, 15, 16, 17, 18, 19, 20, 21, 22, 23 and 24

For maximum effectiveness and longest element life, the windshield and wiper blades should be kept clean. Dirt, tree sap, road tar and so on will cause streaking, smearing and blade deterioration if left on the glass. It is advisable to wash the windshield carefully with a commercial glass cleaner at least once a month. Wipe off the rubber blades with the wet rag afterwards. Do not attempt to move wipers across the windshield by hand; damage to the motor and drive mechanism will result.

To inspect and/or replace the wiper blade elements, place the wiper switch in the **LOW** speed position and the ignition switch in the **ACC** position. When the wiper blades are approximately vertical on the windshield, turn the ignition switch to **OFF**.

Examine the wiper blade elements. If they are found to be cracked, broken or torn, they should be replaced immediately. Replacement intervals will vary with usage, although ozone

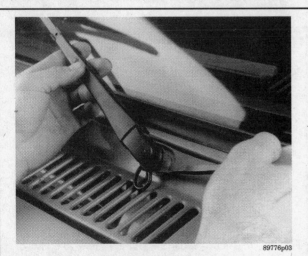

Fig. 12 Remove the wiper arm by prying it gently underneath with a prytool

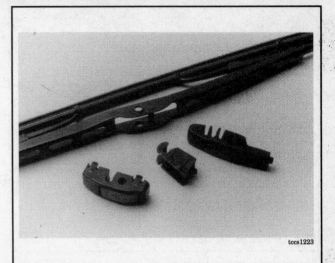

Fig. 13 Bosch® wiper blade and fit kit

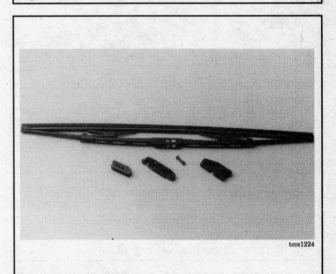

Fig. 14 Lexor® wiper blade and fit kit

deterioration usually limits element life to about one year. If the wiper pattern is smeared or streaked, or if the blade chatters across the glass, the elements should be replaced. It is easiest and most sensible to replace the elements in pairs.

If your vehicle is equipped with aftermarket blades, there are several different types of refills and your vehicle might have any kind. Aftermarket blades and arms rarely use the exact same type blade or refill as the original equipment. Here are some typical aftermarket blades; not all may be available for your vehicle:

The Anco® type uses a release button that is pushed down to allow the refill to slide out of the yoke jaws. The new refill slides back into the frame and locks in place.

Some Trico® refills are removed by locating where the metal backing strip or the refill is wider. Insert a small screwdriver blade between the frame and metal backing strip. Press down to release the refill from the retaining tab.

**Fig. 15** Pylon® wiper blade and adaptor

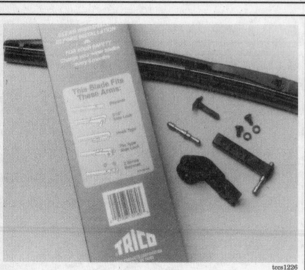

**Fig. 16** Trico® wiper blade and fit kit

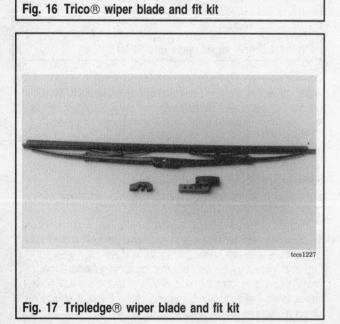

**Fig. 17** Tripledge® wiper blade and fit kit

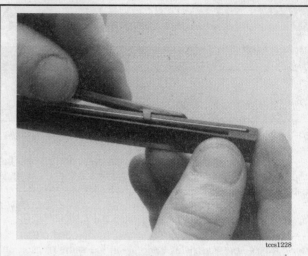

**Fig. 18** To remove and install a Lexor® wiper blade refill, slip out the old insert and slide in a new one

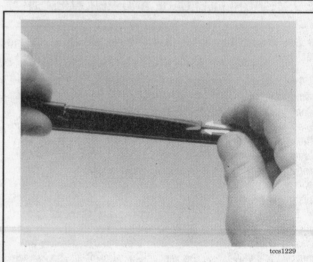

**Fig. 19** On Pylon® inserts, the clip at the end has to be removed prior to sliding the insert off

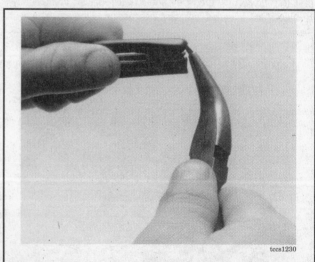

**Fig. 20** On Trico® wiper blades, the tab at the end of the blade must be turned up . . .

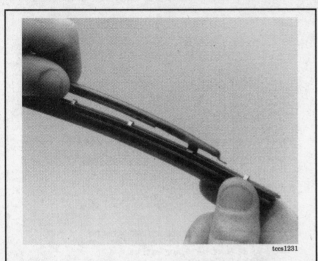

Fig. 21 . . . then the insert can be removed. After installing the replacement insert, bend the tab back

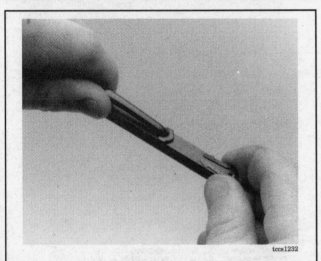

Fig. 22 The Tripledge® wiper blade insert is removed and installed using a securing clip

Other types of Trico® refills have two metal tabs which are unlocked by squeezing them together. The rubber filler can then be withdrawn from the frame jaws. A new refill is installed by inserting the refill into the front frame jaws and sliding it rearward to engage the remaining frame jaws. There are usually four jaws; be certain when installing that the refill is engaged in all of them. At the end of its travel, the tabs will lock into place on the front jaws of the wiper blade frame.

Another type of refill is made from polycarbonate. The refill has a simple locking device at one end which flexes downward out of the groove into which the jaws of the holder fit, allowing easy release. By sliding the new refill through all the jaws and pushing through the slight resistance when it reaches the end of its travel, the refill will lock into position.

To replace the Tridon® refill, it is necessary to remove the wiper blade. This refill has a plastic backing strip with a notch about 1 in. (25mm) from the end. Hold the blade (frame) on a hard surface so that the frame is tightly bowed. Grip the tip of the backing strip and pull up while twisting counterclockwise. The backing strip will snap out of the retaining tab. Do this for the remaining tabs until the refill is free of the blade. The length of these refills is molded into the end and they should be replaced with identical types.

Regardless of the type of refill used, be sure to follow the part manufacturer's instructions closely. Make sure that all of the frame jaws are engaged as the refill is pushed into place and locked. If the metal blade holder and frame are allowed to touch the glass during wiper operation, the glass will be scratched.

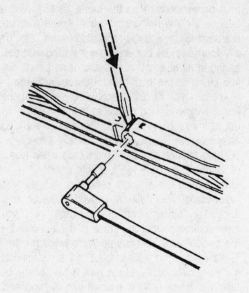

**BLADE REPLACEMENT**

1. CYCLE ARM AND BLADE ASSEMBLY TO UP POSITION—ON THE WINDSHIELD WHERE REMOVAL OF BLADE ASSEMBLY CAN BE PERFORMED WITHOUT DIFFICULTY. TURN IGNITION KEY OFF AT DESIRED POSITION.

2. TO REMOVE BLADE ASSEMBLY, INSERT SCREWDRIVER IN SLOT, PUSH DOWN ON SPRING LOCK AND PULL BLADE ASSEMBLY FROM PIN (VIEW A)

3. TO INSTALL, PUSH THE BLADE ASSEMBLY ON THE PIN SO THAT THE SPRING LOCK ENGAGES THE PIN (VIEW A). BE SURE THE BLADE ASSEMBLY IS SECURELY ATTACHED TO PIN

VIEW A

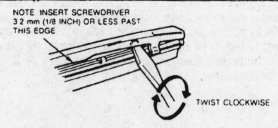

NOTE INSERT SCREWDRIVER 3 2 mm (1/8 INCH) OR LESS PAST THIS EDGE

TWIST CLOCKWISE

**ELEMENT REPLACEMENT**

1 INSERT SCREWDRIVER BETWEEN THE EDGE OF THE SUPER STRUCTURE AND THE BLADE BACKING DRIP (VIEW B) TWIST SCREWDRIVER SLOWLY UNTIL ELEMENT CLEARS ONE SIDE OF THE SUPER STRUCTURE CLAW

2 SLIDE THE ELEMENT INTO THE SUPER STRUCTURE CLAWS

VIEW B

4 INSERT ELEMENT INTO ONE SIDE OF THE END CLAWS (VIEW D) AND WITH A ROCKING MOTION PUSH ELEMENT UPWARD UNTIL IT SNAPS IN (VIEW E)

VIEW D

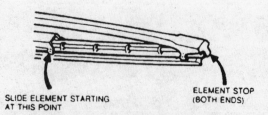

SLIDE ELEMENT STARTING AT THIS POINT

ELEMENT STOP (BOTH ENDS)

3. SLIDE THE ELEMENT INTO THE SUPER STRUCTURE CLAWS, STARTING WITH SECOND SET FROM EITHER END (VIEW C) AND CONTINUE TO SLIDE THE BLADE ELEMENT INTO ALL THE SUPER STRUCTURE CLAWS TO THE ELEMENT STOP (VIEW C)

VIEW C

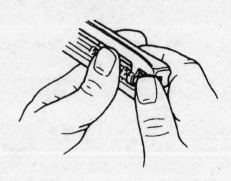

VIEW E

tccs1236

**Fig. 23  Trico® wiper blade insert (element) replacement**

### BLADE REPLACEMENT

1. Cycle arm and blade assembly to a position on the windshield where removal of blade assembly can be performed without difficulty. Turn ignition key off at desired position.
2. To remove blade assembly from wiper arm, pull up on spring lock and pull blade assembly from pin (View A). Be sure spring lock is not pulled excessively or it will become distorted.
3. To install, push the blade assembly onto the pin so that the spring lock engages the pin (View A). Be sure the blade assembly is securely attached to pin.

### ELEMENT REPLACEMENT

1. In the plastic backing strip which is part of the rubber blade assembly, there is an 11.11mm (7/16 inch) long notch located approximately one inch from either end. Locate either notch.
2. Place the frame of the wiper blade assembly on a firm surface with either notched end of the backing strip visible.
3. Grasp the frame portion of the wiper blade assembly and push down until the blade assembly is tightly bowed.
4. With the blade assembly in the bowed position, grasp the tip of the backing strip firmly, pulling up and twisting C.C.W. at the same time. The backing strip will then snap out of the retaining tab on the end of the frame.
5. Lift the wiper blade assembly from the surface and slide the backing strip down the frame until the notch lines up with the next retaining tab, twist slightly, and the backing strip will snap out. Continue this operation with the remaining tabs until the blade element is completely detached from the frame.
6. To install blade element, reverse the above procedure, making sure all six (6) tabs are locked to the backing strip before installing blade to wiper arm.

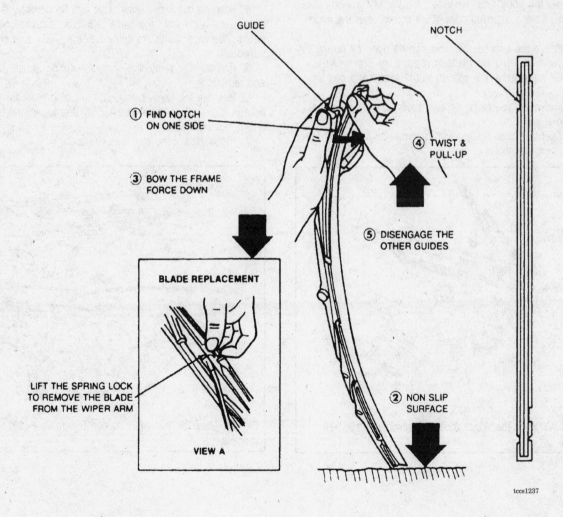

GUIDE

NOTCH

① FIND NOTCH ON ONE SIDE

④ TWIST & PULL-UP

③ BOW THE FRAME FORCE DOWN

⑤ DISENGAGE THE OTHER GUIDES

BLADE REPLACEMENT

LIFT THE SPRING LOCK TO REMOVE THE BLADE FROM THE WIPER ARM

② NON SLIP SURFACE

VIEW A

tccs1237

**Fig. 24 Tridon® wiper blade insert (element) replacement**

## Windshield Wiper Motor

### REMOVAL & INSTALLATION

#### 1967-70 Models
▶ See Figure 25

1. Disconnect the battery ground cable.
2. Disconnect and tag the electrical connections. Disconnect the washer hoses.
3. Loosen the nuts securing the drive link to the wiper motor crank arm. Disconnect the ball joint.
4. Remove the motor attaching screws from the cowl.
5. Remove the motor from its mount.
6. Installation is the reverse of removal.

#### 1971-86 Models
▶ See Figure 26

1. Be sure that the wiper motor arm is in PARK position. The wiper arms should be in their normal OFF position.
2. Open the hood and disconnect the battery ground cable.
3. Remove the exposed cowl cover screws with the hood up.
4. Remove the wiper arms. This can be done by pulling the wiper arms away from the glass to release the clip underneath. The wiper arms are splined to the shafts and can be pulled off.
5. Remove the remaining screws securing the cowl panel and remove it.
6. Loosen the nuts holding the transmission linkage to the wiper motor crank arm.

7. Disconnect the power feed to the wiper arm at the connector next to the radio.
8. Remove the flex hose from the left defroster outlet to gain access to the wiper motor screws.
9. Remove the one screw holding the left hand heater duct to the engine shroud and move the heater duct down and out.
10. Remove the windshield washer hoses from the pump.
11. Remove the 3 screws holding the wiper motor to the cowl and lift the wiper motor out from under the dash.
12. Installation is the reverse of removal. Install the wiper motor in the PARK position.

## Wiper Linkage

### REMOVAL & INSTALLATION

1. Be sure that the wiper motor is in PARK position. The wiper arms should be in their normal OFF position.
2. Open the hood and disconnect the battery ground cable.
3. Remove the exposed cowl cover screws with the hood up.
4. Remove the wiper arms. This can be done by pulling the wiper arms away from the glass to release the clip underneath. The wiper arms are splined to the shafts and can be pulled off.
5. Remove the remaining screws securing the cowl panel and remove it.
6. Remove the screws and nuts securing the transmission linkage to the wiper motor crank arm. Disconnect the ball joint and remove the linkage.
7. Installation is the reverse of removal.

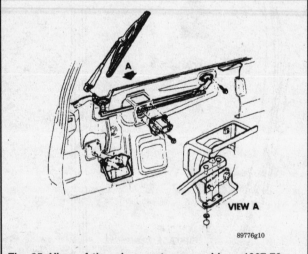

**Fig. 25 View of the wiper motor assembly — 1967-70 models**

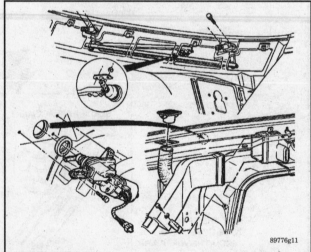

**Fig. 26 View of the wiper motor assembly — 1971-86 models**

## INSTRUMENTS AND SWITCHES

### Instrument Cluster

The entire cluster may be removed from the vehicle for servicing the instruments and gauges. The illuminating and indicator lamps can be removed and replaced without removing the entire cluster. On earlier models, the lamps and bulbs are clip retained and can be easily snapped in or out. Later models use plastic bulb holders that are twist-locked through a laminated plastic printed circuit in the luster housing.

### REMOVAL & INSTALLATION

#### 1967-70 Models

1. Disconnect the battery ground cable.
2. Disconnect the speedometer cable at the head.
3. Remove the two nuts attaching the cluster to the dash panel. The cluster can now be pulled clear of the dash.
4. Disconnect all wires and bulbs, noting their respective locations.
5. Remove the cluster.
6. Installation is the reverse of removal.

#### 1971-86 Models

▶ **See Figure 27**

1. Open the hood and disconnect the battery ground cable.
2. Reach up under the dash and disconnect the speedometer cable by first depressing the tang on the rear of the speedometer head and detaching the cable as the tang is depressed.
3. Unplug the instrument panel harness connector.
4. Disconnect and plug the oil pressure gauge line (if equipped).
5. Remove the nuts from the instrument cluster bezel and remove bezel.

6. Pull the top of the cluster away from instrument panel and lift out the bottom of the cluster.
7. Remove the cluster.
8. Installation is the reverse of removal. The clips at the top of the cluster slip into the openings in the instrument panel after the bottom of the cluster is installed.

### Windshield Wiper/Washer Switch

### REMOVAL & INSTALLATION

#### 1967-72 Models

The windshield wiper switch is mounted on the left side of the instrument panel, and are reached by removing the left side trim panel. Electrical connections must be disconnected at the rear of the switch before removing the switch unit from the dash. Be sure to note how the wires are connected before removing. The switch units are fixed to the instrument panel by two or four screws.

### Headlight Switch

### REMOVAL & INSTALLATION

The headlight switch is mounted on the left-hand side of the instrument panel.
1. Disconnect the negative battery cable.
2. Remove the left instrument panel trim plate.
3. Remove the retaining nut securing the switch, and detach the electrical connector from the back of the switch. The switch can now be removed.
4. Reverse the procedure for installation.

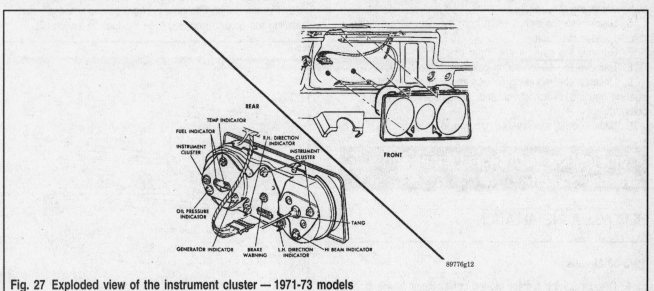

**Fig. 27 Exploded view of the instrument cluster — 1971-73 models**

## Back-Up Light Switch

### REMOVAL & INSTALLATION

#### With Manual Transmission

The back-up light switch is located on the left side of the transmission case. To remove:
1. Disconnect the negative battery cable.
2. Disconnect the back-up switch harness.
3. Remove the back-up switch and the seal.
4. Installation is the reverse of the removal procedure.

#### With Automatic Transmission

The back-up light switch is located on the left side of the transmission case.
1. Disconnect the negative battery cable.
2. Disconnect the back-up switch assembly harness.
3. Place the gear selector in neutral.
4. Squeeze the switch tangs together and lift out the switch assembly.
5. Installation is the reverse of the removal procedure.

## Turn Signal Switch

### REMOVAL & INSTALLATION

#### 1967-72 Models

1. Disconnect the battery ground cable.
2. Remove the steering wheel, preload spring, and cancelling cam.
3. Remove the shift lever roll pin and shift lever (if applicable).
4. Remove the turn signal lever screw and the lever.
5. Push the hazard warning knob in. This must be done to avoid damaging the switch.
6. Disconnect the switch wires from the chassis harness located under the dash.
7. Remove the mast jacket upper bracket.
8. Remove the switch wiring cover from the column.
9. Unscrew the mounting screws and remove the switch, bearing housing, switch cover, and shift housing from the column.
10. Installation is the reverse or removal.

## Combination Turn Signal/Wiper and Washer Switch

### REMOVAL & INSTALLATION

#### 1973-86 Models

1. Disconnect the battery ground cable. Remove the steering wheel.
2. Remove the switch cancelling spring and cam.

3. Remove the column to instrument panel trim plate, if any.
4. Disconnect the switch wiring harness at the half-moon connector.
5. Pry the wiring harness protector out of the column retaining slots.
6. Mark their locations, then remove each wire from the half-moon connector.
7. Remove the turn signal lever screw and the lever.
8. On tilt columns, remove the automatic transmission dial and needle. Remove the cap and bulb from the housing cover. Unscrew and remove the tilt release lever. The directional signal housing cover has to be pulled off the column; there is a special tool used for this.
9. Remove the three switch screws and remove the switch, guiding the wiring harness through the opening.
10. On installation, tape the switch wires and guide them through the housing opening. On tilt columns, the directional signal housing cover must be tapped back into place.

## Ignition Switch

### REMOVAL & INSTALLATION

#### 1967-72 Models

▶ See Figure 28

1. Raise the hood and disconnect the battery ground cable.
2. Remove the lock cylinder by inserting the key in the switch and turning it to the **ACC** position. Insert a piece of stiff wire in the small hole in the cylinder face and push in to depress the plunger. Continue to turn the key counterclockwise until the lock cylinder can be removed.
3. Remove the metallic ignition switch nut.
4. Pull the ignition switch out from behind the dash, and remove the "theft resistant" connector. A screwdriver can be used to unsnap the locking tangs from the connector.
5. Snap the connectors into place on a new switch.
6. Put the switch into position from behind the dash, first installing the ground ring and then the ignition switch nut.

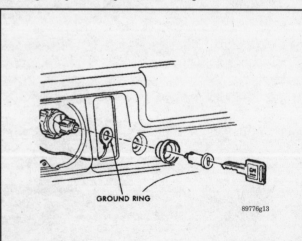

GROUND RING

89776g13

Fig. 28 Exploded view of a common ignition switch — 1967-72 models

7. Install the lock cylinder.
8. Reconnect the battery cable.
9. Installation is the reverse or removal.

**1973-86 Models**

The switch is on the steering column, behind the instrument panel.

1. Lower the steering column, making sure that it is supported.

### ✳✳WARNING

**Extreme care is necessary to prevent damage to the collapsible column.**

2. Make sure the switch is in the **LOCK** position. If the lock cylinder is out, pull the switch rod up to the stop, then go down 1 detent.
3. Remove the two screws and the switch.
4. Before installation, make sure the switch is in the **LOCK** position.
5. Install the switch using the original screws.

### ✳✳CAUTION

**Use of screws that are too long could prevent the column from collapsing on impact.**

6. Replace the column.

## Lock Cylinder

## REMOVAL & INSTALLATION

**1973-78 Models**

1. Remove the steering wheel and turn signal switch.

➡**It is not necessary to completely remove the turn signal switch. Pull the switch over the end of the shaft — no further.**

2. Place the lock cylinder in **RUN** position.

### ✳✳WARNING

**Do not remove the ignition key buzzer.**

3. Insert a small drift pin into the turn signal housing slot. Keeping the drift pin to the right side of the slot, break the housing flash loose and depress the spring latch at the lower end of the lock cylinder. Remove the lock cylinder.

➡**Considerable force may be necessary to break this casting flash, buy be careful not to damage any other parts. When ordering a new lock cylinder, specify a cylinder assembly. This will same assembling the cylinder, washer, sleeve and adapter.**

4. To install, hold the lock cylinder sleeve and rotate the knob clockwise against the stop. Insert the cylinder into the housing, aligning the key and keyway. Hold a 0.07 in. (1.78mm) drill between the lock bezel and housing. Rotate the cylinder counterclockwise, maintaining a light pressure until the drive section of the cylinder mates with the sector. Push in until the snapring pops into the grooves. Remove drill. Check cylinder operation.

➡**The drill prevents forcing the lock cylinder inward beyond its normal position. The buzzer switch and spring latch can hold the lock cylinder in too far. Complete disassembly of the upper bearing housing is necessary to release an improperly installed lock cylinder.**

**1979-86 Models**

1. Remove the steering wheel.
2. Remove the turn signal switch. It is not necessary to completely remove the switch from the column. Pull the switch rearward far enough to slip it over the end of the shaft, but do not pull the harness out of the column.
3. Turn the lock to **RUN**.
4. Remove the lock retaining screw and remove the lock cylinder.

➡**If the retaining screw is dropped on removal, it may fall into the column, requiring complete disassembly of the column to retrieve the screw.**

5. To install, rotate the key to the stop while holding onto the cylinder.
6. Push the lock all the way in.
7. Install the screw. Tighten the screw to 3 ft. lbs. (4 Nm) for regular columns, 2 ft. lbs. (2 Nm) for adjustable columns.
8. Install the turn signal switch and the steering wheel.

## Speedometer Cable

## REMOVAL & INSTALLATION

1. Disconnect the speedometer cable from the rear of the speedometer head. Unscrew through 1972, unclip from 1973.
2. Remove the old cable by pulling it out from the speedometer end of the cable housing. If the old cable is broken, the speedometer cable will have to be disconnected from the transmission and the cable removed from the other end.
3. Lubricate the lower ¾ of the new cable with speedometer cable lubricant and feed the cable into the cable housing.
4. Connect the speedometer cable to the speedometer head and to the transmission if disconnected there.

## LIGHTING

## Headlights

### REMOVAL & INSTALLATION

▶ See Figures 29, 30, 31, 32, 33, 34 and 35

➡Some 1978 and later models have rectangular head-lights. Otherwise the following removal and installation procedures apply.

1. Remove the headlight bezel by releasing the attaching screws.
2. Remove the spring (if any) from the retaining ring and turn the unit to disengage it from the headlamp adjusting screws.

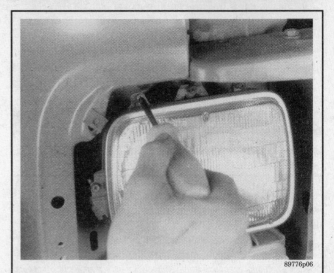

Fig. 31 Remove the headlamp retaining ring screws

Fig. 29 Remove the headlight bezel assembly screws

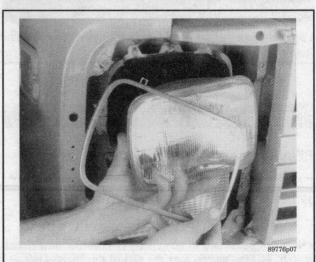

Fig. 32 Hold the headlight and remove the retaining ring

3. Disconnect the wiring harness connector.

➡Do not disturb the adjusting screws.

4. Remove the retaining ring and the headlamp.
5. Position the new sealed beam unit in the retaining ring.

➡The number which is molded into the lens must be at the top.

6. Attach the wiring connector.
7. Install the headlamp assembly, twisting the ring slightly to engage the adjusting screws.
8. Install the retaining ring spring and check the operation of the unit. Install the bezel.

Fig. 30 Remove the headlight bezel assembly

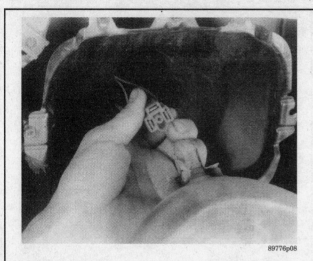
Fig. 33 Slide the headlight forward and disengage the electrical connection

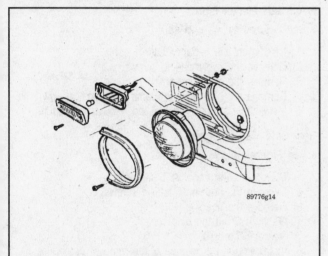
Fig. 34 View of the headlight assembly — 1967-70 models

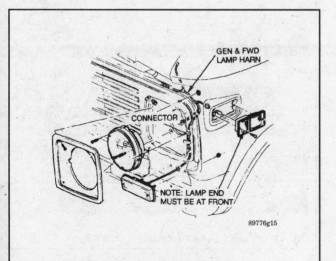
Fig. 35 Headlight assembly on 1971 and later models (rectangular headlights are similar)

## AIMING

▶ See Figures 36 and 37

The headlights must be properly aimed to provide the best, safest road illumination. The lights should be checked for proper aim, and adjusted if necessary, after installing a new sealed beam unit or if the front end sheet metal has been replaced. Certain state and local authorities have requirements for headlight aiming and you should check these before adjusting.

➡The truck's fuel tank should be about half full when adjusting the headlights. Tires should be properly inflated, and if a heavy load is carried, it should remain there.

Horizontal and vertical aiming of each sealed beam unit is provided by two adjusting screws, which move the mounting ring in the body against the tension of the coil spring. There is no adjustment for focus; this is done during headlight manufacturing.

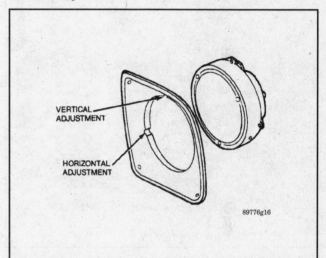
Fig. 36 Common headlight adjusting screw locations on round headlights

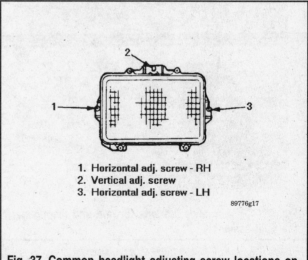
1. Horizontal adj. screw - RH
2. Vertical adj. screw
3. Horizontal adj. screw - LH

Fig. 37 Common headlight adjusting screw locations on rectangular headlights

## Signal and Marker Lights

### REMOVAL & INSTALLATION

#### Front Turn Signal and Parking Lights
▶ See Figures 38, 39 and 40

1. Disconnect the negative battery cable.
2. Remove the four bezel retaining screws.
3. Remove the bezel.
4. Remove the parking lamp retainers.
5. Remove the parking lamp.
6. Disconnect the electrical connector from the parking lamp and install a new bulb.
7. Installation is the reverse of the removal procedure.

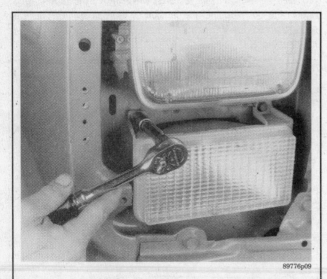

Fig. 38 Remove the lens retainers . . .

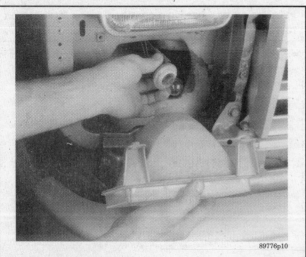

Fig. 39 . . . then slide the lens forward and disengage the bulb assembly

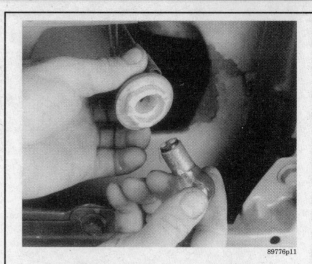

Fig. 40 Depress the bulb and twist it about ⅛ turn counterclockwise, then remove it from the socket

#### Front Side Marker Lights
▶ See Figures 41, 42 and 43

1. Disconnect the negative battery cable.
2. Remove the two retaining screws.
3. Remove the side marker lamp.
4. Remove the bulb from the lamp and install a new bulb.
5. Installation is the reverse of the removal procedure.

#### Rear Side Marker Lights
▶ See Figures 44, 45, 46 and 47

1. Disconnect the negative battery cable.
2. Remove the housing retaining screws.
3. Remove the housing.
4. Gently pull out the bulb socket.
5. Remove the bulb.
6. Installation is the reverse of the removal procedure.

Fig. 41 Unfasten the lens retaining screws

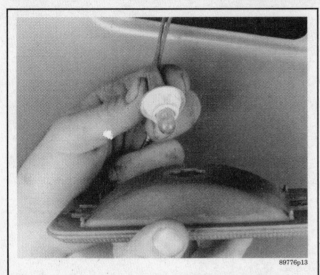
Fig. 42 Remove the bulb assembly from the lens

Fig. 45 . . . then remove the lens assembly

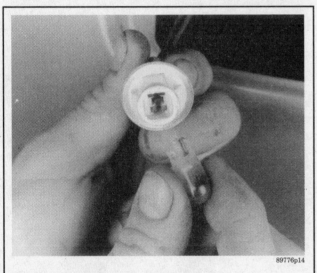
Fig. 43 Pull the bulb from the socket

Fig. 46 Remove the bulb assembly from the lens

Fig. 44 Remove the lens retaining screws . . .

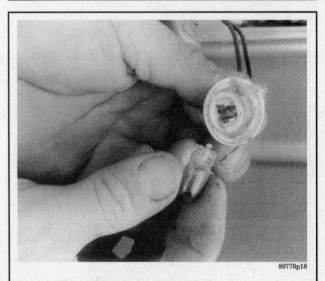
Fig. 47 Pull the bulb from the socket

**Rear Turn Signal, Brake and Parking Lights**

▶ See Figures 48, 49, 50 and 51

1. Disconnect the negative battery cable.
2. Remove the lens housing retaining screws.
3. Remove the lamp housing.
4. Remove the bulb socket by squeezing the retention lock and rotating the socket counterclockwise.
5. Remove the bulb.
6. Installation is the reverse of the removal procedure.

**Dome Light**

▶ See Figures 52 and 53

1. Unsnap the dome lamp lens.
2. Remove the bulb from its socket.
3. Installation is the reverse of removal.

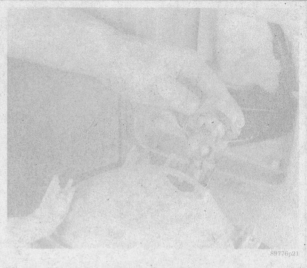

Fig. 50 Disengage the bulb assembly from the lens

Fig. 48 Loosen the lens retaining screws

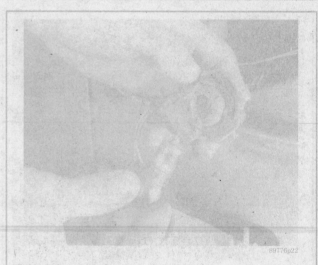

Fig. 51 Depress the bulb and twist it about ⅛ turn counterclockwise, then remove it from the socket

Fig. 49 Slide the lens assembly forward

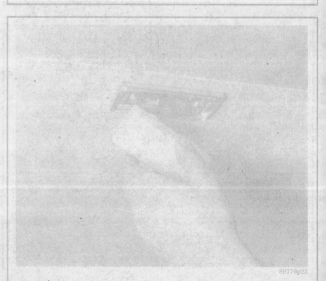

Fig. 52 Remove the dome lamp lens cover

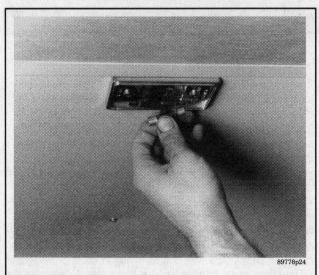
Fig. 53 Unclip the bulb from its socket

## License Plate Lamp

▶ See Figures 54, 55 and 56

1. Unfasten the lamp cover retaining screws.
2. Remove the lamp cover.
3. Remove the license plate lamp bulb from its socket.

Fig. 54 Remove the license plate lamp cover fasteners

Fig. 55 Remove the cover

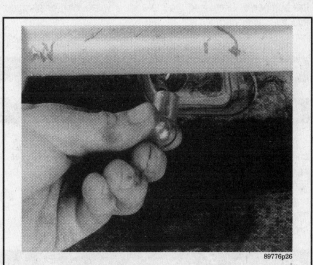
Fig. 56 Slide the bulb assembly forward and disengage the bulb from its socket

## TRAILER WIRING

Wiring the vehicle for towing is fairly easy. There are a number of good wiring kits available and these should be used, rather than trying to design your own.

All trailers will need brake lights and turn signals as well as tail lights and side marker lights. Most areas require extra marker lights for overwide trailers. Also, most areas have recently required back-up lights for trailers, and most trailer manufacturers have been building trailers with back-up lights for several years.

Additionally, some Class I, most Class II and just about all Class III trailers will have electric brakes. Add to this number an accessories wire, to operate trailer internal equipment or to charge the trailer's battery, and you can have as many as seven wires in the harness.

Determine the equipment on your trailer and buy the wiring kit necessary. The kit will contain all the wires needed, plus a plug adapter set which includes the female plug, mounted on the bumper or hitch, and the male plug, wired into, or plugged into the trailer harness.

When installing the kit, follow the manufacturer's instructions. The color coding of the wires is usually standard throughout the industry. One point to note: some domestic vehicles, and most imported vehicles, have separate turn signals. On most domestic vehicles, the brake lights and rear turn signals operate with the same bulb. For those vehicles with separate turn signals, you can purchase an isolation unit so that the brake lights won't blink whenever the turn signals are operated, or, you can go to your local electronics supply house and buy four diodes to wire in series with the brake and turn signal bulbs. Diodes will isolate the brake and turn signals. The choice is yours. The isolation units are simple and quick to install, but far more expensive than the diodes. The diodes, however, require more work to install properly, since they require the cutting of each bulb's wire and soldering in place of the diode.

One, final point, the best kits are those with a spring loaded cover on the vehicle mounted socket. This cover prevents dirt and moisture from corroding the terminals. Never let the vehicle socket hang loosely; always mount it securely to the bumper or hitch.

## CIRCUIT PROTECTION

### Circuit Breakers

A circuit breaker is a electrical switch which breaks the circuit in case of an overload. All models have a circuit breaker in the headlight switch to protect the headlight and parking light systems. An overload may cause the lights to flash on and off. 1974-75 wiper motors have a circuit breaker at the motor. 1975-86 rear mounted air conditioners have a circuit breaker at the firewall.

### Fuses and Flashers

▶ See Figure 57

The fuse block is mounted to the firewall, inside the truck, to the left of the steering column. The turn signal flasher and hazard waring flasher plug into the fuse block. Each fuse receptacle is marked as to the circuits it protects and the correct amperage. In-line fuses are also used to protect some circuits. These are: 1972-86 ammeter, 1973-74 rear air conditioner, and 1975-86 auxiliary heater.

➡A special heavy duty turn signal flasher is required to properly operate the turn signals when a trailer's lights are connected to the system.

89776p28

Fig. 57 The fuse panel is usually located to the left of the steering column inside the vehicle

## WIRING DIAGRAMS

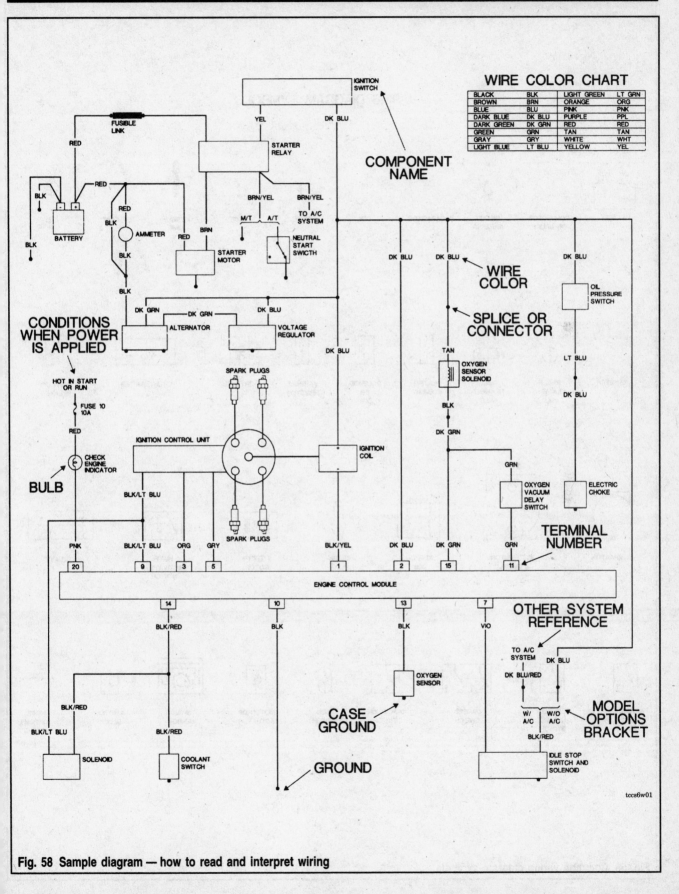

### WIRE COLOR CHART

| BLACK | BLK | LIGHT GREEN | LT GRN |
|---|---|---|---|
| BROWN | BRN | ORANGE | ORG |
| BLUE | BLU | PINK | PNK |
| DARK BLUE | DK BLU | PURPLE | PPL |
| DARK GREEN | DK GRN | RED | RED |
| GREEN | GRN | TAN | TAN |
| GRAY | GRY | WHITE | WHT |
| LIGHT BLUE | LT BLU | YELLOW | YEL |

**Fig. 58 Sample diagram — how to read and interpret wiring**

tccs6w01

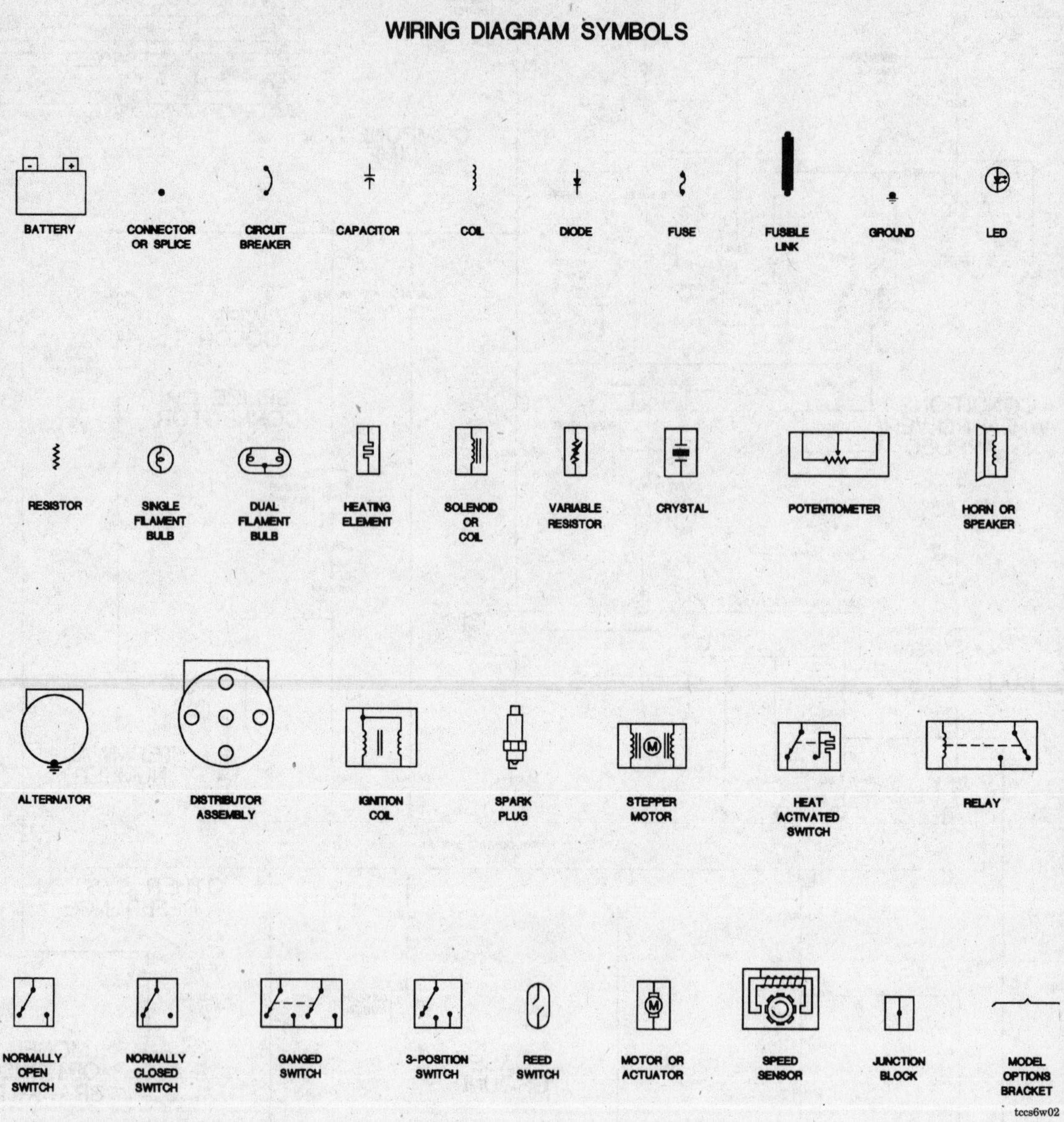

## WIRING DIAGRAM SYMBOLS

| BATTERY | CONNECTOR OR SPLICE | CIRCUIT BREAKER | CAPACITOR | COIL | DIODE | FUSE | FUSIBLE LINK | GROUND | LED |
|---|---|---|---|---|---|---|---|---|---|

| RESISTOR | SINGLE FILAMENT BULB | DUAL FILAMENT BULB | HEATING ELEMENT | SOLENOID OR COIL | VARIABLE RESISTOR | CRYSTAL | POTENTIOMETER | HORN OR SPEAKER |
|---|---|---|---|---|---|---|---|---|

| ALTERNATOR | DISTRIBUTOR ASSEMBLY | IGNITION COIL | SPARK PLUG | STEPPER MOTOR | HEAT ACTIVATED SWITCH | RELAY |
|---|---|---|---|---|---|---|

| NORMALLY OPEN SWITCH | NORMALLY CLOSED SWITCH | GANGED SWITCH | 3-POSITION SWITCH | REED SWITCH | MOTOR OR ACTUATOR | SPEED SENSOR | JUNCTION BLOCK | MODEL OPTIONS BRACKET |
|---|---|---|---|---|---|---|---|---|

tccs6w02

**Fig. 59 Common wiring diagram symbols**

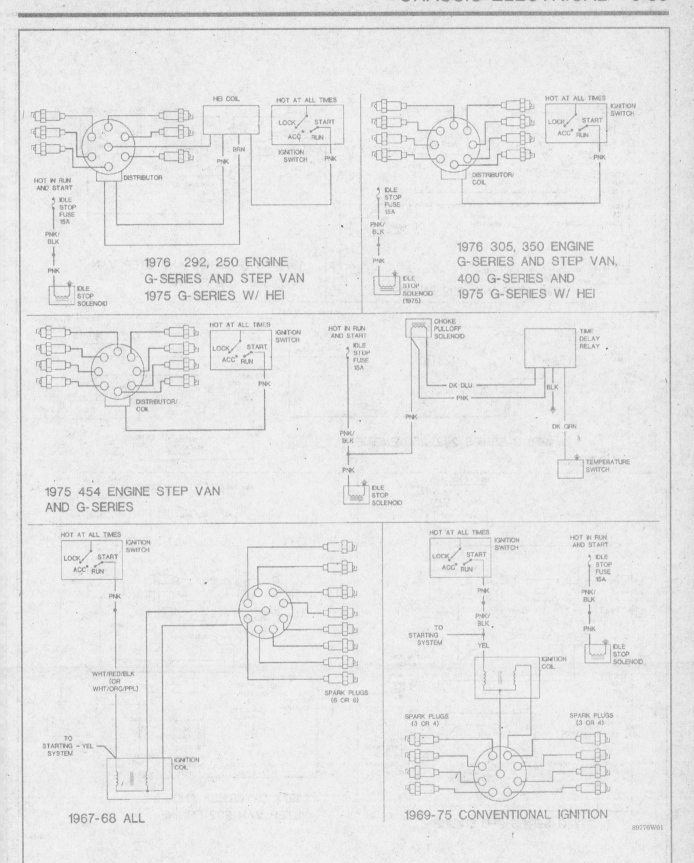

Fig. 60 Engine wiring — 1967-76 G-Series and Step Vans with 194, 230, 250, 292, 305, 307, 350, 400 and 454 cu. in. engines

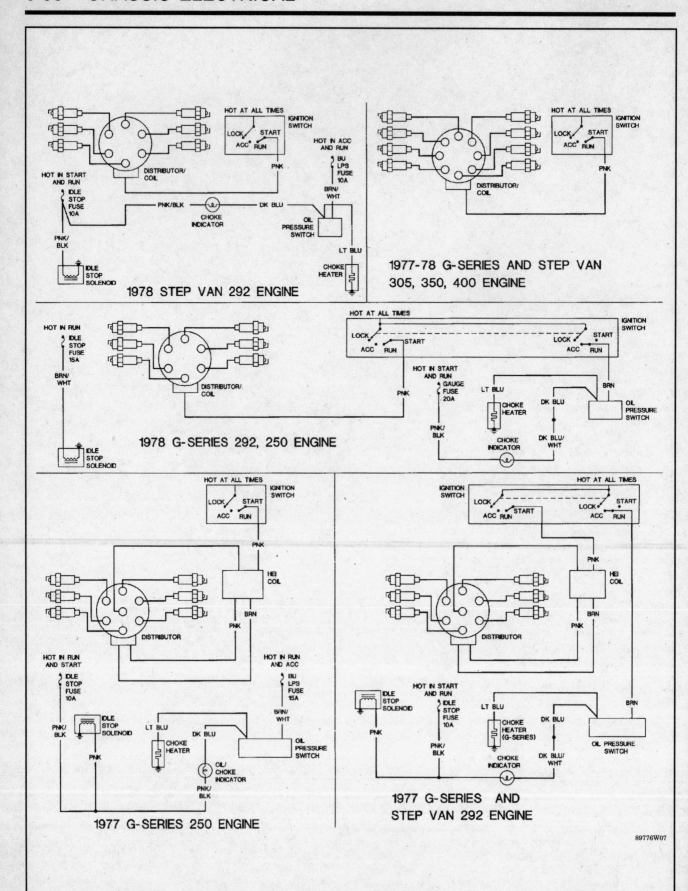

**Fig. 61 Engine wiring — 1977-78 G-Series and Step Vans with 250, 292, 305, 350 and 400 cu. in. engines**

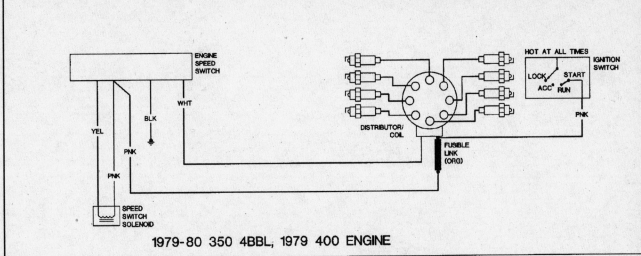

1979-80 350 4BBL, 1979 400 ENGINE

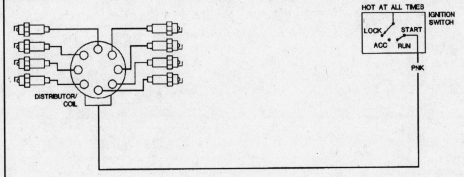

1979-80 305, 350 2BBL ENGINE

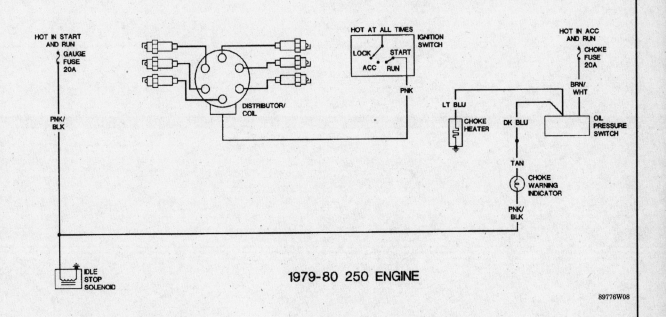

1979-80 250 ENGINE

89776W08

Fig. 62 Engine wiring — 1979-80 G-Series vans with 250, 305, 350 and 400 cu. in. engines

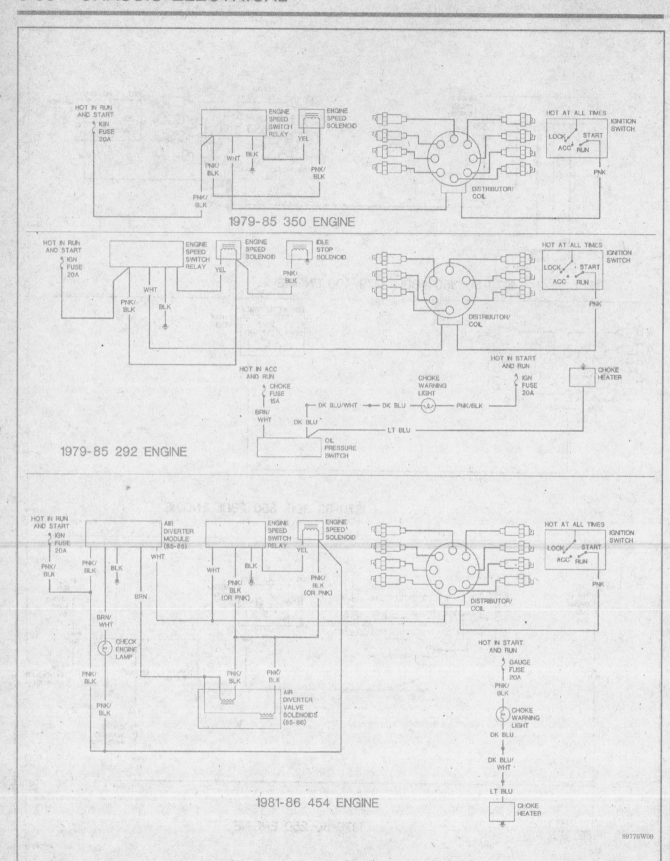

Fig. 63 Engine wiring—1979-85 Step Vans with 292 and 350 cu. in. engines; 1981-86 Step Vans with 454 cu. in. engine

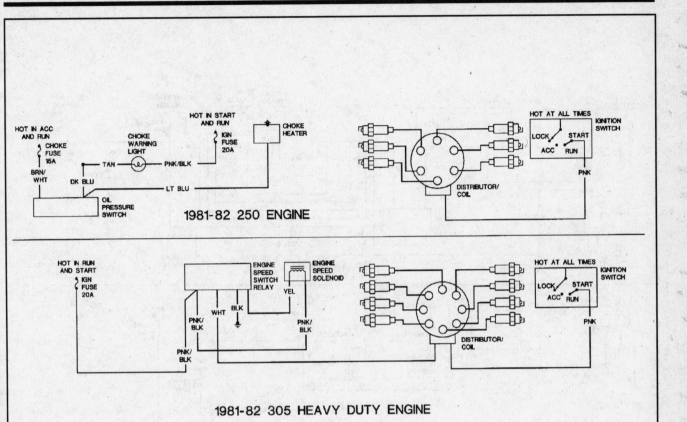

1981-82 250 ENGINE

1981-82 305 HEAVY DUTY ENGINE

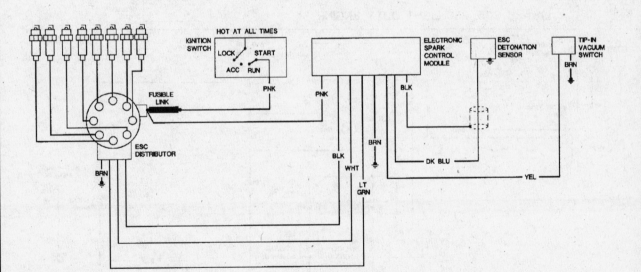

1981-82 305, 350 CALIFORNIA ENGINE

89776W10

**Fig. 64 Engine wiring — 1981-82 G-Series vans with 250 and Heavy Duty 305 cu. in. engines (Federal); 305 and 350 cu. in. engines (California)**

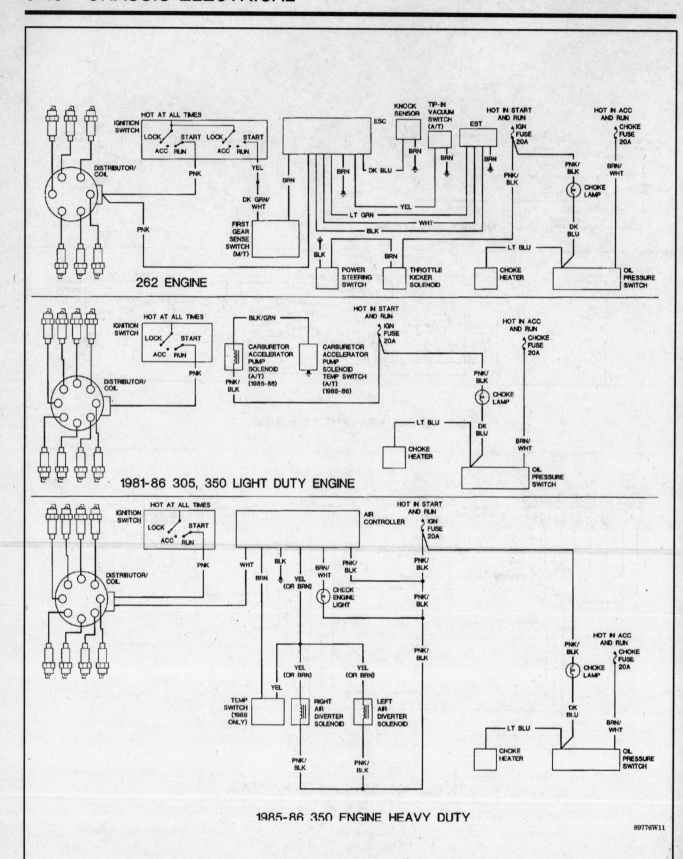

**Fig. 65 Engine wiring — 1981-86 G-Series vans with 262, 305 and Light Duty 350 engines; 1985-88 G-Series vans with Heavy Duty 350 engines (Federal)**

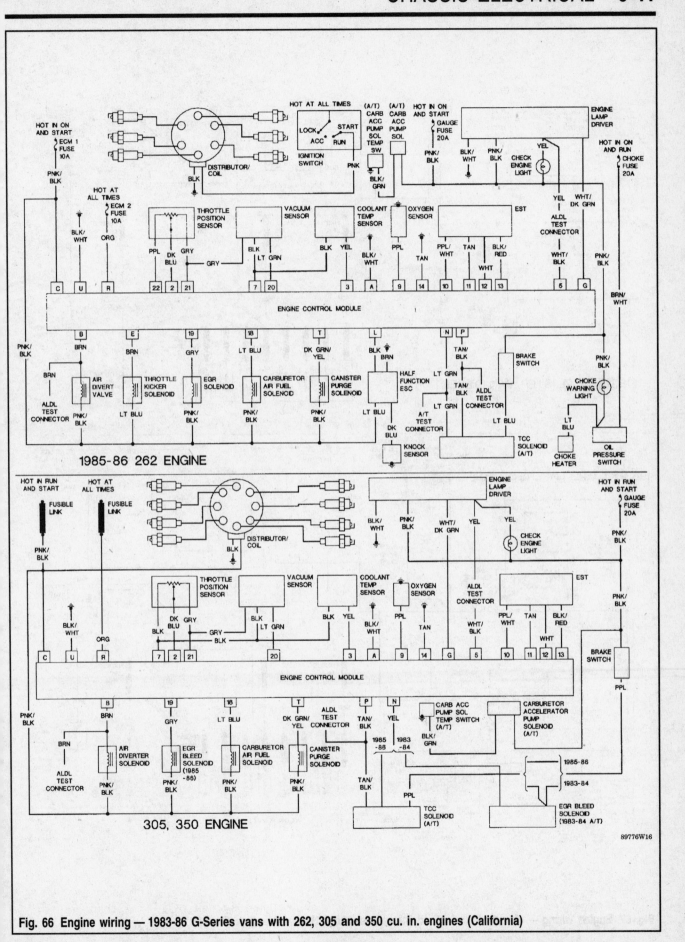

**Fig. 66 Engine wiring — 1983-86 G-Series vans with 262, 305 and 350 cu. in. engines (California)**

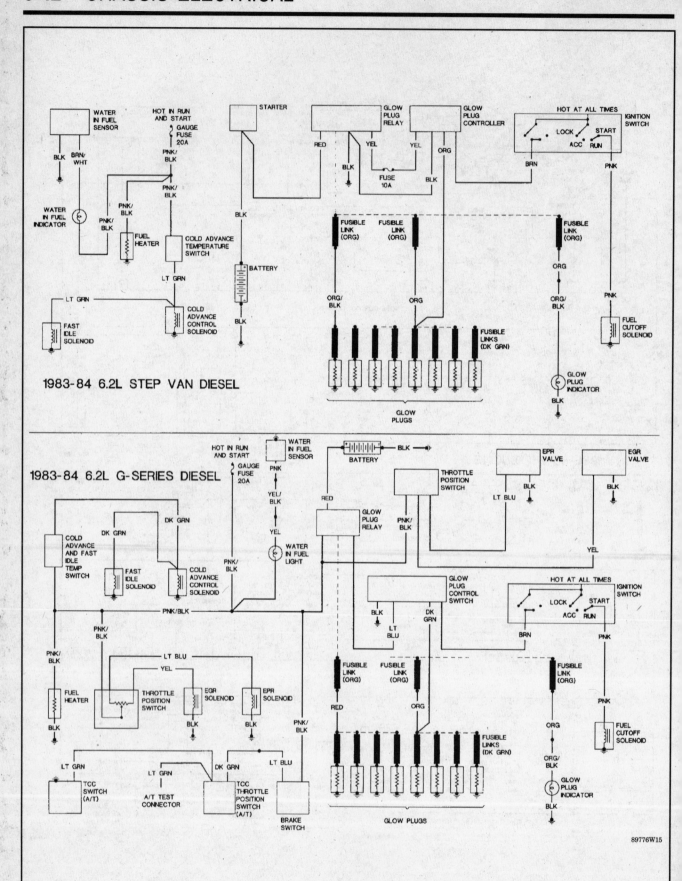

1983-84 6.2L STEP VAN DIESEL

1983-84 6.2L G-SERIES DIESEL

89776W15

**Fig. 67 Engine wiring — 1983-84 G-Series and Step Vans with 6.2L diesel engine (Federal)**

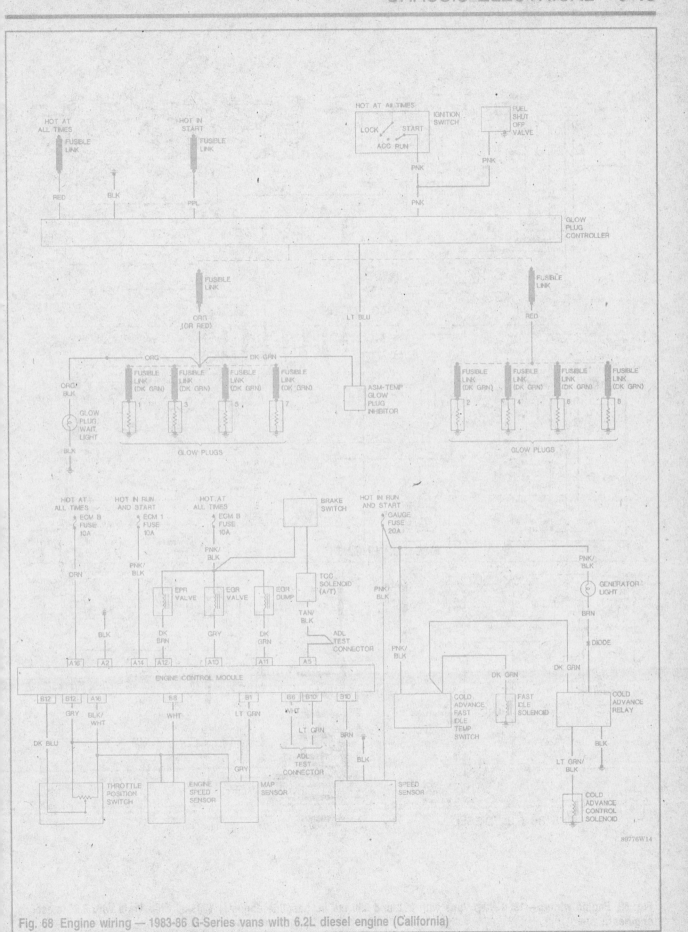

Fig. 68 Engine wiring — 1983-86 G-Series vans with 6.2L diesel engine (California)

89776W14

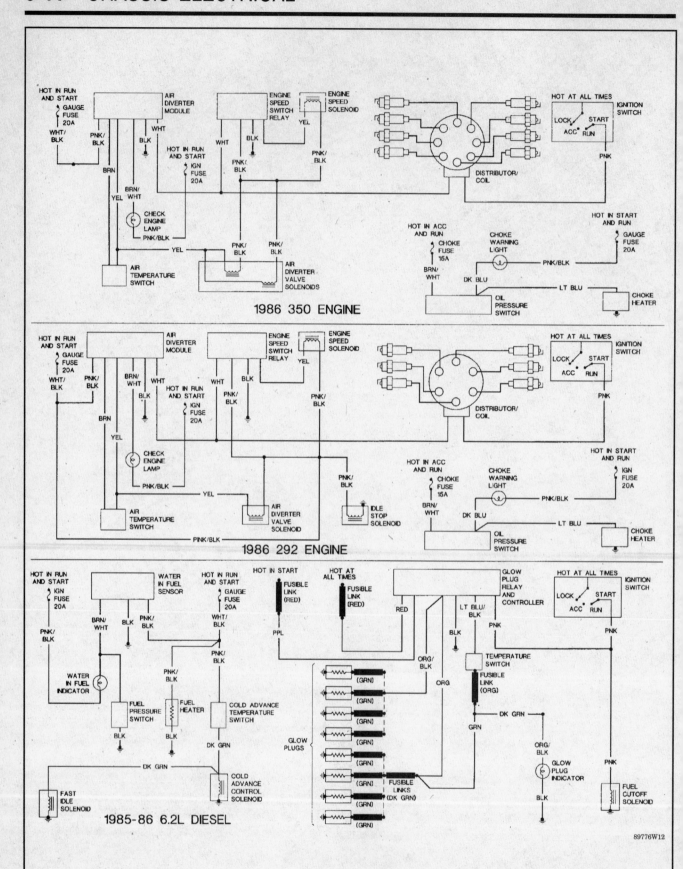

Fig. 69 Engine wiring — 1986 Step Vans with 292 and 350 cu. in. gasoline engines; 1985-86 Step Vans with 6.2L diesel engines

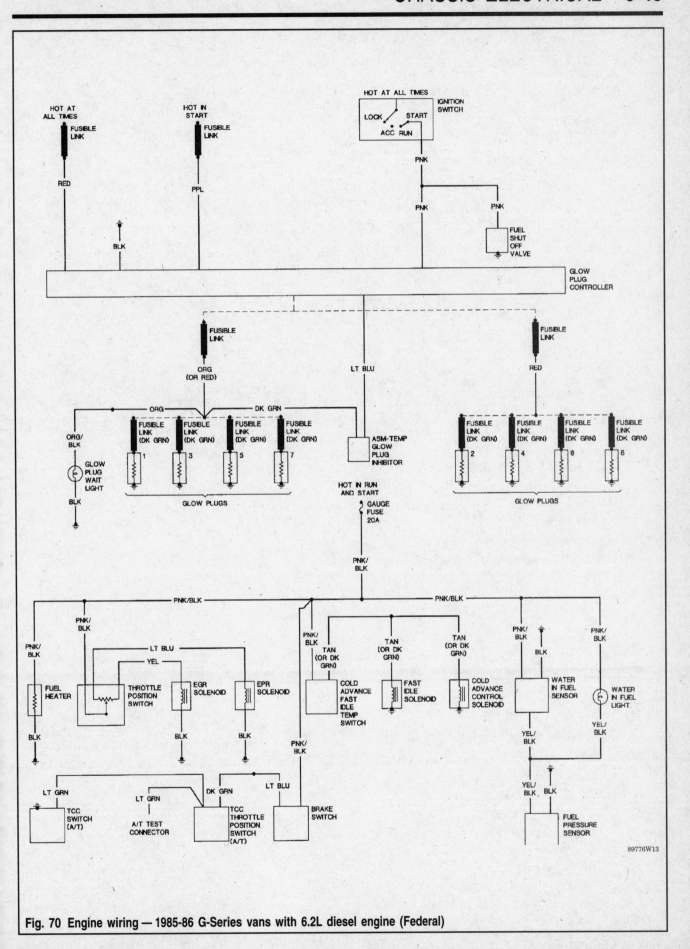

**Fig. 70 Engine wiring — 1985-86 G-Series vans with 6.2L diesel engine (Federal)**

89776W13

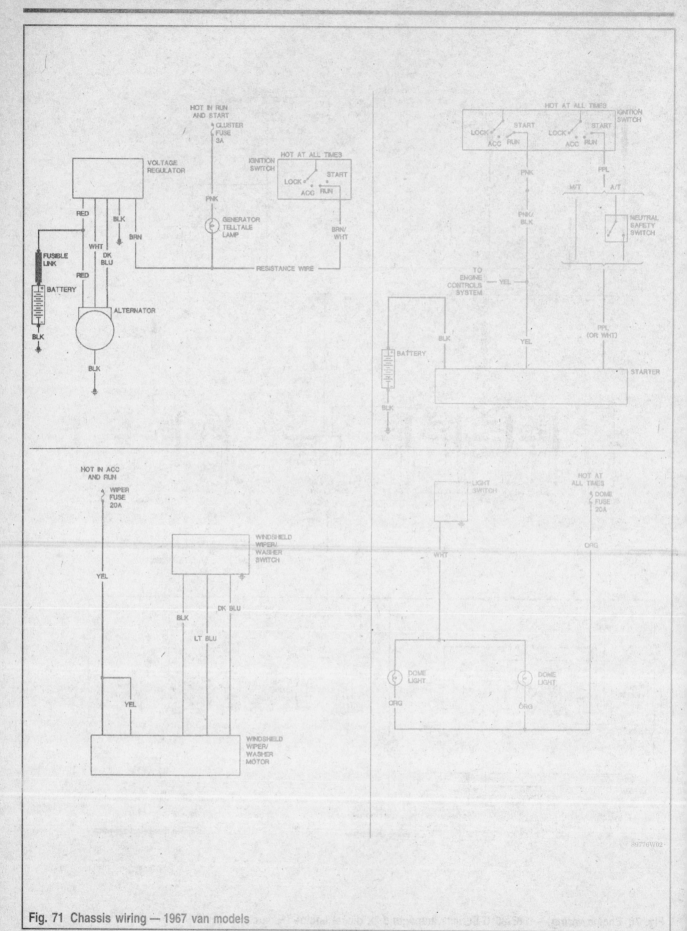

**Fig. 71 Chassis wiring — 1967 van models**

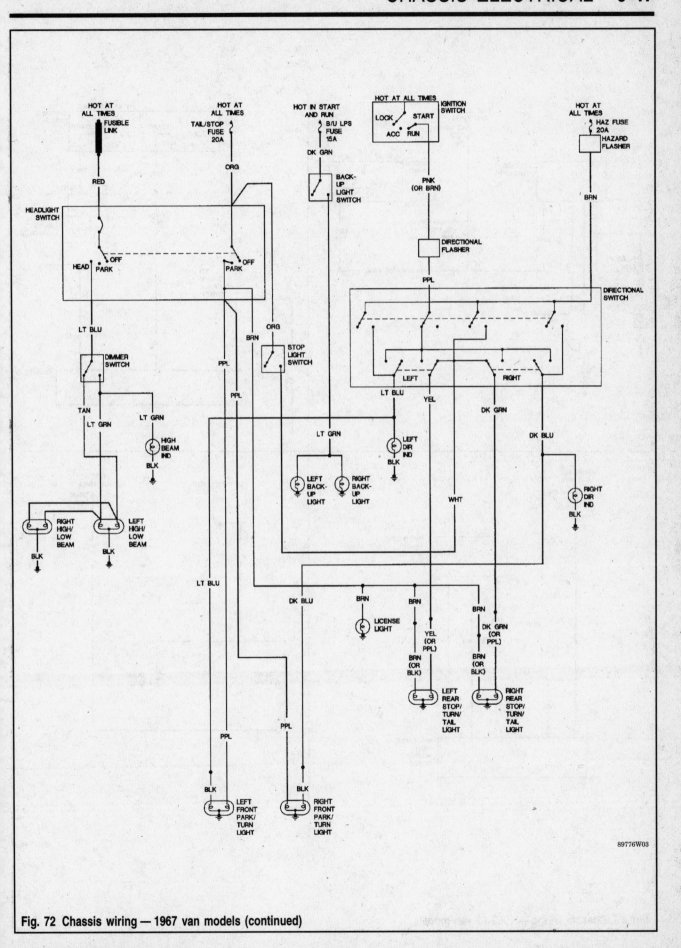

**Fig. 72 Chassis wiring — 1967 van models (continued)**

89776W03

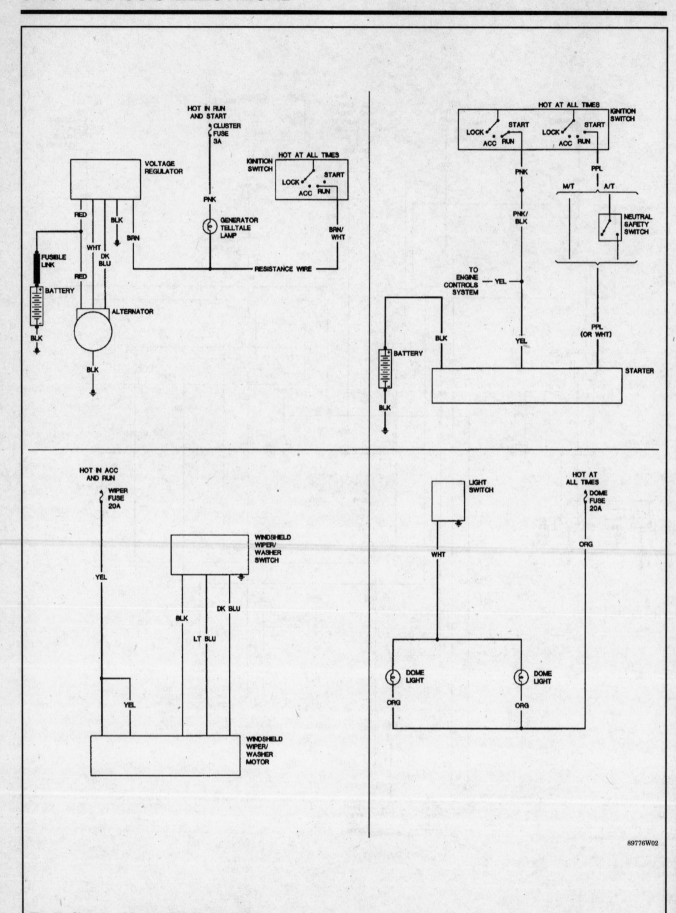

**Fig. 73 Chassis wiring — 1968-72 van models**

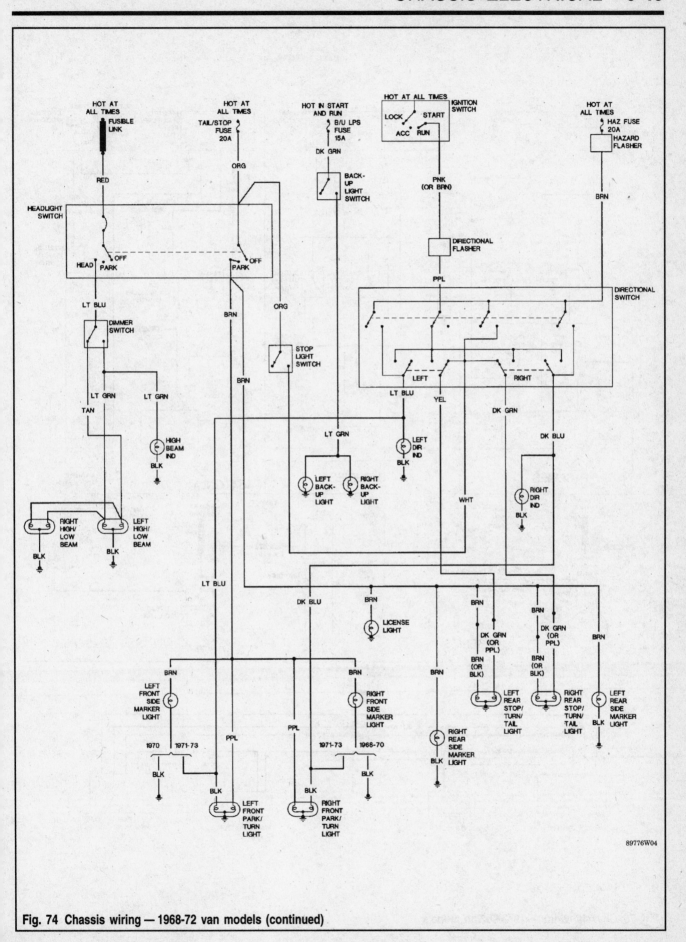

**Fig. 74 Chassis wiring — 1968-72 van models (continued)**

89776W04

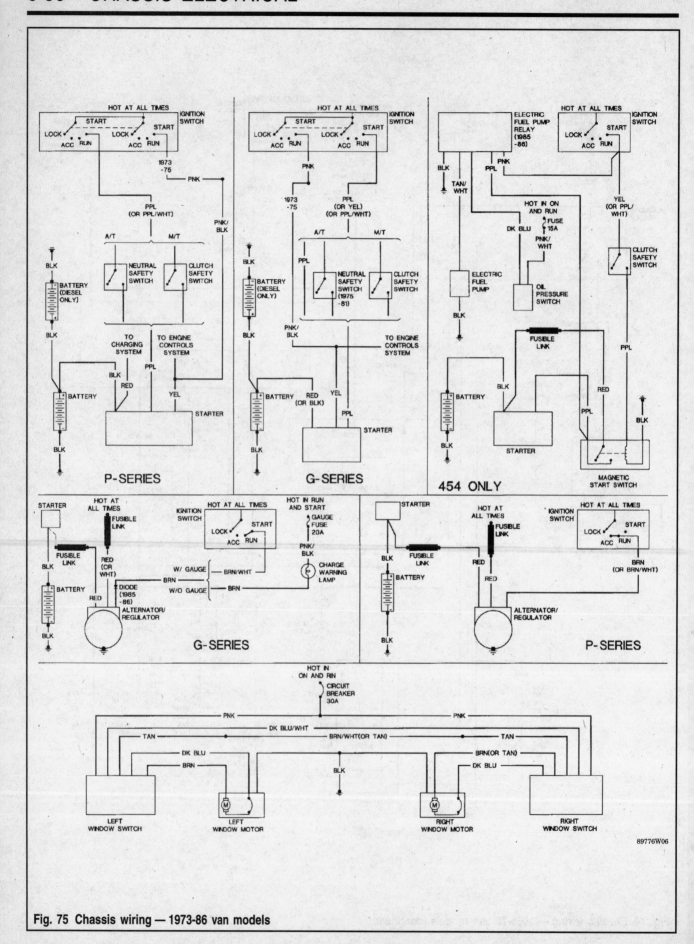

**Fig. 75 Chassis wiring — 1973-86 van models**

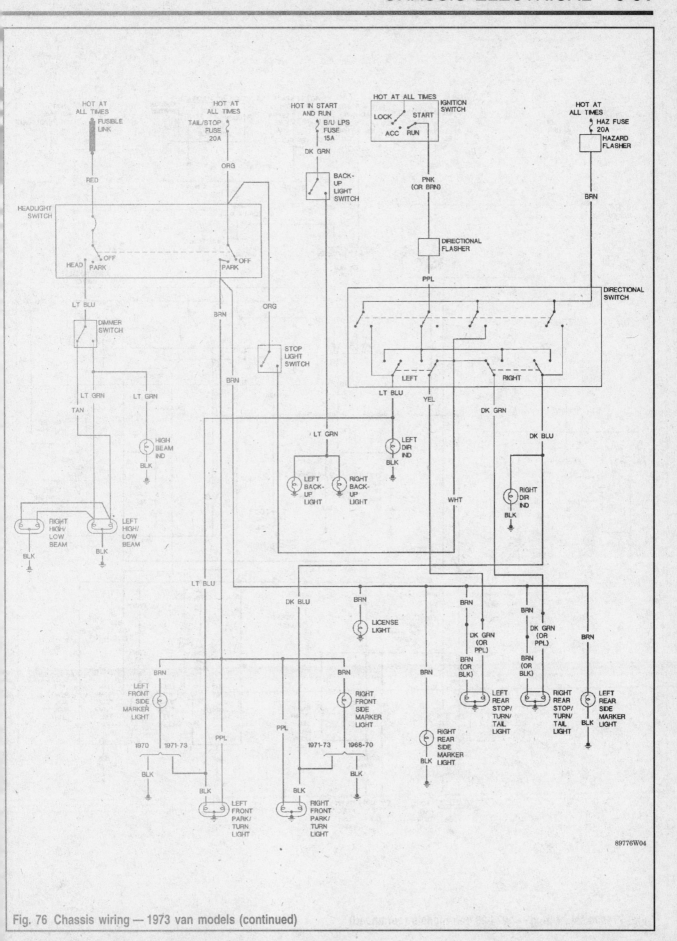

Fig. 76 Chassis wiring — 1973 van models (continued)

89776W04

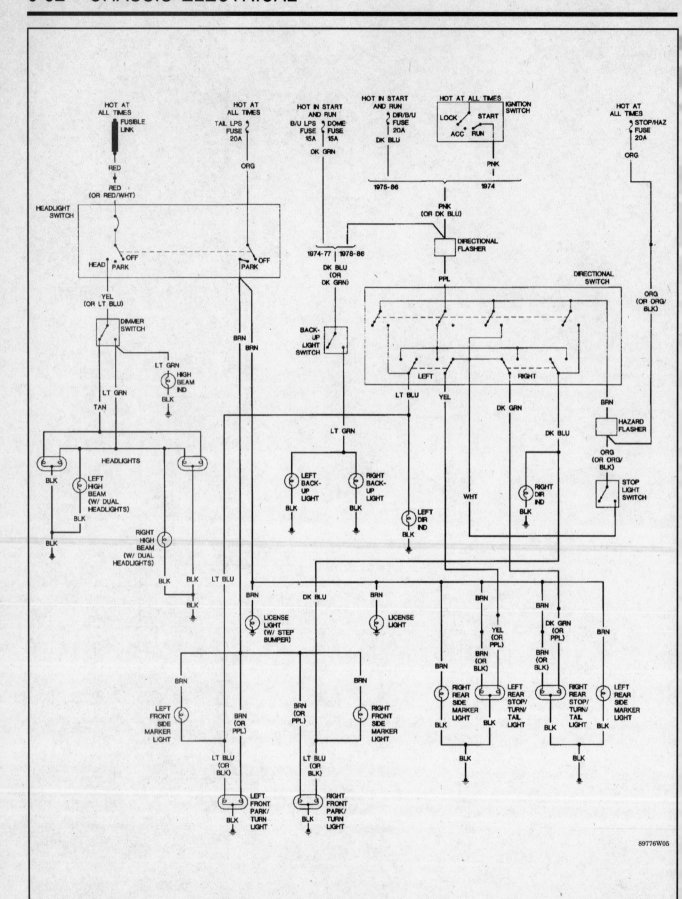

**Fig. 77 Chassis wiring — 1974-86 van models (continued)**

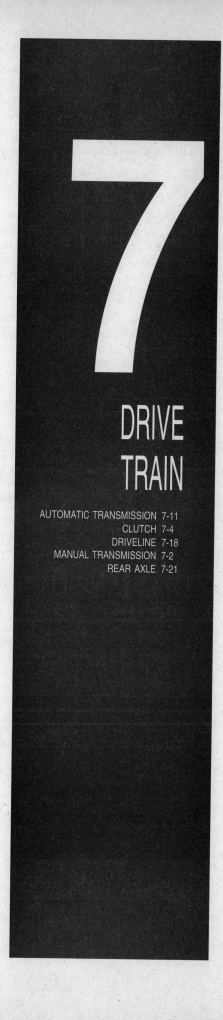

# 7

# DRIVE
# TRAIN

## MANUAL TRANSMISSION

### Understanding the Manual Transmission

Because of the way an internal combustion engine breathes, it can produce torque (or twisting force) only within a narrow speed range. Most overhead valve pushrod engines must turn at about 2500 rpm to produce their peak torque. Often by 4500 rpm, they are producing so little torque that continued increases in engine speed produce no power increases.

The torque peak on overhead camshaft engines is, generally, much higher, but much narrower.

The manual transmission and clutch are employed to vary the relationship between engine RPM and the speed of the wheels so that adequate power can be produced under all circumstances. The clutch allows engine torque to be applied to the transmission input shaft gradually, due to mechanical slippage. The vehicle can, consequently, be started smoothly from a full stop.

The transmission changes the ratio between the rotating speeds of the engine and the wheels by the use of gears. 4-speed or 5-speed transmissions are most common. The lower gears allow full engine power to be applied to the rear wheels during acceleration at low speeds.

The clutch driveplate is a thin disc, the center of which is splined to the transmission input shaft. Both sides of the disc are covered with a layer of material which is similar to brake lining and which is capable of allowing slippage without roughness or excessive noise.

The clutch cover is bolted to the engine flywheel and incorporates a diaphragm spring which provides the pressure to engage the clutch. The cover also houses the pressure plate. When the clutch pedal is released, the driven disc is sandwiched between the pressure plate and the smooth surface of the flywheel, thus forcing the disc to turn at the same speed as the engine crankshaft.

The transmission contains a mainshaft which passes all the way through the transmission, from the clutch to the driveshaft. This shaft is separated at one point, so that front and rear portions can turn at different speeds.

Power is transmitted by a countershaft in the lower gears and reverse. The gears of the countershaft mesh with gears on the mainshaft, allowing power to be carried from one to the other. Countershaft gears are often integral with that shaft, while several of the mainshaft gears can either rotate independently of the shaft or be locked to it. Shifting from one gear to the next causes one of the gears to be freed from rotating with the shaft and locks another to it. Gears are locked and unlocked by internal dog clutches which slide between the center of the gear and the shaft. The forward gears usually employ synchronizers; friction members which smoothly bring gear and shaft to the same speed before the toothed dog clutches are engaged.

### Identification

Most 3-speed transmissions are the very similar Saginaw and Muncie side cover units. These may be told apart by the shape of the side cover. The Saginaw has a single bolt centered at the top edge of the side cover, while the Muncie has two bolts along the top edge. The Muncie was discontinued in 1978. Some 1976-80 models use the top cover Tremec 3-speed. All 3-speeds use side mounted external linkage and a column shift. A column shifted 4-speed Warner T-10 transmission was optional in 1968-69 only.

## Adjustments

### LINKAGE

**3-Speed Column Shift**

◆ See Figure 1

The gearshift linkage should be adjusted each time it is disturbed or removed.

1. Install the control rods to both of the levers and set both shifter levers in the Neutral position.
2. Align both shifter tube levers on the mast jacket in Neutral. Install a 3/16-7/32 in. (4.76-5.56mm) gauge to hold them in place. The gauge is inserted in the holes of the levers.
3. Connect the control rods to the tube levers, making sure that the clamps and tube levers are properly positioned in Neutral.
4. Remove the gauge and move the gearshift lever through all positions to be sure that the adjustment is correct in all positions.

**4-Speed Column Shift**

◆ See Figure 2

➡This procedure applies to 1968-69 models only.

1. Raise and support the van.
2. Place the shifter lever in Neutral.
3. Disconnect the 1st/2nd shift rod from the cross-shaft lever. Disconnect the 3rd/4th shift rod from the transmission lever. Disconnect the reverse cable from the reverse lever, by removing the C-clip. If necessary, manually operate the transmission and put it in Neutral.
4. Remove the engine splash shield. Install a fabricated pin through the upper control shaft bracket into the cutouts in the shaft levers and into the hole in the base of the control shaft.
5. Adjust the swivel on the end of the 1st/2nd rod to freely enter the cross-shaft lever hole. Reconnect the rod to the lever.
6. Adjust the swivel on the end of the 3rd/4th rod to freely enter the transmission lever. Reconnect the rod to the lever.
7. Adjust the swivel on the end of the reverse cable to freely enter the hole in the reverse lever. If there is not enough room for adjustment, move the cable assembly to the front or rear using the cable-to-bracket attaching nuts. Install the washer and C-clip. Tighten the swivel locknut.
8. Remove the fabricated pin, reinstall the splash shields and lower the vehicle.

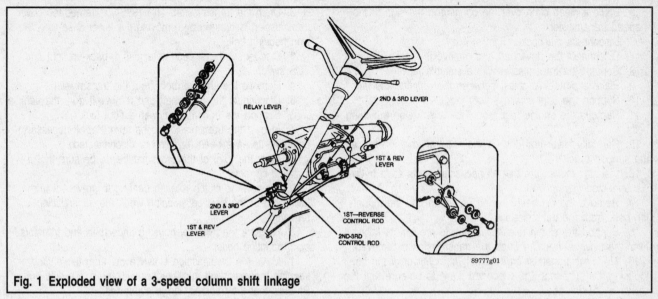

**Fig. 1 Exploded view of a 3-speed column shift linkage**

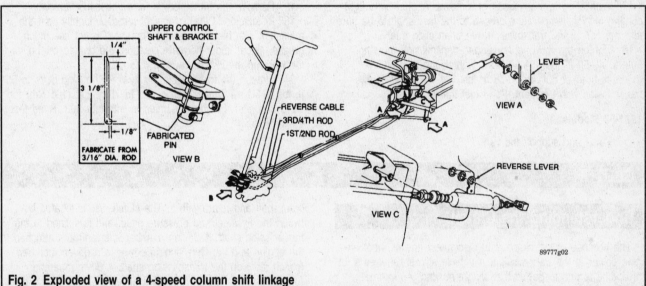

**Fig. 2 Exploded view of a 4-speed column shift linkage**

## Manual Transmission Assembly

### REMOVAL & INSTALLATION

#### 1967 Models

1. Drain the lubricant from the transmission.
2. Remove the driveshaft.
3. Remove the screws holding the steering jacket grommet to the floor and slide the grommet up the jacket out of the way.
4. Remove the accelerator pedal and floor mat.
5. Remove the transmission cover and the floor pans (if equipped).
6. Disconnect the speedometer cable at the transmission rear bearing retainer.
7. Remove the top 2 screws attaching the transmission the bellhousing. Insert 2 guide pins in these holes. They will sup-port the weight of the transmission and keep it level while it is being removed.
8. Remove the flywheel underpan and remove the lower screws attaching the transmission to the bellhousing.
9. Slide the transmission straight back on the guide pins until the mainshaft is free of the splines in the clutch disc.
10. Remove the transmission from the vehicle.
11. Installation is the reverse of removal. Fill the transmission with the specified amount and type of fluid. Road test the vehicle to be sure that the transmission and clutch operate properly.

#### 1968-70 Models

1. Drain the lubricant from the transmission.
2. Disconnect the speedometer cable.
3. Remove the shift controls from the transmission.
4. On vehicles with the 4-speed transmission, remove the floor mat, transmission floor pan cover and place the transmission gearshift in Neutral. Remove the transmission gearshift lever and cover.

5. Place a clean cloth over the opening in the side of the 4-speed transmission.

6. Disconnect the backup light switch.

7. Disconnect the driveshaft and remove it.

8. Support the transmission with a suitable jack.

9. Place a protective shield between the radiator and fan.

10. Support the engine with a floor jack.

11. Remove the engine rear mount-to-transmission attaching bolts.

12. Carefully lower both the engine and transmission to clear the support bracket.

13. Visually, make sure that all necessary parts have been disconnected or removed.

14. Remove the flywheel housing underpan and the mounting bolts from the transmission.

15. Support the clutch release bearing to prevent its falling from the flywheel housing when the transmission is removed.

16. Move the transmission assembly straight out of the belhousing. Be sure that it is supported firmly to be sure that the clutch is not damaged.

17. Installation is the reverse of removal. Apply a very light coating of high temperature grease to the mainshaft to be sure that the clutch and transmission mainshaft slide freely.

18. Tighten the flywheel housing-to-transmission mounting nuts to 40-50 ft. lbs. (54-67 Nm). Tighten the rear engine mount-to-bracket nuts to 55-75 ft. lbs. (74-101 Nm). Fill the transmission with lubricant. Road test the vehicle.

**1971-86 Models**

1. Raise and support the van.

2. Drain the transmission. The 1976-80 Tremec top cover transmission is drained by removing the lower case to extension housing bolt.

3. Disconnect the speedometer cable, back-up light and TCS switch.

4. Remove the shift controls from the transmission.

5. Disconnect the driveshaft and remove it from the vehicle.

6. Support the transmission with a floor jack.

7. Inspect the transmission to be sure that all necessary components have been removed or disconnected.

8. Mark the front of the crossmember to be sure that it is installed correctly.

9. Support the clutch release bearing to prevent it from falling out of the flywheel housing when the transmission is removed.

10. Remove the flywheel housing under pan and transmission mounting bolts.

11. Move the transmission slowly away from the engine, keeping the mainshaft in alignment with the clutch disc hub. Be sure that the transmission is supported.

12. Remove the transmission from under the vehicle.

13. Installation is the reverse of removal. Lightly coat the mainshaft with high temperature grease. Do not use much grease, since, under normal operation, the grease will be thrown onto the clutch, causing it to fail.

14. Tighten the transmission to flywheel housing bolts to 55 ft. lbs. (75 Nm) through 1972, and to 75 ft. lbs. (101 Nm) for 1973 and later. Fill the transmission with lubricant. Road test the vehicle.

# CLUTCH

## Understanding the Clutch

The purpose of the clutch is to disconnect and connect engine power at the transmission. A vehicle at rest requires a lot of engine torque to get all that weight moving. An internal combustion engine does not develop a high starting torque (unlike steam engines) so it must be allowed to operate without any load until it builds up enough torque to move the vehicle. To a point, torque increases with engine rpm. The clutch allows the engine to build up torque by physically disconnecting the engine from the transmission, relieving the engine of any load or resistance.

The transfer of engine power to the transmission (the load) must be smooth and gradual; if it weren't, drive line components would wear out or break quickly. This gradual power transfer is made possible by gradually releasing the clutch pedal. The clutch disc and pressure plate are the connecting link between the engine and transmission. When the clutch pedal is released, the disc and plate contact each other (the clutch is engaged) physically joining the engine and transmission. When the pedal is pushed in, the disc and plate separate (the clutch is disengaged) disconnecting the engine from the transmission.

Most clutch assemblies consists of the flywheel, the clutch disc, the clutch pressure plate, the throw out bearing and fork, the actuating linkage and the pedal. The flywheel and clutch pressure plate (driving members) are connected to the engine

crankshaft and rotate with it. The clutch disc is located between the flywheel and pressure plate, and is splined to the transmission shaft. A driving member is one that is attached to the engine and transfers engine power to a driven member (clutch disc) on the transmission shaft. A driving member (pressure plate) rotates (drives) a driven member (clutch disc) on contact and, in so doing, turns the transmission shaft.

There is a circular diaphragm spring within the pressure plate cover (transmission side). In a relaxed state (when the clutch pedal is fully released) this spring is convex; that is, it is dished outward toward the transmission. Pushing in the clutch pedal actuates the attached linkage. Connected to the other end of this is the throw out fork, which hold the throw out bearing. When the clutch pedal is depressed, the clutch linkage pushes the fork and bearing forward to contact the diaphragm spring of the pressure plate. The outer edges of the spring are secured to the pressure plate and are pivoted on rings so that when the center of the spring is compressed by the throw out bearing, the outer edges bow outward and, by so doing, pull the pressure plate in the same direction - away from the clutch disc. This action separates the disc from the plate, disengaging the clutch and allowing the transmission to be shifted into another gear. A coil type clutch return spring attached to the clutch pedal arm permits full release of the pedal. Releasing the pedal pulls the throw out bearing away from the diaphragm spring resulting in a reversal of spring position. As bearing pressure is gradually released from the spring center, the outer edges of the spring bow outward, pushing the pressure plate into closer contact with the clutch disc. As the disc and plate move closer together, friction between the two increases and slippage is reduced until, when full spring pressure is applied (by fully releasing the pedal) the speed of the disc and plate are the same. This stops all slipping, creating a direct connection between the plate and disc which results in the transfer of power from the engine to the transmission. The clutch disc is now rotating with the pressure plate at engine speed and, because it is splined to the transmission shaft, the shaft now turns at the same engine speed.

The clutch is operating properly if:

1. It will stall the engine when released with the vehicle held stationary.

2. The shift lever can be moved freely between 1st and reverse gears when the vehicle is stationary and the clutch disengaged.

## Adjustments

### LINKAGE AND FREE-PLAY

▶ **See Figure 3**

This adjustment is for the amount of clutch pedal free travel before the throwout bearing contacts the clutch release fingers. It is required periodically to compensate for clutch lining wear. Incorrect adjustment will cause gear grinding and clutch slippage or wear.

➡**If you have a problem with grinding when shifting into gear, shorten the pedal stop bumper to ⅜ in. (9.5mm) and readjust the linkage.**

1. Disconnect the clutch fork return spring at the fork on the clutch housing.

2. Loosen the outer adjusting nut (**A**) and back it off approximately ½ in. (12.7mm) from the swivel.

3. Hold the clutch fork pushrod against the fork to move the throwout bearing against the clutch fingers. The pushrod will slide through the swivel at the cross-shaft.

4. Adjust the inner adjusting nut (**B**) to obtain ³/₁₆-¼ in. (4.76-6.35mm) clearance between nut (**B**) and the swivel. The clearance should be ¼ in. (6.35mm) for 1973 and later models.

5. Release the pushrod, connect the return spring and tighten the outer nut (**A**) to lock the swivel against the inner nut (**B**).

6. Check the free travel at the pedal and readjust as necessary. It should be ¾-1 in. (19-25mm) through 1973 and 1¼-1½ in. (32-38mm) starting in 1974.

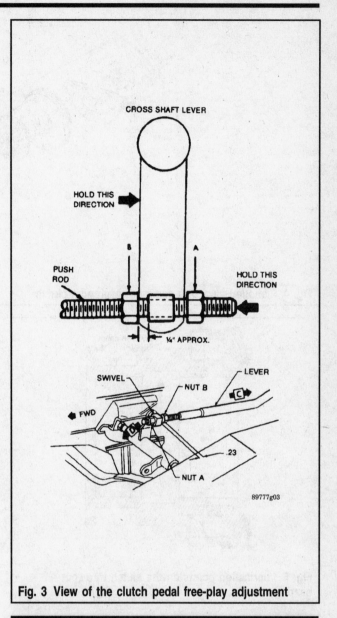

**Fig. 3 View of the clutch pedal free-play adjustment**

## Driven Disc and Pressure Plate

### REMOVAL & INSTALLATION

▶ **See Figures 4, 5, 6, 7, 8, 9, 10, 11, 12, 13 and 14**

### ✳✳CAUTION

**The clutch driven disc may contain asbestos, which has been determined to be a cancer causing agent. Never clean clutch surfaces with compressed air! Avoid inhaling any dust from any clutch surface! When cleaning clutch surfaces, use a commercially available brake cleaning fluid.**

There are two types of clutch pressure plates used, diaphragm and coil spring. In general, the larger heavy duty clutches are usually of the coil spring pressure plate type. Removal and installation details are similar for both types.

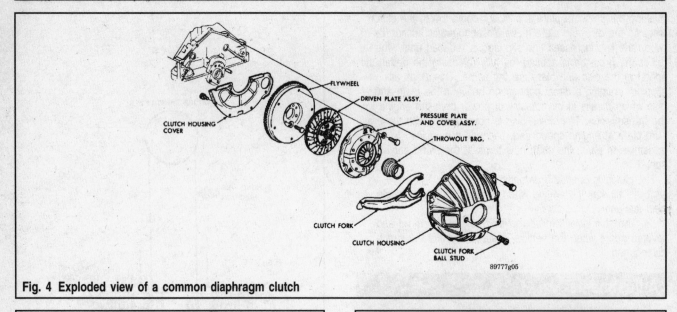

**Fig. 4 Exploded view of a common diaphragm clutch**

FLYWHEEL

DRIVEN PLATE ASSY.

PRESSURE PLATE
AND COVER ASSY.

THROWOUT BRG.

CLUTCH HOUSING
COVER

CLUTCH FORK

CLUTCH HOUSING

CLUTCH FORK
BALL STUD

89777g05

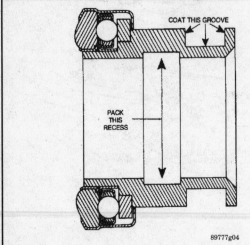

COAT THIS GROOVE

PACK
THIS
RECESS

89777g04

**Fig. 5 Lubrication points on the clutch throwout
bearing**

TCCS7118

**Fig. 7 Carefullt remove the clutch and pressure plate**

TCCS7116

**Fig. 6 Remove the pressure plate bolts in an X pattern**

TCCS7119

**Fig. 8 View of the flywheel once the clutch assembly is
removed**

Fig. 9 Be sure that the flywheel surface is clean, before installing the clutch

Fig. 10 Check across the flywheel surface; it should be flat

Fig. 11 Checking the pressure plate for warpage

Fig. 12 Install a clutch alignment arbor, to align the clutch assembly during installation

Fig. 13 Install a locking agent to the clutch assembly bolts

Fig. 14 Be sure to use a torque wrench to tighten all bolts

### Diaphragm Spring Pressure Plate

1. Remove the transmission as previously outlined.
2. Disconnect the fork pushrod and remove the flywheel housing. Remove the clutch throwout bearing from the fork.
3. Remove the clutch fork by pressing it away from the ball mounting with a screwdriver until the fork snaps loose from the ball or remove the ball stud from the clutch housing.
4. Install a pilot tool (an old mainshaft makes a good pilot tool) to hold the clutch while you are removing it.

➡**Before removing the clutch from the flywheel, match-mark the flywheel, the clutch cover and one of the pressure plate lugs. These parts must be reassembled in their original positions as they are a balanced assembly.**

5. Loosen the clutch attaching bolts one turn at a time to prevent distortion of the clutch cover until the tension is released.
6. Remove the clutch pilot tool and the clutch from the vehicle.

Inspect the flywheel and pressure plate for discoloration, scoring or wear marks. The flywheel can be refaced if necessary, otherwise replace the parts. Also inspect the clutch fork and throwout bearing for looseness or wear. Replace if either is evident.

**To install:**

7. Install the pressure plate in the cover assembly, aligning the notch in the pressure plate with the notch in the cover flange.
8. Install the pressure plate retracting spring, lockwashers, and the drive strap to the pressure plate bolts. Tighten to 11 ft. lbs. (14 Nm).
9. Turn the flywheel until the X mark is at the bottom.
10. Install the clutch disc, pressure plate and cover, using an old mainshaft as an aligning tool.
11. Turn the clutch until the X mark on the clutch cover aligns with the X mark on the flywheel.
12. Install the attaching bolts and tighten them a little at a time in a crisscross pattern until the spring pressure is taken up.
13. Remove the aligning tool.
14. Pack the clutch ball fork seat with a small amount of high temperature grease. Too much grease will cause slippage. Install a new retainer in the groove of the clutch fork, if necessary. Install the retainer with the high side up and the open end on the horizontal.
15. If the clutch fork ball was removed, reinstall it in the clutch housing and snap the clutch fork onto the ball.
16. Lubricate the inside of the throwout bearing collar and the throwout fork groove with a small amount of graphite grease.
17. Install the throwout bearing.
18. Install the flywheel housing and transmission.
19. Further installation is the reverse of removal. Adjust the clutch linkage.

### Coil Spring Pressure Plate

Basically, the same procedures apply to diaphragm clutch removal as to the coil spring clutch removal.

When loosening the clutch holding bolts, loosen them only a turn or two at a time in order to avoid bending the rim of the cover. It will be helpful to place wood or metal spacers, about $^3/_8$ in. (9.5mm) thick, between the clutch levers and the cover to hold the levers down as the holding bolts are being removed or when the clutch is being removed from the engine.

## Master Cylinder

### REMOVAL & INSTALLATION

▶ **See Figures 15 and 16**

1. Disconnect the negative battery cable.
2. Remove the lower steering column covers.
3. Remove the lower left side air conditioning duct (if necessary).
4. Remove the retainer clip and washer from the pushrod.
5. Disconnect the pushrod and remove the wave washer.
6. Disconnect the reservoir hose.
7. Disconnect the secondary cylinder hydraulic line from the master cylinder.
8. Remove the nuts that secure the master cylinder and remove the master cylinder.
9. Scrape all gasket material from the master cylinder and the cowl.
10. Remove the screws that secure the reservoir and remove the reservoir.

### OVERHAUL

1. Remove the adapter and the seal from the master cylinder.
2. Pull the dust cover back and remove the snapring.
3. Shake the pushrod and the plunger out of the master cylinder and remove the following:
   - The front seal
   - The spring
   - The support
   - The rear seal and the shim.

Clean all parts in clean brake fluid. Inspect the cylinder bore and the plunger for scratches, ridges and pitting. Inspect the dust cover for wear and cracking.

4. Lubricate all seals with clean brake fluid.
5. Install the shim and a new seal with the flat against the shim.
6. Install the support and the spring.
7. Install a new seal.
8. Coat the cylinder boar with clean brake fluid and slide the plunger and the pushrod in.
9. Push the pushrod in and install the snapring.
10. Coat the inside of the dust cover with grease and slide it into place.
11. Install a new seal and the adapter, and install the master cylinder.
12. Installation is the reverse of the removal procedure.

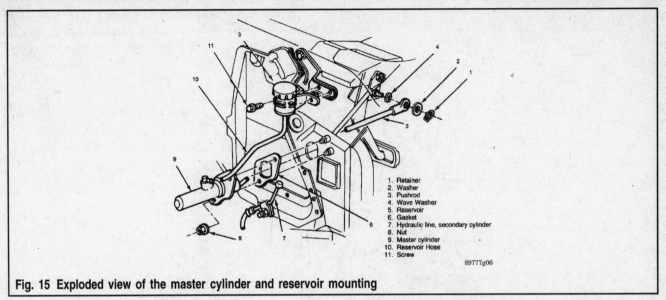

1. Retainer
2. Washer
3. Pushrod
4. Wave Washer
5. Reservoir
6. Gasket
7. Hydraulic line, secondary cylinder
8. Nut
9. Master cylinder
10. Reservoir Hose
11. Screw

89777g06

**Fig. 15 Exploded view of the master cylinder and reservoir mounting**

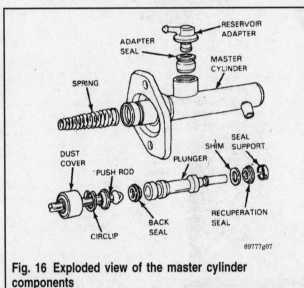

**Fig. 16 Exploded view of the master cylinder components**

## Slave Cylinder

## REMOVAL & INSTALLATION

▶ **See Figures 17 and 18**

1. Disconnect the negative battery cable. Raise and support the vehicle properly.

2. Disconnect the hydraulic line from the slave cylinder.
3. Remove the nuts that secure the slave cylinder and remove the cylinder.
4. Disconnect the hydraulic line from the master cylinder.
5. Remove the nut that secures the hydraulic line and remove the line.
6. Reinstall the nut to hold the speedometer cable in place.

➡**Cover all hydraulic line openings to keep dirt and moisture out of the components.**

## OVERHAUL

1. Remove the pushrod and the dust cover.
2. Remove the snapring and shake the plunger out.
3. Remove the spring and the seal.
   Clean all parts in clean brake fluid. Inspect the cylinder bore and the plunger for scratches, ridges and pitting. Inspect the dust cover for wear and cracking.
4. Coat a new seal with clean brake fluid, slide it into place and install the spring.
5. Coat the hydraulic bore with clean brake fluid and slide the plunger in.
6. Push the plunger in and install the snapring.
7. Coat the inside of the dust cover with grease and slide it into place.
8. Install the pushrod and install the slave cylinder.
9. Installation is the reverse of the removal procedure

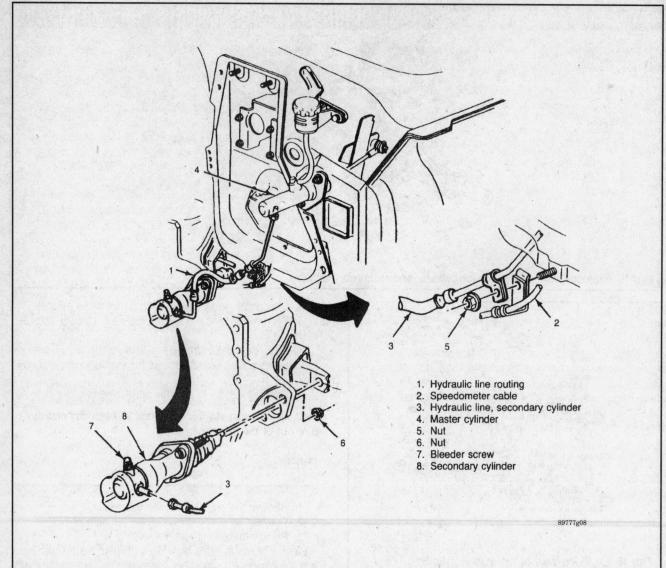

1. Hydraulic line routing
2. Speedometer cable
3. Hydraulic line, secondary cylinder
4. Master cylinder
5. Nut
6. Nut
7. Bleeder screw
8. Secondary cylinder

89777g08

**Fig. 17 Exploded view of the secondary (slave) cylinder mounting and related components**

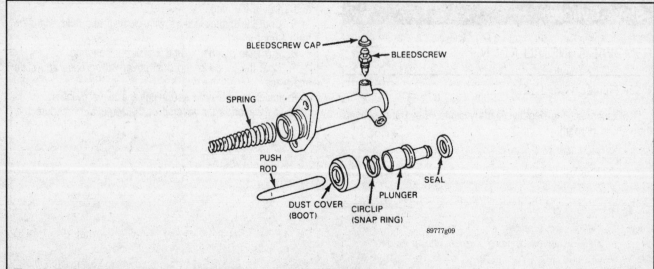

89777g09

**Fig. 18 Exploded view of the secondary (slave) cylinder components**

# AUTOMATIC TRANSMISSION

## Understanding Automatic Transmissions

The automatic transmission allows engine torque and power to be transmitted to the rear wheels within a narrow range of engine operating speeds. It will allow the engine to turn fast enough to produce plenty of power and torque at very low speeds, while keeping it at a sensible rpm at high vehicle speeds (and it does this job without driver assistance). The transmission uses a light fluid as the medium for the transmission of power. This fluid also works in the operation of various hydraulic control circuits and as a lubricant. Because the transmission fluid performs all of these functions, trouble within the unit can easily travel from one part to another. For this reason, and because of the complexity and unusual operating principles of the transmission, a very sound understanding of the basic principles of operation will simplify troubleshooting.

Three automatic transmissions are used. The 2-speed Powerglide was last used in 1971 The 3-speed Turbo Hydra-Matic 350 was introduced in 1969. A heavier duty Turbo Hydra-Matic 400 is used on 1977-86 G-20, G-30 and 3500 350 and 400 V8s. Some 1980 and later transmissions use the Tighten Converter Clutch system. 1982 and later models are available with a Turbo Hydra-Matic 700-R4 4 speed automatic which incorporates the torque converter clutch. No band adjustments are necessary or possible on Turbo Hydra-Matic transmissions; they use clutches instead of bands.

### TORQUE CONVERTER

▶ **See Figure 19**

The torque converter replaces the conventional clutch. It has three functions:

1. It allows the engine to idle with the vehicle at a standstill, even with the transmission in gear.

2. It allows the transmission to shift from range-to-range smoothly, without requiring that the driver close the throttle during the shift.

3. It multiplies engine torque to an increasing extent as vehicle speed drops and throttle opening is increased. This has the effect of making the transmission more responsive and reduces the amount of shifting required.

The torque converter is a metal case which is shaped like a sphere that has been flattened on opposite sides. It is bolted to the rear end of the engine's crankshaft. Generally, the entire metal case rotates at engine speed and serves as the engine's flywheel.

The case contains three sets of blades. One set is attached directly to the case. This set forms the torus or pump. Another set is directly connected to the output shaft, and forms the turbine. The third set is mounted on a hub which, in turn, is mounted on a stationary shaft through a one-way clutch. This third set is known as the stator.

A pump, which is driven by the converter hub at engine speed, keeps the torque converter full of transmission fluid at all times. Fluid flows continuously through the unit to provide cooling.

Under low speed acceleration, the torque converter functions as follows:

The torus is turning faster than the turbine. It picks up fluid at the center of the converter and, through centrifugal force, slings it outward. Since the outer edge of the converter moves faster than the portions at the center, the fluid picks up speed.

The fluid then enters the outer edge of the turbine blades. It then travels back toward the center of the converter case along the turbine blades. In impinging upon the turbine blades, the fluid loses the energy picked up in the torus.

If the fluid was now returned directly into the torus, both halves of the converter would have to turn at approximately the same speed at all times, and torque input and output would both be the same.

In flowing through the torus and turbine, the fluid picks up two types of flow, or flow in two separate directions. It flows through the turbine blades, and it spins with the engine. The stator, whose blades are stationary when the vehicle is being accelerated at low speeds, converts one type of flow into another. Instead of allowing the fluid to flow straight back into the torus, the stator's curved blades turn the fluid almost 90° toward the direction of rotation of the engine. Thus the fluid does not flow as fast toward the torus, but is already spinning when the torus picks it up. This has the effect of allowing the torus to turn much faster than the turbine. This difference in speed may be compared to the difference in speed between the smaller and larger gears in any gear train. The result is that engine power output is higher, and engine torque is multiplied.

As the speed of the turbine increases, the fluid spins faster and faster in the direction of engine rotation. As a result, the ability of the stator to redirect the fluid flow is reduced. Under cruising conditions, the stator is eventually forced to rotate on its one-way clutch in the direction of engine rotation. Under these conditions, the torque converter begins to behave almost like a solid shaft, with the torus and turbine speeds being almost equal.

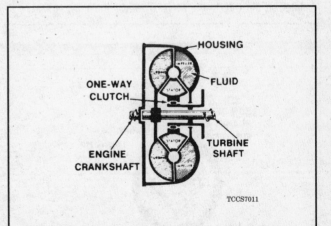

TCCS7011

**Fig. 19 The torque converter housing is rotated by the engine's crankshaft, and turns the impeller — The impeller then spins the turbine, which gives motion to the turbine shaft, driving the gears**

## PLANETARY GEARBOX

▶ **See Figures 20, 21 and 22**

The ability of the torque converter to multiply engine torque is limited. Also, the unit tends to be more efficient when the turbine is rotating at relatively high speeds. Therefore, a planetary gearbox is used to carry the power output of the turbine to the driveshaft.

Planetary gears function very similarly to conventional transmission gears. However, their construction is different in that three elements make up one gear system, and, in that all three elements are different from one another. The three elements are: an outer gear that is shaped like a hoop, with teeth cut into the inner surface; a sun gear, mounted on a shaft and located at the very center of the outer gear; and a set of three planet gears, held by pins in a ring-like planet carrier, meshing with both the sun gear and the outer gear. Either the outer gear or the sun gear may be held stationary, providing more than one possible torque multiplication factor for each set of gears. Also, if all three gears are forced to rotate at the same speed, the gearset forms, in effect, a solid shaft.

Most automatics use the planetary gears to provide various reductions ratios. Bands and clutches are used to hold various portions of the gearsets to the transmission case or to the shaft on which they are mounted. Shifting is accomplished, then, by changing the portion of each planetary gearset which is held to the transmission case or to the shaft.

## SERVOS AND ACCUMULATORS

▶ **See Figure 23**

The servos are hydraulic pistons and cylinders. They resemble the hydraulic actuators used on many other machines, such as bulldozers. Hydraulic fluid enters the cylinder, under pressure, and forces the piston to move to engage the band or clutches.

The accumulators are used to cushion the engagement of the servos. The transmission fluid must pass through the accumulator on the way to the servo. The accumulator housing

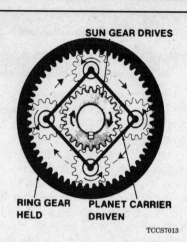

Fig. 21 Planetary gears in the maximum reduction (low) range. The ring gear is held and a lower gear ratio is obtained

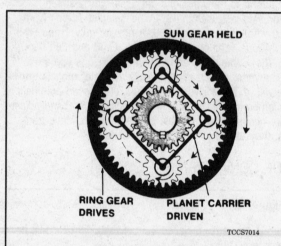

Fig. 22 Planetary gears in the minimum reduction (drive) range. The ring gear is allowed to revolve, providing a higher gear ratio

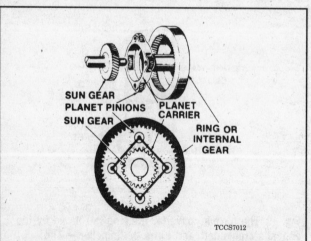

Fig. 20 Planetary gears work in a similar fashion to manual transmission gears, but are composed of three parts

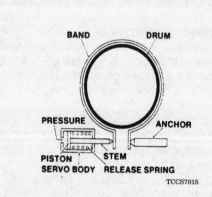

Fig. 23 Servos, operated by pressure, are used to apply or release the bands, to either hold the ring gear or allow it to rotate

contains a thin piston which is sprung away from the discharge passage of the accumulator. When fluid passes through the accumulator on the way to the servo, it must move the piston against spring pressure, and this action smooths out the action of the servo.

## HYDRAULIC CONTROL SYSTEM

The hydraulic pressure used to operate the servos comes from the main transmission oil pump. This fluid is channeled to the various servos through the shift valves. There is generally a manual shift valve which is operated by the transmission selector lever and an automatic shift valve for each automatic upshift the transmission provides.

➡**Many new transmissions are electronically controlled. On these models, electrical solenoids are used to better control the hydraulic fluid. Usually, the solenoids are regulated by an electronic control module.**

There are two pressures which affect the operation of these valves. One is the governor pressure which is effected by vehicle speed. The other is the modulator pressure which is effected by intake manifold vacuum or throttle position. Governor pressure rises with an increase in vehicle speed, and modulator pressure rises as the throttle is opened wider. By responding to these two pressures, the shift valves cause the upshift points to be delayed with increased throttle opening to make the best use of the engine's power output.

Most transmissions also make use of an auxiliary circuit for downshifting. This circuit may be actuated by the throttle linkage the vacuum line which actuates the modulator, by a cable or by a solenoid. It applies pressure to a special downshift surface on the shift valve or valves.

The transmission modulator also governs the line pressure, used to actuate the servos. In this way, the clutches and bands will be actuated with a force matching the torque output of the engine.

## Identification

The transmissions can be quickly identified visually. The word Powerglide is embossed on the right side of the Powerglide case. The Turbo Hydra-Matic 350 has an almost square shaped pan with the right rear corner cut off diagonally; the 400 has an irregularly shaped pan. The Turbo Hydra-Matic 350 has a cable operated downshift linkage connected the the carburetor throttle linkage, while the 400 has an electrical downshift switch on the accelerator linkage.

## Adjustments

### SHIFT LINKAGE

**Powerglide Transmission**
▶ **See Figure 24**

1. Loosen the shift rod adjusting nut at the bottom of the steering column. Set the transmission lever in Drive (D). Deter-

mine Drive by shifting the lever all the way to the right to the Low (L) detent. Rotate it back to the left, one detent, to Drive (D).
2. Attach the control rod to the lever and inner lever of the shaft assembly with the retainers.
3. Assembly the swivel, clamp, grommet, bushing, washers, and nut loosely on the selector lever.
4. Attach the control rod to the outer lever of the shaft assembly with the retainer.
5. Place the selector lever tang in Neutral drive gate of the selector plate assembly and insert the control rod into the swivel.
6. Rotate the lever at the bottom of the column clockwise viewed looking down the steering column, until the tang contacts the Drive side of the Neutral/Drive gate.
7. Tighten the nut.

**Turbo Hydra-Matic Transmissions**

*MODELS THROUGH 1976*
▶ **See Figure 25**

1. Lift the selector lever toward the steering wheel and allow the selector lever to be positioned in Drive by the detent. Do not use the selector lever pointer as a reference.
2. Release the selector lever. The lever should not be able to go into Low unless the lever is lifted.
3. Lift the selector lever toward the steering wheel and allow the lever to be positioned in Neutral by the transmission detent.
4. Release the selector lever. The lever should not be able to engage reverse unless the lever is lifted. A properly adjusted linkage will prevent the lever from moving beyond both the Neutral and Drive detents unless the lever is lifted.
5. If adjustment is required, remove the screw and spring washer from the swivel clamp
6. Set the transmission lever in Neutral by moving it counterclockwise to 1 and then 3 detents clockwise.
7. Put the transmission selector lever in Neutral as determined by the mechanical stop in the steering column.
8. Assembly the swivel spring and washer to the lever and tighten.
9. Readjust the Neutral safety switch if necessary.
10. If the indicator pointer fails to line up properly with the gear symbol, adjust the position of the pointer and scale.

*1977-81 MODELS*
▶ **See Figure 26**

Perform the procedure exactly and in the order presented. Failure to do so may lead to premature transmission failure due to operation without the controls in the full detent position. Such operation will result in reduced oil pressure, and therefore only partial engagement of the drive clutches. Partial engagement of the clutches with sufficient pressure to cause apparent normal operation will result in transmission failure after only a few miles of operation.

1. Remove the nut (F) and slide off the washers, grommet, bushing and clamp (E). Remove swivel (D).
2. Remove the retainer, grommets and the transmission lever (C) from the shaft assembly.
3. Set the transmission lever (C) in the Neutral position either by moving the lever (C) counterclockwise to the L1 posi-

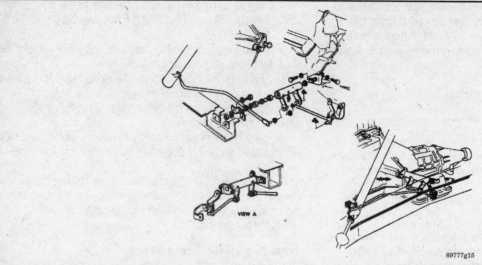

**Fig. 24 Exploded view of the Powerglide shift linkage adjustment**

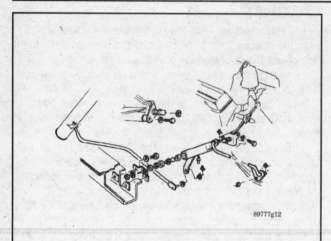

**Fig. 25 Turbo Hydra-Matic shift linkage adjustment — models through 1976**

tion, then clockwise 3 steps to the Neutral position, or by moving the lever (C) clockwise to the Park position, then counterclockwise 2 steps to the Neutral position.

4. Set the column shift lever in the Neutral position by rotating the shift lever until it locks into the stop in the column. Do not use the gear select pointer as a reference to position the column shift lever.

5. Attach rod (A) to the shaft assembly (B) as shown.

6. Slide the swivel (D) and the clamp (E) onto rod (A). Align the column shift lever and loosely attach the assembly.

7. Hold the column shift lever against the Neutral stop, on the Park position side.

8. Tighten the nut (F) to 18 ft. lbs. (24 Nm).

9. Adjust the indicator needle if necessary. It may also be necessary to adjust the neutral start switch.

### 1982 AND LATER MODELS
▶ See Figure 27

1. Set the trans lever (A) in the neutral position by moving it clockwise to the **P** detent, then counterclockwise 2 dents to **N**.

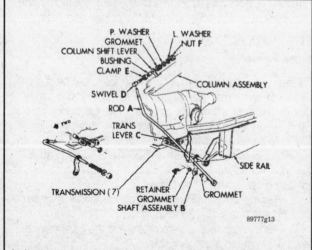

**Fig. 26 Turbo Hydra-Matic shift linkage adjustment — 1977-81 models**

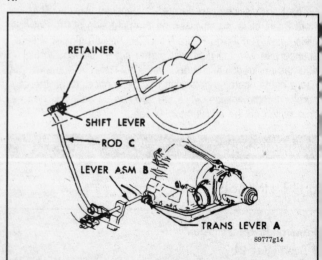

**Fig. 27 Turbo Hydra-Matic shift linkage adjustment — 1982 and later models, column shift shown**

2. Set the column shift lever to the **N** gate notch, by rotating it until the shift lever drops into the **N** gate. Do not use the indicator pointer as a reference to position the shift lever, as this will not be accurate.

3. Attach rod (C) to the transmission shaft assembly as shown.

4. Slide the swivel and clamp onto rod (C) and align it with the column shift lever. Complete the attachment.

5. Hold the column lever against the **N** stop on the **P** position side. Tighten the nut.

## LOW BAND

➡ **Only the Powerglide transmission has bands requiring adjustment; the Turbo Hydra-Matic uses non-adjustable clutches.**

1. Raise and support the vehicle.
2. Place the selector lever in Neutral.
3. Remove the protective cap from the low band adjusting screw on the left side of the transmission.
4. Loosen the adjusting screw locknut ¼ turn and hold it in this position with a wrench.
5. Using an in.lb. torque wrench, adjust the band adjusting screw to 70 in. lbs. (7 Nm), and back the screw off 4 complete turns for a band that has been in operation more than 6000 miles (9654 km), or 3 complete turns for a band that has been in operation less than 6,000 miles.

➡ **The back-off figure is not approximate; it must be exact.**

6. Tighten the adjusting screw locknut.
7. Lower the vehicle and road test.

## Neutral Start Switch

This switch prevents the engine from being started unless the transmission is in Neutral or Park. It is located on the shift linkage on the left side of the transmission. The switch is also used for the back-up lights.

## REMOVAL & INSTALLATION

▶ **See Figure 28**

1. Loosen the clamp on the switch actuating rod on models through 1973 or loosen the switch mounting screws on 1974 and later models.
2. Make sure the transmission is in Neutral.
3. Insert a pin through the hole in the switch actuating arm into the switch body to hold the switch in the Neutral position. Adjust as necessary to make the pin fit.
4. Tighten the adjustment. Remove the pin.
5. Check that the engine can be started only in Park and Neutral and that the backup lights go on only in Reverse. Adjust as necessary.

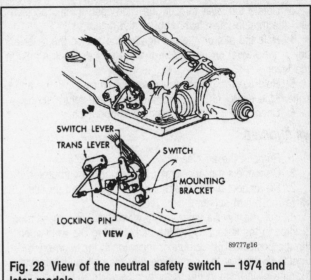

**Fig. 28 View of the neutral safety switch — 1974 and later models**

## Throttle Valve Cable

## ADJUSTMENT

**Powerglide Transmission**

*1967-70 INLINE 6-CYLINDER ENGINE*

1. With the accelerator depressed, the bellcrank on the engine must be in the wide open throttle position.
2. The firewall lever must be ¹⁄₆₄-¹⁄₁₆ in. (0.39-1.6mm) off the lever stop and the transmission lever must be against the transmission internal stop.

*1971 INLINE 6-CYLINDER ENGINE*

▶ **See Figure 29**

1. Remove the air cleaner.
2. Disconnect the throttle return spring.

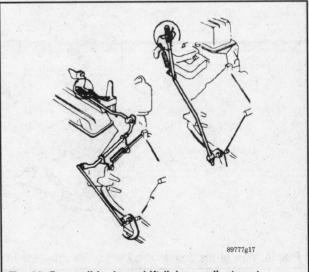

**Fig. 29 Powerglide downshift linkage adjustment**

3. Rotate the lever through the wide open throttle position and the throttle valve lever through the detent.

4. Hold the slot on the rod against the pin on the lever and adjust the swivel on the rod so that it freely enters the hold in the lever.

5. Hold the rod perpendicular to the pin on the lever and tighten the swivel nut. Connect the carburetor return spring.

6. Check the linkage for freedom of operation.

### V8 ENGINES

1. Remove the air cleaner.
2. Disconnect the accelerator linkage at the carburetor.
3. Disconnect the accelerator return spring and throttle valve rod return springs.
4. Pull the throttle valve rod forward until the transmission is through the detent. Open the carburetor to the wide open throttle position. The carburetor must reach the wide open throttle position at the same time that the ball stud contacts the end of the slot in the upper throttle valve rod.
5. Adjust the swivel on the end of the upper throttle valve rod as per Step 4. The allowable tolerance is approximately $\frac{1}{32}$ in. (0.79mm).
6. Connect and adjust the accelerator linkage.
7. Check for freedom of operation. Install the air cleaner.

### Turbo Hydra-Matic 350 Transmission

#### 1969-71 MODELS

▶ See Figure 30

1. Remove the air cleaner.
2. Loosen the detent cable screw.
3. With the choke off and the accelerator linkage adjusted, position the carburetor lever in the wide open position.
4. Pull the detent cable rearward until the wide open throttle stop in the transmission is felt. The cable must be pulled through the detent position to reach the wide open throttle stop.

5. Tighten the detent cable screw and check the linkage for proper operation.

#### 1972 MODELS

1. Remove the air cleaner.
2. Pry up on each side of the snaplock with a screwdriver to release the lock.
3. Compress the locking tabs and disconnect the locking tabs from the bracket.
4. Pull the carburetor to the wide open throttle position against the stop on the carburetor.
5. With the carburetor held in this position, pull the cable housing rearward (through the detent) until the wide open throttle stop in the transmission is felt.
6. Push the snaplock on the cable downward until it is flush with the cable.
7. Do not lubricate the cable. Install the air cleaner.

#### 1973 AND LATER MODELS

▶ See Figure 31

With the snaplock disengaged from the bracket, position the carburetor at the wide open throttle position. Push the snaplock downward until the top is flush with the rest of the cable.

## Downshift Switch

### REMOVAL & INSTALLATION

➡**This procedure applies to Turbo Hydra-Matic 400 transmissions only.**

Unplug the harness from the switch. Remove the fasteners and remove the switch from the linkage. When installing a new downshift switch, press the plunger as far forward as possible. The switch will adjust itself when the accelerator is pressed to the floor.

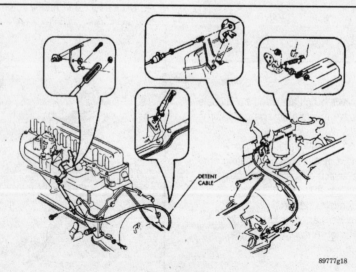

89777g18

**Fig. 30 View of the downshift cable adjustment — 1969-71 models**

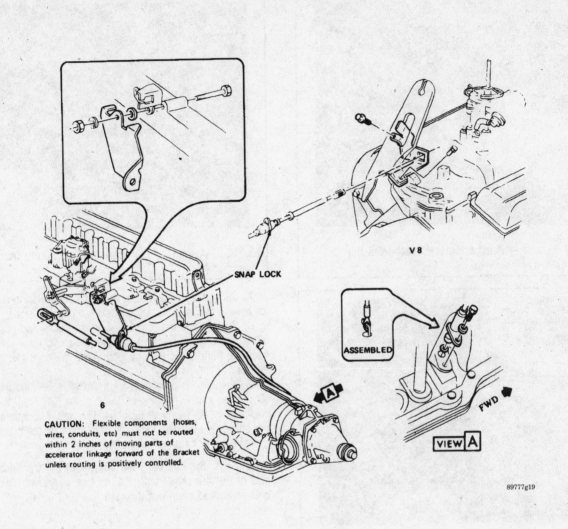

SNAP LOCK

V 8

ASSEMBLED

FWD

VIEW A

6

CAUTION: Flexible components (hoses, wires, conduits, etc) must not be routed within 2 inches of moving parts of accelerator linkage forward of the Bracket unless routing is positively controlled.

89777g19

**Fig. 31 View of the downshift cable with snaplock — 1973 and later models**

## Automatic Transmission Assembly

### REMOVAL & INSTALLATION

◗ See Figures 32, 33, 34 and 35

➡ It would be best to drain the transmission before starting.

1. Disconnect the battery ground cable. Disconnect the downshift cable at the carburetor.
2. Raise and support the truck.
3. Remove the driveshaft, after matchmarking its flange.
4. Disconnect the speedometer cable, downshift cable, vacuum modulator line, shift linkage, and fluid cooler lines at the transmission.
5. Support the transmission and unbolt the rear mount from the crossmember. Remove the crossmember.
6. Remove the converter underpan, matchmark the flywheel and converter, and remove the converter bolts.

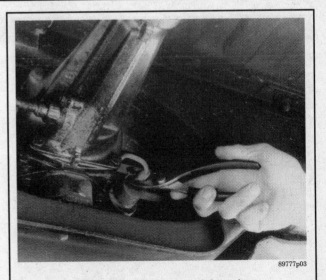

89777p03

**Fig. 32 Disconnect the vacuum modulator hose . . .**

Fig. 33 . . . and the speedometer cable from the transmission

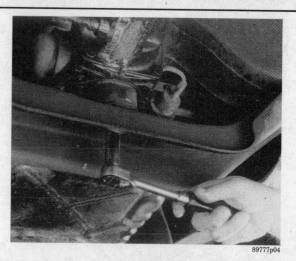

Fig. 35 Unfasten the rear transmission mount from the crossmember

7. Support the engine and lower the transmission slightly for access to the upper transmission to engine bolts.

8. Remove the transmission to engine bolts and pull the transmission back. Remove the filler tube. Rig up a strap or keep the front of the transmission up so the converter doesn't fall out.

9. Reverse the procedure for installation. Bolt the transmission to the engine first tighten to 35 ft. lbs. (47 Nm), then the converter to the flywheel 35 ft. lbs. (47 Nm). Make sure that the converter attaching lugs are flush and that the converter can turn freely before installing the bolts.

➡Lubricate the internal yoke splines at the transmission end of the driveshaft with lithium based grease. The grease should seep out through the vent hole.

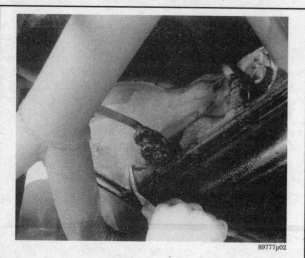

Fig. 34 Pull out the cotter pin, then disconnect the shift linkage from the transmission

## DRIVELINE

Tubular driveshafts are used on all models incorporating needle bearing U-joints. An internally splined sleeve at the forward end compensates for variation in distance between the rear axle and the transmission.

Long wheelbase models use a 2-piece driveshaft with a center support bearing. The front section is supported at the rear end by a rubber cushioned ball bearing mounted in a bracket attached to the frame crossmember. The ball bearing is permanently sealed and lubricated.

## Driveshaft and U-Joints

### REMOVAL & INSTALLATION

▶ See Figures 36, 37, 38, 39 and 40

1. Raise the vehicle and support it on jackstands. There is less chance of lubricant leakage from the rear of the transmission if the rear is raised.

2. Matchmark the driveshaft and rear pinion flange and both halves of 2-piece driveshaft. Remove the U-bolts or straps at the rear axle. Tape the bearing cups to the trunnions.

3. On models with 2-piece driveshaft, remove the bolts attaching the bearing support to the frame crossmember.

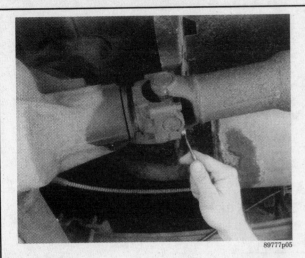

**Fig. 36 Remove the straps retaining the driveshaft to the differential**

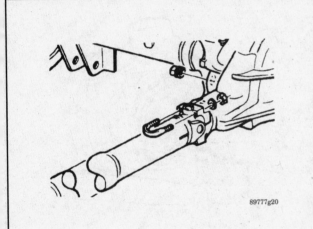

**Fig. 37 View of a common rear driveshaft U-bolt attachment**

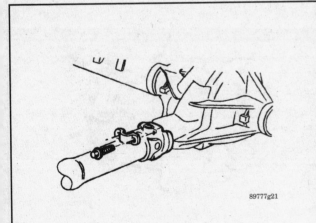

**Fig. 38 View of a common rear driveshaft strap attachment**

4. Slide the driveshaft forward and lower it. Slide the driveshaft toward the rear of the vehicle and disengage the splined sleeve from the output shaft of the transmission.

5. Remove the driveshaft from under the van.

6. Installation is the reverse of removal. Use the matchmarks made previously to help facilitate alignment. For models with 2-piece driveshaft, install the front half into the transmission and install the support to the crossmember. Rotate the shaft so that the front U-joint trunnions so that all are vertical. Rotate the rear shaft 4 splines to the left of the vehicle and connect the front and rear shaft. Some 2-piece driveshafts can only be assembled one way, in which case these instructions can be ignored. Attach the rear U-joint to the axle. On automatic transmission models, lubricate the internal yoke splines at the transmission end of the shaft with lithium base grease. The grease should seep out through the vent hole.

➡A thump in the rear driveshaft sometimes occurs when releasing the brakes after braking to a stop, especially on a downgrade. This is most common with automatic transmission. It is often caused by the driveshaft splines binding and can be cured by removing the driveshaft, inspecting the splines for rough spots or sharp edges, and carefully lubricating. A similar noise may also be caused by the clutch plates in Positraction (through 1973) limited slip rear axles binding. If this isn't caused by wear, it can be cured by draining and refilling the rear axle with the special lubricant and adding Positraction additive, both of which are available from dealers.

## U-JOINT OVERHAUL

U-Joint is mechanic's jargon for universal joint. U-joints should not be confused with U-bolts, which are U-shaped bolts used to hold U-joints in place to the axle or transfer case.

There are two types of U-joints used in these trucks. The first is held together by wire snaprings in the yokes. The second type, first used in 1975, is held together with injection molded plastic retainer rings. This type cannot be reassembled, once disassembled. Repair kits are available, however.

**Snapring Type**
▶ See Figures 41, 42 and 43

These U-joints may be found on all model years.

1. Remove the driveshaft(s) from the truck.
2. Support the lockrings from the yoke and remove the lubrication fitting.
3. Support the yoke in a bench vise. Never clamp the driveshaft tube.
4. Use a socket to press against one trunnion bearing to press the opposite bearing from the yoke.
5. Grasp the cap and work it out.
6. Support the other side of the yoke and press the other bearing cap from the yoke and remove as in Steps 4 and 5.
7. Remove the trunnion from the driveshaft yoke.
8. If equipped with a sliding sleeve, remove the trunnion bearings from the sleeve yoke in the same manner as above. Remove the seal retainer from the end of the sleeve and pull the seal and washer from the retainer.

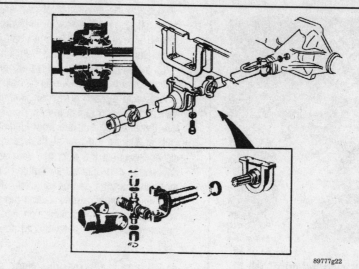

89777g22

Fig. 39 Common two-piece driveshaft mounting

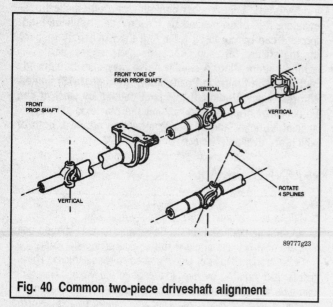

89777g23

Fig. 40 Common two-piece driveshaft alignment

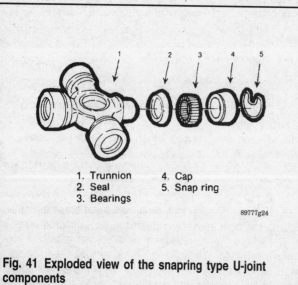

1. Trunnion     4. Cap
2. Seal         5. Snap ring
3. Bearings

89777g24

Fig. 41 Exploded view of the snapring type U-joint components

89777g25

Fig. 42 Installing the trunnion on the driveshaft yoke

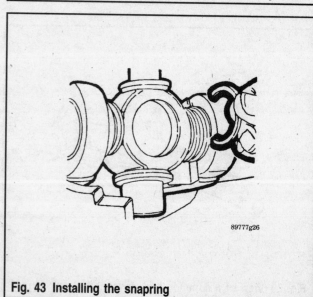

89777g26

Fig. 43 Installing the snapring

9. Disassemble the other U-joint. Clean and check the condition of all parts. You can buy U-joint repair kits to replace all the wearing parts.

**To assemble:**

10. Repack the bearings with grease and replace the trunnion dust seals after any operation that requires disassembly of the U-joint. Be sure that the lubricant reservoir at the end of the trunnion is full of lubricant. Fill the reservoirs with lubricant from the bottom.

11. Install the trunnion into the driveshaft yoke and press the bearings into the yoke over the trunnion hubs as far as it will go.

12. Install the lockrings.

13. Hold the trunnion in one hand and tap the yoke slightly to seat the bearings against the lockrings.

14. Replace the driveshaft.

### Molded Retainer Type

This type is found only on some 1975 and later models. It is held together with injection molded plastic rings.

➡**Don't disassemble these joints unless you have a repair kit. The factory installed joints cannot be reassembled.**

1. Remove the driveshaft.

2. Support the driveshaft in a horizontal position. Place the U-joint so that the lower ear of the shaft yoke is supported by a 1⅛ in. (28mm) socket. Press the lower bearing cup of the yoke ear. This will shear the plastic retaining the lower bearing cup.

➡**Never clamp the driveshaft tubing in a vise.**

3. If the bearing cup is not completely removed, lift the cross, insert a spacer and press the cup completely out.

4. Rotate the driveshaft, shear the opposite plastic retainer, and press the other bearing cup out in the same manner.

5. Remove the cross from the yoke. Production U-joints cannot be reassembled. There are no bearing retainer grooves in the cups. Discard all parts that were removed and substitute those in the overhaul kit.

6. Remove the sheared plastic bearing retainer from the yoke. Drive a small pin or punch through the injection holes to aid in removal.

7. If the other U-joint is to be serviced, remove the bearing cups from the slip yoke in the manner previously described.

8. Be sure that the seals are installed on the service bearing cups to hold the needle bearings in place for handling. Grease the bearings if they aren't pregreased.

**To assemble:**

9. Install one bearing cup partway into one side of the yoke and turn this ear to the bottom.

10. Insert the cross into the yoke so that the trunnion seats freely in the bearing cup.

11. Install the opposite bearing cup partway. Be sure that both trunnions are started straight into the bearing cups.

12. Press against opposite bearing cups, working the cross constantly to be sure that it is free in the cups. If binding occurs, check the needle rollers to be sure that one needle has not become lodged under the end of the trunnion.

13. As soon as one bearing retainer groove is exposed, stop pressing and install the bearing retainer snapring.

14. Continue to press until the opposite bearing retainer can be installed. If difficulty installing the snaprings is encountered, rap the yoke with a hammer to spring the yoke ears slightly.

15. Assemble the other half of the U-joint in the same manner.

16. Check that the cross is free in the cups. If it is too tight, rap the yoke ears again to help seat the bearing retainers.

17. Replace the driveshaft.

## Center Bearing

### REMOVAL & INSTALLATION

Center bearings support the driveline when two or more driveshafts are used. The center bearing is a ball type bearing mounted in a rubber cushion that is attached to the frame crossmember. The bearing is pre-lubricated and sealed by the manufacturer.

The center bearing is secured to the frame crossmember by two bolts, washers and nuts. Support the driveshafts properly and remove the bolts from the center bearing. Remove the rear driveshaft from the axle housing and separate the two shafts. Then slide the center bearing off. Reverse the procedure to install.

Make sure that the driveshafts are properly supported before removing the bolts from the center bearing. The shafts may fall if not supported properly, once the center bearing is unbolted.

## REAR AXLE

## Identification

On 1974 and earlier models the serial number is located on the bottom flange of the differential housing. 1975 and later models have the serial number stamped into the axle shafts, near the differential housing.

## Determining Axle Ratio

Axle ratios offered in these trucks vary from a heavy duty ratio of 4.57:1 to an economy ratio of 2.73:1.

The axle ratio is obtained by dividing the number of teeth on the drive pinion gear into the larger number of teeth on the ring gear. It is always expressed as a proportion and is a simple expression of gear speed reduction and torque multiplication.

To find a unknown axle ratio, make a chalk mark on a tire and on the driveshaft. Move the truck ahead (or back) slowly for one tire rotation and have an observer note the number of driveshaft rotations. The number of driveshaft rotations if the axle ratio. You can get more accuracy by going more than one tire rotation and dividing the result by the number of tire rotations. This can also be done by jacking up both rear wheels and turning them by hand.

The axle ration is also identified by the axle serial number prefix on Chevrolet (GMC) axles. See Section 1 for serial number locations; the prefixes are listed in parts books. Dana axles usually have a tag under one of the cover bolts, giving either the ratio or the number of pinion ring gear teeth.

## Axle Shaft, Bearing, and Seal

### REMOVAL & INSTALLATION

**Semi-Floating Axles**

*EXCEPT 1974-86 LOCKING DIFFERENTIAL*

▶ See Figures 44, 45, 46, 47, 48, 49, 50, 51, 52, 53, 54 and 55

1. Support the axle on jackstands.
2. Remove the wheels and brake drums.

Fig. 46 Using a prytool, separate the cover from the differential case to drain the fluid

Fig. 44 Use a wire brush to clean the dirt and rust from the differential cover

Fig. 47 Remove the cover from the case

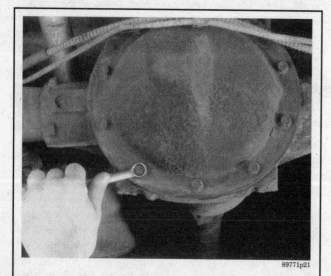

Fig. 45 Unfasten the bolts from the cover

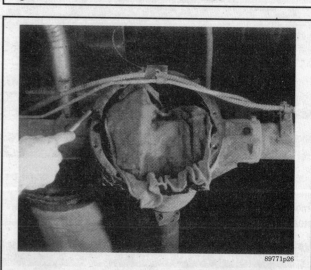

Fig. 48 Cover the differential gears with a rag before cleaning the old gasket from the case

Fig. 49 Unfasten the differential pinion shaft lockscrew

Fig. 50 Remove the lockscrew from the differential

Fig. 51 Remove the pinon shaft

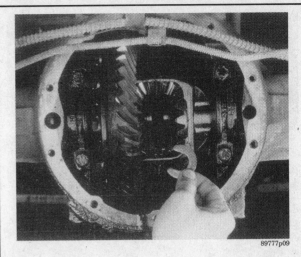

Fig. 52 Remove the C-lock from the inner end of the shaft

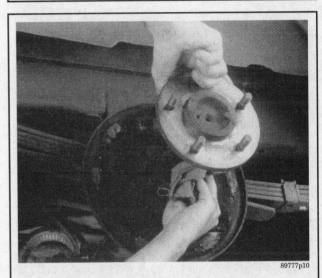

Fig. 53 Remove the axle shaft from the vehicle

Fig. 54 Remove the axle seal using a puller

89777p12

**Fig. 55 Seating a new axle shaft using a seal installer**

3. Clean off the differential cover area, loosen the cover to drain the lubricant, and remove the cover.

4. Turn the differential until you can reach the differential pinion shaft lockscrew. Remove the lockscrew and the pinion shaft.

5. Push in on the axle end. Remove the C-lock from the inner (button) end of the shaft.

6. Remove the shaft, being careful of the oil seal.

7. You can pry the oil seal out of the housing by placing the inner end of the axle shaft behind the steel case of the seal, then prying it out carefully.

8. A puller or a slide hammer is required to remove the bearing from the housing.

9. Pack the new or reused bearing with wheel bearing grease and lubricate the cavity between the seal lips with the same grease.

10. The bearing has to be driven into the housing. Don't use a drift, you might cock the bearing in its bore. Use a piece of pipe or a large socket instead. Drive only on the outer bearing race. In a similar manner, drive the seal in flush with the end of the tube.

11. Slide the shaft into place, turning it slowly until the splines are engaged with the differential. Be careful of the oil seal.

12. Install the C-lock on the inner axle end. Pull the shaft out so that the C-lock seats in the counterbore of the differential side gear.

13. Position the differential pinion shaft through the case and the pinion gears, aligning the lockscrew hole. Install the lockscrew.

14. Install the cover with a new gasket and tighten the bolts evenly in a criss-cross pattern.

15. Fill the axle with lubricant as specified in Section 1.

16. Replace the brake drums and wheels.

### 1974-86 LOCKING DIFFERENTIAL

▶ See Figure 56

This axle uses a thrust block on the differential pinion shaft.

1. Follow Steps 1-3 of the preceding procedure.

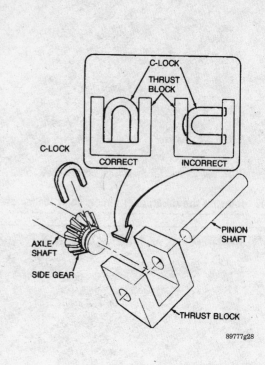

89777g28

**Fig. 56 View of the C-lock and thrust block installation — Eaton locking differential used in 1974 and later models with semi-floating axle**

2. Rotate the differential case so that you can remove the lockscrew and support the pinion shaft so it can't fall into the housing. Remove the differential pinion shaft lockscrew.

3. Carefully pull the pinion shaft partway out and rotate the differential case until the shaft touches the housing at the top.

4. Use a screwdriver to position the C-lock with its open end directly inward. You can't push in the axle shaft till you do this.

5. Push the axle shaft in and remove the C-lock.

6. Follow Steps 6-11 of the preceding procedure.

7. Keep the pinion shaft partway out of the differential case while installing the C-lock on the axle shaft. Put the C-lock on the axle shaft and carefully pull out on the axle shaft until the C-lock is clear of the thrust block.

8. Follow Steps 13-16 of the previous procedure.

### Full-Floating Axles

▶ See Figure 57

The procedures are the same for locking and non-locking axles.

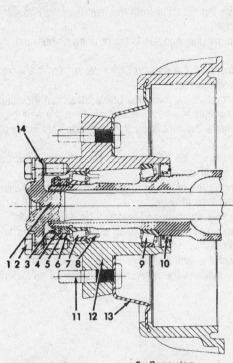

**Fig. 57 View of the full-floating axle bearing and hub components**

1. Axle shaft
2. Shaft-to-hub bolt
3. Locknut
4. Locknut retainer
5. Adjusting nut
6. Thrust washer
7. Hub outer bearing
8. Snap ring
9. Hub inner bearing
10. Oil seal
11. Wheel bolt
12. Hub assembly
13. Drum assembly
14. Gasket

89777g29

The best way to remove the bearings from the wheel hub is with an arbor press. Use of a press reduces the chances of damaging the bearing races, cocking the bearing in its bore, or scoring the hub walls. A local machine shop is probably equipped with the tools to remove and install bearings and seals. However, if one is not available, the hammer and drift method outlined can be used.

1. Support the axles on jackstands.
2. Remove the wheels.
3. Remove the bolts and lock washers that attach the axle shaft flange to the hub.
4. On 1971-72 trucks, install two 1/2x13 in. bolts in the threaded holes provided in the axle shaft flange. By turning these bolts alternately the axle shaft may be easily started and then removed from the housing.
5. On 1973 and later vans, rap on the flange with a soft faced hammer to loosen the shaft. Grip the rib on the end of the flange with a pair of locking pliers and twist to start shaft removal. Remove the shaft from the axle tube.
6. The hub and drum assembly must be removed to remove the bearings and oil seals. You will need a large socket

to remove and later adjust the bearing adjustment nut. There are also special tools available.

7. Disengage the tang of the locknut retainer from the slot or slat of the locknut, then remove the locknut from the housing tube.
8. Disengage the tang of the retainer from the slot or flat of the adjusting nut and remove the retainer from the housing tube.
9. Remove the adjusting nut from the housing tube.
10. Remove the thrust washer from the housing tube.
11. Pull the hub and drum straight off the axle housing.
12. Remove the oil seal and discard.
13. Use a hammer and a long drift to knock the inner bearing, cup, and oil seal from the hub assembly.
14. Remove the outer bearing snapring with a pair of pliers. It may be necessary to tap the bearing outer race away from the retaining ring slightly by tapping on the ring to remove the ring.
15. Drive the outer bearing from the hub with a hammer and drift.
16. To reinstall the bearings, place the outer bearing into the hub. The larger outside diameter of the bearing should face the outer end of the hub. Drive the bearing into the hub using a washer that will cover both the inner and outer races of the bearing. Place a socket on top of this washer, then drive the bearing into place with a series of light taps. If available, an arbor press should be used for this job.
17. Drive the bearing past the snapring groove, and install the snapring. Then, turning the hub assembly over, drive the bearing back against the snapring. Protect the bearing by placing a washer on top of it. You can use the thrust washer that fits between the bearing and the adjusting nut for the job.
18. Place the inner bearing into the hub. The thick edge should be toward the shoulder in the hub. Press the bearing into the hub until it seats against the shoulder, using a washer and socket as outlined earlier. Make certain that the bearing is not cocked and that it is fully seated on the shoulder.
19. Pack the cavity between the oil seal lips with the front wheel bearing grease specified in Section 9, and position it in the hub bore. Carefully press it into place on top of the inner bearing.
20. Pack the wheel bearings with grease, and lightly coat the inside diameter of the hub bearing contact surface and the outside diameter of the axle housing tube.
21. Make sure that the inner bearing, oil seal, axle housing oil deflector, and outer bearing are properly positioned. Install the hub and drum assembly on the axle housing, being careful so as not to damage the oil seal or dislocate other internal components.
22. Install the thrust washer so that the tang on the inside diameter of the washer is in the keyway on the axle housing.
23. Install the adjusting nut. Tighten to 50 ft. lbs. (67 Nm) while rotating the hub. Back off the nut and retighten to 35 ft. lbs. (47 Nm), then back off 1/4 turn.
24. Install the tanged retainer against the inner adjusting nut. Align the adjusting nut so that the short tang of the retainer will engage the nearest slot on the adjusting nut.
25. Install the outer locknut and tighten to 65 ft. lbs. (88 Nm). Bend the long tang of the retainer into the slot of the outer nut. This method of adjustment should provide 0.001-0.010 in. (0.0254-0.254mm) end play.

26. Place a new gasket over the axle shaft and position the axle shaft in the housing so that the shaft splines enter the differential side gear. Position the gasket so that the holes are in alignment, and install the flange-to-hub attaching bolts. Tighten to 90 ft. lbs. (122 Nm) through 1975, 115 ft. lbs. (155 Nm) for 1976 and later.

➡️**To prevent lubricant from leaking through the flange holes, apply a non-hardening sealer to the bolt threads. Use the sealer sparingly.**

27. Replace the wheels.

## Axle Housing

### REMOVAL & INSTALLATION

Raise the vehicle on a hoist and support the axle assembly with a suitable lifting devise. For the 9¾ in. (247.65mm) ring gear and the 10½ in. (266.7mm) ring gear axles, raise the vehicle and place jackstands under the frame side rails for support.

1. Drain the lubricant from the axle housing and remove the driveshaft.
2. Remove the wheel, the brake drum or hub and the drum assembly.
3. Disconnect the parking brake cable from the lever and at the brake flange plate.
4. Disconnect the hydraulic brake lines from the connectors
5. Disconnect the shock absorbers from the axle brackets.
6. Remove the vent hose from the axle vent fitting (if used).
7. Disconnect the height sensing and brake proportional valve linkage (if used).
8. Support the stabilizer shaft assembly with a hydraulic jack and remove (if used).
9. Remove the nuts and washers from the U-bolts.
10. Remove the U-bolts, spring plates and spacers from the axle assembly.
11. Lower the jack and remove the axle assembly.
12. Installation is the reverse of the removal procedure.

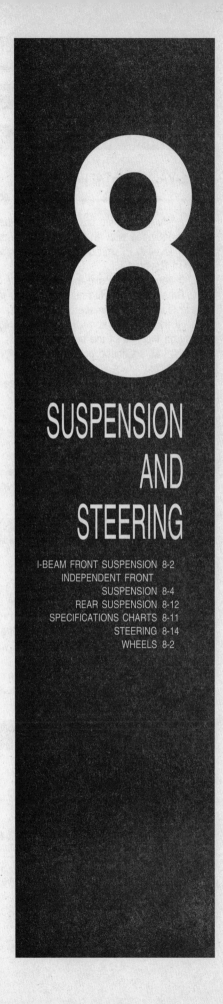

# 8

# SUSPENSION AND STEERING

## WHEELS

### Wheel and Tire

#### REMOVAL & INSTALLATION

1. Apply the parking brake and block the opposite wheel.
2. If equipped with an automatic transmission, place the selector lever in **P**; with a manual transmission, place the shifter in Reverse.
3. If equipped, remove the wheel cover or hub cap.
4. Break loose the lug nuts. If a nut is stuck, never use heat to loosen it or damage to the wheel and bearings may occur. If the nuts are seized, one or two heavy hammer blows directly on the end of the bolt head usually loosens the rust. Be careful as continued pounding will likely damage the brake drum or rotor.
5. Raise the vehicle until the tire is clear of the ground. Support the vehicle safely using jackstands.
6. Remove the lug nuts, then remove the tire and wheel assembly.

**To install:**

7. Make sure the wheel and hub mating surfaces, as well as the wheel lug studs, are clean and free of all foreign material. Always remove rust from the wheel mounting surfaces and the brake rotors/drums. Failure to do so may cause the lug nuts to loosen in service.

8. Position the wheel on the hub or drum and hand-tighten the lug nuts. Make sure that the coned ends face inward.
9. Tighten all the lug nuts, in a crisscross pattern, until they are snug.
10. Remove the supports, if any, and lower the vehicle. Tighten the lug nuts, in a crisscross pattern. Always use a torque wrench to achieve the proper lug nut torque and to prevent stretching the wheel studs.
11. Repeat the torque pattern to assure proper wheel tightening.
12. If equipped, install the hub cab or wheel cover.

#### INSPECTION

Check the wheels for any damage. They must be replaced if they are bent, dented, heavily rusted, have elongated bolt holes, or have excessive lateral or radial run-out. Wheels with excessive run-out may cause a high-speed vehicle vibration.

Replacement wheels must be of the same load capacity, diameter, width, offset and mounting configuration as the original wheels. Using the wrong wheels may affect wheel bearing life, ground and tire clearance, or speedometer and odometer calibrations.

## I-BEAM FRONT SUSPENSION

▶ See Figure 1

Chevrolet and GMC vans from 1967-70 use an I-beam front axle with tapered leaf springs and a single shock absorber at each wheel. The I-beam is a conventional reverse Elliot type using solid kingpins and full-floating steering knuckle bushings. The front wheel spindles are cast integral with the steering knuckles.

A stabilizer (sway) bar is optional to minimize body lean and sway in curves. Heavy duty shock absorbers and springs have been optional on most models.

### Leaf Springs

#### REMOVAL & INSTALLATION

1. Raise and support the van.
2. Support the axle with a floor jack so that the weight is taken off the spring.
3. Remove the spring-to-axle U-bolts.
4. Remove the front and rear spring eye bolts and remove the spring from the van.

5. Installation is the reverse of removal. Position the spring so that the head of the center bolt is indexed with the axle spring seat. After the springs are attache, lower the van to the ground and bounce the front end up and down several times. Then torque the nuts and bolts as follows:
- Leaf Spring U-bolt: 80 ft. lbs. (108 Nm)
- Leaf Spring (front): 75 ft. lbs. (101 Nm)
- Leaf Spring (rear): 50 ft. lbs. (67 Nm)

### Shock Absorbers

#### TESTING

The usual procedure for testing shock absorbers is to stand on the bumper at the end nearest the shock being tested and start the vehicle bouncing up and down. Step off; the vehicle should come to rest within one bounce cycle. The stiffness of the suspension on some models makes this rather difficult, unless you are a very "substantial" individual. Another good test is to drive the vehicle over a bumpy road. Bouncing over bumps is normal, but the shock absorbers should stop the bouncing after the bump is passed, within one or two cycles.

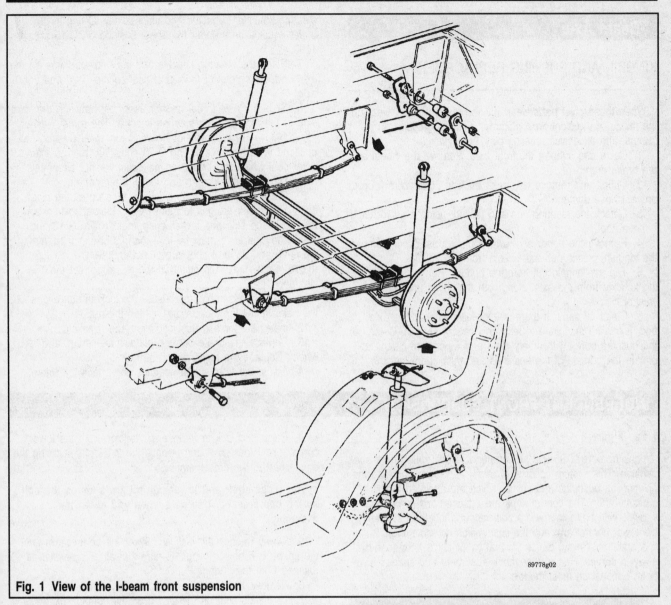

89778g02

**Fig. 1 View of the I-beam front suspension**

## REMOVAL & INSTALLATION

▶ **See Figure 2**

The usual procedure is to replace shock absorbers in axle pairs, to provide equal damping. Heavy duty replacements are available for firmer control.

1. Raise and support the front end as necessary.
2. Remove the bolt and nut from the lower shock end.
3. Remove the upper bolt and nut.
4. Purge the new shock of air by extending it in its normal position and compressing it while inverted. Do this several times. It is normal for there to be more resistance to extension than to compression.
5. Install the shock absorber. Tighten the shock bolts to 75 ft. lbs. (101 Nm) except for the 1967-70 lower bolt; tighten these to 55 ft. lbs. (74 Nm).

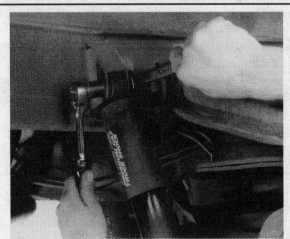

89778p01

**Fig. 2 Remove the upper bolt and nut from the shock absorber**

## I-Beam Axle

### KINGPIN AND BUSHING REPLACEMENT

When these pivot parts wear out, the result is rapid wear on the inside of the front tires, shimmy, a clunking sound on bumps, and excessive steering play.

1. Raise and support the front axle. Remove the wheel and the brake drum.

2. Unbolt and remove the brake backing plate. Wire it up to prevent hose damage.

3. Detach the steering arm and tie rod, using a tie rod stud removal tool.

4. Remove the upper and lower kingpin dust caps. Remove the kingpin lockpin nut and lockpin from the axle.

5. Tap the kingpin out from the bottom. Remove the steering knuckle from the axle, along with the shims and thrust washer.

6. Clean all parts. If there is excessive wear in the axle end, it can be machined to take an oversize kingpin. Clean up the bushing bores with emery cloth and wipe them clean. Lubricate the outside of the bushings and push them into the steering knuckle. Lubricate and place a new O-ring in the upper knuckle bore under the upper bushing on G-10 and 1500.

7. Place the steering knuckle and the original shims on the axle end. Be careful of the upper seal on the G-20 and 2500 axle.

8. Slide the new thrust washer assembly between the lower side of the axle and the steering knuckle. The thrust washer assembly is a bronze washer between tow steel washers, all encased in a dust shield. The G-20 and 2500 has an extra outer seal which must go over the thrust washer assembly.

9. Lubricate the kingpin and install it temporarily.

10. Raise the knuckle with a jack to take up all the clearance. Use feeler gauges to measure the clearance between the top of the axle and the steering knuckle. On G-10 and 1500, the clearance must be less than 0.005 in. (0.127mm). On G-20 and 2500, it should be 0.003-0.008 in (0.0762-0.203mm). Add shims at the top to correct the clearance.

11. On final assembly, make sure the lockpin slot aligns with the hole. Install the lockpin and tighten the nut.

12. Install the kingpin dust caps with new gaskets.

13. Replace the brake backing plate, brake drum, and wheel. Replace the steering and tie rods.

14. Adjust the front wheel bearings and check the toe-in.

## INDEPENDENT FRONT SUSPENSION

▶ **See Figure 3**

Vans from 1971-86 use an independent coil spring front suspension. This system consists of upper and lower control arms pivoting on bushings and shafts, which are attached to the crossmember. The control arms are attached to the steering knuckle with ball joints and a coil spring is located between the lower control arm and the suspension crossmember.

A stabilizer (sway) bar is optional to minimize body lean and sway in curves. Heavy duty shock absorbers and springs have been optional on most models.

## Coil Springs

### REMOVAL & INSTALLATION

### ✳✳CAUTION

**The spring is under a great deal of tension! It's best to use a coil spring compressor when removing the spring. Mishandling the spring could cause it to fly out of its mounting, causing a great deal of personal damage!**

1. Raise and support the van under the frame rails. The control arms should hang free.

2. Disconnect the shock absorber at the lower end and move it aside. Disconnect the stabilizer bar (if any) from the lower control arm.

3. Support the cross-shaft with a jack and install a spring compressor or chain the spring to the control arm as a safety precaution.

4. Raise and jack to remove the tension from the lower control arm cross-shaft and remove the 2 U-bolts securing the cross-shaft to the crossmember.

➡**The cross-shaft and lower control arms keeps the coil spring compressed. Use care when you lower the assembly.**

5. Slowly release the jack and lower the control arm until the spring can be removed. Be sure that all compression is relieved from the spring.

6. Remove the spring.

7. To install, position the spring on the control arm and jack it into position. Use the spring compressor again as a precaution.

8. Position the control arm cross-shaft on the crossmember and install the U-bolts. Be sure that the front indexing hole in the cross-shaft is aligned with the crossmember attaching saddle stud.

9. Further installation is the reverse of removal. Have the front suspension alignment checked.

## Upper Control Arm

### REMOVAL & INSTALLATION

1. Raise and support the van on jackstands.

2. Support the lower control arm with a floor jack.

3. Remove the wheel and tire.

4. Remove the cotter pin from the upper control arm ball stud and loosen the stud nut until the bottom surface of the nut is slightly below the end of the stud.

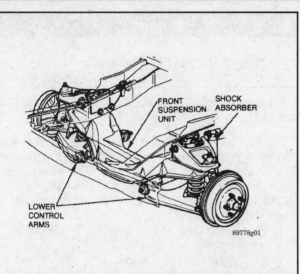

**Fig. 3 View of the independent front suspension**

5. Install a spring compressor on the coil spring for safety.

6. Loosen the upper control arm ball stud in the steering knuckle using a ball joint stud removal tool. Remove the nut from the ball stud and raise the upper arm to clear the steering knuckle. It may be necessary to remove the brake caliper and wire it to the frame to gain clearance. Do not allow the caliper to hang by the brake hose.

7. Remove the nuts securing the control arm shaft studs to the crossmember bracket and remove the control arm.

8. Tape the shims and spacers together and tag for proper reassembly.

9. Installation is the reverse of removal. Place the control arm in position and install the nuts. Before tightening the nuts, insert the caster and camber shims in the same order as when removed. Have the front end alignment checked, and as necessary adjusted.

## Lower Control Arm

### REMOVAL & INSTALLATION

1. Raise and support the van on jackstands.

2. Remove the spring. (Refer to the Coil Spring removal and installation procedure, earlier in this section).

3. Support the inboard end of the control arm after spring removal.

4. Remove the cotter pin from the lower ball stud and loosen the nut.

5. Loosen the lower ball stud in the steering knuckle using a ball joint stud removal tool. When the stud is loose, remove the nut from the stud. It may be necessary to remove the brake caliper and wire it to the frame to gain clearance.

6. Remove the lower control arm.

7. Installation is the reverse of removal.

## Ball Joints

### INSPECTION

▶ **See Figure 4**

Excessive ball joint wear will usually show up as wear on the inside of the front tires. Don't jump to conclusions; front end misalignment can give the same symptom. The lower ball joint gets the most wear due to the distribution of suspension load. The wear limits given are the manufacturer's recommendation; they may not agree with your state's inspection law.

**Upper**

1. Raise and support the van so that the control arms hang free.

2. Remove the wheel.

3. Support the lower control arm with a jackstand and disconnect the upper ball stud from the steering knuckle.

4. On 1971 models, reinstall the nut on the ball stud and measure the torque required to rotate the stud. If it is not within 12-120 inch lbs. (1-13 Nm), replace the joint.

5. On 1972 and later models, the upper ball joint is spring loaded in its socket. If it has any perceptible lateral shake or can be twisted in its socket, it should be replaced.

6. If there are no defects, connect the steering knuckle to the upper stud and torque the nut to 50 ft. lbs. (67 Nm) or 90 ft. lbs. (122 Nm) for G-30 and 3500 models. Tighten the nut further to install the cotter pin but don't exceed 90 ft. lbs. (122 Nm) or 130 ft. lbs. (176 Nm) for G-30 and 3500 models.

**Lower**

1. Support the weight of the control arm at the wheel hub.

2. Measure the distance between the tip of the ball joint stud and the grease fitting below the ball joint.

3. Move the support to the control arm and allow the hub and drum to hang free. Measure the distance again. If the variation between the 2 measurements exceeds 3/32 in. (2.38mm) the ball joint should be replaced.

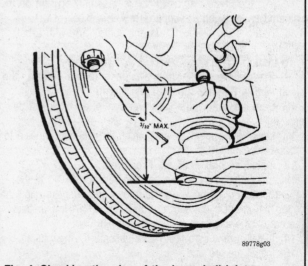

**Fig. 4 Checking the play of the lower ball joint**

## REMOVAL & INSTALLATION

### Upper

1. Raise and support the van.
2. Support the lower control arm with a floor jack.
3. Remove the cotter pin from the upper ball stud and loosen, buy do not remove, the stud nut.
4. Using a ball joint stud removal tool, loosen the ball stud in the steering knuckle. When the stud is loose, remove the tool and the stud nut. It may be necessary to remove the brake caliper and wire it to the frame to gain clearance. Do not allow the caliper to hang by the brake hose.
5. Drill out the rivets. Remove the ball joint assembly.

**To install:**

6. Install the service ball joint, using the nuts supplied. Torque the nuts to 45 ft. lbs. (61 Nm).
7. Torque the ball stud nut as follows: 10 and 1500 Series: 50 ft. lbs. (67 Nm) plus the additional torque to align the cotter pin. Do not exceed 90 ft. lbs. (122 Nm) and never back the nut off to align the pin. 20, 2500, 30, 3500 Series: 90 ft. lbs. (122 Nm) plus additional torque necessary to align the cotter pin. Do not exceed 130 ft. lbs. (176 Nm) and never back off the nut to align the pin.
8. Install a new cotter pin.
9. Install a new lube fitting and lubricate the new joint.
10. If removed, install the brake caliper.
11. Install the tire and lower the van.

### Lower

1. Raise and support the van. Support the lower control arm with a floor jack.
2. Remove the tire and wheel.
3. Remove the lower stud cotter pin and loosen, but do not remove, the stud nut.
4. Loosen the ball joint with a ball joint stud removal tool. It may be necessary to remove the brake caliper and wire it to the frame to gain enough clearance.
5. When the stud is loose, remove the tool and ball stud nut.
6. Install a spring compressor on the coil spring for safety.
7. Pull the brake disc and knuckle assembly up and off the ball stud and support the upper arm with a block of wood.
8. Remove the ball joint from the control arm with a ball joint tool. It must be pressed out.

**To install:**

9. Start the new ball joint into the control arm. Position the bleed vent in the rubber boot facing inward.
10. Seat the ball joint in the lower control arm. It must be pressed in.
11. Lower the upper arm and match the steering knuckle to the lower ball stud.
12. Install the brake caliper, if removed.
13. Install the ball stud nut and torque it to 80-100 ft. lbs. (108-135 Nm) plug the additional torque necessary to align the cotter pin hole. Do not exceed 130 ft. lbs. (176 Nm) or back the nut off the align the holes with the pin.
14. Install a new lube fitting and lubricate the new joint.
15. Install the tire and wheel.
16. Lower the van.

## Front Wheel Bearings

## REMOVAL & INSTALLATION

▶ **See Figures 5, 6, 7, 8, 9, 10, 11, 12, 13, 14, 15, 16, 17 and 18**

Only the front wheel bearings require periodic service. A premium high melting point grease meeting GM specification 6031-M must be used. Long fiber type greases must not be used. This service is recommended at the intervals in the Maintenance Intervals chart or whenever the van has been driven in water up to the hubs.

1. Remove the wheel and tire assembly, and the brake drum or brake caliper.
2. Remove the hub and disc as an assembly. Remove the caliper mounting bolts and insert a block between the brake pads as the caliper is removed. Remove the caliper and wire it

TCCS8024

**Fig. 5 Pry the dust cap from the hub, taking care not to distort or damage its flange**

TCCS8025

**Fig. 6 Once the bent ends are cut, grasp the cotter pin and pull or pry it free of the spindle**

Fig. 7 If difficulty is encountered, gently tap on the pliers with a hammer to help free the cotter pin

Fig. 10 With the nut and washer out of the way, the outer bearing may be removed from the hub

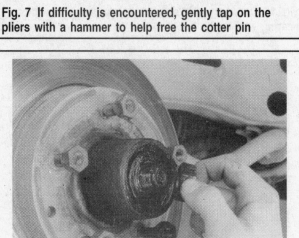

Fig. 8 Loosen and remove the castellated nut from the spindle

Fig. 11 Pull the hub and inner bearing assembly from the spindle

Fig. 9 Remove the washer from the spindle

Fig. 12 Use a small prytool to remove the old inner bearing seal

TCCS8032
**Fig. 13** With the seal removed, the inner bearing may be withdrawn from the hub

TCCS8033
**Fig. 14** Thoroughly pack the bearing with fresh, high temperature wheel bearing grease before installation

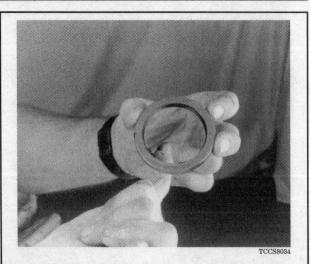
TCCS8034
**Fig. 15** Apply a thin coat of fresh grease to the new inner bearing seal lip

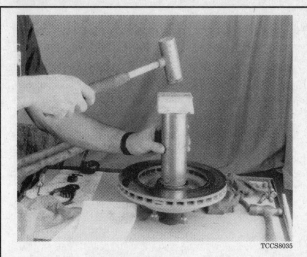
TCCS8035
**Fig. 16** Use a suitably sized driver to install the inner bearing seal to the hub

TCCS8036
**Fig. 17** Tighten the nut to 12 ft. lbs. while gently spinning the wheel, then adjust the bearings

TCCS8037
**Fig. 18** Install the dust cap by tapping on its flange — DO NOT damage the cap by hammering on the center

out of the way. Do not allow the caliper to hang by the brake hose.

3. Pry out the grease cap, cotter pin, spindle nut, and washer, then remove the hub. Do not drop the wheel bearings.

4. Remove the outer roller bearing assembly from the hub. The inner bearing assembly will remain in the hub and may be removed after prying out the inner seal. Discard the seal.

5. Clean all parts in solvent (air dry) and check for excessive wear or damage.

6. Using a hammer and drift, remove the bearings caps from the hub. When installing new cups, make sure that they are not cocked and that they are fully seated against the hub shoulder.

7. Pack both wheel bearings using high melting point wheel bearing grease made for disc brakes. Ordinary grease will melt and ooze out, ruining the pads. Place a healthy globe of grease in the palm of one hand and force the edge of the bearing into it so that the grease fills the bearing. Do this until the wheel bearing is packed. Grease packing tools are available to make this job a lot less messy. There are also tools which make it possible to grease the inner bearing without removing it or the disc from the spindle.

8. Place the inner bearing in the hub and install a new inner seal, making sure that the seal flange faces the bearing cup.

9. Carefully install the wheel hub over the spindle.

10. Using you hands, firmly press the outer bearing into the hub. Install the spindle washer and nut.

11. To adjust the bearings through 1971 models, tighten the adjusting nut to 15 ft. lbs. (20 Nm) while rotating the hub. Back the nut off 1 flat (1/16 turn) and insert a new cotter pin. If the nut and spindle hole do not align, back the nut off slightly. There should be 0.001-0.008 in. (0.0254-0.203mm) end-play in the bearing. This can be measured with a dial indicator, if you wish. Install the dust cap, wheel and tire.

12. To adjust the bearings on 1972 and later models, spin the wheel hub by hand and tighten the nut till it is just snug 12 ft. lbs. (16 Nm). Back off the nut till it is loose, then tighten it finger tight. Loosen the nut until either hole in the spindle lines up with a slot in the nut and insert a new cotter pin. There should be 0.001-0.008 in. (0.0254-0.203mm) end-play in the bearing through 1973, and 0.001-0.005 in. (0.0254-0.127mm) from 1974. This can be measured with a dial indicator, if you wish.

13. Replace the dust cap, wheel and tire.

## Front End Alignment

If the tires are worn unevenly, if the vehicle is not stable on the highway or if the handling seems uneven in spirited driving, wheel alignment should be checked. If an alignment problem is suspected, first check tire inflation and look for other possible causes such as worn suspension and steering components, accident damage or unmatched tires. Repairs may be necessary before the wheels can be properly aligned. Wheel alignment requires sophisticated equipment and can only be performed at a properly equipped shop.

## CASTER

▶ See Figures 19 and 20

Wheel alignment is defined by three different adjustments in three planes. Looking at the vehicle from the side, caster angle describes the steering axis rather than a wheel angle. The steering knuckle is attached to the strut at the top and the control arm at the bottom. The wheel pivots around the line between these points to steer the vehicle. When the upper point is tilted back, this is described as positive caster. Having a positive caster tends to make the wheels self-centering, increasing directional stability. Excessive positive caster makes the wheels hard to steer, while an uneven caster will cause a pull to one side.

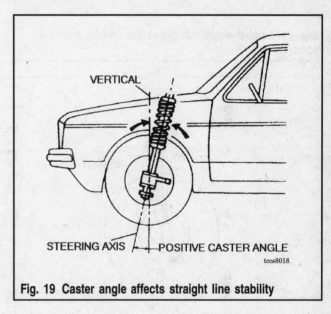

Fig. 19 Caster angle affects straight line stability

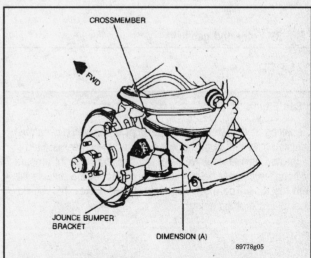

Fig. 20 Bumper stop bracket-to-frame measurement — required for caster setting on 1973-86 models

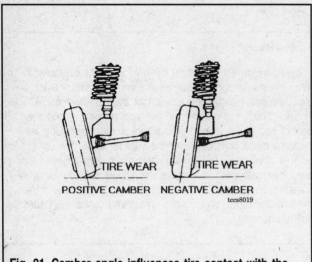

**Fig. 21 Camber angle influences tire contact with the road**

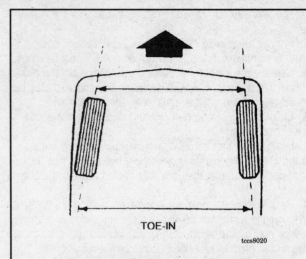

**Fig. 22 Toe-in means the distance between the wheels is closer at the front than at the rear of the wheels**

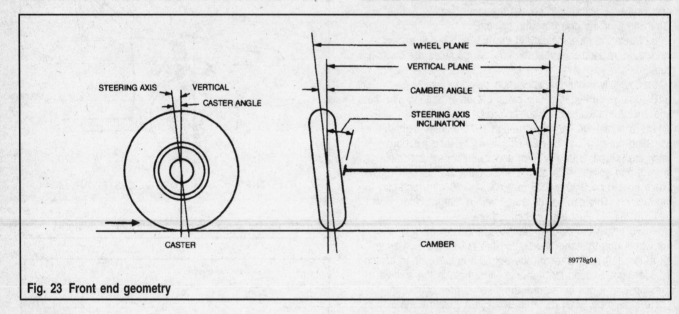

**Fig. 23 Front end geometry**

## CAMBER

▶ See Figure 21

Looking at the wheels from the front of the vehicle, camber adjustment is the tilt of the wheel. When the wheel is tilted in at the top, this is negative camber. In a turn, a slight amount of negative camber helps maximize contact of the outside tire with the road. Too much negative camber makes the vehicle unstable in a straight line.

## TOE-IN

▶ See Figure 22

Looking down at the wheels from above the vehicle, toe alignment is the distance between the front of the wheels relative to the distance between the back of the wheels. If the wheels are closer at the front, they are said to be toed-in or to have a negative toe. A small amount of negative toe enhances directional stability and provides a smoother ride on the highway. On most front wheel drive vehicles, standard toe adjustment is either zero or slightly positive. When power is applied to the front wheels, they tend to toe-in naturally.

## STEERING AXIS OR KINGPIN INCLINATION

▶ See Figure 23

Steering axis inclination (coil spring models) or kingpin inclination (I-beam axles) is the tilt of the steering knuckle or the kingpin. If it is not within specifications, the steering knuckle is bent (coil spring models) and must be replaced, or on I-beam axles, the axle center is bent and must be repaired or replaced. No means of adjustment is provided.

## Wheel Alignment Specifications

| Year | Model | Caster (deg) Range | Caster (deg) Preferred Setting | Camber (deg) Range | Camber (deg) Preferred Setting | Toe-In (in.) | Steering Axis Inclination* (deg) |
|---|---|---|---|---|---|---|---|
| 1967 | All | 2¼P–4¼P | 3¼P | 1¼P–1¾P | 1½P | 1/16–1/8 ① | 7¼ |
| 1968 | All | — | 3¼P | — | 1½P | 3/32–3/16 | 7¼ |
| 1969–70 | All | — | 3¼P | ½P–1½P | 1P | 3/32–3/16 | 7¼ |
| 1971 | All | ¼N–¼P | 0 | 0–½P | ¼P | 1/8–¼ | 8½ |
| 1972 | All | ¼N–¼P | 0 | 0–½P | ¼P | 3/16 | 8½ |
| 1973–80 | All | ② | ② | 0–½P | ¼P | 3/16 | 8½ |
| 1981–86 | All | ② | ② | 0–1P | ½P | 3/16 | 8½ |

—Not Available
* 1967–70—Kingpin inclination
① Per wheel
② Measure the distance from the bump stop bracket to the frame. Read the caster angle from the chart below.

| 1973–80 Bumper stop bracket-to-frame (in.) | | 2½ | 2¾ | 3 | 3¼ | 3½ | 3¾ | 4 | 4¼ | 4½ | 4¾ | 5 |
|---|---|---|---|---|---|---|---|---|---|---|---|---|
| Caster | | 2¼P | 2P | 1½P | 1¼P | 1P | ¾P | ½P | ¼P | 0 | ¼N | ½N |

| 1981–86 Bumper stop bracket-to-frame (in.) | | 1½ | 1¾ | 2 | 2¼ | 2½ | 2¾ | 3 | 3¼ | 3½ | 3¾ | 4 | 4¼ |
|---|---|---|---|---|---|---|---|---|---|---|---|---|---|
| Caster | G10, 20 | 3½P | 3⅓P | 3 1/10P | 2 9/10P | 2 7/10P | — | 2⅖P | 2⅕P | 2 1/10P | 1 9/10P | 1⅘P | 1⅗P |
| | G30 | 2⅘P | 2½P | 2⅕P | 1 9/10P | 1⅗P | — | 1P | 7/10P | ½P | ⅕P | 0 | ⅕N |

89778c01

## REAR SUSPENSION

All vans covered in this manual have a leaf spring rear suspension. Staggered rear shock absorbers are used, starting with 1971 models, to control axle hop on acceleration and braking. Heavy duty shock absorbers and springs have been available on most models.

## Leaf Springs

### REMOVAL & INSTALLATION

#### 1967-70 Models

▶ See Figures 24 and 25

1. Raise and support the vehicle. Position the jackstands under the frame rails.
2. Support the axle with a floor jack so that the weight is taken off the springs.
3. Remove the spring-to-axle U-bolts, spacers and clamp plate.
4. Remove the front bolt from the spring eye and loosen the shackle to withdraw the lower shackle bolt.
5. Remove the spring from the van.
6. Installation is the reverse of removal. Position the spring so that the head of the center bolts is indexed in the axle spring seat. Be sure that the spring spacer is properly positioned. Tighten the U-bolt nuts and front spring bolt to 80 ft. lbs. (108 Nm). Tighten the shackle bolts to 50 ft. lbs. (67 Nm).

#### 1971-86 Models

▶ See Figure 26

1. Raise and support the van.
2. Support the axle so that the weight is taken off the springs.

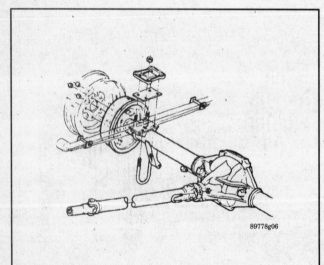

Fig. 24 View of the rear suspension — 1967-70 models

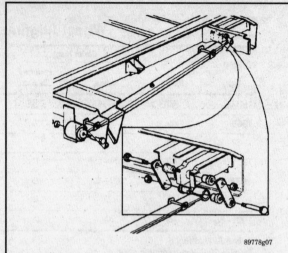

Fig. 25 View of the rear spring shackle — 1967-70 models

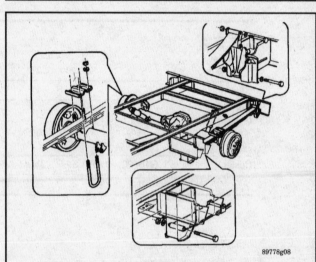

Fig. 26 View of the rear spring assembly and its related components — 1971-86 models

3. Loosen, buy do not remove the spring-to-shackle retaining nut.
4. Remove the nut and bolt securing the shackle to the spring hanger.
5. Remove the nut and bolt securing the spring to the front hanger.
6. Remove the U-bolt retaining nuts and remove the U-bolts and spring plate.
7. Remove the spring.
8. Installation is the reverse of removal. Be sure that the spring is in position at both hangers. The shackle assembly must be attached to the rear spring eye before installing the shackle to the rear hanger. Tighten the U-bolt nuts to 120 ft. lbs. (162 Nm) on G-10, 1500, 20, and 2500 models or 150 ft.

bs. (203 Nm) on G-30 and 3500 models. Torque the front eye bolt and rear shackle bolt to 135 ft. lbs. (183 Nm).

➡Aftermarket kits, consisting of longer axle U-bolts and blocks to be placed between the spring and axle, are available to adjust the rear side height. If this modification is carried to extremes, the front end caster angle and rear end stability will be affected.

## Shock Absorbers

### TESTING

The usual procedure for testing shock absorbers is to stand on the bumper at the end nearest the shock being tested and start the vehicle bouncing up and down. Step off; the vehicle should come to rest within one bounce cycle. The stiffness of the suspension on some models makes this rather difficult, unless you are a very "substantial" individual. Another good test is to drive the vehicle over a bumpy road. Bouncing over bumps is normal, but the shock absorbers should stop the bouncing after the bump is passed, within one or two cycles.

### REMOVAL & INSTALLATION

#### See Figures 27, 28 and 29

The usual procedure is to replace shock absorbers in axle pairs, to provide equal damping. Heavy duty replacements are available for firmer control. Air adjustable shock absorbers can be used to maintain a level rid with heavy loads or when towing.
1. Raise and support the van.
2. Support the rear axle with a floor jack.

3. If the van is equipped with air lift shocks, bleed the air from the lines and disconnect the line from the shock absorber.
4. Disconnect the shock absorber at the top by removing the nuts, washer and bolt.
5. Remove the nut, washer, and bolt from the bottom mount.
6. Remove the shock from the van.

➡Before installation, purge the new shock of air by repeatedly extending it in its normal position and compressing it while inverted. It is normal for there to be more resistance to extension than to compression.

7. Installation if the reverse of removal. If the van is equipped with air lift shock absorbers, inflate them to 10-15 psi minimum air pressure. Torque the shock absorber mounting nuts to 75 ft. lbs. (101 Nm).

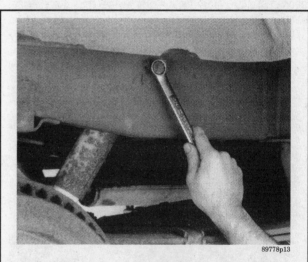

**Fig. 28 Unfasten the top retaining bolt from the rear shock absorber . . .**

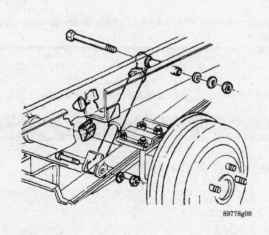

**Fig. 27 View of a common rear shock absorber assembly and its retainers**

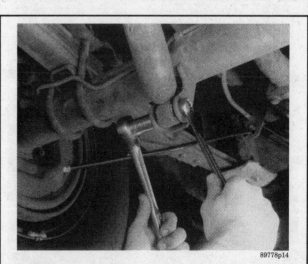

**Fig. 29 . . . then remove the bottom nut, bolt and washer from the shock absorber mount**

## STEERING

### Steering Wheel

#### REMOVAL & INSTALLATION

▶ **See Figures 30, 31, 32, 33 and 34**

1. On 1967-70 models, disconnect the turn signal wiring harness from the chassis wiring harness at the connector.
2. Disconnect the battery ground cable.
3. Remove the horn button, receiving cup, Belleville washer and bushing.
4. Mark the steering wheel-to-steering shaft relationship.
5. On 1975 and later models, remove the snapring from the steering shaft. Remove the nut and washer from the steering shaft.
6. Remove the steering wheel with a puller.

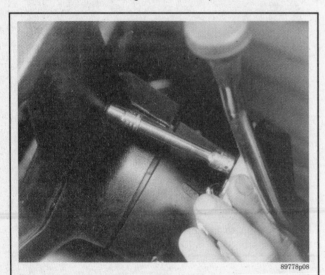

Fig. 30 Remove the horn cap assembly

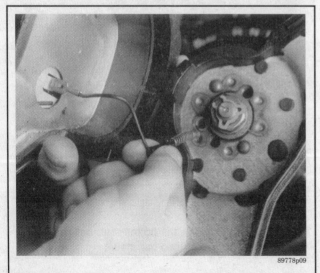

Fig. 31 Disengage the horn electrical connection

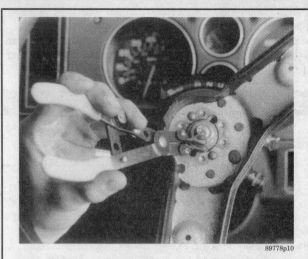

Fig. 32 If equipped, remove the snapring from the steering shaft

Fig. 33 Remove the nut and washer from the steering shaft

7. Installation is the reverse of removal. The turn signal control assembly must be in the Neutral position to prevent damaging the cancelling cam and control assembly.

### Turn Signal Switch

#### REMOVAL & INSTALLATION

**1967-72 Models**

▶ **See Figure 35**

1. Disconnect the battery ground cable.
2. Remove the steering wheel, preload spring, and cancelling cam.
3. Remove the shift lever roll pin and shift lever (if applicable).

89778p12

**Fig. 34 Using a steering wheel puller, remove the steering wheel**

4. Remove the turn signal lever screw and the lever.

5. Push the hazard warning knob in. This must be done to avoid damaging the switch.

6. Disconnect the switch wires from the chassis harness located under the dash.

7. Remove the mast jacket upper bracket.

8. Remove the switch wiring cover from the column.

9. Unscrew the mounting screws and remove the switch, bearing housing, switch cover, and shift housing from the column.

10. Installation is the reverse or removal.

### 1973-86 Models

1. Disconnect the battery ground cable. Remove the steering wheel.

2. Remove the switch cancelling spring and cam.

3. Remove the column to instrument panel trim plate, if any.

4. Disconnect the switch wiring harness at the half-moon connector.

5. Pry the wiring harness protector out of the column retaining slots.

6. Mark their locations, then remove each wire from the half-moon connector.

7. Remove the turn signal lever screw and the lever.

8. On tilt columns, remove the automatic transmission dial and needle. Remove the cap and bulb from the housing cover. Unscrew and remove the tilt release lever. The directional signal housing cover has to be pulled off the column; there is a special tool used for this.

9. Remove the three switch screws and remove the switch, guiding the wiring harness through the opening.

10. On installation, tape the switch wires and guide them through the housing opening. On tilt columns, the directional signal housing cover must be tapped back into place.

## Ignition Switch/Lock Cylinder

For procedures covering the 1967-72 ignition switch, refer to Section 6.

### REMOVAL & INSTALLATION

**1973-78 Models**

▶ See Figure 36

1. Remove the steering wheel and turn signal switch.

➡ **It is not necessary to completely remove the turn signal switch. Pull the switch over the end of the shaft; no further.**

2. Place the lock cylinder in the **RUN** position.

### ✳✳WARNING

**Do not remove the ignition key buzzer.**

3. Insert a small drift pin into the turn signal housing slot. Keeping the drift pin to the right side of the slot, break the

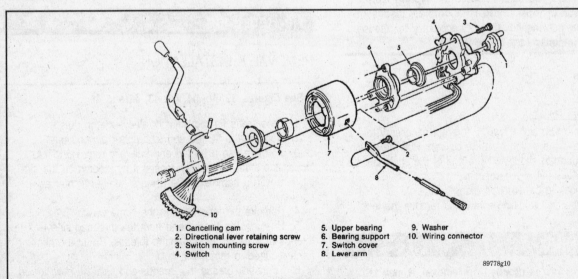

1. Cancelling cam
2. Directional lever retaining screw
3. Switch mounting screw
4. Switch
5. Upper bearing
6. Bearing support
7. Switch cover
8. Lever arm
9. Washer
10. Wiring connector

89778g10

**Fig. 35 Exploded view of the turn signal switch — 1967-72 models**

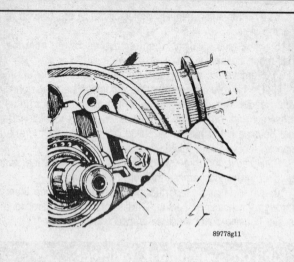

**Fig. 36 Ignition lock cylinder removal — 1973-78 models**

housing flash loose and depress the spring latch at the lower end of the lock cylinder. Remove the lock cylinder.

→Considerable force may be necessary to break this casting flash, but be careful not to damage any other parts. When ordering a new lock cylinder, specify a cylinder assembly. This will save assembling the cylinder, washer, sleeve and adapter.

4. To install, hold the lock cylinder sleeve and rotate the knob clockwise against the stop. Insert the cylinder into the housing, aligning the key and keyway. Hold a 0.070 in. (1.778mm) drill between the lock bezel and housing. Rotate the cylinder counterclockwise, maintaining a light pressure until the drive section of the cylinder mates with the sector. Push in until the snapring pops into the grooves. Remove the drill and check the cylinder operation.

### ✶✶WARNING

The drill prevents forcing the lock cylinder inward beyond its normal position. The buzzer switch and spring latch can hold the lock cylinder in too far. Complete disassembly of the upper bearing housing is necessary to release an improperly installed lock cylinder.

#### 1979-86 Models
▶ See Figure 37

1. Remove the steering wheel.
2. Remove the turn signal switch. It is not necessary to completely remove the switch from the column. Pull the switch rearward far enough to slip it over the end of the shaft, but do not pull the harness out of the column.
3. Turn the lock to the **RUN** position.
4. Remove the lock retaining screw and remove the lock cylinder.

### ✶✶WARNING

If the retaining screw is dropped on removal, it may fall into the column, requiring complete disassembly of the column to retrieve the screw.

5. To install, rotate the key to the stop while holding onto the cylinder.
6. Push the lock all the way in.
7. Install the screw. Tighten the screw to 3 ft. lbs. (4 Nm) for regular columns, or 2 ft. lbs. (2.7 Nm) for adjustable columns.
8. Install the turn signal switch and the steering wheel.

## Ignition Switch

### REMOVAL & INSTALLATION

#### 1973-86 Models
▶ See Figure 38

The switch is on the steering column, behind the instrument panel.
1. Lower the steering column, making sure that it is supported.

### ✶✶WARNING

Extreme care is necessary to prevent damage to the collapsible column.

2. Make sure the switch is in the **LOCK** position. If the lock cylinder is out, pull the switch rod up to the stop, then go down 1 detent.
3. Remove the two screws and the switch.
4. Before installation, make sure the switch is in the **LOCK** position.
5. Install the switch using the original screws.

### ✶✶CAUTION

Use of screws that are too long could prevent the column from collapsing on impact.

6. Replace the column.

## Tie Rod Ends

### REMOVAL & INSTALLATION

▶ See Figures 39, 40, 41, 42, 43, 44 and 45

1. Loosen the tie rod adjuster sleeve clamp nuts.
2. Remove the tie rod end stud cotter pin and nut.
3. You can use a tie rod end ball joint removal tool to loosen the stud, or you can loosen it by tapping on the steering arm with a hammer while using a heavy hammer as a backup.
4. Remove the inner stud in the same way.
5. Unscrew the tie rod end from the threaded sleeve. The threads may be left or right-hand threads. Count the number of turns required to remove it.
6. To install, grease the threads and turn the new tie rod end in as many turns as were needed to remove it. This will give approximately correct toe-in. Tighten the clamp bolts.

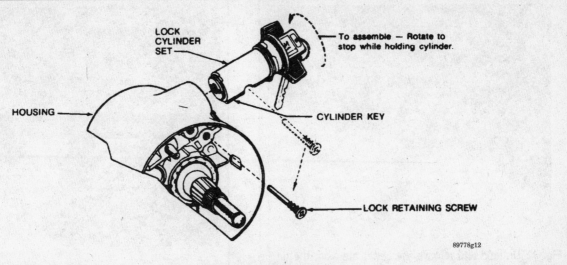

**Fig. 37 Exploded view of the ignition lock cylinder and related components**

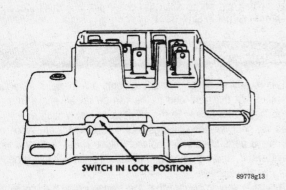

**Fig. 38 View of the ignition switch assembly showing the switch in the LOCK position for removal — 1973 and later models**

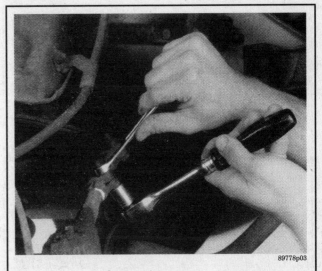

**Fig. 40 Unfasten the tie rod adjusting sleeve retainers**

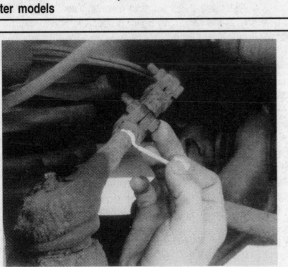

**Fig. 39 Matchmark the old tie rod if you are reusing it; this will aid in installation**

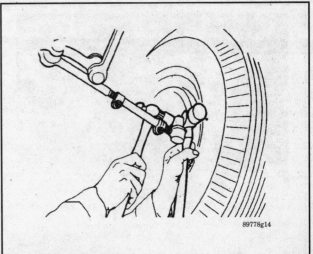

**Fig. 41 When freeing the tie rod end, a second hammer may be used as a backup**

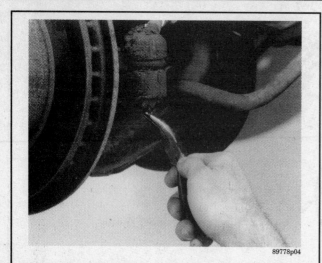

**Fig. 42 Unbend and remove the cotter pin from the tie rod end stud . . .**

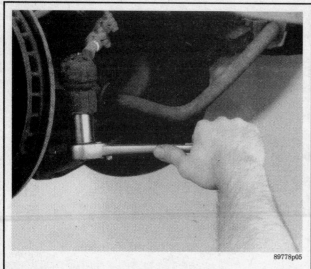

**Fig. 43 . . . then remove the nut**

**Fig. 44 Use a tie rod end ball joint removal tool to loosen the stud . . .**

**Fig. 45 . . . then remove it from the steering arm**

7. Tighten the stud nuts and install new cotter pins. You may tighten the nut to align the cotter pin, buy don't loosen it.

8. Adjust the toe-in.

## Manual Steering Gear

Before any steering gear adjustments are made, it is recommended that the front end of the van be raised and a thorough inspection be made for stiffness or lost motion in the steering gear, steering linkage and front suspension. Worn or damaged parts should be replaced, since a satisfactory adjustment of the steering gear cannot be obtained if bent or badly worn parts exist.

It is also very important that the steering gear be properly aligned in the van. Misalignment of the gear places a stress on the steering worm shaft, therefore a proper adjustment is impossible. To align the steering gear, loosen the steering gear-to-frame mounting bolts to permit the gear to align itself. Check the steering gear to frame mounting seat. If there is a gap at any of the mounting bolts, proper alignment may be obtained by placing shims where excessive gap appears. Tighten the steering gear-to-frame bolts. Alignment of the gear in the van is very important and should be done carefully so that a satisfactory, trouble-free gear adjustment may be obtained.

The steering gear is of the recirculating ball nut type. the ball nut, mounted on the worm gear, is driven by means of steel balls which circulate in helical grooves in both the worm and nut. Ball return guides attached to the nut serve to recirculate the two sets of balls in the grooves. As the steering wheel is turned to the right, the ball nut moves upward. When the wheel is turned to the left, the ball nut moves downward.

The sector teeth on the pinion shaft and the ball nut are designed so that they fit the tightest when the steering wheel is straight ahead. This mesh action is adjusted by an adjusting screw which moves the pinion shaft endwise until the teeth mesh properly. The worm bearing adjuster provides proper preloading of the upper and lower bearings.

Before doing the adjustment procedures given below, ensure that the steering problem is not caused by faulty suspension components, bad front end alignment, etc. Then, proceed with the following adjustments.

## ADJUSTMENTS

### Steering Worm and Sector
▶ See Figures 46 and 47

1. Tighten the worm bearing adjuster plug until all end-play has been removed, then loosen ¼ turn.

2. Use an $^{11}/_{32}$ in. 12 point socket to carefully turn the wormshaft all the way into the right corner then turn back about ½ turn.

3. Tighten the adjuster plug until the proper thrust bearing preload is obtained 5-8 inch lbs. (0.56-0.90 Nm). Tighten the adjuster plug locknut to 85 ft. lbs. (115 Nm).

4. Turn the wormshaft from one stop to the other counting the number of turns. Then turn the shaft back exactly half the number of turns to the center position.

5. Turn the lash (sector shaft) adjuster screw clockwise to remove all lash between the ball nut and sector teeth. Tighten the locknut to 25 ft. lbs. (33 Nm).

6. Using an $^{11}/_{32}$ in. 12 point socket and an inch lb. torque wrench, observe the highest reading while the gear is turned through the center position. It should be 16 inch lbs. or less.

7. If necessary, repeat Steps 5 and 6.

## OVERHAUL

### Steering Gear Disassembly
▶ See Figures 48, 49, 50, 51 and 52

1. Place the steering gear in a vise, clamping onto one of the mounting tabs. The wormshaft should be in a horizontal position.

2. Rotate the wormshaft from stop to stop and count the total number of turns. Turn back exactly halfway, placing the gear on center.

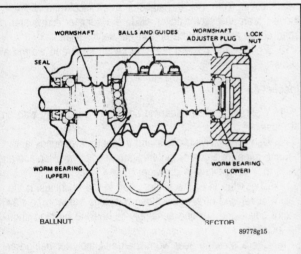

Fig. 46 Cross-section of a Saginaw recirculating ball model steering gear

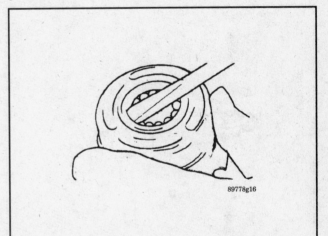

Fig. 48 Removing the bearing retainer from the worm bearing adjuster — Saginaw recirculating ball model steering gear

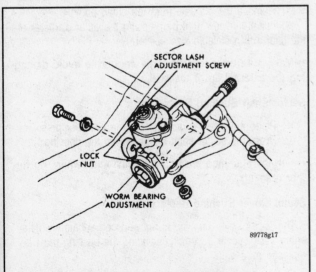

Fig. 47 Common steering gear adjustment points

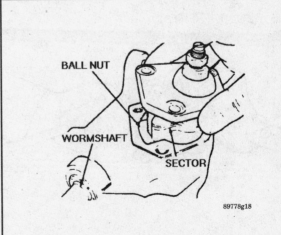

Fig. 49 Removing the sector shaft assembly — Saginaw recirculating ball model steering gear

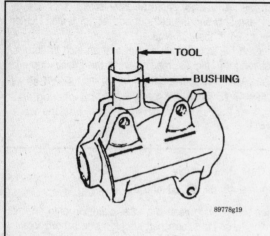

**Fig. 50 Removing the sector shaft bushing — Saginaw recirculating ball model steering gear**

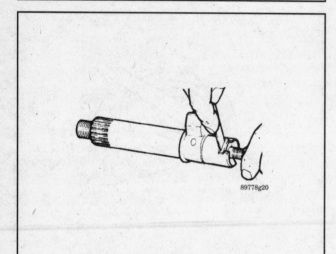

**Fig. 51 Checking the lash adjuster end clearance — Saginaw recirculating ball model steering gear**

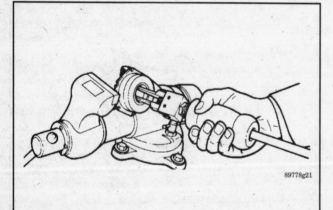

**Fig. 52 Removing the worm shaft lower bearing cup from the adjuster plug — Saginaw recirculating ball model steering gear**

3. Remove the three self locking bolts which attach the sector cover to the housing.

4. Using a plastic hammer, tap lightly on the end of the sector shaft and lift the sector cover and sector shaft assembly from the gear housing.

➡️**It may be necessary to turn the wormshaft by hand until the sector will pass through the opening in the housing.**

5. Remove the locknut from the adjuster plug and remove the adjuster plug assembly.

6. Pull the wormshaft and ball nut an assembly from the housing.

➡️**Damage may be done to the ends of the ball guides if the ball nut is allowed to rotate to the end of the worm.**

7. Remove the worm shaft upper bearing from inside the gear housing.

8. Pry the wormshaft lower bearing retainer from the adjuster plug housing and remove the bearing.

9. Remove the locknut from the lash adjuster screw in the sector cover. Turn the lash adjuster screw clockwise and remove it from the sector cover. Slide the adjuster screw and shim out of the slot in the end of the sector shaft.

10. Pry out and discard both the sector shaft and wormshaft seals.

### Inspection

1. Wash all parts in cleaning solvent and blow dry with an air hose.

2. Use a magnifying glass and inspect the bearings and bearing caps for signs of indentation, or chipping. Replace any parts that show signs of damage.

3. Check the fit of the sector shaft in the bushings in the sector cover and housing. If these bushings are worn, a new sector cover and bushing assembly or housing bushing should be installed.

4. Check steering gear wormshaft assembly for being bent or damaged.

### Shaft Seal Replacement

1. Remove the old seal from the pump body.

2. Install the new seal by pressing the outer diameter of the seal with a suitable size socket.

➡️**Make sure the socket is large enough to avoid damaging the external lip of the seal.**

### Sector Shaft Bushing Replacement

1. Place the steering gear housing in an arbor press.

2. Press the sector shaft bushing from the housing.

➡️**Service bushings are bored to size and require no further reaming.**

### Sector Cover Bushing Replacement

The sector cover bushing is not serviced separately. The entire sector cover assembly including the bushing must be replaced as a unit.

## Ball Nut Service

If there is any indication of binding or tightness when the ball nut is rotated on the worm, the unit should be disassembled, cleaned, inspected and reassembled as follows:

### BALL NUT DISASSEMBLY

1. Remove the screws and clamp retaining the ball guides in the ball nut. Pull the guides out of the ball nut.

2. Turn the ball nut upside down and rotate the wormshaft back and forth until all the balls have dropped out of the ball nut. The ball nut can now be pulled endwise off the worm.

3. Wash all parts in solvent and dry them with air. Use a magnifying glass and inspect the worm and nut grooves and the surface of all balls for signs of indentation. Check all ball guides for damage at the ends. Replace any damaged parts.

### BALL NUT ASSEMBLY

▶ See Figure 53

1. Slip the ball nut over the worm with the ball guide holes up and the shallow end of the ball nut teeth to the left from the steering wheel position. Sight through the ball guide to align the grooves in the worm.

2. Place two ball guide halves together and insert them in the upper circuit in the ball nut. Place the two remaining guides together and insert them in the lower circuit.

3. Count out 25 balls and place them in a suitable container. This is the proper number of balls for one circuit.

4. Load the 25 balls into one of the guide holes while turning the wormshaft gradually away from that hole.

5. Fill the remaining ball circuit in the same manner.

6. Assemble the ball guide clamp to the ball nut and tighten the screws to 18-24 inch lbs. (2-2.7 Nm).

7. Check the assembly by rotating the ball nut on the worm to see that it moves freely.

➡Do not rotate the ball nut to the end of the worm threads as this may damage the ball guides.

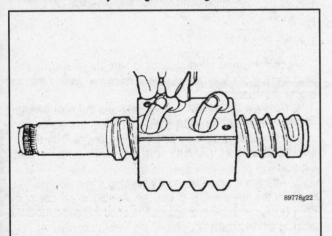

**Fig. 53 Filling the ball circuits — Saginaw recirculating ball model steering gear**

## Steering Gear Assembly

1. Coat the threads of the adjuster plug, sector cover bolts and lash adjuster with a non-drying oil resistant sealing compound.

➡Do not apply compound to the female threads. Use extreme care when applying compound to the bearing adjuster so that it does not come in contact with the wormshaft bearing.

2. Place the steering gear housing in a vise with the wormshaft bore horizontal and the sector cover opening up.

3. Make sure that all seals, bushings and bearing cups are installed in the gear housing and that the ball nut is installed on the wormshaft.

4. Slip the wormshaft upper bearing assembly over the wormshaft and insert the wormshaft and ball nut assembly into the housing, feeding the end of the shaft through the upper ball bearing cup and seal.

5. Place the wormshaft lower bearing assembly in the adjuster plug bearing cup and press the stamped retainer into place with a suitable size socket.

6. Install the adjuster plug and locknut into the lower end of the housing while carefully guiding the end of the wormshaft into the bearing until nearly all end-play has been removed from the wormshaft.

7. Position the lash adjuster including the shim in the slotted end of the sector shaft.

➡End clearance should not be greater than 0.002 in. (0.05mm). If the end clearance is greater than 0.002 in. (0.05mm), a shim package is available with thicknesses of 0.063 in. (1.60mm), 0.065 in. (1.65mm), 0.067 in. (1.70mm) and 0.069 in. (1.75mm).

8. Lubricate the steering gear with 11 oz. (312g) of steering gear grease. Rotate the wormshaft until the ball nut is at the other end of its travel and then pack as much new lubricant into the housing as possible without losing it through the sector shaft opening. Rotate the wormshaft until the ball nut is at the other end of its travel and pack as much lubricant into the opposite end as possible.

9. Rotate the wormshaft until the ball nut is in the center of travel. This is to make sure that the sector shaft and ball nut will engage properly with the center tooth of the sector entering the center tooth space in the ball nut.

10. Insert the sector shaft assembly including lash adjuster screw and shim into the housing so that the center tooth of the sector enters the center tooth space in the ball nut.

11. Pack the remaining portion of the lubricant into the housing and also place some in the sector cover bushing hole.

12. Place the sector cover gasket on the housing.

13. Install the sector cover onto the sector shaft by reaching through the sector cover with a screwdriver and turning the lash adjuster screw counterclockwise until the screw bottoms, then back the screw off ½ turn. Loosely install a new locknut onto the adjuster screw.

14. Install and tighten the sector cover bolt to 30 ft. lbs. (40 Nm).

## REMOVAL & INSTALLATION

1. Set the front wheels in straight ahead position by driving vehicle a short distance on a flat surface.

2. Remove the flexible coupling to steering shaft flange bolts. Mark the relationship of the universal yoke to the wormshaft.

3. Mark the relationship of the Pitman arm to the Pitman shaft. Remove the Pitman shaft nut or Pitman arm pinch bolt, then remove the Pitman arm from the Pitman shaft, using puller J-6632.

4. Remove the steering gear to frame bolts and remove the gear assembly.

5. Remove the flexible coupling pinch bolt and remove the coupling from the steering gear wormshaft.

6. Install the flexible coupling onto the steering gear wormshaft, aligning the flat in the coupling with the flat on the shaft. Push the coupling onto the shaft until the wormshaft bottoms on the coupling reinforcement. Install the pinch bolt and torque to 24 ft. lbs. (32 Nm). The coupling bolt must pass through the shaft undercut.

7. Place the steering gear in position, guiding the coupling bolt into the steering shaft flange.

8. Install the steering gear to frame bolts and torque to 70 ft. lbs. (94 Nm).

9. If flexible coupling alignment pin plastic spacers were used, make sure they are bottomed on the pins, torque the flange bolt nuts to 25 ft. lbs. (33 Nm), and then remove the plastic spacers.

10. If flexible coupling alignment pin plastic spacers were not used, center the pins in the slots in the steering shaft flange and then install and torque the flange bolt nuts to 25 ft. lbs (33 Nm).

11. Install the Pitman arm onto the Pitman shaft, lining up the marks made at removal. Install the Pitman shaft nut torque to 185 ft. lbs. (250 Nm).

## Power Steering System

The procedures for maintaining, adjusting and repairing the power steering system and its components are to be performed only after determining that the steering linkage and front suspension systems are correctly aligned and in good condition. All worn or damaged parts should be replaced before attempting to service the power steering system. After correcting any condition that could affect the power steering, do the preliminary test of the steering system components.

## PRELIMINARY TESTS

### Lubrication

Proper lubrication of the steering linkage and the front suspension components is very important for the proper operation of the steering systems of vans equipped with power steering. Most all power steering systems use the same lubricant in the steering gear box as in the power steering pump reservoir, and the fluid level is maintained at the pump reservoir.

With power cylinder assist power steering, the steering gear is of the standard mechanical type and the lubricating oil is self contained within the gear box and the level is maintained by the removal of a filler plug on the gear box housing. The control valve assembly is mounted on the gear box and is lubricated by power steering oil from the power steering pump reservoir, where the level is maintained.

### Air Bleeding

Air bubbles in the power steering system must be removed from the fluid. Be sure the reservoir is filled to the proper level and the fluid is warmed up to operating temperature. Then, turn the steering wheel through its full travel three or four times until all the air bubbles are removed. Do not hold the steering wheel against its stops. Recheck the fluid level.

### Fluid Level Check

1. Run the engine until the fluid is at the normal operating temperature. Then, turn the steering wheel through its full travel three or four times, and shut off the engine.

2. Check the fluid level in the steering reservoir. If the fluid level is low, add enough fluid to raise the level to the FULL mark on the dipstick or filler tube.

### Pump Belt Check

Inspect the pump belt for cracks, glazing, or worn places. Using a belt tension gauge, check the belt tension for the proper range of adjustment. The amount of tension varies with the make of truck or van and the condition of the belt. New belts (those belts used less than 15 minutes) require a higher figure. The belt deflection method of adjustment may be used only if a belt tension gauge is not available. The belt should be adjusted for a deflection of 1/4-3/8 in. (6.35-9.53mm).

### Fluid Leaks

Check all possible leakage points (hoses, power steering pump, or steering gear) for loss of fluid. Turn the engine on and rotate the steering wheel from stop-to-stop several times. Tighten all loose fittings and replace any defective lines or valve seats.

### Turning Effort

Check the turning effort required to turn the steering wheel after aligning the front wheels and inflating the tires to the proper pressure.

1. With the vehicle on dry pavement and the front wheel straight ahead, set the parking brake and turn the engine on.

2. After a short warm-up period for the engine, turn the steering wheel back and forth several times to warm the steering fluid.

3. Attach a spring scale to the steering wheel rim and measure the pull required to turn the steering wheel one complete revolution in each direction. The effort needed to turn the steering wheel should not exceed the limits specified.

➡This test may be done with the steering wheel removed and a torque wrench applied on the steering wheel nut.

### Power Steering Hose Inspection

Inspect both the input and output hoses of the power steering pump for worn spots, cracks, or signs of leakage. Replace hose if defective, being sure to reconnect the replacement hose properly. Many power steering hoses are identified as to where they are to be connected by special means, such as fittings that will only fit on the correct pump fitting, or hoses of special lengths.

### Test Driving to Check the Power Steering Operation

When test driving to check power steering, drive at a speed between 15 and 20 mph. (24-32 km). Make several turns in each direction. When a turn is completed, the front wheels should return to the straight ahead position with very little help from the driver.

If the front wheels fail to return as they should, and the steering linkage is free, well oiled and properly adjusted, the trouble is probably due to misalignment of the power cylinder or improper adjustment of the spool valve.

## Power Steering Pump

The power steering pump supplies all the power assist used in power steering systems of all designs. There are various designs of pumps used by the truck and van manufacturers but all pumps supply power to operate the steering systems with the least effort. All power steering pumps have a reservoir tank built onto the oil pump. These pumps are driven by belt turned by pulleys on the engine, normally on the front of the crankshaft.

During operation of the engine at idle speed, there is provision for the power steering pump to supply more fluid pressure. During driving speeds or when the van is moving straight ahead, less pressure is needed and the excess is relieved through a pressure relief and flow control valve. The pressure relief part of the valve is inside the flow control and is basically the same for all pumps. The flow control valve regulates, or controls, the constant flow of fluid from the pump as it varies with the demands of the steering gear. The pressure relief valve limits the hydraulic pressure built up when the steering gear is turned against its stops.

During pump disassembly, make sure all work is done on a clean surface. Clean the outside of the pump thoroughly and do not allow dirt of any kind to get inside. Do not immerse the shaft oil seal in solvent.

If replacing the rotor shaft seal, be extremely careful not to scratch the sealing surfaces with tools.

### REMOVAL & INSTALLATION

1. Disconnect the hoses at the pump. When the hoses are disconnected, secure the ends in a raised position to prevent leakage. Cap the ends of the hoses to prevent the entrance of dirt.
2. Cap the pump fittings.
3. Loosen the bracket-to-pump mounting nuts.
4. Remove the pump drive belt.
5. Remove the bracket-to-pump bolts and remove the pump from the van.
6. Installation is the reverse of removal. Fill the reservoir and bleed the pump by turning the pulley counterclockwise (as viewed from the front) until bubbles stop forming. Bleed the system as outlined in the following procedure.

### BLEEDING

1. Fill the reservoir to the proper level and let the fluid remain undisturbed for at least 2 minutes.
2. Start the engine and run it for only about 2 seconds.
3. Add fluid as necessary.
4. Repeat Steps 1-3 until the level remains constant.
5. Raise the front of the vehicle so that the front wheels are off the ground. Set the parking brake and block both rear wheels front and rear. Manual transmissions should be in Neutral; automatic transmissions should be in Park.
6. Start the engine and run it at approximately 1500 rpm.
7. Turn the wheels (off the ground) to the right and left, lightly contacting the stops.
8. Add fluid as necessary.
9. Lower the vehicle and turn the wheels right and left on the ground.
10. Check the level and refill as necessary.
11. If the fluid is extremely foamy, let the van stand for a few minutes with the engine off and repeat the procedure. Check the belt tension and check for a bent or loose pulley. The pulley should not wobble with the engine running.
12. Check that no hoses are contacting any parts of the van, particularly sheet metal.
13. Check the oil level and refill as necessary. This step and the next are very important. When willing, follow Steps 1-10 above
14. Check for air in the fluid. Aerated fluid appears milky. If air is present, repeat the above operation. If it is obvious that the pump will not respond to bleeding after several attempts, a pressure test may be required.

The procedures for maintaining, adjusting, and repairing the power steering systems and components discussed in this section are to be done only after determining that the steering linkages and front suspension systems are correctly aligned and in good condition. All worn or damaged parts should be replaced before attempting to service the power steering system. After correcting any condition that could affect the power steering, do the preliminary tests of the steering system components.

### OVERHAUL

The vane type power steering pump is used in Saginaw steering systems. Centrifugal force moves a number of vanes outward against the pump ring, causing a pumping action of the fluid to the control valve.

**Disassembly**

1. Clean the outside of the pump in a non-toxic solvent before disassembling.
2. Mount the pump in a vise, being careful not to squeeze the front hub too tight.
3. Remove the union and seal.
4. Remove the reservoir retaining studs and separate the reservoir from the housing.
5. Remove the mounting bolt and union O-rings.
6. Remove the filter and filter cage; discard the element.

7. Remove the end plate retaining ring by compressing the retaining ring and then prying it out with a removal tool. The retaining ring may be compressed by inserting a small punch in the 1/8 in.(3mm) diameter hole in the housing and pushing in until the ring clears the groove.

8. Remove the end plate. The end plate is spring loaded and should rise above the housing level. If it is stuck inside the housing, a slight rocking or gentle tapping should free the plate.

9. Remove the shaft woodruff key and tap the end of the shaft gently to free the pressure plate, pump ring, rotor assembly, and thrust plate. Remove these parts as one unit.

10. Remove the end plate O-ring. Separate the pressure plate, pump ring, rotor assembly, and thrust plate.

### Inspection

Clean all metal parts in a non-toxic solvent and inspect them as given below:

1. Check the flow control valve for free movement in the housing bore. If the valve is sticking, see if there is dirt or a rough spot in the bore.

2. Check the cap screw in the end of the flow control valve for looseness. Tighten if necessary being careful not to damage the machined surfaces.

3. Inspect the pressure plate and the pump plate surfaces for flatness and check that there are no cracks or scores in the parts. Do not mistake the normal wear marks for scoring.

4. Check the vanes in the rotor assembly for free movement and that they were installed with the radius edge toward the pump ring.

5. If the flow control valve plunger is defective, install a new part. The valve is factory calibrated and supplied as a unit.

6. Check the driveshaft for worn splines, breaks, bushing material pick-up, etc.

7. Replace all rubber seals and O-rings removed from the pump.

8. Check the reservoir, studs, casting, etc. for burrs and other defects that would impair operation.

### Assembly

1. Install a new shaft seal in the housing and insert the shaft at the hub end of housing, splined end entering mounting face side.

2. Install the thrust plate on the dowel pins with the ported side facing the rear of the pump housing.

3. Install the rotor on the pump shaft over the splined end. Be sure the rotor moves freely on the splines. Countersunk side must be toward the shaft.

4. Install the shaft retaining ring. Install the pump ring on the dowel pins with the rotation arrow toward the rear of the pump housing. Rotation is clockwise as seen from the pulley.

5. Install the vanes in the rotor slots with the radius edge towards the outside.

6. Lubricate the outside diameter and chamfer of the pressure plate with petroleum jelly so as not to damage the O-ring and install the plate on the dowel pins with the ported face toward the pump ring. Seat the pressure plate by placing a large socket on top of the plate and pushing down with the hand.

7. Install the pressure plate spring in the center groove of the plate.

8. Install the end plate O-ring. Lubricate the outside diameter and chamfer of the end plate with petroleum jelly so as not to damage the O-ring and install the end plate in the housing, using an arbor press. Install the end plate retaining ring while pump is in the arbor press. Be sure the ring is in the groove and the ring gap is positioned properly.

9. Install the flow control spring and plunger, hex head screw end in bore first. Install the filter cage, new filter stud seals and union seal.

10. Place the reservoir in the normal position and press down until the reservoir seats on the housing. Check the position of the stud seals and the union seal.

11. Install the studs, union, and driveshaft woodruff key. Support the shaft on the opposite side of the key when tapping the key into place.

## Steering Trouble Diagnosis

**Power Steering**

| Condition | Possible Cause | Correction |
|---|---|---|
| Intermittent or no power assist | 1. Belt slipping and/or low fluid level. | 1. Adjust or replace belt. Add fluid as necessary. |
| | 2. Piston or rod binding in power cylinder. (Linkage type). | 2. Repair or replace piston and rod. |
| | 3. Sliding sleeve stuck in control valve. (Linkage type). | 3. Free-up or replace sleeve. |
| | 4. Improper pump operation. | 4. Refer to "Power Steering Pump." |
| Poor or no recovery from turns | 1. Improper caster setting. | 1. Adjust to specifications. |
| | 2. Steering gear adjustments too tight. | 2. Adjust according to instructions. |
| | 3. Improper spool nut adjustment. (Linkage type). | 3. Adjust according to instructions |
| | 4. Valve spool installed backwards. (Linkage type). | 4. Install valve spool correctly. |
| | 5. Low tire pressure. | 5. Inflate tires to recommended pressure. |
| | 6. Tight steering linkage. | 6. Lubricate as necessary. |
| | 7. King pins frozen. | 7. Lubricate as necessary. |
| Lack of effort (both turns) | 1. Improper sector shaft adjustment. | 1. Adjust Sector Shaft. |
| | 2. Pressure plates on wrong side of reactions rings. | 2. Gear Recondition. |
| Lack of effort (left turn only) | 1. Left turn reaction seal "O" ring worn, damaged or missing. | 1. Gear recondition. |
| | 2. Left turn reaction oil passageway not drilled in housing or cylinder head. | 2. Replace parts as required. |
| | 3. Left turn reaction ring sticking in cylinder head. | 3. Replace parts as required |
| Lack of effort (right turn only) | 1. Right turn U-shaped reaction seal worn, damaged, or missing. | 1. Gear recondition. |
| | 2. Right turn reaction oil passageway not drilled in housing head, or ferrule pin. | 2. Replace parts as required. |
| | 3. Right turn reaction ring sticking in housing head. | 3. Replace parts as required. |

89778c02

## Steering Trouble Diagnosis (cont.)

**Power Steering**

| Condition | Possible Cause | Correction |
|---|---|---|
| Lack of assist (left turn only) | Left turn reaction seal "O" ring worn, damaged, or missing. | Gear recondition. |
| Lack of assist (right turn only) | 1. Right turn U-shaped reaction seal worn, damaged, or missing.<br>2. Worm sealing ring (teflon) worm sleeve seal, ferrule pin "O" ring damaged or worn.<br>3. Excessive internal leakage thru piston end plug and/or side plugs. | 1. Gear recondition.<br>2. Gear recondition.<br>3. Replace worm-piston assembly. |
| Lack of assist (both turns) | 1. Low oil level in pump reservoir (usually accompanied by pump noise).<br>2. Loose pump belt.<br>3. Pump output low.<br>4. Engine idle too low.<br>5. Excessive internal leakage thru piston end plug and/or side plugs. | 1. Fill to proper level.<br>2. Adjust belts.<br>3. Pressure test pump.<br>4. Adjust engine idle.<br>5. Replace worm-piston assembly. |
| Objectionable "hiss" | Noisy valve | Do not replace valve unless "hiss" is extremely objectionable. A replacement valve will also exhibit sight noise and is not always a cure for the objection. |
| Rattle or chuckle noise in steering gear | 1. Gear loose on frame.<br>2. Steering linkages looseness.<br>3. Pressure hose touching other parts of truck.<br>4. Loose Pitman shaft over center adjustment.<br>NOTE: A slight rattle may occur on turns because of increased clearance off the "high point". This is normal and clearance must not be reduced below specified limits to eliminate this slight rattle.<br>5. Loose Pitman arm. | 1. Check gear mounting bolts. Torque bolts to specifications.<br>2. Check linkage pivot points for wear. Replace if necessary.<br>3. Adjust hose position. Do not bend tubing by hand.<br>4. Adjust<br><br><br><br><br><br>5. Torque Pitman arm pinch bolt. |
| Squawk noise in steering gear when turning or recovering from a turn | 1. Dampener O-ring on valve spool cut.<br>2. Loose or worn valve. | 1. Replace dampener O-Ring.<br>2. Replace valve. |
| Chirp noise in steering gear | Gear relief valve. | Replace relief valve. |
| Chirp noise in steering gear | Gear relief valve. | Replace relief valve. |
| Chirp noise in steering pump | Loose belt. | Adjust belt tension. |
| Belt Squeal (Particularly noticeable at full wheel travel and standstill parking) | Loose belt. | Adjust belt tension. |
| Growl noise in steering pump | Excessive back pressure in hoses or steering gear caused by restriction. | Locate restriction and correct. Replace part if necessary. |
| Growl noise in steering pump (particularly noticeable at standstill parking) | 1. Scored pressure plates, thrust plate or rotor.<br>2. Extreme wear of cam ring. | 1. Replace parts and flush system.<br>2. Replace parts. |
| Groan noise in steering pump | 1. Low oil level.<br>2. Air in the oil. Poor pressure hose connection. | 1. Fill reservoir to proper level.<br>2. Torque connector. Bleed system. |
| Rattle or knock noise in steering pump | Loose pump pulley nut. | Torque nut. |

89778c03

## Steering Trouble Diagnosis (cont.)

**Power Steering**

| Condition | Possible Cause | Correction |
|---|---|---|
| Rattle noise in steering pump | 1. Vanes not installed properly.<br>2. Vanes sticking in rotor slots. | 1. Install properly.<br>2. Repair or replace. |
| Swish noise in steering pump | Defective flow control valve. | Replace part. |
| Whine noise in steering pump | Pump shaft bearing scored. | Replace housing and shaft. Flush and bleed system. |
| Intermittent assist | 1. Flow control valve sticking.<br>2. Slipping belt.<br>3. Low fluid level.<br>4. Low pump efficiency. | 1. Pressure test pump and service as necessary.<br>2. Adjust belt.<br>3. Inspect and correct fluid level.<br>4. Pressure test pump and service as necessary. |
| No assist | 1. Pump seizure.<br>2. Broken slipper spring(s).<br>3. Flow control bore plug ring not in place.<br>4. Flow control valve sticking. | 1. Replace pump.<br>2. Recondition pump or replace as necessary.<br>3. Replace snap ring. Inspect groove for depth.<br>4. Pressure test pump and service as necessary. |
| No assist when parking only | 1. Wrong pressure relief valve.<br>2. Broken "O" ring on flow control bore plug.<br>3. Loose pressure relief valve.<br>4. Low pump efficiency | 1. Install proper relief valve.<br>2. Replace "O" ring.<br>3. Tighten valve. DO NOT ADJUST.<br>4. Pressure test pump and service as necessary. |
| Noisy pump | 1. Low fluid level.<br>2. Belt noise.<br>3. Foreign material blocking pump housing oil inlet hole. | 1. Inspect and correct fluid level.<br>2. Inspect for pulley alignment, paint or grease on pulley and correct. Adjust belt.<br>3. Remove reservoir, visually check inlet oil hole and service as necessary. |
| Pump vibration | 1. Pump hose interference with sheet metal or brake lines.<br>2. Belt loose.<br>3. Pulley loose or out of round.<br>4. Crankshaft pulley loose or damaged.<br>5. Bracket pivot bolts loose. | 1. Reroute hoses.<br>2. Adjust belt.<br>3. Replace pulley.<br>4. Replace crankshaft pulley.<br>5. If unable to tighten, replace bracket. |
| Pump leaks | 1. Cap or filler neck leaks.<br>2. Reservoir-solder joints leak.<br>3. Reservoir "O" ring leaking.<br>4. Shaft seal leaking.<br>5. Loose rear bracket bolts.<br>6. Loose or faulty high pressure ferrule.<br>7. Rear bolt holes stripped or casting cracked. | 1. Correct fluid level.<br>2. Resolder or replace reservoir as necessary.<br>3. Inspect sealing area of reservoir. Replace "O" ring or reservoir as necessary.<br>4. Replace seal.<br>5. Tighten bolts.<br>6. Tighten fitting to 24 foot-pounds or replace as necessary.<br>7. Repair, if possible, or replace pump. |
| Hard steering | 1. Low or uneven tire pressure<br>2. Insufficient lubricant in the steering gear housing or in steering linkage.<br>3. Steering gear shaft adjusted too tight.<br>4. Improper caster or toe-in.<br>5. Steering column misaligned.<br>6. Loose, worn or broken pump belt.<br>7. Air in system.<br>8. Low fluid level in the pump reservoir. | 1. Inflate the tires to recommended pressures.<br>2. Lubricate as necessary.<br>3. Adjust according to instructions.<br>4. Align the wheels.<br>5. See "Steering Gear Alignment."<br>6. Adjust or replace belt.<br>7. Bleed air from system.<br>8. Fill to correct level. |

89778c04

## Steering Trouble Diagnosis (cont.)

**Power Steering**

| Condition | Possible Cause | Correction |
|---|---|---|
| | 9. Pump output pressure low. | 9. See "Pressure Test." |
| | 10. Leakage at power cylinder piston rings. (Linkage type). | 10. Replace piston rings and repair as required. |
| | 11. Binding or bent cylinder linkage. (Linkage type). | 11. Replace or repair as required. |
| | 12. Valve spool and/or sleeve sticking. (Linkage type). | 12. Free-up or replace as required. |

89778c05

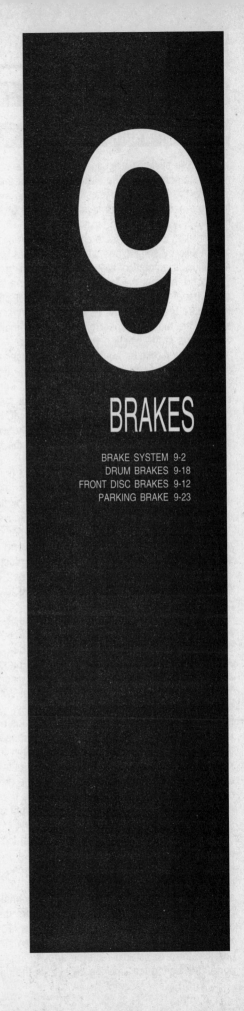

# 9

# BRAKES

## BRAKE SYSTEM

### Basic Operating Principles

Hydraulic systems are used to actuate the brakes of all modern automobiles. The system transports the power required to force the frictional surfaces of the braking system together from the pedal to the individual brake units at each wheel. A hydraulic system is used for two reasons.

First, fluid under pressure can be carried to all parts of an automobile by small pipes and flexible hoses without taking up a significant amount of room or posing routing problems.

Second, a great mechanical advantage can be given to the brake pedal end of the system, and the foot pressure required to actuate the brakes can be reduced by making the surface area of the master cylinder pistons smaller than that of any of the pistons in the wheel cylinders or calipers.

The master cylinder consists of a fluid reservoir along with a double cylinder and piston assembly. Double type master cylinders are designed to separate the front and rear braking systems hydraulically in case of a leak. The master cylinder coverts mechanical motion from the pedal into hydraulic pressure within the lines. This pressure is translated back into mechanical motion at the wheels by either the wheel cylinder (drum brakes) or the caliper (disc brakes).

Steel lines carry the brake fluid to a point on the vehicle's frame near each of the vehicle's wheels. The fluid is then carried to the calipers and wheel cylinders by flexible tubes in order to allow for suspension and steering movements.

In drum brake systems, each wheel cylinder contains two pistons, one at either end, which push outward in opposite directions and force the brake shoe into contact with the drum.

In disc brake systems, the cylinders are part of the calipers. At least one cylinder in each caliper is used to force the brake pads against the disc.

All pistons employ some type of seal, usually made of rubber, to minimize fluid leakage. A rubber dust boot seals the outer end of the cylinder against dust and dirt. The boot fits around the outer end of the piston on disc brake calipers, and around the brake actuating rod on wheel cylinders.

The hydraulic system operates as follows: When at rest, the entire system, from the piston(s) in the master cylinder to those in the wheel cylinders or calipers, is full of brake fluid. Upon application of the brake pedal, fluid trapped in front of the master cylinder piston(s) is forced through the lines to the wheel cylinders. Here, it forces the pistons outward, in the case of drum brakes, and inward toward the disc, in the case of disc brakes. The motion of the pistons is opposed by return springs mounted outside the cylinders in drum brakes, and by spring seals, in disc brakes.

Upon release of the brake pedal, a spring located inside the master cylinder immediately returns the master cylinder pistons to the normal position. The pistons contain check valves and the master cylinder has compensating ports drilled in it. These are uncovered as the pistons reach their normal position. The piston check valves allow fluid to flow toward the wheel cylinders or calipers as the pistons withdraw. Then, as the return springs force the brake pads or shoes into the released position, the excess fluid reservoir through the compensating ports. It is during the time the pedal is in the released position

that any fluid that has leaked out of the system will be replaced through the compensating ports.

Dual circuit master cylinders employ two pistons, located one behind the other, in the same cylinder. The primary piston is actuated directly by mechanical linkage from the brake pedal through the power booster. The secondary piston is actuated by fluid trapped between the two pistons. If a leak develops in front of the secondary piston, it moves forward until it bottoms against the front of the master cylinder, and the fluid trapped between the pistons will operate the rear brakes. If the rear brakes develop a leak, the primary piston will move forward until direct contact with the secondary piston takes place, and it will force the secondary piston to actuate the front brakes. In either case, the brake pedal moves farther when the brakes are applied, and less braking power is available.

All dual circuit systems use a switch to warn the driver when only half of the brake system is operational. This switch is usually located in a valve body which is mounted on the firewall or the frame below the master cylinder. A hydraulic piston receives pressure from both circuits, each circuit's pressure being applied to one end of the piston. When the pressures are in balance, the piston remains stationary. When one circuit has a leak, however, the greater pressure in that circuit during application of the brakes will push the piston to one side, closing the switch and activating the brake warning light.

In disc brake systems, this valve body also contains a metering valve and, in some cases, a proportioning valve. The metering valve keeps pressure from traveling to the disc brakes on the front wheels until the brake shoes on the rear wheels have contacted the drums, ensuring that the front brakes will never be used alone. The proportioning valve controls the pressure to the rear brakes to lessen the chance of rear wheel lock-up during very hard braking.

Warning lights may be tested by depressing the brake pedal and holding it while opening one of the wheel cylinder bleeder screws. If this does not cause the light to go on, substitute a new lamp, make continuity checks, and, finally, replace the switch as necessary.

The hydraulic system may be checked for leaks by applying pressure to the pedal gradually and steadily. If the pedal sinks very slowly to the floor, the system has a leak. This is not to be confused with a springy or spongy feel due to the compression of air within the lines. If the system leaks, there will be a gradual change in the position of the pedal with a constant pressure.

Check for leaks along all lines and at wheel cylinders. If no external leaks are apparent, the problem is inside the master cylinder.

### DISC BRAKES

Instead of the traditional expanding brakes that press outward against a circular drum, disc brake systems utilize a disc (rotor) with brake pads positioned on either side of it. An easily-seen analogy is the hand brake arrangement on a bicycle. The pads squeeze onto the rim of the bike wheel, slowing its motion. Automobile disc brakes use the identical

inciple but apply the braking effort to a separate disc instead
the wheel.

The disc (rotor) is a casting, usually equipped with cooling
s between the two braking surfaces. This enables air to
rculate between the braking surfaces making them less
ensitive to heat buildup and more resistant to fade. Dirt and
ater do not drastically affect braking action since
ontaminants are thrown off by the centrifugal action of the
tor or scraped off the by the pads. Also, the equal clamping
ction of the two brake pads tends to ensure uniform, straight
e stops. Disc brakes are inherently self-adjusting. There are
ree general types of disc brake:
1. A fixed caliper.
2. A floating caliper.
3. A sliding caliper.

The fixed caliper design uses two pistons mounted on either
de of the rotor (in each side of the caliper). The caliper is
ounted rigidly and does not move.

The sliding and floating designs are quite similar. In fact,
ese two types are often lumped together. In both designs,
e pad on the inside of the rotor is moved into contact with
e rotor by hydraulic force. The caliper, which is not held in a
xed position, moves slightly, bringing the outside pad into
ontact with the rotor. There are various methods of attaching
oating calipers. Some pivot at the bottom or top, and some
ide on mounting bolts. In any event, the end result is the
ame.

## RUM BRAKES

Drum brakes employ two brake shoes mounted on a
tationary backing plate. These shoes are positioned inside a
rcular drum which rotates with the wheel assembly. The
hoes are held in place by springs. This allows them to slide
oward the drums (when they are applied) while keeping the
nings and drums in alignment. The shoes are actuated by a
wheel cylinder which is mounted at the top of the backing
late. When the brakes are applied, hydraulic pressure forces
e wheel cylinder's actuating links outward. Since these links
ear directly against the top of the brake shoes, the tops of
e shoes are then forced against the inner side of the drum.
his action forces the bottoms of the two shoes to contact the
rake drum by rotating the entire assembly slightly (known as
ervo action). When pressure within the wheel cylinder is
elaxed, return springs pull the shoes back away from the
rum.

Most modern drum brakes are designed to self-adjust
hemselves during application when the vehicle is moving in
everse. This motion causes both shoes to rotate very slightly
with the drum, rocking an adjusting lever, thereby causing
otation of the adjusting screw. Some drum brake systems are
esigned to self-adjust during application whenever the brakes
are applied. This on-board adjustment system reduces the
eed for maintenance adjustments and keeps both the brake
unction and pedal feel satisfactory.

## Adjustments

### DRUM BRAKES

These brakes are equipped with self-adjusters and no
manual adjustment is necessary, except when brake linings are
replaced. Please refer to the shoe replacement procedures.

### DISC BRAKES

These brakes are inherently self-adjusting and no adjustment
is necessary or possible.

### BRAKE PEDAL

The stop light switch provides for an automatic adjustment
for the brake pedal when it is returned to its stop. With pedal
in fully released position, the stop light switch plunger should
be fully depressed against the pedal shank. Adjust the switch
by moving in or out as necessary.

1. Make certain that the tubular clip is in brake pedal
mounting bracket.

2. With brake pedal depressed, insert switch into tubular
clip until switch body seats on clip. Audible clicks can be
heard as the threaded portion of the switch is pushed through
the clip toward the brake pedal.

3. Pull brake pedal fully rearward against pedal stop until
audible clicking sounds can no longer be heard. Switch will be
moved in tubular clip providing adjustment.

4. Release brake pedal and then repeat Step 3 to assure
that no audible clicking sounds remain.

## Master Cylinder

### REMOVAL & INSTALLATION

▶ See Figures 1, 2, 3, 4 and 5

### ✳✳WARNING

**Do not allow brake fluid to spill on the vehicle's finish, it
will remove the paint. Flush the area with water.**

1. Using a clean cloth, wipe the master cylinder and its
lines to remove excess dirt and then place cloths under the
unit to absorb spilled fluid.

2. Remove the hydraulic lines from the master cylinder and
plug the outlets to prevent the entrance of foreign material.

3. Disconnect the brake pushrod from the brake pedal on
non-power brakes.

4. Remove the attaching bolts and remove the master cylinder from the firewall or the brake booster.

**To install:**

5. Connect the pushrod to the brake pedal with the pin and
retainer.

**Fig. 1 Using an old turkey baster, remove most of the old fluid from the master cylinder**

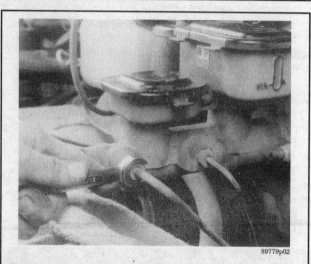

**Fig. 2 Using a flare nut wrench, unfasten the hydraulic lines from the master cylinder**

**Fig. 3 Unfasten the master cylinder-to-booster retainers**

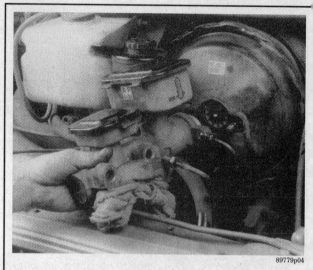

**Fig. 4 Remove the master cylinder from the vehicle**

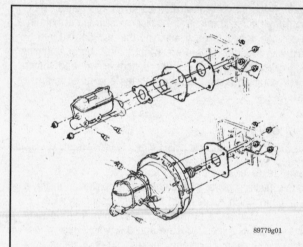

**Fig. 5 Views of the power brake and non-power brake master cylinder mountings**

6. Connect the brake lines and fill the master cylinder reservoirs to the proper levels.

7. Bleed the brake system as outlined in this section.

## OVERHAUL

▶ **See Figures 6 and 7**

In most years, there are 2 sources for master cylinders, Delco-Moraine and Bendix. The Bendix unit can readily be identified by the secondary stop bolt on the bottom, which is not present on the Delco-Moraine unit. Some early models use a Wagner unit which has the cover secured by a bolt. Master cylinders bearing identifying code letters should only be replaced with cylinders bearing the same code letters. Secondary pistons are also coded by rings or grooves on the shank or center section of the piston, and should only be replaced with pistons having the same code. The primary pistons also are of 2 types. One has a deep socket for the pushrod and the other

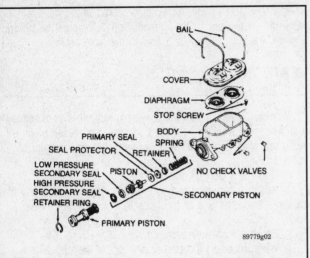

**Fig. 6 Exploded view of a common master cylinder and its internal components**

has a very shallow socket. Be sure to replace pistons with identical parts. Failure to do this could result in a malfunction.

➡This procedure applies to all Delco master cylinders, but not to the Bendix unit used on 1976 and later G-30 and 3500 motorhome models with the Hydro-Boost brake system.

1. Remove the secondary piston stop screw at the bottom of the master cylinder front reservoir.
2. Position the master cylinder in a vise covering the jaws with cloth to prevent damage. (Do not tighten the vise too tightly).
3. Remove the lockring from the inside of the piston bore. Once this is done, the primary piston assembly may be removed.
4. The secondary piston, piston spring, and the retainer may be removed by blowing compressed air through the stop screw hole. If compressed air is not available, the piston may be removed with a small piece of wire. Bend the wire ¼ in.

(6.35mm) from the end to the edge of the secondary piston and pull it from the bore. The brass insert should not be removed unless it is being replaced.

5. Inspect the piston bore for corrosion or other obstructions. Make certain that the outer ports are clean and the fluid reservoirs are free of foreign matter. Check the by-pass and the compensating ports to see if they are clogged.
6. Remove the primary seal, seal protector, and secondary seals from the secondary piston.

Clean all parts in denatured alcohol or brake fluid. Use a soft brush to clean metal parts and compressed air to dry all parts. If corrosion is found inside the housing, either a crocus cloth or fine emery paper can be used to remove these deposits. Remember to wash all parts after this cleaning. Be sure to keep the parts clean until assembly. If there is any doubt of cleanliness, wash the part again. All rubber parts should be clean and free of fluid. Check each rubber part for cuts, nicks, or other damage. If there is any doubt as to the condition of any rubber part, it is best to replace it.

➡Since there are differences between master cylinders, it is important that the assemblies are identified correctly. There is a 2-letter metal stamp located at the end of the master cylinder. If the master cylinder is replaced, it must be replaced with a cylinder with the same markings.

7. Install the new secondary piston assembly.

➡The seal which is nearest the flat end has its lips facing toward the flat end. On Delco units, the seal in the second groove has its lips facing toward the compensating holes of the secondary piston. On Bendix units, the seal is an O-ring.

8. Install the new primary seal and seal protector over the end of the secondary piston opposite the secondary seals. It should be positioned so that the flat side of the seal seats against the flange of the piston with the compensating holes.

➡The seal protector isn't used on 1977 and later models.

9. Install the complete primary piston assembly included in every repair kit.

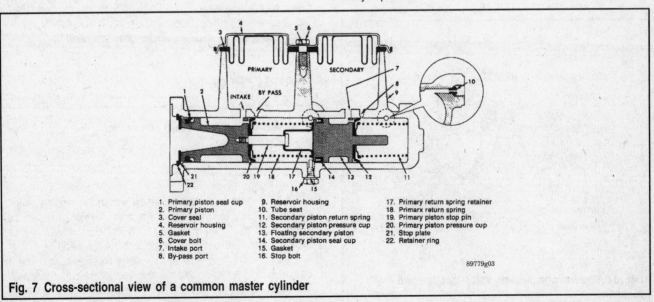

| | |
|---|---|
| 1. Primary piston seal cup | 9. Reservoir housing |
| 2. Primary piston | 10. Tube seat |
| 3. Cover seal | 11. Secondary piston return spring |
| 4. Reservoir housing | 12. Secondary piston pressure cup |
| 5. Gasket | 13. Floating secondary piston |
| 6. Cover bolt | 14. Secondary piston seal cup |
| 7. Intake port | 15. Gasket |
| 8. By-pass port | 16. Stop bolt |

17. Primary return spring retainer
18. Primarx return spring
19. Primary piston stop pin
20. Primary piston pressure cup
21. Stop plate
22. Retainer ring

**Fig. 7 Cross-sectional view of a common master cylinder**

10. Coat the master cylinder bore and the primary and secondary seals with brake fluid. Position the secondary seal spring retainer into the secondary piston spring.

11. Place the retainer and spring over the end of the secondary piston so that the retainer is placed inside the lips of the primary seal.

12. Seat the secondary piston. It may be necessary to manipulate the piston to get it to seat.

13. Position the master cylinder with the open end up and coat the primary and secondary seals on the primary piston with brake fluid. Push the primary piston into the bore of the master cylinder. Hold the piston and position the lockring.

14. Still holding the piston down, install and tighten the stop screw to torque of 25-40 in. lbs. (2-4 Nm).

15. Install the reservoir cover and also the cover on the master cylinder and its retaining clip.

16. Bleed the master cylinder of air by positioning it with the front slightly down, filling it with brake fluid, and working the primary piston until all the bubbles are gone.

## Combination Valve

### OPERATION

▶ **See Figure 8**

This valve is used on all models with disc brakes. It is non-adjustable and non-serviceable. It can be found by following the lines from the master cylinder. The combination valve itself contains a metering valve that restricts flow to the front brakes until the rear brakes overcome the force of their retracting springs to prevent front brake lockup, a pressure differential warning switch which activates a warning light if either the front or rear hydraulic circuit is losing pressure, and a proportioning valve which limits hydraulic pressure to the rear brakes to prevent rear wheel lockup.

The pressure differential warning switch will reset itself automatically when the brakes are used after a malfunction causing the warning light to go on has been corrected.

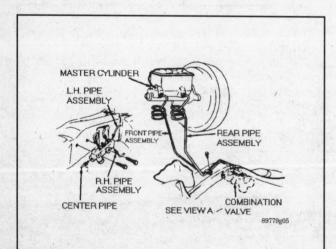

MASTER CYLINDER
L.H. PIPE ASSEMBLY
FRONT PIPE ASSEMBLY
REAR PIPE ASSEMBLY
R.H. PIPE ASSEMBLY
CENTER PIPE
SEE VIEW A
COMBINATION VALVE
89779g05

**Fig. 8 Common combination valve location and mounting**

When the brake hydraulic system is bled of air, the metering valve pin on the end of the combination valve must be hold in a slight amount to allow fluid flow to the front brakes.

### CENTERING THE SWITCH

Whenever work on the brake system is done it is possible that the brake warning light will come on and refuse to go off when the work is finished. In this event, the switch must be centered.

1. Raise and support the truck.

2. Attach a bleeder hose to the rear brake bleed screw and immerse the other end of the hose in a jar of clean brake fluid.

3. Be sure that the master cylinder is full.

4. When bleeding the brakes, the pin in the end of the metering portion of the combination valve must be hold in the open position (with the tool described in the brake bleeding section installed under the pin mounting bolt). Be sure to tighten the bolt after removing the tool.

5. Turn the ignition key **ON**. Open the bleed screw while an assistant applies heavy pressure on the brake pedal. The warning lamp should light. Close the bleed screw before the helper releases the pedal.

To reset the switch, apply heavy pressure to the pedal. This will apply hydraulic pressure to the switch which will re-center it.

6. Repeat Step 5 for the front bleed screw.

7. Turn the ignition **OFF** and lower the truck.

➡ **If the warning lamp does not light during Step 5, the switch is defective and must be replaced.**

## Hydro-Boost System

Diesel engined trucks are equipped with the Bendix Hydro-boost system. This power brake booster obtains hydraulic pressure from the power steering pump, rather than vacuum pressure from the intake manifold as in most gasoline engine brake booster systems. Procedures from removing, overhauling, and replacing the master cylinder are the same as previously outlined. The master cylinder uses the same DOT 3 brake fluid recommended for other systems.

### SYSTEM CHECKS

1. A defective Hydro-Boost cannot cause any of the following conditions:
   a. Noisy brakes
   b. Fading pedal
   c. Pulling brakes.
If any of these occur, check elsewhere in the brake system.

2. Check the fluid level in the master cylinder. It should be within ¼ in. (6.35mm) of the top. If is isn't add only DOT-3 or DOT-4 brake fluid until the correct level is reached.

3. Check the fluid level in the power steering pump. The engine should be at normal running temperature and stopped. The level should register on the pump dipstick. Add power steering fluid to bring the reservoir level up to the correct level.

Low fluid level will result in both poor steering and stopping ability.

## ✳✳WARNING

**The brake hydraulic system uses brake fluid only, while the power steering and Hydro-Boost systems use power steering fluid only. Don't mix the two.**

4. Check the power steering pump belt tension, and inspect all the power steering/Hydro-Boost hoses for kinks or leaks.

5. Check and adjust the engine idle speed, as necessary.

6. Check the power steering pump fluid for bubbles. If air bubbles are present in the fluid, bleed the system:

    a. Fill the power steering pump reservoir to specifications with the engine at normal operating temperature.

    b. With the engine running, rotate the steering wheel through its normal travel 3 or 4 times, without holding the wheel against the stops.

    c. Check the fluid level again.

7. If the problem still exists, go on to the Hydro-Boost test and troubleshooting sections.

## TROUBLESHOOTING

### High Pedal and Steering Effort (Idle)

1. Loosen/broken power steering pump belt
2. Low power steering fluid level
3. Leaking hoses or fittings
4. Low idle speed
5. Hose restriction
6. Defective power steering pump

### High Pedal Effort (Idle)

1. Binding pedal/linkage
2. Fluid contamination
3. Defective Hydro-Boost unit

### Poor Pedal Return

1. Binding pedal linkage
2. Restricted booster return line
3. Internal return system restriction

### Pedal Chatter/Pulsation

1. Power steering pump drive belt slipping
2. Low power steering fluid level
3. Defective power steering pump
4. Defective Hydro-Boost unit

### Brakes Oversensitive

1. Binding linkage
2. Defective Hydro-Boost unit

### Noise

1. Low power steering fluid level
2. Air in the power steering fluid
3. Loose power steering pump drive belt
4. Hose restrictions

## TESTING

### Functional Test

1. Check the brake system for leaks or low fluid level. Correct as necessary.

2. Place the transmission in Neutral and stop the engine. Apply the brakes 4 or 5 times to empty the accumulator.

3. Keep the pedal depressed with moderate pressure 25-40 lbs. (111-177 N) pressure and start the engine.

4. The brake pedal should fall slightly and then push back up against your foot. If no movement is felt, the Hydro-Boost system is not working.

### Accumulator Leak Test

1. Run the engine at normal idle. Turn the steering wheel against one of the stops; hold it there for no longer than 5 seconds. Center the steering wheel and stop the engine.

2. Keep applying the brakes until a hard pedal is obtained. There should be a minimum of 1 power assisted brake application when pedal pressure of 20 25 lbs. is applied.

3. Start the engine and allow it to idle. Rotate the steering wheel against the stop. Listen for a light hissing sound; this is the accumulator being charged. Center the steering wheel and stop the engine.

4. Wait one hour and apply the brakes without starting the engine. As in Step 2, there should be at least 1 stop with power assist. If not, the accumulator is defective and must be replaced.

## SYSTEM BLEEDING

The system should be bled whenever the booster is removed and installed.

1. Fill the power steering pump until the fluid level is at the base of the pump reservoir neck. Disconnect the battery lead from the distributor.

➡**Remove the electrical lead to the fuel solenoid terminal on the injection pump before cranking the engine.**

2. Jack up the front of the car, turn the wheels all the way to the left, and crank the engine for a few seconds.

3. Check steering pump fluid level. If necessary, add fluid to the **Add** mark on the dipstick.

4. Lower the car, connect the battery lead, and start the engine. Check fluid level and add fluid to the **Add** mark is necessary. With the engine running, turn the wheels from side to side to bleed air from the system. Make sure that the fluid level stays above the internal pump casting.

5. The Hydro-Boost system should now be fully bled. If the fluid is foaming after bleeding, stop the engine, let the system set for one hour, then repeat the second part of Step 4.

The preceding procedures should be effective in removing the excess air from the system, however sometimes air may still remain trapped. When this happens the booster may make a gulping noise when the brake is applied. Lightly pumping the brake pedal with the engine running should cause this noise to disappear. After the noise stops, check the pump fluid level and add as necessary.

## OVERHAUL

▶ **See Figure 9**

GMC Hydro-Boost units may be rebuilt. Kits are available through auto parts jobbers and GMC/Chevrolet truck dealers.

➡ **Have a drain pan ready to catch and discard leaking fluid during disassembly.**

Use the accompanying illustration to overhaul the Hydro-Boost system. If replacing the power piston/accumulator, dispose of the old one as shown.

## REMOVAL & INSTALLATION

### Spool Valve Plug and Seal

▶ **See Figures 10 and 11**

1. Turn the engine off and pump the brake pedal 4 or 5 times to deplete the accumulator inside the boost unit.

2. Remove the master cylinder from the boost unit with the brake lines attached. Fasten the master cylinder out of the way with tape or wire.

3. Push the spool valve plug in and use a small screwdriver to carefully remove the retaining ring.

4. Remove the spool valve plug and O-ring.

5. Installation is the reverse of removal. Bleed the system upon installation, following the above bleeding instructions.

### Hydro-Boost Unit

> **✳✳WARNING**
>
> **Power steering fluid and brake fluid cannot be mixed. If brake seals contact the steering fluid or steering seals contact the brake fluid, damage will result.**

1. Turn the engine off and pump the brake pedal 4 or 5 times to deplete the accumulator inside the unit.

2. Remove the two nuts from the master cylinder, and remove the cylinder keeping the brake lines attached. Secure the master cylinder out of the way.

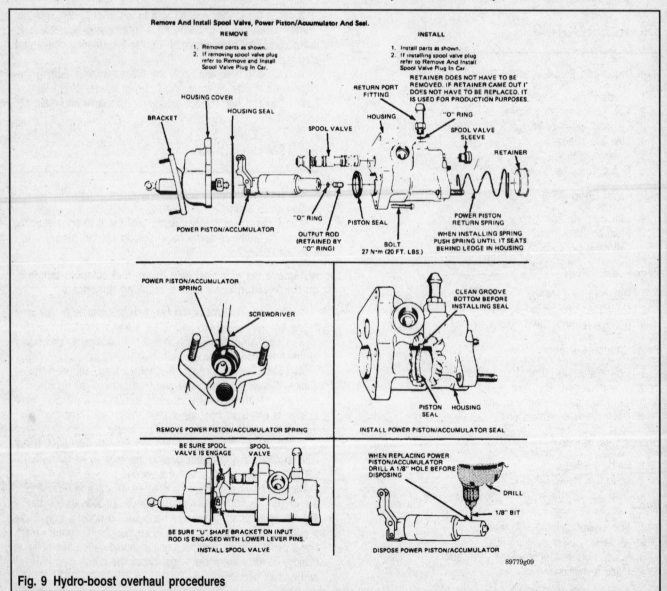

Fig. 9 Hydro-boost overhaul procedures

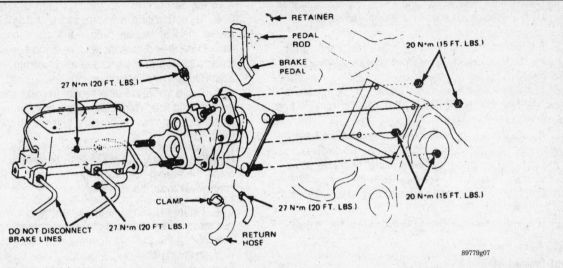

**Fig. 10 Exploded view of the Hydro-booster location and mounting**

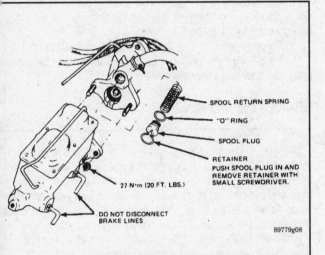

**Fig. 11 Removing the Hydro-boost spool valve and seal**

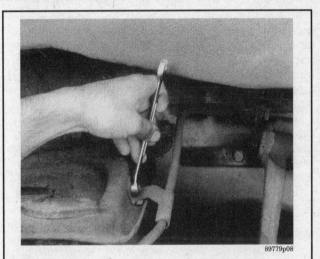

**Fig. 12 Unfasten the retainer from the brake hose bracket**

3. Remove the three hydraulic lines from the booster.
4. Remove the booster unit from the firewall.
5. To install, reverse the removal procedure. Bleed the Hydro-Boost system.

## Brake Hoses and Pipes

### REMOVAL & INSTALLATION

#### Brake Hose
◆ See Figures 12 and 13

1. Raise the end of the vehicle which contains the hose to be repaired, then support the vehicle safely using jackstands.
2. If necessary, remove the wheel for easier access to the hose.

**Fig. 13 Remove the brake hose bracket**

3. Disconnect the hose from the wheel cylinder or caliper and plug the opening to avoid excessive fluid loss or contamination.

4. Disconnect the hose from the brake line and plug the openings to avoid excessive fluid loss or contamination.

**To install:**

5. Install the brake hose to the brake line and tighten to 14 ft. lbs. (19 Nm) for rear brakes or .18 ft. lbs. (24 Nm) for front brakes.

6. If installing a front brake hose, make sure the hose is routed properly, with the loop to the rear of the vehicle.

7. Install the hose to the wheel cylinder or caliper using NEW washers, then tighten the retainer to 36 ft. lbs. (49 Nm).

8. Properly bleed the brake system, then check the connections for leaks.

9. Remove the supports and carefully lower the vehicle.

### Brake Line

▶ See Figure 14

There are 2 options available when replacing a brake line. The first, and probably most preferable, is to replace the entire line using a line of similar length which is already equipped with machined flared ends. Such lines are usually available from auto parts stores and usually require only a minimum of bending in order to properly fit then to the vehicle. The second option is to bend and flare the entire replacement line (or a repair section of line) using the appropriate tools.

Buying a line with machined flares is usually preferable because of the time and effort saved, not to mention the cost of special tools if they are not readily available. Also, machined flares are usually of a much higher quality than those produced by hand flaring tools or kits.

1. Raise the end of the vehicle which contains the hose to be repaired, then support the vehicle safely using jackstands.

2. Remove the components necessary for access to the brake line which is being replaced.

3. Disconnect the fittings at each end of the line, then plug the openings to prevent excessive fluid loss or contamination.

4. Trace the line from 1 end to the other and disconnect the line from any retaining clips, then remove the line from the vehicle.

89779p10

**Fig. 14 Unfasten the brake line from the rear brakes**

**To install:**

5. Try to obtain a replacement line that is the same length as the line that was removed. If the line is longer, you will have to cut it and flare the end, or if you have decided to repair a portion of the line, see the procedure on brake line flaring, later in this section.

6. Use a suitable tubing bender to make the necessary bends in the line. Work slowly and carefully; try to make the bends look as close as possible to those on the line being replaced.

➡ **When bending the brake line, be careful not to kink or crack the line. If the brake line becomes kinked or cracked, it must be replaced.**

7. Before installing the brake line, flush it with brake cleaner to remove any dirt or foreign material.

8. Install the line into the vehicle. Be sure to attach the line to the retaining clips, as necessary. Make sure the replacement brake line does not contact any components that could rub the line and cause a leak.

9. Connect the brake line fittings and tighten to 18 ft. lbs. (24 Nm), except for the rear line-to-hose fitting which should be tightened to 14 ft. lbs. (19 Nm).

10. Properly bleed the brake system and check for leaks.

11. Install any removed components, then remove the supports and carefully lower the vehicle.

## BRAKE LINE FLARING

Use only brake line tubing approved for automotive use; never use copper tubing. Whenever possible, try to work with brake lines that are already cut to the length needed. These lines are available at most auto parts stores and have machine made flares, the quality of which is hard to duplicate with most of the available inexpensive flaring kits.

When the brakes are applied, there is a great amount of pressure developed in the hydraulic system. An improperly formed flare can leak with resultant loss of stopping power. If you have never formed a double-flare, take time to familiarize yourself with the flaring kit; practice forming double-flares on scrap tubing until you are satisfied with the results.

The following procedure applies to the SA9193BR flaring kit, but should be similar to commercially available brake-line flaring kits. If these instructions differ in any way from those in your kit, follow the instructions in the kit.

1. Determine the length necessary for the replacement or repair and allow an additional $\frac{1}{8}$ in. (3.2mm) for each flare. Select a piece of tubing, then cut the brake line to the necessary length using an appropriate saw. Do not use a tubing cutter.

2. Square the end of the tube with a file and chamfer the edges. Remove burrs from the inside and outside diameters of the cut line using a deburring tool.

3. Install the required fittings onto the line.

4. Install SA9193BR, or an equivalent flaring tool, into a vice and install the handle into the operating cam.

5. Loosen the die clamp screw and rotate the locking plate to expose the die carrier opening.

6. Select the required die set (4.75mm DIN) and install in the carrier with the full side of either half facing clamp screw and counter bore of both halves facing punch turret.

7. Insert the prepared line through the rear of the die and push forward until the line end is flush with the die face.

8. Make sure the rear of both halves of the die rest against the hexagon die stops, then rotate the locking plate to the fully closed position and clamp the die firmly by tightening the clamp screw.

9. Rotate the punch turret until the appropriate size (4.75mm DIN) points towards the open end of the line to be flared.

10. Pull the operating handle against the line resistance in order to create the flare, then return the handle to the original position.

11. release the clamp screw and rotate the locking plate to the open position.

12. Remove the die set and line, then separate by gently tapping both halves on the bench. Inspect the flare for proper size and shape. Dimension A should be 0.272-0.286 in. (6.92-7.28mm).

13. If necessary, repeat Steps 2-12 for the other end of the line or for the end of the line which is being repaired.

14. Bend the replacement line or section using SA91108NE, or an equivalent line bending tool.

15. If repairing the original line, join the old and new sections using a female union and tighten.

## Bleeding the Brakes

### SYSTEM BLEEDING

▶ See Figures 15 and 16

The brake system must be bled when any brake line is disconnected or there is air in the system.

### ✲✲WARNING

**Clean, high quality brake fluid is essential to the safe and proper operation of the brake system. You should always buy the highest quality brake fluid that is available. If the brake fluid becomes contaminated, drain and flush the system, then refill the master cylinder with new fluid. Never reuse any brake fluid. Any brake fluid that is removed from the system should be discarded.**

➡**Never bleed a wheel cylinder when a drum is removed.**

1. Clean the master cylinder of excess dirt and remove the cylinder cover and the diaphragm.

2. Fill the master cylinder to the proper level. Check the fluid level periodically during the bleeding process, and replenish it as necessary. Do not allow the master cylinder to run dry, or you will have to start over.

3. Before opening any of the bleeder screws, you may want to give each one a shot of penetrating solvent. This reduces the possibility of breakage when they are unscrewed.

4. Attach a length of vinyl hose to the bleeder screw of the brake to be bled. Insert the other end of the hose into a clear jar half full of brake fluid, so that the end of the hose is

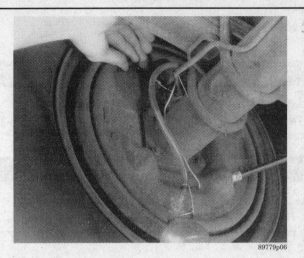

Fig. 15 Attch the hose and bottle to the bleeder screw, then loosen it with a flare nut wrench

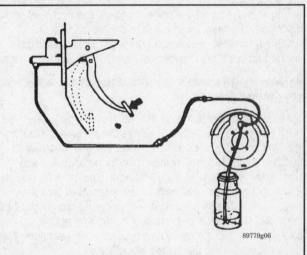

Fig. 16 Have an assistant pump, then hold in the brake pedal while you bleed each wheel

beneath the level of fluid. The correct sequence for bleeding is to work from the brake farthest from the master cylinder to the one closest; right rear, left rear, right front, left front.

5. The combination valve (all vehicles with disc brakes) must be held open during the bleeding process. A clip, tape, or other similar tool (or an assistant) will hold the metering pin in.

6. With power brakes, depress and release the brake pedal three or four times to exhaust any residual vacuum.

7. Have an assistant push down on the brake pedal. Open the bleeder valve slightly. As the pedal reaches the end of its travel, close the bleeder screw. Repeat this process until no air bubbles are visible in the expelled fluid.

➡**Make sure your assistant presses the brake pedal to the floor slowly. Pressing too fast will cause air bubbles to form in the fluid.**

8. Repeat this procedure at each of the brakes. Remember to check the master cylinder level occasionally. Use only fresh

fluid to refill the master cylinder, not the stuff bled from the system.

## FRONT DISC BRAKES

➡These procedures apply to Delco disc brake systems. They do not apply to the Bendix disc brakes used on G-30 and 3500 motorhomes.

### Brake Pads

#### INSPECTION

▶ **See Figures 17 and 18**

Support the front suspension or axle on jackstands and remove the wheels. Look in at the ends of the caliper to check the lining thickness of the outer pad. Look through the inspection hole in the top of the caliper to check the thickness of the inner pad. Minimum acceptable pad thickness is $\frac{1}{32}$ in. (0.79mm) from the rivet heads on original equipment riveted linings and $\frac{1}{2}$ in. (12.7mm) lining thickness on bonded linings.

➡**These manufacturer's specifications may not agree with your state inspection law.**

All original equipment pads are the riveted type; unless you want to remove the pads to measure the actual thickness from the rivet heads, you will have to make the limit for visual inspection $\frac{1}{16}$ in. (1.6mm) or more. The same applies if you don't know what kind of lining you have. The 1974-86 original equipment pads and GM replacement pads have an integral wear sensor. This is a spring steel tab on the rear edge of the inner pad which produces a squeal by rubbing against the rotor to warn that the pads have reached their wear limit. They do not squeal when the brakes are applied.

#### ✳✳WARNING

**The squeal will eventually stop if worn pads aren't replaced. Should this happen, replace the pads immediately to prevent expensive rotor (disc) damage.**

#### REMOVAL & INSTALLATION

The caliper has to be removed to replace the pads. Please refer to the caliper removal and installation procedure. Skip steps 8-10, as there is no need to detach the brake line.

### Caliper

#### REMOVAL & INSTALLATION

▶ **See Figures 19, 20, 21, 22, 23, 24, 25, 26 and 27**

1. Remove the cover on the master cylinder and siphon enough fluid out of the reservoirs to bring the level to $\frac{1}{3}$ full.

9. When the bleed process is complete, refill the master cylinder, install its cover and diaphragm, and discard the fluid bled from the brake system.

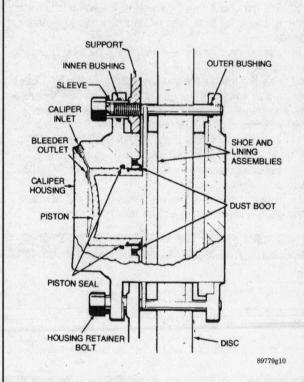

**Fig. 17 View of the disc and caliper components**

This step prevents spilling fluid when the piston is pushed back.

2. Raise and support the vehicle. Remove the front wheels and tires.

3. Push the brake piston back into its bore using a C-clamp to pull the caliper outward.

4. Remove the two bolts which hold the caliper and then lift the caliper off the disc.

#### ✳✳WARNING

**Do not let the caliper assembly hang by the brake hose.**

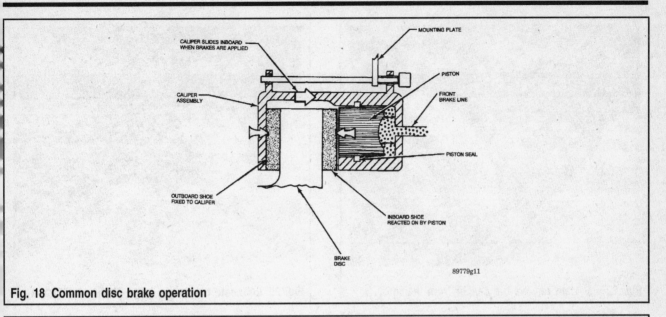

Fig. 18 Common disc brake operation

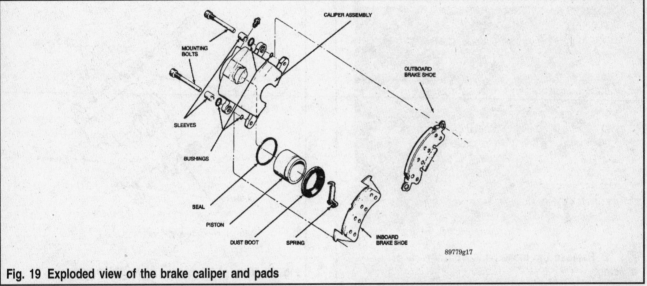

Fig. 19 Exploded view of the brake caliper and pads

Fig. 20 Use a C-clamp to push the piston back into the caliper

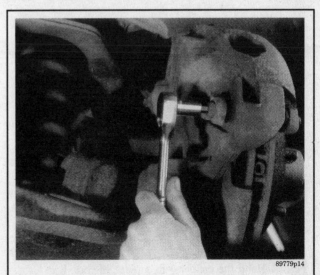

Fig. 21 Loosen and remove the caliper bolts . . .

Fig. 22 . . . then remove the caliper from the rotor

Fig. 23 Remove the brake pads from the caliper assembly

Fig. 24 Hang the caliper with a piece of wire. If necessary, detach the brake hose

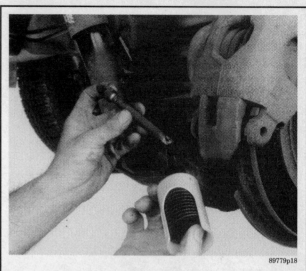

Fig. 25 Lubricate the caliper bolts before installation

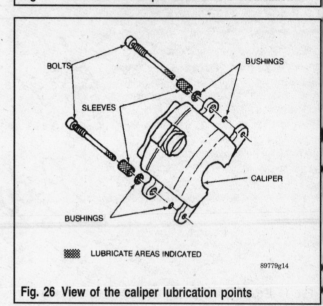

Fig. 26 View of the caliper lubrication points

Fig. 27 Installing the support spring

5. Remove the inboard and outboard shoe.

➡️**If the pads are to be reinstalled, mark them inside and outside.**

6. Remove the pad support spring from the piston.

7. Remove the two sleeves from the inside ears of the caliper and the 4 rubber bushings from the grooves in the caliper ears.

8. Remove the hose from the steel brake line and tape the fittings to prevent foreign material from entering the line or the hoses.

9. Remove the retainer from the hose fitting.

10. Remove the hose from the frame bracket and pull off the caliper with the hose attached.

➡️**Check the inside of the caliper for fluid leakage; if so, the caliper should be overhauled.**

### ✳✳WARNING

**Do not use compressed air to clean the inside of the caliper as this may unseat the dust boot.**

11. Connect the brake line to start reinstallaiton. Lubricate the sleeves, rubber bushings, bushing grooves, and the end of the mounting bolts using silicone lubricant.

12. Install new bushing in the caliper ears along with new sleeves. The sleeve should be replaced so that the end toward the shoe is flush with the machined surface of the ear.

13. Position the support spring and the inner pad into the center cavity of the piston. The outboard pad has ears which are bent over to keep the pad in position while the inboard pad has ears on the top end which fit over the caliper retaining bolts. A spring which is inside the brake piston hold the bottom edge of the inboard pad.

14. Push down on the inner pad until it lays flat against the caliper. It is important to push the piston all the way into the caliper if new linings are installed or the caliper will not fit over the rotor.

15. Position the outboard pad with the ears of the pad over the caliper ears and the tab at the bottom engaged in the caliper cutout.

16. With the two pads in position, place the caliper over the brake disc and align the holes in the caliper with those of the mounting bracket.

### ✳✳WARNING

**Make certain that the brake hose is not twisted or kinked.**

17. Install the mounting bracket bolts through the sleeves in the inboard caliper ears and through the mounting bracket, making sure that the ends of the bolts pass under the retaining ears on the inboard pad.

18. Tighten the mounting bolts to 35 ft. lbs. (47 Nm). Pump the brake pedal to seat the pad against the rotor. Don't do this unless both calipers are in place. Use a pair of channel lock pliers to bend over the upper ears of the outer pad so it isn't loose.

19. Install the front wheel and lower the truck.

20. Add fluid to the master cylinder reservoirs so that they are ¼ in. (6.35mm) from the top.

21. Test the brake pedal by pumping it to obtain a hard pedal. Check the fluid level again and add fluid as necessary. Do not move the vehicle until a hard pedal is obtained.

## OVERHAUL

▶ **See Figures 28, 29, 30, 31 and 32**

### ✳✳WARNING

**Use only denatured alcohol or brake fluid to clean caliper parts. Never use any mineral based cleaning solvents such as gasoline or kerosene as these solvents will deteriorate rubber parts.**

1. Remove the caliper, clean it and place it on a clean and level work surface.

2. Remove the brake hose from the caliper and discard the copper gasket. Check the brake hose for cracks or deterioration. Replace the hose as necessary.

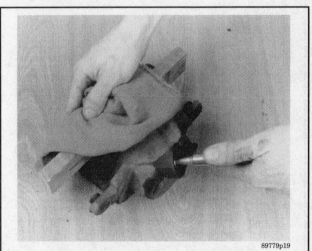

Fig. 28 Apply a small amount of compressed air to push the piston out

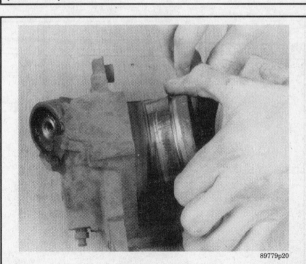

Fig. 29 Grasp the piston and remove it from the caliper bore

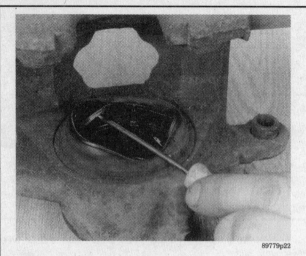

Fig. 30 Use extreme caution when removing the piston seal; DO NOT scratch the caliper bore

Fig. 31 Remove the boot from the caliper housing, taking care not to score or damage the bore

Fig. 32 View of the disassembled caliper and components

3. Drain the brake fluid from the caliper.
4. Pad the interior of the caliper with cloth and then apply compressed air to the caliper inlet hose.

### ✳✳CAUTION

**Do not place hands or fingers in front of the piston in an attempt to catch it. Use just enough air pressure to ease the piston out of the bore.**

5. Remove the piston dust boot by prying it out with a screwdriver. Use caution when performing this procedure.
6. Remove the piston seal from the caliper piston bore using a small piece of wood or plastic. DO NOT use any type of metal tool for this procedure.
7. Remove the bleeder valve from the caliper.
8. Clean all parts in the recommended solvent and dry them completely using compressed air if possible.

➡**The use of shop air hoses may inject oil film into the assembly; use caution when using such hoses.**

9. Examine the mounting bolts for rust or corrosion. Replace them as necessary.
10. Examine the piston for scoring, nicks, or worn plating. If any of these conditions are present, replace them as necessary.

### ✳✳WARNING

**Do not use any type of abrasive on the piston.**

11. Check the piston bore. Small defects can be removed with crocus cloth. If the bore cannot be cleaned in this manner, replace the caliper.
12. Lubricate the piston bore and the new piston seal with brake fluid. Place the seal in the caliper bore groove.
13. Lubricate the piston in the same manner and position the new boot into the groove in the piston so that the fold faces the open end of the piston.
14. Place the piston into the caliper bore using caution not to unseat the seal. Force the piston to the bottom of the bore.
15. Place the dust boot in the caliper counterbore and seat the boot. Make sure that the boot in positioned correctly and evenly.
16. Install the brake hose in the caliper inlet using a new copper gasket.

➡**The hose must be positioned in the caliper locating gate to assure proper positioning of the caliper.**

17. Replace the bleeder screw.
18. Bleed the system.

## Brake Disc (Rotor)

### INSPECTION

The minimum wear thickness, 1.215 in. (30.861mm), is cast into each disc hub. This is a minimum wear dimension and not a refinish dimension. If the thickness of the disc after refinishing will be 1.230 in. (31.242mm) or less, it must be replaced.

efinishing is required whenever the disc surface shows scor-
g or severe rust scale. Scoring not deeper than 0.015 in.
0.381mm) in depth can be corrected by refinishing.

➡Some discs have an anti-squeal groove. This should not
e mistaken for scoring.

## REMOVAL & INSTALLATION

**See Figures 33, 34, 35, 36 and 37**

1. Follow the procedures outlined for removing the caliper
ssembly.
2. Remove the bearing dust cap, cotter pin, center nut, and
uter bearings.
3. Pull the rotor off the spindle and service it, as
ecessary.
To install the unit, reverse the removal procedure. Check the
otor before install it. Pack the inner and outer bearing to the
roper specifications. (See Wheel Bearings).

**Fig. 35** . . . then remove the castellated nut

**Fig. 33 Remove the dust cap using a prytool**

**Fig. 36 Remove the outer bearing assembly** . . .

**Fig. 34 Remove the cotter pin** . . .

**Fig. 37** . . . then remove the rotor

## DRUM BRAKES

### Brake Drum

#### REMOVAL & INSTALLATION

▶ See Figure 38

> **✳✳CAUTION**
>
> Do not blow the brake dust out of the drums with compressed air. It may contain asbestos, which has been found to be a cancer producing agent.

Drums can be removed by raising the vehicle, removing the wheel lugs and the tire, and pulling the drum from the brake assembly. If the brake drums have been scored from worn linings, the brake adjuster must be backed off so that the brake shoes will retract from the drum. To remove the drums from full floating rear axles, follow Steps 1-11 of the Axle Shaft removal and installation procedure in Section 7. Full floating rear axles can readily be identified by the bearing housing protruding through the center of the wheel.

The adjuster can be backed off by inserting a brake adjusting tool through the access hole provided. In some cases the access hole is provided in the brake drum. A metal cover plate is over the hole. This may be removed by using a hammer and chisel.

➡**Make sure all metal particles are removed from the brake drum before reassembly.**

89779p31

**Fig. 38 Slide the brake drum off of the wheel studs on the axle shaft**

To install, reverse the removal procedure.

#### INSPECTION

When the drum is removed, it should be inspected for cracks, scores, or other imperfections. These must be corrected before the drum is replaced.

> **✳✳CAUTION**
>
> If the drum is found to be cracked, replace it. Do not attempt to service a cracked drum.

Minor drum score marks can be removed with fine emery cloth. Heavy score marks must be removed by turning the drum. This is removing metal from the entire inner surface of the drum on a lathe in order to level the surface. Automotive machine shops and some large parts stores are equipped to perform this operation.

If the drum is not scored, it should be polished with fine emery cloth before replacement. If the drum is resurfaced, it should not be enlarged more than 0.060 in. (1.524mm).

➡**Your state inspection law may disagree with this specification.**

It is advisable, while the drums are off, to check them for out-of-round. An inside micrometer is necessary for an exact measurement, therefore unless this tool is available, the drum should be taken to a machine shop to be checked. Any drum which is more than 0.006 in. (0.1524mm) out-of-round will result in an inaccurate brake adjustment and other problems, and should be refinished or replaced.

➡**Make all measurements at right angles to each other and at the open and closed edges of the drum machined surface.**

### Brake Shoes

#### INSPECTION

Remove the drum and inspect the lining thickness on both brake shoes. A front brake lining should be replaced if it is less than 1/8 in. (3mm) thick at the lowest point on the brake shoe. The wear limit for rear brake linings is 1/16 in. (1.5875mm).

➡**Brake shoes should always be replaced in axle sets. The wear specifications given may disagree with your state inspection rules.**

## REMOVAL & INSTALLATION

▶ See Figures 39, 40, 41, 42, 43, 44, 45, 46, 47 and 48

### ✳✳CAUTION

Brake shoes may contain asbestos, which has been determined to be a cancer causing agent. Never clean the brake surfaces with compressed air! Avoid inhaling any dust from any brake surface! When cleaning brake surfaces, use a commercially available brake cleaning fluid.

1. Jack up and securely support the vehicle.
2. Loosen the parking brake equalizer enough to remove all tension on the brake cable (rear brakes only).

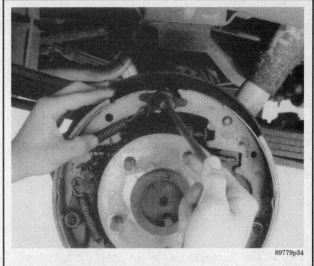
Fig. 41 Remove the second return spring . . . .

Fig. 39 Use an evaporative spray brake cleaner to remove brake dust from the components

Fig. 42 . . . then remove the actuator link

Fig. 40 Use a brake tool to release the return springs

Fig. 43 Remove the shoe guide from the stud at the top of the backing plate

89779p37

**Fig. 44 Use the brake tool to compress the hold-down spring and twist the plate to free the pin**

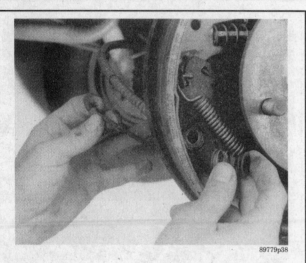

89779p38

**Fig. 45 Once the pin and the slot on top of the plate are aligned, separate the hold-down spring and pin**

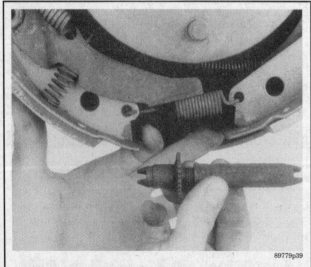

89779p39

**Fig. 46 You can remove the adjuster spring at this time**

89779p40

**Fig. 47 Remove the bottom return spring**

89779p43

**Fig. 48 Remove the parking brake strut and spring**

3. Remove the brake drums.

**☀☀WARNING**

**The brake pedal must not be depressed while the drums are removed.**

4. Using a brake tool, remove the shoe springs. You can do this with ordinary tools, buy it isn't easy.

5. Remove the self-adjuster actuator spring.

6. Remove the link from the secondary shoe by pulling it from the anchor pin.

7. Remove the hold-down pins. These are the brackets which run though the backing plate. They can be removed with a pair of pliers. Reach around the rear of the backing plate and hold the back of the pin. Turn the top of the pin retainer 45° with the plier. This will align the elongated tang with the slot in the retainer. Be careful, as the pin is spring loaded and may fly off when released. Use the same procedure for the other pin assembly.

8. Remove the adjuster actuator assembly.

➤Since the actuator, pivot, and override spring are considered an assembly it is not recommended that they be disassembled.

9. Remove the shoes from the backing plate. Make sure that you have a secure grip on the assembly as the bottom spring will still exert pressure on the shoes. Slowly let the tops of the shoes come together and the tension will decrease and the adjuster and spring may be removed.

➤If the linings are to be reused, mark them for identification.

10. Remove the rear parking brake lever from the secondary shoe. Using a pair of plier, pull back on the spring which surrounds the cable. At the same time, remove the cable from the notch in the shoe bracket. Make sure that the spring does not snap back or injury may result.

11. Use a cloth to remove dirt from the brake drum. Check the drums for scoring and cracks. Have the drums checked for out-of-round and service the drums as necessary.

12. Check the wheel cylinders by carefully pulling the lower edges of the wheel cylinder boots away from the cylinders. If there is excessive leakage, the inside of the cylinder will be moist with fluid. If there is any leakage at all, a cylinder overhaul is in order. DO NOT delay, as a brake failure could result.

➤A small amount of fluid will be present to act as a lubricant for the wheel cylinder pistons.

13. Check the flange plate, which is located around the axle, for leakage of differential lubricant. This condition cannot be overlooked as the lubricant will be absorbed into the brake linings and brake failure will result. Replace the seals as necessary. See Section 7 for details.

➤If new linings are being installed, check them against the old units for length and type.

14. Check the new linings for imperfections.

15. Lightly lubricate the parking brake and cable and the end of the parking brake lever where it enters the shoe. Use high temperature, waterproof, grease or special brake lube.

16. Install the parking brake lever into the secondary shoe with the attaching bolt, spring washer, lockwasher, and nut. It is important that the lever move freely before the shoe is attached. Move the assembly and check for proper action.

17. Lubricate the adjusting screw and make sure that it works freely. Sometimes the adjusting screw will not move due to lack of lubricant or dirt contamination and the brakes will not adjust. In this case, the adjuster should be disassembled, thoroughly cleaned, and lubricated before installation.

18. Connect the brake shoe spring to the bottom portion of both shoes. Make certain that the brake linings are installed in the correct manner, the primary and secondary shoe in the correct position. If you are not sure remove the other brake drum and check it.

19. Install the adjusting mechanism below the spring and separate the top of the shoes.

20. Make the following checks before installation:
a. Be certain that the right hand thread adjusting screw is on the left hand side of the vehicle and the left hand screw is on the right hand side of the vehicle.
b. Make sure that the star adjuster is aligned with the adjusting hole.
c. The adjuster should be installed with the starwheel nearest the secondary shoe and the tension spring away from the adjusting mechanism;
d. If the original linings are being reused, put them back in their original locations.

21. Install the parking brake cable.

22. Position the primary shoe (the shoe with the short lining) first. Secure it with the hold-down pin and with its spring by pushing the pin through the back of the backing plate and, while holding it with one hand, install the spring and the retainer using a pair of needlenose pliers. Install the adjuster actuator assembly.

23. Install the parking brake strut and the strut spring by pulling back the spring with pliers and engaging the end of the cable onto the brake strut and then releasing the spring.

24. Place the small metal guide plate over the anchor pin and position the self-adjuster wire cable eye.

25. Install the actuator return spring. DO NOT pry the actuator lever to install the return spring. Position it using the end of a screwdriver or another suitable tool.

➤If the return springs are bent or in any way distorted, they should be replaced.

26. Using the brake installation tool, place the brake return springs in position. Install the primary spring first over the anchor pin and then place the spring from the secondary show over the wire link end.

27. Pull the brake shoes away from the backing plate and apply a thin coat of high temperature, waterproof, grease or special brake lube in the brake shoe contact points.

28. Once the complete assembly has been installed, check the operation of the self-adjusting mechanism by moving the actuating lever by hand.

29. Adjust the brakes.
a. Turn the star adjuster until the drum slides over the brakes shoes with only a slight drag. Remove the drum:
b. Turn the adjuster back 1¼ turns.

c. Install the drum and wheel and lower the vehicle.

### ✳✳CAUTION

**Avoid overtightening the lug nuts to prevent damage to the brake disc or drum. Alloy wheels can also be cracked by overtightening. Use of a torque wrench is highly recommended.**

➡️**If the adjusting hole in the drum has been punched out, make certain that the insert has been removed from the inside of the drum. Install a rubber hole cover to keep dirt out of the brake assembly. Also, be sure that the drums are installed in the same position as they were when removed, with the locating tang in line with the locating hole in the axle shaft flange.**

d. Make the final adjustment by backing the vehicle and pumping the brakes until the self-adjusting mechanisms adjust to the proper level and the brake pedal reaches satisfactory height.

30. Adjust the parking brake. Details are given later.

### Wheel Cylinders

#### REMOVAL & INSTALLATION

▶ **See Figures 49, 50 and 51**

1. Raise and support the axle.
2. Remove the wheel and tire.
3. Back off the brake adjustment if necessary and remove the drum.
4. Disconnect and plug the brake line.
5. Remove the brake shoe pull-back springs.
6. Remove the screws securing the wheel cylinder to the backing plate. Later models have their wheel cylinders retained by a round retainer. To release the locking tabs, insert two awls (see illustration) into the access slots to bend the tabs back. Install the new retainer over the wheel cylinder abutment using a 1⅛ in. 12 point socket and socket extension.
7. Disengage the wheel cylinder pushrods from the brake shoes and remove the wheel cylinder.
8. Installation is the reverse of removal. Adjust the brakes and bleed the system.

#### OVERHAUL

As with master cylinders, overhaul kits for wheel cylinders are readily available. When rebuidling and installing wheel cylinders, avoid getting any contaminants into the system. Always install clean, new high quality brake fluid. If dirty or improper fluid has been used, it will be necessary to drain the entire system, flush the system with proper brake fluid, replace all rubber components, refill, and bleed the system.

1. Remove the rubber boots from the cylinder ends with pliers. Discard the boots.
2. Remove and discard the pistons and cups.

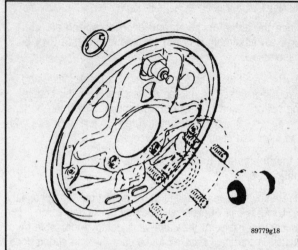

Fig. 49 Later model wheel cylinders are held in place by a retainer (arrow)

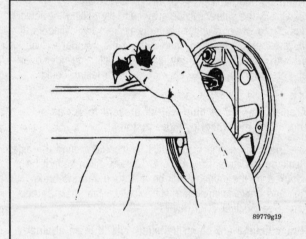

Fig. 50 Bend back the tabs on the retainer using two awls simultaneously

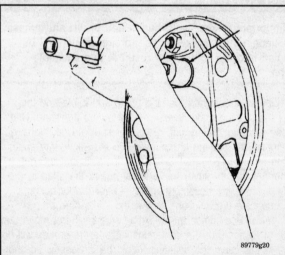

Fig. 51 Install the new retainer over the wheel using a 1⅛ in. 12 point socket and extension

3. Wash the cylinder and metal parts in denatured alcohol or clean brake fluid.

### ✳✳WARNING

**Never use a mineral based solvent such as gasoline, kerosene, or paint thinner for cleaning purposes. These solvents will swell rubber components and quickly deteriorate them.**

## PARKING BRAKE

### Cable

## ADJUSTMENT

▶ See Figure 52

Before attempting parking brake adjustment, make sure that the rear brakes are fully adjusted by making several stops in reverse.

1. Raise and support the rear axle. Release the parking brake.
2. On 1967-70 models, apply the brake 2 notches. On 1971-75 models, apply the pedal 1 click, On 1976 and later models, apply the pedal 4 clicks.
3. Adjust the cable equalizer nut under the truck until a moderate drag can be felt when the rear wheels are turned forward.

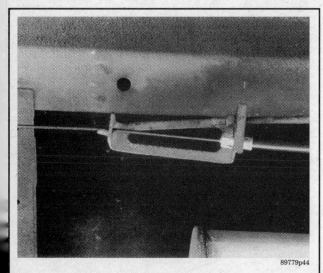

Fig. 52 View of the parking brake equalizer

89779p44

4. Allow the parts to air dry or use compressed air. Do not use rags for cleaning since lint will remain in the cylinder bore.
5. Inspect the piston and replace it if it shows scratches.
6. Lubricate the cylinder bore and counterbore with clean brake fluid.
7. Install the rubber cups (flat side out) and then the pistons (flat side in).
8. Insert new boots into the counterbores by hand. Do not lubricate the boots.

4. Release the parking brake and check that there is no drag when the wheels are turned forward.

➡If the parking brake cable is replaced, pre-stretch it by applying the parking brake hard about three times before attempting adjustment.

## REMOVAL & INSTALLATION

▶ See Figures 53, 54 and 55

### Front Cable

1. Raise vehicle on hoist.
2. Remove adjusting nut from equalizer.
3. Remove retainer clip from rear portion of front cable at frame and from lever arm.
4. Disconnect front brake cable from parking brake pedal or lever assemblies. Remove front brake cable. On some models, it may assist installation of new cable if a heavy cord is tied to other end of cable in order to guide new cable through proper routing.
5. Install cable by reversing removal procedure.
6. Adjust parking brake.

### Center Cable

1. Raise vehicle on hoist.
2. Remove adjusting nut from equalizer.
3. Unhook connector at each end and disengage hooks and guides.
4. Install new cable by reversing removal procedure.
5. Adjust parking brake.
6. Apply parking brake 3 times with heavy pressure and repeat adjustment.

### Rear Cable

1. Raise vehicle on hoist.
2. Remove rear wheel and brake drum.
3. Loosen adjusting nut at equalizer.
4. Disengage rear cable at connector.
5. Bend retainer fingers.
6. Disengage cable at brake shoe operating lever.
7. Install new cable by reversing removal procedure.
8. Adjust parking brake.

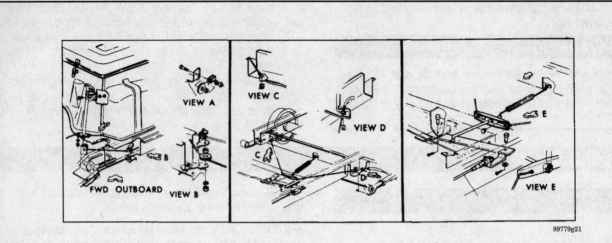

**Fig. 53 Parking brake cables — 1967-70 models**

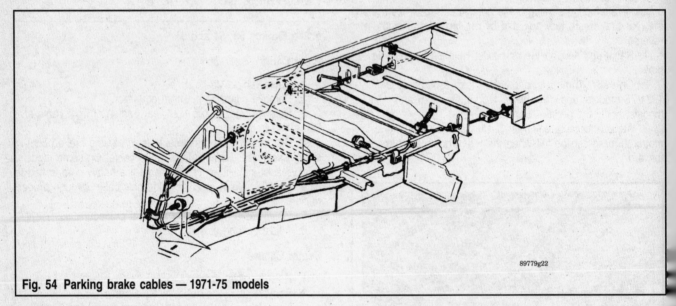

**Fig. 54 Parking brake cables — 1971-75 models**

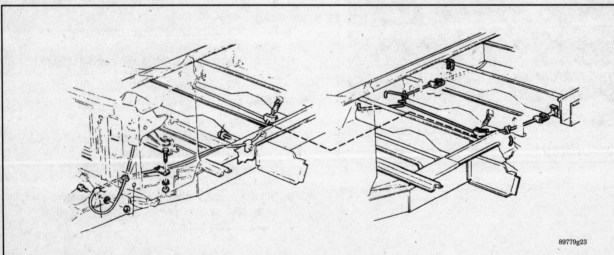

**Fig. 55 Parking brake cables — 1976 and later models**

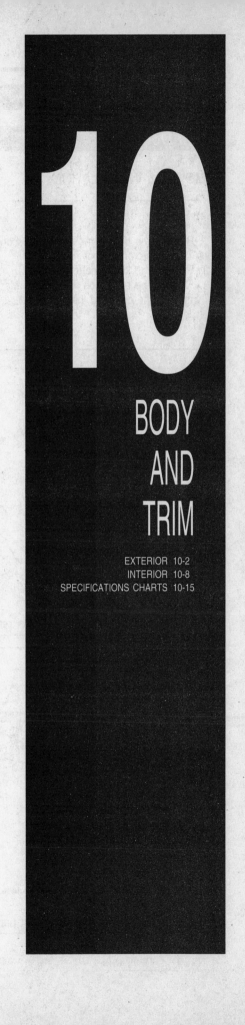

# 10

# BODY AND TRIM

## EXTERIOR

### Front Doors

#### REMOVAL & INSTALLATION

▶ **See Figures 1 and 2**

1. Remove the door trim panel and disconnect the electrical wiring harness from the door (if equipped).
2. Remove the kick panel (if equipped).
3. Remove the hinge bolt cover plate. Mark the position of the hinges on the door and the door pillar.

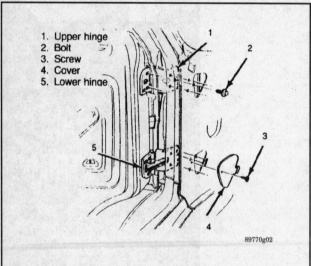

1. Upper hinge
2. Bolt
3. Screw
4. Cover
5. Lower hinge

89770g02

**Fig. 1 View of the door hinges and its retainers**

4. Support the door and remove the door frame-to-hinge bolts.
5. Remove the door from the vehicle.
6. Remove the hinge to door bolts and remove the hinges from the door.
7. Installation is the reverse of the removal procedure.

#### ADJUSTMENT

Special tool J-23457-A #50 Torx Wrench, or its equivalent is required to perform this procedure.

1. Remove the lock striker protector screw.
2. Remove the lock striker protector.
3. Remove the spring.
4. Remove the door striker using tool J-23457-A.
5. Remove the spacer.
6. Remove the kick panel (if equipped).
7. Remove the hinge bolt cover screw.
8. Remove the hinge bolt cover.

Loosen the door hinge bolts as needed to adjust the door. Adjust the door up or down, forward or rearward, and in or out at the door hinges.

9. Adjust the door to obtain a gap of 0.16-0.20 in. (4.1-5.1mm) between the front door and the roof panel.
10. The gap between the rocker panel and the front door at its base should be 0.23-0.27 in. (5.85-6.85mm).
11. Adjust the door to obtain a gap of 0.16-0.20 in. (4.1-5.1mm) between the doors rear edge and the rear door pillar.
12. The gap between the door's front edge and the rear edge of the fender should be 0.16-0.20 in. (4.1-5.1mm).
13. Tighten the door hinge bolts that were loosened.
14. Reverse the removal procedure of the remaining component parts for installation.

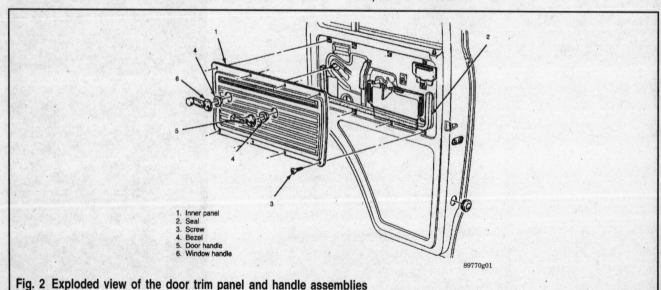

1. Inner panel
2. Seal
3. Screw
4. Bezel
5. Door handle
6. Window handle

89770g01

**Fig. 2 Exploded view of the door trim panel and handle assemblies**

## Sliding Side Door

### REMOVAL & INSTALLATION

▶ See Figures 3, 4 and 5

1. Remove the upper track cover and the hinge cover.
2. Open the door completely. Mark the position of the roller assembly on the door and remove the upper front roller assembly.
3. Remove the upper rear hinge retainer from the hinge.
4. Lift the upper rear hinge off of the track and remove the hinge.
5. Pivot the door away from the vehicle to disengage the rollers and lower the front roller from the track.
6. Remove the door from the vehicle.
7. Installation is the reverse of the removal procedure.

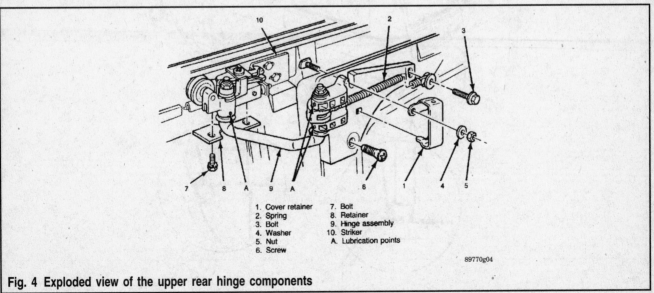

Fig. 5 View of the upper hinge cover

### ADJUSTMENTS

▶ See Figures 5, 6 and 7

**Up and Down**

Special tool J-23457 #50 Torx Wrench, or its equivalent is required to perform this procedure.
1. Remove the upper rear hinge cover.
2. Remove the front lock striker.
3. Remove the rear lock striker using tool J-23457.
4. Remove the rear door wedge assembly.
5. Adjust the rear edge of the door to obtain a gap of 0.16-0.20 in. (4.1-5.1mm) between the top of the door and the roof side rail. This adjustment should provide a gap of 0.23-0.27 in. (5.85-6.85mm) between the bottom of the door and the rocker panel. To accomplish this adjustment, loosen the upper rear hinge to door bolts and align the rear edge of the door up and down. Next, tighten the upper rear hinge to door bolts.

Fig. 3 View of the upper track cover

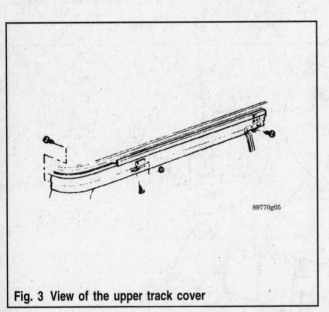

1. Cover retainer
2. Spring
3. Bolt
4. Washer
5. Nut
6. Screw
7. Bolt
8. Retainer
9. Hinge assembly
10. Striker
A. Lubrication points

Fig. 4 Exploded view of the upper rear hinge components

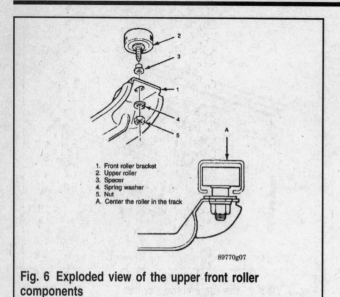

1. Front roller bracket
2. Upper roller
3. Spacer
4. Spring washer
5. Nut
A. Center the roller in the track

89770g07

**Fig. 6 Exploded view of the upper front roller components**

6. Adjust the front edge of the door by loosening the upper front roller bracket to door bolts and the lower hinge to door bolts. Align the door to obtain the same gap as in Step 5, then tighten the lower hinge to door bolt.

7. Adjust the upper front roller bracket up and down so that the roller is centered in the track. The roller must not touch the top or bottom of the track. Tighten the upper front roller bracket to door bolts.

8. Install the previously removed components in the reverse order of their removal.

### In and Out

1. Remove the front lock striker.
2. Loosen the nut retaining the upper front roller to the upper roller bracket.
3. Loosen the lower front roller assembly-to-roller assembly bracket bolts.
4. Loosen the rear door lock striker.
5. Adjust the door in or out until the surface of the door is flush with the surface of the body.
6. Tighten the rear door lock striker.

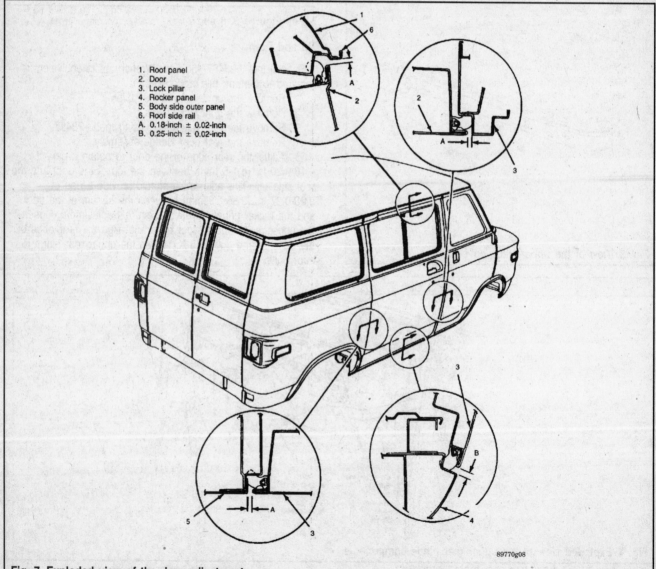

1. Roof panel
2. Door
3. Lock pillar
4. Rocker panel
5. Body side outer panel
6. Roof side rail
A. 0.18-inch ± 0.02-inch
B. 0.25-inch ± 0.02-inch

89770g08

**Fig. 7 Exploded view of the door adjustments**

7. Tighten the lower front roller assembly to roller assembly bracket bolts.

8. Tighten the nut retaining the upper front roller to the upper roller bracket.

9. Install the front lock striker.

### orward and Rearward

1. Mark the position of the front and rear latch strikers on the body pillars.

2. Remove the front and rear lock strikers.

3. Remove the upper front track cover.

4. Loosen the upper rear hinge striker.

5. Adjust the door forward or rearward to obtain a gap of .16-0.20 in. (4.1-5.1mm) between the left and right door edge nd the door pillar.

6. Tighten the upper rear hinge striker.

7. Install the upper front track cover.

8. Install the front and rear lock strikers at the position reviously marked.

### ront Striker

#### See Figure 8

1. Loosen the front latch striker bolts.

2. Slide the door toward the striker.

3. The guide on the door must fit snugly into the rubber ned opening in the striker assembly.

4. Check that the latch fully engages the striker. Add or lelete shims behind the striker to accomplish this adjustment.

5. Tighten the striker bolts.

### ear Striker

#### See Figures 8 and 9

Tool J-23457 Wrench is required to make this adjustment.

1. Loosen the striker using J-23457.

2. Loosen the rear wedge assembly.

3. Center the striker vertically so that the striker properly ngages the door lock. Mark the vertical position of the striker.

4. Adjust the striker in or out to align the surface of the loor flush with the body surface. Mark the position of the striker.

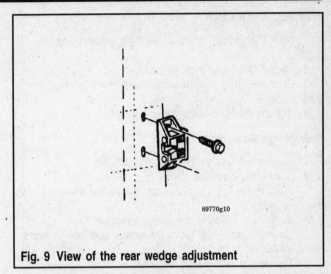

89770g10

**Fig. 9 View of the rear wedge adjustment**

5. Tighten the striker using tool J-23457.

6. Open the door and apply grease to the striker.

7. Close the door and make an impression of the lock on the striker.

8. Open the door and measure the distance from the rear of the striker head to the impression. The distance should be 0.20-0.30 in. (5.1-7.6mm).

9. Adjust the striker by adding or deleting shims. Align the striker to the previously made marks.

10. Tighten the striker using J-23457.

#### Upper Rear Hinge

1. The lower hinge lever should have a gap of 0.10-0.16 in. (2.54-4.06mm) between the outer edge of the lower hinge lever and the striker latch edge. This adjustment is made by adding an equal amount of shims between the guide block and the hinge assembly, and between the roller and the hinge assembly.

2. Adjust the striker up or down to obtain a gap of 0.06 in. (1.5mm) between the lower edge of the striker plate and and the lower edge of the lower hinge lever.

3. Adjust the guide up or down to obtain a gap of 0.02 in. (0.51mm) between the track and the guide.

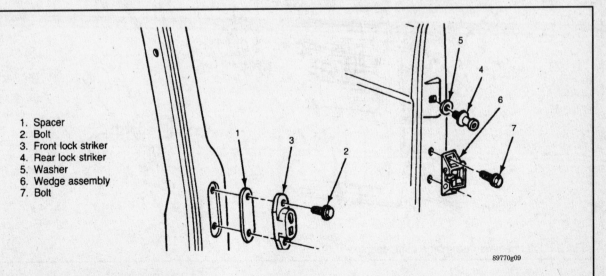

1. Spacer
2. Bolt
3. Front lock striker
4. Rear lock striker
5. Washer
6. Wedge assembly
7. Bolt

89770g09

**Fig. 8 View of the front and rear lock adjustments**

### Door Hold Open Catch

1. Mark the position of the lower roller assembly to the bracket.
2. Loosen the lower roller assembly bolts.
3. Pivot the lower roller assembly to properly engage the latch striker.
4. Tighten the lower roller assembly bolts.

### Rear Wedge Assembly

1. Loosen the rear wedge assembly screws.
2. Completely close the door.
3. From inside the vehicle, center the wedge assembly onto the door wedge.
4. Mark the position of the wedge assembly.
5. Open the door, and move the wedge assembly forward ³/₁₆ in. (4.76mm).
6. Tighten the rear wedge assembly screws.

## Intermediate Door and Hinge

### REMOVAL & INSTALLATION

▶ See Figure 10

1. Open the door, remove the door trim panel and disconnect the electrical wiring harness (if equipped). Then mark the position of the door on the hinges using a wax pencil.
2. Remove the hinge hole plugs on the body side pillar.
3. Remove the strap pin from the bracket, then remove the snapring from the pin, and pull the pin.
4. Support the door safely, and remove the hinge to body pillar bolts.
5. Remove the door from the vehicle.
6. Remove the hinge to door bolts.
7. Remove the hinges from the door.
8. Remove the retainers, seals, and grommets from the door or the hinges.

9. Installation is the reverse of the removal procedure. Make sure to align the hinges with the previously made marks

### ADJUSTMENT

Tool J-23457-A Wrench is required to perform the following adjustments.

1. Remove the door lock striker from the rear intermediate door using J23457-A.
2. Remove the upper and lower rear intermediate door strikers.
3. Loosen the hinge bolts as necessary to adjust the doors
4. Each of the two doors must first be adjusted in the door opening before adjusting the door to door clearance.
5. Adjust the door up and down, forward and rearward, and in and out, at the door hinges.
6. Adjust the door height so that there is a gap of 0.16-0.20 in. (4.1-5.1mm) between the door and the roof panel
7. Adjust the gap between the door and the rocker panel to 0.22-0.26 in. (5.6-6.6mm).
8. Adjust the gap between the doors and the body at the hinge pillars to 0.14-0.18 in. (3.6-4.6mm).
9. Adjust the gap between the front and rear intermediate doors to 0.23-0.27 in. (5.85-6.85mm).
10. Tighten the hinge bolts that were loosened.
11. Install the upper and lower rear intermediate door strikers to the body.
12. Install the door lock striker to the rear intermediate door using J-23457-A.
13. Adjust the upper and lower intermediate door striker to door clearance so that there is 0.172 in. (4.37mm) between the striker and the door latch when the door is in the secondary latch position. (The door is latched but not fully closed.) An ¹¹/₁₆ in. (17.46mm) diameter drill bit may be used to gauge this clearance.
14. Adjust the front intermediate striker on the rear door so that the front door lock properly engages the rear door, and so that the front door is flush with the rear door.

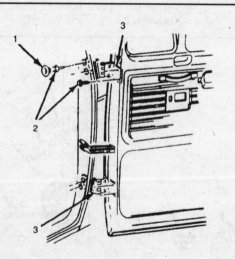
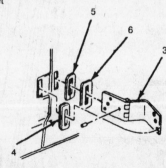

1. Cap
2. Bolt
3. Hinge
4. Grommet
5. Seal
6. Retainer

89770g11

**Fig. 10 Intermediate door hinge components**

## Rear Doors

### REMOVAL & INSTALLATION

▶ See Figure 11

1. Open the door, remove the door trim panel and disconnect the electrical wiring harness (if equipped). Then mark the position of the door on the hinges using a wax pencil.
2. Remove the hinge hole plugs on the body side pillar.
3. Remove the strap pin from the bracket, then remove the snapring from the pin, and pull the pin.
4. Support the door safely, and remove the hinge to body pillar bolts.
5. Remove the door from the vehicle.
6. Remove the hinge to door bolts.
7. Remove the hinges from the door.
8. Remove the retainers, seals, and grommets from the door or the hinges.

9. Installation is the reverse of the removal procedure. Make sure to align the hinges with the previously made marks.

### ADJUSTMENT

Each of the two doors must first be adjusted in the door opening before adjusting the door-to-door clearance.

1. Adjust the door height so that there is a gap of 0.23-0.27 in. (5.85-6.85mm) between the roof panel and the rear door panel.
2. Adjust the gap between the bottom of the door panel (not the bottom of the outer panel) and the platform panel should be 0.23-0.27 in. (5.85-6.85mm). This measurement should be taken on each door individually from the side of the door. The door should be in its normal closed position. The outer rear door panel is 0.58-0.62 in. (14.73-15.75mm) away from the rear platform panel when normally closed.
3. Adjust the rear door outer panel to the body side outer panel gap to 0.14-0.18 in. (3.6-4.6mm).

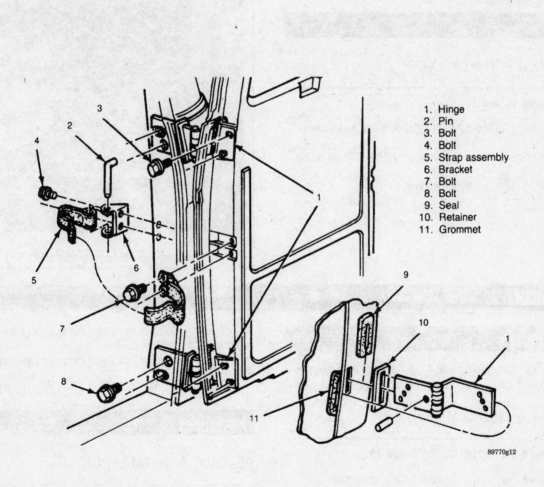

1. Hinge
2. Pin
3. Bolt
4. Bolt
5. Strap assembly
6. Bracket
7. Bolt
8. Bolt
9. Seal
10. Retainer
11. Grommet

89770g12

Fig. 11 Rear door hinge components

4. The door to door clearance between the left and right outer door panels should be 0.23-0.27 in. (5.85-6.85mm).

## Rear Door Striker

### REMOVAL & INSTALLATION

1. Remove the striker-to-door frame bolts.
2. Remove the striker from the door frame.
3. Remove the spacer (if equipped).
4. Install in the reverse order of removal.

### ADJUSTMENT

Adjust the striker to door latch clearance, so that there is 0.172 in. (4.37mm) between the striker and the door latch when the door is in the secondary latch position (the door is latched but not fully closed). An $^{11}/_{16}$ in. (17.46mm) diameter drill bit may be used to gauge this clearance.

## Hood

### REMOVAL & INSTALLATION

▶ See Figures 12 and 13

1. Mark the area around the hinges to make installation easier.
2. Support the hood and remove the hinge to hood frame bolts.
3. Remove the hood from the truck.
4. Installation is the reverse of the removal procedure.

Fig. 12 Mark the hinge-to-hood location

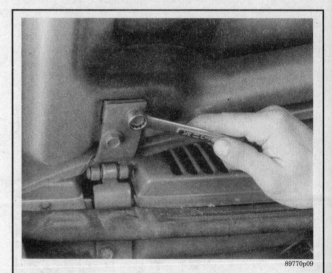

Fig. 13 Unfasten the hinge retaining bolts

## INTERIOR

### Door Panels

Door Handle Clip Remover, tool J-9886-01 or equivalent, is required to perform the following procedure.

### REMOVAL & INSTALLATION

▶ See Figures 14, 15, 16, 17, 18, 19 and 20

1. Remove the window regulator handle using tool J-9886-01.
2. Remove the window regulator handle bezel.
3. Remove the door lock assembly handle using J-9886-01.
4. Remove the control assembly handle bezel.
5. Remove the assist handle (if equipped).
6. Remove the armrest (if equipped).

7. Remove the door trim outer panel screws and pull the panel away from the retainer.
8. Remove the door trim inner panel screws and remove the trim inner panel.
9. Installation is the reverse of the removal procedure.

### Headliner

### REMOVAL & INSTALLATION

▶ See Figure 21

1. Remove the upper window trim that supports the headliner.
2. Pull the headliner bow from the retainer (if equipped).
3. Remove the retainer bolts and the retainers.

Fig. 14 Using a regulator clip tool, disengage the door handle

Fig. 17 . . . then remove the armrest

Fig. 15 Remove the handle and clip

Fig. 18 Unfasten the door panel retaining screws . . .

Fig. 16 Unfasten the armrest retaining screws . . .

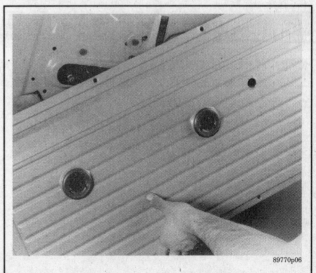

Fig. 19 . . . then remove the door panel

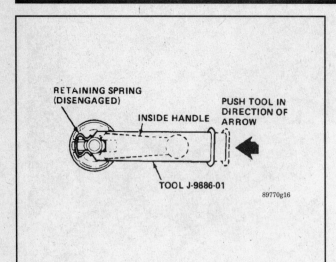

**Fig. 20 Removing the clip retained inside the door handle**

4. Shift the headliner from side to side to disengage the headliner from the clips.
5. Remove the headliner from the vehicle.
6. Install in the reverse order of the removal procedure.

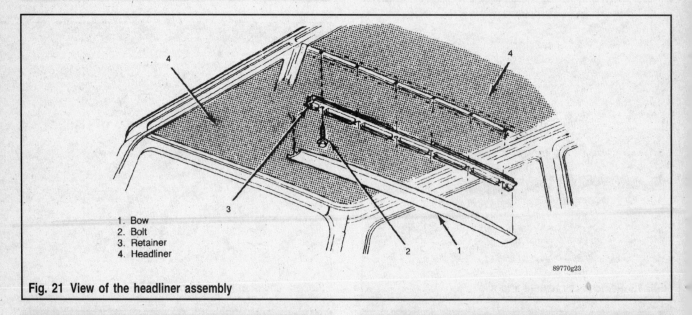

1. Bow
2. Bolt
3. Retainer
4. Headliner

**Fig. 21 View of the headliner assembly**

## Door Locks

### REMOVAL & INSTALLATION

1. Raise the window completely.
2. Remove the door trim panel and the door lock knob.
3. Remove the control assembly.
4. Remove the rear glass run panel.
5. Remove the door lock screws.
6. Remove the lock from the door.
7. Lower the lock in the door far enough to provide clearance for the inside lock rod and install the lock by reversing the removal procedure.

## Door Vent/Window Run Channel Assembly

▶ See Figure 22

The door vent and the window run channel are one assembly. This assembly is fit into the front of the door frame.

### REMOVAL & INSTALLATION

▶ See Figure 23

1. Place the window in the lowered position and remove the door trim panel.
2. Remove the run channel molding. Pull the molding out of the vent assembly only.
3. Remove the door panel to run channel bolt.
4. Remove the door to ventilator screws.

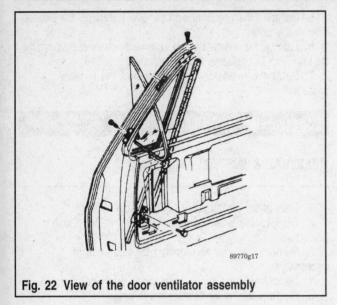

Fig. 22 View of the door ventilator assembly

Fig. 24 Adjusting the ventilator assembly

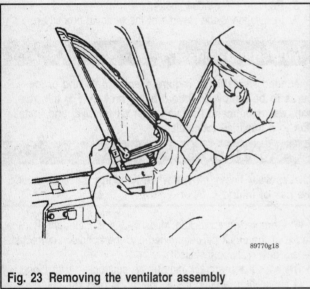

Fig. 23 Removing the ventilator assembly

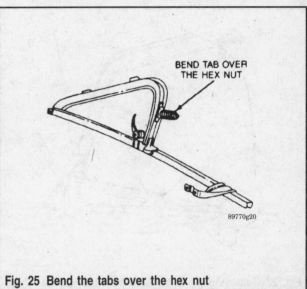

Fig. 25 Bend the tabs over the hex nut

5. Remove the door vent/window run channel assembly from the vehicle by pulling the top of the vent backwards away from the door frame. Then lift and rotate the assembly out of the door.

6. Installation is the reverse of the removal procedure.

## ADJUSTMENT

▶ See Figures 24 and 25

1. Remove the door trim panel.
2. Bend the tabs on the adjustment nut away from the nut.
3. Adjust the vent by placing a wrench on the adjusting nut, and then turning the vent window to the proper tension.
4. Bend the tabs over the adjusting nut and install the door trim panel.

## Door Glass and Regulator

### REMOVAL & INSTALLATION

### ❋❋CAUTION

Always wear heavy gloves when handling glass to minimize the risk of injury.

Door Glass
▶ See Figures 26 and 27

1. Lower the glass to the bottom of the door and remove the door trim panel.
2. Remove the door vent/window channel run assembly.

➡Mask or cover any sharp edges that could scratch the glass.

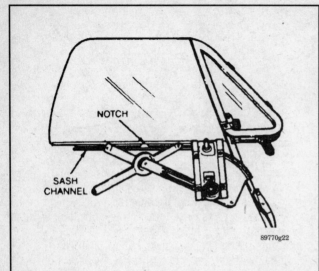

**Fig. 26 View of the door glass and regulator assembly**

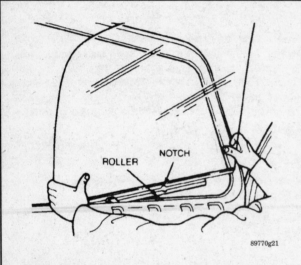

**Fig. 27 Removing the door glass from the vehicle**

3. Slide the glass forward until the front roller is in line with the notch in the sash channel.

4. Disengage the roller from the channel.

5. Push the window forward, then tilt it up until the rear roller is disengaged.

6. Place the window in a level position, and raise it straight up and out of the door.

7. Installation is the reverse of the removal procedure.

### Regulator
♦ See Figure 27

1. Raise the window and tape the glass in the full up position using cloth body tape.

2. Remove the door trim panel and the door panel to regulator bolts.

3. Slide the regulator rearward to disengage the rear roller from the sash channel. Then disengage the lower roller from the regulator rail.

4. Disengage the forward roller from the sash channel at the notch in the sash channel.

5. Collapse the regulator and remove it through the access hole in the door.

6. Lubricate the regulator and the sash channel and regulator rails with Lubriplate® or its equivalent.

7. Install the regulator in the reverse of the removal procedure.

## Electric Window Motor

### REMOVAL & INSTALLATION

1. Disconnect the negative battery cable.

2. Remove the door panel as described in the above procedure.

3. Remove the window regulator for clearance (if necessary).

4. Disconnect the wiring connector to the window motor.

5. Remove the motor to door frame bolts.

6. Remove the window motor.

7. Installation is the reverse of the removal procedure.

## Windshield Glass

➡**Bonded windshields require special tools and procedures to be removed without being broken. For this reason, we recommend that you refer all removal and installation to a qualified technician.**

### ❋❋CAUTION

**Always wear heavy gloves when handling glass to reduce the risk of injury.**

When replacing a cracked windshield, it is important that the cause of the crack be determined and the condition corrected, before new glass is installed.

The cause of the crack may be an obstruction or a high spot somewhere around the flange of the opening; cracking may not occur until pressure from the high spot or obstruction becomes particularly high due to winds, extremes of temperature, or rough terrain.

Suggestions of what to look for are described later in this section, under Inspection.

### REMOVAL

♦ See Figures 28 and 29

When a windshield is broken, the glass may have already have fallen or been removed from the weatherstrip. Often, however, it is necessary to remove a cracked or otherwise imperfect windshield that is still intact. In this case, it is a good practise to crisscross the glass with strips of masking tape before removing the it; this will help hold the glass together and minimize the risk of injury.

If a crack extends to the edge of the glass, mark the point where the crack meets the weather strip. (Use a piece of chalk and mark the point on the cab, next to the weatherstrip.) Later,

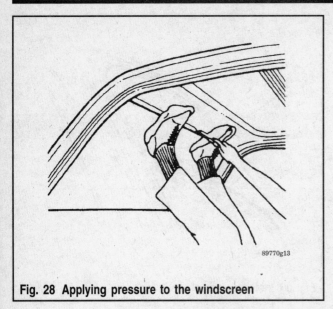

89770g13

**Fig. 28  Applying pressure to the windscreen**

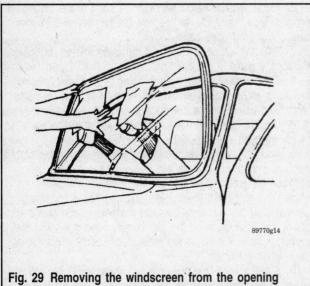

89770g14

**Fig. 29  Removing the windscreen from the opening**

Special tool J-24402-A, Glass Sealant Remover Knife, or its equivalent is required to perform this procedure. To remove the windshield:

1. Place the protective covering around the area where the glass will be removed.

2. Remove the windshield wiper arms, and the interior garnish moldings.

3. Remove the exterior reveal moldings and the support support molding from the urethane adhesive by prying one end of the molding from the adhesive. Pull the free end of the molding away from the windshield or the pinchweld flange until the molding is completely free of the windshield.

4. Using J-24402-A cut the windshield from the urethane adhesive. If the short method of glass replacement is to be used, keep the knife as close to the glass as possible in order to leave a base for the replacement glass.

5. With the help of an assistant, remove the glass.

6. If the original glass is to be reinstalled, place it on a protected bench or a holding or holding fixture. Remove any remaining adhesive with a razor blade or a sharp scraper. Any remaining traces of adhesive material can be removed with denatured alcohol or lacquer thinner.

➡ **When cleaning windshield glass, avoid contacting the edge of the plastic laminate material (on the edge of the glass) with volatile cleaner. Contact may cause discoloration and deterioration of the plastic laminate. Do not use a petroleum based solvent such as gasoline or kerosene. The presence of oil will prevent the adhesion of new material.**

## INSPECTION

An inspection of the windshield opening, the weather strip, and the glass may reveal the cause of a broken windshield. This can help prevent future breakage. If there is no apparent cause of breakage, the weatherstrip should be removed from the flange of the opening and the flange inspected. Look for high weld or solder spots, hardened spot welds sealer, or any other obstruction or irregularity in the flange. Check the weatherstrip for irregularities or obstructions in it.

Check the windshield to be installed to make sure that it does not have any chipped edges. Chipped edges can be ground off, restoring a smooth edge to the glass, and minimizing concentrations of pressure that cause breakage. Remove no more than necessary, in an effort to maintain the original shape of the glass and the proper clearance between it and the flange of the opening.

## INSTALLATION METHODS

There are two methods used for windshield replacement. The short method described previously in the removal procedure is used when the urethane adhesive can be used as a base for the new glass. This method would be used in the case of a cracked glass, if no other service needs to be done to the windshield frame, such as sheet metal or repainting work.

The extended method should be used when work must be done to the windshield frame, such as straightening or repair-

when examining the flange of the opening for a cause of the crack start at the point marked.

The higher the temperature of the work area, the more pliable the weather strip will be. The more pliable the weather strip, the more easily the windshield can be removed.

Before removing the glass, cover the instrument panel, and the surrounding sheet metal with protective covering and remove the wiper arms.

There are two methods of windshield removal, depending on the method of windshield replacement chosen. When using the short method of installation, it is important to cut the glass from the urethane adhesive as close to the glass as possible. This is due to the fact that the urethane adhesive will be used to provide a base for the replacement windshield.

When using the extended method of windshield replacement, all the urethane adhesive must be removed from the pinchweld flange so, the process of cutting the window from the adhesive is less critical.

ing sheet metal, or repainting the windshield frame. In this method, all of the urethane adhesive must be removed from the pinchweld flange.

## INSTALLATION

To replace a urethane adhered windshield, GM adhesive service kit No. 9636067 contains some of the materials needed, and must be used to insure the original integrity of the windshield design. Materials in this kit include:

- One tube of adhesive material
- One dispensing nozzle
- Steel music wire
- Rubber cleaner
- Rubber Primer
- Pinchweld primer
- Blackout primer
- Filler strip (for use on windshield installations for vehicles equipped with embedded windshield antenna)
- Primer applicators

Other materials are required for windshield installation which are not included in the service kit. These include:

- GM rubber lubricant No. 1051717
- Alcohol for cleaning the edge of the glass
- Adhesive dispensing gun J-24811 or its equivalent
- A commercial type razor knife
- Two rubber support spacers

### Extended Method

1. Clean all metal surrounding the windshield opening with a clean alcohol dampened cloth. Allow the alcohol to air dry.

2. Apply the pinchweld primer found in the service kit to the pinchweld area. Do not let any of the primer touch any of the exposed paint because damage to the finish may occur. Allow thirty minutes for the primer to dry.

3. Follow the steps listed under the Short Method for the remainder of the procedure.

### Short Method

▶ **See Figure 30**

1. Install the support molding onto the pinchweld flange from inside the vehicle. The joint of the molding should be located at the bottom center of the moulding.

2. Thoroughly clean the edge of the glass to which the adhesive material will be applied with a clean alcohol dampened cloth. Allow the alcohol to dry.

3. Apply the clear glass primer in the kit to the inner edge of the windshield from the edge of the glass inward 0.04 in. (1.016mm). Apply the primer around the entire perimeter of the glass. Allow the primer to cure for thirty minutes.

4. Apply the blackout primer to the glass in the same area as the clear primer. Allow the blackout primer to dry to the touch.

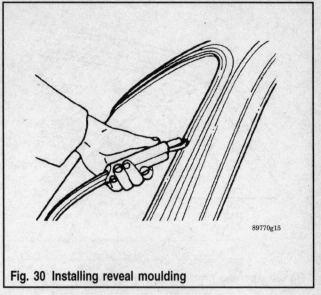

**Fig. 30 Installing reveal moulding**

89770g15

5. Place two rubber blocks onto the base of the pinchweld flange. Place the blocks in line with the last screw on either side of the cowl grille cover.

6. With the aid of a helper, lift the glass into the opening. Center the glass in the opening, on top of the support molding.

7. Check the fit of the revel molding. If necessary remove the glass and cut away additional urethane to give the proper windshield height. Place the glass in the window opening.

8. Cut the tip of the adhesive cartridge approximately ³⁄₁₆ in. (4.76mm) from the end of the tip.

9. Apply the adhesive first in and around the spacer blocks. Apply a smooth continuous bead of adhesive into the gap between the glass edge and the sheet metal. Use a flat bladed tool to paddle the material into position if necessary. Be sure that the adhesive contacts the entire edge of the glass, and extends to fill the gap between the glass and the primer sheet metal (extended method) or solidified urethane base (short method).

10. Spray a mist of water onto the urethane. Water will assist in the curing process. Dry the area where the reveal molding will contact the body and glass.

11. Install new reveal moldings. Remove the protective tape covering the butyl adhesive on the underside of the molding. Push the molding caps onto each end of one of the reveal moldings. Press the lip of the molding into the urethane adhesive while holding it against the edge of the windshield. Take care to seat the molding in the corners. The lip must fully contact the adhesive and the gap must be entirely covered by the crown of the molding. Slide the molding caps onto the adjacent moldings. Use tape to hold the molding in position until the adhesive cures.

12. Install the wiper arms and the interior garnish moldings.

➡**The vehicle should not be driven and should remain at room temperature for six hours to allow the adhesive to cure.**

## How to Remove Stains from Fabric Interior

For rest results, spots and stains should be removed as soon as possible. Never use gasoline, lacquer thinner, acetone, nail polish remover or bleach. Use a 3" x 3" piece of cheesecloth. Squeeze most of the liquid from the fabric and wipe the stained fabric from the outside of the stain toward the center with a lifting motion. Turn the cheesecloth as soon as one side becomes soiled. When using water to remove a stain, be sure to wash the entire section after the spot has been removed to avoid water stains. Encrusted spots can be broken up with a dull knife and vacuumed before removing the stain.

| Type of Stain | How to Remove It |
|---|---|
| Surface spots | Brush the spots out with a small hand brush or use a commercial preparation such as K2R to lift the stain. |
| Mildew | Clean around the mildew with warm suds. Rinse in cold water and soak the mildew area in a solution of 1 part table salt and 2 parts water. Wash with upholstery cleaner. |
| Water stains | Water stains in fabric materials can be removed with a solution made from 1 cup of table salt dissolved in 1 quart of water. Vigorously scrub the solution into the stain and rinse with clear water. Water stains in nylon or other synthetic fabrics should be removed with a commercial type spot remover. |
| Chewing gum, tar, crayons, shoe polish (greasy stains) | Do not use a cleaner that will soften gum or tar. Harden the deposit with an ice cube and scrape away as much as possible with a dull knife. Moisten the remainder with cleaning fluid and scrub clean. |
| Ice cream, candy | Most candy has a sugar base and can be removed with a cloth wrung out in warm water. Oily candy, after cleaning with warm water, should be cleaned with upholstery cleaner. Rinse with warm water and clean the remainder with cleaning fluid. |
| Wine, alcohol, egg, milk, soft drink (non-greasy stains) | Do not use soap. Scrub the stain with a cloth wrung out in warm water. Remove the remainder with cleaning fluid. |
| Grease, oil, lipstick, butter and related stains | Use a spot remover to avoid leaving a ring. Work from the outisde of the stain to the center and dry with a clean cloth when the spot is gone. |
| Headliners (cloth) | Mix a solution of warm water and foam upholstery cleaner to give thick suds. Use only foam—liquid may streak or spot. Clean the entire headliner in one operation using a circular motion with a natural sponge. |
| Headliner (vinyl) | Use a vinyl cleaner with a sponge and wipe clean with a dry cloth. |
| Seats and door panels | Mix 1 pint upholstery cleaner in 1 gallon of water. Do not soak the fabric around the buttons. |
| Leather or vinyl fabric | Use a multi-purpose cleaner full strength and a stiff brush. Let stand 2 minutes and scrub thoroughly. Wipe with a clean, soft rag. |
| Nylon or synthetic fabrics | For normal stains, use the same procedures you would for washing cloth upholstery. If the fabric is extremely dirty, use a multi-purpose cleaner full strength with a stiff scrub brush. Scrub thoroughly in all directions and wipe with a cotton towel or soft rag. |

tccs0g01

## GLOSSARY

**AIR/FUEL RATIO:** The ratio of air-to-gasoline by weight in the fuel mixture drawn into the engine.

**AIR INJECTION:** One method of reducing harmful exhaust emissions by injecting air into each of the exhaust ports of an engine. The fresh air entering the hot exhaust manifold causes any remaining fuel to be burned before it can exit the tailpipe.

**ALTERNATOR:** A device used for converting mechanical energy into electrical energy.

**AMMETER:** An instrument, calibrated in amperes, used to measure the flow of an electrical current in a circuit. Ammeters are always connected in series with the circuit being tested.

**AMPERE:** The rate of flow of electrical current present when one volt of electrical pressure is applied against one ohm of electrical resistance.

**ANALOG COMPUTER:** Any microprocessor that uses similar (analogous) electrical signals to make its calculations.

**ARMATURE:** A laminated, soft iron core wrapped by a wire that converts electrical energy to mechanical energy as in a motor or relay. When rotated in a magnetic field, it changes mechanical energy into electrical energy as in a generator.

**ATMOSPHERIC PRESSURE:** The pressure on the Earth's surface caused by the weight of the air in the atmosphere. At sea level, this pressure is 14.7 psi at 32°F (101 kPa at 0°C).

**ATOMIZATION:** The breaking down of a liquid into a fine mist that can be suspended in air.

**AXIAL PLAY:** Movement parallel to a shaft or bearing bore.

**BACKFIRE:** The sudden combustion of gases in the intake or exhaust system that results in a loud explosion.

**BACKLASH:** The clearance or play between two parts, such as meshed gears.

**BACKPRESSURE:** Restrictions in the exhaust system that slow the exit of exhaust gases from the combustion chamber.

**BAKELITE:** A heat resistant, plastic insulator material commonly used in printed circuit boards and transistorized components.

**BALL BEARING:** A bearing made up of hardened inner and outer races between which hardened steel balls roll.

**BALLAST RESISTOR:** A resistor in the primary ignition circuit that lowers voltage after the engine is started to reduce wear on ignition components.

**BEARING:** A friction reducing, supportive device usually located between a stationary part and a moving part.

**BIMETAL TEMPERATURE SENSOR:** Any sensor or switch made of two dissimilar types of metal that bend when heated or cooled due to the different expansion rates of the alloys. These types of sensors usually function as an on/off switch.

**BLOWBY:** Combustion gases, composed of water vapor and unburned fuel, that leak past the piston rings into the crankcase during normal engine operation. These gases are removed by the PCV system to prevent the buildup of harmful acids in the crankcase.

**BRAKE PAD:** A brake shoe and lining assembly used with disc brakes.

**BRAKE SHOE:** The backing for the brake lining. The term is, however, usually applied to the assembly of the brake backing and lining.

**BUSHING:** A liner, usually removable, for a bearing; an anti-friction liner used in place of a bearing.

**CALIPER:** A hydraulically activated device in a disc brake system, which is mounted straddling the brake rotor (disc). The caliper contains at least one piston and two brake pads. Hydraulic pressure on the piston(s) forces the pads against the rotor.

**CAMSHAFT:** A shaft in the engine on which are the lobes (cams) which operate the valves. The camshaft is driven by the crankshaft, via a belt, chain or gears, at one half the crankshaft speed.

**CAPACITOR:** A device which stores an electrical charge.

**CARBON MONOXIDE (CO):** A colorless, odorless gas given off as a normal byproduct of combustion. It is poisonous and extremely dangerous in confined areas, building up slowly to toxic levels without warning if adequate ventilation is not available.

**CARBURETOR:** A device, usually mounted on the intake manifold of an engine, which mixes the air and fuel in the proper proportion to allow even combustion.

**CATALYTIC CONVERTER:** A device installed in the exhaust system, like a muffler, that converts harmful byproducts of combustion into carbon dioxide and water vapor by means of a heat-producing chemical reaction.

**CENTRIFUGAL ADVANCE:** A mechanical method of advancing the spark timing by using flyweights in the distributor that react to centrifugal force generated by the distributor shaft rotation.

**CHECK VALVE:** Any one-way valve installed to permit the flow of air, fuel or vacuum in one direction only.

**CHOKE:** A device, usually a moveable valve, placed in the intake path of a carburetor to restrict the flow of air.

**CIRCUIT:** Any unbroken path through which an electrical current can flow. Also used to describe fuel flow in some instances.

**CIRCUIT BREAKER:** A switch which protects an electrical circuit from overload by opening the circuit when the current flow exceeds a predetermined level. Some circuit breakers must be reset manually, while most reset automatically.

**COIL (IGNITION):** A transformer in the ignition circuit which steps up the voltage provided to the spark plugs.

**COMBINATION MANIFOLD:** An assembly which includes both the intake and exhaust manifolds in one casting.

**COMBINATION VALVE:** A device used in some fuel systems that routes fuel vapors to a charcoal storage canister instead of venting them into the atmosphere. The valve relieves fuel tank pressure and allows fresh air into the tank as the fuel level drops to prevent a vapor lock situation.

**COMPRESSION RATIO:** The comparison of the total volume of the cylinder and combustion chamber with the piston at BDC and the piston at TDC.

**CONDENSER:** 1. An electrical device which acts to store an electrical charge, preventing voltage surges. 2. A radiator-like device in the air conditioning system in which refrigerant gas condenses into a liquid, giving off heat.

**CONDUCTOR:** Any material through which an electrical current can be transmitted easily.

**CONTINUITY:** Continuous or complete circuit. Can be checked with an ohmmeter.

**COUNTERSHAFT:** An intermediate shaft which is rotated by a mainshaft and transmits, in turn, that rotation to a working part.

**CRANKCASE:** The lower part of an engine in which the crankshaft and related parts operate.

**CRANKSHAFT:** The main driving shaft of an engine which receives reciprocating motion from the pistons and converts it to rotary motion.

**CYLINDER:** In an engine, the round hole in the engine block in which the piston(s) ride.

**CYLINDER BLOCK:** The main structural member of an engine in which is found the cylinders, crankshaft and other principal parts.

**CYLINDER HEAD:** The detachable portion of the engine, usually fastened to the top of the cylinder block and containing all or most of the combustion chambers. On overhead valve engines, it contains the valves and their operating parts. On overhead cam engines, it contains the camshaft as well.

**DEAD CENTER:** The extreme top or bottom of the piston stroke.

**DETONATION:** An unwanted explosion of the air/fuel mixture in the combustion chamber caused by excess heat and compression, advanced timing, or an overly lean mixture. Also referred to as "ping".

**DIAPHRAGM:** A thin, flexible wall separating two cavities, such as in a vacuum advance unit.

**DIESELING:** A condition in which hot spots in the combustion chamber cause the engine to run on after the key is turned off.

**DIFFERENTIAL:** A geared assembly which allows the transmission of motion between drive axles, giving one axle the ability to turn faster than the other.

**DIODE:** An electrical device that will allow current to flow in one direction only.

**DISC BRAKE:** A hydraulic braking assembly consisting of a brake disc, or rotor, mounted on an axle, and a caliper assembly containing, usually two brake pads which are activated by hydraulic pressure. The pads are forced against the sides of the disc, creating friction which slows the vehicle.

**DISTRIBUTOR:** A mechanically driven device on an engine which is responsible for electrically firing the spark plug at a predetermined point of the piston stroke.

**DOWEL PIN:** A pin, inserted in mating holes in two different parts allowing those parts to maintain a fixed relationship.

**DRUM BRAKE:** A braking system which consists of two brake shoes and one or two wheel cylinders, mounted on a fixed backing plate, and a brake drum, mounted on an axle, which revolves around the assembly.

**DWELL:** The rate, measured in degrees of shaft rotation, at which an electrical circuit cycles on and off.

**ELECTRONIC CONTROL UNIT (ECU):** Ignition module, module, amplifier or igniter. See Module for definition.

**ELECTRONIC IGNITION:** A system in which the timing and firing of the spark plugs is controlled by an electronic control unit, usually called a module. These systems have no points or condenser.

**END-PLAY:** The measured amount of axial movement in a shaft.

**ENGINE:** A device that converts heat into mechanical energy.

**EXHAUST MANIFOLD:** A set of cast passages or pipes which conduct exhaust gases from the engine.

**FEELER GAUGE:** A blade, usually metal, of precisely predetermined thickness, used to measure the clearance between two parts.

**FIRING ORDER:** The order in which combustion occurs in the cylinders of an engine. Also the order in which spark is distributed to the plugs by the distributor.

**FLOODING:** The presence of too much fuel in the intake manifold and combustion chamber which prevents the air/fuel mixture from firing, thereby causing a no-start situation.

**FLYWHEEL:** A disc shaped part bolted to the rear end of the crankshaft. Around the outer perimeter is affixed the ring gear. The starter drive engages the ring gear, turning the flywheel, which rotates the crankshaft, imparting the initial starting motion to the engine.

**FOOT POUND (ft. lbs. or sometimes, ft.lb.):** The amount of energy or work needed to raise an item weighing one pound, a distance of one foot.

**FUSE:** A protective device in a circuit which prevents circuit overload by breaking the circuit when a specific amperage is present. The device is constructed around a strip or wire of a lower amperage rating than the circuit it is designed to protect. When an amperage higher than that stamped on the fuse is present in the circuit, the strip or wire melts, opening the circuit.

**GEAR RATIO:** The ratio between the number of teeth on meshing gears.

**GENERATOR:** A device which converts mechanical energy into electrical energy.

**HEAT RANGE:** The measure of a spark plug's ability to dissipate heat from its firing end. The higher the heat range, the hotter the plug fires.

**HUB:** The center part of a wheel or gear.

**HYDROCARBON (HC):** Any chemical compound made up of hydrogen and carbon. A major pollutant formed by the engine as a byproduct of combustion.

**HYDROMETER:** An instrument used to measure the specific gravity of a solution.

**INCH POUND (inch lbs.; sometimes in.lb. or in. lbs.):** One twelfth of a foot pound.

**INDUCTION:** A means of transferring electrical energy in the form of a magnetic field. Principle used in the ignition coil to increase voltage.

**INJECTOR:** A device which receives metered fuel under relatively low pressure and is activated to inject the fuel into the engine under relatively high pressure at a predetermined time.

**INPUT SHAFT:** The shaft to which torque is applied, usually carrying the driving gear or gears.

**INTAKE MANIFOLD:** A casting of passages or pipes used to conduct air or a fuel/air mixture to the cylinders.

**JOURNAL:** The bearing surface within which a shaft operates.

**KEY:** A small block usually fitted in a notch between a shaft and a hub to prevent slippage of the two parts.

**MANIFOLD:** A casting of passages or set of pipes which connect the cylinders to an inlet or outlet source.

**MANIFOLD VACUUM:** Low pressure in an engine intake manifold formed just below the throttle plates. Manifold vacuum is highest at idle and drops under acceleration.

**MASTER CYLINDER:** The primary fluid pressurizing device in a hydraulic system. In automotive use, it is found in brake and hydraulic clutch systems and is pedal activated, either directly or, in a power brake system, through the power booster.

**MODULE:** Electronic control unit, amplifier or igniter of solid state or integrated design which controls the current flow in the ignition primary circuit based on input from the pick-up coil. When the module opens the primary circuit, high secondary voltage is induced in the coil.

**NEEDLE BEARING:** A bearing which consists of a number (usually a large number) of long, thin rollers.

**OHM:($\Omega$)** The unit used to measure the resistance of conductor-to-electrical flow. One ohm is the amount of resistance that limits current flow to one ampere in a circuit with one volt of pressure.

**OHMMETER:** An instrument used for measuring the resistance, in ohms, in an electrical circuit.

**OUTPUT SHAFT:** The shaft which transmits torque from a device, such as a transmission.

**OVERDRIVE:** A gear assembly which produces more shaft revolutions than that transmitted to it.

**OVERHEAD CAMSHAFT (OHC):** An engine configuration in which the camshaft is mounted on top of the cylinder head and operates the valve either directly or by means of rocker arms.

**OVERHEAD VALVE (OHV):** An engine configuration in which all of the valves are located in the cylinder head and the camshaft is located in the cylinder block. The camshaft operates the valves via lifters and pushrods.

**OXIDES OF NITROGEN (NOx):** Chemical compounds of nitrogen produced as a byproduct of combustion. They combine with hydrocarbons to produce smog.

**OXYGEN SENSOR:** Used with the feedback system to sense the presence of oxygen in the exhaust gas and signal the computer which can reference the voltage signal to an air/fuel ratio.

**PINION:** The smaller of two meshing gears.

**PISTON RING:** An open-ended ring which fits into a groove on the outer diameter of the piston. Its chief function is to form a seal between the piston and cylinder wall. Most automotive pistons have three rings: two for compression sealing; one for oil sealing.

**PRELOAD:** A predetermined load placed on a bearing during assembly or by adjustment.

**PRIMARY CIRCUIT:** The low voltage side of the ignition system which consists of the ignition switch, ballast resistor or resistance wire, bypass, coil, electronic control unit and pick-up coil as well as the connecting wires and harnesses.

**PRESS FIT:** The mating of two parts under pressure, due to the inner diameter of one being smaller than the outer diameter of the other, or vice versa; an interference fit.

**RACE:** The surface on the inner or outer ring of a bearing on which the balls, needles or rollers move.

**REGULATOR:** A device which maintains the amperage and/or voltage levels of a circuit at predetermined values.

**RELAY:** A switch which automatically opens and/or closes a circuit.

**RESISTANCE:** The opposition to the flow of current through a circuit or electrical device, and is measured in ohms. Resistance is equal to the voltage divided by the amperage.

**RESISTOR:** A device, usually made of wire, which offers a preset amount of resistance in an electrical circuit.

**RING GEAR:** The name given to a ring-shaped gear attached to a differential case, or affixed to a flywheel or as part of a planetary gear set.

**ROLLER BEARING:** A bearing made up of hardened inner and outer races between which hardened steel rollers move.

**ROTOR:** 1. The disc-shaped part of a disc brake assembly, upon which the brake pads bear; also called, brake disc. 2. The device mounted atop the distributor shaft, which passes current to the distributor cap tower contacts.

**SECONDARY CIRCUIT:** The high voltage side of the ignition system, usually above 20,000 volts. The secondary includes the ignition coil, coil wire, distributor cap and rotor, spark plug wires and spark plugs.

**SENDING UNIT:** A mechanical, electrical, hydraulic or electromagnetic device which transmits information to a gauge.

**SENSOR:** Any device designed to measure engine operating conditions or ambient pressures and temperatures. Usually electronic in nature and designed to send a voltage signal to an on-board computer, some sensors may operate as a simple on/off switch or they may provide a variable voltage signal (like a potentiometer) as conditions or measured parameters change.

**SHIM:** Spacers of precise, predetermined thickness used between parts to establish a proper working relationship.

**SLAVE CYLINDER:** In automotive use, a device in the hydraulic clutch system which is activated by hydraulic force, disengaging the clutch.

**SOLENOID:** A coil used to produce a magnetic field, the effect of which is to produce work.

**SPARK PLUG:** A device screwed into the combustion chamber of a spark ignition engine. The basic construction is a conductive core inside of a ceramic insulator, mounted in an outer conductive base. An electrical charge from the spark plug wire travels along the conductive core and jumps a preset air gap to a grounding point or points at the end of the conductive base. The resultant spark ignites the fuel/air mixture in the combustion chamber.

**SPLINES:** Ridges machined or cast onto the outer diameter of a shaft or inner diameter of a bore to enable parts to mate without rotation.

**TACHOMETER:** A device used to measure the rotary speed of an engine, shaft, gear, etc., usually in rotations per minute.

**THERMOSTAT:** A valve, located in the cooling system of an engine, which is closed when cold and opens gradually in response to engine heating, controlling the temperature of the coolant and rate of coolant flow.

**TOP DEAD CENTER (TDC):** The point at which the piston reaches the top of its travel on the compression stroke.

**TORQUE:** The twisting force applied to an object.

**TORQUE CONVERTER:** A turbine used to transmit power from a driving member to a driven member via hydraulic action, providing changes in drive ratio and torque. In automotive use, it links the driveplate at the rear of the engine to the automatic transmission.

**TRANSDUCER:** A device used to change a force into an electrical signal.

**TRANSISTOR:** A semi-conductor component which can be actuated by a small voltage to perform an electrical switching function.

**TUNE-UP:** A regular maintenance function, usually associated with the replacement and adjustment of parts and components in the electrical and fuel systems of a vehicle for the purpose of attaining optimum performance.

**TURBOCHARGER:** An exhaust driven pump which compresses intake air and forces it into the combustion chambers at higher than atmospheric pressures. The increased air pressure allows more fuel to be burned and results in increased horsepower being produced.

**VACUUM ADVANCE:** A device which advances the ignition timing in response to increased engine vacuum.

**VACUUM GAUGE:** An instrument used to measure the presence of vacuum in a chamber.

**VALVE:** A device which control the pressure, direction of flow or rate of flow of a liquid or gas.

**VALVE CLEARANCE:** The measured gap between the end of the valve stem and the rocker arm, cam lobe or follower that activates the valve.

**VISCOSITY:** The rating of a liquid's internal resistance to flow.

**VOLTMETER:** An instrument used for measuring electrical force in units called volts. Voltmeters are always connected parallel with the circuit being tested.

**WHEEL CYLINDER:** Found in the automotive drum brake assembly, it is a device, actuated by hydraulic pressure, which, through internal pistons, pushes the brake shoes outward against the drums.

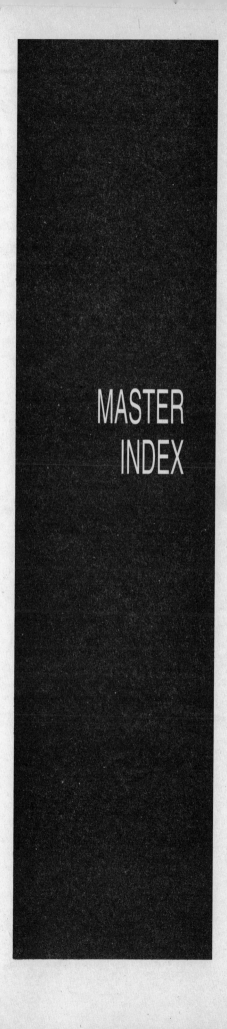

MASTER INDEX